International Politics

Enduring Concepts and Contemporary Issues

Thirteenth Edition

Robert J. Art
Brandeis University

Robert Jervis
Columbia University

D0061248

PEARSON

Boston   Columbus   Indianapolis   New York   San Francisco
Amsterdam   Cape Town   Dubai   London   Madrid   Milan   Munich   Paris   Montréal   Toronto
Delhi   Mexico City   São Paulo   Sydney   Hong Kong   Seoul   Singapore   Taipei   Tokyo

Editor in Chief: Dickson Musselwhite
Publisher: Charlyce Jones Owen
Editorial Assistant: Laura Hernandez
Product Marketing Manager: Tricia Murphy
Field Marketing Manager: Brittany Pogue-Mohammed
Senior Managing Editor: Melissa Feimer
Program Manager: Rob DeGeorge
Project Manager: Joe Scordato
Operations Specialist: Mary Ann Gloriande
Developmental Editor: Maggie Barbieri
Media Editor: Tina Gagliostro
Full-Service Project Management: Chandrasekar Subramanian, SPi Global
Composition: SPi Global
Printer/Binder: R. R. Donnelley & Sons
Cover Printer: Lehigh-Phoenix Color Corp.
Cover Design: Maria Lange
Cover Art Director: Maria Lange
Cover Art: red-feniks/Shutterstock

Library of Congress Cataloging-in-Publication Data
Names: Art, Robert J., editor. | Jervis, Robert - author.
Title: International politics : enduring concepts and contemporary issues /
  [edited by] Robert J. Art, Brandeis University; Robert Jervis, Columbia
  University.
Description: Thirteenth edition. | New York : Pearson, 2016.
Identifiers: LCCN 2016002773 | ISBN 9780134482019
Subjects: LCSH: World politics—1989- | Globalization.
Classification: LCC JZ1242 .I574 2016 | DDC 327--dc23 LC record available at http://lccn.loc.gov/2016002773

10 9 8 7 6 5 4 3 2 1

ISBN 10: 0-13-448201-8
ISBN 13: 978-0-13-448201-9

Brief Contents

Detailed Contents

Preface

The first edition of *International Politics* appeared in 1973, and now, with the 13th edition, it celebrates its 43rd birthday. We are pleased that this reader has been so well received and so long-lived. We hope instructors and students find this edition as useful as they have the previous ones.

New to This Edition

The thirteenth edition retains the four major parts of the previous edition and contains 58 selections, 13 of which are new, making this most recent edition 22% new. The new additions are spread across all four parts of the reader (see below). We also have made two organizational changes. We added a subsection on "Strategic Interaction in Anarchy" in Part I, and consolidated into one subsection the readings on civil wars, human rights, intervention, and international law that appeared in the 12th edition.

Finally, appearing in this edition for the first time are two sets of questions. One set contains 58 questions—one for each of the reader's selections. Each of these questions appears at the end of its corresponding selection. The second set of questions contains only four—one for each of the reader's four major parts. The purpose of the 58 selection questions is to help the student grasp the central argument of each selection by posing a pointed question or questions about it. The purpose of the four parts questions is to help the student tie together all the readings in each part. These two sets of questions, taken together, should help the student master the materials of this reader.

As always, the most important changes in this edition are in the new selections:

- In Part I, we have added three new selections: one by Joseph Nye on the nature of power in international relations; one by John Mearsheimer on anarchy and the struggle for power; and one on game theory by Thomas Schelling.

- In Part II, we added two new selections: one on losing control in crises involving nuclear armed states by Robert Jervis; and another on various scenarios of what the nuclear future might bring by Henry Sokolski.

- Part III contains four new selections: one on the relation between economic interdependence and the likelihood of war by Dale Copeland; one on whether labor or capital does better in the global economy by Erik Brynjolfsson and his associates; another on global financial governance by Erik Heilleiner; and a final one on a new global reserve system to replace the role of the dollar as the world's reserve currency by Joseph Stiglitz.

- Part IV contains four new selections: excerpts from Pope Francis' "Encyclical on the Environment"; a new and updated selection on the United Nations

Security Council by Adam Roberts and Dominik Zaum; one on what is often called "mini-multilateralism," or governance produced by many disparate but interweaving international institutions, by Stewart Patrick; and an essay on the future of the European Union by Stephen Walt.

Features

Originally, we put this reader together to help give the field of international relations greater focus and to bring to students the best articles we could find on the key theoretical concepts in the field. This accounts for the "enduring concepts" in the book's subtitle. A few editions after the first, we then added a separate section on contemporary issues because of our view that these enduring concepts have more meaning for students when applied to salient contemporary issues. All subsequent editions have followed this basic philosophy of combining the best scholarship on theoretical perspectives with that on important contemporary problems.

In constructing the first edition, and in putting together all subsequent editions, including this one, we have tried to create a reader that embodies four features:

- A selection of subjects that, while not exhaustively covering the field of international politics, nevertheless encompasses most of the essential topics that all of us teach in our introductory courses.

- Individual readings that are mainly analytical in content, that take issue with one another, and that thereby introduce the student to the fundamental debates and points of view in the field.

- Editors' introductions to each part that summarize the central concepts the student must master, that organize the central themes of each part, and that relate the readings to one another.

- A book that can be used either as the core around which to design an introductory course or as the primary supplement to enrich an assigned text.

Since the first edition, the field of international relations has experienced a dramatic enrichment in the subjects studied and the quality of works published. Political economy came into its own as an important subfield in the 1970s. New and important works in the field of security studies appeared. The literature on cooperation among states flourished in the early 1980s, and important studies about the environment began to appear in the mid-1980s. Feminist, post-modernist, and constructivist critiques of the mainstream made their appearance also. With the end of the Cold War, these new issues came to the fore: human rights, the tension between state sovereignty and the obligations of the international community, the global environment, civil wars, failed states, nation-building, transnational terrorist groups, and, most recently, the search for new modes of global governance to deal with the collective action problems that are increasingly pressing upon states. The growing diversity of the field has closely mirrored the actual developments in international relations.

Consequently, as for the previous editions, in fashioning the 13th, we have kept in mind both the new developments in world politics and the literature that has accompanied them. Central to this edition, though, as for the other 12, is our belief that the realm of international politics differs fundamentally from that of domestic politics. Therefore, we have continued to put both the developments and the literature in the context of the patterns that still remain valid for understanding the differences between politics in an anarchic environment and politics under a government.

Revel™

Educational technology designed for the way today's students read, think, and learn

When students are engaged deeply, they learn more effectively and perform better in their courses. This simple fact inspired the creation of REVEL: an immersive learning experience designed for the way today's students read, think, and learn. Built in collaboration with educators and students nationwide, REVEL is the newest, fully digital way to deliver respected Pearson content.

REVEL enlivens course content with media interactives and assessments integrated directly within the authors' narrative-that provide opportunities for students to read about and practice course material in tandem. This immersive educational technology boosts student engagement, which leads to better understanding of concepts and improved performance throughout the course.

Learn more about REVEL at www.pearsonhighered.com/REVEL.

Supplements

Pearson is pleased to offer several resources to qualified adopters of *International Politics* and their students that will make teaching and learning from this book even more effective and enjoyable. Several of the supplements for this book are available at the Instructor Resource Center (IRC), an online hub that allows instructors to quickly download book-specific supplements. Please visit the IRC welcome page at www.pearsonhighered.com/irc to register for access.

Instructor's Manual/Test Bank

This resource includes learning objectives, reading guides, multiple-choice questions, true/false questions, and essay questions for each chapter. Available exclusively on the IRC.

Longman Atlas of World Issues (0-205-78020-2)

From population and political systems to energy use and women's rights, the *Longman Atlas of World Issues* features full-color thematic maps that examine the forces shaping the world. Featuring maps from the latest edition of *The Penguin*

State of the World Atlas, this excerpt includes critical thinking exercises to promote a deeper understanding of how geography affects many global issues.

Goode's World Atlas (0-321-65200-2)

First published by Rand McNally in 1923, *Goode's World Atlas* has set the standard for college reference atlases. It features hundreds of physical, political, and thematic maps as well as graphs, tables, and a pronouncing index.

Research and Writing in International Relations (0-205-06065-X)

With current and detailed coverage on how to start research in the discipline's major subfields, this brief and affordable guide offers step-by-step guidance and the essential resources needed to compose political science papers that go beyond description and into systematic and sophisticated inquiry. This text focuses on areas where students often need help—finding a topic, developing a question, reviewing the literature, designing research, and last, writing the paper.

Acknowledgments

In putting together this and previous editions, we received excellent advice from the following colleagues, whom we would like to thank for the time and care they took: Jonathan Acuff, St. Anselm College; Linda S. Adams, Baylor University; David G. Becker, Dartmouth College; Andrew Bennett, Georgetown University; Patrick Bratton, Hawaii Pacific University; Chelsea Brown, Southern Methodist University; James A. Caporaso, University of Washington; Erica Chenoweth, Wesleyan University; Timothy M. Cole, University of Maine; Jane Cramer, University of Oregon; David Edelstein, Georgetown University; Joseph Foudy, Hunter College; Sonia Gardenas, Trinity College; Robert C. Gray, Franklin & Marshall College; Robert J. Griffiths, University of North Carolina at Greensboro; Maia Hallward, Kennesaw State University; James Hentz, Virginia Military Institute; David Houghton, University of Central Florida; Benjamin Judkins, University of Utah; Sean Kay, Ohio Wesleyan University; Mary McCarthy, Drake University; Timothy McKeown, University of North Carolina at Chapel Hill; James A. Mitchell, California State University, Northridge; Ronald Mitchell, University of Oregon; Layna Mosley, University of North Carolina at Chapel Hill; Mueni W. Muiu, Winston-Salem State University; Kathy L. Powers, Pennsylvania State University; Philip Schrodt, University of Kansas; Randall Schweller, The Ohio State University; Margaret E. Scranton, University of Arkansas at Little Rock; Roslin Simowitz, University of Texas at Arlington; Veronica Ward, Utah State University; Ken Wise, Creighton University; and Jeremy Youde, University of Minnesota at Duluth.

Robert J. Art

Robert Jervis

Part I
Anarchy and Its Consequences

 ## LEARNING OBJECTIVES

I.1 Understand power, principle, and legitimacy in statecraft.

I.2 Define anarchy and the anarchic environment of international politics.

I.3 Discuss how international politics exemplifies strategic interaction and the role of game theory.

I.4 Recognize how state actors cope with anarchy and develop patterns that contain the dangers of aggression.

Unlike domestic politics, international politics takes place in an arena that has no central governing body. From this central fact flow important consequences for the behavior of states. In Part I, we explore four of them: the role that principles, legitimacy, and morality can and should play in statecraft; the effects that anarchy has on how states view and relate to one another; the types of strategic interactions that occur among states in anarchy; and the ways that the harsher edges of anarchy can be mitigated, even if not wholly removed.

Power, Principle, and Legitimacy in Statecraft

I.1   Understand power, principle, and legitimacy in statecraft.

Citizens, students, and scholars alike often take up the study of international politics because they want their country to behave in as principled a way as possible. But they soon discover that principle and power, morality and statecraft do not easily mix. Why should this be? Is it inevitable? Can and should states seek to do good in the world? Will they endanger themselves and harm others if they try? These are timeless questions, having been asked by observers of international politics in nearly every previous era. They therefore make a good starting point for thinking about the nature of international politics and the choices states face in our era.

In his history of the Peloponnesian War, the Greek historian Thucydides made the first, and perhaps the most famous, statement about the relation between the prerogatives of power and the dictates of morality. In the Melian dialogue, he argued that "the strong do what they have the power to do and the weak accept what they have to accept" (more frequently stated as "the strong do what they can and the weak suffer what they must"). For Thucydides considerations of power reigned supreme in international politics and were the key to understanding why the war between Athens and Sparta began in the first place. At root, he argued: "what made war inevitable was the growth of Athenian power and the fear which this caused in Sparta." Fearing that Athens' power was growing more quickly than its own, Sparta launched a preventive war to stop Athens from becoming too powerful. Herein lies the first written insight that changes in relative power positions among states, in this case "city-states," can be a cause of war. The forcefulness with which he argued for the "power politics" view of international relations makes Thucydides the first "realist" theorist of international politics. But Ian Hurd shows that in some, if not all international systems, legitimacy plays a powerful role in generating and modifying power.

Hans J. Morgenthau, a leading twentieth-century theorist of international relations, also takes the "power politics" position. He argues that universal standards of morality cannot be an invariable guide to statecraft because there is an "ineluctable tension between the moral command and the requirements of successful political action." Rather than base statecraft on morality, Morgenthau argues that state actors must think and act in terms of power and must do whatever it takes to defend the national interests of their state. J. Ann Tickner, commenting on the primacy of power in Morgenthau's writings, explains that what he considers to be a realistic description of international politics is only a picture of the past and therefore not a prediction about the future, and proposes what she considers to be a feminist alternative. A world in which state actors think of power in terms of collective empowerment, not in terms of leverage over one another, could produce more cooperative outcomes and pose fewer conflicts between the dictates of morality and the power of self-interest. Joseph Nye sees power as central, but notes that it can take multiple forms, including "soft power" that stems from the appeal of a state's culture and values and that can influence not only what others do, but also what they want.

The Meaning of Anarchy

I.2   Define anarchy and the anarchic environment of international politics.

Even those who argue that morality should play a large role in statecraft acknowledge that international politics is not like domestic politics. In the latter, there is government; in the former, there is none. As a consequence, no agency exists above the individual states with authority and power to make laws and settle disputes. States can make commitments and treaties, but no sovereign power ensures compliance and punishes deviations. This—the absence of a supreme power—is what is meant by the anarchic environment of international politics. Anarchy is therefore said to constitute a *state of war*: When all else fails, force is the *ultima ratio*—the final and legitimate arbiter of disputes among states.

The state of war does not mean that every nation is constantly at the brink of war or actually at war with other nations. Most countries, though, do feel threatened by some states at some time, and every state has experienced periods of intense insecurity. No two contiguous states, moreover, have had a history of close, friendly relations uninterrupted by severe tension if not outright war. Because a nation cannot look to a supreme body to enforce laws, nor count on other nations for constant aid and support, it must rely on its own efforts, particularly for defense against attack. Coexistence in an anarchic environment thus requires *self-help*. The psychological outlook that self-help breeds is best described by a saying common among British statesmen since Lord Palmerston: "Great Britain has no permanent enemies or permanent friends, she has only permanent interests."

Although states must provide the wherewithal to achieve their own ends, they do not always reach their foreign policy goals. The goals may be grandiose; the means available, meager. The goals may be attainable; the means selected, inappropriate. But even if the goals are realistic and the means both available and appropriate, a state can be frustrated in pursuit of its ends. The reason is simple but fundamental to an understanding of international politics: What one state does will inevitably impinge on some other states—on some beneficially, but on others adversely. What one state desires, another may covet. What one thinks is just due, another may find threatening. Steps that a state takes to achieve its goals may be rendered useless by the countersteps others take. No state, therefore, can afford to disregard the effects its actions will have on other nations' behavior. In this sense, state behavior is contingent: What one state does is dependent in part upon what others do. Mutual dependence means that each must take the others into account.

Mutual dependence affects nothing more powerfully than it does security— the measures states take to protect their territory. Like other foreign policy goals, the security of one state is contingent upon the behavior of other states. Herein lies the *security dilemma* to which each state is subject: In its efforts to preserve or enhance its own security, one state can take measures that decrease the security of other states and cause them to take countermeasures that neutralize the actions of the first state and that may even menace it. The first state may feel impelled to take further actions, provoking additional countermeasures . . . and so forth. The security dilemma means that an action—reaction spiral can occur between two states or among several of them, forcing each to spend ever larger sums on arms to be no more secure than before. All will run faster merely to stay where they are.

At the heart of the security dilemma are these two constraints: the inherent difficulty in distinguishing between offensive and defensive postures, and the inability of one state to believe or trust that another state's present pacific intentions will remain so. The capability to defend can also provide the capability to attack. In adding to its arms, state A may know that its aim is defensive, that its intentions are peaceful, and therefore that it has no aggressive designs on state B. In a world where states must look to themselves for protection, however, B will examine A's actions carefully and suspiciously. B may think that A will attack it when A's arms become powerful enough and that A's protestations of friendship are designed to lull it into lowering its guard. But even if B believes A's actions are not directed against it, B cannot assume that A's intentions will remain peaceful. Anarchy makes it impossible for A to bind itself to continuing to respect B's interests in the future. B must allow for the possibility that what A can do to it, A sometime might do. The need to assess capabilities along with intentions, or, the equivalent, to allow for a change in intentions, makes state actors profoundly conservative. They prefer to err on the side of safety, to have too much rather than too little. Because security is the basis of existence and the prerequisite for the achievement of all other goals, state actors must be acutely sensitive to the security actions of others. The security dilemma thus means that state actors cannot risk *not* reacting to the security actions of other states, but that in so reacting they can produce circumstances that leave them worse off than before.

The anarchic environment of international politics, then, allows every state to be the final judge of its own interests, but requires that each provide the means to attain them. Because the absence of a central authority permits wars to occur, security considerations become paramount. Because of the effects of the security dilemma, efforts of state leaders to protect their peoples can lead to severe tension and war even when all parties sincerely desire peace. Two states, or two groups of states, each satisfied with the status quo and seeking only security, may not be able to achieve it. Conflicts and wars with no economic or ideological basis can occur. The outbreak of war, therefore, does not necessarily mean that some or all states seek expansion, or that humans have an innate drive for power. That states go to war when none of them wants to, however, does not imply that they never seek war. The security dilemma may explain some wars; it does not explain all wars. States often do experience conflicts of interest over trade, real estate, ideology, and prestige. For example, when someone asked Francis I what differences led to his constant wars with Charles V, he replied: "None whatever. We agree perfectly. We both want control of Italy!" (Cited in Frederick L. Schuman, *International Politics,* 7th ed., New York, 1953, p. 283.) If states cannot obtain what they want by blackmail, bribery, or threats, they may resort to war. Wars can occur when no one wants them; wars usually do occur when someone wants them.

Realists argue that even under propitious circumstances, international cooperation is difficult to achieve because in anarchy, states are often more concerned with relative advantages than with absolute gains. That is, because international politics is a self-help system in which each state must be prepared to rely on its own resources and strength to further its interests, national leaders often seek to become more powerful than their potential adversaries. Cooperation is then made difficult not only by the fear that others will cheat and fail to live up to their agreements, but also by the perceived need to gain a superior position. The reason is not that state actors are concerned with status, but that they fear that arrangements that benefit all, but provide greater benefits to others than to them, will render their country vulnerable to pressure and coercion in the future.

Kenneth N. Waltz develops the above points more fully by analyzing the differences between hierarchic (domestic) and anarchic (international) political systems. He shows why the distribution of capabilities (the relative power positions of states) in anarchic systems is so important and lays out the ways in which political behavior differs in hierarchic and anarchic systems. Anarchy, the security dilemma, and conflicts of interest make international politics difficult, unpleasant, and dangerous.

There is broad agreement among Realists on the consequences of anarchy for states' behavior, but not total agreement. One brand of Realists, who are called the "offensive Realists," argue that the consequences of anarchy go far beyond producing security dilemmas and making cooperation hard to come by. They assert that anarchy forces states, and especially the great powers, to become "power maximizers" because the only way to ensure the states' security is to be the most powerful state in the system. Offensive realism envisions a "dog-eat-dog" world of international politics in which power and fear dominate great power interactions and in which war, or the threat of war, among the great powers or among their proxies is a constant feature of international relations. John J. Mearsheimer lays out the tenets of this brand of realism.

In an anarchic condition, however, the question to ask may not be, "Why does war occur?" but rather "Why does war not occur more frequently than it does?" Instead of asking "Why do states not cooperate more to achieve common interests?" we should ask "Given anarchy and the security dilemma, how is it that states are able to cooperate at all?" Anarchy and the security dilemma do not produce their effects automatically, and it is not self-evident that states are power maximizers. Thus, Alexander Wendt argues that Waltz and other realists have missed the extent to which the unpleasant patterns they describe are "socially constructed"—that is, they stem from the actors' beliefs, perceptions, and interpretations of others' behavior. If national leaders believe that anarchy requires an assertive stance that endangers others, conflict will be generated. But if they think they have more freedom of action and do not take the hostility of others for granted, they may be able to create more peaceful relationships. In this view, structure (anarchy) does not determine state action; agency (human decision) does.

Strategic Interaction in Anarchy

I.3 **Discuss how international politics exemplifies strategic interaction and the role of game theory.**

International politics exemplifies strategic interaction. That is, outcomes are not produced directly by any one state's foreign policy, but by the interaction of the policies of several of them. Each may seek peace and even act in a way that it thinks will bring it about, and yet war can be the result. Intentions and results can be very different, and interaction is central. Interaction is strategic because leaders understand this and when they act have to anticipate how others will behave. Furthermore, they know that others are similarly trying to anticipate what they will do. For example, even if state A is willing to cooperate if it thinks state B will, and state B has the same preference, cooperation will not ensure if A anticipates that B is in fact not likely to cooperate, in part because it thinks that B doubts that A state will cooperate. (This is a version of Rousseau's "Stag Hunt.)

Strategic interaction is best understood through game theory, which is explained in his selection by Thomas C. Schelling, who won a Nobel Prize for his work in this area. In the same vein James Fearon shows that if states were fully rational and informed, wars should not occur because both sides would prefer a peaceful compromise to the identical settlement that actually was reached after mutually costly fighting. The test of war is necessary not because of the conflict of interest itself, but because in the absence of an international authority states cannot commit themselves to living up to their agreements (a problem of anarchy) and cannot credibly reveal their intentions and capabilities to others (a problem of strategic interaction).

Robert Jervis shows a different facet of strategic interaction in arguing that the extent to which states can make themselves more secure without menacing others depends in large part on whether offensive postures can be distinguished from defensive ones and whether the offense is believed to be more efficacious than the defense. In a world where defense is thought to be easier than offense, the security dilemma is mitigated and, consequently, states are more secure and the hard edge of anarchy is softened. The reverse is true if offense is thought to be easier: the security dilemma operates powerfully, and, consequently, states are less secure and the effects of anarchy cut deeply.

The Mitigation of Anarchy

I.4   Recognize how state actors cope with anarchy and develop patterns that contain the dangers of aggression.

Even realists note that conflict and warfare are not constant characteristics of international politics. Most states remain at peace with most others most of the time. State actors have developed a number of ways of coping with anarchy; of gaining more than a modicum of security; of regulating their competition with other states; and of developing patterns that contain, but do not eliminate, the dangers of aggression.

Robert Jervis shows that the impact of anarchy and the security dilemma on the possibilities for cooperation is not constant but varies with both the circumstances states find themselves in and the strategies they follow. Even when states have benign intentions, cooperation is most difficult when the gains from exploiting the other are high and the costs of being exploited are also great. Here it is very tempting to try to take advantage of the other and symmetrically dangerous to trust the other side, which feels the same incentives. It is also not conducive to cooperation if the outcome of both sides working together is only slightly better than mutual competition. Conversely, a reversal of these incentives makes cooperation under anarchy easier and more likely. These are not only conditions that states can find themselves in; they can guide states that seek to cooperate. For example, to minimize the danger of exploitation states can divide a large transactions into a series of smaller ones in which the gains from cheating and the losses from being cheated on are relatively slight at each state. They can also increase transparency to clarify whether each state has cooperated in its previous moves, stake their reputations on living up to their pledges to cooperate, and small states can seek to have larger ones step in if they break their promises. Efforts to do this also signal a state's desire to cooperate and can increase trust. None of this is foolproof, of course, but it can reduce the danger that the policies states follow in anarchy and the security dilemma will generate rather than ameliorate conflict.

The kind of state we are dealing with may make a big difference. Most strikingly, it appears that democracies may never have gone to war against each other. This is not to say, as Woodrow Wilson did, that democracies are inherently peaceful. They seem to fight as many wars as do dictatorships. But, as Michael W. Doyle shows, they do not fight each other. If this is correct—and, of course, both the evidence and the reasons are open to dispute—it implies that anarchy and the security dilemma do not prevent peaceful and even harmonious relations among states that share certain common values and beliefs.

Democracies are relatively recent developments. For a longer period of time, two specific devices—international law and diplomacy—have proved useful in resolving conflicts among states. Although not enforced by a world government, international law can provide norms for behavior and mechanisms for settling disputes. The effectiveness of international law derives from the willingness of states to observe it. Its power extends no further than the disposition of states "to agree to agree." Where less than vital interests are at stake, state actors may accept settlements that are not entirely satisfactory because they think the precedents or principles justify the compromises made. Much of international law reflects a consensus among states on what is of equal benefit to all, as, for example, the rules regulating international communications. Diplomacy, too, can facilitate coopera-tion and resolve disputes. If diplomacy is skillful, and the legitimate interests of the parties in dispute are taken into account, understandings can often be reached on issues that might otherwise lead to war. These points and others are explored more fully by Stanley Hoffmann and Hans J. Morgenthau.

National leaders use these two traditional tools within a balance-of-power system. Much maligned by President Wilson and his followers and misunder-stood by many others, balance of power refers to the way in which stability is achieved through the conflicting efforts of individual states, whether or not any or all of them deliberately pursue that goal. Just as Adam Smith argued that if every individual pursued his or her own self-interest, the interaction of individual egoisms would enhance national wealth, so international relations theorists have argued that even if every state seeks power at the expense of the others, no one state will likely dominate. In both cases a general good can be the unintended product of selfish individual actions. Moreover, even if most states desire only to keep what they have, their own interests dictate that they band together to resist any state or coalition of states that threatens to dominate them.

The balance-of-power system is likely to prevent any one state acquiring hegemony. It will not, however, benefit all states equally nor maintain the peace permanently. Rewards will be unequal because of inequalities in power and expertise. Wars will occur because they are one means by which states can preserve what they have or acquire what they covet. Small states may even be eliminated by their more powerful neighbors. The international system will be unstable, however, only if states flock to what they think is the strongest side. What is called *bandwagoning* or the *domino theory* argues that the international system is precarious because successful aggression will attract many followers, either out of fear or out of a desire to share the spoils of victory. Stephen M. Walt disagrees, drawing on balance-of-power theory and historical evidence, to argue that rather than bandwagoning, under most conditions states balance against emerging threats. They do not throw in their lot with the stronger side. Instead, they join with others to prevent any state from becoming so strong that it could dominate the system.

Power balancing is a strategy followed by individual states acting on their own. Other ways of coping with anarchy, which may supplement or exist alongside this impulse, are more explicitly collective. David C. Kang shows that before Western influences impinged, East Asian politics did not conform to either bandwagoning or balancing or indeed to other standard views of how states in anarchy "should" behave. Instead they adopted a hierarchical order under a Chinese leadership that was based as much on cultural legitimacy as on military or economic power. In other circumstances, regimes and institutions can help overcome anarchy and facilitate cooperation. When states agree on the principles, rules, and norms that should govern behavior, they can often ameliorate the security dilemma and increase the scope for cooperation. Institutions may not only embody common understandings but, as Robert O. Keohane argues, they can also help states work toward mutually desired outcomes by providing a framework for long-run agreements, making it easier for each state to see whether others are living up to their promises, and increasing the costs the state will pay if it cheats. In the final section of this reader we will discuss how institutions can contribute to global governance under current conditions.

Part I Questions for Review

Does a focus on anarchy lead us to exaggerate the role and extent of conflict, especially violent conflict, in international relations? Have some of the ways that states have conceived of anarchy and tried to cope with it inadvertently increased conflict?

Chapter 1
Power, Principle, and Legitimacy in Statecraft

The Melian Dialogue

THUCYDIDES

Next summer Alcibiades sailed to Argos with twenty ships and seized 300 Argive citizens who were still suspected of being pro-Spartan. These were put by the Athenians into the nearby islands under Athenian control.

The Athenians also made an expedition against the island of Melos. They had thirty of their own ships, six from Chios, and two from Lesbos; 1,200 hoplites, 300 archers, and twenty mounted archers, all from Athens; and about 1,500 hoplites from the allies and the islanders.

The Melians are a colony from Sparta. They had refused to join the Athenian empire like the other islanders, and at first had remained neutral without helping either side; but afterwards, when the Athenians had brought force to bear on them by laying waste their land, they had become open enemies of Athens.

Now the generals Cleomedes, the son of Lycomedes, and Tisias, the son of Tisimachus, encamped with the above force in Melian territory and, before doing any harm to the land, first of all sent representatives to negotiate. The Melians did not invite these representatives to speak before the people, but asked them to make the statement for which they had come in front of the governing body and the few. The Athenian representatives then spoke as follows:

'So we are not to speak before the people, no doubt in case the mass of the people should hear once and for all and without interruption an argument from us which is both persuasive and incontrovertible, and should so be led astray. This, we realize, is your motive in bringing us here to speak before the few. Now suppose that you who sit here should make assurance doubly sure. Suppose that you, too, should refrain from dealing with every point in detail in a set speech, and should instead interrupt us whenever we say something controversial and deal with that before going on to the next point? Tell us first whether you approve of this suggestion of ours.'

The Council of the Melians replied as follows:

'No one can object to each of us putting forward our own views in a calm atmosphere. That is perfectly reasonable. What is scarcely consistent with such a proposal is the present threat, indeed the certainty, of your making war on us. We see that you have come prepared to judge the argument yourselves, and that the likely end of it all will be either war, if we prove that we are in the right, and so refuse to surrender, or else slavery.'

Athenians: If you are going to spend the time in enumerating your suspicions about the future, or if you have met here for any other reason except to look the facts in the face and on the basis of these facts to consider how you can save your city from destruction, there is no point in our going on with this discussion. If, however, you will do as we suggest, then we will speak on.

Melians: It is natural and understandable that people who are placed as we are should have recourse to all kinds of arguments and different points of view. However, you are right in saying that we are met together here to discuss the safety of our country and, if you will have it so, the discussion shall proceed on the lines that you have laid down.

Athenians: Then we on our side will use no fine phrases saying, for example, that we have a right to our empire because we defeated the Persians, or that we have come against you now because of the injuries you have done us—a great mass of words that nobody would believe. And we ask you on your side not to imagine that you will influence us by saying that you, though a colony of Sparta, have not joined Sparta in the war, or that you have never done us any harm. Instead we recommend that you should try to get what it is possible for you to get, taking into consideration what we both really do think; since you know as well as we do that, when these matters are discussed by practical people, the standard of justice depends on the equality of power to compel and that in fact the strong do what they have the power to do and the weak accept what they have to accept.

Melians: Then in our view (since you force us to leave justice out of account and to confine ourselves to self-interest)—in our view it is at any rate useful that you should not destroy a principle that is to the general good of all men—namely, that in the case of all who fall into danger there should be such a thing as fair play and just dealing, and that such people should be allowed to use and to profit by arguments that fall short of a mathematical accuracy. And this is a principle which affects you as much as anybody, since your own fall would be visited by the most terrible vengeance and would be an example to the world.

Athenians: As for us, even assuming that our empire does come to an end, we are not despondent about what would happen next. One is not so much frightened of being conquered by a power which rules over others, as Sparta does (not that we are concerned with Sparta now), as of what would happen if a ruling power is attacked and defeated by its own subjects. So far as this point is concerned, you can leave it to us to face the risks involved. What we shall do now is to show you that it is for the good of our own empire that we are here and that it is for the preservation of your city that we shall say what we are going to say. We do not want any trouble in bringing you into our empire, and we want you to be spared for the good both of yourselves and of ourselves.

Melians: And how could it be just as good for us to be the slaves as for you to be the masters?

Athenians: You, by giving in, would save yourselves from disaster; we, by not destroying you, would be able to profit from you.

Melians: So you would not agree to our being neutral, friends instead of enemies, but allies of neither side?

Athenians: No, because it is not so much your hostility that injures us; it is rather the case that, if we were on friendly terms with you, our subjects would regard that as a sign of weakness in us, whereas your hatred is evidence of our power.

Melians: Is that your subjects' idea of fair play—that no distinction should be made between people who are quite unconnected with you and people who are mostly your own colonists or else rebels whom you have conquered?

Athenians: So far as right and wrong are concerned they think that there is no difference between the two, that those who still preserve their independence do so because they are strong, and that if we fail to attack them it is because we are afraid. So that by conquering you we shall increase not only the size but the security of our empire. We rule the sea and you are islanders, and weaker islanders too than the others; it is therefore particularly important that you should not escape.

Melians: But do you think there is no security for you in what we suggest? For here again, since you will not let us mention justice, but tell us to give in to your interests, we, too, must tell you what our interests are and, if yours and ours happen to coincide, we must try to persuade you of the fact. Is it not certain that you will make enemies of all states who are at present neutral, when they see what is happening here and naturally conclude that in course of time you will attack them too? Does not this mean that you are strengthening the enemies you have already and are forcing others to become your enemies even against their intentions and their inclinations?

Athenians: As a matter of fact we are not so much frightened of states on the continent. They have their liberty, and this means that it will be a long time before they begin to take precautions against us. We are more concerned about islanders like yourselves, who are still unsubdued, or subjects who have already become embittered by the constraint which our empire imposes on them. These are the people who are most likely to act in a reckless manner and to bring themselves and us, too, into the most obvious danger.

Melians: Then surely, if such hazards are taken by you to keep your empire and by your subjects to escape from it, we who are still free would show ourselves great cowards and weaklings if we failed to face everything that comes rather than submit to slavery.

Athenians: No, not if you are sensible. This is no fair fight, with honour on one side and shame on the other. It is rather a question of saving your lives and not resisting those who are far too strong for you.

Melians: Yet we know that in war fortune sometimes makes the odds more level than could be expected from the difference in numbers of the two sides. And if we surrender, then all our hope is lost at once, whereas, so long as we remain in action, there is still a hope that we may yet stand upright.

Athenians: Hope, that comforter in danger! If one already has solid advantages to fall back upon, one can indulge in hope. It may do harm, but will not destroy one. But hope is by nature an expensive commodity, and those who are risking their all on one cast find out what it means only when they are already ruined; it never fails them in the period when such a knowledge would enable them to take precautions. Do not let this happen to you, you who are weak and whose fate depends on a single movement of the scale. And do not be like those people who, as so commonly happens, miss the chance of saving themselves in a human and practical way, and, when every clear and distinct hope has left them in their adversity, turn to what is blind and vague, to prophecies and oracles and such things which by encouraging hope lead men to ruin.

Melians: It is difficult, and you may be sure that we know it, for us to oppose your power and fortune, unless the terms be equal. Nevertheless we trust that the gods will give us fortune as good as yours, because we are standing for what is right against what is wrong; and as for what we lack in power, we trust that it will be made up for by our alliance with the Spartans, who are bound, if for no other reason, then for honour's sake, and because we are their kinsmen, to come to our help. Our confidence, therefore, is not so entirely irrational as you think.

Athenians: So far as the favour of the gods is concerned, we think we have as much right to that as you have. Our aims and our actions are perfectly consistent with the beliefs men hold about the gods and with the principles which govern their own conduct. Our opinion of the gods and our knowledge of men lead us to conclude that it is a general and necessary law of nature to rule whatever one can. This is not a law that we made ourselves, nor were we the first to act upon it when it was made. We found it already in existence, and we shall leave it to exist forever among those who come after us. We are merely acting in accordance with it, and we know that you or anybody else with the same power as ours would be acting in precisely the same way. And therefore, so far as the gods are concerned, we see no good reason why we should fear to be at a disadvantage. But with regard to your views about Sparta and your confidence that she, out of a sense of honour, will come to your aid, we must say that we congratulate you on your simplicity but do not envy you your folly. In matters that concern themselves or their own constitution the Spartans are quite remarkably good; as for their relations with others, that is a long story, but it can be expressed shortly and clearly by saying that of all people we know the Spartans are most conspicuous for believing that what they like doing is honourable and what suits their interests is just. And this kind of attitude is not going to be of much help to you in your absurd quest for safety at the moment.

Melians: But this is the very point where we can feel most sure. Their own self-interest will make them refuse to betray their own colonists, the Melians, for that would mean losing the confidence of their friends among the Hellenes and doing good to their enemies.

Athenians: You seem to forget that if one follows one's self-interest one wants to be safe, whereas the path of justice and honour involves one in danger. And, where danger is concerned, the Spartans are not, as a rule, very venturesome.

Melians: But we think that they would even endanger themselves for our sake and count the risk more worth taking than in the case of others, because we are so close to the Peloponnese that they could operate more easily, and because they can depend on us more than on others, since we are of the same race and share the same feelings.

Athenians: Goodwill shown by the party that is asking for help does not mean security for the prospective ally. What is looked for is a positive preponderance of power in action. And the Spartans pay attention to this point even more than others do. Certainly they distrust their own native resources so much that when they attack a neighbour they bring a great army of allies with them. It is hardly likely therefore that, while we are in control of the sea, they will cross over to an island.

Melians: But they still might send others. The Cretan sea is a wide one, and it is harder for those who control it to intercept others than for those who want to slip through to do so safely. And even if they were to fail in this, they would turn against your own land and against those of your allies left unvisited by Brasidas. So, instead of troubling about a country which has nothing to do with you, you will find trouble nearer home, among your allies, and in your own country.

Athenians: It is a possibility, something that has in fact happened before. It may happen in your case, but you are well aware that the Athenians have never yet relinquished a single siege operation through fear of others. But we are somewhat shocked to find that, though you announced your intention of discussing how you could preserve yourselves, in all this talk you have said absolutely nothing which could justify a man in thinking that he could be preserved. Your chief points are concerned with what you hope may happen in the future, while your actual resources are too scanty to give you a chance of survival against the forces that are opposed to you at this moment. You will therefore be showing an extraordinary lack of common sense if, after you have asked us to retire from this meeting, you still fail to reach a conclusion wiser than anything you have mentioned so far. Do not be led astray by a false sense of honour—a thing which often brings men to ruin when they are faced with an obvious danger that somehow affects their pride. For in many cases men have still been able to see the dangers ahead of them, but this thing called dishonour, this word, by its own force of seduction, has drawn them into a state where they have surrendered to an idea, while in fact they have fallen voluntarily into irrevocable disaster, in dishonour that is all the more dishonourable because it has come to them from their own folly rather than their misfortune. You, if you take the right view, will be careful to avoid this. You will see that there is nothing disgraceful in giving way to the greatest city in Hellas when she is offering you such reasonable terms—alliance on a tribute-paying basis and liberty to enjoy your own property. And, when you are allowed to choose between war and safety, you will not be so insensitively arrogant as to make the wrong choice. This is the safe rule—to stand up to one's equals, to behave with deference towards one's superiors, and to treat one's inferiors with moderation. Think it over again, then, when we have withdrawn from the meeting, and let this be a point that constantly recurs to your minds—that you are discussing the fate of your country, that you have only one country, and that its future for good or ill depends on this one single decision which you are going to make.

The Athenians then withdrew from the discussion. The Melians, left to themselves, reached a conclusion which was much the same as they had indicated in their previous replies. Their answer was as follows:

'Our decision, Athenians, is just the same as it was at first. We are not prepared to give up in a short moment the liberty which our city has enjoyed from its foundation for 700 years. We put our trust in the fortune that the gods will send and which has saved us up to now, and in the help of men—that is, of the Spartans; and so we shall try to save ourselves. But we invite you to allow us to be friends of yours and enemies to neither side, to make a treaty which shall be agreeable to both you and us, and so to leave our country.'

The Melians made this reply, and the Athenians, just as they were breaking off the discussion, said:

'Well, at any rate, judging from this decision of yours, you seem to us quite unique in your ability to consider the future as something more certain than what is before your eyes, and to see uncertainties as realities, simply because you would like them to be so. As you have staked most on and trusted most in Spartans, luck, and hopes, so in all these you will find yourselves most completely deluded.'

The Athenian representatives then went back to the army, and the Athenian generals, finding that the Melians would not submit, immediately commenced hostilities and built a wall completely round the city of Melos, dividing the work out among the various states. Later they left behind a garrison of some of their own and some allied troops to blockade the place by land and sea, and with the greater part of their army returned home. The force left behind stayed on and continued with the siege.

About the same time the Argives invaded Phliasia and were ambushed by the Phliasians and the exiles from Argos, losing about eighty men.

Then, too, the Athenians at Pylos captured a great quantity of plunder from Spartan territory. Not even after this did the Spartans renounce the treaty and make war, but they issued a proclamation saying that any of their people who wished to do so were free to make raids on the Athenians. The Corinthians also made some attacks on the Athenians because of private quarrels of their own, but the rest of the Peloponnesians stayed quiet.

Meanwhile the Melians made a night attack and captured the part of the Athenian lines opposite the market-place. They killed some of the troops, and then, after bringing in corn and everything else useful that they could lay their hands on, retired again and made no further move, while the Athenians took measures to make their blockade more efficient in future. So the summer came to an end.

In the following winter the Spartans planned to invade the territory of Argos, but when the sacrifices for crossing the frontier turned out unfavourably, they gave up the expedition. The fact that they had intended to invade made the Argives suspect certain people in their city, some of whom they arrested, though others succeeded in escaping.

About this same time the Melians again captured another part of the Athenian lines where there were only a few of the garrison on guard. As a result of this, another force came out afterwards from Athens under the command of Philocrates, the son of Demeas. Siege operations were now carried on vigorously and, as there was also some treachery from inside, the Melians surrendered unconditionally to the Athenians, who put to death all the men of military age whom they took, and sold the women and children as slaves. Melos itself they took over for themselves, sending out later a colony of 500 men.

Questions for Review

The Athenians say that they are acting as powerful states as they always have and as any others would do in their circumstances. Is this an adequate explanation for their behavior? Is it an adequate justification?

Legitimacy in International Politics

Ian Hurd

What motivates states to follow international norms, rules, and commitments? All social systems must confront what we might call the problem of social control— that is, how to get actors to comply with society's rules—but the problem is particularly acute for international relations, because the international social system does not possess an overarching center of political power to enforce rules. . . .

Consider three generic reasons why an actor might obey a rule: (1) because the actor fears the punishment of rule enforcers, (2) because the actor sees the rule in its own self-interest, and (3) because the actor feels the rule is legitimate and ought to be obeyed. The trait distinguishing the superior from the subordinate is different in each case. In the first, it is asymmetry of physical capacity; in the second, a particular distribution of incentives; and in the third, a normative structure of status and legitimacy. . . . These devices recur in combination across all social systems where rules exist to influence behavior, ranging from the governing of children in the classroom, to the internal structure of organized crime syndicates, to the international system of states. Where rules or norms exist, compliance with them may be achieved by one or a combination of these devices. Studies of domestic political sociology rotate around them, with scholars arguing variously for making one of the three devices foundational or combining them in assorted ways. It is generally seen as natural that a social system may exhibit each at different moments or locations.

In international relations studies, talking about compliance secured by either coercion or self-interest is uncontroversial, and well-developed bodies of literature—falling roughly into the neorealist and rationalist-neoliberal schools, respectively—elaborate each of these notions. However, the idea that states' compliance with international rules is a function of the legitimacy of the rules or of their source gets less attention; and when it is attended to, scholars generally fail to spell out the process by which it operates. . . .

There is no obvious reason, either theoretical or empirical, why the study of the international system should be limited to only two of these three mechanisms and that to do so means missing significant features of the system. This should be a matter of empirical study, not assumption. . . .

Legitimacy, as I use it here, refers to the normative belief by an actor that a rule or institution ought to be obeyed. It is a subjective quality, relational between actor and institution, and defined by the actor's *perception* of the institution. The actor's perception may come from the substance of the rule or from the procedure or source by which it was constituted. Such a perception affects behavior because it is internalized by the actor and helps to define how the actor sees its interests. . . .

Seeing the international system as governed by institutions of legitimate authority opens several very interesting avenues for research, three of which I will sketch here. First, what is the process by which a particular norm, rule, or institution comes to be seen as legitimate? States are somewhat discriminating in which rules they accept as legitimate (although they are not completely free agents in this regard), and so not all potential norms are internalized. Much more could be known about how a given norm comes to be accepted or not. For instance, could we say that the international market has recently become legitimate and so authoritative in this sense? This direction is suggested by recent work on how elements of the international economy have become "disembedded" from domestic political control. A related puzzle, much discussed in studies of domestic institutions, particularly courts, is how a political institution might alter its behavior in order to make itself more *authoritative* (and thus effective). Two international institutions, the International Court of Justice and the UN Security Council, seem quite aware that their present actions have consequences for their future legitimacy and that their legitimacy affects their power and effectiveness. These two areas, international courts and international markets, are fertile ground for the further study of legitimacy and legitimation of international institutions. Moreover, because the process of legitimation is never monolithic, the legitimation of these institutions has generated counteractive delegitimizing efforts. In the case of the Security Council [from 1992 to 2011], Libya . . . pursued a determined strategy to delegitimize the UN sanctions against it by portraying the council as unrepresentative of the will of the wider international community.

The legitimacy pull of the UN Security Council can be demonstrated by Japan's response to sanctions on North Korea in 1994. While the UN Security Council was considering imposing sanctions on North Korea for its surreptitious nuclear program, Japan expressed its opposition to sanctions both publicly and in informal consultations with the Security Council. An essential element in any sanctions program would have been to forbid the remittances of Koreans living in Japan back to North Korea; these remittances accounted for between $600 million and $1.8 billion of North Korea's annual gross national product of $20 billion. For this and other reasons, Japan opposed strong sanctions and worked hard to delay, diminish, or defeat the proposal. Yet at the same time, the Japanese government publicly stated that notwithstanding its opposition, it would abide by the final decision of the council.[1] On the one hand, given the legal status of Security Council resolutions one might expect nothing less than full compliance by member states. But on the other, and more realistically, this is a strong sign that Japan accepted the legitimacy of a Security Council decision, even with a medium probability of an adverse outcome, and even without formal Japanese presence in the deliberations of the council.[2] This strong, public, and a priori commitment to the rule of law in international affairs may have been motivated by a desire to appear a "good community member" (and so improve Japan's case for permanent membership in a reformed Security Council) or by an actual normative commitment to the rules as they are. In either case, Japan was conscious that the international community holds Security Council decisions as legitimate and sees compliance with them as the duty of a good international citizen. This has been particularly true since the late 1980s with the increase in consensus and consultations in the Security Council.

A second area for further research is the role of power (material and ideological) in making an institution legitimate. It is well known that the process of internalizing community norms is rife with considerations of power, both in determining what norms exist in the community and which norms a particular actor might latch on to, but at the same time this process is different from simple coercion. Power is involved in creating the realm of the apparently "normal" as well as in reproducing and challenging its hegemony through ideology and institutions. Here, my only aim has been to make the case that legitimate authority exists in international relations and show what difference this makes, not delve into the process by which an institution *became* legitimate. This second task is important and requires extending the application of writers like Antonio Gramsci, Michel Foucault, and Pierre Bourdieu to international relations.

Finally, what happens in the international setting to the safeguards we generally expect of our governing institutions, such as representativeness and accountability? If international institutions can be authoritative, how do we make them accountable? Certain international institutions, such as the UN, are already recognized as sufficiently governmental that they are expected to be somewhat democratic, but international democracy and accountability will have to be much more widely promoted once we recognize that any institution that is accepted as legitimate stands in a position of authority over states and thus exercises power.

Questions for Review

How is legitimacy established? Under what circumstances does it override considerations of the sort that Thucydides (in the last reading) and Morgenthau (in the next reading) enumerate?

Notes

1 *New York Times*, 3 June 1994. A1.
2 *New York Times*, 9 June 1994, A1.

Six Principles of Political Realism

HANS J. MORGENTHAU

1. Political realism believes that politics, like society in general, is governed by objective laws that have their roots in human nature. In order to improve society it is first necessary to understand the laws by which society lives. The operation of these laws being impervious to our preferences, men will challenge them only as the risk of failure.

   Realism, believing as it does in the objectivity of the laws of politics, must also believe in the possibility of developing a rational theory that reflects, however imperfectly and one-sidedly, these objective laws. It believes also, then, in the possibility of distinguishing in politics between truth and opinion—between what is true objectively and rationally, supported by evidence and illuminated by reason, and what is only a subjective judgment, divorced from the facts as they are and informed by prejudice and wishful thinking.

   Human nature, in which the laws of politics have their roots, has not changed since the classical philosophies of China, India, and Greece endeavored to discover these laws. Hence, novelty is not necessarily a virtue in political theory, nor is old age a defect. The fact that a theory of politics, if there be such a theory, has never been heard of before tends to create a presumption against, rather than in favor of, its soundness. Conversely, the fact that a theory of politics was developed hundreds or even thousands of years ago—as was the theory of the balance of power—does not create a presumption that it must be outmoded and obsolete. . . .

For realism, theory consists in ascertaining facts and giving them meaning through reason. It assumes that the character of a foreign policy can be ascertained only through the examination of the political acts performed and of the foreseeable consequences of these acts. Thus we can find out what statesmen have actually done, and from the foreseeable consequences of their acts we can surmise what their objectives might have been.

Yet examination of the facts is not enough. To give meaning to the factual raw material of foreign policy, we must approach political reality with a kind of rational outline, a map that suggests to us the possible meanings of foreign policy. In other words, we put ourselves in the position of a statesman who must meet a certain problem of foreign policy under certain circumstances, and we ask ourselves what the rational alternatives are from which a states-man may choose who must meet this problem under these circumstances (presuming always that he acts in a rational manner), and which of these rational alternatives this particular statesman, acting under these circum-stances, is likely to choose. It is the testing of this rational hypothesis against the actual facts and their consequences that gives theoretical meaning to the facts of international politics.

2. The main signpost that helps political realism to find its way through the landscape of international politics is the concept of interest defined in terms of power. This concept provides the link between reason trying to understand international politics and the facts to be understood. It sets politics as an autonomous sphere of action and understanding apart from other spheres, such as economics (understood in terms of interest defined as wealth), ethics, aesthetics, or religion. Without such a concept a theory of politics, interna-tional or domestic, would be altogether impossible, for without it we could not distinguish between political and nonpolitical facts, nor could we bring at least a measure of systematic order to the political sphere.

We assume that statesmen think and act in terms of interest defined as power, and the evidence of history bears that assumption out. That assump-tion allows us to retrace and anticipate, as it were, the steps a statesman— past, present, or future—has taken or will take on the political scene. We look over his shoulder when he writes his dispatches; we listen in on his conversation with other statesmen; we read and anticipate his very thoughts. Thinking in terms of interest defined as power, we think as he does, and as disinterested observers we understand his thoughts and actions perhaps better than he, the actor on the political scene, does himself.

The concept of interest defined as power imposes intellectual disci-pline upon the observer, infuses rational order into the subject matter of politics, and thus makes the theoretical understanding of politics possible. On the side of the actor, it provides for rational discipline in action and creates that astounding continuity in foreign policy which makes American, British, or Russian foreign policy appear as an intelligible, rational continuum, by and large consistent within itself, regardless of the different motives, preferences, and intellectual and moral qualities of successive statesmen. A realist theory of international politics, then, will guard against two popular fallacies: the concern with motives and the concern with ideological preferences.

To search for the clue to foreign policy exclusively in the motives of statesmen is both futile and deceptive. It is futile because motives are the most illusive of psychological data, distorted as they are, frequently beyond recognition, by the interests and emotions of actor and observer alike. Do we really know what our own motives are? And what do we know of the motives of others?

Yet even if we had access to the real motives of statesmen, that knowledge would help us little in understanding foreign policies, and might well lead us astray. It is true that the knowledge of the statesman's motives may give us one among many clues as to what the direction of his foreign policy might be. It cannot give us, however, the one clue by which to predict his foreign policies. History shows no exact and necessary correlation between the quality of motives and the quality of foreign policy. This is true in both moral and political terms.

We cannot conclude from the good intentions of a statesman that his foreign policies will be either morally praiseworthy or politically successful. Judging his motives, we can say that he will not intentionally pursue policies that are morally wrong, but we can say nothing about the probability of their success. If we want to know the moral and political qualities of his actions, we must know them, not his motives. How often have statesmen been motivated by the desire to improve the world, and ended by making it worse? And how often have they sought one goal and ended by achieving something they neither expected nor desired? . . .

A realist theory of international politics will also avoid the other popular fallacy of equating the foreign policies of a statesman with his philosophic or political sympathies, and of deducing the former from the latter. Statesmen, especially under contemporary conditions, may well make a habit of presenting their foreign policies in terms of their philosophic and political sympathies in order to gain popular support for them. Yet they will distinguish with Lincoln between their "*official* duty," which is to think and act in terms of the national interest, and their "*personal* wish," which is to see their own moral values and political principles realized throughout the world. Political realism does not require, nor does it condone, indifference to political ideals and moral principles, but it requires indeed a sharp distinction between the desirable and the possible—between what is desirable everywhere and at all times and what is possible under the concrete circumstances of time and place.

It stands to reason that not all foreign policies have always followed so rational an objective, and unemotional a course. The contingent elements of personality, prejudice, and subjective preference, and of all the weaknesses of intellect and will which flesh is heir to, are bound to deflect foreign policies from their rational course. Especially where foreign policy is conducted under the conditions of democratic control, the need to marshal popular emotions to the support of foreign policy cannot fail to impair the rationality of foreign policy itself. Yet a theory of foreign policy which aims at rationality must for the time being, as it were, abstract from these irrational elements and seek to paint a picture of foreign policy which presents the rational essence to be found in experience, without the contingent deviations from rationality which are also found in experience. . . .

The difference between international politics as it actually is and a rational theory derived from it is like the difference between a photograph and a painted portrait. The photograph shows everything that can be seen by the naked eye; the painted portrait does not show everything that can be seen by the naked eye, but it shows, or at least seeks to show, one thing that the naked eye cannot see: the human essence of the person portrayed.

Political realism contains not only a theoretical but also a normative element. It knows that political reality is replete with contingencies and systemic irrationalities and points to the typical influences they exert upon foreign policy. Yet it shares with all social theory the need, for the sake of theoretical understanding, to stress the rational elements of political reality; for it is these rational elements that make reality intelligible for theory. Political realism presents the theoretical construct of a rational foreign policy which experience can never completely achieve.

At the same time political realism considers a rational foreign policy to be good foreign policy; for only a rational foreign policy minimizes risks and maximizes benefits and, hence, complies both with the moral precept of prudence and the political requirement of success. Political realism wants the photographic picture of the political world to resemble as much as possible its painted portrait. Aware of the inevitable gap between good—that is, rational—foreign policy and foreign policy as it actually is, political realism maintains not only that theory must focus upon the rational elements of political reality, but also that foreign policy ought to be rational in view of its own moral and practical purposes.

Hence, it is no argument against the theory here presented that actual foreign policy does not or cannot live up to it. That argument misunderstands the intention of this book, which is to present not an indiscriminate description of political reality, but a rational theory of international politics. Far from being invalidated by the fact that, for instance, a perfect balance of power policy will scarcely be found in reality, it assumes that reality, being deficient in this respect, must be understood and evaluated as an approximation to an ideal system of balance of power.

3. Realism assumes that its key concept of interest defined as power is an objective category which is universally valid, but it does not endow that concept with a meaning that is fixed once and for all. The idea of interest is indeed of the essence of politics and is unaffected by the circumstances of time and place. Thucydides' statement, born of the experiences of ancient Greece, that "identity of interests is the surest of bonds whether between states or individuals" was taken up in the nineteenth century by Lord Salisbury's remark that "the only bond of union that endures" among nations is "the absence of all clashing interests." It was erected into a general principle of government by George Washington:

> A small knowledge of human nature will convince us, that, with far the greatest part of mankind, interest is the governing principle; and that almost every man is more or less, under its influence. Motives of public virtue may for a time, or in particular instances, actuate men to the observance of a conduct purely disinterested; but they are not of themselves sufficient to produce persevering conformity to the refined dictates and obligations of social duty. Few men are capable of making a continual sacrifice of all views of private interest, or advantage, to the common good. It is vain to exclaim against the depravity of human nature on this account; the fact is so, the experience of every age and nation has proved it and we must in a great measure, change the constitution of man, before we can make it otherwise. No institution, not built on the presumptive truth of these maxims can succeed.[1]

> It was echoed and enlarged upon in our century by Max Weber's observation:

> Interests (material and ideal), not ideas, dominate directly the actions of men. Yet the "images of the world" created by these ideas have very often served as switches determining the tracks on which the dynamism of interests kept actions moving.[2]

Yet the kind of interest determining political action in a particular period of history depends upon the political and cultural context within which foreign policy is formulated. The goals that might be pursued by nations in their foreign policy can run the whole gamut of objectives any nation has ever pursued or might possibly pursue.

The same observations apply to the concept of power. Its content and the manner of its use are determined by the political and cultural environment. Power may comprise anything that establishes and maintains the control of man over man. Thus power covers all social relationships which serve that end, from physical violence to the most subtle psychological ties by which one mind controls another. Power covers the domination of man by man, both when it is disciplined by moral ends and controlled by constitutional safeguards, as in Western democracies, and when it is that untamed and barbaric force which finds its laws in nothing but its own strength and its sole justification in its aggrandizement.

Political realism does not assume that the contemporary conditions under which foreign policy operates, with their extreme instability and the ever present threat of large-scale violence, cannot be changed. The balance of power, for instance, is indeed a perennial element of all pluralistic societies, as the authors of *The Federalist* papers well knew; yet it is capable of operating, as it does in the United States, under the conditions of relative stability and peaceful conflict. If the factors that have given rise to these conditions can be duplicated on the international scene, similar conditions of stability and peace will then prevail there, as they have over long stretches of history among certain nations.

What is true of the general character of international relations is also true of the nation state as the ultimate point of reference of contemporary foreign policy. While the realist indeed believes that interest is the perennial standard by which political action must be judged and directed, the contemporary connection between interest and the nation state is a product of history, and is therefore bound to disappear in the course of history. Nothing in the realist position militates against the assumption that the present division of the political world into nation states will be replaced by larger units of a quite different character, more in keeping with the technical potentialities and the moral requirements of the contemporary world.

The realist parts company with other schools of thought before the all-important question of how the contemporary world is to be transformed. The realist is persuaded that this transformation can be achieved only through the workmanlike manipulation of the perennial forces that have shaped the past as they will the future. The realist cannot be persuaded that we can bring about that transformation by confronting a political reality that has its own laws with an abstract ideal that refuses to take those laws into account.

4. Political realism is aware of the moral significance of political action. It is also aware of the ineluctable tension between the moral command and the requirements of successful political action. And it is unwilling to gloss over and obliterate that tension and thus to obfuscate both the moral and the political issue by making it appear as though the stark facts of politics were morally more satisfying than they actually are, and the moral law less exacting than it actually is.

Realism maintains that universal moral principles cannot be applied to the actions of states in their abstract universal formulation, but that they must be filtered through the concrete circumstances of time and place. The individual may say for himself: "*Fiat justitia, pereat mundus* (Let justice be done, even if the world perish)," but the state has no right to say so in the name of those who are in its care. Both individual and state must judge political action by universal moral principles, such as that of liberty. Yet while the individual has a moral right to sacrifice himself in defense of such a moral principle, the state has no right to let its moral disapprobation of the infringement of liberty get in the way of successful political action, itself inspired by the moral principle of national survival. There can be no political morality without prudence; that is, without consideration of the political consequences of seemingly moral action. Realism, then, considers prudence—the weighing of the consequences of alternative political actions—to be the supreme virtue in politics. Ethics in the abstract judges action by its conformity with the moral law; political ethics judges action by its political consequences. Classical and medieval philosophy knew this, and so did Lincoln when he said:

> I do the very best I know how, the very best I can, and I mean to keep doing so until the end. If the end brings me out all right, what is said against me won't amount to anything. If the end brings me out wrong, ten angels swearing I was right would make no difference.

5. Political realism refuses to identify the moral aspirations of a particular nation with the moral laws that govern the universe. As it distinguishes between truth and opinion, so it distinguishes between truth and idolatry. All nations are tempted—and few have been able to resist the temptation for long—to clothe their own particular aspirations and actions in the moral purposes of the universe. To know that nations are subject to the moral law is one thing, while to pretend to know with certainty what is good and evil in the relations among nations is quite another. There is a world of difference between the belief that all nations stand under the judgement of God, inscrutable to the human mind, and the blasphemous conviction that God is always on one's side and that what one wills oneself cannot fail to be willed by God also.

The lighthearted equation between a particular nationalism and the counsels of Providence is morally indefensible, for it is that very sin of pride against which the Greek tragedians and the Biblical prophets have warned rulers and ruled. That equation is also politically pernicious, for it is liable to engender the distortion in judgement which, in the blindness of crusading frenzy, destroys nations and civilizations—in the name of moral principle, ideal, or God himself.

On the other hand, it is exactly the concept of interest defined in terms of power that saves us from both that moral excess and that political folly. For if we look at all nations, our own included, as political entities pursuing their respective interests defined in terms of power, we are able to do justice to all of them. And we are able to do justice to all of them in a dual sense: We are able to judge other nations as we judge our own and, having judged them in this fashion, we are then capable of pursuing policies that respect the interests of other nations, while protecting and promoting those of our own. Moderation in policy cannot fail to reflect the moderation of moral judgment.

6. The difference, then, between political realism and other schools of thought is real, and it is profound. However much the theory of political realism may have been misunderstood and misinterpreted, there is no gainsaying its distinctive intellectual and moral attitude to matters political.

Intellectually, the political realist maintains the autonomy of the political sphere, as the economist, the lawyer, the moralist maintain theirs. He thinks in terms of interest defined as power, as the economist thinks in terms of interest defined as wealth; the lawyer, of the conformity of action with legal rules; the moralist, of the conformity of action with moral principles. The economist asks, "How does this policy affect the wealth of society, or a segment of it?" The lawyer asks: "Is this policy in accord with the rules of law?" The moralist asks: "Is this policy in accord with moral principles?" And the political realist asks: "How does this policy affect the power of the nation?" (Or of the federal government, of Congress, of the party, of agriculture, as the case may be.)

The political realist is not unaware of the existence and relevance of standards of thought other than political ones. As a political realist, he cannot but subordinate these other standards to those of politics. And he parts company with other schools when they impose standards of thought appropriate to other spheres upon the political sphere. . . .

This realist defense of the autonomy of the political sphere against its subversion by other modes of thought does not imply disregard for the existence and importance of these other modes of thought. It rather implies that each should be assigned its proper sphere and function. Political realism is based upon a pluralistic conception of human nature. Real man is a composite of "economic man," "political man," "moral man," "religious man," etc. A man who was nothing but "political man" would be a beast, for he would be completely lacking in moral restraints. A man who was nothing but "moral man" would be a fool, for he would be completely lacking in prudence. A man who was nothing but "religious man" would be a saint, for he would be completely lacking in worldly desires.

Recognizing that these different facets of human nature exist, political realism also recognizes that in order to understand one of them one has to deal with it on its own terms. That is to say, if I want to understand "religious man," I must for the time being abstract from the other aspects of human nature and deal with its religious aspect as if it were the only one. Furthermore, I must apply to the religious sphere the standards of thought appropriate to it, always remaining aware of the existence of other standards and their actual influence upon the religious qualities of man. What is true of this facet of human nature is true of all the others. No modern economist, for instance, would conceive of his science and its relations to other sciences of man in any other way. It is exactly through such a process of emancipation from other standards of thought, and the development of one appropriate to its subject matter, that economics has developed as an autonomous theory of the economic activities of man. To contribute to a similar development in the field of politics is indeed the purpose of political realism.

It is in the nature of things that a theory of politics which is based upon such principles will not meet with unanimous approval—nor does, for that matter, such a foreign policy. For theory and policy alike run counter to two trends in our culture which are not able to reconcile themselves to the assumptions and results of a rational, objective theory of politics. One of these trends disparages the role of power in society on grounds that stem from the experience and philosophy of the nineteenth century; we shall address ourselves to this tendency later in greater detail. The other trend, opposed to the realist theory and practice of politics, stems from the very relationship that exists, and must exist, between the human mind and the political sphere. . . . The human mind in its day-by-day operations cannot bear to look the truth of politics straight in the face. It must disguise, distort, belittle, and embellish the truth—the more so, the more the individual is actively involved in the processes of politics, and particularly in those of international politics. For only by deceiving himself about the nature of politics and the role he plays on the political scene is man able to live contentedly as a political animal with himself and his fellow men.

Thus it is inevitable that a theory which tries to understand international politics as it actually is and as it ought to be in view of its intrinsic nature, rather than as people would like to see it, must overcome a psychological resistance that most other branches of learning need not face.

Questions for Review

Is a particular conception of human nature really necessary for these six principles? Is Morgenthau claiming that his six principles accurately describe the way states behave or is he claiming that they outline how they should behave—or both?

Notes

1 *The Writings of George Washington,* edited by John C. Fitzpatrick (Washington: United States Printing Office, 1931–44), Vol. X, p. 363.

2 Marianne Weber, *Max Weber* (Tuebingen: J. C. B. Mohr, 1926), pp. 347–8. See also Max Weber, *Gesammelte Aufsätze zur Religionssoziologie* (Tuebingen: J. C. B. Mohr, 1920), p. 252.

A Critique of Morgenthau's Principles of Political Realism

J. ANN TICKNER

> It is not in giving life but in risking life that man is raised above the animal: that is why superiority has been accorded in humanity not to the sex that brings forth but to that which kills.
>
> —SIMONE DE BEAUVOIR[1]

International politics is a man's world, a world of power and conflict in which warfare is a privileged activity. Traditionally, diplomacy, military service and the science of international politics have been largely male domains. In the past women have rarely been included in the ranks of professional diplomats or the military; of the relatively few women who specialize in the academic discipline of international relations, few are security specialists. Women political scientists who do study international relations tend to focus on areas such as international political economy, North–South relations and matters of distributive justice.

Today, in the United States, where women are entering the military and the foreign service in greater numbers than ever before, they are rarely to be found in positions of military leadership or at the top of the foreign policy establishment.[2] One notable exception, Jeane Kirkpatrick, who was U.S. ambassador to the United Nations in the early 1980s, has described herself as "a mouse in a man's world"; for, in spite of her authoritative and forceful public style and strong conservative credentials, Kirkpatrick maintains that she failed to win the respect or attention of her male colleagues on matters of foreign policy.[3]

Kirkpatrick's story could serve to illustrate the discrimination that women often encounter when they rise to high political office. However, the doubts as to whether a woman would be strong enough to press the nuclear button (an issue raised when a tearful Patricia Schroeder was pictured sobbing on her husband's shoulder as she bowed out of the 1988 U.S. presidential race), suggest that there may be an even more fundamental barrier to women's entry into the highest ranks of the military or of foreign policy making. Nuclear strategy, with its vocabulary of power, threat, force and deterrence, has a distinctly masculine ring;[4] moreover women are stereotypically judged to be lacking in qualities which these terms evoke. It has also been suggested that, although more women are entering the world of public policy, they are more comfortable dealing with domestic issues such as social welfare that are more compatible with their nurturing skills. Yet the large number of women in the ranks of the peace movement suggests that women are not uninterested in issues of war and peace, although their frequent dissent from national security policy has often branded them as naive, uninformed or even unpatriotic.

In this chapter I propose to explore the question of why international politics is perceived as a man's world and why women remain so underrepresented in the higher echelons of the foreign policy establishment, the military and the academic discipline of international relations. Since I believe that there is something about this field that renders it particularly inhospitable and unattractive to women, I intend to focus on the nature of the discipline itself rather than on possible strategies to remove barriers to women's access to high policy positions. As I have already suggested, the issues that are given priority in foreign policy are issues with which men have had a special affinity. Moreover, if it is primarily men who are describing these issues and constructing theories to explain the workings of the international system, might we not expect to find a masculine perspective in the academic discipline also? If this were so then it could be argued that the exclusion of women has operated not only at the level of discrimination but also through a process of self-selection which begins with the way in which we are taught about international relations.

In order to investigate this claim that the discipline of international relations, as it has traditionally been defined by realism, is based on a masculine world view, I propose to examine the six principles of political realism formulated by Hans J. Morgenthau in his classic work *Politics Among Nations*. I shall use some ideas from feminist theory to show that the way in which Morgenthau describes and explains international politics, and the prescriptions that ensue are embedded in a masculine perspective. Then I shall suggest some ways in which feminist theory might help us begin to conceptualize a worldview from a feminine perspective and to formulate a feminist epistemology of international relations. Drawing on these observations I shall conclude with a reformulation of Morgenthau's six principles. Male critics of contemporary realism have already raised many of the same questions about realism that I shall address. However, in undertaking this exercise, I hope to make a link between a growing critical perspective on international relations theory and feminist writers interested in global issues. Adding a feminist perspective to its discourse could also help to make the field of international relations more accessible to women scholars and practitioners.

Hans J. Morgenthau's Principles of Political Realism: A Masculine Perspective?

I have chosen to focus on Hans J. Morgenthau's six principles of political realism because they represent one of the most important statements of contemporary realism from which several generations of scholars and practitioners of international relations in the United States have been nourished. Although Morgenthau has frequently been criticized for his lack of scientific rigour and ambiguous use of language, these six principles have significantly framed the way in which the majority of international relations scholars and practitioners in the West have thought about international politics since 1945.[5]

Morgenthau's principles of political realism can be summarized as follows:

1. Politics, like society in general, is governed by objective laws that have their roots in human nature, which is unchanging: therefore it is possible to develop a rational theory that reflects these objective laws.

2. The main signpost of political realism is the concept of interest defined in terms of power which infuses rational order into the subject matter of politics, and thus makes the theoretical understanding of politics possible. Political realism stresses the rational, objective and unemotional.

3. Realism assumes that interest defined as power is an objective category which is universally valid but not with a meaning that is fixed once and for all. Power is the control of man over man.

4. Political realism is aware of the moral significance of political action. It is also aware of the tension between the moral command and the requirements of successful political action.

5. Political realism refuses to identify the moral aspirations of a particular nation with the moral laws that govern the universe. It is the concept of interest defined in terms of power that saves us from moral excess and political folly.

6. The political realist maintains the autonomy of the political sphere; he asks "How does this policy affect the power of the nation?" Political realism is based on a pluralistic conception of human nature. A man who was nothing but "political man" would be a beast, for he would be completely lacking in moral restraints. But, in order to develop an autonomous theory of political behaviour, "political man" must be abstracted from other aspects of human nature.[6]

I am not going to argue that Morgenthau is incorrect in his portrayal of the international system. I do believe, however, that it is a partial description of international politics because it is based on assumptions about human nature that are partial and that privilege masculinity. First, it is necessary to define masculinity and femininity. According to almost all feminist theorists, masculinity and femininity refer to a set of socially constructed categories, which vary in time and place, rather than to biological determinants. In the West, conceptual dichotomies such as objectivity vs. subjectivity, reason vs. emotion, mind vs. body, culture vs. nature, self vs. other or autonomy vs. relatedness, knowing vs. being and public vs. private have typically been used to describe male/female differences by feminists and non-feminists alike.[7] In the United States, psychological tests conducted across different socioeconomic groups confirm that individuals perceive these dichotomies as masculine and feminine and also that the characteristics associated with masculinity are more highly valued by men and women alike.[8] It is important to stress, however, that these characteristics are stereotypical; they do not necessarily describe individual men or women, who can exhibit characteristics and modes of thought associated with the opposite sex.

Using a vocabulary that contains many of the words associated with masculinity as I have identified it, Morgenthau asserts that it is possible to develop a rational (and unemotional) theory of international politics based on objective laws that have their roots in human nature. Since Morgenthau wrote the first edition of *Politics Among Nations* in 1948, this search for an objective science of international politics based on the model of the natural sciences has been an important part of the realist and neorealist agenda. In her feminist critique of the natural sciences, Evelyn Fox Keller points out that most scientific communities share the "assumption that the universe they study is directly accessible, represented by concepts and shaped not by language but only by the demands of logic and experiment."[9] The laws of nature, according to this view of science, are "beyond the relativity of language." Like most feminists, Keller rejects this view of science which, she asserts, imposes a coercive, hierarchical and conformist pattern on scientific inquiry. Feminists in general are sceptical about the possibility of finding a universal and objective foundation for knowledge, which Morgenthau claims is possible. Most share the belief that knowledge is socially constructed: since it is language that transmits knowledge, the use of language and its claims to objectivity must continually be questioned.

Keller argues that objectivity, as it is usually defined in our culture, is associated with masculinity. She identifies it as "a network of interactions between gender development, a belief system that equates objectivity with masculinity, and a set of cultural values that simultaneously (and cojointly) elevates what is defined as scientific and what is defined as masculine."[10] Keller links the separation of self from other, an important stage of masculine gender development, with this notion of objectivity. Translated into scientific inquiry this becomes the striving for the separation of subject and object, an important goal of modern science and one which, Keller asserts, is based on the need for control; hence objectivity becomes associated with power and domination.

The need for control has been an important motivating force for modern realism. To begin his search for an objective, rational theory of international politics, which could impose order on a chaotic and conflictual world, Morgenthau constructs an abstraction which he calls political man, a beast completely lacking in moral restraints. Morgenthau is deeply aware that real men, like real states, are both moral and bestial but, because states do not live up to the universal moral laws that govern the universe, those who behave morally in international politics are doomed to failure because of the immoral actions of others. To solve this tension Morgenthau postulates a realm of international politics in which the amoral behaviour of political man is not only permissible but prudent. It is a Hobbesian world, separate and distinct from the world of domestic order. In it, states may act like beasts, for survival depends on a maximization of power and a willingness to fight.

Having long argued that the personal is political, most feminist theory would reject the validity of constructing an autonomous political sphere around which boundaries of permissible modes of conduct have been drawn. As Keller maintains, "the demarcation between public and private not only defines and defends the boundaries of the political but also helps form its content and style."[11] Morgenthau's political man is a social construct based on a partial representation of human nature. One might well ask where the women were in Hobbes's state of nature; presumably they must have been involved in reproduction and chil-drearing, rather than warfare, if life was to go on for more than one generation.[12] Morgenthau's emphasis on the conflictual aspects of the international system contributes to a tendency, shared by other realists, to de-emphasize elements of cooperation and regeneration which are also aspects of international relations.[13]

Morgenthau's construction of an amoral realm of international power politics is an attempt to resolve what he sees as a fundamental tension between the moral laws that govern the universe and the requirements of successful political action in a world where states use morality as a cloak to justify the pursuit of their own national interests. Morgenthau's universalistic morality postulates the highest form of morality as an abstract ideal, similar to the Golden Rule, to which states seldom adhere: the morality of states, by contrast, is an instrumental morality guided by self-interest.

Morgenthau's hierarchical ordering of morality contains parallels with the work of psychologist Lawrence Kohlberg. Based on a study of the moral develop-ment of 84 American boys, Kohlberg concludes that the highest stage of human moral development (which he calls stage 6) is the ability to recognize abstract uni-versal principles of justice; lower on the scale (stage 2) is an instrumental morality concerned with serving one's own interests while recognizing that others have interests too. Between these two is an interpersonal morality which is contextual and characterized by sensitivity to the needs of others (stage 3).[14]

In her critique of Kohlberg's stages of moral development, Carol Gilligan argues that they are based on a masculine conception of morality. On Kohlberg's scale women rarely rise above the third or contextual stage. Gilligan claims that this is not a sign of inferiority but of difference. Since women are socialized into a mode of thinking which is contextual and narrative, rather than formal and abstract, they tend to see issues in contextual rather than in abstract terms.[15] In international relations the tendency to think about morality either in terms of abstract, universal and unattainable standards or as purely instrumental, as Morgenthau does, detracts from our ability to tolerate cultural differences and to seek potential for building community in spite of these differences.

Using examples from feminist literature I have suggested that Morgenthau's attempt to construct an objective, universal theory of international politics is rooted in assumptions about human nature and morality that, in modern West-ern culture, are associated with masculinity. Further evidence that Morgenthau's principles are not the basis for a universalistic and objective theory is contained in his frequent references to the failure of what he calls the "legalistic–moralistic" or idealist approach to world politics which he claims was largely responsible for both the world wars. Having laid the blame for the Second World War on the misguided morality of appeasement, Morgenthau's *realpolitik* prescriptions for successful political action appear as prescriptions for avoiding the mistakes of the 1930s rather than as prescriptions with timeless applicability.

If Morgenthau's world view is embedded in the traumas of the Second World War, are his prescriptions still valid as we move further away from this event? I share with other critics of realism the view that, in a rapidly changing world, we must begin to search for modes of behaviour different from those prescribed by Morgenthau. Given that any war between the major powers is likely to be nuclear, increasing security by increasing power could be suicidal.[16] Moreover, the nation state, the primary constitutive element of the international system for Morgenthau and other realists, is no longer able to deal with an increasingly pluralistic array of problems ranging from economic interdependence to environmental degradation. Could feminist theory make a contribution to international relations theory by constructing an alternative, feminist perspective on international politics that might help us to search for more appropriate solutions?

A Feminist Perspective on International Relations?

If the way in which we describe reality has an effect on the ways we perceive and act upon our environment, new perspectives might lead us to consider alternative courses of action. With this in mind I shall first examine two important concepts in international relations, power and security, from a feminist perspective and then discuss some feminist approaches to conflict resolution.

Morgenthau's definition of power, the control of man over man, is typical of the way power is usually defined in international relations. Nancy Hartsock argues that this type of power-as-domination has always been associated with masculinity, since the exercise of power has generally been a masculine activity: rarely have women exercised legitimized power in the public domain. When women write about power they stress energy, capacity and potential, says Hartsock. She notes that women theorists, even when they have little else in common, offer similar definitions of power which differ substantially from the understanding of power as domination.[17]

Hannah Arendt, frequently cited by feminists writing about power, defines power as the human ability to act in concert, or to take action in connection with others who share similar concerns.[18] This definition of power is similar to that of psychologist David McClelland's portrayal of female power, which he describes as shared rather than assertive.[19] Jane Jaquette argues that, since women have had less access to the instruments of coercion, they have been more apt to rely on power as persuasion; she compares women's domestic activities to coalition building.[20]

All of these writers are portraying power as a relationship of mutual enablement. Tying her definition of female power to international relations, Jaquette sees similarities between female strategies of persuasion and strategies of small states operating from a position of weakness in the international system. There are also examples of states' behaviour that contain elements of the female strategy of coalition building. One such example is the Southern African Development Coordination Conference (SADCC), which is designed to build regional infrastructure based on mutual cooperation and collective self-reliance in order to decrease dependence on the South African economy. Another is the European Community, which has had considerable success in building mutual cooperation in an area of the world whose history would not predict such a course of events.[21] It is rare, however, that cooperative outcomes in international relations are described in these terms, although Karl Deutsch's notion of pluralistic security communities might be one such example where power is associated with building community.[22] I am not denying that power as domination is a pervasive reality in international relations. However, there are also instances of cooperation in interstate relations, which tend to be obscured when power is seen solely as domination. Thinking about power in this multidimensional sense may help us to think constructively about the potential for cooperation as well as conflict, an aspect of international relations generally played down by realism.

Redefining national security is another way in which feminist theory could contribute to new thinking about international relations.[23] Traditionally in the West, the concept of national security has been tied to military strength and its role in the physical protection of the nation state from external threats. Morgenthau's notion of defending the national interest in terms of power is consistent with this definition. But this traditional definition of national security is partial at best in today's world.[24] The technologically advanced states are highly interdependent, and rely on weapons whose effects would be equally devastating to winners and losers alike. For them to defend national security by relying on war as the last resort no longer appears very useful. Moreover, if one thinks of security in North–South rather than East–West terms, for a large portion of the world's population security has as much to do with the satisfaction of basic material needs as with military threats. According to Johan Galtung's notion of structural violence, to suffer a lower life expectancy by virtue of one's place of birth is a form of violence whose effects can be as devastating as war.[25]

Basic needs satisfaction has a great deal to do with women, but only recently have women's roles as providers of basic needs, and in development more generally, become visible as important components in development strategies.[26] Traditionally the development literature has focused on aspects of the development process that are in the public sphere, are technologically complex and are usually undertaken by men. Thinking about the role of women in development and the way in which we can define development and basic needs satisfaction to be inclusive of women's roles and needs are topics that deserve higher priority on the international agenda. Typically, however, this is an area about which traditional international relations theory, with the priority it gives to order over justice, has had very little to say.

A further threat to national security, more broadly defined, which has also been missing from the agenda of traditional international relations, concerns the environment. Carolyn Merchant argues that a mechanistic view of nature, contained in modern science, has helped to guide an industrial and technological development which has resulted in environmental damage that has now become a matter of global concern. In the introduction to her book *The Death of Nature*, Merchant suggests that, "Women and nature have an age-old association—an affiliation that has persisted throughout culture, language, and history."[27] Hence she maintains that the ecology movement, which is growing up in response to environmental threats, and the women's movement are deeply interconnected. Both stress living in equilibrium with nature rather than dominating it, both see nature as a living non-hierarchical entity in which each part is mutually dependent on the whole. Ecologists, as well as many feminists, are now suggesting that only such a fundamental change of world view will allow the human species to survive the damage it is inflicting on the environment.

Thinking about military, economic and environmental security in interdependent terms suggests the need for new methods of conflict resolution that seek to achieve mutually beneficial, rather than zero sum, outcomes. One such method comes from Sara Ruddick's work on "maternal thinking."[28] Ruddick describes maternal thinking as focused on the preservation of life and the growth of children. To foster a domestic environment conducive to these goals, tranquility must be preserved by avoiding conflict where possible, engaging in it non-violently and restoring community when it is over. In such an environment the ends for which disputes are fought are subordinate to the means by which they are resolved. This method of conflict resolution involves making contextual judgments rather than appealing to absolute standards and thus has much in common with Gilligan's definition of female morality.

While non-violent resolution of conflict in the domestic sphere is a widely accepted norm, passive resistance in the public realm is regarded as deviant. But, as Ruddick argues, the peaceful resolution of conflict by mothers does not usually extend to the children of one's enemies, an important reason why women have been ready to support men's wars.[29] The question for Ruddick then becomes how to get maternal thinking, a mode of thinking which she believes can be found in men as well as women, out into the public realm. Ruddick believes that finding a common humanity among one's opponents has become a condition of survival in the nuclear age when the notion of winners and losers has become questionable.[30] Portraying the adversary as less than human has all too often been a technique of the nation state to command loyalty and to increase its legitimacy in the eyes of its citizens. Such behaviour in an age of weapons of mass destruction may be self-defeating.

We might also look to Gilligan's work for a feminist perspective on conflict resolution. Reporting on a study of playground behaviour of American boys and girls, Gilligan argues that girls are less able to tolerate high levels of conflict, and more likely than boys to play games that involve taking turns and in which the success of one does not depend on the failure of another.[31] While Gilligan's study does not take into account attitudes toward other groups (racial, ethnic, economic or national), it does suggest the validity of investigating whether girls are socialized to use different modes of problem solving when dealing with conflict, and whether such behaviour might be useful in thinking about international conflict resolution.

Toward a Feminist Epistemology of International Relations

I am deeply aware that there is no *one* feminist approach but many, which come out of various disciplines and intellectual traditions. Yet there are common themes in the different feminist literatures that I have reviewed which could help us to begin to formulate a feminist epistemology of international relations. Morgenthau encourages us to try to stand back from the world and to think about theory building in terms of constructing a rational outline or map that has universal applications. In contrast, the feminist literature reviewed here emphasizes connection and contingency. Keller argues for a form of knowledge, which she calls "dynamic objectivity," "that grants to the world around us its independent integrity, but does so in a way that remains cognizant of, indeed relies on, our connectivity with that world."[32] Keller illustrates this mode of thinking in her study of Barbara McClintock, whose work on genetic transposition won her a Nobel prize after many years of marginalization by the scientific community.[33] McClintock, Keller argues, was a scientist with a respect for complexity, diversity and individual difference whose methodology allowed her data to speak rather than imposing explanations on it.

Keller's portrayal of McClintock's science contains parallels with what Sandra Harding calls an African world view.[34] Harding tells us that the Western liberal notion of rational economic man, an individualist and a welfare maximizer, similar to the image of rational political man on which realism has based its theoretical investigations, does not make any sense in the African world view where the individual is seen as part of the social order acting within that order rather than upon it. Harding believes that this view of human behaviour has much in common with a feminist perspective. If we combine this view of human behaviour with Merchant's holistic perspective which stresses the interconnectedness of all things, including nature, it may help us to begin to think from a more global perspective. Such a perspective appreciates cultural diversity but at the same time recognizes a growing interdependence, which makes anachronistic the exclusionary thinking fostered by the nation state system.

Keller's dynamic objectivity, Harding's African world view and Merchant's ecological thinking all point us in the direction of an appreciation of the "other" as a subject whose views are as legitimate as our own, a way of thinking that has been sadly lacking in the history of international relations. Just as Keller cautions us against the construction of a feminist science which could perpetuate similar exclusionary attitudes, Harding warns us against schema that contrast people by race, gender or class and that originate within projects of social domination. Feminist thinkers generally dislike dichotomization and the distancing of subject from object that goes with abstract thinking, both of which, they believe, encourage a we/they attitude characteristic of international relations. Instead, feminist literature urges us to construct epistemologies that value ambiguity and difference. These qualities could stand us in good stead as we begin to build a human or ungendered theory of international relations which contains elements of both masculine and feminine modes of thought.

Morgenthau's Principles of Political Realism: A Feminist Reformulation

The first part of this paper used feminist theory to develop a critique of Morgenthau's principles of political realism in order to demonstrate how the theory and practice of international relations may exhibit a masculine bias. The second part suggested some contributions that feminist theory might make to reconceptualizing some important elements in international relations and to thinking about a feminist epistemology. Drawing on these observations, this conclusion will present a feminist reformulation of Morgenthau's six principles of political realism, outlined earlier in this paper, which might help us to begin to think differently about international relations. I shall not use the term realism since feminists believe that there are multiple realities: a truly realistic picture of international politics must recognize elements of cooperation as well as conflict, morality as well as *realpolitik*, and the strivings for justice as well as order.[35] This reformulation may help us to think in these multidimensional terms.

1. A feminist perspective believes that objectivity, as it is culturally defined, is associated with masculinity. Therefore, supposedly "objective" laws of human nature are based on a partial, masculine view of human nature. Human nature is both masculine and feminine; it contains elements of social reproduction and development as well as political domination. Dynamic objectivity offers us a more connected view of objectivity with less potential for domination.

2. A feminist perspective believes that the national interest is multidimensional and contextually contingent. Therefore, it cannot be defined solely in terms of power. In the contemporary world the national interest demands cooperative rather than zero sum solutions to a set of interdependent global problems which include nuclear war, economic well-being and environmental degradation.

3. Power cannot be infused with meaning that is universally valid. Power as domination and control privileges masculinity and ignores the possibility of collective empowerment, another aspect of power often associated with femininity.

4. A feminist perspective rejects the possibility of separating moral command from political action. All political action has moral significance. The realist agenda for maximizing order through power and control gives priority to the moral command of order over those of justice and the satisfaction of basic needs necessary to ensure social reproduction.

5. While recognizing that the moral aspirations of particular nations cannot be equated with universal moral principles, a feminist perspective seeks to find common moral elements in human aspirations which could become the basis for de-escalating international conflict and building international community.

6. A feminist perspective denies the autonomy of the political. Since autonomy is associated with masculinity in Western culture, disciplinary efforts to construct a world view which does not rest on a pluralistic conception of human nature are partial and masculine. Building boundaries around a narrowly defined political realm defines political in a way that excludes the concerns and contributions of women.

To construct this feminist alternative is not to deny the validity of Morgenthau's work. But adding a feminist perspective to the epistemology of international relations is a stage through which we must pass if we are to think about constructing an ungendered or human science of international politics which is sensitive to, but goes beyond, both masculine and feminine perspectives. Such inclusionary thinking, as Simone de Beauvoir tells us, values the bringing forth of life as much as the risking of life; it is becoming imperative in a world in which the technology of war and a fragile natural environment threaten human existence. An ungendered, or human, discourse becomes possible only when women are adequately represented in the discipline and when there is equal respect for the contributions of women and men alike.

Questions for Review

Is Tickner claiming that women act differently from men and that if more leaders were female world politics would be very different? What evidence would indicate that Tickner's view is more accurate than Morgenthau's?

Notes

An earlier version of this paper was presented at a symposium on Gender and International Relations at the London School of Economics in June 1988. I would like to thank the editors of *Millennium*, who organized this symposium, for encouraging me to undertake this rewriting. I am also grateful to Hayward Alker Jr. and Susan Okin for their careful reading of the manuscript and helpful suggestions.

1 Quoted in Sandra Harding, *The Science Question in Feminism* (Ithaca, N.Y.: Cornell University Press, 1986), p. 148.

2 In 1987 only 4.8 percent of the top career Foreign Service employees were women. Statement of Patricia Schroeder before the Committee on Foreign Affairs, U.S. House of Representatives, p. 4 *Women's Perspectives on U.S. Foreign Policy: A Compilation of Views* (Washington, D.C.: U.S. Government Printing Office, 1988). For an analysis of women's roles in the American military, see Cynthia Enloe, *Does Khaki Become You? The Militarisation of Women's Lives* (London: Pluto Press, 1983).

3 Edward P. Crapol (ed.), *Women and American Foreign Policy* (Westport, Conn.: Greenwood Press, 1987), p. 167.

4 For an analysis of the role of masculine language in shaping strategic thinking see Carol Cohn, "Sex and Death in the Rational World of Defense Intellectuals," *Signs: Journal of Women in Culture and Society* (Vol. 12, No. 4, Summer 1987).

5 The claim for the dominance of the realist paradigm is supported by John A. Vasquez, "Colouring It Morgenthau: New Evidence for an Old Thesis on Quantitative International Studies," *British Journal of International Studies* (Vol. 3, No. 5, October 1979), pp. 210–28. For a critique of Morgenthau's ambiguous use of language see Inis L. Claude Jr., *Power and International Relations* (New York: Random House, 1962), especially pp. 25–37.

6 These are drawn from Hans Morgenthau, *Politics Among Nations: The Struggle for Power and Peace,* 5th revised edition (New York: Alfred Knopf, 1973), pp. 4–15. I am aware that these principles embody only a partial statement of Morgenthau's very rich study of international politics, a study which deserves a much more detailed analysis than I can give here.

7 This list is a composite of the male/female dichotomies which appear in Evelyn Fox Keller's *Reflections on Gender and Science* (New Haven, Conn.: Yale University Press, 1985) and Harding, *op. cit.*

8 Inge K. Broverman, Susan R. Vogel, Donald M. Broverman, Frank E. Clarkson and Paul S. Rosenkranz, "Sex-role Stereotypes: A Current Appraisal," *Journal of Social Issues* (Vol. 28, No. 2, 1972), pp. 59–78. Replication of this research in the 1980s confirms that these perceptions still hold.

9 Keller, *op. cit.*, p. 130.

10 *Ibid.*, p. 89.

11 *Ibid.*, p. 9.

12 Sara Ann Ketchum, "Female Culture, Woman Culture and Conceptual Change: Toward a Philosophy of Women's Studies," *Social Theory and Practice* (Vol. 6, No. 2, Summer 1980).

13 Others have questioned whether Hobbes's state of nature provides an accurate description of the international system. See, for example. Charles Beitz, *Political Theory and International Relations* (Princeton, N.J.: Princeton University Press, 1979), pp. 35–50; and Stanley Hoffmann, *Duties Beyond Borders* (Syracuse, N.Y.: Syracuse University Press, 1981), chap. 1.

14 Kohlberg's stages of moral development are described and discussed in Robert Kegan, *The Evolving Self: Problem and Process in Human Development* (Cambridge, Mass.: Harvard University Press, 1982), chap. 2.

15 Carol Gilligan, *In a Different Voice: Psychological Theory and Women's Development* (Cambridge, Mass.: Harvard University Press, 1982). See chap. 1 for Gilligan's critique of Kohlberg.

16 There is evidence that, toward the end of his life, Morgenthau himself was aware that his own prescriptions were becoming anachronistic. In a seminar presentation in 1978 he suggested that power politics as the guiding principle for the conduct of international relations had become fatally defective. For a description of this seminar presentation see Francis Anthony Boyle, *World Politics and International Law* (Durham, N.C.: Duke University Press, 1985), pp. 70–4.

17 Nancy C. M. Hartsock, *Money, Sex and Power: Toward a Feminist Historical Materialism* (Boston: Northeastern University Press, 1983), p. 210.

18 Hannah Arendt, *On Violence* (New York: Harcourt, Brace and World, 1969), p. 44. Arendt's definition of power, as it relates to international relations, is discussed more extensively in Jean Bethke Elshtain's "Reflections on War and Political Discourse: Realism, Just War, and Feminism in a Nuclear Age," *Political Theory* (Vol. 13, No. 1, February 1985), pp. 39–57.

19 David McClelland, "Power and the Feminine Role," in David McClelland, *Power: The Inner Experience* (New York: Wiley, 1975).

20 Jane S. Jaquette, "Power as Ideology: A Feminist Analysis," in Judith H. Stiehm (ed.), *Women's Views of the Political World of Men* (Dobbs Ferry, N.Y.: Transnational Publishers, 1984).

21 These examples are cited by Christine Sylvester, "The Emperor's Theories and Transformations: Looking at the Field through Feminist Lenses," in Dennis Pirages and Christine Sylvester (eds.), *Transformations in the Global Political Economy* (Basingstoke UK: Macmillan, 1989).

22 Karl W. Deutsch et al., *Political Community and the North Atlantic Area* (Princeton, N.J.: Princeton University Press, 1957).

23 New thinking is a term that is also being used in the Soviet Union to describe foreign policy reformulations under Gorbachev. There are indications that the Soviets are beginning to conceptualize security in the multidimensional terms described here. See Margot Light, *The Soviet Theory of International Relations* (New York: St. Martin's Press, 1988), chap. 10.

24 This is the argument made by Edward Azar and Chung-in Moon, "Third World National Security: Toward a New Conceptual Framework," *International Interactions* (Vol. 11, No. 2, 1984), pp. 103–35.

25 Johan Galtung, "Violence, Peace, and Peace Research," in Galtung, *Essays in Peace Research,* Vol. I (Copenhagen: Christian Ejlers, 1975).

26 See, for example, Gita Sen and Caren Grown, *Development, Crises and Alternative Visions: Third World Women's Perspectives* (New York: Monthly Review Press, 1987). This is an example of a growing literature on women and development which deserves more attention from the international relations community.

27 Carolyn Merchant, *The Death of Nature: Women, Ecology and the Scientific Revolution* (New York: Harper and Row, 1982), p. xv.

28 Sara Ruddick, "Maternal Thinking" and "Preservative Love and Military Destruction: Some Reflections on Mothering and Peace," in Joyce Treblicot, *Mothering: Essays in Feminist Theory* (Totowa, N.J.: Rowman and Allenhead, 1984).

29 For a more extensive analysis of this issue see Jean Bethke Elshtain, *Women and War* (New York: Basic Books, 1987).

30 This type of conflict resolution contains similarities with the problem solving approach of Edward Azar, John Burton and Herbert Kelman. See, for example, Edward E. Azar and John W. Burton, *International Conflict Resolution: Theory and Practice* (Brighton UK: Wheatsheaf, 1986) and Herbert C. Kelman, "Interactive Problem Solving: A Social-Psychological Approach to Conflict Resolution," in W. Klassen (ed.), *Dialogue Toward Inter-Faith Understanding* (Tantur/Jerusalem: Ecumenical Institute for Theoretical Research, 1986), pp. 293–314.

31 Gilligan, *op. cit.,* pp. 9–10.

32 Keller, *op. cit.,* p. 117.

33 Evelyn Fox Keller, *A Feeling for the Organism: The Life and Work of Barbara McClintock* (New York: Freeman, 1983).

34 Harding, *op. cit.,* chap. 7.

35 "Utopia and reality are . . . the two facets of political science. Sound political thought and sound political life will be found only where both have their place": E. H. Carr, *The Twenty Years Crisis: 1919–1939* (New York: Harper and Row, 1964), p. 10.

What Is Power in Global Affairs?

JOSEPH S. NYE, JR.

Many analysts reject the "elements of national power" approach as misleading and inferior to the behavioral or relational approach that became dominant among social science analysis in the latter half of the twentieth century. Strictly speaking, the skeptics are correct. Power resources are simply the tangible and intangible raw materials or vehicles that underlie power relationships, and whether a given set of resources produces preferred outcomes or not depends upon behavior in context. The vehicle is not the power relationship. Knowing the horsepower and mileage of a vehicle does not tell us whether it will get to the preferred destination.

In practice, discussions of power in global affairs involve both definitions. Many of the terms that we use daily, such as "military power" and "economic power," are hybrids that combine both resources and behaviors. So long as that is the case, we must make clear whether we are speaking of behavioral- or resource-based definitions of power, and we must be aware of the imperfect relation between them. For example, when people speak of the rising power of China or India, they tend to point to the large populations and increased economic or military resources of those countries. But whether the capacity that those resources imply can actually be converted into preferred outcomes will depend upon the contexts and the country's skill in converting resources into strategies that will produce preferred outcomes. These different definitions are summarized in Figure 1.1. The figure also illustrates the more careful relational definition in which power is the ability to alter others' behavior to produce preferred outcomes.

POWER DEFINED AS RESOURCES

context   skill

Power = resources → conversion strategy → preferred outcomes

POWER DEFINED AS BEHAVIORAL OUTCOMES

Power = affect others → re: something → by means → to preferred outcomes
(scope)   (domain)   (coercion, reward, attraction)

Figure 1.1 Power as Resources and Power as Behavioral Outcomes

This is what people are getting at when they say things like "Power doesn't necessarily lead to influence" (though for reasons already explained, that formulation is confusing).

In the end, because it is outcomes, not resources, that we care about, we must pay more attention to contexts and strategies. Power-conversion strategies turn out to be a critical variable that does not receive enough attention. Strategies relate means to ends, and those that combine hard and soft power resources successfully in different contexts are the key to smart power.

Three Aspects of Relational Power

In addition to the distinction between resource and relational definitions of power, it is useful to distinguish three different aspects of relational power: commanding change, controlling agendas, and establishing preferences. All too often these are conflated. For example, a recent book on foreign policy defines power as "getting people or groups to do something they don't want to do." But such a narrow approach can lead to mistakes.

The ability to command others to change their behavior against their initial preferences is one important dimension of relational power, but not the only one. Another dimension is the ability to affect others' preferences so that they want what you want and you need not command them to change. . . . This co-optive power contrasts with and complements command power. It is a mistake to think that power consists of just ordering others to change. You can affect their behavior by shaping their preferences in ways that produce what you want rather than relying on carrots and sticks to change their behavior "when push comes to shove." Sometimes you can get the outcomes you want without pushing or shoving. Ignoring this dimension by using a too narrow definition of power can lead to a poorly shaped foreign policy.

The first aspect, or "face," of power was defined by Yale political scientist Robert Dahl in studies of New Haven in the 1950s, and it is widely used today even though it covers only part of power behavior. This face of power focuses on the ability to get others to act in ways that are contrary to their initial preferences and strategies. To measure or judge power, you have to know how strong another person's or nation's initial preferences were and how much they were changed by your efforts. . . .

In the 1960s, shortly after Dahl developed his widely accepted definition, political scientists Peter Bachrach and Morton Baratz pointed out that Dahl's definition missed what they called the "second face of power." Dahl ignored the dimension of framing and agenda-setting. If ideas and institutions can be used to frame the agenda for action in a way that make others' preferences seem irrelevant or out of bounds, then it may never be necessary to push or shove them. In other words, it may be possible to shape others' preferences by affecting their expectations of what is legitimate or feasible. Agenda-framing focuses on the ability to keep issues off the table, or as Sherlock Holmes might put it, dogs that fail to bark.

Powerful actors can make sure that the less powerful are never invited to the table, or if they get there, the rules of the game have already been set by those who arrived first. . . . Those who are subject to this second face of power may or may not be aware of it. If they accept the legitimacy of the institutions or the social discourse that framed the agenda, they may not feel unduly constrained by the second face of power. But if the agenda of action is constrained by threats of coercion or promises of payments, then it is just an instance of the first face of power. The target's acquiescence in the legitimacy of the agenda is what makes this face of power co-optive and partly constitutive of soft power—the ability to get what you want by the co-optive means of framing the agenda, persuading, and eliciting positive attraction.

Still later, in the 1970s, sociologist Steven Lukes pointed out that ideas and beliefs also help shape others' *initial* preferences. In Dahl's approach, I can exercise power over you by getting you to do what you would otherwise not want to do; in other words, by changing your situation, I can make you change your preferred strategy. But I can also exercise power over you by determining your very wants. I can shape your basic or initial preferences, not merely change the situation in a way that makes you change your strategy for achieving your preferences.

This dimension of power is missed by Dahl's definition. A teenage boy may carefully choose a fashionable shirt to wear to school to attract a girl, but the teenager may not be aware that the reason the shirt is so fashionable is that a national retailer recently launched a major advertising campaign. Both his preference and that of the other teenagers have been formed by an unseen actor who has shaped the structure of preferences. If you can get others to want the same outcomes that you want, it will not be necessary to override their initial desires. Lukes called this the "third face of power." . . .

Table 1.1 Three Aspects of Relational Power

FIRST FACE: A uses threats or rewards to change B's behavior against B's initial preferences and strategies. B knows this and feels the effect of A's power.

SECOND FACE: A controls the agenda of actions in a way that limits B's choices of strategy. B may or may not know this and be aware of A's power.

THIRD FACE: A helps to create and shape B's basic beliefs, perceptions, and preferences. B is unlikely to be aware of this or to realize the effect of A's power.

Some theorists have called these the public, hidden, and invisible faces of power, reflecting the degrees of difficulty that the target has in discovering the source of power. The second and third faces embody aspects of structural power. A structure is simply an arrangement of all the parts of a whole. Humans are embedded in complex structures of culture, social relations, and power that affect and constrain them. . . . Some exercises of power reflect the intentional decisions of particular actors, whereas others are the product of unintended consequences and larger social forces. . . .

Command power (the first face) is very visible and readily grasped. It is the basis for hard power—the ability to get desired outcomes through coercion and payment. The co-optive power of faces two and three is more subtle and therefore less visible. It contributes to soft power, the ability to get preferred outcomes through the co-optive means of agenda-setting, persuasion, and attraction. All too often policymakers have focused solely on hard command power to compel others to act against their preferences and have ignored the soft power that comes from preference formation. But when co-opting is possible, policymakers can save on carrots and sticks.

In global politics, some goals that states seek are more susceptible to the second and third than to the first face of power. Arnold Wolfers once distinguished between what he called possession goals—specific and often tangible objectives—and milieu goals, which are often structural and intangible. For example, access to resources or basing rights or a trade agreement is a possession goal, whereas promoting an open trade system, free markets, democracy, or human rights is a milieu goal. In the terminology used previously, we can think of states having specific goals and general or structural goals. Focusing solely on command power and the first face of power may mislead us about how to promote such goals. For example, in the promotion of democracy, military means alone are less successful than military means combined with soft power approaches—as the United States discovered in Iraq. And the soft power of attraction and persuasion can have both agentic and structural dimensions. For example, a country can try to attract others through actions such as public diplomacy, but it may also attract others through the structural effects of its example or what can be called the "shining city on the hill" effect.

Another reason not to collapse all three faces of power into the first is that doing so diminishes attention to networks, which are an important type of structural power in the twenty-first century. Networks are becoming increasingly important in an information age, and positioning in social networks can be an important power resource. For example, in a hub-and-spokes network, power can derive from being the hub of communications. If you communicate with your other friends through me, that gives me power. If the points on the rim are not directly connected to each other, their dependence on communication through the hub can shape their agenda. For example, even after independence, many communications among former French African colonies ran through Paris, and that increased French power to shape their agenda. . . .

For policy purposes, it can be useful to think of the three faces of power in a reverse sequence from the order in which they were invented by social scientists.

A policymaker should consider preference formation and agenda-framing as means of shaping the environment before turning to the first, or command, face of power. In short, those who insist on collapsing the second and third dimensions of power into the first will miss an increasingly important aspect of power in this century. . . .

Realism and the Full Spectrum of Power Behavior

Realism assumes that in the anarchic conditions of world politics, where there is no higher international government authority above states, they must rely on their own devices to preserve their independence, and that when push comes to shove, the ultima ratio is the use of force. Realism portrays the world in terms of sovereign states aiming to preserve their security, with military force as their ultimate instrument. Thus, war has been a constant aspect of international affairs over the centuries. Realists come in many sizes and shapes, but all tend to argue that global politics is power politics. In this they are right, but some limit their understanding by conceiving of power too narrowly. A pragmatic or common-sense realist takes into account the full spectrum of power resources, including ideas, persuasion, and attraction. Many classical realists of the past understood the role of soft power better than some of their modern progeny.

Realism represents a good first cut at portraying some aspects of international relations. But as we have seen, states are no longer the only important actors in global affairs; security is not the only major outcome that they seek, and force is not the only or always the best instrument available to achieve those outcomes. Indeed, these conditions of complex interdependence are typical of relations among advanced postindustrial countries such as the United States, Canada, Europe, Australia, and Japan. Mutual democracy, liberal culture, and a deep network of transnational ties mean that anarchy has very different effects than realism predicts. In such conditions, a smart power strategy has a much higher mixture of the second and third faces of power.

It is not solely in relations among advanced countries, however, that soft power plays an important role. In an information age, communications strategies become more important, and outcomes are shaped not merely by whose army wins but also by whose story wins. In the fight against terrorism, for example, it is essential to have a narrative that appeals to the mainstream and prevents its recruitment by radicals. In the battle against insurgencies, kinetic military force must be accompanied by soft power instruments that help to win over the hearts and minds (shape the preferences) of the majority of the population. . . .

Soft Power Behavior and Resources

Some critics complain that the prevailing definition of soft power has become fuzzy. . . . But these critics are mistaken because they confuse the actions of a state seeking to achieve desired outcomes with the resources used to produce them. Many types of *resources* can contribute to soft power, but that does not mean that soft power is any type of *behavior*. The use of force, payment, and some agenda-setting based on them I call hard power. Agenda-setting that is regarded as legitimate by the target, positive attraction, and persuasion are the parts of the spectrum of behaviors I include in soft power. Hard power is push; soft power is pull. Fully defined, soft power is the ability to affect others through the co-optive means of framing the agenda, persuading, and eliciting positive attraction in order to obtain preferred outcomes.

Here is a representation of a spectrum of power behaviors:

H A R D	Command → Coerce Threaten Pay Sanction Frame Persuade Attract ← Co-opt	S O F T

In general, the types of resources associated with hard power include tangibles such as force and money. The types of resources associated with soft power often include intangible factors such as institutions, ideas, values, culture, and the perceived legitimacy of policies. But the relationship is not perfect. Intangible resources such as patriotism, morale, and legitimacy strongly affect the military capacity to fight and win. And threats to use force are intangible, even though they are a dimension of hard power.

If we remember the distinction between power resources and power behavior, we realize that the resources often associated with hard power behavior can also produce soft power behavior depending on the context and how they are used. Command power can create resources that in turn can create soft power at a later phase—for example, institutions that will provide soft power resources in the future. Similarly, co-optive behavior can be used to generate hard power resources in the form of military alliance or economic aid. A tangible hard power resource such as a military unit can produce both command behavior (by winning a battle) and co-optive behavior (by attracting) depending on how it is used. And because attraction depends upon the mind of the perceiver, the subject's perceptions play a significant role in whether given resources produce hard or soft power behavior.

For example, naval forces can be used to win battles (hard power) or win hearts and minds (soft power) depending on what the target and what the issue are. The U.S. Navy's help in providing relief to Indonesia after the 2004 East Asian tsunami had a strong effect on increasing Indonesians' attraction to the United States. . . . Similarly, successful economic performance such as that of China can produce both the hard power of sanctions and restricted market access and the soft power of attraction and emulation of success.

Some analysts have misinterpreted soft power as a synonym for culture and then gone on to downgrade its importance. . . . But this criticism confuses the resources that may produce behavior with the behavior itself. Whether the possession of power resources actually produces favorable behavior depends upon the context and the skills of the agent in converting the resources into behavioral outcomes. Eating sushi, trading Pokemon cards, or hiring a Japanese pitcher (as the Boston Red Sox did) does not necessarily convey power to Japan. But this is not unique to soft power resources. Having a larger tank army may produce victory if a battle is fought in a desert, but not if it is fought in a swamp. Similarly, a nice smile can be a soft power resource, and you may be more inclined to do something for me if I smile whenever we meet, but if I smile at your mother's funeral, it may destroy soft power rather than create it.

Soft Power and Smart Power

. . . I developed the term "smart power" in 2004 to counter the misperception that soft power alone can produce effective foreign policy. I defined smart power as the ability to combine hard and soft power resources into effective strategies. Unlike soft power, smart power is an evaluative as well as a descriptive concept. Soft power can be good or bad from a normative perspective, depending on how it is used. Smart power has the evaluation built into the definition. Critics who say "smart power—which can be dubbed Soft Power 2.0—has superseded Soft Power 1.0 in the U.S. foreign policy lexicon" are simply mistaken. A more accurate criticism is that because the concept (unlike that of soft power) has a normative dimension, it often lends itself to slogans, though that need not be the case.

Smart power is available to all states (and nonstate actors), not just the United States. For example . . . small states have often developed smart power strategies. Norway, with 5 million people, has enhanced its attractiveness with legitimizing policies in peacemaking and development assistance, while also being an active and effective participant in NATO. And at the other extreme in terms of population size, China, a rising power in economic and military resources, has deliberately decided to invest in soft power resources so as to make its hard power look less threatening to its neighbors and thus develop a smart strategy.

Smart power goes to the heart of the problem of power conversion. As we saw earlier, some countries and actors may be endowed with greater power resources than others, yet not be very effective in converting the full range of their power resources into strategies that produce the outcomes they seek. Some argue that with an inefficient eighteenth-century government structure, the United States is weak in power conversion. Others respond that much of American strength is generated outside of government by the nation's open economy and civil society. And it may be that power conversion is easier when a country has a surplus of assets and can afford to absorb the costs of mistakes. But the first steps to smart power and effective power-conversion strategies are understanding the full range of power resources and recognizing the problems of combining them effectively in various contexts. . . .

Questions for Review

How are the "faces of power" and the distinction between "hard" and "soft" power related? How has soft power been used to set the international agenda?

Chapter 2
The Meaning of Anarchy

The Anarchic Structure of World Politics

Kenneth N. Waltz

Political Structures

Only through some sort of systems theory can international politics be understood. To be a success, such a theory has to show how international politics can be conceived of as a domain distinct from the economic, social, and other international domains that one may conceive of. To mark international-political systems off from other international systems, and to distinguish systems-level from unit-level forces, requires showing how political structures are generated and how they affect, and are affected by, the units of the system. How can we conceive of international politics as a distinct system? What is it that intervenes between interacting units and the results that their acts and interactions produce? To answer these questions, this chapter first examines the concept of social structure and then defines structure as a concept appropriate for national and for international politics.

A system is composed of a structure and of interacting units. The structure is the system-wide component that makes it possible to think of the system as a whole. The problem is . . . to contrive a definition of structure free of the attributes and the interactions of units. Definitions of structure must leave aside, or abstract from, the characteristics of units, their behavior, and their interactions. Why must those obviously important matters be omitted? They must be omitted so that we can distinguish between variables at the level of the units and variables at the level of the system. The problem is to develop theoretically useful concepts to replace the vague and varying systemic notions that are customarily employed—notions such as environment, situation, context, and milieu. Structure is a useful concept if it gives clear and fixed meaning to such vague and varying terms.

We know what we have to omit from any definition of structure if the definition is to be useful theoretically. Abstracting from the attributes of units means leaving aside questions about the kinds of political leaders, social and economic institutions, and ideological commitments states may have.

Abstracting from relations means leaving aside questions about the cultural, economic, political, and military interactions of states. To say what is to be left out does not indicate what is to be put in. The negative point is important nevertheless because the instruction to omit attributes is often violated and the instruction to omit interactions almost always goes unobserved. But if attributes and interactions are omitted, what is left? The question is answered by considering the double meaning of the term "relation." As S. F. Nadel points out, ordinary language obscures a distinction that is important in theory. "Relation" is used to mean both the interaction of units and the positions they occupy vis-à-vis each other.[1] To define a structure requires ignoring how units relate with one another (how they interact) and concentrating on how they stand in relation to one another (how they are arranged or positioned). Interactions, as I have insisted, take place at the level of the units. How units stand in relation to one another, the way they are arranged or positioned, is not a property of the units. The arrangement of units is a property of the system.

By leaving aside the personality of actors, their behavior, and their interactions, one arrives at a purely positional picture of society. Three propositions follow from this. First, structures may endure while personality, behavior, and interactions vary widely. Structure is sharply distinguished from actions and interactions. Second, a structural definition applies to realms of widely different substance so long as the arrangement of parts is similar.[2] Third, because this is so, theories developed for one realm may with some modification be applicable to other realms as well. . . .

The concept of structure is based on the fact that units differently juxtaposed and combined behave differently and in interacting produce different outcomes. I first want to show how internal political structure can be defined. In a book on international-political theory, domestic political structure has to be examined in order to draw a distinction between expectations about behavior and outcomes in the internal and external realms. Moreover, considering domestic political structure now will make the elusive international-political structure easier to catch later on.

Structure defines the arrangement, or the ordering, of the parts of a system. Structure is not a collection of political institutions but rather the arrangement of them. How is the arrangement defined? The constitution of a state describes some parts of the arrangement, but political structures as they develop are not identical with formal constitutions. In defining structures, the first question to answer is this: What is the principle by which the parts are arranged?

Domestic politics is hierarchically ordered. The units—institutions and agencies—stand vis-à-vis each other in relations of super- and subordination. The ordering principle of a system gives the first, and basic, bit of information about how the parts of a realm are related to each other. In a polity the hierarchy of offices is by no means completely articulated, nor are all ambiguities about relations of super- and subordination removed. Nevertheless, political actors are formally differentiated according to the degrees of their authority, and their distinct functions are specified. By "specified" I do not mean that the law of the land fully describes the duties that different agencies perform, but only that broad agreement prevails on the tasks that various parts of a government are to undertake and on the extent of the power they legitimately wield. Thus Congress supplies the military forces; the President commands them. Congress makes the laws; the executive branch enforces them; agencies administer laws; judges interpret them. Such specification of roles and differentiation of functions is found in any state, the more fully so as the state is more highly developed. The specification of functions of formally differentiated parts gives the second bit of structural information. This second part of the definition adds some content to the structure, but only enough to say more fully how the units stand in relation to one another. The roles and the functions of the British Prime Minister and Parliament, for example, differ from those of the American President and Congress. When offices are juxtaposed and functions are combined in different ways, different behaviors and outcomes result, as I shall shortly show.

The placement of units in relation to one another is not fully defined by a system's ordering principle and by the formal differentiation of its parts. The standing of the units also changes with changes in their relative capabilities. In the performance of their functions, agencies may gain capabilities or lose them. The relation of Prime Minister to Parliament and of President to Congress depends on, and varies with, their relative capabilities. The third part of the definition of structure acknowledges that even while specified functions remain unchanged, units come to stand in different relation to each other through changes in relative capability.

A domestic political structure is thus defined: first, according to the principle by which it is ordered; second, by specification of the functions of formally differentiated units; and third, by the distribution of capabilities across those units. Structure is a highly abstract notion, but the definition of structure does not abstract from everything. To do so would be to leave everything aside and to include nothing at all. The three-part definition of structure includes only what is required to show how the units of the system are positioned or arranged. Everything else is omitted. Concern for tradition and culture, analysis of the character and personality of political actors, consideration of the conflictive and accommodative processes of politics, description of the making and execution of policy—all such matters are left aside. Their omission does not imply their unimportance. They are omitted because we want to figure out the expected effects of structure on process and of process on structure. That can be done only if structure and process are distinctly defined.

I defined domestic political structures first by the principle according to which they are organized or ordered, second by the differentiation of units and the specification of their functions, and third by the distribution of capabilities across units. Let us see how the three terms of the definition apply to international politics.

1. Ordering Principles

Structural questions are questions about the arrangement of the parts of a system. The parts of domestic political systems stand in relations of super- and subordination. Some are entitled to command; others are required to obey. Domestic systems are centralized and hierarchic. The parts of international-political systems stand in relations of coordination. Formally, each is the equal of all the others. None is entitled to command; none is required to obey. International systems are decentralized and anarchic. The ordering principles of the two structures are distinctly different, indeed, contrary to each other. Domestic political structures have governmental institutions and offices as their concrete counterparts. International politics, in contrast, has been called "politics in the absence of government."[3] International organizations do exist, and in ever-growing numbers. Supranational agents able to act effectively, however, either themselves acquire some of the attributes and capabilities of states, as did the medieval papacy in the era of Innocent III, or they soon reveal their inability to act in important ways except with the support, or at least the acquiescence, of the principal states concerned with the matters at hand. Whatever elements of authority emerge internationally are barely once removed from the capability that provides the foundation for the appearance of those elements. Authority quickly reduces to a particular expression of capability. In the absence of agents with system-wide authority, formal relations of super- and subordination fail to develop.

The first term of a structural definition states the principle by which the system is ordered. Structure is an organizational concept. The prominent characteristic of international politics, however, seems to be the lack of order and of organization. How can one think of international politics as being any kind of an order at all? The anarchy of politics internationally is often referred to. If structure is an organizational concept, the terms "structure" and "anarchy" seem to be in contradiction. If international politics is "politics in the absence of government," what are we in the presence of? In looking for international structure, one is brought face to face with the invisible, an uncomfortable position to be in.

The problem is this: how to conceive of an order without an orderer and of organizational effects where formal organization is lacking. Because these are difficult questions, I shall answer them through analogy with microeconomic theory. Reasoning by analogy is helpful where one can move from a domain for which theory is well developed to one where it is not. Reasoning by analogy is permissible where different domains are structurally similar.

Classical economic theory, developed by Adam Smith and his followers, is microtheory. Political scientists tend to think that microtheory is theory about small-scale matters, a usage that ill accords with its established meaning. The term "micro" in economic theory indicates the way in which the theory is constructed rather than the scope of the matters it pertains to. Microeconomic theory describes how an order is spontaneously formed from the self-interested acts and interactions of individual units—in this case, persons and firms. The theory then turns upon the two central concepts of the economic units and of the market. Economic units and economic markets are concepts, not descriptive realities or concrete entities. This must be emphasized since from the early eighteenth century to the present, from the sociologist Auguste Comte to the psychologist George Katona, economic theory has been faulted because its assumptions fail to correspond with realities.[4] Unrealistically, economic theorists conceive of an economy operating in isolation from its society and polity. Unrealistically, economists assume that the economic world is the world of the world. Unrealistically, economists think of the acting unit, the famous "economic man," as a single-minded profit maximizer. They single out one aspect of man and leave aside the wondrous variety of human life. As any moderately sensible economist knows, "economic man" does not exist. Anyone who asks businessmen how they make their decisions will find that the assumption that men are economic maximizers grossly distorts their characters. The assumption that men behave as economic men, which is known to be false as a descriptive statement, turns out to be useful in the construction of theory.

Markets are the second major concept invented by microeconomic theorists. Two general questions must be asked about markets: How are they formed? How do they work? The answer to the first question is this: The market of a decentralized economy is individualist in origin, spontaneously generated, and unintended. The market arises out of the activities of separate units—persons and firms—whose aims and efforts are directed not toward creating an order but rather toward fulfilling their own internally defined interests by whatever means they can muster. The individual unit acts for itself. From the coaction of like units emerges a structure that affects and constrains all of them. Once formed, a market becomes a force in itself, and a force that the constitutive units acting singly or in small numbers cannot control. Instead, in lesser or greater degree as market conditions vary, the creators become the creatures of the market that their activity gave rise to. Adam Smith's great achievement was to show how self-interested, greed-driven actions may produce good social outcomes if only political and social conditions permit free competition. If a laissez-faire economy is harmonious, it is so because the intentions of actors do not correspond with the outcomes their actions produce. What intervenes between the actors and the objects of their action in order to thwart their purposes? To account for the unexpectedly favorable outcomes of selfish acts, the concept of a market is brought into play. Each unit seeks its own good; the result of a number of units simultaneously doing so transcends the motives and the aims of the separate units. Each would like to work less hard and price his product higher. Taken together, all have to work harder and price their products lower. Each firm seeks to increase its profit; the result of many firms doing so drives the profit rate downward. Each man seeks his own end, and, in doing so, produces a result that was no part of his intention. Out of the mean ambition of its members, the greater good of society is produced.

The market is a cause interposed between the economic actors and the results they produce. It conditions their calculations, their behaviors, and their interactions. It is not an agent in the sense of *A* being the agent that produces outcome *X*. Rather it is a structural cause. A market constrains the units that comprise it from taking certain actions and disposes them toward taking others. The market, created by self-directed interacting economic units, selects behaviors according to their consequences. The market rewards some with high profits and assigns others to bankruptcy. Since a market is not an institution or an agent in any concrete or palpable sense, such statements become impressive only if they can be reliably inferred from a theory as part of a set of more elaborate expectations. They can be. Microeconomic theory explains how an economy operates and why certain effects are to be expected. . . .

International-political systems, like economic markets, are formed by the coaction of self-regarding units. International structures are defined in terms of the primary political units of an era, be they city states, empires, or nations. Structures emerge from the coexistence of states. No state intends to participate in the formation of a structure by which it and others will be constrained. International-political systems, like economic markets, are individualist in origin, spontaneously generated, and unintended. In both systems, structures are formed by the coaction of their units. Whether those units live, prosper, or die depends on their own efforts. Both systems are formed and maintained on a principle of self-help that applies to the units. . . .

In a microtheory, whether of international politics or of economics, the motivation of the actors is assumed rather than realistically described. I assume that states seek to ensure their survival. The assumption is a radical simplification made for the sake of constructing theory. The question to ask of the assumption, as ever, is not whether it is true but whether it is the most sensible and useful one that can be made. Whether it is a useful assumption depends on whether a theory based on the assumption can be contrived, a theory from which important consequences not otherwise obvious can be inferred. Whether it is a sensible assumption can be directly discussed.

Beyond the survival motive, the aims of states may be endlessly varied; they may range from the ambition to conquer the world to the desire merely to be left alone. Survival is a prerequisite to achieving any goals that states may have, other than the goal of promoting their own disappearance as political entities. The survival motive is taken as the ground of action in a world where the security of states is not assured, rather than as a realistic description of the impulse that lies behind every act of state. The assumption allows for the fact that no state always acts exclusively to ensure its survival. It allows for the fact that some states may persistently seek goals that they value more highly than survival; they may, for example, prefer amalgamation with other states to their own survival in form. It allows for the fact that in pursuit of its security no state will act with perfect knowledge and wisdom—if indeed we could know what those terms might mean. . . .

Actors may perceive the structure that constrains them and understand how it serves to reward some kinds of behavior and to penalize others. But then again they either may not see it or, seeing it, may for any of many reasons fail to conform their actions to the patterns that are most often rewarded and least often punished. To say that "the structure selects" means simply that those who conform to accepted and successful practices more often rise to the top and are likelier to stay there. The game one has to win is defined by the structure that determines the kind of player who is likely to prosper. . . .

2. The Character of the Units

The second term in the definition of domestic political structure specifies the functions performed by differentiated units. Hierarchy entails relations of super- and subordination among a system's parts, and that implies their differentiation. In defining domestic political structure the second term, like the first and third, is needed because each term points to a possible source of structural variation. The states that are the units of international-political systems are not formally differentiated by the functions they perform. Anarchy entails relations of coordination among a system's units, and that implies their sameness. The second term is not needed in defining international-political structure, because, so long as anarchy endures, states remain like units. International structures vary only through a change of organizing principle or, failing that, through variations in the capabilities of units. Nevertheless I shall discuss these like units here, because it is by their interactions that international-politics structures are generated.

Two questions arise: Why should states be taken as the units of the system? Given a wide variety of states, how can one call them "like units"? Questioning the choice of states as the primary units of international-political systems became popular in the 1960s and 1970s as it was at the turn of the century. Once one understands what is logically involved, the issue is easily resolved. Those who question the state-centric view do so for two main reasons. First, states are not the only actors of importance on the international scene. Second, states are declining in importance, and other actors are gaining, or so it is said. Neither reason is cogent, as the following discussion shows.

States are not and never have been the only international actors. But then structures are defined not by all of the actors that flourish within them but by the major ones. In defining a system's structure one chooses one or some of the infinitely many objects comprising the system and defines its structure in terms of them. For international-political systems, as for any system, one must first decide which units to take as being the parts of the system. Here the economic analogy will help again. The structure of a market is defined by the number of firms competing. If many roughly equal firms contend, a condition of perfect competition is approximated. If a few firms dominate the market, competition is said to be oligopolistic even though many smaller firms may also be in the field. But we are told that definitions of this sort cannot be applied to international politics because of the interpenetration of states, because of their inability to control the environment of their action, and because rising multinational corporations and other nonstate actors are difficult to regulate and may rival some states in influence. The importance of nonstate actors and the extent of transnational activities are obvious. The conclusion that the state-centric conception of international politics is made obsolete by them does not follow. That economists and economically minded politics scientists have thought that it does is ironic. The irony lies in the fact that all of the reasons given for scrapping the state-centric concept can be related more strongly and applied to firms. Firms competing with numerous others have no hope of controlling their market, and oligopolistic firms constantly struggle with imperfect success to do so. Firms interpenetrate, merge, and buy each other up at a merry pace. Moreover, firms are constantly threatened and regulated by, shall we say, "nonfirm" actors. Some governments encourage concentration; others work to prevent it. The market structure of parts of an economy may move from a wider to a narrower competition or may move in the opposite direction, but whatever the extent and the frequency of change, market structures, generated by the interaction of firms, are defined in terms of them.

Just as economists define markets in terms of firms, so I define international-political structures in terms of states. If Charles P. Kindleberger were right in saying that "the nation-state is just about through as an economic unit,"[5] then the structure of international politics would have to be redefined. That would be necessary because economic capabilities cannot be separated from the other capabilities of states. The distinction frequently drawn between matters of high and low politics is misplaced. States use economic means for military and political ends; and military and political means for the achievement of economic interests.

An amended version of Kindleberger's statement may hold: Some states may be nearly washed up as economic entities, and others not. That poses no problem for international-political theory since international politics is mostly about inequalities anyway. So long as the major states are the major actors, the structure of international politics is defined in terms of them. That theoretical statement is of course borne out in practice. States set the scene in which they, along with nonstate actors, state their dramas or carry on their humdrum affairs. Though they may choose to interfere little in the affairs of nonstate actors for long periods of time, states nevertheless set the terms of intercourse, whether by passively permitting informal rules to develop or by actively intervening to change rules that no longer suit them. When the crunch comes, states remake the rules by which other actors operate. Indeed, one may be struck by the ability of weak states to impede the operation of strong international corporations and by the attention the latter pay to the wishes of the former. . . .

States are the units whose interactions form the structure of international-political systems. They will long remain so. The death rate among states is remarkably low. Few states die; many firms do. . . . To call states "like units" is to say that each state is like all other states in being an autonomous political unit. It is another way of saying that states are sovereign. But sovereignty is also a bothersome concept. Many believe, as the anthropologist M. G. Smith has said, that "in a system of sovereign states no state is sovereign."[6] The error lies in identifying the sovereignty of states with their ability to do as they wish. To say that states are sovereign is not to say that they can do as they please, that they are free of others' influence, that they are able to get what they want. Sovereign states may be hardpressed all around, constrained to act in ways they would like to avoid, and able to do hardly anything just as they would like to. The sovereignty of states has never entailed their insulation from the effects of other states' actions. To be sovereign and to be dependent are not contradictory conditions. Sovereign states have seldom led free and easy lives. What then is sovereignty? To say that a state is sovereign means that it decides for itself how it will cope with its internal and external problems, including whether or not to seek assistance from others and in doing so to limit its freedom by making commitments to them. States develop their own strategies, chart their own courses, make their own decisions about how to meet whatever needs they experience and whatever desires they develop. It is no more contradictory to say that sovereign states are always constrained and often tightly so than it is to say that free individuals often make decisions under the heavy pressure of events.

Each state, like every other state, is a sovereign political entity. And yet the differences across states, from Costa Rica to the Soviet Union, from Gambia to the United States, are immense. States are alike, and they are also different. So are corporations, apples, universities, and people. Whenever we put two or more objects in the same category, we are saying that they are alike not in all respects but in some. No two objects in this world are identical, yet they can often be usefully compared and combined. "You can't add apples and oranges" is an old saying that seems to be especially popular among salesmen who do not want you to compare their wares with others. But we all know that the trick of adding dissimilar objects is to express the result in terms of a category that comprises them. Three apples plus four oranges equals seven pieces of fruit. The only interesting question is whether the category that classifies objects according to their common qualities is useful. One can add up a large number of widely varied objects and say that one has eight million things, but seldom need one do that.

States vary widely in size, wealth, power, and form. And yet variations in these and in other respects are variations among like units. In what way are they like units? How can they be placed in a single category? States are alike in the tasks that they face, though not in their abilities to perform them. The differences are of capability, not of function. States perform or try to perform tasks, most of which are common to all of them; the ends they aspire to are similar. Each state duplicates the activities of other states at least to a considerable extent. Each state has its agencies for making, executing, and interpreting laws and regulations, for raising revenues, and for defending itself. Each state supplies out of its own resources and by its own means most of the food, clothing, housing, transportation, and amenities consumed and used by its citizens. All states, except the smallest ones, do much more of their business at home than abroad. One has to be impressed with the functional similarity of states and, now more than ever before, with the similar lines their development follows. From the rich to the poor states, from the old to the new ones, nearly all of them take a larger hand in matters of economic regulation, of education, health, and housing, of culture and the arts, and so on almost endlessly. The increase of the activities of states is a strong and strikingly uniform international trend. The functions of states are similar, and distinctions among them arise principally from their varied capabilities. International politics consists of like units duplicating one another's activities.

3. The Distribution of Capabilities

The parts of a hierarchic system are related to one another in ways that are determined both by their functional differentiation and by the extent of their capabilities. The units of an anarchic system are functionally undifferentiated. The units of such an order are then distinguished primarily by their greater or lesser capabilities for performing similar tasks. This states formally what students of international politics have long noticed. The great powers of an era have always been marked off from others by practitioners and theorists alike. Students of national government make such distinctions as that between parliamentary and presidential systems; governmental systems differ in form. Students of international politics make distinctions between international-political systems only according to the number of their great powers. The structure of a system changes with changes in the distribution of capabilities across the system's units. And changes in structure change expectations about how the units of the system will behave and about the outcomes their interactions will produce. Domestically, the differentiated parts of a system may perform similar tasks. We know from observing the American government that executives sometimes legislate and legislatures sometimes execute. Internationally, like units sometimes perform different tasks . . . but two problems should be considered.

The first problem is this: Capability tells us something about units. Defining structure partly in terms of the distribution of capabilities seems to violate my instruction to keep unit attributes out of structural definitions. As I remarked earlier, structure is a highly but not entirely abstract concept. The maximum of abstraction allows a minimum of content, and that minimum is what is needed to enable one to say how the units stand in relation to one another. States are differently placed by their power. And yet one may wonder why only *capability* is included in the third part of the definition, and not such characteristics as ideology, form of government, peacefulness, bellicosity, or whatever. The answer is this: Power is estimated by comparing the capabilities of a number of units. Although capabilities are attributes of units, the distribution of capabilities across units is not. The distribution of capabilities is not a unit attribute, but rather a system-wide concept. . . .

The second problem is this: Though relations defined in terms of interactions must be excluded from structural definitions, relations defined in terms of grouping of states do seem to tell us something about how states are placed in the system. Why not specify how states stand in relation to one another by considering the alliances they form? Would doing so not be comparable to defining national political structures partly in terms of how presidents and prime ministers are related to other political agents? It would not be. Nationally as internationally, structural definitions deal with the relation of agents and agencies in terms of the organization of realms and not in terms of the accommodations and conflicts that may occur within them or the groupings that may now and then form. Parts of a government may draw together or pull apart, may oppose each other or cooperate in greater or lesser degree. These are the relations that form and dissolve within a system rather than structural alterations that mark a change from one system to another. This is made clear by the example that runs nicely parallel to the case of alliances. Distinguishing systems of political parties according to their number is common. A multiparty system changes if, say, eight parties become two, but not if two groupings of the eight form merely for the occasion of fighting an election. By the same logic, an international-political system in which three or more great powers have split into two alliances remains a multipolar system—structurally distinct from a bipolar system, a system in which no third power is able to challenge the top two. . . .

In defining international-political structures we take states with whatever traditions, habits, objectives, desires, and forms of government they may have. We do not ask whether states are revolutionary or legitimate, authoritarian or democratic, ideological or pragmatic. We abstract from every attribute of states except their capabilities. Nor in thinking about structure do we ask about the relations of states—their feelings of friendship and hostility, their diplomatic exchanges, the alliances they form, and the extent of the contacts and exchanges among them. We ask what range of expectations arises merely from looking at the type of order that prevails among them and at the distribution of capabilities within that order. We abstract from any particular qualities of states and from all of their concrete connections. What emerges is a positional picture, a general description of the ordered overall arrangement of a society written in terms of the placement of units rather than in terms of their qualities. . . .

Anarchic Structures and Balances of Power

[We must now] examine the characteristics of anarchy and the expectations about outcomes associated with anarchic realms. . . . [This] is best accomplished by drawing some comparisons between behavior and outcomes in anarchic and hierarchic realms.

4. Violence at Home and Abroad

The state among states, it is often said, conducts its affairs in the brooding shadow of violence. Because some states may at any time use force, all states must be prepared to do so—or live at the mercy of their militarily more vigorous neighbors. Among states, the state of nature is a state of war. This is meant not in the sense that war constantly occurs but in the sense that, with each state deciding for itself whether or not to use force, war may at any time break out. Whether in the family, the community, or the world at large, contact without at least occasional conflict is inconceivable; and the hope that in the absence of an agent to manage or to manipulate conflicting parties the use of force will always be avoided cannot be realistically entertained. Among men as among states, anarchy, or the absence of government, is associated with the occurrence of violence.

The threat of violence and the recurrent use of force are said to distinguish international from national affairs. But in the history of the world surely most rulers have had to bear in mind that their subjects might use force to resist or overthrow them. If the absence of government is associated with the threat of violence, so also is its presence. A haphazard list of national tragedies illustrates the point all too well. The most destructive wars of the hundred years following the defeat of Napoleon took place not among states but *within* them. Estimates of deaths in China's Taiping Rebellion, which began in 1851 and lasted 13 years, range as high as 20 million. In the American Civil War some 600 thousand people lost their lives. In more recent history, forced collectivation and Stalin's purges eliminated 5 million Russians, and Hitler exterminated 6 million Jews. In some Latin American countries, coups d'état and rebellions have been normal features of national life. Between 1948 and 1957, for example, 200 thousand Colombians were killed in civil strife. In the middle 1970s most inhabitants of Idi Amin's Uganda must have felt their lives becoming nasty, brutish, and short, quite as in Thomas Hobbes's state of nature. If such cases constitute aberrations, they are uncomfortably common ones. We easily lose sight of the fact that struggles to achieve and maintain power, to establish order, and to contrive a kind of justice within states may be bloodier than wars among them.

If anarchy is identified with chaos, destruction, and death, then the distinction between anarchy and government does not tell us much. Which is more precarious: the life of a state among states, or of a government in relation to its subjects? The answer varies with time and place. Among some states at some times, the actual or expected occurrence of violence is low. Within some states at some times, the actual or expected occurrence of violence is high. The use of force, or the constant fear of its use, are not sufficient grounds for distinguishing international from domestic affairs. If the possible and the actual use of force mark both national and international orders, then no durable distinction between the two realms can be drawn in terms of the use or the nonuse of force. No human order is proof against violence.

To discover qualitative differences between internal and external affairs one must look for a criterion other than the occurrence of violence. The distinction between international and national realms of politics is not found in the use or the nonuse of force but in their different structures. But if the dangers of being violently attacked are greater, say, in taking an evening stroll through downtown Detroit than they are in picnicking along the French and German border, what practical difference does the difference of structure make? Nationally as internationally, contact generates conflict and at times issues in violence.

The difference between national and international politics lies not in the use of force but in the different modes of organization for doing something about it. A government, ruling by some standard of legitimacy, arrogates to itself the right to use force—that is, to apply a variety of sanctions to control the use of force by its subjects. If some use private force, others may appeal to the government. A government has no monopoly on the use of force, as is all too evident. An effective government, however, has a monopoly on the *legitimate* use of force, and legitimate here means that public agents are organized to prevent and to counter the private use of force. Citizens need not prepare to defend themselves. Public agencies do that. A national system is not one of self-help. The international system is.

5. Interdependence and Integration

The political significance of interdependence varies depending on whether a realm is organized, with relations of authority specified and established, or remains formally unorganized. Insofar as a realm is formally organized, its units are free to specialize, to pursue their own interests without concern for developing the means of maintaining their identity and preserving their security in the presence of others. They are free to specialize because they have no reason to fear the increased interdependence that goes with specialization. If those who specialize most benefit most, then competition in specialization ensues. Goods are manufactured, grain is produced, law and order are maintained, commerce is conducted, and financial services are provided by people who ever more narrowly specialize. In simple economic terms, the cobbler depends on the tailor for his pants and the tailor on the cobbler for his shoes, and each would be ill-clad without the services of the other. In simple political terms, Kansas depends on Washington for protection and regulation and Washington depends on Kansas for beef and wheat. In saying that in such situations interdependence is close, one need not maintain that the one part could not learn to live without the other. One need only say that the cost of breaking the interdependent relation would be high. Persons and institutions depend heavily on one another because of the different tasks they perform and the different goods they produce and exchange. The parts of a polity bind themselves together by their differences.[7]

Differences between national and international structures are reflected in the ways the units of each system define their ends and develop the means for reaching them. In anarchic realms, like units coact. In hierarchic realms, unlike units interact. In an anarchic realm, the units are functionally similar and tend to remain so. Like units work to maintain a measure of independence and may even strive for autarchy. In a hierarchic realm, the units are differentiated, and they tend to increase the extent of their specialization. Differentiated units become closely interdependent, the more closely so as their specialization proceeds. Because of the difference of structure, interdependence within and interdependence among nations are two distinct concepts. So as to follow the logicians' admonition to keep a single meaning for a given term throughout one's discourse, I shall use "integration" to describe the condition within nations and "interdependence" to describe the condition among them.

Although states are like units functionally, they differ vastly in their capabilities. Out of such differences something of a division of labor develops. The division of labor across nations, however, is slight in comparison with the highly articulated division of labor within them. Integration draws the parts of a nation closely together. Interdependence among nations leaves them loosely connected. Although the integration of nations is often talked about, it seldom takes place. Nations could mutually enrich themselves by further dividing not just the labor that goes into the production of goods but also some of the other tasks they perform, such as political management and military defense. Why does their integration not take place? The structure of international politics limits the cooperation of states in two ways.

In a self-help system each of the units spends a portion of its effort, not in forwarding its own good, but in providing the means of protecting itself against others. Specialization in a system of divided labor works to everyone's advantage, though not equally so. Inequality in the expected distribution of the increased product works strongly against extension of the division of labor internationally. When faced with the possibility of cooperating for mutual gain, states that feel insecure must ask how the gain will be divided. They are compelled to ask not "Will both of us gain?" but "Who will gain more?" If an expected gain is to be divided, say, in the ratio of two to one, one state may use its disproportionate gain to implement a policy intended to damage or destroy the other. Even the prospect of large absolute gains for both parties does not elicit their cooperation so long as each fears how the other will use its increased capabilities. Notice that the impediments to collaboration may not lie in the character and the immediate intention of either party. Instead, the condition of insecurity—at the least, the uncertainty of each about the other's future intentions and actions—works against their cooperation. . . .

A state worries about a division of possible gains that may favor others more than itself. That is the first way in which the structure of international politics limits the cooperation of states. A state also worries lest it become dependent on others through cooperative endeavors and exchanges of goods and services. That is the second way in which the structure of international politics limits the cooperation of states. The more a state specializes, the more it relies on others to supply the materials and goods that it is not producing. The larger a state's imports and exports, the more it depends on others. The world's well-being would be increased if an ever more elaborate division of labor were developed, but states would thereby place themselves in situations of ever closer interdependence. Some states may not resist that. For small and ill-endowed states the costs of doing so are excessively high. But states that can resist becoming ever more enmeshed with others ordinarily do so in either or both of two ways. States that are heavily dependent, or closely interdependent, worry about securing that which they depend on. The high interdependence of states means that the states in question experience, or are subject to, the common vulnerability that high interdependence entails. Like other organizations, states seek to control what they depend on or to lessen the extent of their dependency. This simple thought explains quite a bit of the behavior of states: their imperial thrusts to widen the scope of their control and their autarchic strivings toward greater self-sufficiency.

Structures encourage certain behaviors and penalize those who do not respond to the encouragement. Nationally, many lament the extreme development of the division of labor, a development that results in the allocation of ever narrower tasks to individuals. And yet specialization proceeds, and its extent is a measure of the development of societies. In a formally organized realm a premium is put on each unit's being able to specialize in order to increase its value to others in a system of divided labor. The domestic imperative is "specialize"! Internationally, many lament the resources states spend unproductively for their own defense and the opportunities they miss to enhance the welfare of their people through cooperation with other states. And yet the ways of states change little. In an unorganized realm each unit's incentive is to put itself in a position to be able to take care of itself since no one else can be counted on to do so. The international imperative is "take care of yourself"! Some leaders of nations may understand that the well-being of all of them would increase through their participation in a fuller division of labor. But to act on the idea would be to act on a domestic imperative, an imperative that does not run internationally. What one might want to do in the absence of structural constraints is different from what one is encouraged to do in their presence. States do not willingly place themselves in situations of increased dependence. In a self-help system, considerations of security subordinate economic gain to political interest. . . .

6. Structures and Strategies

That motives and outcomes may well be disjoined should now be easily seen. Structures cause nations to have consequences they were not intended to have. Surely most of the actors will notice that, and at least some of them will be able to figure out why. They may develop a pretty good sense of just how structures work their effects. Will they not then be able to achieve their original ends by appropriately adjusting their strategies? Unfortunately, they often cannot. To show why this is so I shall give only a few examples; once the point is made, the reader will easily think of others.

If shortage of a commodity is expected, all are collectively better off if they buy less of it in order to moderate price increases and to distribute shortages equitably. But because some will be better off if they lay in extra supplies quickly, all have a strong incentive to do so. If one expects others to make a run on a bank, one's prudent course is to run faster than they do even while knowing that if few others run, the bank will remain solvent, and if many run, it will fail. In such cases, pursuit of individual interest produces collective results that nobody wants, yet individuals by behaving differently will hurt themselves without altering outcomes. These two much used examples establish the main point. Some courses of action cannot sensibly follow unless you and I are pretty sure that many others will as well. . . .

We may well notice that our behavior produces unwanted outcomes, but we are also likely to see that such instances as these are examples of what Alfred E. Kahn describes as "large" changes that are brought about by the accumulation of "small" decisions. In such situations people are victims of the "tyranny of small decisions," a phrase suggesting that "if one hundred consumers choose option x, and this causes the market to make decision X (where X equals $100x$), it is not necessarily true that those same consumers would have voted for that outcome if that large decision had ever been presented for their explicit consideration."[8] If the market does not present the large question for decision, then individuals are doomed to making decisions that are sensible within their narrow contexts even though they know all the while that in making such decisions they are bringing about a result that most of them do not want. Either that or they organize to overcome some of the effects of the market by changing its structure—for example, by bringing consumer units roughly up to the size of the units that are making producers' decisions. This nicely makes the point: So long as one leaves the structure unaffected it is not possible for changes in the intentions and the actions of particular actors to produce desirable outcomes or to avoid undesirable ones. . . . The only remedies for strong structural effects are structural changes.

Structural constraints cannot be wished away, although many fail to understand this. In every age and place, the units of self-help systems—nations, corporations, or whatever—are told that the greater good, along with their own, requires them to act for the sake of the system and not for their own narrowly defined advantage. In the 1950s, as fear of the world's destruction in nuclear war grew, some concluded that the alternative to world destruction was world disarmament. In the 1970s, with the rapid growth of population, poverty, and pollution, some concluded, as one political scientist put it, that "states must meet the needs of the political ecosystem in its global dimensions or court annihilation."[9] The international interest must be served; and if that means anything at all, it means that national interests are subordinate to it. The problems are found at the global level. Solutions to the problems continue to depend on national policies. What are the conditions that would make nations more or less willing to obey the injunctions that are so often laid on them? How can they resolve the tension between pursuing their own interests and acting for the sake of the system? No one has shown how that can be done, although many wring their hands and plead for rational behavior. The very problem, however, is that rational behavior, given structural constraints, does not lead to the wanted results. With each country constrained to take care of itself, no one can take care of the system.[10]

A strong sense of peril and doom may lead to a clear definition of ends that must be achieved. Their achievement is not thereby made possible. The possibility of effective action depends on the ability to provide necessary means. It depends even more so on the existence of conditions that permit nations and other organizations to follow appropriate policies and strategies. World-shaking problems cry for global solutions, but there is no global agency to provide them. Necessities do not create possibilities. Wishing that final causes were efficient ones does not make them so.

Great tasks can be accomplished only by agents of great capability. That is why states, and especially the major ones, are called on to do what is necessary for the world's survival. But states have to do whatever they think necessary for their own preservation, since no one can be relied on to do it for them. Why the advice to place the international interest above national interests is meaningless can be explained precisely in terms of the distinction between micro- and macrotheories. . . .

Some have hoped that changes in the awareness and purpose, in the organization and ideology of states would change the quality of international life. Over the centuries states have changed in many ways, but the quality of international life has remained much the same. States may seek reasonable and worthy ends, but they cannot figure out how to reach them. The problem is not in their stupidity or ill will, although one does not want to claim that those qualities are lacking. The depth of the difficulty is not understood until one realizes that intelligence and goodwill cannot discover and act on adequate programs. Early in the 20th century Winston Churchill observed that the British-German naval race promised disaster *and* that Britain had no realistic choice other than to run it. States facing global problems are like individual consumers trapped by the "tyranny of small decisions." States, like consumers, can get out of the trap only by changing the structure of their field of activity. The message bears repeating: The only remedy for a strong structural effect is a structural change.

7. The Virtues of Anarchy

To achieve their objectives and maintain their security, units in a condition of anarchy—be they people, corporations, states, or whatever—must rely on the means they can generate and the arrangements they can make for themselves. Self-help is necessarily the principle of action in an anarchic order. A self-help situation is one of high risk—of bankruptcy in the economic realm and of war in a world of free states. It is also one in which organizational costs are low. Within an economy or within an international order, risks may be avoided or lessened by moving from a situation of coordinate action to one of super- and subordination, that is, by erecting agencies with effective authority and extending a system of rules. Government emerges where the functions of regulation and management themselves become distinct and specialized tasks. The costs of maintaining a hierarchic order are frequently ignored by those who deplore its absence. Organizations have at least two aims: to get something done and to maintain themselves as organizations. Many of their activities are directed toward the second purpose. The leaders of organizations, and political leaders preeminently, are not masters of the matters their organizations deal with. They have become leaders not by being experts on one thing or another but by excelling in the organizational arts—in maintaining control of a group's members, in eliciting predictable and satisfactory efforts from them, in holding a group together. In making political decisions, the first and most important concern is not to achieve the aims the members of an organization may have but to secure the continuity and health of the organization itself.[11]

Along with the advantages of hierarchic orders go the costs. In hierarchic orders, moreover, the means of control become an object of struggle. Substantive issues become entwined with efforts to influence or control the controllers. The hierarchic ordering of politics adds one to the already numerous objects of struggle, and the object added is at a new order of magnitude.

If the risks of war are unbearably high, can they be reduced by organizing to manage the affairs of nations? At a minimum, management requires controlling the military forces that are at the disposal of states. Within nations, organizations have to work to maintain themselves. As organizations, nations, in working to maintain themselves, sometimes have to use force against dissident elements and areas. As hierarchical systems, governments nationally or globally are disrupted by the defection of major parts. In a society of states with little coherence, attempts at world government would founder on the inability of an emerging central authority to mobilize the resources needed to create and maintain the unity of the system by regulating and managing its parts. The prospect of world government would be an invitation to prepare for world civil war. . . . States cannot entrust managerial powers to a central agency unless that agency is able to protect its client states. The more powerful the clients and the more the power of each of them appears as a threat to the others, the greater the power lodged in the center must be. The greater the power of the center, the stronger the incentive for states to engage in a struggle to control it.

States, like people, are insecure in proportion to the extent of their freedom. If freedom is wanted, insecurity must be accepted. Organizations that establish relations of authority and control may increase insecurity as they decrease freedom. If might does not make right, whether among people or states, then some institution or agency has intervened to lift them out of nature's realm. The more influential the agency, the stronger the desire to control it becomes. In contrast, units in an anarchic order act for their own sakes and not for the sake of preserving an organization and furthering their fortunes within it. Force is used for one's own interest. In the absence of organization, people or states are free to leave one another alone. Even when they do not do so, they are better able, in the absence of the politics of the organization, to concentrate on the politics of the problem and to aim for a minimum agreement that will permit their separate existence rather than a maximum agreement for the sake of maintaining unity. If might decides, then bloody struggles over right can more easily be avoided.

Nationally, the force of a government is exercised in the name of right and justice. Internationally, the force of a state is employed for the sake of its own protection and advantage. Rebels challenge a government's claim to authority; they question the rightfulness of its rule. Wars among states cannot settle questions of authority and right; they can only determine the allocation of gains and losses among contenders and settle for a time the question of who is the stronger.

Nationally, relations of authority are established. Internationally, only relations of strength result. Nationally, private force used against a government threatens the political system. Force used by a state—a public body—is, from the international perspective, the private use of force; but there is no government to overthrow and no governmental apparatus to capture. Short of a drive toward world hegemony, the private use of force does not threaten the system of international politics, only some of its members. War pits some states against others in a struggle among similarly constituted entities. The power of the strong may deter the weak from asserting their claims, not because the weak recognize a kind of rightfulness of rule on the part of the strong, but simply because it is not sensible to tangle with them. Conversely, the weak may enjoy considerable freedom of action if they are so far removed in their capabilities from the strong that the latter are not much bothered by their actions or much concerned by marginal increases in their capabilities.

National politics is the realm of authority, of administration, and of law. International politics is the realm of power, of struggle, and of accommodation. The international realm is preeminently a political one. The national realm is variously described as being hierarchic, vertical, centralized, heterogeneous, directed, and contrived; the international realm, as being anarchic, horizontal, decentralized, homogeneous, undirected, and mutually adaptive. The more centralized the order, the nearer to the top the locus of decisions ascends. Internationally, decisions are made at the bottom level, there being scarcely any other. In the vertical–horizontal dichotomy, international structures assume the prone position. Adjustments are made internationally, but they are made without a formal or authoritative adjuster. Adjustment and accommodation proceed by mutual adaptation.[12] Action and reaction, and reaction to the reaction, proceed by a piecemeal process. The parties feel each other out, so to speak, and define a situation simultaneously with its development. Among coordinate units, adjustment is achieved and accommodations arrived at by the exchange of "considerations," in a condition, as Chester Barnard put it, "in which the duty of command and the desire to obey are essentially absent."[13] Where the contest is over considerations, the parties seek to maintain or improve their positions by maneuvering, by bargaining, or by fighting. The manner and intensity of the competition is determined by the desires and the abilities of parties that are at once separate and interacting.

Whether or not by force, each state plots the course it thinks will best serve its interests. If force is used by one state or its use is expected, the recourse of other states is to use force or be prepared to use it singly or in combination. No appeal can be made to a higher entity clothed with the authority and equipped with the ability to act on its own initiative. Under such conditions the possibility that force will be used by one or another of the parties looms always as a threat in the background. In politics force is said to be the *ultima ratio*. In international politics force serves, not only as the *ultima ratio,* but indeed as the first and constant one. To limit force to being the *ultima ratio* of politics implies, in the words of Ortega y Gasset, "the previous submission of force to methods of reason."[14] The constant possibility that force will be used limits manipulations, moderates demands, and serves as an incentive for the settlement of disputes. One who knows that pressing too hard may lead to war has strong reason to consider whether possible gains are worth the risks entailed. The threat of force internationally is comparable to the role of the strike in labor and management bargaining. "The few strikes that take place are in a sense," as Livernash has said, "the cost of the strike option which produces settlements in the large mass of negotiations."[15] Even if workers seldom strike, their doing so is always a possibility. The possibility of industrial dispute, leading to long and costly strikes encourages labor and management to face difficult issues, to try to understand each other's problems, and to work hard to find accommodations. The possibility that conflicts among nations may lead to long and costly wars has similarly sobering effects.

8. Anarchy and Hierarchy

I have described anarchies and hierarchies as though every political order were of one type or the other. Many, and I suppose most, political scientists who write of structures allow for a greater, and sometimes for a bewildering, variety of types. Anarchy is seen as one end of a continuum whose other end is marked by the presence of a legitimate and competent government. International politics is then described as being flecked with particles of government and alloyed with elements of community—supranational organizations whether universal or regional, alliances, multinational corporations, networks of trade, and whatnot. International-political systems are thought of as being more or less anarchic.

Those who view the world as a modified anarchy do so, it seems, for two reasons. First, anarchy is taken to mean not just the absence of government but also the presence of disorder and chaos. Since world politics, although not reliably peaceful, falls short of unrelieved chaos, students are inclined to see a lessening of anarchy in each outbreak of peace. Since world politics, although not formally organized, is not entirely without institutions and orderly procedures, students are inclined to see a lessening of anarchy when alliances form, when transactions across national borders increase, and when international agencies multiply. Such views confuse structure with process, and I have drawn attention to that error often enough.

Second, the two simple categories of anarchy and hierarchy do not seem to accommodate the infinite social variety our senses record. Why insist on reducing the types of structure to two instead of allowing for a greater variety? Anarchies are ordered by the juxtaposition of similar units, but those similar units are not identical. Some specialization by function develops among them. Hierarchies are ordered by the social division of labor among units specializing in different tasks, but the resemblance of units does not vanish. Much duplication of effort continues. All societies are organized segmentally or hierarchically in greater or lesser degree. Why not, then, define additional social types according to the mixture of organizing principles they embody? One might conceive of some societies approaching the purely anarchic, of others approaching the purely hierarchic, and of still others reflecting specified mixes of the two organizational types. In anarchies the exact likeness of units and the determination of relations by capability alone would describe a realm wholly of politics and power with none of the interaction of units guided by administration and conditioned by authority. In hierarchies the complete differentiation of parts and the full specification of their functions would produce a realm wholly of authority and administration with none of the interaction of parts affected by politics and power. Although such pure orders do not exist, to distinguish realms by their organizing principles is nevertheless proper and important.

Increasing the number of categories would bring the classification of societies closer to reality. But that would be to move away from a theory claiming explanatory power to a less theoretical system promising greater descriptive accuracy. One who wishes to explain rather than to describe should resist moving in that direction if resistance is reasonable. Is it? What does one gain by insisting on two types when admitting three or four would still be to simplify boldly? One gains clarity and economy of concepts. A new concept should be introduced only to cover matters that existing concepts do not reach. If some societies are neither anarchic or hierarchic, if their structures are defined by some third ordering principle, then we would have to define a third system.[16] All societies are mixed. Elements in them represent both of the ordering principles. That does not mean that some societies are ordered according to a third principle. Usually one can easily identify the principle by which a society is ordered. The appearance of anarchic sectors within hierarchies does not alter and should not obscure the ordering principle of the larger system, for those sectors are anarchic only within limits. The attributes and behavior of the units populating those sectors within the larger system differ, moreover, from what they should be and how they would behave outside of it. Firms in oligopolistic markets again are perfect examples of this. They struggle against one another, but because they need not prepare to defend themselves physically, they can afford to specialize and to participate more fully in the division of economic labor than states can. Nor do the states that populate an anarchic world find it impossible to work with one another, to make agreements limiting their arms, and to cooperate in establishing organizations. Hierarchic elements within international structures limit and restrain the exercise of sovereignty but only in ways strongly conditioned by the anarchy of the larger system. The anarchy of that order strongly affects the likelihood of cooperation, the extent of arms agreements, and the jurisdiction of international organizations. . . .

Questions for Review·

How can an abstract characteristic like anarchy be a force in world politics? Are domestic and international politics as different as Waltz implies?

Notes

1 S. F. Nadel, *The Theory of Social Structure* (Glencoe, Ill.: Free Press, 1957), pp. 8–11.

2 Ibid., pp. 104–9.

3 William T. R. Fox, "The Uses of International Relations Theory," in William T. R. Fox, ed., *Theoretical Aspects of International Relations* (Notre Dame, Ind.: University of Notre Dame Press, 1959), p. 35.

4 Marriet Martineau, *The Positive Philosophy of Auguste Comte: Freely Translated and Condensed,* 3rd ed. (London: Kegan Paul, Trench, Trubner, 1983), Vol. 2, pp. 51–53; George Katona, "Rational Behavior and Economic Behavior," *Psychological Review* 60 (September 1953).

5 Charles P. Kindleberger, *American Business Abroad* (New Haven, Ct.: Yale University Press, 1969), p. 207.

6 Smith should know better. Translated into terms that he has himself so effectively used, to say that states are sovereign is to say that they are segments of a plural society. See his "A Structural Approach to Comparative Politics" in David Easton, ed., *Varieties of Politics Theories* (Englewood Cliffs, N.J.: Prentice Hall, 1966), p. 122 cf. his "On Segmentary Lineage Systems," *Journal of the Royal Anthropological Society of Great Britain and Ireland* 86 (July–December 1956).

7 Émile Durkheim, *The Division of Labor in Society,* trans. George Simpson (New York: Free Press, 1964), p. 212.

8 Alfred E. Kahn, "The Tyranny of Small Decisions: Market Failure, Imperfections and Limits of Econometrics," in Bruce M. Russett, ed., *Economic Theories of International Relations* (Chicago, Ill.: Markham, 1966), p. 23.

9 Richard W. Sterling, *Macropolitics: International Relations in a Global Society* (New York: Knopf, 1974), p. 336.

10 Put differently, states face a "prisoners' dilemma." If each of two parties follows his own interest, both end up worse off than if each acted to achieve joint interests. For thorough examination of the logic of such situations, see Glenn H. Snyder and Paul Diesing, *Conflict among Nations* (Princeton, N.J.: Princeton University Press, 1977); for brief and suggestive international applications, see Robert Jervis, "Cooperation under the Security Dilemma," *World Politics* 30 (January 1978).

11 Cf. Paul Diesing, *Reason in Society* (Urbana, Ill.: University of Illinois Press, 1962), pp. 198–204; Anthony Downs, *Inside Bureaucracy* (Boston: Little, Brown, 1967), pp. 262–70.

12 Cf. Chester I. Barnard, "On Planning for World Government," in Chester I. Barnard, ed., *Organization and Management* (Cambridge, Mass.: Harvard University Press, 1948), pp. 148–52; Michael Polanyi, "The Growth of Thought in Society," *Economica* 8 (November 1941), pp. 428–56.

13 Barnard, "On Planning," pp. 150–51.

14 Quoted in Chalmers A. Johnson, *Revolutionary Change* (Boston: Little, Brown, 1966), p. 13.

15 E. R. Livernash, "The Relation of Power to the Structure and Process of Collective Bargaining," in Bruce M. Russett, ed., *Economic Theories of International Politics* (Chicago, Ill.: Markham, 1963), p. 430.

16 Émile Durkheim's depiction of solidary and mechanical societies still provides the best explication of the two ordering principles, and his logic in limiting the types of society to two continues to be compelling despite the efforts of his many critics to overthrow it (see esp. *The Division of Labor in Society*).

Anarchy and the Struggle for Power

JOHN J. MEARSHEIMER

Great powers, I argue, are always searching for opportunities to gain power over their rivals, with hegemony as their final goal. This perspective does not allow for status quo powers, except for the unusual state that achieves preponderance. Instead, the system is populated with great powers that have revisionist intentions at their core. This chapter presents a theory that explains this competition for power. Specifically, I attempt to show that there is a compelling logic behind my claim that great powers seek to maximize their share of world power. . . .

Why States Pursue Power

My explanation for why great powers vie with each other for power and strive for hegemony is derived from five assumptions about the international system. None of these assumptions alone mandates that states behave competitively. Taken together, however, they depict a world in which states have considerable reason to think and sometimes behave aggressively. In particular, the system encourages states to look for opportunities to maximize their power vis-à-vis other states. . . .

The first assumption is that the international system is anarchic, which does not mean that it is chaotic or riven by disorder. It is easy to draw that conclusion, since realism depicts a world characterized by security competition and war. By itself, however, the realist notion of anarchy has nothing to do with conflict; it is an ordering principle, which says that the system comprises independent states that have no central authority above them. Sovereignty, in other words, inheres in states because there is no higher ruling body in the international system. There is no "government over governments."

The second assumption is that great powers inherently possess some offensive military capability, which gives them the wherewithal to hurt and possibly destroy each other. States are potentially dangerous to each other, although some states have more military might than others and are therefore more dangerous. A state's military power is usually identified with the particular weaponry at its disposal, although even if there were no weapons, the individuals in those states could still would countenance attacking the United States, which is far more powerful than its neighbors. The ideal situation is to be the hegemon in the system. . . . Survival would then be almost guaranteed.

Consequently, states pay close attention to how power is distributed among them, and they make a special effort to maximize their share of world power. Specifically, they look for opportunities to alter the balance of power by acquiring additional increments of power at the expense of potential rivals. States employ a variety of means—economic, diplomatic, and military—to shift the balance of power in their favor, even if doing so makes other states suspicious or even hostile. Because one state's gain in power is another state's loss, great powers tend to have a zero-sum mentality when dealing with each other. The trick, of course, is to be the winner in this competition and to dominate the other states in the system. Thus, the claim that states maximize relative power is tantamount to arguing that states are disposed to think offensively toward other states, even though their ultimate motive is simply to survive. In short, great powers have aggressive intentions.

Even when a great power achieves a distinct military advantage over its rivals, it continues looking for chances to gain more power. The pursuit of power stops only when hegemony is achieved. The idea that a great power might feel secure without dominating the system, provided it has an "appropriate amount" of power, is not persuasive, for two reasons. First, it is difficult to assess how much relative power one state must have over its rivals before it is secure. Is twice as much power an appropriate threshold? Or is three times as much power the magic number? The root of the problem is that power calculations alone do not determine which side wins a war. Clever strategies, for example, sometimes allow less powerful states to defeat more powerful foes.

Second, determining how much power is enough becomes even more complicated when great powers contemplate how power will be distributed among them ten or twenty years down the road. The capabilities of individual states vary over time, sometimes markedly, and it is often difficult to predict the direction and scope of change in the balance of power. Remember, few in the West anticipated the collapse of the Soviet Union before it happened. In fact, during the first half of the Cold War, many in the West feared that the Soviet economy would eventually generate greater wealth than the American economy, which would cause a marked power shift against the United States and its allies. What the future holds for China and Russia and what the balance of power will look like in 2020 is difficult to foresee.

Given the difficulty of determining how much power is enough for today and tomorrow, great powers recognize that the best way to ensure their security is to achieve hegemony now, thus eliminating any possibility of a challenge by another great power. Only a misguided state would pass up an opportunity to be the hegemon in the system because it thought it already had sufficient power to survive. But even if a great power does not have the wherewithal to achieve hegemony (and that is usually the case), it will still act offensively to amass as much power as it can, because states are almost always better off with more rather than less power. In short, states do not become status quo powers until they completely dominate the system.

All states are influenced by this logic, which means that not only do they look for opportunities to take advantage of one another, they also work to ensure that other states do not take advantage of them. After all, rival states are driven by the same logic, and most states are likely to recognize their own motives at play in the actions of other states. In short, states ultimately pay attention to defense as well as offense. They think about conquest themselves, and they work to check aggressor states from gaining power at their expense. This inexorably leads to a world of constant security competition, where states are willing to lie, cheat, and use brute force if it helps them gain advantage over their rivals. Peace, if one defines that concept as a state of tranquility or mutual concord, is not likely to break out in this world. . . .

It should be apparent from this discussion that saying that states are power maximizers is tantamount to saying that they care about relative power, not absolute power. There is an important distinction here, because states concerned about relative power behave differently than do states interested in absolute power. States that maximize relative power are concerned primarily with the distribution of material capabilities. In particular, they try to gain as large a power advantage as possible over potential rivals, because power is the best means to survival in a dangerous world. Thus, states motivated by relative power concerns are likely to forgo large gains in their own power, if such gains give rival states even greater power, for smaller national gains that nevertheless provide them with a power advantage over their rivals. States that maximize absolute power, on the other hand, care only about the size of their own gains, not those of other states. They are not motivated by balance-of-power logic but instead are concerned with amassing power without regard to how much power other states control. They would jump at the opportunity for large gains, even if a rival gained more in the deal. Power, according to this logic, is not a means to an end (survival), but an end in itself.

Calculated Aggression

There is obviously little room for status quo powers in a world where states are inclined to look for opportunities to gain more power. Nevertheless, great powers cannot always act on their offensive intentions, because behavior is influenced not only by what states want, but also by their capacity to realize these desires. Every state might want to be king of the hill, but not every state has the wherewithal to compete for that lofty position, much less achieve it. Much depends on how military might is distributed among the great powers. A great power that has a marked power advantage over its rivals is likely to behave more aggressively, because it has the capability as well as the incentive to do so.

By contrast, great powers facing powerful opponents will be less inclined to consider offensive action and more concerned with defending the existing balance of power from threats by their more powerful opponents. Let there be an opportunity for those weaker states to revise the balance in their own favor, however, and they will take advantage of it.

In short, great powers are not mindless aggressors so bent on gaining power that they charge headlong into losing wars or pursue Pyrrhic victories. On the contrary, before great powers take offensive actions, they think carefully about the balance of power and about how other states will react to their moves. They weigh the costs and risks of offense against the likely benefits. If the benefits do not outweigh the risks, they sit tight and wait for a more propitious moment. Nor do states start arms races that are unlikely to improve their overall position. . . . States sometimes limit defense spending either because spending more would bring no strategic advantage or because spending more would weaken the economy and undermine the state's power in the long run. To paraphrase Clint Eastwood, a state has to know its limitations to survive in the international system.

Nevertheless, great powers miscalculate from time to time because they invariably make important decisions on the basis of imperfect information. States hardly ever have complete information about any situation they confront. There are two dimensions to this problem. Potential adversaries have incentives to misrepresent their own strength or weakness, and to conceal their true aims. For example, a weaker state trying to deter a stronger state is likely to exaggerate its own power to discourage the potential aggressor from attacking. On the other hand, a state bent on aggression is likely to emphasize its peaceful goals while exaggerating its military weakness, so that the potential victim does not build up its own arms and thus leaves itself vulnerable to attack. Probably no national leader was better at practicing this kind of deception than Adolf Hitler.

But even if disinformation was not a problem, great powers are often unsure about how their own military forces, as well as the adversary's, will perform on the battlefield. For example, it is sometimes difficult to determine in advance how new weapons and untested combat units will perform in the face of enemy fire. Peace time maneuvers and war games are helpful but imperfect indicators of what is likely to happen in actual combat. Fighting wars is a complicated business in which it is often difficult to predict outcomes. . . .

Great powers are also sometimes unsure about the resolve of opposing states as well as allies. For example, Germany believed that if it went to war against France and Russia in the summer of 1914, the United Kingdom would probably stay out of the fight. Saddam Hussein expected the United States to stand aside when he invaded Kuwait in August 1990. Both aggressors guessed wrong, but each had good reason to think that its initial judgment was correct. In the 1930s, Adolf Hitler believed that his great-power rivals would be easy to exploit and isolate because each had little interest in fighting Germany and instead was determined to get someone else to assume that burden. He guessed right. In short, great powers constantly find themselves confronting situations in which they have to make important decisions with incomplete information. Not surprisingly, they sometimes make faulty judgments and end up doing themselves serious harm.

Some defensive realists go so far as to suggest that the constraints of the international system are so powerful that offense rarely succeeds, and that aggressive great powers invariably end up being punished. . . . They emphasize that (1) threatened states balance against aggressors and ultimately crush them, and (2) there is an offense-defense balance that is usually heavily tilted toward the defense, thus making conquest especially difficult. Great powers, therefore, should be content with the existing balance of power and not try to change it by force. . . .

There is no question that systemic factors constrain aggression, especially balancing by threatened states. But defensive realists exaggerate those restraining forces. Indeed, the historical record provides little support for their claim that offense rarely succeeds. One study estimates that there were 63 wars between 1815 and 1980, and the initiator won 39 times, which translates into about a 60 percent success rate. . . . In short, the historical record shows that offense sometimes succeeds and sometimes does not. The trick for a sophisticated power maximizer is to figure out when to raise and when to fold.

Hegemony's Limits

Great powers, as I have emphasized, strive to gain power over their rivals and hopefully become hegemons. Once a state achieves that exalted position, it becomes a status quo power. More needs to be said, however, about the meaning of hegemony.

A hegemon is a state that is so powerful that it dominates all the other states in the system. No other state has the military wherewithal to put up a serious fight against it. In essence, a hegemon is the only great power in the system. A state that is substantially more powerful than the other great powers in the system is not a hegemon, because it faces, by definition, other great powers. The United Kingdom in the mid-nineteenth century, for example, is sometimes called a hegemon. But it was not a hegemon, because there were four other great powers in Europe at the time—Austria, France, Prussia, and Russia—and the United Kingdom did not dominate them in any meaningful way. In fact, during that period, the United Kingdom considered France to be a serious threat to the balance of power. Europe in the nineteenth century was multipolar, not unipolar.

Hegemony means domination of the system, which is usually interpreted to mean the entire world. It is possible, however, to apply the concept of a system more narrowly and use it to describe particular regions, such as Europe, Northeast Asia, and the Western Hemisphere. Thus, one can distinguish between *global hegemons*, which dominate the world, and *regional hegemons*, which dominate distinct geographical areas. The United States has been a regional hegemon in the Western Hemisphere for at least the past one hundred years. No other state in the Americas has sufficient military might to challenge it, which is why the United States is widely recognized as the only great power in its region. . . .

Power and Fear

That great powers fear each other is a central aspect of life in the international system. But as noted, the level of fear varies from case to case. For example, the Soviet Union worried much less about Germany in 1930 than it did in 1939. How much states fear each other matters greatly, because the amount of fear between them largely determines the severity of their security competition, as well as the probability that they will fight a war. The more profound the fear is, the more intense is the security competition, and the more likely is war. The logic is straightforward: a scared state will look especially hard for ways to enhance its security, and it will be disposed to pursue risky policies to achieve that end. Therefore, it is important to understand what causes states to fear each other more or less intensely.

Fear among great powers derives from the fact that they invariably have some offensive military capability that they can use against each other, and the fact that one can never be certain that other states do not intend to use that power against oneself. Moreover, because states operate in an anarchic system, there is no night watchman to whom they can turn for help if another great power attacks them. Although anarchy and uncertainty about other states' intentions create an irreducible level of fear among states that leads to power-maximizing behavior, they cannot account for why sometimes that level of fear is greater than at other times. The reason is that anarchy and the difficulty of discerning state intentions are constant facts of life, and constants cannot explain variation. The capability that states have to threaten each other, however, varies from case to case, and it is the key factor that drives fear levels up and down. Specifically, the more power a state possesses, the more fear it generates among its rivals. Germany, for example, was much more powerful at the end of the 1930s than it was at the decade's beginning, which is why the Soviets became increasingly fearful of Germany over the course of that decade. . . .

The Hierarchy of State Goals

Survival is the number one goal of great powers, according to my theory. In practice, however, states pursue non-security goals as well. For example, great powers invariably seek greater economic prosperity to enhance the welfare of their citizenry. They sometimes seek to promote a particular ideology abroad, as happened during the Cold War when the United States tried to spread democracy around the world and the Soviet Union tried to sell communism. National unification is another goal that sometimes motivates states, as it did with Prussia and Italy in the nineteenth century and Germany after the Cold War. Great powers also occasionally try to foster human rights around the globe. States might pursue any of these, as well as a number of other non-security goals.

Offensive realism certainly recognizes that great powers might pursue these non-security goals, but it has little to say about them, save for one important point: states can pursue them as long as the requisite behavior does not conflict with balance-of-power logic, which is often the case. Indeed, the pursuit of these non-security goals sometimes complements the hunt for relative power. For example, Nazi Germany expanded into eastern Europe for both ideological and realist reasons, and the superpowers competed with each other during the Cold War for similar reasons. Furthermore, greater economic prosperity invariably means greater wealth, which has significant implications for security, because wealth is the foundation of military power. Wealthy states can afford powerful military forces, which enhance a state's prospects for survival. . . .

Sometimes the pursuit of non-security goals has hardly any effect on the balance of power, one way or the other. Human rights interventions usually fit this description, because they tend to be small-scale operations that cost little and do not detract from a great power's prospects for survival. For better or for worse, states are rarely willing to expend blood and treasure to protect foreign populations from gross abuses, including genocide. For instance, despite claims that American foreign policy is infused with moralism, Somalia (1992–93) is the only instance during the past one hundred years in which U.S. soldiers were killed in action on a humanitarian mission. And in that case, the loss of a mere eighteen soldiers in an infamous firefight in October 1993 so traumatized American policymakers that they immediately pulled all U.S. troops out of Somalia and then refused to intervene in Rwanda in the spring of 1994, when ethnic Hutu went on a genocidal rampage against their Tutsi neighbors. Stopping that genocide would have been relatively easy and it would have had virtually no effect on the position of the United States in the balance of power. Yet nothing was done. In short, although realism does not prescribe human rights interventions, it does not necessarily proscribe them.

But sometimes the pursuit of non-security goals conflicts with balance-of-power logic, in which case states usually act according to the dictates of realism. For example, despite the U.S. commitment to spreading democracy across the globe, it helped overthrow democratically elected governments and embraced a number of authoritarian regimes during the Cold War, when American policymakers felt that these actions would help contain the Soviet Union. In World War II, the liberal democracies put aside their antipathy for communism and formed an alliance with the Soviet Union against Nazi Germany. "I can't take communism," Franklin Roosevelt emphasized, but to defeat Hitler "I would hold hands with the Devil." In the same way, Stalin repeatedly demonstrated that when his ideological preferences clashed with power considerations, the latter won out. To take the most blatant example of his realism, the Soviet Union formed a non-aggression pact with Nazi Germany in August 1939—the infamous Molotov-Ribbentrop Pact—in hopes that the agreement would at least temporarily satisfy Hitler's territorial ambitions in eastern Europe and turn the Wehrmacht toward France and the United Kingdom. When great powers confront a serious threat, in short, they pay little attention to ideology as they search for alliance partners.

Security also trumps wealth when those two goals conflict, because "defence," as Adam Smith wrote in *The Wealth of Nations*, "is of much more importance than opulence." Smith provides a good illustration of how states behave when forced to choose between wealth and relative power. In 1651, England put into effect the famous Navigation Act, protectionist legislation designed to damage Holland's commerce and ultimately cripple the Dutch economy. The legislation mandated that all goods imported into England be carried either in English ships or ships owned by the country that originally produced the goods. Since the Dutch produced few goods themselves, this measure would badly damage their shipping, the central ingredient in their economic success. Of course, the Navigation Act would hurt England's economy as well, mainly because it would rob England of the benefits of free trade. "The act of navigation," Smith wrote, "is not favorable to foreign commerce, or to the growth of that opulence that can arise from it." Nevertheless, Smith considered the legislation "the wisest of all the commercial regulations of England" because it did more damage to the Dutch economy than to the English economy, and in the mid-seventeenth century Holland was "the only naval power which could endanger the security of England." . . .

Cooperation among States

One might conclude from the preceding discussion that my theory does not allow for any cooperation among the great powers. But this conclusion would be wrong. States can cooperate, although cooperation is sometimes difficult to achieve and always difficult to sustain. Two factors inhibit cooperation: considerations about relative gains and concern about cheating. Ultimately, great powers live in a fundamentally competitive world where they view each other as real, or at least potential, enemies, and they therefore look to gain power at each other's expense.

Any two states contemplating cooperation must consider how profits or gains will be distributed between them. They can think about the division in terms of either absolute or relative gains (recall the distinction made earlier between pursuing either absolute power or relative power; the concept here is the same). With absolute gains, each side is concerned with maximizing its own profits and cares little about how much the other side gains or loses in the deal. Each side cares about the other only to the extent that the other side's behavior affects its own prospects for achieving maximum profits. With relative gains, on the other hand, each side considers not only its own individual gain, but also how well it fares compared to the other side.

Because great powers care deeply about the balance of power, their thinking focuses on relative gains when they consider cooperating with other states. For sure, each state tries to maximize its absolute gains; still, it is more important for a state to make sure that it does no worse, and perhaps better, than the other state in any agreement. Cooperation is more difficult to achieve, however, when states are attuned to relative gains rather than absolute gains. This is because states concerned about absolute gains have to make sure that if the pie is expanding, they are getting at least some portion of the increase, whereas states that worry about relative gains must pay careful attention to how the pie is divided, which complicates cooperative efforts.

Concerns about cheating also hinder cooperation. Great powers are often reluctant to enter into cooperative agreements for fear that the other side will cheat on the agreement and gain a significant advantage. This concern is especially acute in the military realm, causing a "special peril of defection," because the nature of military weaponry allows for rapid shifts in the balance of power. Such a development could create a window of opportunity for the state that cheats to inflict a decisive defeat on its victim.

These barriers to cooperation notwithstanding, great powers do cooperate in a realist world. Balance-of-power logic often causes great powers to form alliances and cooperate against common enemies. The United Kingdom, France, and Russia, for example, were allies against Germany before and during World War I. States sometimes cooperate to gang up on a third state, as Germany and the Soviet Union did against Poland in 1939. More recently, Serbia and Croatia agreed to conquer and divide Bosnia between them, although the United States and its European allies prevented them from executing their agreement. Rivals as well as allies cooperate. After all, deals can be struck that roughly reflect the distribution of power and satisfy concerns about cheating. The various arms control agreements signed by the superpowers during the Cold War illustrate this point.

The bottom line, however, is that cooperation takes place in a world that is competitive at its core—one where states have powerful incentives to take advantage of other states. This point is graphically highlighted by the state of European politics in the forty years before World War I. The great powers cooperated frequently during this period, but that did not stop them from going to war on August 1, 1914. The United States and the Soviet Union also cooperated considerably during World War II, but that cooperation did not prevent the outbreak of the Cold War shortly after Germany and Japan were defeated. Perhaps most amazingly, there was significant economic and military cooperation between Nazi Germany and the Soviet Union during the two years before the Wehrmacht attacked the Red Army. No amount of cooperation can eliminate the dominating logic of security competition. Genuine peace, or a world in which states do not compete for power, is not likely as long as the state system remains anarchic.

Questions for Review

What room does Mearsheimer see for cooperation among the great powers? Why do he and Wendt (in the next reading) reach such different conclusions?

Anarchy Is What States Make of It

ALEXANDER WENDT

Classical realists such as Thomas Hobbes, Reinhold Niebuhr, and Hans J. Morgenthau attributed egoism and power politics primarily to human nature, whereas structural realists or neorealists emphasize anarchy. The difference stems in part from different interpretations of anarchy's causal powers. Kenneth Waltz's work is important for both. In *Man, the State, and War,* he defines anarchy as a condition of possibility for or "permissive" cause of war, arguing that "wars occur because there is nothing to prevent them."[1] It is the human nature or domestic politics of predator states, however, that provide the initial impetus or "efficient" cause of conflict which forces other states to respond in kind. . . . But . . . In Waltz's *Theory of International Politics* . . . the logic of anarchy seems by itself to constitute self-help and power politics as necessary features of world politics.[2] . . .

Waltz defines political structure in three dimensions: ordering principles (in this case, anarchy), principles of differentiation (which here drop out), and the distribution of capabilities.[3] By itself, this definition predicts little about state behavior. It does not predict whether two states will be friends or foes, will recognize each other's sovereignty, will have dynastic ties, will be revisionist or status quo powers, and so on. These factors, which are fundamentally intersubjective, affect states' security interests and thus the character of their interaction under anarchy. . . . Put more generally, without assumptions about the structure of identities and interests in the system, Waltz's definition of structure cannot predict the content or dynamics of anarchy. Self-help is one such intersubjective structure and, as such, does the decisive explanatory work in the theory. The question is whether self-help is a logical or contingent feature of anarchy. In this section, I develop the concept of a "structure of identity and interest" and show that no particular one follows logically from anarchy.

A fundamental principle of constructivist social theory is that people act toward objects, including other actors, on the basis of the meanings that the objects have for them. States act differently toward enemies than they do toward friends because enemies are threatening and friends are not. Anarchy and the distribution of power are insufficient to tell us which is which. U.S. military power has a different significance for Canada than for Cuba, despite their similar "structural" positions, just as British missiles have a different significance for the United States than do Soviet missiles. The distribution of power may always affect states' calculations, but how it does so depends on the intersubjective understandings and expectations, on the "distribution of knowledge," that constitute their conceptions of self and other.[4] If society "forgets" what a university is, the powers and practices of professor and student cease to exist; if the United States and Soviet Union decide that they are no longer enemies, "the Cold War is over." It is collective meanings that constitute the structures which organize our actions.

Actors acquire identities—relatively stable, role-specific understandings and expectations about self—by participating in such collective meanings. Identities are inherently relational: "Identity, with its appropriate attachments of psychological reality, is always identity within a specific, socially constructed world," Peter Berger argues.[5] Each person has many identities linked to institutional roles, such as brother, son, teacher, and citizen. Similarly, a state may have multiple identities as "sovereign," "leader of the free world," "imperial power," and so on. The commitment to and the salience of particular identities vary, but each identity is an inherently social definition of the actor grounded in the theories which actors collectively hold about themselves and one another and which constitute the structure of the social world.

Identities are the basis of interests. Actors do not have a "portfolio" of interests that they carry around independent of social context; instead, they define their interests on the process of defining situations. . . . Sometimes situations are unprecedented in our experience, and in these cases we have to construct their meaning, and thus our interests, by analogy or invent them de novo. More often they have routine qualities in which we assign meanings on the basis of institutionally defined roles. When we say that professors have an "interest" in teaching, research, or going on leave, we are saying that to function in the role identity of "professor," they have to define certain situations as calling for certain actions. This does not mean that they will necessarily do so (expectations and competence do not equal performance), but if they do not, they will not get tenure. The absence or failure of roles makes defining situations and interests more difficult, and identity confusion may result. This seems to be happening today in the United States and the former Soviet Union: Without the cold war's mutual attributions of threat and hostility to define their identities, these states seem unsure of what their "interests" should be.

An institution is a relatively stable set or "structure" of identities and interests. Such structures are often codified in formal rules and norms, but these have motivational force only in virtue of actors' socialization to and participation in collective knowledge. Institutions are fundamentally cognitive entities that do not exist apart from actors' ideas about how the world works. This does not mean that institutions are not real or objective, that they are "nothing but" beliefs. As collective knowledge, they are experienced as having an existence "over and above the individuals who happen to embody them at the moment."[6] In this way, institutions come to confront individuals as more or less coercive social facts, but they are still a function of what actors collectively "know." Identities and such collective cognitions do not exist apart from each other; they are "mutually constitutive." On this view, institutionalization is a process of internalizing new identities and interests, not something occurring outside them and affecting only behavior; socialization is a cognitive process, not just a behavioral one. Conceived in this way, institutions may be cooperative or conflictual, a point sometimes lost in scholarship on international regimes, which tends to equate institutions with cooperation. There are important differences between conflictual and cooperative institutions to be sure, but all relatively stable self-other relations—even those of "enemies"—are defined intersubjectively.

Self-help is an institution, one of various structures of identity and interest that may exist under anarchy. Processes of identity formation under anarchy are concerned first and foremost with preservation or "security" of the self. Concepts of security therefore differ in the extent to which and the manner in which, the self is identified cognitively with the other, and, I want to suggest, it is upon this cognitive variation that the meaning of anarchy and the distribution of power depends. Let me illustrate with a standard continuum of security systems.

At one end is the "competitive" security system, in which states identify negatively with each other's security so that ego's gain is seen as alter's loss. Negative identification under anarchy constitutes systems of "realist" power politics: risk-averse actors that infer intentions from capabilities and worry about relative gains and losses. At the limit—in the Hobbesian war of all against all—collective action is nearly impossible in such a system because each actor must constantly fear being stabbed in the back.

In the middle is the "individualistic" security system, in which states are indifferent to the relationship between their own and others' security. This constitutes "neoliberal" systems: States are still self-regarding about their security but are concerned primarily with absolute gains rather than relative gains. One's position in the distribution of power is less important, and collective action is more possible (though still subject to free riding because states continue to be "egoists").

Competitive and individualistic systems are both "self-help" forms of anarchy in the sense that states do not positively identify the security of self with that of others but instead treat security as the individual responsibility of each. Given the lack of a positive cognitive identification on the basis of which to build security regimes, power politics within such systems will necessarily consist of efforts to manipulate others to satisfy self-regarding interests.

This contrasts with the "cooperative" security system, in which states identify positively with one another so that the security of each is perceived as the responsibility of all. This is not self-help in any interesting sense, since the "self" in terms of which interests are defined is the community; national interests are international interests. In practice, of course, the extent to which states identify with the community varies from the limited form found in "concerts" to the full-blown form seen in "collective security" arrangements. Depending on how well developed the collective self is, it will produce security practices that are in varying degrees altruistic or prosocial. This makes collective action less dependent on the presence of active threats and less prone to free riding. Moreover, it restructures efforts to advance one's objectives, or "power politics," in terms of shared norms rather than relative power.

On this view, the tendency in international relations scholarship to view power and institutions as two opposing explanations of foreign policy is therefore misleading, since anarchy and the distribution of power only have meaning for state action in virtue of the understandings and expectations that constitute institutional identities and interests. Self-help is one such institution, constituting one kind of anarchy but not the only kind. Waltz's three-part definition of structure therefore seems underspecified. In order to go from structure to action, we need to add a fourth: the intersubjectively constituted structure of identities and interests in the system.

This has an important implication for the way in which we conceive of states in the state of nature before their first encounter with each other. Because states do not have conceptions of self and other, and thus security interests, apart from or prior to interaction, we assume too much about the state of nature if we concur with Waltz that, in virtue of anarchy, "international political systems, like economic markets, are formed by the coaction of self-regarding units."[7] We also assume too much if we argue that, in virtue of anarchy, states in the state of nature necessarily face a "stag hunt" or "security dilemma."[8] These claims presuppose a history of interaction in which actors have acquired "selfish" identities and interests; before interaction (and still in abstraction from first- and second-image factors) they would have no experience upon which to base such definitions of self and other. To assume otherwise is to attribute to states in the state of nature qualities that they can only possess in society. Self-help is an institution, not a constitutive feature of anarchy.

What, then, *is* a constitutive feature of the state of nature before interaction? Two things are left if we strip away those properties of the self which presuppose interaction with others. The first is the material substrate of agency, including its intrinsic capabilities. For human beings, this is the body; for states, it is an organizational apparatus of governance. In effect, I am suggesting for rhetorical purposes that the raw material out of which members of the state system are constituted is created by domestic society before states enter the constitutive process of international society, although this process implies neither stable territoriality nor sovereignty, which are internationally negotiated terms of individuality (as discussed further below). The second is a desire to preserve this material substrate, to survive. This does not entail "self-regardingness," however, since actors do not have a self prior to interaction with another; how they view the meaning and requirements of this survival therefore depends on the processes by which conceptions of self evolve.

This may all seem very arcane, but there is an important issue at stake: Are the foreign policy identities and interests of states exogenous or endogenous to the state system? The former is the answer of an individualistic or undersocialized systemic theory for which rationalism is appropriate; the latter is the answer of a fully socialized systemic theory. Waltz seems to offer the latter and proposes two mechanisms, competition and socialization, by which structure conditions state action.[9] The content of his argument about this conditioning, however, presupposes a self-help system that is not itself a constitutive feature of anarchy. As James Morrow points out, Waltz's two mechanisms condition behavior, not identity and interest. . . . [10]

If self-help is not a constitutive feature of anarchy, it must emerge causally from processes in which anarchy plays only a permissive role. This reflects a second principle of constructivism: that the meanings in terms of which action is organized arise out of interaction. . . .

Consider two actors—ego and alter—encountering each other for the first time.[11] Each wants to survive and has certain material capabilities, but neither actor has biological or domestic imperatives for power, glory, or conquest . . . and there is no history of security or insecurity between the two. What should they do? Realists would probably argue that each should act on the basis of worst-case assumptions about the other's intentions, justifying such an attitude as prudent in view of the possibility of death from making a mistake. Such a possibility always exists, even in civil society; however, society would be impossible if people made decisions purely on the basis of worst-case possibilities. Instead, most decisions are and should be made on the basis of probabilities, and these are produced by interaction, by what actors *do.*

In the beginning is ego's gesture, which may consist, for example, of an advance, a retreat, a brandishing of arms, a laying down of arms, or an attack. For ego, this gesture represents the basis on which it is prepared to respond to alter. This basis is unknown to alter, however, and so it must make an inference or "attribution" about ego's intentions and, in particular, given that this is anarchy, about whether ego is a threat. The content of this inference will largely depend on two considerations. The first is the gesture's and ego's physical qualities, which are in part contrived by ego and which include the direction of movement, noise, numbers, and immediate consequences of the gesture. The second consideration concerns what alter would intend by such qualities were it to make such a gesture itself. Alter may make an attributional "error" in its inference about ego's intent, but there is also no reason for it to assume a priori—before the gesture—that ego is threatening, since it is only through a process of signaling and interpreting that the costs and probabilities of being wrong can be determined. Social threats are constructed, not natural.

Consider an example. Would we assume, a priori, that we were about to be attacked if we are ever contacted by members of an alien civilization? I think not. We would be highly alert, of course, but whether we placed our military forces on alert or launched an attack would depend on how we interpreted the import of their first gesture for our security—if only to avoid making an immediate enemy out of what may be a dangerous adversary. The possibility of error, in other words, does not force us to act on the assumption that the aliens are threatening: Action depends on the probabilities we assign, and these are in key part a function of what the aliens do; prior to their gesture, we have no systemic basis for assigning probabilities. If their first gesture is to appear with a thousand spaceships and destroy New York, we will define the situation as threatening and respond accordingly. But if they appear with one spaceship, saying what seems to be "we come in peace," we will feel "reassured" and will probably respond with a gesture intended to reassure them, even if this gesture is not necessarily interpreted by them as such.

This process of signaling, interpreting, and responding completes a "social act" and begins the process of creating intersubjective meanings. It advances the same way. The first social act creates expectations on both sides about each other's future behavior: potentially mistaken and certainly tentative, but expectations nonetheless. Based on this tentative knowledge, ego makes a new gesture, again signifying the basis on which it will respond to alter, and again alter responds, adding to the pool of knowledge each has about the other, and so on over time. The mechanism here is reinforcement; interaction rewards actors for holding certain ideas about each other and discourages them from holding others. If repeated long enough, these "reciprocal typifications" will create relatively stable concepts of self and other regarding the issue at stake in the interaction.[12]

Competitive systems of interaction are prone to security "dilemmas," in which the efforts of actors to enhance their security unilaterally threatens the security of the others, perpetuating distrust and alienation. The forms of identity and interest that constitute such dilemmas, however, are themselves ongoing effects of, not exogenous to, the interaction; identities are produced in and through "situated activity."[13] We do not *begin* our relationship with the aliens in a security dilemma; security dilemmas are not given by anarchy or nature. . . .

The mirror theory of identity formation is a crude account of how the process of creating identities and interests might work, but it does not tell us why a system of states—such as, arguably, our own—would have ended up with self-regarding and not collective identities. In this section, I examine an efficient cause, predation, which, in conjunction with anarchy as a permissive cause, may generate a self-help system. In so doing, however, I show the key role that the structure of identities and interests plays in mediating anarchy's explanatory role.

The predator argument is straightforward and compelling. For whatever reasons—biology, domestic politics, or systemic victimization—some states may become predisposed toward aggression. The aggressive behavior of these predators or "bad apples" forces other states to engage in competitive power politics, to meet fire with fire, since failure to do so may degrade or destroy them. One predator will best a hundred pacifists because anarchy provides no guarantees. This argument is powerful in part because it is so weak: Rather than making the strong assumption that all states are inherently power-seeking (a purely reductionist theory of power politics), it assumes that just one is power-seeking and that the others have to follow suit because anarchy permits the one to exploit them.

In making this argument, it is important to reiterate that the possibility of predation does not in itself force states to anticipate it a priori with competitive power politics of their own. The possibility of predation does not mean that "war may at any moment occur"; it may in fact be extremely unlikely. Once a predator emerges, however, it may condition identity and interest formation in the following manner.

In an anarchy of two, if ego is predatory, alter must either define its security in self-help terms or pay the price. . . . The timing of the emergence of predation relative to the history of identity formation in the community is therefore crucial to anarchy's explanatory role as a permissive cause. Predation will always lead victims to defend themselves, but whether defense will be collective or not depends on the history of interaction within the potential collective as much as on the ambitions of the predator. Will the disappearance of the Soviet threat renew old insecurities among the members of the North Atlantic Treaty Organization? Perhaps, but not if they have reasons independent of that threat for identifying their security with one another. Identities and interests are relationship-specific, not intrinsic attributes of a "portfolio"; states may be competitive in some relationships and solidary in others . . .

The source of predation also matters. If it stems from unit-level causes that are immune to systemic impacts (causes such as human nature or domestic politics taken in isolation), then it functions in a manner analogous to a "genetic trait" in the constructed world of the state system. Even if successful, this trait does not select for other predators in an evolutionary sense so much as it teaches other states to respond in kind, but since traits cannot be unlearned, the other states will continue competitive behavior until the predator is either destroyed or transformed from within. However, in the more likely event that predation stems at least in part from prior systemic interaction—perhaps as a result of being victimized in the past (one thinks here of Nazi Germany or the Soviet Union)—then it is more a response to a learned identity and, as such, might be transformed by future social interaction in the form of appeasement, reassurances that security needs will be met, systemic effects on domestic politics, and so on. In this case, in other words, there is more hope that process can transform a bad apple into a good one. . . .

This raises anew the question of exactly how much and what kind of role human nature and domestic politics play in world politics. The greater and more destructive this role, the more significant predation will be, and the less amenable anarchy will be to formation of collective identities. Classical realists, of course, assumed that human nature was possessed by an inherent lust for power or glory. My argument suggests that assumptions such as this were made for a reason: An unchanging Hobbesian man provides the powerful efficient cause necessary for a relentless pessimism about world politics that anarchic structure alone, or even structure plus intermittent predation, cannot supply. . . .

Assuming for now that systemic theories of identity formation in world politics are worth pursuing, let me conclude by suggesting that the realist–rationalist alliance "reifies" self-help in the sense of treating it as something separate from the practices by which it is produced and sustained. Peter Berger and Thomas Luckmann define reification as follows: "[It] is the apprehension of the products of human activity *as if* they were something else than human products—such as facts of nature, results of cosmic laws, or manifestations of divine will. Reification implies that man is capable of forgetting his own authorship of the human world, and further, that the dialectic between man, the producer, and his products is lost to consciousness. The reified world is . . . experienced by man as a strange facticity, an *opus alienum* over which he has no control rather than as the *opus proprium* of his own productive activity."[14] By denying or bracketing states' collective authorship of their identities and interests, in other words, the realist–rationalist alliance denies or brackets the fact that competitive power politics help create a very "problem of order" they are supposed to solve—that realism is a self-fulfilling prophecy. Far from being exogenously given, the intersubjective knowledge that constitutes competitive identities and interests is constructed every day by processes of "social will formation."[15] It is what states have made of themselves.

Questions for Review

In Wendt's framework, how much freedom does an individual state have to define and redefine anarchy? Can we find variation in time and place in how states have thought about the absence of a governing authority?

Notes

1 Kenneth Waltz, *Man, the State, and War* (New York: Columbia University Press, 1959), p. 232.

2 Kenneth Waltz, *Theory of International Politics* (Boston: Addison-Wesley, 1979).

3 Waltz, *Theory of International Politics*, pp. 79–101.

4 The phrase "distribution of knowledge" is Barry Barnes's, as discussed in his work *The Nature of Power* (Cambridge: Polity Press, 1988); see also Peter Berger and Thomas Luckmann, *The Social Construction of Reality* (New York: Anchor Books, 1966).

5 Berger, "Identity as a Problem in the Sociology of Knowledge," *European Journal of Sociology*, 7, 1 (1966), 111.

6 Berger and Luckmann, p. 58.

7 Waltz, *Theory of International Politics*, p. 91.

8 See Waltz, *Man, the State, and War*; and Robert Jervis, "Cooperation Under the Security Dilemma," *World Politics* 30 (January 1978), 167–214.

9 Waltz, *Theory of International Politics*, pp. 74–77.

10 See James Morrow, "Social Choice and System Structure in World Politics," *World Politics* 41 (October 1988), 89.

11 This situation is not entirely metaphorical in world politics, since throughout history states have "discovered" each other, generating an instant anarchy as it were. A systematic empirical study of first contacts would be interesting.

12 On "reciprocal typifications," see Berger and Luckmann, pp. 54–58.

13 See C. Norman Alexander and Mary Glenn Wiley, "Situated Activity and Identity Formation," in Morris Rosenberg and Ralph Turner, eds., *Social Psychology: Sociological Perspectives* (New York: Basic Books, 1981), pp. 269–89.

14 See Berger and Luckmann, p. 89.

15 See Richard Ashley, "Social Will and International Anarchy," in Hayward Alker and Richard Ashley, eds., *After Realism*, work in progress, Massachusetts Institute of Technology, Cambridge, and Arizona State University, Tempe, 1992.

Chapter 3
Strategic Interaction in Anarchy

Game Theory: A Practitioner's Approach

THOMAS C. SCHELLING

> To a practitioner in the social sciences, game theory primarily helps to identify *situations* in which interdependent decisions are somehow problematic; *solutions* often require venturing into the social sciences. Game theory is usually about *anticipating* each other's choices; it can also cope with *influencing* other's choices. To a social scientist the great contribution of game theory is probably the payoff matrix, an accounting device comparable to the equals sign in algebra.

In 2005 I received an award "for having deepened our understanding of conflict and cooperation through game-theoretic analysis". Does that make me a game theorist? If so, what defines a game theorist?

Notice that "game theory," in contrast to almost any other discipline you might think of, has "theory" in the name of the subject. There are economists, only some of whom are economic theorists; statisticians, only some of whom are statistical theorists; physicists, only some of whom are theoretical physicists; and so on through most disciplines. But game theory has "theory" in its name. So is a game theorist, like an economist who uses economic theory, someone who *uses* game theory or is a game theorist, like an economic *theorist* who produces economic theory, someone who *produces theory* of the game-theory type?

I am not, or only somewhat, a producer of game-theory theory; I am a user of (elementary) game theory. So I call myself a practitioner, a user, not a creator. (Roger Myerson, in response to the paragraph above, suggested "game analyst" for people like me.)

There are two definitions of game theory. There is a soft one and a hard one. According to the soft one, game theory is the study of how two or more entities – people, governments, organizations – make choices among actions in situations where the outcomes depend on the choices both or all of them make, where each has his or her or its own preferences among the possible outcomes – how they should (might) rationally make their interdependent choices. Each individual needs to anticipate the decisions the others are making. But that means that each needs to anticipate what the others are *anticipating*. And that means anticipating what the others anticipate oneself to be anticipating! This may sound like an infinite regress, but essentially it only means finding a set of expectations that are consistent with each other. Somehow a common expectation of the "expectable" outcome must be recognized and acted on.

I digressed to introduce what I consider the most helpful invention of game theory *for the social sciences*, the "payoff matrix". (Anyone who wants to argue that the concept of "equilibrium" is the greatest concept will find me willing to argue.) The payoff matrix is usually for two-party situations; it's hard to display three dimensions (although in certain symmetrical situations among many players, a 2×n matrix can often be helpful). It can display multiple choice situations. A two-party two-choice situation may look like this:

"COLUMN"

(chooses a or b)

		a	b	
	:-------------------:			:
	:	3 :	4 :	
A	: 3	: 1	:	
	-------------------			:
	:	1 :	2 :	
B	: 4	: 2	:	
	:-------------------:			

"ROW" (chooses A or B)

There are four possible outcomes. Each player values the outcomes in the order 4, 3, 2, 1, 4 being most preferred, 1 least preferred. ROW's preferences ("payoffs") are in the lower left corner of each cell: row B column a is his favourite, row A column b his least. COLUMN's preferences are in the upper right of each cell. In the abstract logic of game theory, this is a game if we specify the order of moves. Let it be that choices are simultaneous. We are invited to find the "solution".

Note: this "game" includes only ordinal preferences, that is, the order of preference. It doesn't show whether the worst outcome is much worse than the next to last, compared with the first and second. It also has a somewhat deceptive symmetry, since both players have only the 4, 3, 2, 1 designators of preference, We might have had, for ROW, the numbers 10, 9, 6, 0, and for COLUMN the numbers 10, 3, 2, 1. These cardinal (absolute) numbers would give us more information; whether we need the greater information to "solve" the game we don't know yet.

Now, my purpose here is not to illustrate how we might try to "solve" the little game above, but to raise the question, "Is this mathematics?"

My answer is "no", Any possible analysis requires only the ability to tell whether one number is larger than another – not even arithmetic – or in the second case of 10, 9, 6, 0, how much larger – no multiplication, let alone any differential equations! Yet an impressive body of useful game-theory analysis, especially in the social sciences, has been based on simple 2×2 matrices no more complicated than the one above. (Recognizing that 5 is larger than 2 may by definition be mathematics, but not in ordinary parlance.)

A Game and Some Characteristics

Actually the one presented above is almost surely the simple matrix most examined in the literature of the social sciences. And it illustrates some useful concepts. One is *"dominance"*: one choice is better than the other no matter what the other party chooses. ROW prefers 4 to 3, and 2 to 1, and so may choose row *B* without regard to COLUMN's choice, and similarly for COLUMN's preference for column *b*. Another is *"equilibrium"*: if both choose *B* and *b*, neither regrets the choice, neither would unilaterally opt to change it. A third may be called *"payoff dominance"*: the payoffs in *A, a* are preferred by both parties to the payoffs they choose in *B, b*; so the outcome they achieve is *"nonoptimal"* but in the absence of some ability to concert they can't get to *A, a*. And that little matrix illustrates the tendency for most situations to involve a combination of conflict and common interest. Their favourite outcomes differ – *B, a* versus *A, b* – but they have a common interest in getting, if possible, *A, a* instead of *B, b*.

Within the confines of abstract game theory, the lower-right cell in the matrix above, yielding the "dominated" but equilibrium outcome, *B, b*, is usually considered the *"solution"*. Social scientists have devoted a great literature to exploring alternatives to that solution, but they have done so by putting that matrix into some kind of social context, such as communication and contract enforcement, or unilateral promises, or repeated play and reputation, that is, moving into the empirical social sciences and treating that matrix as a kind of core of the situation but not the whole game.

Let me offer another matrix, which will underlie the exposition to come.

```
                          "COLUMN"

                      (chooses a or b)
                        a       b
                    -------------------
                    :      2 :   4 :
              A   : 2      : 3    :
                    -------------------
              B   :      3 :   1 :
                    : 4      : 1    :
                    -------------------
```
"ROW" (chooses *A* or *B*)

This one provides neither party a dominant choice; rather the choices are *"contingent"*, the best choice for either depends on what the other chooses. And there are *two equilibria*! Lower left and upper right are both outcomes from which neither would unilaterally change. This matrix, like the earlier one, is symmetrical: each faces a choice identical to the other's. If this is a game that has a "solution", what could the solution be?

A possibility is that, not knowing what COLUMN will do, row should play it safe with the upper row. But if that were a convincing strategy, COLUMN should know it and, expecting row *A*, would choose column *b*, and both would be better off, ROW even better of the two of them. But why not expect COLUMN to be the one to play it safe at a? In that case ROW would choose B, making both better off, COLUMN more so than ROW. But who should decide to let the other play it safe? If both "play it safe", they end up at A, a, second worst for both of them. That doesn't appear a promising basis for a "solution".

What I'm going to argue in a moment is that game theory provides a neat way to identify the quantitative characteristics – or, as above, with only the numbers 4, 3, 2, 1, qualitative (ordinal) characteristics – of a situation, but the solution may require going beyond the abstract characterization in search of more information. What kinds of information? I'm going to propose culture, institutions, precedents, reputations, identifications, even signalling or conversation. And I'm going to use a variation on the above matrix, with cardinal (absolute) values, rather than ordinal, as below:

"COLUMN"

(chooses a or b)

		a	b
A		8 :	10 :
	: 8	: 9	:
B		9 :	1 :
	: 10	: 1	:

"ROW" (chooses A or B)

This matrix is symmetrical: each faces identical choices and outcomes. One outcome is very bad. Two are equilibria: they are clearly the best outcomes, but which should be chosen?

(In some situations there are many, even infinitely many, equilibria, sometimes with identical payoffs; the problem then, if choices must be taken independently without communication, is one of pure coordination, to identify some hint or signal or suggestion or precedent or "rule" that both parties, or all parties, recognize as a common expectation. An example: I've arranged for all the students in my class to be admitted to special seating at the inaugural parade in Washington. They will be recognized because, as I told them, they will all give the same password. But I neglected to give them the password! I've told the person in charge that my students can be easily identified because they will all give the same password. My students have no way of communicating with each other; they must all give the same password to be admitted. How do they all choose the same password? Classroom experience finds most of them able to "solve" this problem.)

A non-equilibrium is at upper left. Evidently there is a basis for playing it safe, to avoid the lower right. But if either could be expected to play it safe, or for any other reason to choose A or a, the other should make both better off by choosing B or, as the case may be, b. If each expects the other to play it safe, they choose B and b, and get a very bad outcome.

A Situation, Exemplified by the "Game"

Now I want to give an "interpretation" of that matrix, a very common situation that all of us are acquainted with, have encountered numerous times, and see what a "solution" – either an expectable outcome or a somehow preferred outcome – might depend on.

Here's the interpretation. Two cars approach an intersection at right angles to each other, one to the other's left, one to the other's right, going at similar speeds and evidently going to arrive at the intersection simultaneously at those speeds. If both continue without slowing, they will arrive at the same time and some sort of collision, or at least a jolting stop, is inevitable. If both slow down, both lose time, and they still haven't "solved" the problem. (We then have another "game" to play: both stopped, waiting for the other.) If either one slows down while the other proceeds at speed, they get a "solution" in the sense that there is no superior alternative, each gets at least his second best, but one loses a little time relative to the other.

Each needs to anticipate whether the other will slow down or continue at the same speed. And their expectations have to be consistent: if each expects the other to slow down, they will collide (or come to a jolting stop); if each expects the other to continue at speed, they lose time unnecessarily. If one slows down and the other continues, they have "cooperated". A favourable outcome is necessarily asymmetrical: in the abstract we don't know which of the two, out of generosity, modesty or caution will slow down or how the other may come to believe he or she can proceed with confidence.

The answer is not in the matrix. The *question* is nicely formulated in the matrix, the *answer* is not.

So where is the answer? Or where do we look for it? Where do the two drivers look for it? How likely are they to find *the* solution, or *a* solution?

There are some interesting possibilities. One is that something in the situation points to an obvious pair of choices. We can call that pair of choices a "solution". For example, maybe if one were going too fast to stop in time and the other could see that only he could avert collision, the latter would know that only he could "solve" the problem. But I proposed they were going at the same speed.

Maybe there is a "clue" that both can recognize: one's type of vehicle or one's style of driving indicates recklessness and the other chooses caution. Maybe, at their speeds, the danger is not bodily injury but only damage to the car, and one car is new and expensive and the other is old and already out of shape and has little to lose in collision at moderate speed. Maybe it is visible that one car carries children and the other only the driver, and the latter knows that the car with children will cautiously slow down.

Another possibility is that there is a rule, some convention, known to both drivers and known to be known to both, that indicates who is to slow down. "Ladies first" may be a possibility, if gender is visible. That the car to the other's right has the privilege may be a known rule. Of course, red and green lights can provide a rule known to all drivers. Some of these rules may need enforcement; some may depend on courtesy and good citizenship. And some may be self enforcing. The red and green lights make it dangerous to claim an intersection when the light is red: the other car will be expecting clear passage. (The coloured lights probably need no legal status; all that's required is the discriminating signal.) Similarly, the rule that the car to the other's right goes first may be so well known that it is dangerous to contest it. If it is widely believed that taxis are willing to risk moderate damage to the vehicle in order to complete the journey quickly, and especially if it is known that taxi drivers believe in the universality of that belief, taxis will take the right of way and others will acknowledge it by slowing down.

Of course, "ladies first", or "taxis first", or "new car slows down" is an asymmetric solution, a discriminatory solution, but even the one discriminated against benefits from there being a recognizable solution.

I had an experience in Beijing a quarter-century ago that dramatized the self-enforcement concept. Bicycles were swarming on a wide avenue and I tried to cross, watching the oncoming bicycles with a view to navigating safely among them. At one point it became clear to me that I'd better halt briefly. The result was 14 cyclists tumbling to the pavement. I was later told the "rule". Keep moving at constant speed in a straight line and pay no attention to the bicycles; they will be counting on your steady movement in a straight line, and any departure will only confuse them and cause the kind of multiple collisions I had innocently provoked.

Then there is the possibility of signalling. A nice asymmetrical possibility is putting one's hand out the window and gesturing to the other to proceed: only the driver on the other's right can do that, the other driver's left hand would not be visible to the driver on the right [in the USA].

An interesting question is whether cooperation could be more effective if drivers approaching the intersection could speak to each other. The technology surely exists, though it's not generally available. My suspicion is that with communication the bargaining may not prove efficient. Both parties may be demanding; both may declare unilaterally, both may be so generous that both offer to slow down like two people waiting for each other to be the first through a door. Too many options may make it harder to concert on one.

One car – we hope it's not both – might have an indicator, perhaps on the windshield or on the license plate, indicating "I always slow down" or "I always demand right-of-way". Is this a credible declaration? I believe it must be: if the car says it slows down, the driver certainly doesn't want the other to slow down, and if the car claims right-of-way, it certainly doesn't intend to slow down. Deception doesn't lead to solution.

(We might add another option: speed up. This would be effective if the other driver either slowed down or maintained speed, but the enhanced risk if both speed up might seem to make it too dangerous to be worth considering. Still, if it is so dangerous that no sensible driver would consider it, maybe that makes it a safe option! Game theory suggests that if it is so risky it has to be considered. It is somewhat like Yogi Berra's remark, "Nobody goes there any more, it's too crowded".)

Anticipate vs. Influence

In the work for which I received the award, my interest has been less in problems of reciprocal anticipation, like the one we just worked, than in how the parties may attempt to influence each other's behaviour, the choices each other makes. (Even in our little traffic example, we saw the possibility of signalling.) This subject arises in behaviour among nations, in industrial disputes, in criminal law, in bargaining over a purchase, in encouraging and disciplining children or pets, in extortion and blackmail, and even, as we saw, in negotiating automobile (or bicycle) traffic.

An important way of influencing another's behaviour, I observed, was by influencing the other's expectation of one's own behaviour. And that, I observed, was often accomplished by determining one's own behaviour in advance, in a manner visible to the other, or communicable to the other in a credible way. And one could attempt to determine one's own behaviour either unconditionally or conditional on the other's response. I was especially impressed with the role of *commitment*, of becoming *committed* to a course of action: "I'm going through" in our traffic example, or "I'm slowing down".

In the traffic example, "I'm going through" was believable because it wouldn't serve the driver's purpose unless it were the driver's evident intention. And it was an unconditional commitment, not one contingent on the other's slowing down.

But "come one step closer and I'll shoot" may require convincing that the gun is real, that the gun is loaded, and that one actually would dare to fire at the target. And it is conditional: it implies "and if you don't, I won't". It is what I call a "threat". In calling it a threat I mean that what is threatened is what one would prefer not to do. If one would actually prefer to shoot in that contingency – that the intruder keep coming – it would be a warning, a statement revealing a truth that the intruder surely wants to know. (Bluffing, of course, is always a possibility; one can fire a shot to prove the gun is loaded, but the willingness to shoot is not so easily proven.)

Another commitment is the *promise*. A promise may be conditional or unconditional. "If you clean your room I'll take you to the ball game", or "I'll be home in time to take you to the ball game". The latter will assure that the child will be home.

What is interesting is how difficult it may be to take a firm unconditional commitment, to issue a believable threat, or to make a believable promise. I'll illustrate some of these points using one of the matrices above, but to illustrate the importance, and the possible difficulty, of making appropriate believable promises, let me describe a television show by Alfred Hitchcock.

An old man passes a jeweller's store in the darkness of early morning just as three men emerge with bags in their hands. They've evidently robbed the store. Just as they are about to get into their getaway car the leader turns back to the old man and says, "Sorry, old man, but we can't afford to leave any witnesses alive". The old man says he wouldn't tell anything; the robber says that the old man could identify them if they were ever caught, and they can't afford that possibility. The old man says, "Wait, there must be some alternative. Does anyone have a knife?" When someone produces a scissors he says, "Put my eyes out". One way to make a promise believable is to make it impossible to renege – if you can find a way!

To show how promises may afford a "solution," let's look at that original matrix above, the one that led to an inferior outcome. Here it is again:

"COLUMN"

(chooses *a* or *b*)

```
                                    a      b

                                 :------------------:
                                 :     3:    4:
                          A   : 3      : 1   :
"ROW" (chooses A or B)           ------------------:
                          B   :    1:    2:
                                 : 4      : 2   :
                                 :------------------:
```

It doesn't matter who has to choose first, or who gets to choose first, or whether they choose simultaneously; the outcome is ineluctably at the lower right, with payoffs of 2 and 2, *as long as all they care about is the numerical payoffs.* But suppose ROW can make a believable promise, and so can COLUMN. Here's what ROW can propose (and, to make it simple, let's assume that all he has to do is to say "I promise"). He says, "I promise that if you promise to choose *a* I shall choose *A'*. Note that this is a conditional promise: he doesn't promise to choose *A*, he promises to choose *A if* COLUMN makes a corresponding (unconditional) promise to choose *a* before ROW makes his choice. Both have to be capable of believable promises. But if they have or can arrange that capability they can "solve" the problem presented by the matrix.

My interest is mainly in how and when and under what circumstances some individuals – people, governments, corporations, unions, political parties – can actually make believable promises. But it is important to see, as in the above matrix, what a great difference it can make.

For an extended discussion of who can make believable promises, threats, or unconditional commitments, in what circumstances and within what institutions, I must refer you to a book of mine, *The Strategy of Conflict* (Schelling, 1960). Here I'll just mention a sample of circumstances. Begin with the promise.

In the movie, *The Princess Bride*, the reluctant maiden is wed to the evil prince in a bumbling ceremony that is interrupted by an attack on the castle. In the confusion she meets the hero, whom she loves, and confesses that all hope is lost, she is married. The hero demands, "Did you say "I do""? After some reflection she is pretty sure that that part of the ceremony got omitted in the battle for the castle. Then you are not married. You can't be if you didn't say "I do".. "I do" in a marriage ceremony is part of a formula – a "performative utterance" in the terminology of Austin (1962) and a "speech act" in the terminology of Searle (1969) – that changes the legal status of the woman's relation to the man who must also say "I do" (and not merely "yes"):

But even a child, told he or she will receive a specific reward for good behaviour, is likely to say, "Promise?". Uttering the word "promise" affects one's relation to the child; merely offering the reward is somewhat less serious than is promising. And failure to keep the promise makes future attempts at promise less rewarding.

Signing, with witnesses, a legal contract is a method of reciprocal promising. Having a reputation for keeping promises is an asset; issuing a promise stakes that reputation on the fulfilment. Being known to believe in a deity that enforces promises provides one a capacity to invoke penalty on defections; "cross my heart and hope to die" or "may God strike me dead" can be credible. Offering a tangible pledge, as a forfeit, may work; one offers one's guitar to the pawnshop to guarantee repayment of the loan. In earlier times, hostages were offered, or exchanged.

There are occasionally "mechanisms" for arranging commitments. In the 1930s many national labour unions in the USA with numerous locals that might find themselves engaged in a strike arranged "strike insurance", according to which any local union engaged, in a strike could count on financial contributions from all the other locals, to help avert the worst consequences of lost wages. The intention, I understand, was originally only to share the burdens among the locals. But the effect was to make striking so much less costly to the striking union that its threat to persist in the strike became much more credible than if there had been no financial recourse. The bargaining position – the "commitment" to persevere – was thus enhanced.

In 1950 President Truman proposed that the Congress authorize the stationing of seven army divisions in Germany, to bolster NATO's defence. The question arose, could seven added divisions make enough difference to a possible successful defence against a Soviet-bloc invasion? Secretary of State Dean Acheson, questioned by the U.S. Senate, explained that what the seven divisions could do was not to make possible an effective defence of Western Europe; that was not feasible for the time being. What they could do was to guarantee that if 300 000 American young men were killed or captured, the war could not stop there; it would escalate ineluctably to a higher level of warfare. They were the commitment, the pledge, the hostages.

Questions for Review

Why does Schelling think that game theory is useful for understanding international politics? Do you think that his approach is so abstract that it squeezes the life out of the subject matter?

Rationalist Explanations for War

James D. Fearon

The central puzzle about war, and also the main reason we study it, is that wars are costly but nonetheless wars recur. Scholars have attempted to resolve the puzzle with three types of argument. First, one can argue that people (and state leaders in particular) are sometimes or always irrational. . . . Second, one can argue that the leaders who order war enjoy its benefits but do not pay the costs, which are suffered by soldiers and citizens. Third, one can argue that even rational leaders who consider the risks and costs of war may end up fighting nonetheless. This article focuses on arguments of the third sort, which I will call rationalist explanations. . . .

My main argument is that on close inspection none of the principal rationalist arguments advanced in the literature holds up as an explanation because none addresses or adequately resolves the central puzzle, namely, that war is costly and risky, so rational states should have incentives to locate negotiated settlements that all would prefer to the gamble of war. The common flaw of the standard rationalist arguments is that they fail either to address or to explain adequately what prevents leaders from reaching *ex ante* (prewar) bargains that would avoid the costs and risks of fighting. A coherent rationalist explanation for war must do more than give reasons why armed conflict might appear an attractive option to a rational leader under some circumstances—it must show why states are unable to locate an alternative outcome that both would prefer to a fight. . . .

If these standard arguments do not resolve the puzzle on rationalist terms, what does? I propose that there are three defensible answers, which take the form of general mechanisms, or causal logics, that operate in a variety of more specific international contexts. In the first mechanism, rational leaders may be unable to locate a mutually preferable negotiated settlement due to *private information* about relative capabilities or resolve and *incentives to misrepresent* such information. Leaders know things about their military capabilities and willingness to fight that other states do not know, and in bargaining situations they can have incentives to misrepresent such private information in order to gain a better deal. . . .

Second, rationally led states may be unable to arrange a settlement that both would prefer to war due to *commitment problems*, situations in which mutually preferable bargains are unattainable because one or more states would have an incentive to renege on the terms. . . .

The third sort of rationalist explanation I find less compelling than the first two, although it is logically tenable. States might be unable to locate a peaceful settlement both prefer due to *issue indivisibilities*. Perhaps some issues, by their very natures, simply will not admit compromise. Though neither example is wholly convincing, issues that might exhibit indivisibility include abortion in domestic politics and the problem of which prince sits on the throne of, say, Spain, in eighteenth- or nineteenth-century international politics. . . .

The Puzzle

Most historians and political scientists who study war dismiss as naive the view that all wars must be unwanted because they entail destruction and suffering. Instead, most agree that while a few wars may have been unwanted by the leaders who brought them about—World War I is sometimes given as an example—many or perhaps most wars were simply wanted. The leaders involved viewed war as a costly but worthwhile gamble.

Moreover, many scholars believe that wanted wars are easily explained from a rationalist perspective. Wanted wars are thought to be Pareto-efficient—they occur when no negotiated settlements exist that both sides would prefer to the gamble of military conflict. Conventional wisdom holds that while this situation may be tragic, it is entirely possible between states led by rational leaders who consider the costs and risks of fighting. Unwanted wars, which take place despite the existence of settlements both sides preferred to conflict, are thought to pose more of a puzzle, but one that is resolvable and also fairly rare.

The conventional distinction between wanted and unwanted wars misunderstands the puzzle posed by war. The reason is that the standard conception does not distinguish between two types of efficiency—*ex ante* and *ex post*. As long as both sides suffer some costs for fighting, then war is always inefficient *ex post*—both sides would have been better off if they could have achieved the same final resolution without suffering the costs (or by paying lower costs). This is true even if the costs of fighting are small, or if one or both sides viewed the potential benefits as greater than the costs, since there are still costs. Unless states enjoy the activity of fighting for its own sake, as a consumption good, then war is inefficient *ex post*.

From a rationalist perspective, the central puzzle about war is precisely this *ex post* inefficiency. Before fighting, both sides know that war will entail some costs, and even if they expect offsetting benefits they still have an incentive to avoid the costs. The central question, then, is what prevents states in a dispute from reaching an *ex ante* agreement that avoids the costs they know will be paid *ex post* if they go to war? Giving a rationalist explanation for war amounts to answering this question. . . .

War Due to Private Information and Incentives to Misrepresent

Two commonly employed rationalist explanations in the literature directly address the preceding question. Both turn on the claim that war can be and often is the product of rational miscalculation. One explanation holds that a state's leaders may rationally overestimate their chance of military victory against an adversary, so producing a disagreement about relative power that only war can resolve. The other argues that rationally led states may lack information about an adversary's willingness to fight over some interest and so may challenge in the mistaken belief that war will not follow. . . .

While these ideas point toward a tenable rationalist explanation for war, neither goes far enough and neither works by itself. Both neglect the fact that states can in principle communicate with each other and so avoid a costly miscalculation of relative power or will. The cause of war cannot be simply lack of information, but whatever it is that prevents its disclosure. I argue that the fact that states have incentives to misrepresent their positions is crucial here, explaining on rationalist terms why diplomacy may not allow rational states to clarify disagreements about relative power or to avoid the miscalculation of resolve. . . .

In a rationalist framework, disagreements about relative power and uncertainty about a potential opponent's willingness to fight must have the same source: leaders' private information about factors affecting the likely course of a war or their resolve to fight over specific interests. In order to avoid war's *ex post* inefficiency, leaders have incentives to share any such private information, which would have the effect of revealing peaceful settlements that lie within the bargaining range. So, to explain how war could occur between states led by rational leaders who consider the costs of fighting, we need to explain what would prevent them from sharing such private information.

Incentives to Misrepresent in Bargaining

Prewar bargaining may fail to locate an outcome in the bargaining range because of strategic incentives to withhold or misrepresent private information. While states have an incentive to avoid the costs of war, they also wish to obtain a favorable resolution of the issues. This latter desire can give them an incentive to exaggerate their true willingness or capability to fight, if by doing so they might deter future challenges or persuade the other side to make concessions. States can also have an incentive to conceal their capabilities or resolve, if they are concerned that revelation would make them militarily (and hence politically) vulnerable or would reduce the chances for a successful first strike. Similarly, states may conceal their true willingness to fight in order to avoid appearing as the aggressor.

Combined with the fact of private information, these various incentives to misrepresent can explain why even rational leaders may be unable to avoid the miscalculations of relative will and power that can cause war. . . .

The July crisis of World War I provides several examples of how incentives to misrepresent can make miscalculations of resolve hard to dispel. Soon after German leaders secretly endorsed Austrian plans to crush Serbia, they received both direct and indirect verbal indications from St. Petersburg that Russia would fight rather than acquiesce.[1] For example, on 21 July, the Russian Foreign Minister told the German ambassador that "Russia would not be able to tolerate Austria-Hungary's using threatening language to Serbia or taking military measures."[2] Such verbal statements had little effect on German leaders' beliefs, however, since they knew Russian leaders had a strategic incentive to misrepresent. On 18 July in a cable explaining Berlin's policy to Ambassador Lichnowsky in London, Secretary of State Jagow wrote that "there is certain to be some blustering in St. Petersburg."[3] Similarly, when on 26 July Lichnowsky began to report that Britain might join with France and Russia in the event of war, German Chancellor Bethmann Hollweg told his personal assistant of the "danger that France and England will commit their support to Russia in order not to alienate it, perhaps without really believing that for us mobilization means war, thinking of it as a bluff which they answer with a counterbluff."[4]

At the same time, the Chancellor had an incentive to misrepresent the strength and nature of German support for Austria's plans. Bethmann correctly anticipated that revealing this information would make Germany appear the aggressor, which might undermine Social Democratic support for his policies in Germany as well as turn British public opinion more solidly against his state. This incentive led the Chancellor to avoid making direct or pointed inquiries about England's attitude in case of war. The incentive also led him to pretend to go along with the British Foreign Secretary's proposals for a conference to mediate the dispute. In consequence, Lord Grey may not have grasped the need for a stronger warning to Germany until fairly late in the crisis (on 29 July), by which time diplomatic and military actions had made backing off more difficult for both Austria and Germany.

In July 1914, incentives to misrepresent private information fostered and supported miscalculations of willingness to fight. Miscalculations of relative power can arise from this same source. On the one hand, states at times have an incentive to exaggerate their capabilities in an attempt to do better in bargaining. On the other hand, they can also have the well-known incentive to withhold information about capabilities and strategy. Presumably because of the strongly zero-sum aspect of military engagements, a state that has superior knowledge of an adversary's war plans may do better in war and thus in prewar bargaining—hence, states rarely publicize war plans. While the theoretical logic has not been worked out, it seems plausible that states' incentives to conceal information about capabilities and strategy could help explain some disagreements about relative power.

The 1904 war between Japan and Russia serves to illustrate this scenario. On the eve of the war, Russian leaders believed that their military could almost certainly defeat Japan. In this conviction they differed little from the view of most European observers. By contrast, at the imperial council of 4 February that decided for war, the Japanese chief of staff estimated a fifty-fifty chance of prevailing, if their attack began immediately. Thus Japanese and Russian leaders disagreed about relative power—their estimates of the likelihood of victory summed to greater than 1. . . .

The disagreement arose in substantial part from Japanese private information about their military capabilities and how they compared with Russia's. A far superior intelligence service had provided the Japanese military with a clear picture of Russian strengths and weaknesses in Northeast Asia and enabled them to develop an effective offensive strategy. . . .

If by communicating this private information the Japanese could have led the Russians to see that their chances of victory were smaller than expected, they might have done so. . . . However, it was unthinkable for the Japanese to reveal such information or convince the Russians even if they did. In the first place, the Japanese could not simply make announcements about the quality of their forces, since the Russians would have had no reason to believe them. Second, explaining how they planned to win a war might seriously compromise any such attempt by changing the likelihood that they would win; there is a trade-off between revealing information about resolve or capabilities to influence bargaining and reducing the advantages of a first strike.

In sum, the combination of private information about relative power or will and the strategic incentive to misrepresent these afford a tenable rationalist explanation for war. While states always have incentives to locate a peaceful bargain cheaper than war, they also always have incentives to do well in the bargaining. Given the fact of private information about capabilities or resolve, these incentives mean that states cannot always use quiet diplomatic conversations to discover mutually preferable settlements. It may be that the only way to surmount this barrier to communication is to take actions that produce a real risk of inefficient war. . . .

War as a Consequence of Commitment Problems

This section considers a second and quite different rationalist mechanism by which war may occur even though the states in dispute share the same assessment of the bargaining range. Even if private information and incentives to misrepresent it do not tempt states into a risky process of discovery or foster costly investments in reputation, states may be unable to settle on an efficient bargained outcome when for structural reasons they cannot trust each other to uphold the deal. . . .

Preemptive War and Offensive Advantages

Consider the problem faced by two gunslingers with the following preferences. Each would most prefer to kill the other by stealth, facing no risk of retaliation, but each prefers that both live in peace to a gunfight in which each risks death. There is a bargain here that both sides prefer to "war"—namely, that each leaves the other alone—but without the enforcement capabilities of a third party, such as an effective sheriff, they may not be able to attain it. Given their preferences, neither person can credibly commit not to defect from the bargain by trying to shoot the other in the back. Note that no matter how far the shadow of the future extends, iteration (or repeat play) will not make cooperation possible in strategic situations of this sort. Because being the "sucker" here may mean being permanently eliminated, strategies of conditional cooperation such as tit-for-tat are infeasible. Thus, if we can find a plausible analogy in international relations, this example might afford a coherent rationalist explanation for war.

Preemptive war scenarios provide the analogy. If geography or military technology happened to create large first-strike or offensive advantages, then states might face the same problem as the gunslingers. . . .

Preventive War as a Commitment Problem

Empirically, preventive motivations seem more prevalent and important than preemptive concerns. In his diplomatic history of Europe from 1848 to 1918, A.J.P. Taylor argued that "every war between the Great Powers [in this period] started as a preventive war, not a war of conquest."[5] In this subsection I argue that within a rationalist framework, preventive war is properly understood as arising from a commitment problem occasioned by anarchy and briefly discuss some empirical implications of this view. . . .[6]

While preventive war arises here from states' inability to trust each other to keep to a bargain, the lack of trust is not due to states' uncertainty about present or future motivations, as in typical security-dilemma and spiral-model accounts. In my argument, states understand each other's motivations perfectly well—there is no private information—and they further understand that each would like to avoid the costs of war—they are not ineluctably greedy. Lack of trust arises here from the situation, a structure of preferences and opportunities, that gives one party an incentive to renege. . . .

Preventive motivations figured in the origins of World War I and are useful to illustrate these points. One of the reasons that German leaders were willing to run serious risks of global conflict in 1914 was that they feared the consequences of further growth of Russian military power, which appeared to them to be on a dangerous upward trajectory. Even if the increase in Russian power had not led Russia to attack Austria and Germany at some point in the future—war still being a costly option—greater Russian power would have allowed St. Petersburg to pursue a more aggressive foreign policy in the Balkans and the Near East, where Austria and Russia had conflicting interests. Austrian and German leaders greatly feared the consequences of such a (pro-Slav) Russian foreign policy for the domestic stability of the Austro-Hungarian Empire, thus giving them incentives for a preventive attack on Russia.

By the argument made above, the states should in principle have had incentives to cut a multiperiod deal both sides would have preferred to preventive war. For example, fearing preventive attack by Austria and Germany, Russian leaders might have wished to have committed themselves not to push so hard in the Balkans as to endanger the Dual Monarchy. But such a deal would be so obviously unenforceable as to not be worth proposing. Leaving aside the serious monitoring difficulties, once Russia had become stronger militarily, Austria would have no choice but to acquiesce to a somewhat more aggressive Russian policy in the Balkans. And so Russia would be drawn to pursue it, regardless of its overall motivation or desire for conquest of Austria-Hungary. . . .

Commitment, Strategic Territory, and the Problem of Appeasement

The objects over which states bargain frequently are themselves sources of military power. Territory is the most important example, since it may provide economic resources that can be used for the military or be strategically located, meaning that its control greatly increases a state's chances for successful attack or defense. Territory is probably also the main issue over which states fight wars.

In international bargaining on issues with this property, a commitment problem can operate that makes mutually preferable negotiated solutions unattainable. The problem is similar to that underlying preventive war. Here, both sides might prefer some package of territorial concessions to a fight, but if the territory in question is strategically vital or economically important, its transfer could radically increase one side's future bargaining leverage (think of the Golan Heights).

In principle, one state might prefer war to the status quo but be unable to commit not to exploit the large increase in bargaining leverage it would gain from limited territorial concessions. Thus the other state might prefer war to limited concessions (appeasement), so it might appear that the issues in dispute were indivisible. But the underlying cause of war in this instance is not indivisibility per se but rather the inability of states to make credible commitments under anarchy.

As an example, the 1939 Winter War between Finland and the Soviet Union followed on the refusal of the Finnish government to cede some tiny islands in the Gulf of Finland that Stalin seems to have viewed as necessary for the defense of Leningrad in the event of a European war. One of the main reasons the Finns were so reluctant to grant these concessions was that they believed they could not trust Stalin not to use these advantages to pressure Finland for more in the future. So it is possible that Stalin's inability to commit himself not to attempt to carry out in Finland the program he had just applied in the Baltic states may have led or contributed to a costly war both sides clearly wished to avoid.

Conclusion

The article has developed two major claims. First, under broad conditions the fact that fighting is costly and risky implies that there should exist negotiated agreements that rationally led states in dispute would prefer to war. This claim runs directly counter to the conventional view that rational states can and often do face a situation of deadlock, in which war occurs because no mutually preferable bargain exists.

Second, essentially two mechanisms, or causal logics, explain why rationally led states are sometimes unable to locate or agree on such a bargain: (1) the combination of private information about resolve or capability and incentives to misrepresent these, and (2) states' inability, in specific circumstances, to commit to uphold a deal. Historical examples were intended to suggest that both mechanisms can claim empirical relevance.

I conclude by anticipating two criticisms. First, I am not saying that explanations for war based on irrationality or "pathological" domestic politics are less empirically relevant. Doubtless they are important, but we cannot say how so or in what measure if we have not clearly specified the causal mechanisms making for war in the "ideal" case of rational unitary states. In fact, a better understanding of what the assumption of rationality really implies for explaining war may actually raise our estimate of the importance of particular irrational and second-image factors.

For example, once the distinction is made clear, bounded rationality may appear a more important cause of disagreements about relative power than private information about military capabilities. If private information about capabilities was often a major factor influencing the odds of victory, then we would expect rational leaders to update their war estimates during international crises; a tough bargaining stand by an adversary would signal that the adversary was militarily stronger than expected. Diplomatic records should then contain evidence of leaders reasoning as follows: "The fact that the other side is not backing down means that we are probably less likely to win at war than we initially thought." I do not know of a single clear instance of this sort of updating in any international crisis, even though updating about an opponent's resolve, or willingness to fight, is very common.

Second, one might argue that since both anarchy and private information plus incentives to misrepresent are constant features of international politics, neither can explain why states fail to strike a bargain preferable to war in one instance but not another. This argument is correct. But the task of specifying the causal mechanisms that explain the occurrence of war must precede the identification of factors that lead the mechanisms to produce one outcome rather than another in particular settings. That is, specific models in which commitment or information problems operate allow one to analyze how different variables (such as power shifts and cost-benefit ratios in the preventive war model) make for war in some cases rather than others.

Questions for Review

Fearon's arguments are developed within a set of assumptions about rationality; do you think this approach yields a good explanation for world politics? How important—and how accurate—do you think private information is?

Notes

1 Luigi Albertini, *The Origins of the War of 1914*, vol. 2 (London: Oxford University Press, 1953), pp. 183–87.

2 Ibid., p. 187.

3 Ibid., p. 158. For the full text of the cable, see Karl Kautsky, comp., *German Documents Relating to the Outbreak of the World War* (New York: Oxford University Press, 1924), doc. no. 71, p. 130.

4 Konrad Jarausch, "The Illusion of Limited War: Chancellor Bethmann Hollweg's Calculated Risk," *Central European History* 2 (March 1969), pp. 48–76. The quotation is drawn from p. 65.

5 Taylor, *The Struggle for Mastery in Europe, 1848–1918* (London: Oxford University Press, 1954), p. 166.

6 To my knowledge, Van Evera is the only scholar whose treatment of preventive war analyzes at some length how issues of credible commitment intervene. The issue is raised by both Snyder and Levy. See Van Evera, "Causes of War," pp. 62–64; Jack Snyder, "Perceptions of the Security Dilemma in 1914," in Robert Jervis, Richard Ned Lebow, and Janice Gross Stein, eds., *Psychology and Deterrence* (Baltimore, Md.: Johns Hopkins University Press, 1985), p. 160; and Jack Levy, "Declining Power and the Preventive Motivation for War," *World Politics* 40 (October 1987), p. 96.

Offense, Defense, and the Security Dilemma

Robert Jervis

Another approach starts with the central point of the security dilemma—that an increase in one state's security decreases the security of others—and examines the conditions under which this proposition holds. Two crucial variables are involved: whether defensive weapons and policies can be distinguished from offensive ones, and whether the defense or the offense has the advantage. The definitions are not always clear, and many cases are difficult to judge, but these two variables shed a great deal of light on the question of whether status-quo powers will adopt compatible security policies. All the variables discussed so far leave the heart of the problem untouched. But when defensive weapons differ from offensive ones, it is possible for a state to make itself more secure without making others less secure. And when the defense has the advantage over the offense, a large increase in one state's security only slightly decreases the security of the others, and status-quo powers can all enjoy a high level of security and largely escape from the state of nature.

Offense–Defense Balance

When we say that the offense has the advantage, we simply mean that it is easier to destroy the other's army and take its territory than it is to defend one's own. When the defense has the advantage, it is easier to protect and to hold than it is to move forward, destroy, and take. If effective defenses can be erected quickly, an attacker may be able to keep territory he has taken in an initial victory. Thus, the dominance of the defense made it very hard for Britain and France to push Germany out of France in World War I. But when superior defenses are difficult for an aggressor to improvise on the battlefield and must be constructed during peacetime, they provide no direct assistance to him.

The security dilemma is at its most vicious when commitments, strategy, or technology dictate that the only route to security lies through expansion. Status-quo powers must then act like aggressors: the fact that they would gladly agree to forego the opportunity for expansion in return for guarantees for their security has no implications for their behavior. Even if expansion is not sought as a goal in itself, there will be quick and drastic changes in the distribution of territory and influence. Conversely, when the defense has the advantage, status-quo states can make themselves more secure without gravely endangering others.[1] Indeed, if the defense has enough of an advantage and if the states are of roughly equal size, not only will the security dilemma cease to inhibit status-quo states from cooperating, but aggression will be next to impossible, thus rendering international anarchy relatively unimportant. If states cannot conquer each other, then the lack of sovereignty, although it presents problems of collective goods in a number of areas, no longer forces states to devote their primary attention to self-preservation. Although, if force were not usable, there would be fewer restraints on the use of nonmilitary instruments, these are rarely powerful enough to threaten the vital interests of a major state.

Two questions of the offense-defense balance can be separated. First, does the state have to spend more or less than one dollar on defensive forces to offset each dollar spent by the other side on forces that could be used to attack? If the state has one dollar to spend on increasing its security, should it put it into offensive or defensive forces? Second, with a given inventory of forces, is it better to attack or to defend? Is there an incentive to strike first or to absorb the other's blow? These two aspects are often linked: If each dollar spent on offense can overcome each dollar spent on defense, and if both sides have the same defense budgets, then both are likely to build offensive forces and find it attractive to attack rather than to wait for the adversary to strike.

These aspects affect the security dilemma in different ways. The first has its greatest impact on arms races. If the defense has the advantage, and if the status-quo powers have reasonable subjective security requirements, they can probably avoid an arms race. Although an increase in one side's arms and security will still decrease the other's security, the former's increase will be larger than the latter's decrease. So if one side increases its arms, the other can bring its security back up to its previous level by adding a smaller amount to its forces. And if the first side reacts to this change, its increase will also be smaller than the stimulus that produced it. Thus a stable equilibrium will be reached. Shifting from dynamics to statics, each side can be quite secure with forces roughly equal to those of the other. Indeed, if the defense is much more potent than the offense, each side can be willing to have forces much smaller than the other's, and can be indifferent to a wide range of the other's defense policies.

The second aspect—whether it is better to attack or to defend—-influences short-run stability. When the offense has the advantage, a state's reaction to international tension will increase the chances of war. The incentives for pre-emption and the "reciprocal fear of surprise attack" in this situation have been made clear by analyses of the dangers that exist when two countries have first-strike capabilities.[2] There is no way for the state to increase its security without menacing, or even attacking, the other. Even Bismarck, who once called preventive war "committing suicide from fear of death," said that "no government, if it regards war as inevitable even if it does not want it, would be so foolish as to leave to the enemy the choice of time and occasion and to wait for the moment which is most convenient for the enemy."[3] In another arena, the same dilemma applies to the policeman in a dark alley confronting a suspected criminal who appears to be holding a weapon. Though racism may indeed be present, the security dilemma can account for many of the tragic shootings of innocent people in the ghettos.

Beliefs about the course of a war in which the offense has the advantage further deepen the security dilemma. When there are incentives to strike first, a successful attack will usually so weaken the other side that victory will be relatively quick, bloodless, and decisive. It is in these periods when conquest is possible and attractive that states consolidate power internally—for instance, by destroying the feudal barons—and expand externally. There are several consequences that decrease the chance of cooperation among status-quo states. First, war will be profitable for the winner. The costs will be low and the benefits high. Of course, losers will suffer; the fear of losing could induce states to try to form stable cooperative arrangements, but the temptation of victory will make this particularly difficult. Second, because wars are expected to be both frequent and short, there will be incentives for high levels of arms, and quick and strong reaction to the other's increases in arms. The state cannot afford to wait until there is unambiguous evidence that the other is building new weapons. Even large states that have faith in their economic strength cannot wait, because the war will be over before their products can reach the army. Third, when wars are quick, states will have to recruit allies in advance.[4] Without the opportunity for bargaining and realignments during the opening stages of hostilities, peacetime diplomacy loses a degree of the fluidity that facilitates balance-of-power policies. Because alliances must be secured during peacetime, the international system is more likely to become bipolar. It is hard to say whether war therefore becomes more or less likely, but this bipolarity increases tension between the two camps and makes it harder for status-quo states to gain the benefits of cooperation. Fourth, if wars are frequent, statesmen's perceptual thresholds will be adjusted accordingly and they will be quick to perceive ambiguous evidence as indicating that others are aggressive. Thus, there will be more cases of status-quo powers arming against each other in the incorrect belief that the other is hostile.

When the defense has the advantage, all the foregoing is reversed. The state that fears attack does not preempt—since that would be a wasteful use of its military resources—but rather prepares to receive an attack. Doing so does not decrease the security of others, and several states can do it simultaneously; the situation will therefore be stable, and status-quo powers will be able to cooperate. When Herman Kahn argues that ultimatums "are vastly too dangerous to give because . . . they are quite likely to touch off a pre-emptive strike,"[5] he incorrectly assumes that it is always advantageous to strike first.

More is involved than short-run dynamics. When the defense is dominant, wars are likely to become stalemates and can be won only at enormous cost. Relatively small and weak states can hold off larger and stronger ones, or can deter attack by raising the costs of conquest to an unacceptable level. States then approach equality in what they can do to each other. Like the .45-caliber pistol in the American West, fortifications were the "great equalizer" in some periods. Changes in the status quo are less frequent and cooperation is more common wherever the security dilemma is thereby reduced.

Many of these arguments can be illustrated by the major powers' policies in the periods preceding the two world wars. Bismarck's wars surprised statesmen by showing that the offense had the advantage, and by being quick, relatively cheap, and quite decisive. Falling into a common error, observers projected this pattern into the future.[6] The resulting expectations had several effects. First, states sought semi-permanent allies. In the early stages of the Franco-Prussian War, Napoleon III had thought that there would be plenty of time to recruit Austria to his side. Now, others were not going to repeat this mistake. Second, defense budgets were high and reacted quite sharply to increases on the other side. It is not surprising that Richardson's theory of arms races fits this period well. Third, most decision makers thought that the next European war would not cost much blood and treasure.[7] That is one reason why war was generally seen as inevitable and why mass opinion was so bellicose. Fourth, once war seemed likely, there were strong pressures to preempt. Both sides believed that whoever moved first could penetrate the other deep enough to disrupt mobilization and thus gain an insurmountable advantage. (There was no such belief about the use of naval forces. Although Churchill made an ill-advised speech saying that if German ships "do not come out and fight in time of war they will be dug out like rats in a hole,"[8] everyone knew that submarines, mines and coastal fortifications made this impossible. So at the start of the war each navy prepared to defend itself rather than attack, and the short-run destabilizing forces that launched the armies toward each other did not operate.)[9] Furthermore, each side knew that the other saw the situation the same way, thus increasing the perceived danger that the other would attack, and giving each added reasons to precipitate a war if conditions seemed favorable. In the long and the short run, there were thus both offensive and defensive incentives to strike. This situation casts light on the common question about German motives in 1914: "Did Germany unleash the war deliberately to become a world power or did she support Austria merely to defend a weakening ally," thereby protecting her own position?[10] To some extent, this question is misleading. Because of the perceived advantage of the offense, war was seen as the best route both to gaining expansion and to avoiding drastic loss of influence. There seemed to be no way for Germany merely to retain and safeguard her existing position.

Of course the war showed these beliefs to have been wrong on all points. Trenches and machine guns gave the defense an overwhelming advantage. The fighting became deadlocked and produced horrendous casualties. It made no sense for the combatants to bleed themselves to death. If they had known the power of the defense beforehand, they would have rushed for their own trenches rather than for the enemy's territory. Each side could have done this without increasing the other's incentives to strike. War might have broken out anyway; but at least the pressures of time and the fear of allowing the other to get the first blow would not have contributed to this end. And, had both sides known the costs of the war, they would have negotiated much more seriously. The obvious question is why the states did not seek a negotiated settlement as soon as the shape of the war became clear. Schlieffen had said that if his plan failed, peace should be sought.[11] The answer is complex, uncertain, and largely outside of the scope of our concerns. But part of the reason was the hope and sometimes the expectation that breakthroughs could be made and the dominance of the offensive restored. Without that hope, the political and psychological pressures to fight to a decisive victory might have been overcome.

The politics of the interwar period were shaped by the memories of the previous conflict and the belief that any future war would resemble it. Political and military lessons reinforced each other in ameliorating the security dilemma. Because it was believed that the First World War had been a mistake that could have been avoided by skillful conciliation, both Britain and, to a lesser extent, France were highly sensitive to the possibility that interwar Germany was not a real threat to peace, and alert to the danger that reacting quickly and strongly to her arms could create unnecessary conflict. And because Britain and France expected the defense to continue to dominate, they concluded that it was safe to adopt a more relaxed and nonthreatening military posture.[12] Britain also felt less need to maintain tight alliance bonds. The Allies' military posture then constituted only a slight danger to Germany; had the latter been content with the status quo, it would have been easy for both sides to have felt secure behind their lines of fortifications. Of course the Germans were not content, so it is not surprising that they devoted their money and attention to finding ways out of a defense-dominated stalemate. *Blitzkrieg* tactics were necessary if they were to use force to change the status quo.

The initial stages of the war on the Western Front also contrasted with the First World War. Only with the new air arm were there any incentives to strike first, and these forces were too weak to carry out the grandiose plans that had been both dreamed and feared. The armies, still the main instrument, rushed to defensive positions. Perhaps the allies could have successfully attacked while the Germans were occupied in Poland.[13] But belief in the defense was so great that this was never seriously contemplated. Three months after the start of the war, the French Prime Minister summed up the view held by almost everyone but Hitler: on the Western Front there is "deadlock. Two Forces of equal strength and the one that attacks seeing such enormous casualties that it cannot move without endangering the continuation of the war or of the aftermath."[14] The Allies were caught in a dilemma they never fully recognized, let alone solved. On the one hand, they had very high war aims; although unconditional surrender had not yet been adopted, the British had decided from the start that the removal of Hitler was a necessary condition for peace.[15] On the other hand, there were no realistic plans or instruments for allowing the Allies to impose their will on the other side. The British Chief of the Imperial General Staff noted, "The French have no intention of carrying out an offensive for years, if at all"; the British were only slightly bolder.[16] So the Allies looked to a long war that would wear the Germans down, cause civilian suffering through shortages, and eventually undermine Hitler. There was little analysis to support this view—and indeed it probably was not supportable—but as long as the defense was dominant and the numbers on each side relatively equal, what else could the Allies do?

To summarize, the security dilemma was much less powerful after World War I than it had been before. In the later period, the expected power of the defense allowed status-quo states to pursue compatible security policies and avoid arms races. Furthermore, high tension and fear of war did not set off short-run dynamics by which each state, trying to increase its security, inadvertently acted to make war more likely. The expected high costs of war, however, led the Allies to believe that no sane German leader would run the risks entailed in an attempt to dominate the Continent, and discouraged them from risking war themselves.

Technology and Geography

Technology and geography are the two main factors that determine whether the offense or the defense has the advantage. As Brodie notes, "On the tactical level, as a rule, few physical factors favor the attacker but many favor the defender. The defender usually has the advantage of cover. He characteristically fires from behind some form of shelter while his opponent crosses open ground."[17] Anything that increases the amount of ground the attacker has to cross, or impedes his progress across it, or makes him more vulnerable while crossing, increases the advantage accruing to the defense. When states are separated by barriers that produce these effects, the security dilemma is eased, since both can have forces adequate for defense without being able to attack. Impenetrable barriers would actually prevent war; in reality, decision makers have to settle for a good deal less. Buffer zones slow the attacker's progress; they thereby give the defender time to prepare, increase problems of logistics, and reduce the number of soldiers available for the final assault. At the end of the nineteenth century, Arthur Balfour noted Afghanistan's "non-conducting" qualities. "So long as it possesses few roads, and no railroads, it will be impossible for Russia to make effective use of her great numerical superiority at any point immediately vital to the Empire." The Russians valued buffers for the same reasons; it is not surprising that when Persia was being divided into Russian and British spheres of influence some years later, the Russians sought assurances that the British would refrain from building potentially menacing railroads in their sphere. Indeed, since railroad construction radically altered the abilities of countries to defend themselves and to attack others, many diplomatic notes and much intelligence activity in the late nineteenth century centered on this subject.[18]

Oceans, large rivers, and mountain ranges serve the same function as buffer zones. Being hard to cross, they allow defense against superior numbers. The defender has merely to stay on his side of the barrier and so can utilize all the men he can bring up to it. The attacker's men, however, can cross only a few at a time, and they are very vulnerable when doing so. If all states were self-sufficient islands, anarchy would be much less of a problem. A small investment in shore defenses and a small army would be sufficient to repel invasion. Only very weak states would be vulnerable, and only very large ones could menace others. As noted above, the United States, and to a lesser extent Great Britain, have partly been able to escape from the state of nature because their geographical positions approximated this ideal.

Although geography cannot be changed to conform to borders, borders can and do change to conform to geography. Borders across which an attack is easy tend to be unstable. States living within them are likely to expand or be absorbed. Frequent wars are almost inevitable since attacking will often seem the best way to protect what one has. This process will stop, or at least slow down, when the state's borders reach—by expansion or contraction—a line of natural obstacles. Security without attack will then be possible. Furthermore, these lines constitute salient solutions to bargaining problems and, to the extent that they are barriers to migration, are likely to divide ethnic groups, thereby raising the costs and lowering the incentives for conquest.

Attachment to one's state and its land reinforce one quasi-geographical aid to the defense. Conquest usually becomes more difficult the deeper the attacker pushes into the other's territory. Nationalism spurs the defenders to fight harder; advancing not only lengthens the attacker's supply lines, but takes him through unfamiliar and often devastated lands that require troops for garrison duty. These stabilizing dynamics will not operate, however, if the defender's war matériel is situated near its borders, or if the people do not care about their state, but only about being on the winning side. In such cases, positive feedback will be at work and initial defeats will be insurmountable.[19]

Imitating geography, men have tried to create barriers. Treaties may provide for demilitarized zones on both sides of the border, although such zones will rarely be deep enough to provide more than warning. Even this was not possible in Europe, but the Russians adopted a gauge for their railroads that was broader than that of the neighboring states, thereby complicating the logistics problems of any attacker—including Russia.

Perhaps the most ambitious and at least temporarily successful attempts to construct a system that would aid the defenses of both sides were the interwar naval treaties, as they affected Japanese-American relations. As mentioned earlier, the problem was that the United States could not defend the Philippines without denying Japan the ability to protect her home islands.[20] (In 1941 this dilemma became insoluble when Japan sought to extend her control to Malaya and the Dutch East Indies. If the Philippines had been invulnerable, they could have provided a secure base from which the United States could interdict Japanese shipping between the homeland and the areas she was trying to conquer.) In the 1920s and early 1930s each side would have been willing to grant the other security for its possessions in return for a reciprocal grant, and the Washington Naval Conference agreements were designed to approach this goal. As a Japanese diplomat later put it, their country's "fundamental principle" was to have "a strength insufficient for attack and adequate for defense."[21] Thus Japan agreed in 1922 to accept a navy only three-fifths as large as that of the United States, and the United States agreed not to fortify its Pacific islands.[22] (Japan had earlier been forced to agree not to fortify the islands she had taken from Germany in World War I.) Japan's navy would not be large enough to defeat America's anywhere other than close to the home islands. Although the Japanese could still take the Philippines, not only would they be unable to move farther, but they might be weakened enough by their efforts to be vulnerable to counterattack. Japan, however, gained security. An American attack was rendered more difficult because the American bases were unprotected and because, until 1930, Japan was allowed unlimited numbers of cruisers, destroyers, and submarines that could weaken the American fleet as it made its way across the ocean.[23]

The other major determinant of the offense-defense balance is technology. When weapons are highly vulnerable, they must be employed before they are attacked. Others can remain quite invulnerable in their bases. The former characteristics are embodied in unprotected missiles and many kinds of bombers. (It should be noted that it is not vulnerability *per se* that is crucial, but the location of the vulnerability. Bombers and missiles that are easy to destroy only after having been launched toward their targets do not create destabilizing dynamics.) Incentives to strike first are usually absent for naval forces that are threatened by a naval attack. Like missiles in hardened silos, they are usually well protected when in their bases. Both sides can then simultaneously be prepared to defend themselves successfully.

In ground warfare under some conditions, forts, trenches, and small groups of men in prepared positions can hold off large numbers of attackers. Less frequently, a few attackers can storm the defenses. By and large, it is a contest between fortifications and supporting light weapons on the one hand, and mobility and heavier weapons that clear the way for the attack on the other. As the erroneous views held before the two world wars show, there is no simple way to determine which is dominant. "[T]hese oscillations are not smooth and predictable like those of a swinging pendulum. They are uneven in both extent and time. Some occur in the course of a single battle or campaign, others in the course of a war, still others during a series of wars." Longer-term oscillations can also be detected:

> The early Gothic age, from the twelfth to the late thirteenth century, with its wonderful cathedrals and fortified places, was a period during which the attackers in Europe generally met serious and increasing difficulties, because the improvement in the strength of fortresses outran the advance in the power of destruction. Later, with the spread of firearms at the end of the fifteenth century, old fortresses lost their power to resist. An age ensued during which the offense possessed, apart from short-term setbacks, new advantages. Then, during the seventeenth century, especially after about 1660, and until at least the outbreak of the War of the Austrian Succession in 1740, the defense regained much of the ground it had lost since the great medieval fortresses had proved unable to meet the bombardment of the new and more numerous artillery.[24]

Another scholar has continued the argument: "The offensive gained an advantage with new forms of heavy mobile artillery in the nineteenth century, but the stalemate of World War I created the impression that the defense again had an advantage; the German invasion in World War II, however, indicated the offensive superiority of highly mechanized armies in the field."[25]

The situation today with respect to conventional weapons is unclear. Until recently it was believed that tanks and tactical air power gave the attacker an advantage. The initial analyses of the 1973 Arab-Israeli war indicated that new anti-tank and anti-aircraft weapons have restored the primacy of the defense. These weapons are cheap, easy to use, and can destroy a high proportion of the attacking vehicles and planes that are sighted. It then would make sense for a status-quo power to buy lots of $20,000 missiles rather than buy a few half-million dollar fighter-bombers. Defense would be possible even against a large and well-equipped force; states that care primarily about self-protection would not need to engage in arms races. But further examinations of the new technologies and the history of the October War cast doubt on these optimistic conclusions and leave us unable to render any firm judgment.[26]

Concerning nuclear weapons, it is generally agreed that defense is impossible—a triumph not of the offense, but of deterrence. Attack makes no sense, not because it can be beaten off, but because the attacker will be destroyed in turn. In terms of the questions under consideration here, the result is the equivalent of the primacy of the defense. First, security is relatively cheap. Less than one percent of the G.N.P. is devoted to deterring a direct attack on the United States; most of it is spent on acquiring redundant systems to provide a lot of insurance against the worst conceivable contingencies. Second, both sides can simultaneously gain security in the form of second-strike capability. Third, and related to the foregoing, second-strike capability can be maintained in the face of wide variations in the other side's military posture. There is no purely military reason why each side has to react quickly and strongly to the other's increases in arms. Any spending that the other devotes to trying to achieve first-strike capability can be neutralized by the state's spending much smaller sums on protecting its second-strike capability. Fourth, there are no incentives to strike first in a crisis.

Important problems remain, of course. Both sides have interests that go well beyond defense of the homeland. The protection of these interests creates conflicts even if neither side desires expansion. Furthermore, the shift from defense to deterrence has greatly increased the importance and perceptions of resolve. Security now rests on each side's belief that the other would prefer to run high risks of total destruction rather than sacrifice its vital interests. Aspects of the security dilemma thus appear in a new form. Are weapons procurements used as an index of resolve? Must they be so used? If one side fails to respond to the other's buildup, will it appear weak and thereby invite predation? Can both sides simultaneously have images of high resolve or is there a zero-sum element involved? Although these problems are real, they are not as severe as those in the prenuclear era: There are many indices of resolve, and states do not so much judge images of resolve in the abstract as ask how likely it is that the other will stand firm in a particular dispute. Since states are most likely to stand firm on matters which concern them most, it is quite possible for both to demonstrate their resolve to protect their own security simultaneously.

Offense–Defense Differentiation

The other major variable that affects how strongly the security dilemma operates is whether weapons and policies that protect the state also provide the capability for attack. If they do not, the basic postulate of the security dilemma no longer applies. A state can increase its own security without decreasing that of others. The advantage of the defense can only ameliorate the security dilemma. A differentiation between offensive and defensive stances comes close to abolishing it. Such differentiation does not mean, however, that all security problems will be abolished. If the offense has the advantage, conquest and aggression will still be possible. And if the offense's advantage is great enough, status-quo powers may find it too expensive to protect themselves by defensive forces and decide to procure offensive weapons even though this will menace others. Furthermore, states will still have to worry that even if the other's military posture shows that it is peaceful now, it may develop aggressive intentions in the future.

Assuming that the defense is at least as potent as the offense, the differentiation between them allows status-quo states to behave in ways that are clearly different from those of aggressors. Three beneficial consequences follow. First, status-quo powers can identify each other, thus laying the foundations for cooperation. Conflicts growing out of the mistaken belief that the other side is expansionist will be less frequent. Second, status-quo states will obtain advance warning when others plan aggression. Before a state can attack, it has to develop and deploy offensive weapons. If procurement of these weapons cannot be disguised and takes a fair amount of time, as it almost always does, a status-quo state will have the time to take countermeasures. It need not maintain a high level of defensive arms as long as its potential adversaries are adopting a peaceful posture. (Although being so armed should not, with the one important exception noted below, alarm other status-quo powers.) States do, in fact, pay special attention to actions that they believe would not be taken by a status-quo state because they feel that states exhibiting such behavior are aggressive. Thus the seizure or development of transportation facilities will alarm others more if these facilities have no commercial value, and therefore can only be wanted for military reasons. In 1906, the British rejected a Russian protest about their activities in a district of Persia by claiming that this area was "only of [strategic] importance [to the Russians] if they wished to attack the Indian frontier, or to put pressure upon us by making us think that they intend to attack it."[27]

The same inferences are drawn when a state acquires more weapons than observers feel are needed for defense. Thus, the Japanese spokesman at the 1930 London naval conference said that his country was alarmed by the American refusal to give Japan a 70 percent ratio (in place of a 60 percent ratio) in heavy cruisers: "As long as America held that ten percent advantage, it was possible for her to attack. So when America insisted on sixty percent instead of seventy percent, the idea would exist that they were trying to keep that possibility, and the Japanese people could not accept that."[28] Similarly, when Mussolini told

Chamberlain in January 1939 that Hitler's arms program was motivated by defensive considerations, the Prime Minister replied that "German military forces were now so strong as to make it impossible for any Power or combination of Powers to attack her successfully. She could not want any further armaments for defensive purposes; what then did she want them for?"[29]

Of course these inferences can be wrong—as they are especially likely to be because states underestimate the degree to which they menace others.[30] And when they are wrong, the security dilemma is deepened. Because the state thinks it has received notice that the other is aggressive, its own arms building will be less restrained and the chances of cooperation will be decreased. But the dangers of incorrect inferences should not obscure the main point: When offensive and defensive postures are different, much of the uncertainty about the other's intentions that contributes to the security dilemma is removed.

The third beneficial consequence of a difference between offensive and defensive weapons is that if all states support the status quo, an obvious arms control agreement is a ban on weapons that are useful for attacking. As President Roosevelt put it in his message to the Geneva Disarmament Conference in 1933: "If all nations will agree wholly to eliminate from possession and use the weapons which make possible a successful attack, defenses automatically will become impregnable, and the frontiers and independence of every nation will become secure."[31] The fact that such treaties have been rare—the Washington naval agreements discussed above and the anti-ABM treaty can be cited as examples—shows either that states are not always willing to guarantee the security of others, or that it is hard to distinguish offensive from defensive weapons.

Is such a distinction possible? Salvador de Madariaga, the Spanish statesman active in the disarmament negotiations of the interwar years, thought not: "A weapon is either offensive or defensive according to which end of it you are looking at." The French Foreign Minister agreed (although French policy did not always follow this view): "Every arm can be employed offensively or defensively in turn. . . . The only way to discover whether arms are intended for purely defensive purposes or are held in a spirit of aggression is in all cases to enquire into the intentions of the country concerned." Some evidence for the validity of this argument is provided by the fact that much time in these unsuccessful negotiations was devoted to separating offensive from defensive weapons. Indeed, no simple and unambiguous definition is possible and in many cases no judgment can be reached. Before the American entry into World War I, Woodrow Wilson wanted to arm merchantmen only with guns in the back of the ship so they could not initiate a fight, but this expedient cannot be applied to more common forms of armaments.[32]

There are several problems. Even when a differentiation is possible, a status-quo power will want offensive arms under any of three conditions: (1) If the offense has a great advantage over the defense, protection through defensive forces will be too expensive. (2) Status-quo states may need offensive weapons to regain territory lost in the opening stages of war. It might be possible, however, for a state to wait to procure these weapons until war seems likely, and they might be needed only in relatively small numbers, unless the aggressor was able to construct strong defenses quickly in the occupied areas. (3) The state may feel that it must be prepared to take the offensive either because the other side will make peace only if it loses territory or because the state has commitments to attack if the other makes war on a third party. As noted above, status-quo states with extensive commitments are often forced to behave like aggressors. Even when they lack such commitments, status-quo states must worry about the possibility that if they are able to hold off an attack, they will still not be able to end the war unless they move into the other's territory to damage its military forces and inflict pain. Many American naval officers after the Civil War, for example, believed that "only by destroying the commerce of the opponent could the United States bring him to terms."[33]

A further complication is introduced by the fact that aggressors as well as status-quo powers require defensive forces as a prelude to acquiring offensive ones, to protect one frontier while attacking another, or for insurance in case the war goes badly. Criminals as well as policemen can use bulletproof vests. Hitler as well as Maginot built a line of forts. Indeed, Churchill reports that in 1936 the German Foreign Minister said: "As soon as our fortifications are constructed [on our western borders] and the countries in Central Europe realize that France cannot enter German territory, all these countries will begin to feel very differently about their foreign policies, and a new constellation will develop."[34] So a state may not necessarily be reassured if its neighbor constructs strong defenses.

More central difficulties are created by the fact that whether a weapon is offensive or defensive often depends on the particular situation—for instance, the geographical setting and the way in which the weapon is used. "Tanks. . . . spearheaded the fateful German thrust through the Ardennes in 1940, but if the French had disposed of a properly concentrated armored reserve, it would have provided the best means for their cutting off the penetration and turning into a disaster for the Germans what became instead an overwhelming victory."[35] Anti-aircraft weapons seem obviously defensive—to be used, they must wait for the other side to come to them. But the Egyptian attack on Israel in 1973 would have been impossible without effective air defenses that covered the battlefield. Nevertheless, some distinctions are possible. Sir John Simon, then the British Foreign Secretary, in response to the views cited earlier, stated that just because a fine line could not be drawn, "that was no reason for saying that there were not stretches of territory on either side which all practical men and women knew to be well on this or that side of the line." Although there are almost no weapons and strategies that are useful only for attacking, there are some that are almost exclusively defensive. Aggressors could want them for protection, but a state that relied mostly on them could not menace others. More frequently, we cannot "determine the absolute character of a weapon, but [we can] make a comparison. . . [and] discover whether or not the offensive potentialities predominate, whether a weapon is more useful in attack or in defense."[36]

The essence of defense is keeping the other side out of your territory. A purely defensive weapon is one that can do this without being able to penetrate the enemy's land. Thus a committee of military experts in an interwar disarmament conference declared that armaments "incapable of mobility by means of self-contained power," or movable only after long delay, were "only capable of being used for the defense of a State's territory."[37] The most obvious examples are fortifications. They can shelter attacking forces, especially when they are built right along the frontier,[38] but they cannot occupy enemy territory. A state with only a strong line of forts, fixed guns, and a small army to man them would not be much of a menace. Anything else that can serve only as a barrier against attacking troops is similarly defensive. In this category are systems that provide warning of an attack, the Russian's adoption of a different railroad gauge, and nuclear land mines that can seal off invasion routes.

If total immobility clearly defines a system that is defensive only, limited mobility is unfortunately ambiguous. As noted above, short-range fighter aircraft and anti-aircraft missiles can be used to cover an attack. And, unlike forts, they can advance with the troops. Still, their inability to reach deep into enemy territory does make them more useful for the defense than for the offense. Thus, the United States and Israel would have been more alarmed in the early 1970s had the Russians provided the Egyptians with long-range instead of short-range aircraft. Naval forces are particularly difficult to classify in these terms, but those that are very short-legged can be used only for coastal defense.

Any forces that for various reasons fight well only when on their own soil in effect lack mobility and therefore are defensive. The most extreme example would be passive resistance. Noncooperation can thwart an aggressor, but it is very hard for large numbers of people to cross the border and stage a sit-in on another's territory. Morocco's recent march on the Spanish Sahara approached this tactic, but its success depended on special circumstances. Similarly, guerrilla warfare is defensive to the extent to which it requires civilian support that is likely to be forthcoming only in opposition to a foreign invasion. Indeed, if guerrilla warfare were easily exportable and if it took ten defenders to destroy each guerrilla, then this weapon would not only be one which could be used as easily to attack the other's territory as to defend one's own, but one in which the offense had the advantage: so the security dilemma would operate especially strongly.

If guerrillas are unable to fight on foreign soil, other kinds of armies may be unwilling to do so. An army imbued with the idea that only defensive wars were just would fight less effectively, if at all, if the goal were conquest. Citizen militias may lack both the ability and the will for aggression. The weapons employed, the short term of service, the time required for mobilization, and the spirit of repelling attacks on the homeland, all lend themselves much more to defense than to attacks on foreign territory.[39]

Less idealistic motives can produce the same result. A leading student of medieval warfare has described the armies of that period as follows: "Assembled with difficulty, insubordinate, unable to maneuver, ready to melt away from its standard the moment that its short period of service was over, a feudal force presented an assemblage of unsoldierlike qualities such as have seldom been known to coexist. Primarily intended to defend its own borders from the Magyar, the Northman, or the Saracen . . . , the institution was utterly unadapted to take the offensive."[40] Some political groupings can be similarly described. International coalitions are more readily held together by fear than by hope of gain. Thus Castlereagh was not being entirely self-serving when in 1816 he argued that the Quadruple Alliance "could only have owed its origin to a sense of common danger; in its very nature it must be conservative; it cannot threaten either the security or the liberties of other States."[41] It is no accident that most of the major campaigns of expansion have been waged by one dominant nation (for example, Napoleon's France and Hitler's Germany), and that coalitions among relative equals are usually found defending the status quo. Most gains from conquest are too uncertain and raise too many questions of future squabbles among the victors to hold an alliance together for long. Although defensive coalitions are by no means easy to maintain—-conflicting national objectives and the free-rider problem partly explain why three of them dissolved before Napoleon was defeated—the common interest of seeing that no state dominates provides a strong incentive for solidarity.

Weapons that are particularly effective in reducing fortifications and barriers are of great value to the offense. This is not to deny that a defensive power will want some of those weapons if the other side has them: Brodie is certainly correct to argue that while their tanks allowed the Germans to conquer France, properly used French tanks could have halted the attack. But France would not have needed these weapons if Germany had not acquired them, whereas even if France had no tanks, Germany could not have foregone them since they provided the only chance of breaking through the French lines. Mobile heavy artillery is, similarly, especially useful in destroying fortifications. The defender, while needing artillery to fight off attacking troops or to counterattack, can usually use lighter guns since they do not need to penetrate such massive obstacles. So it is not surprising that one of the few things that most nations at the interwar disarmament conferences were able to agree on was that heavy tanks and mobile heavy guns were particularly valuable to a state planning an attack.[42]

Weapons and strategies that depend for their effectiveness on surprise are almost always offensive. That fact was recognized by some of the delegates to the interwar disarmament conferences and is the principle behind the common national ban on concealed weapons. An earlier representative of this widespread view was the mid-nineteenth-century Philadelphia newspaper that argued: "As a measure of defense, knives, dirks, and sword canes are entirely useless. They are fit only for attack, and all such attacks are of murderous character. Whoever carries such a weapon has prepared himself for homicide."[43]

It is, of course, not always possible to distinguish between forces that are most effective for holding territory and forces optimally designed for taking it. Such a distinction could not have been made for the strategies and weapons in Europe during most of the period between the Franco-Prussian War and World War I. Neither naval forces nor tactical air forces can be readily classified in these terms. But the point here is that when such a distinction is possible, the central characteristic of the security dilemma no longer holds, and one of the most troublesome consequences of anarchy is removed.

Offense-Defense Differentiation and Strategic Nuclear Weapons

In the interwar period, most statesmen held the reasonable position that weapons that threatened civilians were offensive.[44] But when neither side can protect its civilians, a counter-city posture is defensive because the state can credibly threaten to retaliate only in response to an attack on itself or its closest allies. The costs of this strike are so high that the state could not threaten to use it for the less-than-vital interest of compelling the other to abandon an established position.

In the context of deterrence, offensive weapons are those that provide defense. In the now familiar reversal of common sense, the state that could take its population out of hostage, either by active or passive defense or by destroying the other's strategic weapons on the ground, would be able to alter the status quo. The desire to prevent such a situation was one of the rationales for the anti-ABM agreements; it explains why some arms controllers opposed building ABMs to protect cities, but favored sites that covered ICBM fields. Similarly, many analysts wanted to limit warhead accuracy and favored multiple re-entry vehicles (MRVs), but opposed multiple independently targetable re-entry vehicles (MIRVs). The former are more useful than single warheads for penetrating city defenses, and ensure that the state has a second-strike capability. MIRVs enhance counterforce capabilities. . . .

What is most important for the argument here is that land-based ICBMs are both offensive and defensive, but when both sides rely on Polaris-type systems (SLBMs), offense and defense use different weapons. ICBMs can be used either to destroy the other's cities in retaliation or to initiate hostilities by attacking the other's strategic missiles. Some measures—for instance, hardening of missile sites and warning systems—are purely defensive, since they do not make a first strike easier. Others are predominantly offensive—for instance, passive or active city defenses, and highly accurate warheads. But ICBMs themselves are useful for both purposes. And because states seek a high level of insurance, the desire for protection as well as the contemplation of a counterforce strike can explain the acquisition of extremely large numbers of missiles. So it is very difficult to infer the other's intentions from its military posture. Each side's efforts to increase its own security by procuring more missiles decreases, to an extent determined by the relative efficacy of the offense and the defense, the other side's security. That is not the case when both sides use SLBMs. The point is not that sea-based systems are less vulnerable than land-based ones (this bears on the offense-defense ratio) but that SLBMs are defensive, retaliatory weapons. . . . SLBMs are not the main instrument of attack against other SLBMs. The hardest problem confronting a state that wants to take its cities out of hostage is to locate the other's SLBMs, a job that requires not SLBMs but anti-submarine weapons. A state might use SLBMs to attack the other's submarines (although other weapons would probably be more efficient), but without anti-submarine warfare (ASW) capability the task cannot be performed. A status-quo state that wanted to forego offensive capability could simply forego ASW research and procurement. . . .

When both sides rely on ICBMs, one side's missiles can attack the other's, and so the state cannot be indifferent to the other's building program. But because one side's SLBMs do not menace the other's, each side can build as many as it wants and the other need not respond. Each side's decision on the size of its force depends on technical questions, its judgment about how much destruction is enough to deter, and the amount of insurance it is willing to pay for—and these considerations are independent of the size of the other's strategic force. Thus the crucial nexus in the arms race is severed. . . .

Four Worlds

The two variables we have been discussing—whether the offense or the defense has the advantage, and whether offensive postures can be distinguished from defensive ones—can be combined to yield four possible worlds.

The first world is the worst for status-quo states. These is no way to get security without menacing others, and security through defense is terribly difficult to obtain. Because offensive and defensive postures are the same, status-quo states acquire the same kind of arms that are sought by aggressors. And because the offense has the advantage over the defense, attacking is the best route to protecting what you have; status-quo states will therefore behave like aggressors. The situation will be unstable. Arms races are likely. Incentives to strike first will turn crises into wars. Decisive victories and conquests will be common. States will grow and shrink rapidly, and it will be hard for any state to maintain its size and influence without trying to increase them. Cooperation among status-quo powers will be extremely hard to achieve.

There are no cases that totally fit this picture, but it bears more than a passing resemblance to Europe before World War I. Britain and Germany, although in many respects natural allies, ended up as enemies. Of course much of the explanation lies in Germany's ill-chosen policy. And from the perspective of our theory, the powers' ability to avoid war in a series of earlier crises cannot be easily explained. Nevertheless, much of the behavior in this period was the product of technology and beliefs that magnified the security dilemma. Decision makers thought that the offense had a big advantage and saw little difference between offensive and defensive military postures. The era was characterized by arms races. And once war seemed likely, mobilization races created powerful incentives to strike first.

In the nuclear era, the first world would be one in which each side relied on vulnerable weapons that were aimed at similar forces and each side understood the situation. In this case, the incentives to strike first would be very high—so high that status-quo powers as well as aggressors would be sorely tempted to preempt. And since the forces could be used to change the status quo as well as to preserve it, there would be no way for both sides to increase their security simultaneously. Now the familiar logic of deterrence leads both sides to see the dangers in this world. Indeed, the new understanding of this situation was one reason why vulnerable bombers and missiles were replaced. Ironically, the 1950s would have been more hazardous if the decision makers had been aware of the dangers of their posture and had therefore felt greater pressure to strike first.

In the second world, the security dilemma operates because offensive and defensive postures cannot be distinguished; but it does not operate as strongly as in the first world because the defense has the advantage, and so an increment in one side's strength increases its security more than it decreases the other's. So, if both sides have reasonable subjective security requirements, are of roughly equal power, and the variables discussed earlier are favorable, it is quite likely that status-quo states can adopt compatible security policies. Although a state will not be able to judge the other's intentions from the kinds of weapons it procures, the level of arms spending will give important evidence. Of course a state that seeks a high level of arms might be not an aggressor but merely an insecure state, which if conciliated will reduce its arms, and if confronted will reply in kind. To assume that the apparently excessive level of arms indicates aggressiveness could therefore lead to a response that would deepen the dilemma and create needless conflict. But empathy and skillful statesmanship can reduce this danger. Furthermore, the advantageous position of the defense means that a status-quo state can often maintain a high degree of security with a level of arms lower than that of its expected adversary. Such a state demonstrates that it lacks the ability or desire to alter the status quo, at least at the present time. The strength of the defense also allows states to react slowly and with restraint when they fear that others are menacing them. So, although status-quo powers will to some extent be threatening to others, that extent will be limited.

This world is the one that comes closest to matching most periods in history. Attacking is usually harder than defending because of the strength of fortifications and obstacles. But purely defensive postures are rarely possible because fortifications are usually supplemented by armies and mobile guns which can support an attack. In the nuclear era, this world would be one in which both sides relied on relatively invulnerable ICBMs and believed that limited nuclear war was impossible. Assuming no MIRVs, it would take more than one attacking missile to destroy one of the adversary's. Preemption is therefore unattractive. If both sides have large inventories, they can ignore all but drastic increases on the other side. A world of either ICBMs or SLBMs in which both sides adopted the policy of limited nuclear war would probably fit in this category too. The means of preserving the status quo would also be the means of changing it, as we discussed earlier. And the defense usually would have the advantage, because compellence is more difficult than deterrence. Although a state might succeed in changing the status quo on issues that matter much more to it than to others, status-quo powers could deter major provocations under most circumstances.

In the third world there may be no security dilemma, but there are security problems. Because states can procure defensive systems that do not threaten others, the dilemma need not operate. But because the offense has the advantage, aggression is possible, and perhaps easy. If the offense has less of an advantage, stability and cooperation are likely because the status-quo states will procure defensive forces. They need not react to others who are similarly armed, but can wait for the warning they would receive if others started to deploy offensive weapons. But each state will have to watch the others carefully, and there is room for false suspicions. The costliness of the defense and the allure of the offense can lead to unnecessary mistrust, hostility, and war, unless some of the variables discussed earlier are operating to restrain defection.

Table 1

	Offense Has the Advantage	Defense Has the Advantage
	1	2
Offensive posture not distinguishable from defensive one	Doubly dangerous	Security dilemma, but security requirements may be compatible
	3	4
Offensive posture distinguishable from defensive one	No security dilemma, but aggression possible	Doubly stable
	Status-quo states can follow different policy than aggressors	
	Warning given	

A hypothetical nuclear world that would fit this description would be one in which both sides relied on SLBMs, but in which ASW techniques were very effective. Offense and defense would be different, but the former would have the advantage. This situation is not likely to occur; but if it did, a status-quo state could show its lack of desire to exploit the other by refraining from threatening its submarines. The desire to have more protecting you than merely the other side's fear of retaliation is a strong one, however, and a state that knows that it would not expand even if its cities were safe is likely to believe that the other would not feel threatened by its ASW program. It is easy to see how such a world could become unstable, and how spirals of tensions and conflict could develop.

The fourth world is doubly safe. The differentiation between offensive and defensive systems permits a way out of the security dilemma; the advantage of the defense disposes of the problems discussed in the previous paragraphs. There is no reason for a status-quo power to be tempted to procure offensive forces, and aggressors give notice of their intentions by the posture they adopt. Indeed, if the advantage of the defense is great enough, there are no security problems. The loss of the ultimate form of the power to alter the status quo would allow greater scope for the exercise of nonmilitary means and probably would tend to freeze the distribution of values.

This world would have existed in the first decade of the twentieth century if the decision makers had understood the available technology. In that case, the European powers would have followed different policies both in the long run and in the summer of 1914. Even Germany, facing powerful enemies on both sides, could have made herself secure by developing strong defenses. France could also have made her frontier almost impregnable. Furthermore, when crises arose, no one would have had incentives to strike first. There would have been no competitive mobilization races reducing the time available for negotiations.

In the nuclear era, this world would be one in which the superpowers relied on SLBMs, ASW technology was not up to its task, and limited nuclear options were not taken seriously. . . . Because the problem of violence below the nuclear threshold would remain, on issues other than defense of the homeland, there would still be security dilemmas and security problems. But the world would nevertheless be safer than it has usually been.

Questions for Review

Is the security dilemma a basic cause of conflict in international politics? Is it ever possible to distinguish offensive weapons and political strategies from defensive ones?

Notes

1 Thus, when Wolfers argues that a status-quo state that settles for rough equality of power with its adversary, rather than seeking preponderance, may be able to convince the other to reciprocate by showing that it wants only to protect itself, not menace the other, he assumes that the defense has an advantage. See Arnold Wolfers, *Discord and Collaboration* (Baltimore: Johns Hopkins Press, 1962), p. 126.

2 Thomas Schelling, *The Strategy of Conflict* (New York: Oxford University Press, 1963), chap. 9.

3 Quoted in Fritz Fischer, *War of Illusions* (New York: Norton, 1975), pp. 377, 461.

4 George Quester, *Offense and Defense in the International System* (New York: John Wiley, 1977), p. 105.

5 Herman Kahn, *On Thermonuclear War* (Princeton, N.J.: Princeton University Press, 1960), p. 211 (also see p. 144).

6 For a general discussion of such mistaken learning from the past, see Jervis, *Perception and Misperception in International Relations* (Princeton, N.J.: Princeton University Press, 1976), chap. 6. The important and still not completely understood question of why this belief formed and was maintained throughout the war is examined in Bernard Brodie, *War and Politics* (New York: Macmillan, 1973), pp. 262–70; Brodie, "Technological Change, Strategic Doctrine, and Political Outcomes," in Klaus Knorr, ed., *Historical Dimensions of National Security Problems* (Lawrence: University Press of Kansas, 1976), pp. 290–92; and Douglas Porch, "The French Army and the Spirit of the Offensive, 1900–14," in Brian Bond and Ian Roy, eds., *War and Society* (New York: Holmes & Meier, 1975), pp. 117–43.

7 Some were not so optimistic. Grey's remark is well-known: "The lamps are going out all over Europe; we shall not see them lit again in our life-time." The German Prime Minister, Bethmann Hollweg, also feared the consequences of the war. But the controlling view was that it would certainly pay for the winner.

8 Quoted in Martin Gilbert, *Winston S. Churchill*, III, *The Challenge of War, 1914–1916* (Boston: Houghton Mifflin, 1971), p. 84.

9 Quester (fn. 4), pp. 98–99. Robert Art, *The Influence of Foreign Policy on Seapower*, II (Beverly Hills: Sage Professional Papers in International Studies Series, 1973), pp. 14–18, 26–28.

10 Konrad Jarausch, "The Illusion of Limited War: Chancellor Bethmann Hollweg's Calculated Risk, July 1914," *Central European History*, II (March 1969): p. 50.

11 Brodie, *War and Politics* (New York: Macmillan, 1973), p. 58.

12 President Roosevelt and the American delegates to the League of Nations Disarmament Conference maintained that the tank and the mobile heavy artillery had reestablished the dominance of the offensive, thus making disarmament more urgent (Marion Boggs, *Attempts to Define and Limit "Aggressive" Armament in Diplomacy and Strategy* [Columbia: University of Missouri Studies, XVI, No. 1, 1941]: pp. 31, 108), but this was a minority position and may not even have been believed by the Americans. The reduced prestige and influence of the military, and the high pressures to cut government spending throughout this period also contributed to the lowering of defense budgets.

13 Jon Kimche, *The Unfought Battle* (New York: Stein, 1968); Nicholas William Bethell, *The War Hitler Won: The Fall of Poland, September 1939* (New York: Holt, 1972); Alan Alexandroff and Richard Rosecrance, "Deterrence in 1939," *World Politics*, XXIX (April 1977): pp. 404–24.

14 Roderick Macleod and Denis Kelly, eds., *Time Unguarded: The Ironside Diaries, 1937–1940* (New York: McKay, 1962), p. 173.

15 For a short time, as France was falling, the British Cabinet did discuss reaching a negotiated peace with Hitler. The official history downplays this, but it is covered in P. M. H. Bell, *A Certain Eventuality* (Farnborough, England: Saxon House, 1974), pp. 40–48.

16 MacLeod and Kelly (fn. 14), p. 174. In flat contradiction to common sense and almost everything they believed about modern warfare, the Allies planned an expedition to Scandinavia to cut the supply of iron ore to Germany and to aid Finland against the Russians. But the dominant mood was the one described above.

17 Brodie (fn. 11), p. 179.

18 Arthur Balfour, "Memorandum," Committee on Imperial Defence, April 30, 1903, pp. 2–3; see the telegrams by Sir Arthur Nicolson, in G. P. Gooch and Harold Temperley, eds., *British Documents on the Origins of the War*, Vol. 4 (London: H.M.S.O., 1929), pp. 429, 524. These barriers do not prevent the passage of long-range aircraft; but even in the air, distance usually aids the defender.

19 See, for example, the discussion of warfare among Chinese warlords in Hsi-Sheng Chi, "The Chinese Warlord System as an International System," in Morton Kaplan, ed., *New Approaches to International Relations* (New York: St. Martin's, 1968), pp. 405–25.

20 Some American decision makers, including military officers, thought that the best way out of the dilemma was to abandon the Philippines.

21 Quoted in Elting Morison, *Turmoil and Tradition: A Study of the Life and Times of Henry L. Stimson* (Boston: Houghton Mifflin, 1960), p. 326.

22 The United States "refused to consider limitations on Hawaiian defenses, since these works posed no threat to Japan." William Braisted, *The United States Navy in the Pacific, 1909–1922* (Austin: University of Texas Press, 1971), p. 612.

23 That is part of the reason why the Japanese admirals strongly objected when the civilian leaders decided to accept a seven-to-ten ratio in lighter craft in 1930. Stephen Pelz, *Race to Pearl Harbor* (Cambridge, Mass.: Harvard University Press, 1974), p. 3.

24 John Nef, *War and Human Progress* (New York: Norton, 1963), p. 185. Also see *ibid.*, pp. 237, 242–43, and 323; C. W. Oman, *The Art of War in the Middle Ages* (Ithaca, N.Y.: Cornell University Press, 1953), pp. 70–72; John Beeler, *Warfare in Feudal Europe, 730–1200* (Ithaca, N.Y.: Cornell University Press, 1971), pp. 212–14; Michael Howard, *War in European History* (London: Oxford University Press, 1976), pp. 33–37.

25 Quincy Wright, *A Study of War* (abridged ed.; Chicago: University of Chicago Press, 1964), p. 142. Also see pp. 63–70, 74–75. There are important exceptions to these generalizations—the American Civil War, for instance, falls in the middle of the period Wright says is dominated by the offense.

26 Geoffrey Kemp, Robert Pfaltzgraff, and Uri Ra'anan, eds., *The Other Arms Race* (Lexington, Mass.: D.C. Heath, 1975); James Foster, "The Future of Conventional Arms Control," *Policy Sciences*, No. 8 (Spring 1977): pp. 1–19.

27 Richard Challener, *Admirals, Generals, and American Foreign Policy, 1898–1914* (Princeton, N.J.: Princeton University Press, 1973); Grey to Nicolson, in Gooch and Temperley (fn. 18), p. 414.

28 Quoted in James Crowley, *Japan's Quest for Autonomy* (Princeton, N.J.: Princeton University Press, 1966), p. 49. American naval officers agreed with the Japanese that a ten-to-six ratio would endanger Japan's supremacy in her home waters.

29 E. L. Woodward and R. Butler, ed., *Documents on British Foreign Policy, 1919–1939*. 3d ser. III (London: H.M.S.O., 1950), p. 526.

30 Jervis (fn. 6), pp. 69–72, 352–55.

31 Quoted in Merze Tate, *The United States and Armaments* (Cambridge, Mass.: Harvard University Press, 1948), p. 108.

32 Boggs (fn. 12), pp. 15, 40.

33 Kenneth Hagan, *American Gunboat Diplomacy and the Old Navy, 1877–1899* (Westport, Conn.: Greenwood Press, 1973), p. 20.

34 Winston Churchill, *The Gathering Storm* (Boston: Houghton, 1948), p. 206.

35 Brodie, *War and Politics* (fn. 6), p. 325.

36 Boggs (fn. 12), pp. 42, 83. For a good argument about the possible differentiation between offensive and defensive weapons in the 1930s, see Basil Liddell Hart, "Aggression and the Problem of Weapons," *English Review,* 55 (July 1932): pp. 71–78.

37 Quoted in Boggs (fn. 12), p. 39.

38 On these grounds, the Germans claimed in 1932 that the French forts were offensive (*ibid.*, p. 49). Similarly, fortified forward naval bases can be necessary for launching an attack; see Braisted (fn. 22), p. 643.

39 The French made this argument in the interwar period; see Richard Challener, *The French Theory of the Nation in Arms* (New York: Columbia University Press, 1955), pp. 181–82. The Germans disagreed; see Boggs (fn. 12), pp. 44–45.

40 Oman (fn. 24), pp. 57–58.

41 Quoted in Charles Webster, *The Foreign Policy of Castlereagh,* II, *1815–1822* (London: G. Bell and Sons, 1963), p. 510.

42 Boggs (fn. 12), pp. 14–15, 47–48, 60.

43 Quoted in Philip Jordan, *Frontier Law and Order* (Lincoln: University of Nebraska Press, 1970), p. 7 also see pp. 16–17.

44 Boggs (fn. 12), pp. 20, 28.

Chapter 4
The Mitigation of Anarchy

Cooperation under the Security Dilemma

By Robert Jervis

I. Anarchy and the Security Dilemma

The lack of an international sovereign not only permits wars to occur, but also makes it difficult for states that are satisfied with the status quo to arrive at goals that they recognize as being in their common interest. Because there are no institutions or authorities that can make and enforce international laws, the policies of cooperation that will bring mutual rewards if others cooperate may bring disaster if they do not. Because states are aware of this, anarchy encourages behavior that leaves all concerned worse off than they could be, even in the extreme case in which all states would like to freeze the status quo. This is true of the men in Rousseau's "Stag Hunt." If they cooperate to trap the stag, they will all eat well. But if one person defects to chase a rabbit—which he likes less than stag—none of the others will get anything. Thus, all actors have the same preference order, and there is a solution that gives each his first choice: (1) cooperate and trap the stag (the international analogue being cooperation and disarmament); (2) chase a rabbit while others remain at their posts (maintain a high level of arms while others are disarmed); (3) all chase rabbits (arms competition and high risk of war); and (4) stay at the original position while another chases a rabbit (being disarmed while others are armed).[1] Unless each person thinks that the others will cooperate, he himself will not. And why might he fear that any other person would do something that would sacrifice his own first choice? The other might not understand the situation, or might not be able to control his impulses if he saw a rabbit, or might fear that some other member of the group is unreliable. If the person voices any of these suspicions, others are more likely to fear that he will defect, thus making them more likely to defect, thus making it more rational for him to defect. Of course in this simple case—and in many that are more realistic—there are a number of arrangements that could permit cooperation. But the main point remains: although actors may know that they seek a common goal, they may not be able to reach it.

Even when there is a solution that is everyone's first choice, the international case is characterized by three difficulties not present in the Stag Hunt. First, to the incentives to defect given above must be added the potent fear that even if the other state now supports the staus quo, it may become dissatisfied later. No matter how much decision makers are committed to the status quo, they cannot bind themselves and their successors to the same path. Minds can be changed, new leaders can come to power, values can shift, new opportunities and dangers can arise.

The second problem arises from a possible solution. In order to protect their possessions, states often seek to control resources or land outside their own territory. Countries that are not self-sufficient must try to assure that the necessary supplies will continue to flow in wartime. This was part of the explanation for Japan's drive into China and Southeast Asia before World War II. If there were an international authority that could guarantee access, this motive for control would disappear. But since there is not, even a state that would prefer the status quo to increasing its area of control may pursue the latter policy.

When there are believed to be tight linkages between domestic and foreign policy or between the domestic politics of two states, the quest for security may drive states to interfere pre-emptively in the domestic politics of others in order to provide an ideological buffer zone. Thus, Metternich's justification for supervising the politics of the Italian states has been summarized as follows:

W. G. Nicholson, "Memorandum on Seistan and Other Points Raised in the Discussion on the Defence of India," (Committee of Imperial Defence, March 20, 1903). It should be noted that the possibility of neither side building railways was not mentioned, thus strongly biasing the analysis.

Every state is absolutely sovereign in its internal affairs. But this implies that every state must do nothing to interfere in the internal affairs of any other. However, any false or pernicious step taken by any state in its internal affairs may disturb the repose of another state, and this consequent disturbance of another state's repose constitutes an interference in that state's internal affairs. Therefore, every state—or rather, every sovereign of a great power—has the duty, in the name of the sacred right of independence of every state, to supervise the governments of smaller states and to prevent them from taking false and pernicious steps in their internal affairs.[2]

More frequently, the concern is with direct attack. In order to protect themselves, states seek to control, or at least to neutralize, areas on their borders. But attempts to establish buffer zones can alarm others who have stakes there, who fear that undesirable precedents will be set, or who believe that their own vulnerability will be increased. When buffers are are sought in areas empty of great powers, expansion tends to feed on itself in order to protect what is acquired, as was often noted by those who opposed colonial expansion. [Arthur] Balfour's complaint [in 1918] was typical: "Every time I come to a discussion—at intervals of, say, five years—I find there is a new sphere which we have got to guard, which is supposed to protect the gateways of India. Those gateways are getting further and further away from India, and I do not know how far west they are going to be brought by the General Staff."[3]

Though this process is most clearly visible when it involves territorial expansion, it often operates with the increase of less tangible power and influence. The expansion of power usually brings with it an expansion of responsibilities and commitments; to meet them, still greater power is required. The state will take many positions that are subject to challenge. It will be involved with a wide range of controversial issues unrelated to its core values. And retreats that would be seen as normal if made by a small power would be taken as an index of weakness inviting predation if made by a large one.

The third problem present in international politics but not in the Stag Hunt is the security dilemma: many of the means by which a state tries to increase its security decrease the security of others. In domestic society, there are several ways to increase the safety of one's person and property without endangering others. One can move to a safer neighborhood, put bars on the windows, avoid dark streets, and keep a distance from suspicious-looking characters. Of course these measures are not convenient, cheap, or certain of success. But no one save criminals need be alarmed if a person takes them. In international politics, however, one state's gain in security often inadvertently threatens others. In explaining British policy on naval disarmament in the interwar period to the Japanese, Ramsey MacDonald said that "Nobody wanted Japan to be insecure."[4] But the problem was not with British desires, but with the consequences of her policy. In earlier periods, too, Britain had needed a navy large enough to keep the shipping lanes open. But such a navy could not avoid being a menace to any other state with a coast that could be raided, trade that could be interdicted, or colonies that could be isolated. When Germany started building a powerful navy before World War I, Britain objected that it could only be an offensive weapon aimed at her. As Sir Edward Grey, the Foreign Secretary, put it to King Edward VII: "If the German Fleet ever becomes superior to ours, the German Army can conquer this country. There is no corresponding risk of this kind to Germany; for however superior our Fleet was, no naval victory could bring us any nearer to Berlin." The English position was half correct: Germany's navy was an anti-British instrument. But the British often overlooked what the Germans knew full well: "in every quarrel with England, German colonies and trade were . . . hostages for England to take." Thus, whether she intended it or not, the British Navy constituted an important instrument of coercion.[5]

II. What Makes Cooperation More Likely?

Given this gloomy picture, the obvious question is, why are we not all dead? Or, to put it less starkly, what kinds of variables ameliorate the impact of anarchy and the security dilemma? The workings of several can be seen in terms of the Stag Hunt or repeated plays of the Prisoner's Dilemma. The Prisoner's Dilemma differs from the Stag Hunt in that there is no solution that is in the best interests of all the participants; there are offensive as well as defensive incentives to defect from the coalition with the others; and, if the game is to be played only once, the only rational response is to defect. But if the game is repeated indefinitely, the latter characteristic no longer holds and we can analyze the game in terms similar to those applied to the Stag Hunt. It would be in the interest of each actor to have others deprived of the power to defect; each would be willing to sacrifice this ability if others were similarly restrained. But if the others are not, then it is in the actor's interest to retain the power to defect. The game theory matrices for these two situations are given below, with the numbers in the boxes being the order of the actors' preferences.

STAG HUNT

	A COOPERATE	A DEFECT
B COOPERATE	1 1	2 4
B DEFECT	4 2	3 3

PRISONER'S DILEMMA

	A COOPERATE	A DEFECT
B COOPERATE	2 2	1 4
B DEFECT	4 1	3 3

We can see the logical possibilities by rephrasing our question: "Given either of the above situations, what makes it more or less likely that the players will cooperate and arrive at CC?" The chances of achieving this outcome will be increased by: (1) anything that increases incentives to cooperate by increasing the gains of mutual cooperation (CC) and/or decreasing the costs the actor will pay if he cooperates and the other does not (CD); (2) anything that decreases the incentives for defecting by decreasing the gains of taking advantage of the other (DC) and/or increasing the costs of mutual noncooperation (DD); (3) anything that increases each side's expectation that the other will cooperate.

The Costs of Being Exploited (CD)

The fear of being exploited (that is, the cost of CD) most strongly drives the security dilemma; one of the main reasons why international life is not more nasty, brutish, and short is that states are not as vulnerable as men are in a state of nature. People are easy to kill, but as Adam Smith replied to a friend who feared that the Napoleonic Wars would ruin England, "Sir, there is a great deal of ruin in a nation."[6] The easier it is to destroy a state, the greater the reason for it either to join a larger and more secure unit, or else to be especially suspicious of others, to require a large army, and, if conditions are favorable, to attack at the slightest provocation rather than wait to be attacked. If the failure to eat that day—be it venison or rabbit—means that he will starve, a person is likely to defect in the Stag Hunt even if he really likes venison and has a high level of trust in his colleagues. (Defection is especially likely if the others are also starving or if they know that he is.) By contrast, if the costs of CD are lower, if people are well-fed or states are resilient, they can afford to take a more relaxed view of threats.

A relatively low cost of CD has the effect of transforming the game from one in which both players make their choices simultaneously to one in which an actor can make his choice after the other has moved. He will not have to defect out of fear that the other will, but can wait to see what the other will do. States that can afford to be cheated in a bargain or that cannot be destroyed by a surprise attack can more easily trust others and need not act at the first, and ambiguous, sign of menace. Because they have a margin of time and error, they need not match, or more than match, any others' arms in peacetime. They can mobilize in the prewar period or even at the start of the war itself, and still survive. For example, those who opposed a crash program to develop the H-bomb felt that the U.S. margin of safety was large enough so that even if Russia managed to gain a lead in the race, America would not be endangered. The program's advocates disagreed: "If we let the Russians get the super first, catastrophe becomes all but certain."[7]

When the costs of CD are tolerable, not only is security easier to attain but, what is even more imporant here, the relatively low level of arms and relatively passive foreign policy that a status-quo power will be able to adopt are less likely to threaten others. Thus it is easier for status-quo states to act on their common interests if they are hard to conquer. All other things being equal, a world of small states will feel the effects of anarchy much more than a world of large ones. Defensible borders, large size, and protection against sudden attack not only aid the state, but facilitate cooperation that can benefit all states.

Of course, if one state gains invulnerability by being more powerful than most others, the problem will remain because its security provides a base from which it can exploit others. When the price a state will pay for DD is low, it leaves others with few hostages for its good behavior. Others who are more vulnerable will grow apprehensive, which will lead them to acquire more arms and will reduce the chances of cooperation. The best situation is one in which a state will not suffer greatly if others exploit it, for example, by cheating on an arms control agreement (that is, the costs of CD are low); but it will pay a high long-run price if cooperation with the others breaks down—for example, if agreements cease functioning or if there is a long war (that is, the costs of DD are high). The state's invulnerability is then mostly passive; it provides some protection, but it cannot be used to menace others. As we will discuss below, this situation is approximated when it is easier for states to defend themselves than to attack others, or when mutual deterrence obtains because neither side can protect itself.

The differences between highly vulnerable and less vulnerable states are illustrated by the contrasting policies of Britain and Austria after the Napoleonic Wars. Britain's geographic isolation and political stability allowed her to take a fairly relaxed view of disturbances on the Continent. Minor wars and small changes in territory or in the distribution of power did not affect her vital interests. An adversary who was out to overthrow the system could be stopped after he had made his intentions clear. And revolutions within other states were no menace, since they would not set off unrest within England. Austria, surrounded by strong powers, was not so fortunate; her policy had to be more closely attuned to all conflicts. By the time an aggressor-state had clearly shown its colors, Austria would be gravely threatened. And foreign revolutions, be they democratic or nationalistic, would encourage groups in Austria to upset the existing order. So it is not surprising that Metternich propounded the doctrine summarized earlier, which defended Austria's right to interfere in the internal affairs of others, and that British leaders rejected this view. Similarly, Austria wanted the Congress system to be a relatively tight one, regulating most disputes. The British favored a less centralized system. In other words, in order to protect herself, Austria had either to threaten or to harm others, whereas Britain did not. For Austria and her neighbors the security dilemma was acute; for Britain it was not.

The ultimate cost of CD is of course loss of sovereignty. This cost can vary from situation to situation. The lower it is (for instance, because the two states have compatible ideologies, are similar ethnically, have a common culture, or because the citizens of the losing state expect economic benefits), the less the impact of the security dilemma; the greater the costs, the greater the impact of the dilemma. Here is another reason why extreme differences in values and ideologies exacerbate international conflict.

It is through the lowering of the costs of CD that the proposed Rhodesian "safety net"— guaranteeing that whites who leave the country will receive fair payment for their property—would have the paradoxical effect of making it more likely that the whites will stay. This is less puzzling when we see that the whites are in a multi-person Prisoner's Dilemma with each other. Assume that all whites are willing to stay if most of the others stay; but, in the absence of guarantees, if there is going to be a mass exodus, all want to be among the first to leave (because late-leavers will get less for their property and will have more trouble finding a country to take them in). Then the problem is to avoid a self-fulfilling prophecy in which each person rushes to defect because he fears others are going to. In narrowing the gap between the payoff for leaving first (DC) and leaving last (CD) by reducing the cost of the latter, the guarantees make it easier for the whites to cooperate among themselves and stay.

Subjective Security Demands. Decision makers act in terms of the vulnerability they feel, which can differ from the actual situation; we must therefore examine the decision makers' subjective security requirements. Two dimensions are involved. First, even if they agree about the objective situation, people can differ about how much security they desire—or, to put it more precisely, about the price they are willing to pay to gain increments of security. The more states value their security above all else (that is, see a prohibitively high cost in CD), the more they are likely to be sensitive to even minimal threats, and to demand high levels of arms. And if arms are positively valued because of pressures from a military-industrial complex, it will be especially hard for status-quo powers to cooperate. By contrast, the security dilemma will not operate as strongly when pressing domestic concerns increase the opportunity costs of armaments. In this case, the net advantage of exploiting the other (DC) will be less, and the costs of arms races (that is, one aspect of DD) will be greater; therefore the state will behave as though it were relatively invulnerable.

The second aspect of subjective security is the perception of threat (that is, the estimate of whether the other will cooperate). A state that is predisposed to see either a specific other state as an adversary, or others in general as a menace, will react more strongly and more quickly than a state that sees its environment as benign. Indeed, when a state believes that another not only is not likely to be an adversary, but has sufficient interests in common with it to be an ally, then it will actually welcome an increase in the other's power.

British and French foreign policies in the interwar years illustrate these points. After the rise of Hitler, Britain and France felt that increases in each other's arms increased rather than decreased their own security. The differing policies that these states followed toward Germany can be explained by their differences on both dimensions of the variable of subjective security. Throughout the period, France perceived Germany as more of a threat than England did. The British were more optimistic and argued that conciliation could turn Germany into a supporter of the status quo. Furthermore, in the years immediately following World War I, France had been more willing to forego other values in order to increase her security and had therefore followed a more belligerent policy than England, maintaining a larger army and moving quickly to counter German assertiveness. As this example shows, one cannot easily say how much subjective security a state should seek. High security requirements make it very difficult to capitalize on a common interest and run the danger of setting off spirals of arms races and hostility. The French may have paid this price in the 1920s. Low security requirements avoid this trap, but run the risk of having too few arms and of trying to conciliate an aggressor.

One aspect of subjective security related to the predisposition to perceive threat is the state's view of how many enemies it must be prepared to fight. A state can be relaxed about increases in another's arms if it believes that there is a functioning collective security system. The chances of peace are increased in a world in which the prevailing international system is valued in its own right, not only because most states restrain their ambitions and those who do not are deterred (these are the usual claims for a Concert system), but also because of the decreased chances that the status-quo states will engage in unnecessary conflict out of the quest for security. Indeed, if there were complete faith in collective security, no state would want an army. By contrast, the security dilemma is insoluble when each state fears that many others, far from coming to its aid, are likely to join in any attack. Winston Churchill, as First Lord of the Admiralty, was setting a high security requirement when he noted [before World War I]:

> Besides the Great Powers, there are many small states who are buying or building great ships of war and whose vessels may by purchase, by some diplomatic combination, or by duress, be brought into the line against us. None of these powers need, like us, navies to defend their actual safety of independence. They build them so as to play a part in world affairs. It is sport to them. It is death to us.[8]

It takes great effort for any one state to be able to protect itself alone against an attack by several neighbors. More importantly, it is next to impossible for all states in the system to have this capability. Thus, a state's expectation that allies will be available and that only a few others will be able to join against it is almost a necessary condition for security requirements to be compatible.

Gains from Cooperation and Costs of a Breakdown (CC and DD)

The main costs of a policy of reacting quickly and severely to increases in the other's arms are not the price of one's own arms, but rather the sacrifice of the potential gains from cooperation (CC) and the increase in the dangers of needless arms races and wars (DD). The greater these costs, the greater the incentives to try cooperation and wait for fairly unambiguous evidence before assuming that the other must be checked by force. Wars would be much more frequent—even if the first choice of all states was the status quo—if they were less risky and costly, and if peaceful intercourse did not provide rich benefits. Ethiopia . . . asked for guarantees that the Territory of Afars and Issas would not join a hostile alliance against it when it gained independence. A spokesman for the Territory replied that this was not necessary: Ethiopia "already had the best possible guarantee in the railroad" that links the two countries and provides indispensable revenue for the Territory.[9]

The basic points are well known and so we can move to elaboration. First, most statesmen know that to enter a war is to set off a chain of unpredictable and uncontrollable events. Even if everything they see points to a quick victory, they are likely to hesitate before all the uncertainties. And if the battlefield often produces startling results, so do the council chambers. The state may be deserted by allies or attacked by neutrals. Or the postwar alignment may rob it of the fruits of victory, as happened to Japan in 1895. Second, the domestic costs of wars must be weighed. Even strong states can be undermined by dissatisfaction with the way the war is run and by the necessary mobilization of men and ideas. Memories of such disruptions were one of the main reasons for the era of relative peace that followed the Napoleonic Wars. Liberal statesmen feared that large armies would lead to despotism; conservative leaders feared that wars would lead to revolution. (The other side of this coin is that when there are domestic consequences of foreign conflict that are positively valued, the net cost of conflict is lowered and cooperation becomes more difficult.) Third—turning to the advantages of cooperation—for states with large and diverse economies the gains from economic exchange are rarely if ever sufficient to prevent war. Norman Angell was wrong about World War I being impossible because of economic ties among the powers; and before World War II, the U.S. was Japan's most important trading partner. Fourth, the gains from cooperation can be increased, not only if each side gets more of the traditional values such as wealth, but also if each comes to value the other's well-being positively. Mutual cooperation will then have a double payoff: in addition to the direct gains, there will be the satisfaction of seeing the other prosper.[10]

While high costs of war and gains from cooperation will ameliorate the impact of the security dilemma, they can create a different problem. If the costs are high enough so that DD is the last choice for both sides, the game will shift to "Chicken." This game differs from the Stag Hunt in that each actor seeks to exploit the other; it differs from Prisoner's Dilemma in that both actors share an interest in avoiding mutual non-cooperation. In Chicken, if you think the other side is going to defect, you have to cooperate because, although being exploited (CD) is bad, it is not as bad as a total breakdown (DD). As the familiar logic of deterrence shows, the actor must then try to convince his adversary that he is going to stand firm (defect) and that the only way the other can avoid disaster is to back down (cooperate). Commitment, the rationality of irrationality, manipulating the communications system, and pretending not to understand the situation, are among the tactics used to reach this goal. The same logic applies when both sides are enjoying great benefits from cooperation. The side that can credibly threaten to disrupt the relationship unless its demands are met can exploit the other. This situation may not be stable, since the frequent use of threats may be incompatible with the maintenance of a cooperative relationship. Still, [French president Charles] de Gaulle's successful threats to break up the Common Market unless his partners acceded to his wishes remind us that the shared benefits of cooperation as well as the shared costs of defection can provide the basis for exploitation. Similarly, one reason for the collapse of the Franco-British entente more than a hundred years earlier was that decision makers on both sides felt confident that their own country could safely pursue a policy that was against the other's interest because the other could not afford to destroy the highly valued relationship.[11] Because statesmen realize that the growth of positive interdependence can provide others with new levers of influence over them, they may resist such developments more than would be expected from the theories that stress the advantages of cooperation.

Gains from Exploitation (DC)

Defecting not only avoids the danger that a state will be exploited (CD), but brings positive advantages by exploiting the other (DC) The lower these possible gains, the greater the chances of cooperation. Even a relatively satisfied state can be tempted to expand by the hope of gaining major values. The temptation will be less when the state sees other ways of reaching its goals, and/or places a low value on what exploitation could bring. The gains may be low either because the immediate advantage provided by DC (for example, having more arms than the other side) cannot be translated into a political advantage (for example, gains in territory), or because the political advantage itself is not highly valued. For instance, a state may not seek to annex additional territory because the latter lacks raw materials, is inhabited by people of a different ethnic group, would be costly to garrison, or would be hard to assimilate without disturbing domestic politics and values. A state can reduce the incentives that another state has to attack it, by not being a threat to the latter and by providing goods and services that would be lost were the other to attempt exploitation. . . .

The Probability That the Other Will Cooperate

The variables discussed so far influence the payoffs for each of the four possible outcomes. To decide what to do, the state has to go further and calculate the expected value of cooperating or defecting. Because such calculations involve estimating the probability that the other will cooperate, the state will have to judge how the variables discussed so far act on the other. To encourage the other to cooperate, a state may try to manipulate these variables. It can lower the other's incentives to defect by decreasing what it could gain by exploiting the state (DC)—the details would be similar to those discussed in the previous paragraph—and it can raise the costs of deadlock (DD). But if the state cannot make DD the worst outcome for the other, coercion is likely to be ineffective in the short run because the other can respond by refusing to cooperate, and dangerous in the long run because the other is likely to become convinced that the state is aggressive. So the state will have to concentrate on making cooperation more attractive. One way to do this is to decrease the costs the other will pay if it cooperates and the state defects (CD). Thus, the state could try to make the other less vulnerable. It was for this reason that in the late 1950's and early 1960's some American defense analysts argued that it would be good for both sides if the Russians developed hardened missiles. Of course, decreasing the other's vulnerability also decreases the state's ability to coerce it, and opens the possibility that the other will use this protection as a shield behind which to engage in actions inimical to the state. But by sacrificing some ability to harm the other, the state can increase the chances of mutually beneficial cooperation.

The state can also try to increase the gains that will accrue to the other from mutual cooperation (CC). Although the state will of course gain if it receives a share of any new benefits, even an increment that accrues entirely to the other will aid the state by increasing the likelihood that the other will cooperate.[12]

This line of argument can be continued through the infinite regressions that game theory has made familiar. If the other is ready to cooperate when it thinks the state will, the state can increase the chances of CC by showing that it *is* planning to cooperate. Thus the state should understate the gains it would make if it exploited the other (DC) and the costs it would pay if the other exploited it (CD), and stress or exaggerate the gains it would make under mutual cooperation (CC) and the costs it would pay if there is deadlock (DD). The state will also want to convince the other that it thinks that the other is likely to cooperate. If the other believes these things, it will see that the state has strong incentives to cooperate, and so it will cooperate in turn. One point should be emphasized. Because the other, like the state, may be driven to defect by the fear that it will be exploited if it does not, the state should try to reassure it that this will not happen. Thus, when Khrushchev indicated his willingness to withdraw his missiles from Cuba, he simultaneously stressed to Kennedy that "we are of sound mind and understand perfectly well" that Russia could not launch a successful attack against the U.S., and therefore that there was no reason for the U.S. to contemplate a defensive, pre-emptive strike of its own.[13]

There is, however, a danger. If the other thinks that the state has little choice but to cooperate, it can credibly threaten to defect unless the state provides it with additional benefits. Great advantages of mutual cooperation, like high costs of war, provide a lever for competitive bargaining. Furthermore, for a state to stress how much it gains from cooperation may be to imply that it is gaining much more than the other and to suggest that the benefits should be distributed more equitably.

When each side is ready to cooperate if it expects the other to, inspection devices can ameliorate the security dilemma. Of course, even a perfect inspection system cannot guarantee that the other will not later develop aggressive intentions and the military means to act on them. But by relieving immediate worries and providing warning of coming dangers, inspection can meet a significant part of the felt need to protect oneself against future threats, and so make current cooperation more feasible. Similar functions are served by breaking up one large transaction into a series of smaller ones. At each transaction each can see whether the other has cooperated; and its losses, if the other defects, will be small. And since what either side would gain by one defection is slight compared to the benefits of continued cooperation, the prospects of cooperation are high. Conflicts and wars among status-quo powers would be much more common were it not for the fact that international politics is usually a series of small transactions.

How a statesman interprets the other's past behavior and how he projects it into the future is influenced by his understanding of the security dilemma and his ability to place himself in the other's shoes. The dilemma will operate much more strongly if statesmen do not understand it, and do not see that their arms—sought only to secure the status quo—may alarm others and that others may arm, not because they are contemplating aggression, but because they fear attack from the first state. These two failures of empathy are linked. A state which thinks that the other knows that it wants only to preserve the status quo and that its arms are meant only for self-preservation will conclude that the other side will react to its arms by increasing its own capability only if it is aggressive itself. Since the other side is not menaced, there is no legitimate reason for it to object to the first state's arms; therefore, objection proves that the other is aggressive . . . .

Statesmen who do not understand the security dilemma will think that the money spent is the only cost of building up their arms. This belief removes one important restraint on arms spending. Furthermore, it is also likely to lead states to set their security requirements too high. Since they do not understand that trying to increase one's security can actually decrease it, they will overestimate the amount of security that is attainable; they will think that when in doubt they can "play it safe" by increasing their arms. Thus it is very likely that two states which support the status quo but do not understand the security dilemma will end up, if not in a war, then at least in a relationship of higher conflict than is required by the objective situation.

The belief that an increase in military strength always leads to an increase in security is often linked to the belief that the only route to security is through military strength. As a consequence, a whole range of meliorative policies will be downgraded. Decision makers who do not believe that adopting a more conciliatory posture, meeting the other's legitimate grievances, or developing mutual gains from cooperation can increase their state's security, will not devote much attention or effort to these possibilities.

On the other hand, a heightened sensitivity to the security dilemma makes it more likely that the state will treat an aggressor as though it were an insecure defender of the status quo. Partly because of their views about the causes of World War I, the British were predisposed to believe that Hitler sought only the rectification of legitimate and limited grievances and that security could best be gained by constructing an equitable international system. As a result they pursued a policy which, although well designed to avoid the danger of creating unnecessary conflict with a status-quo Germany, helped destroy Europe.

Geography, Commitments, Beliefs, and Security through Expansion

A final consideration does not easily fit in the matrix we have been using, although it can be seen as an aspect of vulnerability and of the costs of CD. Situations vary in the ease or difficulty with which all states can simultaneously achieve a high degree of security. The influence of military technology on this variable is the subject of the next section. Here we want to treat the impact of beliefs, geography, and commitments (many of which can be considered to be modifications of geography, since they bind states to defend areas outside their homelands). In the crowded continent of Europe, security requirements were hard to mesh. Being surrounded by powerful states, Germany's problem—or the problem created by Germany—was always great and was even worse when her relations with both France and Russia were bad, such as before World War I. In that case, even a status-quo Germany, if she could not change the political situation, would almost have been forced to adopt something like the Schlieffen Plan [that required taking the offensive]. Because she could not hold off both of her enemies, she had to be prepared to defeat one quickly and then deal with the other in a more leisurely fashion. If France or Russia stayed out of a war between the other state and Germany, they would allow Germany to dominate the Continent (even if that was not Germany's aim). They therefore had to deny Germany this ability, thus making Germany less secure. Although Germany's arrogant and erratic behavior, coupled with the desire for an unreasonably high level of security (which amounted to the desire to escape from her geographic plight), compounded the problem, even wise German statesmen would have been hard put to gain a high degree of security without alarming their neighbors.

A similar situation arose for France after World War I. She was committed to protecting her allies in Eastern Europe, a commitment she could meet only by taking the offensive against Germany. But since there was no way to guarantee that France might not later seek expansion, a France that could successfully launch an attack in response to a German move into Eastern Europe would constitute a potential danger to German core values. Similarly, a United States credibly able to threaten retaliation with strategic nuclear weapons if the Soviet Union attacks

Western Europe also constitutes a menace, albeit a reduced one, to the Soviet ability to maintain the status quo . . . .

For the United States, the problem posed by the need to protect Europe is an exception. Throughout most of its history, this country has been in a much more favorable position: relatively self-sufficient and secure from invasion, it has not only been able to get security relatively cheaply, but by doing so, did not menace others. But ambitions and commitments have changed this situation. After the American conquest of the Philippines, "neither the United States nor Japan could assure protection for their territories by military and naval means without compromising the defenses of the other. This problem would plague American and Japanese statesmen down to 1941."[14] Furthermore, to the extent that Japan could protect herself, she could resist American threats to go to war if Japan did not respect China's independence. These complications were minor compared to those that followed World War II. A world power cannot help but have the ability to harm many others that is out of proportion to the others' ability to harm it.

Britain had been able to gain security without menacing others to a greater degree than the Continental powers, though to a lesser one than the United States. But the acquisition of colonies and a dependence on foreign trade sacrificed her relative invulnerability of being an island. Once she took India, she had to consider Russia as a neighbor; the latter was expanding in Central Asia, thus making it much more difficult for both countries to feel secure. The need to maintain reliable sea lanes to India meant that no state could be allowed to menace South Africa and, later, Egypt. But the need to protect these two areas brought new fears, new obligations, and new security requirements that conflicted with those of other European nations. Furthermore, once Britain needed a flow of imports during both peace and wartime, she required a navy that could prevent a blockade. A navy sufficient for that task could not help but be a threat to any other state that had valuable trade.

A related problem is raised by the fact that defending the status quo often means protecting more than territory. Nonterritorial interests, norms, and the structure of the international system must be maintained. If all status-quo powers agree on these values and interpret them in compatible ways, problems will be minimized. But the potential for conflict is great, and the policies followed are likely to exacerbate the security dilemma. The greater the range of interests that have to be protected, the more likely it is that national efforts to maintain the status quo will clash. As a French spokesman put it in 1930: "Security! The term signifies more indeed than the maintenance of a people's homeland, or even of their territories beyond the seas. It also means the maintenance of the world's respect for them, the maintenance of their economic interests, everything in a word, which goes to make up the grandeur, the life itself, of the nation."[15] When security is thought of in this sense, it almost automatically has a competitive connotation. It involves asserting one state's will over others, showing a high degree of leadership if not dominance, and displaying a prickly demeanor. The resulting behavior will almost surely clash with that of others who define their security in the same way.

The problem will be almost insoluble if statesmen believe that their security requires the threatening or attacking of others. "That which stops growing begins to rot," declared a minister to Catherine the Great.[16] More common is the belief that if the other is secure, it will be emboldened to act against one's own state's interests, and the belief that in a war it will not be enough for the state to protect itself: it must be able to take the war to the other's homeland. These convictions make it very difficult for status-quo states to develop compatible security policies, for they lead the state to conclude that its security requires that others be rendered insecure.

Questions for Review

If Jervis correctly outlines ways in which states can cooperate despite anarchy, why is conflict so common? What assumptions does he make that you might want to question?

Notes

1 This kind of rank-ordering is not entirely an analyst's invention, as is shown by the following section of a British army memo of 1903 dealing with British and Russian railroad construction near the Persia-Afghanistan border:

The conditions of the problem may . . . be briefly summarized as follows:

a) If we make a railway to Seistan while Russia remains inactive, we gain a considerable defensive advantage at considerable financial cost;

b) If Russia makes a railway to Seistan, while we remain inactive, she gains a considerable offensive advantage at considerable financial cost;

c) If both we and Russia make railways to Seistan, the defensive and offensive advantages may be held to neutralize each other; in other words, we shall have spent a good deal of money and be no better off than we are at present. On the other hand, we shall be no worse off, whereas under alternative (b) we shall be much worse off. Consequently, the theoretical balance of advantage lies with the proposed railway extension from Quetta to Seistan.

2 Paul Schroeder, *Metternich's Diplomacy at Its Zenith, 1820–1823* (Westport, Conn.: Greenwood Press 1969), 126.

3 Quoted in Michael Howard, *The Continental Commitment* (Harmondsworth, England: Penguin 1974), 67.

4 Quoted in Gerald Wheeler, *Prelude to Pearl Harbor* (Columbia: University of Missouri Press 1963), 167.

5 Quoted in Leonard Wainstein, "The Dreadnought Gap," in Robert Art and Kenneth Waltz, eds., The Use of Force (Boston: Little, Brown 1971), 155;

Raymond Sontag, *European Diplomatic History, 1871–1932* (New York: Appleton-Century-Crofts 1933), 147.

6 Quoted in Bernard Brodie, *Strategy in the Missile Age* (Princeton: Princeton University Press 1959), 6.

7 Herbert York, *The Advisors: Oppenheimer, Teller, and the Superbomb* (San Francisco: Freeman. 1976), 56–60.

8 Quoted in Peter Gretton, *Former Naval Person* (London: Cassell 1968), 151.

9 Michael Kaufman, "Tension Increases in French Colony," *New York Times*, July 11, 1976.

10 Experimental support for this argument is summarized in Morton Deutsch, *The Resolution of Conflict* (New Haven: Yale University Press 1973), 181–95.

11 Roger Bullen, *Palmerston, Guizot, and the Collapse of the Entente Cordiale* (London: Athlone Press 1974), 81, 88, 93, 212. For a different view of this case, see Stanley Mellon, "Entente, Diplomacy, and Fantasy," *Reviews in European History*, II (September 1976), 376–80.

12 This assumes, however, that these benefits to the other will not so improve the other's power position that it will be more able to menace the state in the future.

13 Walter LaFeber, ed., *The Dynamics of World Power; A Documentary History of United States Foreign Policy 1945–1973*, II: *Eastern Europe and the Soviet Union* (New York: Chelsea House in association with McGraw-Hill 1973), 700.

14 William Braisted, *The United States Navy in the Pacific, 1897–1909* (Austin: University of Texas Press 1958), 240.

15 Jules Cambon, "The Permanent Bases of French Foreign Policy," *Foreign Affairs*, VIII (January 1930), 185.

16 Quoted in Adam Ulam, *Expansion and Co-Existence* (New York: Praeger 1968), 5.

Kant, Liberal Legacies, and Foreign Affairs

MICHAEL W. DOYLE

I

What difference do liberal principles and institutions make to the conduct of the foreign affairs of liberal states? A thicket of conflicting judgments suggests that the legacies of liberalism have not been clearly appreciated. For many citizens of liberal states, liberal principles and institutions have so fully absorbed domestic politics that their influence on foreign affairs tends to be either overlooked altogether or, when perceived, exaggerated. Liberalism becomes either unselfconsciously patriotic or inherently "peace-loving." For many scholars and diplomats, the relations among independent states appear to differ so significantly from domestic politics that influences of liberal principles and domestic liberal institutions are denied or denigrated. They judge that international relations are governed by perceptions of national security and the balance of power; liberal principles and institutions, when they do intrude, confuse and disrupt the pursuit of balance-of-power politics.

Although liberalism is misinterpreted from both these points of view, a crucial aspect of the liberal legacy is captured by each. Liberalism is a distinct ideology and set of institutions that has shaped the perceptions of and capacities for, foreign relations of political societies that range from social welfare or social democratic to laissez faire. It defines much of the content of the liberal patriot's nationalism. Liberalism does appear to disrupt the pursuit of balance-of-power politics. Thus its foreign relations cannot be adequately explained (or prescribed) by a sole reliance on the balance of power. But liberalism is not inherently "peace-loving"; nor is it consistently restrained or peaceful in intent. Furthermore, liberal practice may reduce the probability that states will successfully exercise the consistent restraint and peaceful intentions that a world peace may well require in the nuclear age. Yet the peaceful intent and restraint that liberalism does manifest in limited aspects of its foreign affairs announces the possibility of a world peace this side of the grave or of world conquest. It has strengthened the prospects for a world peace established by the steady expansion of a separate peace among liberal societies. . . .

II

Liberalism has been identified with an essential principle—the importance of the freedom of the individual. Above all, this is a belief in the importance of moral freedom, of the right to be treated and a duty to treat others as ethical subjects, and not as objects or means only. This principle has generated rights and institutions.

A commitment to a threefold set of rights forms the foundation of liberalism. Liberalism calls for freedom from arbitrary authority, often called "negative freedom," which includes freedom of conscience, a free press and free speech, equality under the law, and the right to hold, and therefore to exchange, property without fear of arbitrary seizure. Liberalism also calls for those rights necessary to protect and promote the capacity and opportunity for freedom, the "positive freedoms." Such social and economic rights as equality of opportunity in education and rights to health care and employment, necessary for effective self-expression and participation, are thus among liberal rights. A third liberal right, democratic participation or representation, is necessary to guarantee the other two. To ensure that morally autonomous individuals remain free in those areas of social action where public authority is needed, public legislation has to express the will of the citizens making laws for their own community.

These three sets of rights, taken together, seem to meet the challenge that Kant identified:

> To organize a group of rational beings who demand general laws for their survival, but of whom each inclines toward exempting himself, and to establish their constitution in such a way that, in spite of the fact their private attitudes are opposed, these private attitudes mutually impede each other in such a manner that [their] public behavior is the same as if they did not have such evil attitudes.[1]

But the dilemma within liberalism is how to reconcile the three sets of liberal rights. The right to private property, for example, can conflict with equality of opportunity and both rights can be violated by democratic legislation. During the 180 years since Kant wrote, the liberal tradition has evolved two high roads to individual freedom and social order; one is laissez-faire, or "conservative," liberalism and the other is social welfare, or social democratic, or "liberal," liberalism. Both reconcile these conflicting rights (though in differing ways) by successfully organizing free individuals into a political order.

The political order of laissez-faire and social welfare liberals is marked by a shared commitment to four essential institutions. First, citizens possess juridical equality and other fundamental civil rights such as freedom of religion and the press. Second, the effective sovereigns of the state are representative legislatures deriving their authority from the consent of the electorate and exercising their authority free from all restraint apart from the requirement that basic civic rights be preserved. Most pertinently for the impact of liberalism on foreign affairs, the state is subject to neither the external authority of other states nor to the internal authority of special prerogatives held, for example, by monarchs or military castes over foreign policy. Third, the economy rests on a recognition of the rights of private property including the ownership of means of production. Property is justified by individual acquisition (for example, by labor) or by social agreement or social utility. This excludes state socialism or state capitalism, but it need not exclude market socialism or various forms of the mixed economy. Fourth, economic decisions are predominantly shaped by the forces of supply and demand, domestically and internationally, and are free from strict control by bureaucracies. . . .

III

In foreign affairs liberalism has shown, as it has in the domestic realm, serious weaknesses. But unlike liberalism's domestic realm, its foreign affairs have experienced startling but less than fully appreciated successes. Together they shape an unrecognized dilemma, for both these successes and weaknesses in large part spring from the same cause: the international implications of liberal principles and institutions.

The basic postulate of liberal international theory holds that states have the right to be free from foreign intervention. Since morally autonomous citizens hold rights to liberty, the states that democratically represent them have the right to exercise political independence. Mutual respect for these rights then becomes the touchstone of international liberal theory. When states respect each other's rights, individuals are free to establish private international ties without state interference. Profitable exchange between merchants and educational exchanges among scholars then create a web of mutual advantages and commitments that bolsters sentiments of public respect.

These conventions of mutual respect have formed a cooperative foundation for relations among liberal democracies of a remarkably effective kind. *Even though liberal states have become involved in numerous wars with nonliberal states, constitutionally secure liberal states have yet to engage in war with one another.*[2] No one should argue that such wars are impossible; but preliminary evidence does appear to indicate that there exists a significant predisposition against warfare between liberal states. Indeed, threats of war also have been regarded as illegitimate. A liberal zone of peace, a pacific union, has been maintained and has expanded despite numerous particular conflicts of economic and strategic interest. . . .

Statistically, war between any two states (in any single year or other short period of time) is a low probability event. War between any two adjacent states, considered over a long period of time, may be somewhat more probable. The apparent absence of war among the more clearly liberal states, whether adjacent or not, for almost two hundred years thus has some significance. Politically more significant, perhaps, is that, when states are forced to decide, by the pressure of an impinging world war, on which side of a world contest they will fight, liberal states wind up all on the same side, despite the real complexity of the historical, economic, and political factors that affect their foreign policies. And historically, we should recall that medieval and early modern Europe were the warring cockpits of states, wherein France and England and the Low Countries engaged in near constant strife. Then in the late eighteenth century there began to emerge liberal regimes. At first hesitant and confused, and later clear and confident as liberal regimes gained deeper domestic foundations and longer international experience, a pacific union of these liberal states became established.

The realist model of international relations, which provides a plausible explanation of the general insecurity of states, offers little guidance in explaining the pacification of the liberal world. Realism, in its classical formation, holds that the state is and should be formally sovereign, effectively unbounded by individual rights nationally and thus capable of determining its own scope of authority. (This determination can be made democratically, oligarchically, or autocratically.) Internationally, the sovereign state exists in an anarchical society in which it is radically independent, neither bounded nor protected by international "law" or treaties or duties, and hence, insecure. Hobbes, one of the seventeenth-century founders of the realist approach, drew the international implications of realism when he argued that the existence of international anarchy, the very independence of states, best accounts for the competition, the fear, and the temptation toward preventive war that characterize international relations. Politics among nations is not a continuous combat, but it is in this view a "state of war . . . a tract of time, wherein the will to contend by battle is sufficiently known."[3] . . .

Finding that all states, including liberal states, do engage in war, the realist concludes that the effects of differing domestic regimes (whether liberal or not) are overridden by the international anarchy under which all states live.[4] . . . But the ends that shape the international state of war are decreed for the realist by the anarchy of the international order and the fundamental quest for power that directs the policy of all states, irrespective of differences in their domestic regimes. As Rousseau argued, international peace therefore depends on the abolition of international relations either by the achievement of a world state or by a radical isolationism (Corsica). Realists judge neither to be possible.

Recent additions to game theory specify some of the circumstances under which prudence could lead to peace. Experience; geography; expectations of cooperation and belief patterns; and the differing payoffs to cooperation (peace) or conflict associated with various types of military technology all appear to influence the calculus.[5] But when it comes to acquiring the techniques of peaceable interaction, nations appear to be slow, or at least erratic, learners. The balance of power (more below) is regarded as a primary lesson in the realist primer, but centuries of experience did not prevent either France (Louis XIV, Napoleon I) or Germany (Wilhelm II, Hitler) from attempting to conquer Europe, twice each. Yet some, very new, black African states appear to have achieved a twenty-year-old system of impressively effective standards of mutual toleration. These standards are not completely effective (as in Tanzania's invasion of Uganda); but they have confounded expectations of a scramble to redivide Africa.[6] Geography—"insular security" and "continental insecurity"—may affect foreign policy attitudes; but it does not appear to determine behavior, as the bellicose records of England and Japan suggest. Beliefs, expectations, and attitudes of leaders and masses should influence strategic behavior. . . . Nevertheless, it would be difficult to determine if liberal leaders have had more peaceable attitudes than leaders who lead nonliberal states. But even if one did make that discovery, he also would have to account for why these peaceable attitudes only appear to be effective in relations with other liberals (since wars with nonliberals have not been uniformly defensive). . . .

Second, at the level of social determinants, some might argue that relations among any group of states with similar social structures or with compatible values would be peaceful. But again, the evidence for feudal societies, communist societies, fascist societies, or socialist societies does not support this conclusion. Feudal warfare was frequent and very much a sport of the monarchs and nobility. There have not been enough truly totalitarian, fascist powers (nor have they lasted long enough) to test fairly their pacific compatibility; but fascist powers in the wider sense of nationalist, capitalist, military dictatorships fought each other in the 1930s. Communist powers have engaged in wars more recently in East Asia. And we have not had enough socialist societies to consider the relevance of socialist pacification. The more abstract category of pluralism does not suffice.

Certainly Germany was pluralist when it engaged in war with liberal states in 1914; Japan as well in 1941. But they were not liberal.

And third, at the level of interstate relations, neither specific regional attributes nor historic alliances or friendships can account for the wide reach of the liberal peace. The peace extends as far as, and no further than, the relations among liberal states, not including nonliberal states in an otherwise liberal region (such as the north Atlantic in the 1930s) nor excluding liberal states in a nonliberal region (such as Central America or Africa).

At this level, Raymond Aron has identified three types of interstate peace: empire, hegemony, and equilibrium.[7] An empire generally succeeds in creating an internal peace, but this is not an explanation of peace among independent liberal states. Hegemony can create peace by over-awing potential rivals. Although far from perfect and certainly precarious, United States hegemony, as Aron notes, might account for the interstate peace in South America in the postwar period during the height of the Cold War conflict. However, the liberal peace cannot be attributed merely to effective international policing by a predominant hegemon—Britain in the nineteenth century, the United States in the postwar period. Even though a hegemon might well have an interest in enforcing a peace for the sake of commerce or investments or as a means of enhancing its prestige or security, hegemons such as seventeenth-century France were not peace-enforcing police, and the liberal peace persisted in the interwar period when international society lacked a predominant hegemonic power. Moreover, this explanation overestimates hegemonic control in both periods. Neither England nor the United States was able to prevent direct challenges to its interests (colonial competition in the nineteenth century, Middle East diplomacy and conflicts over trading with the enemy in the postwar period). Where then was the capacity to prevent all armed conflicts between liberal regimes, many of which were remote and others strategically or economically insignificant? Liberal hegemony and leadership are important, but they are not sufficient to explain a liberal peace. . . .

Finally, some realists might suggest that the liberal peace simply reflects the absence of deep conflicts of interest among liberal states. Wars occur outside the liberal zone because conflicts of interest are deeper there. But this argument does nothing more than raise the question of why liberal states have fewer or less fundamental conflicts of interest with other liberal states than liberal states have with nonliberal, or nonliberal states have with other nonliberals. We must therefore examine the workings of liberalism among its own kind—a special pacification of the "state of war" resting on liberalism and nothing either more specific or more general.

IV

Most liberal theorists have offered inadequate guidance in understanding the exceptional nature of liberal pacification. Some have argued that democratic states would be inherently peaceful simply and solely because in these states citizens rule the polity and bear the costs of wars. Unlike monarchs, citizens are not able to indulge their aggressive passions and have the consequences suffered by someone else. Other liberals have argued that laissez-faire capitalism contains an inherent tendency toward rationalism, and that, since war is irrational, liberal capitalisms will be pacifistic. Others still, such as Montesquieu, claim that "commerce is the cure for the most destructive prejudices," and "Peace is the natural effect of trade."[8] While these developments can help account for the liberal peace, they do not explain the fact that liberal states are peaceful only in relations with other liberal states. France and England fought expansionist, colonial wars throughout the nineteenth century (in the 1830s and 1840s against Algeria and China); the United States fought a similar war with Mexico in 1848 and intervened again in 1914 under president Wilson. Liberal states are as aggressive and war prone as any other form of government or society in their relations with nonliberal states.

Immanuel Kant offers the best guidance. "Perpetual Peace," written in 1795, predicts the ever-widening pacification of the liberal pacific union, explains that pacification, and at the same time suggests why liberal states are not pacific in their relations with nonliberal states. . . .

Kant shows how republics, once established, lead to peaceful relations. He argues that once the aggressive interests of absolutist monarchies are tamed and once the habit of respect for individual rights is engrained by republican government, wars would appear as the disaster to the people's welfare that he and the other liberals thought them to be. The fundamental reason is this:

> If the consent of the citizens is required in order to decide that war should be declared (and in this constitution it cannot but be the case), nothing is more natural than that they would be very cautious in commencing such a poor game, decreeing for themselves all the calamities of war. Among the latter would be: having to fight, having to pay the costs of war from their own resources, having painfully to repair the devastation war leaves behind, and, to fill up the measure of evils, load themselves with a heavy national debt that would embitter peace itself and that can never be liquidated on account of constant wars in the future. But, on the other hand, in a constitution which is not republican, and under which the subjects are not citizens, a declaration of war is the easiest thing in the world to decide upon, because war does not require of the ruler, who is the proprietor and not a member of the state, the least sacrifice of the pleasure of his table, the chase, his country houses, his court functions, and the like. He may, therefore, resolve on war as on a pleasure party for the most trivial reasons, and with perfect indifference leave the justification which decency requires to the diplomatic corps who are ever ready to provide it.[9]

One could add to Kant's list another source of pacification specific to liberal constitutions. The regular rotation of office in liberal democratic polities is a nontrivial device that helps ensure that personal animosities among heads of government provide no lasting, escalating source of tension.

These domestic republican restraints do not end war. If they did, liberal states would not be warlike, which is far from the case. They do introduce Kant's "caution" in place of monarchical caprice. Liberal wars are only fought for popular, liberal purposes. To see how this removes the occasion of wars among liberal states and not wars between liberal and nonliberal states, we need to shift our attention from constitutional law to international law, Kant's second source.

Complementing the constitutional guarantee of caution, *international law* adds a second source—a guarantee of respect. The separation of nations that asocial sociability encourages is reinforced by the development of separate languages and religions. These further guarantee a world of separate states—an essential condition needed to avoid a "global, soul-less despotism." Yet, at the same time, they also morally integrate liberal states "as culture progresses and men gradually come closer together toward a greater agreement on principles for peace and understanding."[10] As republics emerge (the first source) and as culture progresses, an understanding of the legitimate rights of all citizens and of all republics comes into play; and this, now that caution characterizes policy, sets up the moral foundations for the liberal peace. Correspondingly, international law highlights the importance of Kantian publicity. Domestically, publicity helps ensure that the officials of republics act according to the principles they profess to hold just and according to the interests of the electors they claim to represent. Internationally, free speech and the effective communication of accurate conceptions of the political life of foreign peoples is essential to establish and preserve the understanding on which the guarantee of respect depends. In short, domestically just republics, which rest on consent, presume foreign republics to be also consensual, just, and therefore deserving of accommodation. The experience of cooperation helps engender further cooperative behavior when the consequences of state policy are unclear but (potentially) mutually beneficial.[11]

Lastly, *cosmopolitan law* adds material incentives to moral commitments. The cosmopolitan right to hospitality permits the "spirit of commerce" sooner or later to take hold of every nation, thus impelling states to promote peace and to try to avert war.

Liberal economic theory holds that these cosmopolitan ties derive from a cooperative international division of labor and free trade according to comparative advantage. Each economy is said to be better off than it would have been under autarky; each thus acquires an incentive to avoid policies that would lead the other to break these economic ties. Since keeping open markets rests upon the assumption that the next set of transactions will also be determined by prices rather than coercion, a sense of mutual security is vital to avoid security-motivated searches for economic autarky. Thus, avoiding a challenge to another liberal state's security or even enhancing each other's security by means of alliance naturally follows economic interdependence.

A further cosmopolitan source of liberal peace is that the international market removes difficult decisions of production and distribution from the direct sphere of state policy. A foreign state thus does not appear directly responsible for these outcomes; states can stand aside from, and to some degree above, these contentious market rivalries and be ready to step in to resolve crises. Furthermore, the interdependence of commerce and the connections of state officials help create crosscutting transnational ties that serve as lobbies for mutual accommodation. According to modern liberal scholars, international financiers and transnational, bureaucratic, and domestic organizations create interests in favor of accommodation and have ensured by their variety that no single conflict sours an entire relationship.[12]

No one of these constitutional, international or cosmopolitan sources is alone sufficient, but together (and only where together) they plausibly connect the characteristics of liberal politics and economies with sustained liberal peace. Liberal states have not escaped from the realists' "security dilemma," the insecurity caused by anarchy in the world political system considered as a whole. But the effects of international anarchy have been tamed in the relations among states of a similarly liberal character. Alliances of purely mutual strategic interest among liberal and nonliberal states have been broken, economic ties between liberal and nonliberal states have proven fragile, but the political bond of liberal rights and interests has proven a remarkably firm foundation for mutual nonaggression. A separate peace exists among liberal states.

Table 1 Wars Involving Liberal Regimes

Period	Liberal Regimes and the Pacific Union (by Date "Liberal")[a]	Total Number
18th century	Swiss Cantons[b] French Republic 1790–1795, the United States[b] 1776–	3
1800–1850	Swiss Confederation, the United States France 1830–1849 Belgium 1830– Great Britain 1832– Netherlands 1848– Piedmont 1848– Denmark 1849–	8
1850–1900	Switzerland, the United States, Belgium, Great Britain, Netherlands Piedmont 1861, Italy 1861– Denmark 1866 Sweden 1864– Greece 1864– Canada 1867– France 1871– Argentina 1880– Chile 1891–	13

(Continued)

Period	Liberal Regimes and the Pacific Union (by Date "Liberal")[a]	Total Number
1900–1945	Switzerland, the United States, Great Britain, Sweden, Canada Greece 1911, 1928–1936 Italy 1922 Belgium 1940 Netherlands 1940 Argentina 1943 France 1940 Chile 1924, 1932 Australia 1901– Norway 1905–1940 New Zealand 1907– Colombia 1910–1949 Denmark 1914–1940 Poland 1917–1935 Latvia 1922–1934 Germany 1918–1932 Austria 1918–1934 Estonia 1919–1934 Finland 1919– Uruguay 1919– Costa Rica 1919– Czechoslovakia 1920–1939 Ireland 1920– Mexico 1928– Lebanon 1944–	29
1945[c]	Switzerland, the United States, Great Britain, Sweden, Canada, Australia, New Zealand, Finland, Ireland, Mexico Uruguay 1973 Chile 1973 Lebanon 1975 Costa Rica 1948, 1953– Iceland 1944– France 1945– Denmark 1945– Norway 1945– Austria 1945– Brazil 1945–1954, 1955–1964 Belgium 1946– Luxemburg 1946– Netherlands 1946– Italy 1946– Philippines 1946–1972 India 1947–1975, 1977– Sri Lanka 1948–1961, 1963–1977, 1978– Ecuador 1948–1963, 1979– Israel 1949– West Germany 1949– Peru 1950–1962, 1963–1968, 1980– El Salvador 1950–1961 Turkey 1950–1960, 1966–1971 Japan 1951– Bolivia 1956–1969 Colombia 1958– Venezuela 1959– Nigeria 1961–1964, 1979– Jamaica 1962–	49

Period	Liberal Regimes and the Pacific Union (by Date "Liberal")[a]	Total Number
	Trinidad 1962– Senegal 1963– Malaysia 1963– South Korea 1963–1972 Botswana 1966– Singapore 1965– Greece 1975– Portugal 1976– Spain 1978– Dominican Republic 1978–	

[a]I have drawn up this approximate list of "Liberal Regimes" according to the four institutions described as essential: market and private property economies; politics that are extremely sovereign; citizens who possess juridical rights; and "republican" (whether republican or monarchical), representative, government. This latter includes the requirement that the legislative branch have an effective role in public policy and be formally and competitively, either potentially or actually, elected. Furthermore, I have taken into account whether male suffrage is wide (that is, 30 percent) or open to "achievement" by inhabitants (for example, to poll-tax payers or householders) of the national or metropolitan territory. Female suffrage is granted within a generation of its being demanded; and representative government is internally sovereign (for example, including and especially over military and foreign affairs) as well as stable (in existence for at least three years).

[b]There are domestic variations within these liberal regimes. For example, Switzerland was liberal only in certain cantons; the United States was liberal only north of the Mason-Dixon line until 1865, when it became liberal throughout. These lists also exclude ancient "republics," since none appear to fit Kant's criteria. See Stephen Holmes, "Aristippus in and out of Athens," *American Political Science Review* 73, No. 1 (March 1979).

[c]Selected list, excludes liberal regimes with populations less than one million.

SOURCES: Arthur Banks and W. Overstreet, eds., *The Political Handbook of the World*, 1980 (New York: McGraw-Hill, 1980); Foreign and Commonwealth Office, *A Year Book of the Commonwealth* 1980 (London: HMSO, 1980); *Europa Yearbook 1981* (London: Europe, 1981); W. L. Langer, *An Encyclopedia of World History* (Boston: Houghton-Mifflin, 1968); Department of State, *Country Reports on Human Rights Practices* (Washington, D.C.: U.S. Government Printing Office, 1981); and *Freedom at Issue*, No. 54 (January–February 1980).

Table 2 International Wars Listed Chronologically

British-Maharattan (1817–1818)

Greek (1821–1828)

Franco-Spanish (1823)

First Anglo-Burmese (1823–1826)

Japanese (1825–1830)

Russo-Persian (1826–1828)

Russo-Turkish (1828–1829)

First Polish (1831)

First Syrian (1831–1832)

Texan (1835–1836)

First British-Afghan (1838–1842)

Second Syrian (1839–1840)

Franco-Algerian (1839–1847)

Peruvian-Bolivian (1841)

First British-Sikh (1845–1846)

Mexican-American (1846–1848)

Austro-Sardinian (1848–1849)

First Schleswig-Holstein (1848–1849)

Hungarian (1848–1849)

Second British-Sikh (1848–1849)

(Continued)

Roman Republic (1849)

La Plata (1851–1852)

First Turco-Montenegran (1852–1853)

Crimean (1853–1856)

Sepoy (1857–1859)

Second Turco-Montenegran (1858–1859)

Italian Unification (1859)

Spanish-Moroccan (1859–1860)

Italo-Roman (1860)

Italo-Sicilian (1860–1861)

Franco-Mexican (1862–1867)

Ecuadorian-Colombian (1863)

Second Polish (1863–1864)

Spanish-Santo Dominican (1863–1865)

Second Schleswig-Holstein (1864)

Lopez (1864–1870)

Spanish-Chilean (1865–1866)

Seven Weeks (1866)

Ten Years (1868–1878)

Franco-Prussian (1870–1871)

Dutch-Achinese (1873–1878)

Balkan (1875–1877)

Russo-Turkish (1877–1878)

Bosnian (1878)

Second British-Afghan (1878–1880)

Pacific (1879–1880)

British-Zulu (1879)

Franco-Indochinese (1882–1884)

Mahdist (1882–1885)

Sino-French (1884–1885)

Central American (1885)

Serbo-Bulgarian (1885)

Sino-Japanese (1894–1895)

Franco-Madagascan (1894–1895)

Cuban (1895–1896)

Italo-Ethiopian (1895–1896)

First Philippine (1896–1898)

Greco-Turkish (1897)

Spanish-American (1898)

Second Philippine (1899–1902)

Boer (1899–1902)

Boxer Rebellion (1900)

Ilinden (1903)

Russo-Japanese (1904–1905)

Central American (1906)

Central American (1907)

Spanish-Moroccan (1909–1910)

Italo-Turkish (1911–1912)

First Balkan (1912–1913)

Second Balkan (1913)

World War I (1914–1918)

Russian Nationalities (1917–1921)

Russo-Polish (1919–1920)

Hungarian-Allies (1919)

Greco-Turkish (1919–1922)

Riffian (1921–1926)

Druze (1925–1927)

Sino-Soviet (1929)

Manchurian (1931–1933)

Chaco (1932–1935)

Italo-Ethiopian (1935–1936)

Sino-Japanese (1937–1941)

Changkufeng (1938)

Nomohan (1939)

World War II (1939–1945)

Russo-Finnish (1939–1940)

Franco-Thai (1940–1941)

Indonesian (1945–1946)

Indochinese (1945–1954)

Palestine (1948–1949)

Hyderabad (1948)

Madagascan (1947–1948)

First Kashmir (1947–1949)

Korean (1950–1953)

Algerian (1954–1962)

Russo-Hungarian (1956)

Sinai (1956)

Tibetan (1956–1959)

Sino-Indian (1962)

Vietnamese (1965–1975)

Second Kashmir (1965)

Six Day (1967)

Israeli-Egyptian (1969–1970)

Football (1969)

Bangladesh (1971)

Philippine-MNLF (1972–)

(Continued)

Yom Kippur (1973)
Turco-Cypriot (1974)
Ethiopian-Eritrean (1974–1991)*
Vietnamese-Cambodian (1975–1991)*
Timor (1975–1999)*
Saharan (1975–1991)*
Ogaden (1976–1979)*
Ugandan-Tanzanian (1978–1979)
Sino-Vietnamese (1979)
Russo-Afghan (1979–1989)
Irani-Iraqi (1980–1988)

SOURCE: From Melvin Small, *Resort to Arms: International Civil Wars, 1816–1980*. Copyright © 1982. Reproduced with permission of Sage Publications Inc Books in the format Textbook via Copyright Clearance Center. This is a partial list of international wars fought between 1816 and 1980. In Appendices A and B of Resort to Arms, Small and Singer identify a total of 575 wars in this period, but approximately 159 of them appear to be largely domestic or civil wars. This definition of war excludes covert interventions, some of which have been directed by liberal regimes against other liberal regimes. One example is the United States' effort to destabilize the Chilean election and Allende's government. Nonetheless, it is significant . . . that such interventions are not pursued publicly as acknowledged policy. The covert destabilization campaign against Chile is recounted in U.S. Congress, Senate, Select Committee to Study Governmental Operations with Respect to Intelligence Activities, Covert Action in Chile, 1963–73, 94th Congress, 1st Session (Washington, D.C.: U.S. Government Printing Office, 1975).
*Ending date supplied by the editor

Questions for Review

Doyle wrote this article in 1983; has the subsequent history borne out his arguments? What is the relationship between a state being liberal and its being democratic?

Notes

1 Immanuel Kant, "Perpetual Peace" (1795), in *The Philosophy of Kant*, ed. Carl J. Friedrich (New York: Modern Library, 1949), p. 453.

2 There appear to be some exceptions to the tendency for liberal states not to engage in a war with each other. Peru and Ecuador, for example, entered into conflict. But for each, the war came within one to three years after the establishment of a liberal regime, that is, before the pacifying effects of liberalism could become deeply ingrained. The Palestinians and the Israelis clashed frequently along the Lebanese border, which Lebanon could not hold secure from either belligerent. But at the beginning of the 1967 War, Lebanon seems to have sent a flight of its own jets into Israel. The jets were repulsed. Alone among Israel's Arab neighbors, Lebanon engaged in no further hostilities with Israel.

3 Thomas Hobbes, *Leviathan* (New York: Penguin, 1980), I, chap. 13, 62, p. 186.

4 Kenneth N. Waltz, *Man, the State, and War* (New York: Columbia University Press, 1954, 1959), pp. 120–23; and see his *Theory of International Politics* (Reading, Mass.: Addison-Wesley, 1979). The classic sources of this form of Realism are Hobbes and, more particularly, Rousseau's "Essay on St. Pierre's Peace Project" and his "State of War" in *A Lasting Peace* (London: Constable, 1917), E. H. Carr's *The Twenty Year's Crisis: 1919–1939* (London: Macmillan & Co., 1951), and the works of Hans Morgenthau.

5 Jervis, "Cooperation under the Security Dilemma," *World Politics* 30, no. 1 (January 1978), pp. 172–86.

6 Robert H. Jackson and Carl G. Rosberg, "Why West Africa's Weak States Persist," *World Politics* 35, No. 1 (October 1962).

7 Raymond Aron, *Peace and War* (New York: Praeger, 1968), pp. 151–54.

8 The incompatibility of democracy and war is forcefully asserted by Paine in *The Rights of Man*. The connection between liberal capitalism, democracy, and peace is argued by, among others, Joseph Schumpeter in *Imperialism and Social Classes* (New York: Meridian, 1955); and Montesquieu, *Spirit of the Laws* I, bk. 20, chap. 1. This literature is surveyed and analyzed by Albert Hirschman, "Rival Interpretations of Market Society: Civilizing, Destructive, or Feeble?" *Journal of Economic Literature* 20 (December 1982).

9 Immanuel Kant, "Perpetual Peace," in *The Enlightenment*, ed. Peter Gay (New York: Simon & Schuster, 1974), pp. 790–92.

10 Kant, *The Philosophy of Kant*, p. 454. These factors also have a bearing on Karl Deutsch's "compatibility of values" and "predictability of behavior."

11 A highly stylized version of this effect can be found in the realist's "Prisoners' Dilemma" game. There, a failure of mutual trust and the incentives to enhance one's own position produce a noncooperative solution that makes both parties worse off. Contrarily, cooperation, a commitment to avoid exploiting the other party, produces joint gains. The significance of the game in this context is the character of its participants. The "prisoners" are presumed to be felonious, unrelated apart from their partnership in crime, and lacking in mutual trust—competitive nation-states in an anarchic world. A similar game between fraternal or sororal twins—Kant's republics—would be likely to lead to different results. See Robert Jervis, "Hypotheses on Misperception," *World Politics* 20, No. 3 (April 1968), for an exposition of the role of presumptions; and "Cooperation under the Security Dilemma," *World Politics* 30, No. 2 (January 1978), for the factors realists see as mitigating the security dilemma caused by anarchy.Also, expectations (including theory and history) can influence behavior, making liberal states expect (and fulfill) pacific policies toward each other. These effects are explored at a theoretical level in R. Dacey, "Some Implications of 'Theory Absorption' for Economic Theory and the Economics Information," in *Philosophical Dimensions of Economics*, ed. J. Pitt (Dordrecht, Holland: D. Reidel, 1980).

12 Karl Polanyi, *The Great Transformation* (Boston: Beacon Press, 1944), chaps. 1–2 and Samuel Huntington and Z. Brzezinski, *Political Power: USA/USSR* (New York: Viking Press, 1963, 1964), chap. 9. And see Richard Neustadt, *Alliance Politics* (New York: Columbia University Press, 1970) for a detailed case study of interliberal politics.

Alliances: Balancing and Bandwagoning

Stephen M. Walt

When confronted by a significant external threat, states may either balance or bandwagon. Balancing is defined as allying with others against the prevailing threat; bandwagoning refers to alignment with the source of danger. Thus two distinct hypotheses about how states will select their alliance partners can be identified on the basis of whether the states ally against or with the principal external threat.[1]

These two hypotheses depict very different worlds. If balancing is more common than bandwagoning, then states are more secure, because aggressors will face combined opposition. But if bandwagoning is the dominant tendency, then security is scarce, because successful aggressors will attract additional allies, enhancing their power while reducing that of their opponents. . . .

Balancing Behavior

The belief that states form alliances in order to prevent stronger powers from dominating them lies at the heart of traditional balance-of-power theory. According to this view, states join alliances to protect themselves from states or coalitions whose superior resources could pose a threat. States choose to balance for two main reasons.

First, they place their survival at risk if they fail to curb a potential hegemon before it becomes too strong. To ally with the dominant power means placing one's trust in its continued benevolence. The safer strategy is to join with those who cannot readily dominate their allies, in order to avoid being dominated by those who can. As Winston Churchill explained Britain's traditional alliance policy: "For four hundred years the foreign policy of England has been to oppose the strongest, most aggressive, most dominating power on the Continent. . . . [I]t would have been easy . . . and tempting to join with the stronger and share the fruits of his conquest. However, we always took the harder course, joined with the less strong powers, . . . and thus defeated the Continental military tyrant whoever he was."[2] More recently, Henry Kissinger advocated a rapprochement with China, because he believed that in a triangular relationship, it was better to align with the weaker side.

Second, joining the weaker side increases the new member's influence within the alliance, because the weaker side has greater need for assistance. Allying with the strong side, by contrast, gives the new member little influence (because it adds relatively less to the coalition) and leaves it vulnerable to the whims of its partners. Joining the weaker side should be the preferred choice.

Bandwagoning Behavior

The belief that states will balance is unsurprising, given the many familiar examples of states joining together to resist a threatening state or coalition. Yet, despite the powerful evidence that history provides in support of the balancing hypothesis, the belief that the opposite response is more likely is widespread. According to one scholar: "In international politics, nothing succeeds like success. Momentum accrues to the gainer and accelerates his movement. The appearance of irreversibility in his gains enfeebles one side and stimulates the other all the more. The bandwagon collects those on the sidelines."[3]

The bandwagoning hypothesis is especially popular with statesmen seeking to justify overseas involvements or increased military budgets. For example, German admiral Alfred von Tirpitz's famous risk theory rested on this type of logic. By building a great battle fleet, Tirpitz argued, Germany could force England into neutrality or alliance with her by posing a threat to England's vital maritime supremacy.

Bandwagoning beliefs have also been a recurring theme throughout the Cold War. Soviet efforts to intimidate both Norway and Turkey into not joining NATO reveal the Soviet conviction that states will accommodate readily to threats, although these moves merely encouraged Norway and Turkey to align more closely with the West.[4] Soviet officials made a similar error in believing that the growth of Soviet military power in the 1960s and 1970s would lead to a permanent shift in the correlation of forces against the West. Instead, it contributed to a Sino-American rapprochement in the 1970s and the largest peacetime increase in U.S. military power in the 1980s.

American officials have been equally fond of bandwagoning notions. According to NSC–68, the classified study that helped justify a major U.S. military buildup in the 1950s: "In the absence of an affirmative decision [to increase U.S. military capabilities] . . . our friends will become more than a liability to us, they will become a positive increment to Soviet power."[5] President John F. Kennedy once claimed that "if the United States were to falter, the whole world . . . would inevitably begin to move toward the Communist bloc."[6] And though Henry Kissinger often argued that the United States should form balancing alliances to contain the Soviet Union, he apparently believed that U.S. allies were likely to bandwagon. As he put it, "If leaders around the world . . . assume that the U.S. lacked either the forces or the will . . . they will accommodate themselves to what they will regard as the dominant trend."[7] Ronald Reagan's claim, "If we cannot defend ourselves [in Central America] . . . then we cannot expect to prevail elsewhere. . . . [O]ur credibility will collapse and our alliances will crumble," reveals the same logic in a familiar role—that of justifying overseas intervention.[8]

Balancing and bandwagoning are usually framed solely in terms of capabilities. Balancing is alignment with the weaker side, bandwagoning with the stronger. This conception should be revised, however, to account for the other factors that statesmen consider when deciding with whom to ally. Although power is an important part of the equation, it is not the only one. It is more accurate to say that states tend to ally with or against the foreign power that poses the greatest threat. For example, states may balance by allying with other strong states if a weaker power is more dangerous for other reasons. Thus the coalitions that defeated Germany in World War I and World War II were vastly superior in total resources, but they came together when it became clear that the aggressive aims of the Wilhelmines and Nazis posed the greater danger. Because balancing and bandwagoning are more accurately viewed as a response to threats, it is important to consider other factors that will affect the level of threat that states may pose: aggregate power, geographic proximity, offensive power, and aggressive intentions. . . .

By defining the basic hypotheses in terms of threats rather than power alone, we gain a more complete picture of the factors that statesmen will consider when making alliance choices. One cannot determine a priori, however, which sources of threat will be most important in any given case; one can say only that all of them are likely to play a role. And the greater the threat, the greater the probability that the vulnerable state will seek an alliance.

The Implications of Balancing and Bandwagoning

The two general hypotheses of balancing and bandwagoning paint starkly contrasting pictures of international politics. Resolving the question of which hypothesis is more accurate is especially important, because each implies very different policy prescriptions. What sort of world does each depict, and what policies are implied?

If balancing is the dominant tendency, then threatening states will provoke others to align against them. Because those who seek to dominate others will attract widespread opposition, status quo states can take a relatively sanguine view of threats. Credibility is less important in a balancing world, because one's allies will resist threatening states out of their own self-interest, not because they expect others to do it for them. Thus the fear of allies defecting will decline. Moreover, if balancing is the norm and if statesmen understand this tendency, aggression will be discouraged because those who contemplate it will anticipate resistance.

In a balancing world, policies that convey restraint and benevolence are best. Strong states may be valued as allies because they have much to offer their partners, but they must take particular care to avoid appearing aggressive. Foreign and defense policies that minimize the threat one poses to others make the most sense in such a world.

A bandwagoning world, by contrast, is much more competitive. If states tend to ally with those who seem most dangerous, then great powers will be rewarded if they appear both strong and potentially aggressive. International rivalries will be more intense, because a single defeat may signal the decline of one side and the ascendancy of the other. This situation is especially alarming in a bandwagoning world, because additional defections and a further decline in position are to be expected. Moreover, if statesmen believe that bandwagoning is widespread, they will be more inclined to use force. This tendency is true for both aggressors and status quo powers. The former will use force because they will assume that others will be unlikely to balance against them and because they can attract more allies through belligerence or brinkmanship. The latter will follow suit because they will fear the gains their opponents will make by appearing powerful and resolute.[9]

Finally, misperceiving the relative propensity to balance or bandwagon is dangerous, because the policies that are appropriate for one situation will backfire in the other. If statesmen follow the balancing prescription in a bandwagoning world, their moderate responses and relaxed view of threats will encourage their allies to defect, leaving them isolated against an overwhelming coalition. Conversely, following the bandwagoning prescription in a world of balancers (employing power and threats frequently) will lead others to oppose you more and more vigorously.[10]

These concerns are not merely theoretical. In the 1930s, France failed to recognize that her allies in the Little Entente were prone to bandwagon, a tendency that French military and diplomatic policies reinforced. As noted earlier, Soviet attempts to intimidate Turkey and Norway after World War II reveal the opposite error; they merely provoked a greater U.S. commitment to these regions and cemented their entry into NATO. Likewise, the self-encircling bellicosity of Wilhelmine Germany and Imperial Japan reflected the assumption, prevalent in both states, that bandwagoning was the dominant tendency in international affairs.

When Do States Balance? When Do They Bandwagon?

These examples highlight the importance of identifying whether states are more likely to balance or bandwagon and which sources of threat have the greatest impact on the decision. . . . In general, we should expect balancing behavior to be much more common than bandwagoning, and we should expect bandwagoning to occur only under certain identifiable conditions.

Although many statesmen fear that potential allies will align with the strongest side, this fear receives little support from most of international history. For example, every attempt to achieve hegemony in Europe since the Thirty Years' War has been thwarted by a defensive coalition formed precisely for the purpose of defeating the potential hegemon. Other examples are equally telling. Although isolated cases of bandwagoning do occur, the great powers have shown a remarkable tendency to ignore other temptations and follow the balancing prescription when necessary.

This tendency should not surprise us. Balancing should be preferred for the simple reason that no statesman can be completely sure of what another will do. Bandwagoning is dangerous because it increases the resources available to a threatening power and requires placing trust in its continued forbearance. Because perceptions are unreliable and intentions can change, it is safer to balance against potential threats than to rely on the hope that a state will remain benevolently disposed.

But if balancing is to be expected, bandwagoning remains a possibility. Several factors may affect the relative propensity for states to select this course.

Strong versus Weak States

In general, the weaker the state, the more likely it is to bandwagon rather than balance. This situation occurs because weak states add little to the strength of a defensive coalition but incur the wrath of the more threatening states nonetheless. Because weak states can do little to affect the outcome (and may suffer grievously in the process), they must choose the winning side. Only when their decision can affect the outcome is it rational for them to join the weaker alliance. By contrast, strong states can turn a losing coalition into a winning one. And because their decision may mean the difference between victory and defeat, they are likely to be amply rewarded for their contribution.

Weak states are also likely to be especially sensitive to proximate power. Where great powers have both global interests and global capabilities, weak states will be concerned primarily with events in their immediate vicinity. Moreover, weak states can be expected to balance when threatened by states with roughly equal capabilities but they will be tempted to bandwagon when threatened by a great power. Obviously, when the great power is capable of rapid and effective action (i.e., when its offensive capabilities are especially strong), this temptation will be even greater.

The Availability of Allies

States will also be tempted to bandwagon when allies are simply unavailable. This statement is not simply tautological, because states may balance by mobilizing their own resources instead of relying on allied support. They are more likely to do so, however, when they are confident that allied assistance will be available. Thus a further prerequisite for balancing behavior is an effective system of diplomatic communication. The ability to communicate enables potential allies to recognize their shared interests and coordinate their responses. If weak states see no possibility of outside assistance, however, they may be forced to accommodate the most imminent threat. Thus the first Shah of Iran saw the British withdrawal from Kandahar in 1881 as a signal to bandwagon with Russia. As he told the British representative, all he had received from Great Britain was "good advice and honeyed words—nothing else."[11] Finland's policy of partial alignment with the Soviet Union suggests the same lesson. When Finland joined forces with Nazi Germany during World War II, it alienated the potential allies (the United States and Great Britain) that might otherwise have helped protect it from Soviet pressure after the war.

Of course, excessive confidence in allied support will encourage weak states to free-ride, relying on the efforts of others to provide security. Free-riding is the optimal policy for a weak state, because its efforts will contribute little in any case. Among the great powers, the belief that allies are readily available encourages buck-passing; states that are threatened strive to pass to others the burdens of standing up to the aggressor. Neither response is a form of bandwagoning, but both suggest that effective balancing behavior is more likely to occur when members of an alliance are not convinced that their partners are unconditionally loyal.

Taken together, these factors help explain the formation of spheres of influence surrounding the great powers. Although strong neighbors of strong states are likely to balance, small and weak neighbors of the great powers may be more inclined to bandwagon. Because they will be the first victims of expansion, because they lack the capabilities to stand alone, and because a defensive alliance may operate too slowly to do them much good, accommodating a threatening great power may be tempting.

Peace and War

Finally, the context in which alliance choices are made will affect decisions to balance or bandwagon. States are more likely to balance in peacetime or in the early stages of a war, as they seek to deter or defeat the powers posing the greatest threat. But once the outcome appears certain, some will be tempted to defect from the losing side at an opportune moment. Thus both Rumania and Bulgaria allied with Nazi Germany initially and then abandoned Germany for the Allies, as the tides of war ebbed and flowed across Europe in World War II.

The restoration of peace, however, restores the incentive to balance. As many observers have noted, victorious coalitions are likely to disintegrate with the conclusion of peace. Prominent examples include Austria and Prussia after their war with Denmark in 1864, Britain and France after World War I, the Soviet Union and the United States after World War II, and China and Vietnam after the U.S. withdrawal from Vietnam. This recurring pattern provides further support for the proposition that balancing is the dominant tendency in international politics and that bandwagoning is the opportunistic exception.

Summary of Hypotheses on Balancing and Bandwagoning

Hypotheses on Balancing

1. *General form:* States facing an external threat will align with others to oppose the states posing the threat.

2. The greater the threatening state's aggregate power, the greater the tendency for others to align against it.

3. The nearer a powerful state, the greater the tendency for those nearby to align against it. Therefore, neighboring states are less likely to be allies than are states separated by at least one other power.

4. The greater a state's offensive capabilities, the greater the tendency for others to align against it. Therefore, states with offensively oriented military capabilities are likely to provoke other states to form defensive coalitions.

5. The more aggressive a state's perceived intentions, the more likely others are to align against that state.

6. Alliances formed during wartime will disintegrate when the enemy is defeated.

Hypotheses on Bandwagoning

The hypotheses on bandwagoning are the opposite of those on balancing.

1. *General form:* States facing an external threat will ally with the most threatening power.

2. The greater a state's aggregate capabilities, the greater the tendency for others to align with it.

3. The nearer a powerful state, the greater the tendency for those nearby to align with it.

4. The greater a state's offensive capabilities, the greater the tendency for others to align with it.

5. The more aggressive a state's perceived intentions, the less likely other states are to align against it.

6. Alliances formed to oppose a threat will disintegrate when the threat becomes serious.

Hypotheses on the Conditions Favoring Balancing or Bandwagoning

1. Balancing is more common than bandwagoning.

2. The stronger the state, the greater its tendency to balance. Weak states will balance against other weak states but may bandwagon when threatened by great powers.

3. The greater the probability of allied support, the greater the tendency to balance. When adequate allied support is certain, however, the tendency for free-riding or buck-passing increases.

4. The more unalterably aggressive a state is perceived to be, the greater the tendency for others to balance against it.

5. In wartime, the closer one side is to victory, the greater the tendency for others to bandwagon with it.

Questions for Review

Are balancing and bandwagoning the only alternatives for states? Do we expect the same pattern Walt sees in a world with only one superpower?

Notes

1 My use of the terms *balancing* and *bandwagoning* follows that of Kenneth Waltz (who credits it to Stephen Van Evera) in his *Theory of International Politics* (Reading, Mass., 1979). Arnold Wolfers uses a similar terminology in his essay "The Balance of Power in Theory and Practice," in *Discord and Collaboration: Essays on International Politics* (Baltimore, Md., 1962), pp. 122–24.

2 Winston S. Churchill, *The Second World War*, vol. 1: *The Gathering Storm* (Boston, 1948), pp. 207–8.

3 W. Scott Thompson, "The Communist International System," *Orbis* 20, no. 4 (1977).

4 For the effects of the Soviet pressure on Turkey, see George Lenczowski, *The Middle East in World Affairs*, 4th ed. (Ithaca, 1980), pp. 134–38; and Bruce R. Kuniholm, *The Origins of the Cold War in the Near East* (Princeton, N.J., 1980), pp. 355–78. For

the Norwegian response to Soviet pressure, see Herbert Feis, *From Trust to Terror: The Onset of the Cold War, 1945–50* (New York, 1970), p. 381 and Geir Lundestad, *America, Scandinavia, and the Cold War: 1945–1949* (New York, 1980), pp. 308–9.

5 NSC–68 ("United States Objectives and Programs for National Security"), reprinted in Gaddis and Etzold, *Containment*, p. 404. Similar passages can be found on pp. 389, 414, and 434.

6 Quoted in Seyom Brown, *The Faces of Power: Constancy and Change in United States Foreign Policy from Truman to Johnson* (New York, 1968), p. 217.

7 Quoted in U.S. House Committee on Foreign Affairs, *The Soviet Union and the Third World: Watershed in Great Power Policy?* 97th Cong., 1st sess., 1977, pp. 157–58.

8 *New York Times*, April 28, 1983, p. A12. In the same speech, Reagan also said: "If Central America were to fall, what would the consequences be for our position in Asia and Europe and for alliances such as NATO? . . . Which ally, which friend would trust us then?"

9 It is worth noting that Napoleon and Hitler underestimated the costs of aggression by assuming that their potential enemies would bandwagon. After Munich, for example, Hitler dismissed the possibility of opposition by claiming that British and French statesmen were "little worms." Napoleon apparently believed that England could not "reasonably make war on us unaided" and assumed that the Peace of Amiens guaranteed that England had abandoned its opposition to France. Because Hitler and Napoleon believed in a bandwagoning world, they were excessively eager to go to war.

10 This situation is analogous to Robert Jervis's distinction between the deterrence model and the spiral model. The former calls for opposition to a suspected aggressor, the latter for appeasement. Balancing and bandwagoning are the alliance equivalents of deterring and appeasing. See Robert Jervis, *Perception and Misperception in International Politics* (Princeton, N.J., 1976), chap. 3.

11 Quoted in C. J. Lowe, *The Reluctant Imperialists* (New York, 1967), p. 85.

Hierarchy and Hegemony in International Politics

David C. Kang

Introduction

In 1592, the Japanese general Hideyoshi invaded Korea, transporting over 160,000 troops on approximately seven hundred ships. He eventually mobilized a half million troops, intending to continue on to conquer China. Over sixty thousand Korean soldiers, eventually supported by over one hundred thousand Ming Chinese forces, defended the Korean peninsula. After six years of war, the Japanese retreated, and Hideyoshi died, having failed spectacularly in his quest.

The Imjin War "easily dwarfed those of their European contemporaries" and involved men and material five to ten times the scale of the Spanish Armada of

1588, which has been described as the "greatest military force ever assembled" in Renaissance Europe.[1] That in itself should be sufficient cause for international-relations scholars to explore the war's causes and consequences. Yet even more important for the study of international relations is that Hideyoshi's invasion of Korea marked the *only* military conflict between Japan, Korea, and China for over six centuries. For three hundred years both before and after the Imjin War, Japan was a part of the Chinese world. That the three major powers in East Asia—and indeed, much of the rest of the system—could peacefully coexist for such an extended span of time, despite having the military and technological capability to wage war on a massive scale, raises the question of why stability was the norm in East Asian international relations.

In fact, from 1368 to 1841—from the founding of the Ming dynasty to the Opium wars between Britain and China—there were only two wars between China, Korea, Vietnam, and Japan: China's invasion of Vietnam (1407–1428) and Japan's invasion of Korea (1592–1598). Apart from those two episodes, these four major territorial and centralized states developed and maintained peaceful and long-lasting relations with one another, and the more powerful these states became, the more stable were their relations. China was clearly the dominant military, cultural, and economic power in the system, but its goals did not include expansion against its established neighboring states. By the fourteenth century, these Sinicized states had evolved a set of international rules and institutions known as the "tribute system," with China clearly the hegemon and operating under a presumption of inequality, which resulted in a clear hierarchy and lasting peace. These smaller Sinicized states of the region emulated Chinese practices and to varying degrees accepted Chinese centrality. Cultural, diplomatic, and economic relations between the states in the region were both extensive and intensive.

Built on a mix of legitimate authority and material power, the tribute system provided a normative social order that also contained credible commitments by China not to exploit secondary states that accepted its authority. This order was explicit and formally unequal, but it was also informally equal: secondary states were not allowed to call themselves nor did they believe themselves equal with China, yet they had substantial latitude in their actual behavior. China stood at the top of the hierarchy, and there was no intellectual challenge to the rules of the game until the late nineteenth century and the arrival of the Western powers. Korean, Vietnamese, and even Japanese elites consciously copied Chinese institutional and discursive practices in part to craft stable relations with China, not to challenge them.

The East Asian historical experience was markedly different from the European historical experience, both in its fundamental rules and in the level of conflict among the major actors. The European "Westphalian" system emphasized a formal equality between states and balance-of-power politics; it was also marked by incessant interstate conflict. The East Asian "tribute system" emphasized formal inequality between states and a clear hierarchy, and it was marked by centuries of stability among the core participants. Although there has been a tendency to view the European experience as universal, studying the East Asian historical experience as an international system both allows us to ask new questions about East Asia and gives us a new perspective on our own contemporary geopolitical system. Much of world history has involved hegemons building hierarchies and establishing order, and studying these relations in different historical contexts promises to provide new insights into contemporary issues. . . .

Indeed, we tend to take for granted the current set of rules, ideas, and institutions as the natural or inevitable way that countries interact with one another: passports that define citizenship, nation-states as the only legitimate political actor allowed to conducted diplomatic relations, borders between nation-states that are measured to the inch, and, perhaps most centrally, the idea of balance-of-power politics as the basic and enduring pattern of international relations. After all, this characterizes much of contemporary international relations.

Yet this current international system is actually a recent phenomenon in the scope of world history. These international rules and norms arose among European powers only beginning in the seventeenth century. In 1648, the great powers of Europe signed a series of treaties creating a set of rules governing international relations that became known as the "peace of Westphalia." Over the next few centuries, the European powers gradually regularized, ritualized, and institutionalized these Westphalian definitions of sovereignty, diplomacy, nationality, and commercial exchange. For example, although diplomats and merchants occasionally carried various types of identifying credentials before the nineteenth century, it was not until 1856 that the U.S. Congress passed a law giving the Department of State the sole power to issue an official documentation of citizenship, and only after World War I did passports become commonplace.

One outgrowth of this particular Western system of international relations is that equality is taken for granted both as a normative goal and as an underlying and enduring reality of international politics. In this current system, all nation-states are considered equal and are granted identical rights no matter how large the disparity in wealth or size. . . . In international relations, the idea of equality is most clearly expressed in the belief that the balance of power is a fundamental process: too powerful a state will threaten other states and cause them to band together to oppose the powerful state. This idea—that international relations are most stable when states are roughly equal—conditions much of our thinking about how international politics functions. In this way, the European experience, in which a number of similarly sized states engaged in centuries of incessant interstate conflict, is now presumed to be the universal norm. . . .

But these patterns, ideas, and institutions are actually specific ideas from a specific time and place, an Enlightenment notion from the eighteenth century, and there is as much inequality as equality in international relations, both now and in the past. In fact, there are actually two enduring patterns to international relations, not just the balance of power: the opposite idea—that inequality can be stable—also exists. Known as "hegemony," the idea is that under certain conditions, a dominant state can stabilize the system by providing leadership. Both equality and inequality could be stable under certain conditions and unstable under other conditions. Important for us is to realize that even "anarchic" systems differ, and different anarchic systems develop different rules, norms, and institutions that help structure and guide behavior. . . .

The historical East Asian international system . . . contains three overarching themes. First, almost all the actors in East Asia accepted a set of unquestioned rules and institutions about the basic ways in which international relations worked. Known as the *tribute system,* and involving in particular a hierarchic rank ordering based on status, these rules were taken for granted as the way in which political actors interacted with one another. Largely derived from Chinese ideas over the centuries, by the fourteenth century these ideas and institutions had become the rules of the game. This does not mean, however, that the tribute system was identically and consistently applied by every state in every situation—far from it. Like the basic rules and institutions of the Westphalian system today, different states modified, abandoned, and used these ideas in a flexible manner depending on situation and circumstance. The tribute system did, however, form the core organizing principles of the system, and these principles endured for centuries as the basis for international interaction throughout East Asia.

Within this system, cultural achievement in the form of status was as important a goal as was military or economic power. The status hierarchy and rank order were key components of this system, and ranking did not necessarily derive from political, economic, or military power. China was the hegemon, and its status derived from its cultural achievements and social recognition by other political actors, not from its raw size or its military or economic power. All the political units in the system played by these rules. Even political units that rejected Confucian notions of cultural achievement—such as the nomads—accepted the larger rules of the game, the way hierarchy was defined, and the manner in which international relations was conducted, and they defined their own ideals and cultures in opposition to the dominant ideas and institutions of the time. Movement up and down the hierarchy occurred within the rules, and it was not until the arrival of Western powers in the nineteenth century that there appeared an alternative set of rules for how to conduct international relations.

Second, within this larger set of rules and institutions existed a smaller *Confucian society* made up of China, Korea, Vietnam, and Japan. I use the term "society" to mean a self-conscious political grouping where shared ideas, norms, and interests determine membership in the group. Their interests may not be identical, and indeed the goals of the group members can often conflict, but they share the same basic understandings about what the criteria for membership in the group are, the values and norms of the group, and how status is measured.

These four states accepted Chinese ideas and were culturally similar, and although many other political units existed in the system and used the larger rules of the game, it was essentially these four states that formed an inner circle based largely on Confucian ideas. . . .

Finally, these rules and norms were consequential for diplomacy, war, trade, and cultural exchange between political units in East Asia. Far more than a thin veneer of meaningless social lubricants, the tribute system and its ideas and institutions formed the basis for relations between states. The tribute system, with its inherent notions of inequality and its many rules and responsibilities for managing relations among unequals, provided a set of tools for resolving conflicting goals and interests short of resorting to war.

Questions for Review

Is hegemony a true alternative to anarchy in world politics? Is the behavior of China (and perhaps the other states in Asia) influenced by notions of hierarchy?

Notes

1 Kenneth Swope, "Crouching Tigers, Hidden Weapons," *Journal of Military History*, vol. 69, January 2005, p. 13.

The Future of Diplomacy

Hans J. Morgenthau

Four Tasks of Diplomacy

. . . Diplomacy [is] an element of national power. The importance of diplomacy for the preservation of international peace is but a particular aspect of that general function. For a diplomacy that ends in war has failed in its primary objective: the promotion of the national interest by peaceful means. This has always been so and is particularly so in view of the destructive potentialities of total war.

Taken in its widest meaning, comprising the whole range of foreign policy, the task of diplomacy is fourfold: (1) Diplomacy must determine its objectives in the light of the power actually and potentially available for the pursuit of these objectives. (2) Diplomacy must assess the objectives of other nations and the power actually and potentially available for the pursuit of these objectives. (3) Diplomacy must determine to what extent these different objectives are compatible with each other. (4) Diplomacy must employ the means suited to the pursuit of its objectives. Failure in any one of these tasks may jeopardize the success of foreign policy and with it the peace of the world.

A nation that sets itself goals which it has not the power to attain may have to face the risk of war on two counts. Such a nation is likely to dissipate its strength and not to be strong enough at all points of friction to deter a hostile nation from challenging it beyond endurance. The failure of its foreign policy may force the nation to retrace its steps and to redefine its objectives in view of its actual strength. Yet it is more likely that, under the pressure of an inflamed public opinion, such a nation will go forward on the road toward an unattainable goal, strain all its resources to achieve it, and finally, confounding the national interest with that goal, seek in war the solution to a problem that cannot be solved by peaceful means.

A nation will also invite war if its diplomacy wrongly assesses the objectives of other nations and the power at their disposal. . . . A nation that mistakes a policy of imperialism for a policy of the status quo will be unprepared to meet the threat to its own existence which the other nation's policy entails. Its weakness will invite attack and may make war inevitable. A nation that mistakes a policy of the status quo for a policy of imperialism will evoke through its disproportionate reaction the very danger of war which it is trying to avoid. For as A mistakes B's policy for imperialism, so B might mistake A's defensive reaction for imperialism. Thus both nations, each intent upon forestalling imaginary aggression from the other side, will rush to arms. Similarly, the confusion of one type of imperialism with another may call for disproportionate reaction and thus evoke the risk of war.

As for the assessment of the power of other nations, either to overrate or to underrate it may be equally fatal to the cause of peace. By overrating the power of B, A may prefer to yield to B's demands until, finally, A is forced to fight for its very existence under the most unfavorable conditions. By underrating the power of B, A may become overconfident in its assumed superiority. A may advance demands and impose conditions upon B which the latter is supposedly too weak to resist. Unsuspecting B's actual power of resistance, A may be faced with the alternative of either retreating and conceding defeat or of advancing and risking war.

A nation that seeks to pursue an intelligent and peaceful foreign policy cannot cease comparing its own objectives and the objectives of other nations in the light of their compatibility. If they are compatible, no problem arises. If they are not compatible, nation A must determine whether its objectives are so vital to itself that they must be pursued despite that incompatibility with the objectives of B. If it is found that A's vital interests can be safeguarded without the attainment of these objectives, they ought to be abandoned. On the other hand, if A finds that these objectives are essential for its vital interests, A must then ask itself whether B's objectives, incompatible with its own, are essential for B's vital interests. If the answer seems to be in the negative, A must try to induce B to abandon its objectives, offering B equivalents not vital to A. In other words, through diplomatic bargaining, the give and take of compromise, a way must be sought by which the interests of A and B can be reconciled.

Finally, if the incompatible objectives of A and B should prove to be vital to either side, a way might still be sought in which the vital interests of A and B might be redefined, reconciled, and their objectives thus made compatible with each other. Here, however—even provided that both sides pursue intelligent and peaceful policies—A and B are moving dangerously close to the brink of war.

It is the final task of an intelligent diplomacy, intent upon preserving peace, to choose the appropriate means for pursuing its objectives. The means at the disposal of diplomacy are three: persuasion, compromise, and threat of force. No diplomacy relying only upon the threat of force can claim to be both intelligent and peaceful. No diplomacy that would stake everything on persuasion and compromise deserves to be called intelligent. Rarely, if ever, in the conduct of the foreign policy of a great power is there justification for using only one method to the exclusion of the others. Generally, the diplomatic representative of a great power, in order to be able to serve both the interests of his country and the interests of peace, must at the same time use persuasion, hold out the advantages of a compromise, and impress the other side with the military strength of his country.

The art of diplomacy consists in putting the right emphasis at any particular moment on each of these three means at its disposal. A diplomacy that has been successfully discharged in its other functions may well fail in advancing the national interest and preserving peace if it stresses persuasion when the give and take of compromise is primarily required by the circumstances of the case. A diplomacy that puts most of its eggs in the basket of compromise when the military might of the nation should be predominantly displayed, or stresses military might when the political situation calls for persuasion and compromise, will likewise fail. . . .

The Promise of Diplomacy: Its Nine Rules[1]

Diplomacy could revive if it would part with [the] vices, which in recent years have well-nigh destroyed its usefulness, and if it would restore the techniques which have controlled the mutual relations of nations since time immemorial. By doing so, however, diplomacy would realize only one of the preconditions for the preservation of peace. The contribution of a revived diplomacy to the cause of peace would depend upon the methods and purposes of its use. . . .

We have already formulated the four main tasks with which a foreign policy must cope successfully in order to be able to promote the national interest and preserve peace. It remains for us now to reformulate those tasks in the light of the special problems with which contemporary world politics confront diplomacy. . . .

The main reason for [the] threatening aspect of contemporary world politics [lies] in the character of modern war, which has changed profoundly under the impact of nationalistic universalism* and modern technology. The effects of modern technology cannot be undone. The only variable that remains subject

---

*[Editors' Note: By this term Professor Morgenthau refers to the injection of ideology into international politics and to each nation's claim that its own ethical code would serve as the basis of international conduct for all nations.]

to deliberate manipulation is the new moral force of nationalistic universalism. The attempt to reverse the trend toward war through the techniques of a revived diplomacy must start with this phenomenon. That means, in negative terms, that a revived diplomacy will have a chance to preserve peace only when it is not used as the instrument of a political religion aiming at universal dominion.

Four Fundamental Rules

DIPLOMACY MUST BE DIVESTED OF THE CRUSADING SPIRIT This is the first of the rules that diplomacy can neglect only at the risk of war. In the words of William Graham Sumner:

> If you want war, nourish a doctrine. Doctrines are the most frightful tyrants to which men ever are subject, because doctrines get inside of a man's own reason and betray him against himself. Civilised men have done their fiercest fighting for doctrines. The reconquest of the Holy Sepulcher, "the balance of power," "no universal dominion," "trade follows the flag," "he who holds the land will hold the sea," "the throne and the altar," the revolution, the faith—these are the things for which men have given their lives. . . . Now when any doctrine arrives at that degree of authority, the name of it is a club which any demagogue may swing over you at any time and apropos of anything. In order to describe a doctrine, we must have recourse to theological language. A doctrine is an article of faith. It is something which you are bound to believe, not because you have some rational grounds for believing it is true, but because you belong to such and such a church or denomination. . . . A policy in a state we can understand; for instance, it was the policy of the United States at the end of the eighteenth century to get the free navigation of the Mississippi to its mouth, even at the expense of war with Spain. That policy had reason and justice in it; it was founded in our interests; it had positive form and definite scope. A doctrine is an abstract principle; it is necessarily absolute in its scope and abstruse in its terms; it is metaphysical assertion. It is never true, because it is absolute, and the affairs of men are all conditioned and relative. . . . Now to turn back to politics, just think what an abomination in statecraft an abstract doctrine must be. Any politician or editor can, at any moment, put a new extension on it. The people acquiesce in the doctrine and applaud it because they hear the politicians and editors repeat it, and the politicians and editors repeat it because they think it is popular. So it grows. . . . It may mean anything or nothing, at any moment, and no one knows how it will be. You accede to it now, within the vague limits of what you suppose it to be; therefore, you will have to accede to it tomorrow when the same name is made to cover something which you never have heard or thought of. If you allow a political catchword to go on and grow, you will awaken some day to find it standing over you, the arbiter of your destiny, against which you are powerless, as men are powerless against delusions. . . . What can be more contrary to sound statesmanship and common sense than to put forth an abstract assertion which has no definite relation to any interest

of ours now at stake, but which has in it any number of possibilities of producing complications which we cannot foresee, but which are sure to be embarrassing when they arise![2]

The Wars of Religion have shown that the attempt to impose one's own religion as the only true one upon the rest of the world is as futile as it is costly. A century of almost unprecedented bloodshed, devastation, and barbarization was needed to convince the contestants that the two religions could live together in mutual toleration. The two political religions of our time have taken the place of the two great Christian denominations of the sixteenth and seventeenth centuries. Will the political religions of our time need the lesson of the Thirty Years' War, or will they rid themselves in time of the universalistic aspirations that inevitably issue in inconclusive war?

Upon the answer to that question depends the cause of peace. For only if it is answered in the affirmative can a moral consensus, emerging from shared convictions and common values, develop—a moral consensus within which a peace-preserving diplomacy will have a chance to grow. Only then will diplomacy have a chance to face the concrete political problems that require peaceful solution. If the objectives of foreign policy are not to be defined in terms of a world-embracing political religion, how are they to be defined? This is a fundamental problem to be solved once the crusading aspirations of nationalistic universalism have been discarded.

THE OBJECTIVES OF FOREIGN POLICY MUST BE DEFINED IN TERMS OF THE NATIONAL INTEREST AND MUST BE SUPPORTED WITH ADEQUATE POWER   This is the second rule of a peace-preserving diplomacy. The national interest of a peace-loving nation can only be defined in terms of national security, and national security must be defined as integrity of the national territory and of its institutions. National security, then, is the irreducible minimum that diplomacy must defend with adequate power without compromise. But diplomacy must ever be alive to the radical transformation that national security has undergone under the impact of the nuclear age. Until the advent of that age, a nation could use its diplomacy to purchase its security at the expense of another nation. Today, short of a radical change in the atomic balance of power in favor of a particular nation, diplomacy, in order to make one nation secure from nuclear destruction, must make them all secure. With the national interest defined in such restrictive and transcendent terms, diplomacy must observe the third of its rules.

DIPLOMACY MUST LOOK AT THE POLITICAL SCENE FROM THE POINT OF VIEW OF OTHER NATIONS   "Nothing is so fatal to a nation as an extreme of self-partiality, and the total want of consideration of what others will naturally hope or fear."[3] What are the national interests of other nations in terms of national security and are they compatible with one's own? The definition of the national interest in terms of national security is easier, and the interests of the two opposing nations are more likely to be compatible in a bipolar system than in any other system of the balance of power. The bipolar system, as we have seen, is more unsafe from the point of view of peace than any other, when both blocs are in competitive contact throughout the world and the ambition of both is fired by the crusading zeal of a universal mission. " . . . Vicinity, or nearness of situation, constitutes nations natural enemies."[4]

Yet once they have defined their national interests in terms of national security, they can draw back from their outlying positions, located close to, or within, the sphere of national security of the other side, and retreat into their respective spheres, each self-contained within its orbit. Those outlying positions add nothing to national security; they are but liabilities, positions that cannot be held in case of war. Each bloc will be the more secure the wider it makes the distance that separates both spheres of national security. Each side can draw a line far distant from each other, making it understood that to touch or even to approach it means war. What then about the interjacent spaces, stretching between the two lines of demarcation? Here the fourth rule of diplomacy applies.

NATIONS MUST BE WILLING TO COMPROMISE ON ALL ISSUES THAT ARE NOT VITAL TO THEM   All government, indeed every human benefit and enjoyment, every virtue and every prudent act, is founded on compromise and barter. We balance inconveniences; we give and take; we remit some rights, that we may enjoy others; and we choose rather to be happy citizens than subtle disputants. As we must give away some natural liberties, for the advantages to be derived from the communion and fellowship of a great empire. But, in all fair dealings, the thing bought must bear some proportion to the purchase paid. None will barter away the immediate jewel of his soul.[5] Here diplomacy meets its most difficult task. For minds not beclouded by the crusading zeal of a political religion and capable of viewing the national interests of both sides with objectivity, the delimitation of these vital interests should not prove too difficult. Compromise on secondary issues is a different matter. Here the task is not to separate and define interests that by their very nature already tend toward separation and definition, but to keep in balance interests that touch each other at many points and may be intertwined beyond the possibility of separation. It is an immense task to allow the other side a certain influence in those interjacent spaces without allowing them to be absorbed into the orbit of the other side. It is hardly a less immense task to keep the other side's influence as small as possible in the regions close to one's own security zone without absorbing those regions into one's own orbit. For the performance of these tasks, no formula stands ready for automatic application. It is only through a continuous process of adaptation, supported both by firmness and self-restraint, that compromise on secondary issues can be made to work. It is, however, possible to indicate a priori what approaches will facilitate or hamper the success of policies of compromise.

First of all, it is worth noting to what extent the success of compromise—that is, compliance with the fourth rule—depends upon compliance with the other three rules, which in turn are similarly interdependent. As the compliance with the second rule depends upon the realization of the first, so the third rule must await its realization from compliance with the second. A nation can only take a rational view of its national interests after it has parted company with the crusading spirit of a political creed. A nation is able to consider the national interests of the other side with objectivity only after it has become secure in what it considers its own national interests. Compromise on any issue, however minor, is impossible so long as both sides are not secure in their national interests. Thus nations cannot hope to comply with the fourth rule if they are not willing to comply with the other three. Both morality and expediency require compliance with these four fundamental rules.

Compliance makes compromise possible, but it does not assure its success. To give compromise, made possible through compliance with the first three rules, a chance to succeed, five other rules must be observed.

Five Prerequisites of Compromise

GIVE UP THE SHADOW OF WORTHLESS RIGHTS FOR THE SUBSTANCE OF REAL ADVANTAGE   A diplomacy that thinks in legalistic and propagandistic terms is particularly tempted to insist upon the letter of the law, as it interprets the law, and to lose sight of the consequences such insistence may have for its own nation and for humanity. Since there are rights to be defended, this kind of diplomacy thinks that the issue cannot be compromised. Yet the choice that confronts the diplomat is not between legality and illegality, but between political wisdom and political folly. "The question with me," said Edmund Burke, "is not whether you have a right to render your people miserable, but whether it is not your interest to make them happy. It is not what a lawyer tells me I *may* do, but what humanity, reason and justice tell me I ought to do."[6]

NEVER PUT YOURSELF IN A POSITION FROM WHICH YOU CANNOT RETREAT WITHOUT LOSING FACE AND FROM WHICH YOU CANNOT ADVANCE WITHOUT GRAVE RISKS   The violation of this rule often results from disregard for the preceding one. A diplomacy that confounds the shadow of legal right with the actuality of political advantage is likely to find itself in a position where it may have a legal right, but no political business, to be. In other words, a nation may identify itself with a position, which it may or may not have a right to hold, regardless of the political consequences. And again compromise becomes a difficult matter. A nation cannot retreat from that position without incurring a serious loss of prestige. It cannot advance from that position without exposing itself to political risks, perhaps even the risk of war. That heedless rush into untenable positions and, more particularly, the stubborn refusal to extricate oneself from them in time is the earmark of incompetent diplomacy. Its classic examples are the policy of Napoleon III on the eve of the Franco-Prussian War of 1870 and the policies of Austria and Germany on the eve of the First World War. These examples also show how closely the risk of war is allied with the violation of this rule.

NEVER ALLOW A WEAK ALLY TO MAKE DECISIONS FOR YOU   Strong nations that are oblivious to the preceding rules are particularly susceptible to violating this one. They lose their freedom of action by identifying their own national interests completely with those of the weak ally. Secure in the support of its powerful friend, the weak ally can choose the objectives and methods of its foreign policy to suit itself. The powerful nation then finds that it must support interests not its own and that it is unable to compromise on issues that are vital not to itself, but only to its ally.

The classic example of the violation of this rule is to be found in the way in which Turkey forced the hand of Great Britain and France on the eve of the Crimean War in 1853. The Concert of Europe had virtually agreed upon a compromise settling the conflict between Russia and Turkey, when Turkey, knowing that the Western powers would support it in a war with Russia, did its best to provoke that war and thus involved Great Britain and France in it against their will. Thus Turkey went far in deciding the issue of war and peace for Great Britain and France according to its own national interests. Great Britain and France had to accept that decision even though their national interests did not require war with Russia and they had almost succeeded in preventing its outbreak. They had surrendered their freedom of action to a weak ally, which used its control over their policies for its own purposes.

THE ARMED FORCES ARE THE INSTRUMENT OF FOREIGN POLICY, NOT ITS MASTER   No successful and no peaceful foreign policy is possible without observance of this rule. No nation can pursue a policy of compromise with the military determining the ends and means of foreign policy. The armed forces are instruments of war; foreign policy is an instrument of peace. It is true that the ultimate objectives of the conduct of war and of the conduct of foreign policy are identical: Both serve the national interest. Both, however, differ fundamentally in their immediate objective, in the means they employ, and in the modes of thought they bring to bear upon their respective tasks.

The objective of war is simple and unconditional: to break the will of the enemy. Its methods are equally simple and unconditional: to bring the greatest amount of violence to bear upon the most vulnerable spot in the enemy's armor. Consequently, the military leader must think in absolute terms. He lives in the present and in the immediate future. The sole question before him is how to win victories as cheaply and quickly as possible and how to avoid defeat.

The objective of foreign policy is relative and conditional: to bend, not to break, the will of the other side as far as necessary in order to safeguard one's own vital interests without hurting those of the other side. The methods of foreign policy are relative and conditional: not to advance by destroying the obstacles in one's way, but to retreat before them, to circumvent them, to maneuver around them, to soften and dissolve them slowly by means of persuasion, negotiation, and pressure. In consequence, the mind of the diplomat is complicated and subtle. It sees the issue in hand as a moment in history, and beyond the victory of tomorrow it anticipates the incalculable possibilities of the future. In the words of Bolingbroke:

> Here let me only say, that the glory of taking towns, and winning battles, is to be measured by the utility that results from those victories. Victories that bring honour to the arms, may bring shame to the councils, of a nation. To win a battle, to take a town, is the glory of a general, and of an army. . . . But the glow of a nation is to proportion the ends she proposes, to her interest and her strength; the means she employs to the ends she proposes, and the vigour she exerts to both.[7]

To surrender the conduct of foreign affairs to the military, then, is to destroy the possibility of compromise and thus surrender the cause of peace. The military mind knows how to operate between the absolutes of victory and defeat. It knows nothing of that patient intricate and subtle maneuvering of diplomacy, whose main purpose is to avoid the absolutes of victory and defeat and meet the other side on the middle ground of negotiated compromise. A foreign policy conducted by military men according to the rules of the military art can only end in war, for "what we prepare for is what we shall get."[8]

For nations conscious of the potentialities of modern war, peace must be the goal of their foreign policies. Foreign policy must be conducted in such a way as to make the preservation of peace possible and not make the outbreak of war inevitable. In a society of sovereign nations, military force is a necessary instrument of foreign policy. Yet the instrument of foreign policy should not become the master of foreign policy. As war is fought in order to make peace possible, foreign policy should be conducted in order to make peace permanent. For the performance of both tasks, the subordination of the military under the civilian authorities which are constitutionally responsible for the conduct of foreign affairs is an indispensable prerequisite.

THE GOVERNMENT IS THE LEADER OF PUBLIC OPINION, NOT ITS SLAVE   Those responsible for the conduct of foreign policy will not be able to comply with the foregoing principles of diplomacy if they do not keep this principle constantly in mind. As has been pointed out above in greater detail, the rational requirements of good foreign policy cannot from the outset count upon the support of a public opinion whose preferences are emotional rather than rational. This is bound to be particularly true of a foreign policy whose goal is compromise, and which, therefore, must concede some of the objectives of the other side and give up some of its own. Especially when foreign policy is conducted under conditions of democratic control and is inspired by the crusading zeal of a political religion, statesmen are always tempted to sacrifice the requirements of good foreign policy to the applause of the masses. On the other hand, the statesmen who would defend the integrity of these requirements against even the slightest contamination with popular passion would seal his own doom as a political leader and, with it, the doom of his foreign policy, for he would lose the popular support which put and keeps him in power.

The statesman, then, is allowed neither to surrender to popular passions nor disregard them. He must strike a prudent balance between adapting himself to them and marshaling them to the support of his policies. In one word, he must lead. He must perform that highest feat of statesmanship: trimming his sails to the winds of popular passion while using them to carry the ship to the port of good foreign policy, on however roundabout and zigzag a course.

Conclusion

The road to international peace which we have outlined cannot compete in inspirational qualities with the simple and fascinating formulae that for a century and a half have fired the imagination of a war-weary world. There is something spectacular in the radial simplicity of a formula that with one sweep seems to dispose of the problem of war once and for all. This has been the promise of such solutions as free trade, arbitration, disarmament, collective security, universal socialism, international government, and the world state. There is nothing spectacular, fascinating, or inspiring, at least for the people at large, in the business of diplomacy.

We have made the point, however, that these solutions, insofar as they deal with the real problem and not merely with some of its symptoms, presuppose the existence of an integrated international society, which actually does not exist. To bring into existence such an international society and keep it in being, the accommodating techniques of diplomacy are required. As the integration of domestic society and its peace develop from the unspectacular and almost unnoticed day-by-day operations of the techniques of accommodation and change, so the ultimate ideal of international life—that is, to transcend itself in a supranational society—must await its realization from the techniques of persuasion, negotiation, and pressure, which are the traditional instruments of diplomacy.

The reader who has followed us to this point may well ask: But has not diplomacy failed in preventing war in the past? To that legitimate question two answers can be given.

Diplomacy has failed many times, and it has succeeded many times, in its peace-preserving task. It has failed sometimes because nobody wanted it to succeed. We have seen how different in their objectives and methods the limited wars of the past have been from the total war of our time. When war was the normal activity of kings, the task of diplomacy was not to prevent it, but to bring it about at the most propitious moment.

On the other hand, when nations have used diplomacy for the purpose of preventing war, they have often succeeded. The outstanding example of a successful war-preventing diplomacy in modern times is the Congress of Berlin of 1878. By the peaceful means of an accommodating diplomacy, that Congress settled, or at least made susceptible of settlement, the issues that had separated Great Britain and Russia since the end of the Napoleonic Wars. During the better part of the nineteenth century, the conflict between Great Britain and Russia over the Balkans, the Dardanelles, and the Eastern Mediterranean hung like a suspended sword over the peace of the world. Yet, during the fifty years following the Crimean War, though hostilities between Great Britain and Russia threatened to break out time and again, they never actually did break out. The main credit for the preservation of peace must go to the techniques of an accommodating diplomacy which culminated in the Congress of Berlin. When British Prime Minister Disraeli returned from that Congress to London, he declared with pride that he was bringing home "peace . . . with honor." In fact, he had brought peace for later generations, too; for a century there has been no war between Great Britain and Russia.

We have, however, recognized the precariousness of peace in a society of sovereign nations. The continuing success of diplomacy in preserving peace depends, as we have seen, upon extraordinary moral and intellectual qualities that all the leading participants must possess. A mistake in the evaluation of one of the elements of national power, made by one or the other of the leading statesmen, may spell the difference between peace and war. So may an accident spoiling a plan or a power calculation.

Diplomacy is the best means of preserving peace which a society of sovereign nations has to offer, but, especially under the conditions of contemporary world politics and of contemporary war, it is not good enough. It is only when nations have surrendered to a higher authority the means of destruction which modern technology has put in their hands—when they have given up their sovereignty— that international peace can be made as secure as domestic peace. Diplomacy can make peace more secure than it is today, and the world state can make peace more secure than it would be if nations were to abide by the rules of diplomacy. Yet, as there can be no permanent peace without a world state, there can be no world state without the peace-preserving and community-building processes of diplomacy. For the world state to be more than a dim vision, the accommodating processes of diplomacy, mitigating and minimizing conflicts, must be revived. Whatever one's conception of the ultimate state of international affairs may be, in the recognition of that need and in the demand that it be met all men of good will can join.

Questions for Review

How do you reconcile Morgenthau's praise of diplomacy with his six principles of realism? His rules are couched in terms of what states "must" do; what determines whether they follow these instructions or not?

Notes

1 We by no means intend to give here an exhaustive account of rules of diplomacy. We propose to discuss only those which seem to have a special bearing upon the contemporary situation.

2 "War." *Essays of William Graham Sumner* (New Haven, Conn.: Yale University Press, 1934), Vol. I, pp. 169 ff.

3 Edmund Burke, "Remarks on the Policy of the Allies with Respect to France" (1793), *Works*, Vol. IV (Boston: Little, Brown and Company, 1889), p. 447.

4 *The Federalist Papers*, No. 6.

5 Edmund Burke, "Speech on the Conciliation with America," *loc. cit.*, Vol. II, p. 169.

6 "Speech on Conciliation with the Colonies" (1775), *The Works of Edmund Burke*, Vol. II (Boston: Little, Brown and Company, 1865), p. 140.

7 *Bolingbroke's Defense of the Treaty of Utrecht* (Cambridge: Cambridge University Press, 1932), p. 95.

8 William Graham Sumner, *op. cit.*, p. 173.

The Uses and Limits of International Law

STANLEY HOFFMANN

The student of international law who examines its functions in the present international system and in the foreign policy of states will, unless he takes refuge in the comforting seclusion from reality that the pure theory of law once provided, be reduced to one of three attitudes. He will become a cynic, if he chooses to stress, like Giraudoux in *Tiger at the Gates*, the way in which legal claims are shaped to support any position a state deems useful or necessary on nonlegal grounds, or if he gets fascinated by the combination of cacophony and silence that characterizes international law as a system of world public order. He will become a hypocrite, if he chooses to rationalize either the conflicting interpretations and uses of law by states as a somehow converging effort destined to lead to some such system endowed with sufficient stability and solidity, or else if he endorses one particular construction (that of his own statesmen) as a privileged and enlightened contribution to the achievement of such a system. He will be overcome by consternation, if he reflects upon the gap between, on the one hand, the ideal of a world in which traditional self-help will be at least moderated by procedures and rules made even more indispensable by the proliferation both of states and of lethal weapons, and, on the other hand, the realities of inexpiable conflicts, sacred egoisms, and mutual recriminations. . . .

1. Some of the functions of international law constitute *assets both for the policy maker and from the viewpoint of world order*, i.e., of providing the international milieu with a framework of predictability and with procedures for the transaction of interstate business.

   a. International law is an instrument of *communication*. To present one's claims in legal terms means, 1, to signal to one's partner or opponent which "basic conduct norms" (to use Professor Scheinman's expression) one considers relevant or essential, and 2, to indicate which procedures one intends to follow and would like the other side to follow. At a time when both the size of a highly heterogeneous international milieu and the imperatives of prudence in the resort to force make communication essential and often turn international relations into a psychological contest, international law provides a kind of common language that does not amount to a common code of legitimacy yet can serve as a joint frame of reference. (One must however remember, 1, that communication is no guarantee against misperception, and 2, that what is being communicated may well determine the other side's response to the message: If "we" communicate to "them" an understanding of the situation that threatens their basic values or goals—like our interpretation of the war in South Vietnam as a case of aggression—there will be no joint frame of reference at all, and in fact the competition may become fiercer.)

b. International law affords means of *channeling conflict*—of diverting inevitable tensions and clashes from the resort to force. Whenever there have been strong independent reasons for avoiding armed conflict—in an international system in which the superpowers in particular have excellent reasons for "managing" their confrontations, either by keeping them nonviolent, or by using proxies—international law has provided statesmen both with alibis for shunning force and with alternatives to violence. . . . In Berlin, both the Soviets and the West shaped their moves in such a way as to leave to the other side full responsibility for a first use of force, and to avoid the kind of frontal collision with the other side's legal claim that could have obliged the opponent to resort to force in order not to lose power or face. Thus, today as in earlier periods, law can indeed . . . serve as an alternative to confrontation whenever states are eager or forced to look for an alternative.

2. International law also plays various useful roles in the policy process, which however do not ipso facto contribute to world order. Here, we are concerned with *law as a tool of policy* in the competition of state visions, objectives, and tactics.

   a. The establishment of a network of rights and obligations, or the resort to legal arguments can be useful for the *protection or enhancement of a position:* if one wants to give oneself a full range of means with which to buttress a threatened status quo (cf. the position of the West in Berlin [during cold war]; this is also what treaties of alliance frequently are for); if one wants to enhance one's power in a way that is demonstrably authorized by principles in international law (cf. Nasser's claim when he nationalized the Suez Canal, and Sukarno's invocation of the principle of self-determination against Malaysia); if one wants to restore a political position badly battered by an adversary's move, so that the resort to legal arguments becomes part of a strategy of restoring the status quo ante (Western position during the Berlin blockade; Kennedy's strategy during the Cuban missile crisis; Western powers' attempts during the first phase of the Suez crisis; Soviet tactics in the U.N. General Assembly debates on the financing of peace-keeping operations).

b. In all those instances, policy makers use law as a way of putting pressure on an opponent by *mobilizing international support* behind the legal rules invoked: law serves as a focal point, as the tool for "internationalizing" a national interest and as the cement of a political coalition. States that may have political misgivings about pledging direct support to a certain power whose interests only partly coincide with theirs, or because they do not want to antagonize another power thereby, may find it both easier and useful to rally to the defense of a legal principle in whose maintenance or promotion they may have a stake.

c. A policy maker who ignores international law leaves the field of political-competition-through-legal-manipulation open to his opponents or rivals. International law provides one of the numerous *chessboards* on which state contests occur.

3. Obviously, this indicates not only that to the statesmen international law provides an instrument rather than a guide for action, but also that this tool is often *not used*, when resort to it would hamper the state's interest as defined by the policy maker.

a. One of the reasons why international law often serves as a technique of political mobilization is the appeal of reciprocity: "You must support my invocation of the rule against him, because if you let the rule be violated at my expense, someday it may be breached at yours; and we both have an interest in its preservation." But *reciprocity cuts both ways:* My using a certain legal argument to buttress my case against him may encourage him, now or later, to resort to the same argument against me; I may therefore be unwise to play on a chessboard in which, given the solemn and abstract nature of legal rights and obligations, I may not be able to make the kind of distinction between my (good) case and your (bad) one that can best be made by resort to ad hoc, political and circumstantial evidence that is irrelevant or ruled out in legal argumentation. Thus . . . during the Cuban crisis, when the United States tried to distinguish between Soviet missiles in Cuba and American ones in Turkey in order to build its case and get support, America's use of the OAS [Organization of American States] Charter as the legal basis for its "quarantine" established a dangerous precedent which the Soviets could use some day, against the U.S. or its allies, on behalf of the Warsaw Pact. And in the tragicomedy of the battle over Article 19 of the U.N.

Charter, one reason why the U.S. finally climbed down from its high legal horse and gave up the attempt to deprive the Soviets of their right to vote, unless they paid their share, was the growing awareness of the peril which the principle of the exercise of the U.N. taxing power by the General Assembly could constitute some day for the United States if it lost control of the Assembly.

b. One of the things that international law "communicates" is the solemnity of a commitment: a treaty, or a provision of the Charter, serves as a kind of tripwire or burglar alarm. When it fails to deter, the victim and third parties have a fateful choice between upholding the legal principle by all means, at the cost of a possible escalation in violence, and choosing to settle the dispute more peacefully, at the cost of *fuzzing the legal issue.* For excellent political reasons, the latter course is frequently adopted . . . in the form of dropping any reference to the legal principle at stake. . . .

c. The very *ambiguity* of international law, which in many essential areas displays either gaping holes or conflicting principles, allows policy makers in an emergency to act as if international law were irrelevant—as if it were neither a restraint nor a guide. . . .

d. However, precisely because there is a legal chessboard for state competition, the fact that international law does not, in a crisis, really restrict one's freedom of action, does not mean that one will forgo legal rationalizations of the moves selected. Here we come to the last set of considerations about the role of law:

4. The resort to legal arguments by policy makers may be *detrimental to world order and thereby counterproductive for the state* that used such arguments.

a. In the legal vacuum or confusion which prevails in areas as vital to states as internal war or the use of force, each state tries to justify its conduct with legal rationalizations. The result is a kind of *escalation of claims and counterclaims,* whose consequence, in turn, is both a further devaluation of international law and a "credibility gap" at the expense of those states who have debased the currency. America's rather indiscriminate resort to highly debatable legal arguments to support its Vietnam policy is a case in point. The unsubtle reduction of international law to a mere storehouse of convenient *ex post* justifications (as in the case of British intervention at Suez, or American interventions in Santo Domingo and Vietnam) undermines the very pretense of contributing to world order with which these states have tried to justify their unilateral acts.

b. Much of contemporary international law authorizes states to *increase their power.* In this connection, Nasser's nationalization of the Suez Canal Company was probably quite legal, and those who accept the rather tortured argument put forth by the State Department legal advisers to justify the Cuban "quarantine" have concluded that this partial blockade was authorized by the OAS Charter and not in contradiction with the U.N. Charter. Yet it is obvious that a full exploitation by all states of all permissions granted by international law would be a perfect recipe for chaos.

c. *Attempts to enforce or to strengthen international law,* far from consolidating a system of desirable restraints on state (mis)behavior, may actually *backfire* if the political conditions are not ripe. This is the central lesson of the long story of the financing of U.N. peace-keeping operations. American self-intoxication with the importance of the rule of law, fed by misleading analogies between the U.N. Charter and the U.S. Constitution, resulted ultimately in a weakening of the influence of the World Court (which largely followed America's line of reasoning), and in an overplaying of America's hand during the "non-session" of the General Assembly in the fall of 1964 and winter of 1965.

These are sobering considerations. But what they tell us is not, as so many political scientists seem to believe, that international law is, at best, a farce, and, at worst, even a potential danger; what they tell us is that *the nature of the international system condemns international law to all the weaknesses and perversions that it is so easy to deride.* International law is merely a magnifying mirror that reflects faithfully and cruelly the essence and the logic of international politics. In a fragmented world, there is no "global perspective" from which anyone can authoritatively assess, endorse, or reject the separate national efforts at making international law serve national interests above all. Like the somber universe of Albert Camus' Caligula, this is a judgeless world where no one is innocent. . . .

The permanent plight of international law is that, now as before, it shows on its body of rules all the scars inflicted by the international state of war. The tragedy of contemporary international law is that of a double divorce: first, between the old liberal dream of a world rule of law, and the realities of an international system of multiple minidramas that always threaten to become major catastrophes; second, between the old dream and the new requirements of moderation which in the circumstances of the present system suggest a *down-playing* of formal law in the realm of peace-and-war issues, and an *upgrading* of more flexible techniques, until the system has become less fierce. The interest of international law for the political scientist is that there is no better way of grasping the continuing differences between order within a national society and the fragile order of international affairs than to study how and when states use legal language, symbols, and documents, and with what results. . . .

Questions for Review

If international law cannot be enforced, how can it influence states? Is international law essentially a Western invention and a tool for Western dominance?

International Institutions: Can Interdependence Work?

Robert O. Keohane

To analyze world politics in the [current era] is to discuss international institutions: the rules that govern elements of world politics and the organizations that help implement those rules. . . . Under what conditions should China be admitted to the World Trade Organization (WTO)? How many billions of dollars does the International Monetary Fund (IMF) need at its disposal to remain an effective "lender of last resort" for countries such as Indonesia, Korea, and Thailand that were threatened in 1997 with financial collapse? Will the tentative Kyoto Protocol on Climate Change be renegotiated, ratified, and implemented effectively? Can future United Nations peacekeeping practices—in contrast to the UN fiascoes in Bosnia and Somalia—be made more effective?

These questions help illustrate the growing importance of international institutions for maintaining world order. . . . Superpowers need general rules because they seek to influence events around the world. Even an unchallenged superpower such as the United States would be unable to achieve its goals through the bilateral exercise of influence: the costs of such massive "arm-twisting" would be too great.

International institutions are increasingly important, but they are not always successful. Ineffective institutions such as the United Nations Industrial Development Organization or the Organization of African Unity exist alongside effectual ones such as the Montreal Protocol on Substances that Deplete the Ozone Layer and the European Union. In recent years, we have gained insight into what makes some institutions more capable than others—how such institutions best promote cooperation among states and what mechanics of bargaining they use. But our knowledge is incomplete, and as the world moves toward new forms of global regulation and governance, the increasing impact of international institutions has raised new questions about how these institutions themselves are governed.

Theory and Reality, 1919–89

Academic "scribblers" did not always have to pay much attention to international institutions. The 1919 Versailles Treaty constituted an attempt to construct an institution for multilateral diplomacy—the League of Nations. But the rejection of the League Covenant by the U.S. Senate ensured that until World War II the most important negotiations in world politics—from the secret German-Russian deals of the 1920s to the 1938 Munich conference—took place on an ad hoc basis. Only after the United Nations was founded in 1945, with strong support from the United States and a multiplicity of specialized agencies performing different tasks, did international institutions begin to command substantial international attention. . . .

[After 1945], however, even the most powerful states [came to] rely increasingly on international institutions. . . . From the late 1960s onward, the Treaty on the Non-Proliferation of Nuclear Weapons was the chief vehicle for efforts to prevent the dangerous spread of nuclear weapons. NATO was not only the most successful multilateral alliance in history but also the most highly institutionalized, with a secretary-general, a permanent staff, and elaborate rules governing relations among members. From its founding in 1947 through the Uruguay Round that concluded in 1993, the General Agreement on Tariffs and Trade (GATT) presided over a series of trade rounds that have reduced import tariffs among industrialized countries by up to 90 percent, boosting international trade. After a shaky start in the 1940s, the IMF had—by the 1960s—become the centerpiece of efforts by the major capitalist democracies to regulate their monetary affairs. When that function atrophied with the onset of flexible exchange rates in the 1970s, it became their leading agent for financing and promoting economic development in Africa, Asia, and Latin America. The sheer number of inter-governmental organizations also rose dramatically—from about 30 in 1910 to 70 in 1940 to more than 1,000 by 1981.

The exchange rate and oil crises of the early 1970s helped bring perceptions in line with reality. Suddenly, both top policymakers and academic observers in the United States realized that global issues required systematic policy coordination and that such coordination required institutions. In 1974, then secretary of state Henry Kissinger, who had paid little attention to international institutions, helped establish the International Energy Agency to enable Western countries to deal cooperatively with the threat of future oil embargoes like the 1973 OPEC embargo of the Netherlands and United States. And the Ford administration sought to construct a new international monetary regime based on flexible rather than pegged exchange rates. Confronted with complex interdependence and the efforts of states to manage it, political scientists began to redefine the study of international institutions, broadening it to encompass what they called "international regimes"—structures of rules and norms that could be more or less informal. The international trade regime, for example, did not have strong formal rules or integrated, centralized management; rather, it provided a set of interlocking institutions, including regular meetings of the GATT contracting parties, formal dispute settlement arrangements, and delegation of technical tasks to a secretariat, which gradually developed a body of case law and practice. . . .

In the 1980s, research on international regimes moved from attempts to describe the phenomena of interdependence and international regimes to closer analysis of the conditions under which countries cooperate. How does cooperation occur among sovereign states and how do international institutions affect it? From the standpoint of political realism, both the reliance placed by states on certain international institutions and the explosion in their numbers were puzzling. Why should international institutions exist at all in a world dominated by sovereign states? This question seemed unanswerable if institutions were seen as opposed to, or above, the state but not if they were viewed as devices to help states accomplish their objectives.

The new research on international institutions broke decisively with legalism—the view that law can be effective regardless of political conditions—as well as with the idealism associated with the field's origins. Instead, scholars adopted the assumptions of realism, accepting that relative state power and competing interests were key factors in world politics, but at the same time drawing new conclusions about the influence of institutions on the process. Institutions create the capability for states to cooperate in mutually beneficial ways by reducing the costs of making and enforcing agreements—what economists refer to as "transaction costs." They rarely engage in centralized enforcement of agreements, but they do reinforce practices of reciprocity, which provide incentives for governments to keep their own commitments to ensure that others do so as well. Even powerful states have an interest, most of the time, in following the rules of well-established international institutions, since general conformity to rules makes the behavior of other states more predictable.

This scholarship drew heavily on the twin concepts of uncertainty and credibility. Theorists increasingly recognized that the preferences of states amount to "private information"—that absent full transparency, states are uncertain about what their partners and rivals value at any given time. They naturally respond to uncertainty by being less willing to enter into agreements, since they are unsure how their partners will later interpret the terms of such agreements. International institutions can reduce this uncertainty by promoting negotiations in which transparency is encouraged; by dealing with a series of issues over many years and under similar rules, thus encouraging honesty in order to preserve future reputation; and by systematically monitoring the compliance of governments with their commitments.

Even if a government genuinely desires an international agreement, it may be unable to persuade its partners that it will, in the future, be willing and able to implement it. Successful international negotiations may therefore require changes in domestic institutions. For instance, without "fast-track" authority on trade, the United States' negotiating partners have no assurance that Congress will refrain from adding new provisions to trade agreements as a condition for their ratification. Hence, other states are reluctant to enter into trade negotiations with the United States since they may be confronted, at the end of tortuous negotiations, with a redesigned agreement less favorable to them than the draft they initialed. By the same token, without fast-track authority, no promise by the U.S. government to abide by negotiated terms has much credibility, due to the president's lack of control over Congress.

In short, this new school of thought argued that, rather than imposing themselves on states, international institutions should respond to the demand by states for cooperative ways to fulfill their own purposes. By reducing uncertainty and the costs of making and enforcing agreements, international institutions help states achieve collective gains.

Yesterday's Controversies: 1989–95

This new institutionalism was not without its critics, who focused their attacks on three perceived shortcomings: First, they claimed that international institutions are fundamentally insignificant since states wield the only real power in world politics. They emphasized the weakness of efforts by the UN or League of Nations to achieve collective security against aggression by great powers, and they pointed to the dominant role of major contributors in international economic organizations. Hence, any effects of these international institutions were attributed more to the efforts of their great power backers than to the institutions themselves.

This argument was overstated. Of course, great powers such as the United States exercise enormous influence within international institutions. But the policies that emerge from these institutions are different from those that the United States would have adopted unilaterally. . . . Where agreement by many states is necessary for policy to be effective, even the United States finds it useful to compromise on substance to obtain the institutional seal of approval. Therefore, the decision-making procedures and general rules of international institutions matter. They affect both the substance of policy and the degree to which other states accept it.

The second counterargument focused on "anarchy": the absence of a world government or effective international legal system to which victims of injustice can appeal. As a result of anarchy, critics argued, states prefer relative gains (i.e., doing better than other states) to absolute gains. They seek to protect their power and status and will resist even mutually beneficial cooperation if their partners are likely to benefit more than they are. For instance, throughout the American-Soviet arms race, both sides focused on their relative positions—who was ahead or threatening to gain a decisive advantage—rather than on their own levels of armaments. Similar dynamics appear on certain economic issues, such as the fierce Euro-American competition (i.e., Airbus Industrie versus Boeing) in the production of large passenger jets.

Scholarly disputes about the "relative gains question" were intense but short-lived. It turned out that the question needed to be reframed: not, "do states seek relative or absolute gains?" but "under what conditions do they forego even mutually beneficial cooperation to preserve their relative power and status?" When there are only two major players, and one side's gains may decisively change power relationships, relative gains loom large: in arms races, for example, or monopolistic competition (as between Airbus and Boeing). Most issues of potential cooperation, however, from trade liberalization to climate change, involve multilateral negotiations that make relative gains hard to calculate and entail little risk of decisive power shifts for one side over another. Therefore, states can be expected most of the time to seek to enhance their own welfare without being worried that others will also make advances. So the relative gains argument merely highlights the difficulties of cooperation where there is tough bilateral competition; it does not by any means undermine prospects for cooperation in general.

The third objection to theories of cooperation was less radical but more enduring. Theorists of cooperation had recognized that cooperation is not harmonious: it emerges out of discord and takes place through tough bargaining. Nevertheless, they claimed that the potential joint gains from such cooperation explained the dramatic increases in the number and scope of cooperative multilateral institutions. Critics pointed out, however, that bargaining problems could produce obstacles to achieving joint gains. For instance, whether the Kyoto Protocol can lead to a global agreement is questionable in part because developing countries refused to accept binding limits on their emissions and the U.S. Senate declared its unwillingness to ratify any agreement not containing such commitments by developing countries. Both sides staked out tough bargaining positions, hindering efforts at credible compromise. As a result of these bargaining problems, the fact that possible deals could produce joint gains does not assure that cooperative solutions will be reached. The tactics of political actors and the information they have available about one another are both key aspects of a process that does not necessarily lead to cooperation. Institutions may help provide "focal points," on which competing actors may agree, but new issues often lack such institutions. In this case, both the pace and the extent of cooperation become more problematic.

Today's Debates

The general problem of bargaining raises specific issues about how institutions affect international negotiations, which always involve a mixture of discord and potential cooperation. Thinking about bargaining leads to concerns about subjectivity, since bargaining depends so heavily on the beliefs of the parties involved. And the most fundamental question scholars wish to answer concerns effectiveness: What structures, processes, and practices make international institutions more or less capable of affecting policies—and outcomes—in desired ways?

The impact of institutional arrangements on bargaining remains puzzling. We understand from observation, from game theory, and from explorations of bargaining in a variety of contexts that outcomes depend on more than the resources available to the actors or the pay-offs they receive. Institutions affect bargaining patterns in complex and nuanced ways. Who, for example, has authority over the agenda? In the 1980s, Jacques Delors used his authority as head of the European Commission to structure the agenda of the European Community, thus leading to the Single European Act and the Maastricht Treaty. What voting or consensus arrangements are used and who interprets ambiguities? At the Kyoto Conference, agreement on a rule of "consensus" did not prevent the conference chair from ignoring objections as he gaveled through provision after provision in the final session. Can disgruntled participants block implementation of formally ratified agreements? In the GATT, until 1993, losers could prevent the findings of dispute resolution panels from being implemented; but in the WTO, panel recommendations take effect unless there is a consensus not to implement them. Asking such questions systematically about international institutions may well yield significant new insights in future years.

Institutional maneuvers take place within a larger ideological context that helps define which purposes such institutions pursue and which practices they find acceptable. The Mandates System of the League of Nations depended in part on specific institutional arrangements, but more fundamental was the shared understanding that continued European rule over non-European peoples was acceptable. No system of rule by Europeans over non-Europeans could remain legitimate after the collapse of that consensus during the 15 years following World War II. . . .

The procedures and rules of international institutions create informational structures. They determine what principles are acceptable as the basis for reducing conflicts and whether governmental actions are legitimate or illegitimate. Consequently, they help shape actors' expectations. For instance, trade conflicts are increasingly ritualized in a process of protesting in the WTO—promising tough action on behalf of one's own industries, engaging in quasi-judicial dispute resolution procedures, claiming victory if possible, or complaining about defeat when necessary. There is much sound and fury, but regularly institutionalized processes usually relegate conflict to the realm of dramatic expression. Institutions thereby create differentiated information. "Insiders" can interpret the language directed toward "outsiders" and use their own understandings to interpret, or manipulate, others' beliefs.

Finally, students of international institutions continue to try to understand why some institutions are so much more effective than others. Variation in the coherence of institutional policy or members' conformity with institutional rules is partially accounted for by the degree of common interests and the distribution of power among members. Institutions whose members share social values and have similar political systems—such as NATO or the European Union—are likely to be stronger than those such as the Organization for Security and Cooperation in Europe or the Association of South East Asian Nations, whose more diverse membership does not necessarily have the same kind of deep common interests. Additionally, the character of domestic politics, . . . has a substantial impact on international institutions. The distribution of power is also important. Institutions dominated by a small number of members—for example, the IMF, with its weighted voting system—can typically take more decisive action than those where influence is more widely diffused, such as the UN General Assembly.

Overcoming the Democratic Deficit

Even as scholars pursue these areas of inquiry, they are in danger of overlooking a major normative issue: the "democratic deficit" that exists in many of the world's most important international institutions. As illustrated most recently by the far-reaching interventions of the IMF in East Asia, the globalization of the world economy and the expanding role of international institutions are creating a powerful form of global regulation. Major international institutions are increasingly laying down rules and guidelines that governments, if they wish to attract foreign investment and generate growth, must follow. But these international institutions are managed by technocrats and supervised by high governmental officials. That is, they are run by élites. Only in the most attenuated sense is democratic control exercised over major international organizations. Key negotiations in the WTO are made in closed sessions. The IMF negotiates in secret with potential borrowers, and it has only begun in the last few months to provide the conditions it imposes on recipients. . . .

Admittedly, democracy does not always work well. American politicians regularly engage in diatribes against international institutions, playing on the dismay of a vocal segment of their electorates at the excessive number of foreigners in the United Nations. More seriously, an argument can be made that the IMF, like central banks, can only be effective if it is insulated from direct democratic control. Ever since 1787, however, practitioners and theorists have explored how authoritative decision making can be combined with accountability to publics and indirect democratic control. The U.S. Constitution is based on such a theory—the idea that popular sovereignty, though essential, is best exercised indirectly, through rather elaborate institutions. An issue that scholars should now explore is how to devise international institutions that are not only competent and effective but also accountable, at least ultimately, to democratic publics.

One possible response is to say that all is well, since international institutions are responsible to governments—which, in turn, are accountable in democracies to their own people. International regulation simply adds another link to the chain of delegation. But long chains of delegation, in which the public affects action only at several removes, reduce actual public authority. If the terms of multilateral cooperation are to reflect the interests of broader democratic publics rather than just those of narrow élites, traditional patterns of delegation will have to be supplemented by other means of ensuring greater accountability to public opinion.

One promising approach would be to seek to invigorate transnational society in the form of networks among individuals and nongovernmental organizations. The growth of such networks—of scientists, professionals in various fields, and human rights and environmental activists—has been aided greatly by the fax machine and the Internet and by institutional arrangements that incorporate these networks into decision making. For example, natural and social scientists developed the scientific consensus underlying the Kyoto Protocol through the Intergovernmental Panel on Climate Change (IPCC) whose scientific work was organized by scientists who did not have to answer to any governments. The Kyoto Protocol was negotiated, but governments opposed to effective action on climate change could not hope to renegotiate the scientific guidelines set by the IPCC. . . .

Therefore, the future accountability of international institutions to their publics may rest only partly on delegation through formal democratic institutions. Its other pillar may be voluntary pluralism under conditions of maximum transparency. International policies may increasingly be monitored by loose groupings of scientists or other professionals, or by issue advocacy networks such as Amnesty International and Greenpeace, whose members, scattered around the world, will be linked even more closely by modern information technology. Accountability will be enhanced not only by chains of official responsibility, but by the requirement of transparency. Official actions, negotiated among state representatives in international organizations, will be subjected to scrutiny by transnational networks.

Such transparency, however, represents nongovernmental organizations and networks more than ordinary people, who may be as excluded from élite networks as they are from government circles. That is, transnational civil society may be a necessary but insufficient condition for democratic accountability. Democracies should insist that, wherever feasible, international organizations maintain sufficient transparency for transnational networks of advocacy groups, domestic legislators, and democratic publics to evaluate their actions. But proponents of democratic accountability should also seek counterparts to the mechanisms of control embedded in national democratic institutions. Governors of the Federal Reserve Board are, after all, nominated by the president and confirmed by the Senate, even if they exercise great authority during their terms of office. If Madison, Hamilton, and Jay could invent indirect mechanisms of popular control in the *Federalist Papers* two centuries ago, it should not be beyond our competence to devise comparable mechanisms at the global level in the twenty-first century.

Questions for Review

Does Keohane's argument for the importance of institutions contradict claims for the importance of anarchy? How do Keohane's arguments fit with or contradict those of Kang?

Part II
The Uses of Force

Learning Objectives

II.1 Explore how force has been and can be used in a changing world.

II.2 Discuss how the utility of force depends not only on the costs and perceived benefits of fighting but on a number of other factors as well.

II.3 Understand the implications of a nuclear future with regard to both superpowers and smaller countries.

With the end of both the Cold War and the Soviet Union, the nightmare of an all-out nuclear war between the superpowers that so dominated world politics since 1945 ended. Notwithstanding the rising tensions between the United States, on the one hand, and China and Russia, on the other, it is not likely that a new danger of the same magnitude will arise, at least for the economically developed democracies of North America, Japan, and Western Europe. Indeed, for the first time since the formation of these nation-states, the citizens of these countries may live out their lives without worrying that they or their children will have to die or kill in a major war.

This fact, however, does not mean that we should no longer be concerned with how states use force. Even if the optimistic prediction is correct, we still need to understand previous eras in which warfare played such a large role. We cannot understand the course of the Cold War without studying the role nuclear weapons played in it. Moreover, an understanding of the role that nuclear weapons played in that era is central for determining the role they will play in this era. This is true for no other reason than that national leaders' views of the present are heavily influenced by their reading of the past. Furthermore, even within the developed rich world, where a great power war is unlikely, military power still remains useful to the conduct of statecraft. If it were not, these states would have already disarmed. They have not because the use of force must always be available, even if it is not always necessary. For much of the rest of the world, unfortunately, circumstances are different. Threats to the security of states remain real, and war among them has not been abolished. For all states, then—those likely to enjoy peace and those that will have to endure war—what has changed is not so much the utility of military power as how it can be usefully employed. Most obviously, the attacks of September 11, 2001, and the subsequent American "global war on terror" have shown the potency of an old form of force that has been given new life by modern technologies. People have been killed by terrorism from time immemorial, but now attacks can do much greater damage, not only by killing more people but by disrupting entire societies. And as the drone strikes in Afghanistan and Pakistan and the raid that killed Osama Bin Laden show, counterterrorism often involves not only intelligence and protection, but violence as well. These new forms of force call for new understandings and new countermeasures, many of them subject to fierce debate.

The Political Uses of Force

II.1   Explore how force has been and can be used in a changing world.

The use of force almost always represents the partial failure of a policy. The exception, of course, is the case in which fighting is valued for its own sake—when it is believed that war brings out heroic values and purifies individuals and cultures, or when fighting is seen as entertainment. Changes in states' values and the increased destructiveness of war, however, have led state actors to view armed conflicts as the last resort. Threats are a second choice to diplomatic maneuvers; actual use of force follows only if the threats fail.

Because of the high costs of violence, its use is tempered by restraints and bargaining. As bloody as most wars are, they could always be bloodier. Brutalities are limited in part by the combatants' shared interests, if not by their scruples. Even if two states differ enough to go to war, it does not necessarily follow that they have no common interests. Only when everything that is good for one side is bad for the other (a "zero-sum" situation) do the opponents gain nothing by bargaining. In most cases, however, certain outcomes are clearly bad for both sides; therefore, even though they are at war, each side shares an interest in avoiding them.

The shared nature of the interest, as Thomas C. Schelling points out, stems from the fact that it is easier to destroy than to create. Force can be used to take—or to bargain. If you can take what you want, you do not need your adversary's cooperation and do not have to bargain with him. A country may use force to seize disputed territory just as a robber may kill you to get your wallet. Most of the things people and nations want, however, cannot be taken in this way. A nation not only wants to take territory, it wants to govern and exploit it. A nation may want others to stop menacing it; it may even want others to adopt its values. Brute force alone cannot achieve these goals. A nation that wants to stop others from menacing it may not want to fight them in order to remove the threat. A nation that wants others to adopt its values cannot impose them solely through conquest. Where the cooperation of an adversary is needed, bargaining will ensue. The robber does not need the cooperation of his victim if he kills him to get his wallet. However, the thief who must obtain the combination of a safe from the hostage who carries it only in his head does need such cooperation. The thief may use force to demonstrate that the hostage can lose his life if he does not surrender the combination. But the thief no more wishes to kill the hostage and lose the combination than the hostage wishes to die. The hostage may trade the combination for his life. The bargain may be unequal or unfair, but it is still a bargain.

The mutual avoidance of certain outcomes explains why past wars have not been as bloody as they could have been; but an analysis of why wars were not more destructive should not blind us to the factors that made them as destructive as they were. By 1914, for example, all the statesmen of Europe believed a war inevitable, and all were ready to exploit it. None, however, imagined the staggering losses that their respective nations would inflict and bear in the field, or the extent to which noncombatants would be attacked. Yet by the second year of World War I, the same men were accepting the deaths of hundreds or thousands for a few yards' gain in the front lines; and by the end of the war, they were planning large-scale aerial gas attacks on each other's major cities. The German bombing of Guernica in 1937 and Rotterdam in 1940 shocked statesmen and citizens alike, but by the middle of World War II both were accepting as routine the total destruction of German and Japanese cities.

Three factors largely account for the increasing destructiveness of the wars of the last two centuries. First was the steady technological improvement in weaponry. Weapons such as machine guns, submarines, poison gas, and aircraft made it feasible to maim or kill large numbers of people quickly. The rapidity of destruction that is possible with nuclear weapons is only the most recent, albeit biggest, advance. Second was the growth in the capacity, and thus the need, of states to field ever larger numbers of forces. As states became more industrialized and centralized, they acquired the wealth and developed the administrative apparatus to move men on a grand scale. Concomitant with the increase in military potential was the necessity to realize this potential. As soon as one state expanded the forces at its disposal, all other states had to follow suit. Thus, when Prussia instituted universal conscription and the general-staff system, and then demonstrated their advantages with swift victories over Austria and France, the rest of the continent quickly adopted its methods. An increase in the potential power of states led to an increase in their standing power.

Third was the gradual "democratization" of war: the expansion of the battle-field and hence the indiscriminate mass killing of noncombatants. Everyone, citizens and soldiers alike, began fighting and dying. World War II, with its extensive use of airpower, marked not the debut but the zenith of this mass killing. As war changed from the province of the princes to the burden of the masses, the distinction between combatants and noncombatants increasingly blurred. Most wars of the eighteenth century did impinge upon the citizenry, but mainly financially; few civilians died in them. With the widespread use of conscription in the nineteenth and twentieth centuries, however, more citizens became soldiers. With the advent of industrialization and with the increasing division of labor, the citizens who did not fight remained behind to produce weapons. Now, a nation not only had to conquer its enemy's armies, but also had to destroy the industrial plant that supplied their weapons. Gradually, the total energy of a country was diverted into waging wars, and as the costs of wars increased, so did the justifications given for them and the benefits claimed to derive from them. The greater the sacrifices asked, the larger the victory spoils demanded. Because wars became literally wars of, by, and for the people, governments depended increasingly on the support of their citizens. As wars became democratized, so too did they become popularized and propagandized.

The readings in the first section explore how force has been and can be used in a changing world. Robert J. Art notes that the threat and use of force has four distinct functions and shows how their relative importance varies from one situation to another. Thomas C. Schelling examines the differences between the uses of conventional and nuclear weapons and the links between force and foreign policy goals. Terrorism has never been absent from world politics, and Bruce Hoffman discusses its changing forms and purposes, and distinguishes terrorism from guerrilla warfare and criminal activity.

The Utility of Force Today

II.2 Discuss how the utility of force depends not only on the costs and perceived benefits of fighting but on a number of other factors as well.

It is a mistake to examine the possible use of force in a vacuum. As Clausewitz stressed, force is an instrument for reaching political goals. Its utility, as well as the likelihood of its use, depends not only on the costs and perceived benefits of fighting but on the general political context, the values statesmen and citizens hold, the alternative policy instruments available, and the objectives sought.

Realism, represented in many of the readings in Part I, stresses the importance of military power. The three readings in this section demonstrate the continuing relevance of force to political outcomes. Robert J. Art argues that military power is fungible—that is, it can be used to reach a number of goals, even for a state such as the United States that lacks strong state enemies. Erica Chenoweth and Maria Stephan show that nonviolent movements are very potent, generally a more effective way to remove repressive regimes than are armed insurgencies. Despite the fighting in Syria, Iraq, and Afghanistan, what is striking is that in many ways the world has become more peaceful, as is discussed further in Part IV. The data through 2010 summarized by the World Bank show a striking decline in both international and civil wars in recent years, although transnational criminal violence, often associated with trafficking in drugs and humans, has increased. When large-scale violence does occur, economic development can be crippled for years, which means that decreases are even more valuable than the immediate saving of lives and sparing of misery would indicate.

The Nuclear Future

II.3 Understand the implications of a nuclear future with regard to both superpowers and smaller countries.

During the Cold War, nuclear weapons, it was argued, helped make competition between the two superpowers safer than it would otherwise have been. That is, nuclear weapons made the two superpowers scared, not safe, and this restrained them. Each had to worry that if it pushed the other too far, matters could get out of hand and escalate to nuclear war. Each learned, especially after the Cuban missile crisis of 1962, not to push the other to the point where it faced the choice of upping the ante and risking loss of control, or backing down and risking humiliation. Rules of the road between the two superpowers gradually developed, and their subsequent competition proved safer in the last 28 years of the Cold War than it had been in the first 15.

How relevant for today is the superpower experience with nuclear weapons? Will states that experience intense political conflicts with one another be deterred from pushing one another too far? Or will they be less restrained than were the superpowers and find themselves in the horror of escalating to the use of nuclear weapons? How valid a model is the U.S.–Soviet experience for dyadic conflicts today? Building on the work of Schelling, Robert Jervis argues that although during the Cold War lack of credibility inhibited the threat to start a nuclear war, what was very potent was the threat to take actions that were dangerous because they set in motion actions and interactions that neither superpower could be sure it could control. The same mechanisms operate today. Henry Sokolski explains that while nuclear weapons do not loom as large as they did in the Cold War, not only have they not gone away, but they are of increasing importance and we need to understand the complex arguments that are being made about them. Thomas C. Schelling argues that perhaps the most popular argument—that nuclear weapons should be abolished—is not only unlikely to persuade power-holders, but would lead to a world that is more, not less dangerous than the current one because of the potential for destabilizing arms races.

Part II Questions for Review

What are the political implications of the changes in technology over time that have affected the forms of violence at the disposal of states and non-state actors? Are there any general principles that can be discerned in the application of violence, or does the great variety in actors and circumstances make generalizations impossible?

Chapter 5
The Political Uses of Force

The Four Functions of Force

Robert J. Art

In view of what is likely to be before us, it is vital to think carefully and precisely about the uses and limits of military power. That is the purpose of this essay. It is intended as a backdrop for policy debates, not a prescription of specific policies. It consciously eschews elaborate detail on the requisite military forces for scenarios *a . . . n* and focuses instead on what military power has and has not done, can and cannot do. Every model of how the world works has policy implications. But not every policy is based on a clear view of how the world works. What, then, are the uses to which military power can be put? How have nuclear weapons affected these uses? And what is the future of force in a world of nuclear parity and increasing economic interdependence?

What Are the Uses of Force?

The goals that states pursue range widely and vary considerably from case to case. Military power is more useful for realizing some goals than others, though it is generally considered of some use by most states for all of the goals that they hold. If we attempt, however, to be descriptively accurate, to enumerate all of the purposes for which states use force, we shall simply end up with a bewildering list. Descriptive accuracy is not a virtue *per se* for analysis. In fact, descriptive accuracy is generally bought at the cost of analytical utility. (A concept that is descriptively accurate is usually analytically useless.) Therefore, rather than compile an exhaustive list of such purposes, I have selected four categories that themselves analytically exhaust the functions that force can serve: defense, deterrence, compellence, and "swaggering."

Not all four functions are necessarily well or equally served by a given military posture. In fact, usually only the great powers have the wherewithal to develop military forces that can serve more than two functions at once. Even then, this is achieved only vis-à-vis smaller powers, not vis-à-vis the other great ones. The measure of the capabilities of a state's military forces must be made relative to those of another state, not with reference to some absolute scale.

A state that can compel another state can also defend against it and usually deter it. A state that can defend against another state cannot thereby automatically deter or compel it. A state can deter another state without having the ability to either defend against or compel it. A state that can swagger vis-à-vis another may or may not be able to perform any of the other three functions relative to it. Where feasible, defense is the goal that all states aim for first. If defense is not possible, deterrence is generally the next priority. Swaggering is the function most difficult to pin down analytically; deterrence, the one whose achievement is the most difficult to demonstrate; compellence, the easiest to demonstrate but among the hardest to achieve. The following discussion develops these points more fully.

The *defensive* use of force is the deployment of military power so as to be able to do two things—to ward off an attack and to minimize damage to oneself if attacked. For defensive purposes, a state will direct its forces against those of a potential or actual attacker, but not against his unarmed population. For defensive purposes, a state can deploy its forces in place prior to an attack, use them after an attack has occurred to repel it, or strike first if it believes that an attack upon it is imminent or inevitable. The defensive use of force can thus involve both peaceful and physical employment and both repellent (second) strikes and offensive (first) strikes. If a state strikes first when it believes an attack upon it is imminent, it is launching a preemptive blow. If it strikes first when it believes an attack is inevitable but not momentary, it is launching a preventive blow. Preemptive and preventive blows are undertaken when a state calculates, first, that others plan to attack it and, second, that to delay in striking offensively is against its interests. A state preempts in order to wrest the advantage of the first strike from an opponent. A state launches a preventive attack because it believes that others will attack it when the balance of forces turns in their favor and therefore attacks while the balance of forces is in its favor. In both cases it is better to strike first than to be struck first. The major distinction between preemption and prevention is the calculation about when an opponent's attack will occur. For preemption, it is a matter of hours, days, or even a few weeks at the most; for prevention, months or even a few years. In the case of preemption, the state has almost no control over the timing of its attack; in the case of prevention, the state can in a more leisurely way contemplate the timing of its attack. For both cases, it is the belief in the certainty of war that governs the offensive, defensive attack. For both cases, the maxim, "the best defense is a good offense," makes good sense.

The *deterrent* use of force is the deployment of military power so as to be able to prevent an adversary from doing something that one does not want him to do and that he might otherwise be tempted to do by threatening him with unacceptable punishment if he does it. Deterrence is thus the threat of retaliation. Its purpose is to prevent something undesirable from happening. The threat of punishment is directed at the adversary's population and/or industrial infrastructure.

The effectiveness of the threat depends upon a state's ability to convince a potential adversary that it has both the will and power to punish him severely if he undertakes the undesirable action in question. Deterrence therefore employs force peacefully. It is the threat to resort to force in order to punish that is the essence of deterrence. If the threat has to be carried out, deterrence by definition has failed. A deterrent threat is made precisely with the intent that it will not have to be carried out. Threats are made to prevent actions from being undertaken. If the threat has to be implemented, the action has already been undertaken. Hence deterrence can be judged successful only if the retaliatory threats have not been implemented.

Deterrence and defense are alike in that both are intended to protect the state or its closest allies from physical attacks. The purpose of both is dissuasion—persuading others *not* to undertake actions harmful to oneself. The defensive use of force dissuades by convincing an adversary that he cannot conquer one's military forces. The deterrent use of force dissuades by convincing the adversary that his population and territory will suffer terrible damage if he initiates the undesirable action. Defense dissuades by presenting an unvanquishable military force. Deterrence dissuades by presenting the certainty of retaliatory devastation.

Defense is possible without deterrence, and deterrence is possible without defense. A state can have the military wherewithal to repel an invasion without also being able to threaten devastation to the invader's population or territory. Similarly, a state can have the wherewithal credibly to threaten an adversary with such devastation and yet be unable to repel his invading force. Defense, therefore, does not necessarily buy deterrence, nor deterrence defense. A state that can defend itself from attack, moreover, will have little need to develop the wherewithal to deter. If physical attacks can be repelled or if the damage from them drastically minimized, the incentive to develop a retaliatory capability is low. A state that cannot defend itself, however, will try to develop an effective deterrent if that be possible. No state will leave its population and territory open to attack if it has the means to redress the situation. Whether a given state can defend or deter or do both vis-à-vis another depends upon two factors: (1) the quantitative balance of forces between it and its adversary; and (2) the qualitative balance of forces, that is, whether the extant military technology favors the offense or the defense. These two factors are situation-specific and therefore require careful analysis of the case at hand.

The *compellent* use of force is the deployment of military power so as to be able either to stop an adversary from doing something that he has already undertaken or to get him to do something that he has not yet undertaken. Compellence, in Schelling's words, "involves initiating an action . . . that can cease, or become harmless, only if the opponent responds." Compellence can employ force either physically or peacefully. A state can start actually harming another with physical destruction until the latter abides by the former's wishes. Or, a state can take actions against another that do not cause physical harm but that require the latter to pay some type of significant price until it changes its behavior. America's bombing of North Vietnam in early 1965 was an example of physical compellence; Tirpitz's building of a German fleet aimed against England's in the two decades before World War I, an example of peaceful compellence. In the first case, the United States started bombing North Vietnam in order to compel it to stop assisting the Vietcong forces in South Vietnam. In the latter case, Germany built a battlefleet that in an engagement threatened to cripple England's in order to compel her to make a general political settlement advantageous to Germany. In both cases, one state initiated some type of action against another precisely so as to be able to stop it, to bargain it away for the appropriate response from the "put upon" state.

The distinction between compellence and deterrence is one between the active and passive use of force. The success of a deterrent threat is measured by its not having to be used. The success of a compellent action is measured by how closely and quickly the adversary conforms to one's stipulated wishes. In the case of successful deterrence, one is trying to demonstrate a negative, to show why something did not happen. It can never be clear whether one's actions were crucial to, or irrelevant to, why another state chose *not* to do something. In the case of successful compellence, the clear sequence of actions and reactions lends a compelling plausibility to the centrality of one's actions. Figure 1 illustrates the distinction. In successful compellence, state B can claim that its pressure deflected state A from its course of action. In successful deterrence, state B has no change in state A's behavior to point to, but instead must resort to claiming that its threats were responsible for the continuity in A's behavior. State A may have changed its behavior for reasons other than state B's compellent action. State A may have continued with its same behavior for reasons other than state B's deterrent threat. "Proving" the importance of B's influence on A for either case is not easy, but it is more plausible to claim that

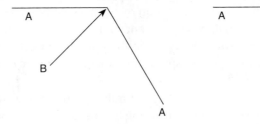

COMPELLENCE	DETERRENCE
(1) A is doing something that B cannot tolerate	(1) A is presently not doing anything that B finds intolerable
(2) B initiates action against A in order to get him to stop his intolerable actions	(2) B tells A that if A changes his behavior and does something intolerable, B will punish him
(3) A stops his intolerable actions and B stops his (or both cease simultaneously)	(3) A continues not to do anything B finds intolerable

Figure 1

B influenced A when there is a change in A's behavior than when there is not. Explaining why something did not happen is more difficult than explaining why something did.

Compellence may be easier to demonstrate than deterrence, but it is harder to achieve. Schelling argues that compellent actions tend to be vaguer in their objectives than deterrent threats and for that reason more difficult to attain. If an adversary has a hard time understanding what it is that one wished him to do, his compliance with one's wishes is made more difficult. There is, however, no inherent reason why a compellent action must be vaguer than a deterrent threat with regard to how clearly the adversary understands what is wanted from him. "Do not attack me" is not any clearer in its ultimate meaning than "stop attacking my friend." A state can be as confused or as clear about what it wishes to prevent as it can be about what it wishes to stop. The clarity, or lack of it, of the objectives of compellent actions and deterrent threats does not vary according to whether the given action is compellent or deterrent in nature, but rather according to a welter of particularities associated with the given action. Some objectives, for example, are inherently clearer and hence easier to perceive than others. Some statesmen communicate more clearly than others. Some states have more power to bring to bear for a given objective than others. It is the specifics of a given situation, not any intrinsic difference between compellence and deterrence, that determines the clarity with which an objective is perceived.

We must, therefore, look elsewhere for the reason as to why compellence is comparatively harder to achieve than deterrence. It lies, not in what one asks another to do, but in *how* one asks. With deterrence, state B asks something of state A in this fashion: "Do not take action X; for if you do, I will bash you over the head with this club." With compellence, state B asks something of state A in this fashion: "I am now going to bash you over the head with this club and will continue to do so until you do what I want." In the former case, state A can easily deny with great plausibility any intention of having planned to take action X. In the latter case, state A cannot deny either that it is engaged in a given course of action or that it is being subjected to pressure by state B. If they are to be successful, compellent actions require a state to alter its behavior in a manner quite visible to all in response to an equally visible forceful initiative taken by another state. In contrast to compellent actions, deterrent threats are both easier to appear to have ignored or easier to acquiesce to without great loss of face. In contrast to deterrent threats, compellent actions more directly engage the prestige and the passions of the put-upon state. Less prestige is lost in not doing something than in clearly altering behavior due to pressure from another. In the case of compellence, a state has publicly committed its prestige and resources to a given line of conduct that it is now asked to give up. This is not so for deterrence. Thus, compellence is intrinsically harder to attain than deterrence, not because its objectives are vaguer, but because it demands more humiliation from the compelled state.

The fourth purpose to which military power can be put is the most difficult to be precise about. *Swaggering* is in part a residual category, the deployment of military power for purposes other than defense, deterrence, or compellence. Force is not aimed directly at dissuading another state from attacking, at repelling attacks, nor at compelling it to do something specific. The objectives for swaggering are more diffuse, ill-defined, and problematic than that. Swaggering almost always involves only the peaceful use of force and is expressed usually in one of two ways: displaying one's military might at military exercises and national demonstrations and buying or building the era's most prestigious weapons. The swagger use of force is the most egoistic: It aims to enhance the national pride of a people or to satisfy the personal ambitions of its ruler. A state or statesman swaggers in order to look and feel more powerful and important, to be taken seriously by others in the councils of international decision making, to enhance the nation's image in the eyes of others. If its image is enhanced, the nation's defense, deterrent, and compellent capabilities may also be enhanced; but swaggering is not undertaken solely or even primarily for these specific purposes. Swaggering is pursued because it offers to bring prestige "on the cheap." Swaggering is pursued because of the fundamental yearning of states and statesmen for respect and prestige. Swaggering is more something to be enjoyed for itself than to be employed for a specific, consciously thought-out end.

And yet, the instrumental role of swaggering cannot be totally discounted because of the fundamental relation between force and foreign policy that it obtains in an anarchic environment. Because there is a connection between the military might that a nation is thought to possess and the success that it achieves in attaining its objectives, the enhancement of a state's stature in the eyes of others can always be justified on *realpolitik* lines. If swaggering causes other states to take one's interests more seriously into account, then the general interests of the state will benefit. Even in its instrumental role, however, swaggering is undertaken less for any given end than for all ends. The swaggering function of military power is thus at one and the same time the most comprehensive and the most diffuse, the most versatile in its effects and the least focused in its immediate aims, the most instrumental in the long run and the least instrumental in the short run, easy to justify on hardheaded grounds and often undertaken on emotional grounds. Swaggering mixes the rational and irrational more than the other three functions of military power and, for that reason, remains both pervasive in international relations and elusive to describe.

Defense, deterrence, compellence, and swaggering—these are the four general purposes for which force can be employed. Discriminating among them analytically, however, is easier than applying them in practice. This is due to two factors. First, we need to know the motives behind an act in order to judge its purpose; but the problem is that motives cannot be readily inferred from actions because several motives can be served by the same action. But neither can one readily infer the motives of a state from what it publicly or officially proclaims them to be. Such statements should not necessarily be taken at face value because of the role that bluff and dissimulation play in statecraft. Such statements are also often concocted with domestic political, not foreign audiences in mind, or else are deliberate exercises in studied ambiguity. Motives are important in order to interpret actions, but neither actions nor words always clearly delineate motives.

It is, moreover, especially difficult to distinguish defensive from compellent actions and deterrent from swaggering ones unless we know the reasons for which they were undertaken. Peaceful defensive preparations often look largely the same as peaceful compellent ones. Defensive attacks are nearly indistinguishable from compellent ones. Is he who attacks first the defender or the compeller? Deterrence and swaggering both involve the acquisition and display of an era's prestigious weapons. Are such weapons acquired to enhance prestige or to dissuade an attack?

Second, to make matters worse, consider the following example. Germany launched an attack upon France and Russia at the end of July 1914 and thereby began World War I. There are two schools of thought as to why Germany did this. One holds that its motives were aggressive—territorial aggrandizement, economic gain, and elevation to the status of a world empire. Another holds that her motives were preventive and hence defensive. She struck first because she feared encirclement, slow strangulation, and then inevitable attack by her two powerful neighbors, foes whom she felt were daily increasing their military might faster than she was. She struck while she had the chance to win.

It is not simple to decide which school is the more nearly correct because both can marshall evidence to build a powerful case. Assume for the moment, though, that the second is closer to the truth. There are then two possibilities to consider: (1) Germany launched an attack because it *was* the case that her foes were planning to attack her ultimately, and Germany had the evidence to prove it; or (2) Germany felt she had reasonable evidence of her foes' *intent* to attack her eventually, but in fact her evidence was wrong because she misperceived their intent from their actions. If the first was the case, then we must ask this question: How responsible was Germany's diplomacy in the fifteen years before 1914, aggressive and blundering as it was, in breeding hostility in her neighbors? Germany attacked in the knowledge that they would eventually have struck her, but if her fifteen-year diplomatic record was a significant factor in causing them to lay these plans, must we conclude that Germany in 1914 was merely acting defensively? Must we confine our judgment about the defensive or aggressive nature of the act to the month or even the year in which it occurred? If not, how many years back in history do we go in order to make a judgment? If the second was the case, then we must ask this question: If Germany attacked in the belief, mistakenly as it turns out, that she would be attacked, must we conclude that Germany was acting defensively? Must we confine our judgment about the defensive or aggressive nature of the act simply to Germany's beliefs about others' intent, without reference to their actual intent?

It is not easy to answer these questions. Fortunately, we do not have to. Asking them is enough because it illustrates that an assessment of the *legitimacy* of a state's motives in using force is integral to the task of determining what its motives are. One cannot, that is, specify motives without at the same time making judgments about their legitimacy. The root cause of this need lies in the nature of state action. In anarchy every state is a valid judge of the legitimacy of its goals because there is no supranational authority to enforce agreed upon rules. Because of the lack of universal standards, we are forced to examine each case within its given context and to make individual judgments about the meaning of the particulars. When individual judgment is exercised, individuals may well differ. Definitive answers are more likely to be the exception rather than the rule.

Where does all of this leave us? Our four categories tell us what are the four possible purposes for which states can employ military power. The attributes of each alert us to the types of evidence for which to search. But because the context of an action is crucial in order to judge its ultimate purpose, these four categories cannot be applied mindlessly and ahistorically. Each state's purpose in using force in a given instance must fall into one of these four categories. We know *a priori* what the possibilities are. Which one it is, is an exercise in judgment, an exercise that depends as much upon the particulars of the given case as it does upon the general features of the given category . . . (see Table 1).

Table 1 The Purposes of Force

Type	Purpose	Mode	Targets	Characteristics
Defensive	Fend off attacks and/or reduce damage of an attack	Peaceful and physical	Primarily military	Defensive preparations can have dissuasion value;
			Secondarily industrial	Defensive preparations can look aggressive;
				First strikes can be taken for defense.
Deterrent	Prevent adversary from initiating an action	Peaceful	Primarily civilian	Threats of retaliation made as not to have to be carried out;
			Secondarily industrial	
			Tertiarily military	Second strike preparations can be viewed as first strike preparations.
Compellent	Get adversary to stop doing something or start doing something	Peaceful and physical	All three with no clear ranking	Easy to recognize but hard to achieve;

Type	Purpose	Mode	Targets	Characteristics
				Compellent actions can be justified on defensive grounds.
Swaggering	Enhance prestige	Peaceful	None	Difficult to describe because of instrumental and irrational nature;
				Swaggering can be threatening.

Questions for Review

Can defensive uses of military power be easily distinguished from compellent ones? Can deterrence, which involves preserving the status quo, look like compellence to a state that finds the status quo disadvantageous?

The Diplomacy of Violence

THOMAS C. SCHELLING

The usual distinction between diplomacy and force is not merely in the instruments, words or bullets, but in the relation between adversaries—in the interplay of motives and the role of communication, understandings, compromise, and restraint. Diplomacy is bargaining; it seeks outcomes that, though not ideal for either party, are better for both than some of the alternatives. In diplomacy each party somewhat controls what the other wants, and can get more by compromise, exchange, or collaboration than by taking things in his own hands and ignoring the other's wishes. The bargaining can be polite or rude, entail threats as well as offers, assume a status quo or ignore all rights and privileges, and assume mistrust rather than trust. But whether polite or impolite, constructive or aggressive, respectful or vicious, whether it occurs among friends or antagonists and whether or not there is a basis for trust and goodwill, there must be some common interest, if only in the avoidance of mutual damage, and an awareness of the need to make the other party prefer an outcome acceptable to oneself.

With enough military force a country may not need to bargain. Some things a country wants it can take, and some things it has it can keep, by sheer strength, skill, and ingenuity. It can do this *forcibly*, accommodating only to opposing strength, skill, and ingenuity and without trying to appeal to an enemy's wishes. Forcibly a country can repel and expel, penetrate and occupy, seize, exterminate, disarm and disable, confine, deny access, and directly frustrate intrusion or attack.

It can, that is, if it has enough strength. "Enough" depends on how much an opponent has.

There is something else, though, that force can do. It is less military, less heroic, less impersonal, and less unilateral; it is uglier, and has received less attention in Western military strategy. In addition to seizing and holding, disarming and confining, penetrating and obstructing, and all that, military force can be used to *hurt*. In addition to taking and protecting things of value it can destroy value. In addition to weakening an enemy militarily it can cause an enemy plain suffering. . . .

The Contrast of Brute Force with Coercion

There is a difference between taking what you want and making someone give it to you, between fending off assault and making someone afraid to assault you, between holding what people are trying to take and making them afraid to take it, between losing what someone can forcibly take and giving it up to avoid risk or damage. It is the difference between defense and deterrence, between brute force and intimidation, between conquest and blackmail, between action and threats. It is the difference between the unilateral, "undiplomatic" recourse to strength, and coercive diplomacy based on the power to hurt.

The contrasts are several. The purely "military" or "undiplomatic" recourse to forcible action is concerned with enemy strength, not enemy interests; the coercive use of the power to hurt, though, is the very exploitation of enemy wants and fears. And brute strength is usually measured relative to enemy strength, the one directly opposing the other, while the power to hurt is typically not reduced by the enemy's power to hurt in return. Opposing strengths may cancel each other, pain and grief do not. The willingness to hurt, the credibility of a threat, and the ability to exploit the power to hurt will indeed depend on how much the adversary can hurt in return but there is little or nothing about an adversary's pain or grief that directly reduces one's own. Two sides cannot both overcome each other with superior strength; they may both be able to hurt each other. With strength they can dispute objects of value; with sheer violence they can destroy them.

And brute force succeeds when it is used, whereas the power to hurt is most successful when held in reserve. It is the *threat* of damage, or of more damage to come, that can make someone yield or comply. It is *latent* violence that can influence someone's choice—violence that can still be withheld or inflicted or that a victim believes can be withheld or inflicted. The threat of pain tries to structure someone's motives, while brute force tries to overcome his strength. Unhappily, the power to hurt is often communicated by some performance of it. Whether it is sheer terroristic violence to induce an irrational response, or cool premeditated violence to persuade somebody that you mean it and may do it again, it is not the pain and damage itself but its influence on somebody's behavior that matters.

It is the expectation of *more* violence that gets the wanted behavior, if the power to hurt can get it at all.

To exploit a capacity for hurting and inflicting damage one needs to know what an adversary treasures and what scares him and one needs the adversary to understand what behavior of his will cause the violence to be inflicted and what will cause it to be withheld. The victim has to know what is wanted, and he may have to be assured of what is not wanted. The pain and suffering have to appear *contingent* on his behavior; it is not the threat alone that is effective—the threat of pain or loss if he fails to comply—but the corresponding assurance, possibly an implicit one, that he can avoid the pain or loss if he does comply. The prospect of certain death may stun him, but it gives him no choice.

Coercion by threat of damage also requires that our interests and our opponent's not be absolutely opposed. If his pain were our greatest delight and our satisfaction his great woe, we would just proceed to hurt and to frustrate each other. It is when his pain gives us little or no satisfaction compared with what he can do for us, and the action or inaction that satisfies us costs him less than the pain we can cause, that there is room for coercion. Coercion requires finding a bargain, arranging for him to be better off doing what we want—worse off not . . . doing what we want—when he takes the threatened penalty into account. . . .

This difference between coercion and brute force is as often in the intent as in the instrument. To hunt down Comanches and to exterminate them was brute force; to raid their villages to make them behave was coercive diplomacy, based on the power to hurt. The pain and loss to the Indians might have looked much the same one way as the other; the difference was one of purpose and effect. If Indians were killed because they were in the way, or somebody wanted their land, or the authorities despaired of making them behave and could not confine them and decided to exterminate them, that was pure unilateral force. If *some* Indians were killed to make *other* Indians behave, that was coercive violence—or intended to be, whether or not it was effective. The Germans at Verdun perceived themselves to be chewing up hundreds of thousands of French soldiers in a gruesome "meatgrinder." If the purpose was to eliminate a military obstacle—the French infantryman, viewed as a military "asset" rather than as a warm human being—the offensive at Verdun was a unilateral exercise of military force. If instead the object was to make the loss of young men—not of impersonal "effectives," but of sons, husbands, fathers and the pride of French manhood—so anguishing as to be unendurable, to make surrender a welcome relief and to spoil the foretaste of an Allied victory, then it was an exercise in coercion, in applied violence, intended to offer relief upon accommodation. And of course, since any use of force tends to be brutal, thoughtless, vengeful, or plain obstinate, the motives themselves can be mixed and confused. The fact that heroism and brutality can be either coercive diplomacy or a contest in pure strength does not promise that the distinction will be made, and the strategies enlightened by the distinction, every time some vicious enterprise gets launched. . . .

War appears to be, or threatens to be, not so much a contest of strength as one of endurance, nerve, obstinacy, and pain. It appears to be, and threatens to be, not so much a contest of military strength as a bargaining process—dirty, extortionate, and often quite reluctant bargaining on one side or both—nevertheless a bargaining process.

The difference cannot quite be expressed as one between the *use* of force and the *threat* of force. The actions involved in forcible accomplishment, on the one hand, and in fulfilling a threat, on the other, can be quite different. Sometimes the most effective direct action inflicts enough cost or pain on the enemy to serve as a threat, sometimes not. The United States threatens the Soviet Union with virtual destruction of its society in the event of a surprise attack on the United States; a hundred million deaths are awesome as pure damage, but they are useless in stopping the Soviet attack—especially if the threat is to do it all afterward anyway. So it is worthwhile to keep the concepts distinct—to distinguish forcible action from the threat of pain—recognizing that some actions serve as both a means of forcible accomplishment and a means of inflicting pure damage; some do not. Hostages tend to entail almost pure pain and damage, as do all forms of reprisal after the fact. Some modes of self-defense may exact so little in blood or treasure as to entail negligible violence; and some forcible actions entail so much violence that their threat can be effective by itself.

The power to hurt, though it can usually accomplish nothing directly, is potentially more versatile than a straightforward capacity for forcible accomplishment. By force alone we cannot even lead a horse to water—we have to drag him—much less make him drink. Any affirmative action, any collaboration, almost anything but physical exclusion, expulsion, or extermination, requires that an opponent or a victim do something, even if only to stop or get out. The threat of pain and damage may make him want to do it, and anything he can do is potentially susceptible to inducement. Brute force can only accomplish what requires no collaboration. The principle is illustrated by a technique of unarmed combat: One can disable a man by various stunning, fracturing, or killing blows, but to take him to jail one has to exploit the man's own efforts. "Come-along" holds are those that threaten pain or disablement, giving relief as long as the victim complies, giving him the option of using his own legs to get to jail. . . .

The fact that violence—pure pain and damage—can be used or threatened to coerce and to deter, to intimidate and to blackmail, to demoralize and to paralyze, in a conscious process of dirty bargaining, does not by any means imply that violence is not often wanton and meaningless or, even when purposive, in danger of getting out of hand. Ancient wars were often quite "total" for the loser, the men being put to death, the women sold as slaves, the boys castrated, the cattle slaughtered, and the buildings leveled, for the sake of revenge, justice, personal gain, or merely custom. If an enemy bombs a city, by design or by carelessness, we usually bomb his if we can. In the excitement and fatigue of warfare, revenge is one of the few satisfactions that can be savored. . . . Pure violence, like fire, can be harnessed to a purpose; that does not mean that behind every holocaust is a shrewd intention successfully fulfilled.

But if the occurrence of violence does not always bespeak a shrewd purpose, the absence of pain and destruction is no sign that violence was idle. Violence is most purposive and most successful when it is threatened and not used. Successful threats are those that do not have to be carried out. . . .

The Strategic Role of Pain and Damage

Pure violence, nonmilitary violence, appears most conspicuously in relations between unequal countries, where there is no substantial military challenge and the outcome of military engagement is not in question: Hitler could make his threats contemptuously and brutally against Austria; he could make them, if he wished, in a more refined way against Denmark. It is noteworthy that it was Hitler, not his generals, who used this kind of language; proud military establishments do not like to think of themselves as extortionists. Their favorite job is to deliver victory, to dispose of opposing military force and to leave most of the civilian violence to politics and diplomacy. But if there is no room for doubt how a contest in strength will come out, it may be possible to bypass the military stage altogether and to proceed at once to the coercive bargaining.

A typical confrontation of unequal forces occurs at the *end* of a war, between victor and vanquished. Where Austria was vulnerable before a shot was fired, France was vulnerable after its military shield had collapsed in 1940. Surrender negotiations are the place where the threat of civil violence can come to the fore. Surrender negotiations are often so one-sided, or the potential violence so unmistakable, that bargaining succeeds and the violence remains in reserve. But the fact that most of the actual damage was done during the military stage of the war, prior to victory and defeat, does not mean that violence was idle in the aftermath, only that it was latent and the threat of it successful. . . .

The Russians crushed Budapest in 1956 and cowed Poland and other neighboring countries. There was a lag of ten years between military victory and this show of violence, but the principle was the one [just] explained. . . . Military victory is often the prelude to violence, not the end of it, and the fact that successful violence is usually held in reserve should not deceive us about the role it plays.

What about pure violence during war itself, the infliction of pain and suffering as a military technique? Is the threat of pain involved only in the political use of victory, or is it a decisive technique of war itself?

Evidently between unequal powers it has been part of warfare. Colonial conquest has often been a matter of "punitive expeditions" rather than genuine military engagements. If the tribesmen escape into the brush you can burn their villages without them until they assent to receive what, in strikingly modern language, used to be known as the Queen's "protection." . . .

Pure hurting, as a military tactic, appeared in some of the military actions against the plains Indians. In 1868, during the war with the Cheyennes, General Sheridan decided that his best hope was to attack the Indians in their winter camps. His reasoning was that the Indians could maraud as they pleased during the seasons when their ponies could subsist on grass, and in the winter hide away in remote places. "To disabuse their minds from the idea that they were secure from punishment, and to strike at a period when they were helpless to move their stock and villages, a winter campaign was projected against the large bands hiding away in the Indian territory."[1]

These were not military engagements; they were punitive attacks on people. They were an effort to subdue by the use of violence, without a futile attempt to draw the enemy's military forces into decisive battle. They were "massive retaliation" on a diminutive scale, with local effects not unlike those of Hiroshima. The Indians themselves totally lacked organization and discipline, and typically could not afford enough ammunitions for target practice and were no military match for the cavalry; their own rudimentary strategy was at best one of harassment and reprisal. Half a century of Indian fighting in the West left us a legacy of cavalry tactics; but it is hard to find a serious treatise on American strategy against the Indians or Indian strategy against the whites. The twentieth is not the first century in which "retaliation" has been part of our strategy, but it is the first in which we have systematically recognized it. . . .

Making it "terrible beyond endurance" is what we associate with Algeria and Palestine, the crushing of Budapest, and the tribal warfare in Central Africa. But in the great wars of the last hundred years it was usually military victory, not the hurting of the people, that was decisive; General Sherman's attempt to make war hell for the Southern people did not come to epitomize military strategy for the century to follow. To seek out and destroy the enemy's military force, to achieve a crushing victory over enemy armies, was still the avowed purpose and the central aim of American strategy in both world wars. Military action was seen as an *alternative* to bargaining, not a *process* of bargaining.

The reason is not that civilized countries are so averse to hurting people that they prefer "purely military" wars. (Nor were all of the participants in these wars entirely civilized.) The reason is apparently that the technology and geography of warfare, at least for a war between anything like equal powers during the century ending in World War II, kept coercive violence from being decisive before military victory was achieved. Blockade indeed was aimed at the whole enemy nation, not concentrated on its military forces; the German civilians who died of influenza in the First World War were victims directed at the whole country. It has never been quite clear whether blockade—of the South in the Civil War or of the Central Powers in both world wars, or submarine warfare against Britain—was expected to make war unendurable for the people or just to weaken the enemy forces by denying economic support. Both arguments were made, but there was no need to be clear about the purpose as long as either purpose was regarded as legitimate and either might be served. "Strategic bombing" of enemy homelands was also occasionally rationalized in terms of the pain and privation it could inflict on people and the civil damage it could do to the nation, as an effort to display either to the population or to the enemy leadership that surrender was better than persistence in view of the damage that could be done. It was also rationalized in more "military" terms, as a way of selectively denying war material to the troops or as a way of generally weakening the economy on which the military effort rested.

But terrorism—as violence intended to coerce the enemy rather than to weaken him militarily—blockade and strategic bombing by themselves were not quite up to the job in either world war in Europe. (They might have been sufficient in the war with Japan after straightforward military action had brought American aircraft into range.) Airplanes could not quite make punitive, coercive violence decisive in Europe, at least on a tolerable time schedule, and preclude the need to defeat or to destroy enemy forces as long as they had nothing but conventional explosives and incendiaries to carry. Hitler's V–1 buzz bomb and his V–2 rocket are fairly pure cases of weapons whose purpose was to intimidate, to hurt Britain itself rather than Allied military forces. What the V–2 needed was a punitive payload worth carrying, and the Germans did not have it. Some of the expectations in the 1920s and the 1930s that another major war would be one of pure civilian violence, of shock and terror from the skies, were not borne out by the available technology. The threat of punitive violence kept occupied countries quiescent; but the wars were won in Europe on the basis of brute strength and skill and not by intimidation, not by the threat of civilian violence but by the application of military force. Military victory was still the price of admission. Latent violence against people was reserved for the politics of surrender and occupation.

The great exception was the two atomic bombs on Japanese cities. These were weapons of terror and shock. They hurt, and promised more hurt, and that was their purpose. The few "small" weapons we had were undoubtedly of some direct military value but their enormous advantage was in pure violence. In a military sense the United States could gain a little by destruction of two Japanese industrial cities; in a civilian sense, the Japanese could lose much. The bomb that hit Hiroshima was a threat aimed at all of Japan. The political target of the bomb was not the dead of Hiroshima or the factories they worked in, but the survivors of Tokyo. The two bombs were in the tradition of Sheridan against the Comanches and Sherman in Georgia. Whether in the end those two bombs saved lives or wasted them, Japanese lives or American lives; whether punitive coercive violence is uglier than straightforward military force or more civilized; whether terror is more or less humane than military destruction; we can at least perceive that the bombs on Hiroshima and Nagasaki represented violence against the country itself and not mainly an attack on Japan's material strength. The effect of the bombs, and their purpose, was not mainly the military destruction they accomplished but the pain and the shock and the promise of more.

The Nuclear Contribution to Terror and Violence

Man has, it is said, for the first time in history enough military power to eliminate his species from the earth, weapons against which there is no conceivable defense. War has become, it is said, so destructive and terrible that it ceases to be an instrument of national power. "For the first time in human history," says Max Lerner in a book whose title, *The Age of Overkill,* conveys the point, "men have bottled up a power . . . which they have thus far not dared to use." And Soviet military authorities, whose party dislikes having to accommodate an entire theory of history to a single technological event, have had to re-examine a set of principles that had been given the embarrassing name of "permanently operating factors" in warfare. Indeed, our era is epitomized by words like "the first time in human history," and by the abdication of what was "permanent."

For dramatic impact these statements are splendid. Some of them display a tendency, not at all necessary, to belittle the catastrophe of earlier wars. They may exaggerate the historical novelty of deterrence and the balance of terror.[2] More important, they do not help to identify just what is new about war when so much destructive energy can be packed in warheads at a price that permits advanced countries to have them in large numbers. Nuclear warheads are incomparably more devastating than anything packaged before. What does that imply about war?

It is not true that for the first time in history man has the capability to destroy a large fraction, even the major part, of the human race. Japan was defenseless by August 1945. With a combination of bombing and blockade, eventually invasion, and if necessary the deliberate spread of disease, the United States could probably have exterminated the population of the Japanese islands without nuclear weapons. . . .

It is a grisly thing to talk about. We did not do it and it is not imaginable that we would have done it. We had no reason; if we had had a reason, we would not have the persistence of purpose once the fury of war had been dissipated in victory and we had taken on the task of the executioner. If we and our enemies might do such a thing to each other now, and to others as well, it is not because nuclear weapons have for the first time made it feasible.

Nuclear weapons can do it quickly. . . . To compress a catastrophic war within the span of time that a man can stay awake drastically changes the politics of war, the process of decision, the possibility of central control and restraint, the motivations of people in charge, and the capacity to think and reflect while war is in progress. It *is* imaginable that we might destroy 200,000,000 Russians in a war of the present, though not 80,000,000 Japanese in a war of the past. It is not only imaginable, it is imagined. It is imaginable because it could be done "in a moment, in the twinkling of an eye, at the last trumpet."

This may be why there is so little discussion of how an all-out war might be brought to a close. People do not expect it to be "brought" to a close, but just to come to an end when everything has been spent. It is also why the idea of "limited war" has become so explicit in recent years. Earlier wars, like the World Wars I and II or the Franco-Prussian War, were limited by *termination,* by an ending that occurred before the period of greatest potential violence, by negotiation that brought the *threat* of pain and privation to bear but often precluded the massive *exercise* of civilian violence. With nuclear weapons available, the restraint of violence cannot await the outcome of a contest of military strength; restraint, to occur at all, must occur during war itself.

This is a difference between nuclear weapons and bayonets. It is not in the number of people they can eventually kill but in the speed with which it can be done, in the centralization of decision, in the divorce of the war from political process, and in computerized programs that threaten to take the war out of human hands once it begins.

That nuclear weapons make it *possible* to compress the fury of global war into a few hours does not mean that they make it *inevitable.* We have still to ask whether that is the way a major nuclear war would be fought, or ought to be fought. Nevertheless, that the whole war might go off like one big string of firecrackers makes a critical difference between our conception of nuclear war and the world wars we have experienced. . . .

There is another difference. In the past it has usually been the victors who could do what they pleased to the enemy. War has often been "total war" for the loser. With deadly monotony the Persians, Greeks and Romans "put to death all men of military age, and sold the women and children into slavery," leaving the defeated territory nothing but its name until new settlers arrived sometime later. But the defeated could not do the same to their victors. The boys could be castrated and sold only after the war had been won, and only on the side that lost it. The power to hurt could be brought to bear only after military strength had achieved victory. The same sequence characterized the great wars of this century; for reasons of technology and geography, military force has usually had to penetrate, to exhaust, or to collapse opposing military force—to achieve military victory—before it could be brought to bear on the enemy nation itself. The Allies in World War I could not inflict coercive pain and suffering directly on the Germans in a decisive way until they could defeat the German army; and the Germans could not coerce the French people with bayonets unless they first beat the Allied troops that stood in their way. With two-dimensional warfare, there is a tendency for troops to confront each other, shielding their own lands while attempting to press into each other. Small penetrations could not do major damage to the people; large penetrations were so destructive of military organization that they usually ended the military phase of the war.

Nuclear weapons make it possible to do monstrous violence to the enemy without first achieving victory. With nuclear weapons and today's means of delivery, one expects to penetrate an enemy homeland without first collapsing his military force. What nuclear weapons have done, or appear to do, is to promote this kind of warfare to first place. Nuclear weapons threaten to make war less military, and are responsible for the lowered status of "military victory" at the present time. *Victory is no longer a prerequisite for hurting the enemy.* And it is no assurance against being terribly hurt. One need not wait until he has won the war before inflicting "unendurable" damages on his enemy. One need not wait until he has lost the war. There was a time when the assurance of victory—false or genuine assurance—could make national leaders not just willing but sometimes enthusiastic about war. Not now.

Not only *can* nuclear weapons hurt the enemy before the war has been won, and perhaps hurt decisively enough to make the military engagement academic, but it is widely assumed that in a major war that is *all* they can do. Major war is often discussed as though it would be only a contest in national destruction. If this is indeed the case—if the destruction of cities and their populations has become, with nuclear weapons, the primary object in an all-out war the sequence of war has been reversed. Instead of destroying enemy forces as a prelude to imposing one's will on the enemy nation, one would have to destroy the nation as a means or a prelude to destroying the enemy forces. If one cannot disable enemy forces without virtually destroying the country, the victor does not even have the option of sparing the conquered nation. He has already destroyed it. Even with blockade and strategic bombing it could be supposed that a country would be defeated before it was destroyed, or would elect surrender before annihilation had gone far. In the Civil War it could be hoped that the South would become too weak to fight before it became too weak to survive. For "all-out" war, nuclear weapons threaten to reverse this sequence.

So nuclear weapons do make a difference, marking an epoch in warfare. The difference is not just in the amount of destruction that can be accomplished but in the role of destruction and in the decision process. Nuclear weapons can change the speed of events, the control of events, the sequence of events, the relation of victor to vanquished, and the relation of homeland to fighting front. Deterrence rests today on the threat of pain and extinction, not just on the threat of military defeat. We may argue about the wisdom of announcing "unconditional surrender" as an aim in the last major war, but seem to expect "unconditional destruction" as a matter of course in another one.

Something like the same destruction always *could* be done. With nuclear weapons there is an expectation that it would be done. . . . What is new is . . . the idea that major war might be just a contest in the killing of countries, or not even a contest but just two parallel exercises in devastation.

That is the difference nuclear weapons make. At least they *may* make the difference. They also may not. If the weapons themselves are vulnerable to attack, or the machines that carry them, a successful surprise might eliminate the opponent's means of retribution. That an enormous explosion can be packaged in a single bomb does not by itself guarantee that the victor will receive deadly punishment. Two gunfighters facing each other in a Western town had an unquestioned capacity to kill one another; that did not guarantee that both would die in a gunfight—only the slower of the two. Less deadly weapons, permitting an injured one to shoot back before he died, might have been more conducive to a restraining balance of terror, or of caution. The very efficiency of nuclear weapons could make them ideal for starting war, if they can suddenly eliminate the enemy's capability to shoot back.

And there is a contrary possibility: that nuclear weapons are not vulnerable to attack and prove not to be terribly effective against each other, posing no need to shoot them quickly for fear they will be destroyed before they are launched, and with no task available but the systematic destruction of the enemy country and no necessary reason to do it fast rather than slowly. Imagine that nuclear destruction had to go slowly—that the bombs could be dropped only one per day. The prospect would look very different, something like the most terroristic guerrilla warfare on a massive scale. It happens that nuclear war does not have to go slowly; but it may also not have to go speedily. The mere existence of nuclear weapons does not itself determine that everything must go off in a blinding flash, any more than that it must go slowly. Nuclear weapons do not simplify things quite that much. . . .

In World Wars I and II one went to work on enemy military forces, not his people, because until the enemy's military forces had been taken care of there was typically not anything decisive that one could do to the enemy nation itself. The Germans did not, in World War I, refrain from bayoneting French citizens by the millions in the hopes that the Allies would abstain from shooting up the German population. They could not get at the French citizens until they had breached the Allied lines. Hitler tried to terrorize London and did not make it. The Allied air forces took the war straight to Hitler's territory, with at least some thought of doing in Germany what Sherman recognized he was doing in Georgia; but with the bombing technology of World War II one could not afford to bypass the troops and go exclusively for enemy populations—not, anyway, in Germany. With nuclear weapons one has that alternative.

To concentrate on the enemy's military installations while deliberately holding in reserve a massive capacity for destroying his cities, for exterminating his people and eliminating his society, on condition that the enemy observe similar restraint with respect to one's own society is not the "conventional approach." In World Wars I and II the first order of business was to destroy enemy armed forces because that was the only promising way to make him surrender. To fight a purely military engagement "all-out" while holding in reserve a decisive capacity for violence, on condition the enemy do likewise, is not the way military operations have traditionally been approached.

. . . In the present era noncombatants appear to be not only deliberate targets but primary targets. . . . In fact, noncombatants appeared to be primary targets at both ends of the scale of warfare; thermonuclear war threatened to be a contest in the destruction of cities and populations; and, at the other end of the scale, insurgency is almost entirely terroristic. We live in an era of dirty war.

Why is this so? Is war properly a military affair among combatants, and is it a depravity peculiar to the twentieth century that we cannot keep it within decent bounds? Or is war inherently dirty?

To answer this question it is useful to distinguish three stages in the involvement of noncombatants—of plain people and their possessions—in the fury of war. These stages are worth distinguishing; but their sequence is merely descriptive of Western Europe during the past three hundred years, not a historical generalization. The first stage is that in which the people may get hurt by inconsiderate combatants. This is the status that people had during the period of "civilized warfare" that the International Committee had in mind.

From about 1648 to the Napoleonic era, war in much of Western Europe was something superimposed on society. It was a contest engaged in by monarchies for stakes that were measured in territories, and, occasionally, money or dynastic claims. The troops were mostly mercenaries and the motivation for war was confined to the aristocratic elite. Monarchs fought for bits of territory, but the residents of disputed terrain were more concerned with protecting their crops and their daughters from marauding troops than with whom they owed allegiance to. They were, as Quincy Wright remarked in his classic *Study of War,* little concerned that the territory in which they lived had a new sovereign.[3] Furthermore, as far as the King of Prussia and the Emperor of Austria were concerned, the loyalty and enthusiasm of the Bohemian farmer were not decisive considerations. It is an exaggeration to refer to European war during this period as a sport of kings, but not a gross exaggeration. And the military logistics of those days confined military operations to a scale that did not require the enthusiasm of a multitude.

Hurting people was not a decisive instrument in warfare. Hurting people or destroying property only reduced the value of things that were being fought over, to the disadvantage of both sides. Furthermore, the monarchs who conducted wars often did not want to discredit the social institutions they shared with their enemies. Bypassing an enemy monarch and taking the war straight to his people would have had revolutionary implications. Destroying the opposing monarchy was often not in the interest of either side; opposing sovereigns had much more in common with each other than with their own subjects, and to discredit the claims of a monarchy might have produced a disastrous backlash. It is not surprising—or, if it is surprising, not altogether astonishing—that on the European continent in that particular era war was fairly well confined to military activity.

One could still, in those days and in that part of the world, be concerned for the rights of noncombatants and hope to devise rules that both sides in the war might observe. The rules might well be observed because both sides had something to gain from preserving social order and not destroying the enemy. Rules might be a nuisance, but if they restricted both sides the disadvantages might cancel out.

This was changed during the Napoleonic wars. In Napoleon's France, people cared about the outcome. The nation was mobilized. The war was a national effort, not just an activity of the elite. It was both political and military genius on the part of Napoleon and his ministers that an entire nation could be mobilized for war. Propaganda became a tool of warfare, and war became vulgarized.

Many writers deplored this popularization of war, this involvement of the democratic masses. In fact, the horrors we attribute to thermonuclear war were already foreseen by many commentators, some before the First World War and more after it, but the new "weapon" to which these terrors were ascribed was people, millions of people, passionately engaged in national wars, spending themselves in a quest for total victory and desperate to avoid total defeat. Today we are impressed that a small number of highly trained pilots can carry enough energy to blast and burn tens of millions of people and the buildings they live in; two or three generations ago there was concern that tens of millions of people using bayonets and barbed wire, machine guns and shrapnel, could create the same kind of destruction and disorder.

That was the second stage in the relation of people to war, the second in Europe since the middle of the seventeenth century. In the first stage people had been neutral but their welfare might be disregarded; in the second stage people were involved because it was *their* war. Some fought, some produced materials of war, some produced food, and some took care of children; but they were all part of a war-making nation. When Hitler attacked Poland in 1939, the Poles had reason to care about the outcome. When Churchill said the British would fight on the beaches, he spoke for the British and not for a mercenary army. The war was about something that mattered. If people would rather fight a dirty war than lose a clean one, the war will be between nations and not just between governments. If people have an influence on whether the war is continued or on the terms of a truce, making the war hurt people serves a purpose. It is a dirty purpose, but war itself is often about something dirty. The Poles and the Norwegians, the Russians and the British, had reason to believe that if they lost the war the consequences would be dirty. This is so evident in modern civil wars—civil wars that involve popular feelings—that we expect them to be bloody and violent. To hope that they would be fought cleanly with no violence to people would be a little like hoping for a clean race riot.

There is another way to put it that helps to bring out the sequence of events. If a modern war were a clean one, the violence would not be ruled out but merely saved for the postwar period. Once the army has been defeated in the clean war, the victorious enemy can be as brutally coercive as he wishes. A clean war would determine which side gets to use its power to hurt coercively after victory, and it is likely to be worth some violence to avoid being the loser.

"Surrender" is the process following military hostilities in which the power to hurt is brought to bear. If surrender negotiations are successful and not followed by overt violence, it is because the capacity to inflict pain and damage was successfully used in the bargaining process. On the losing side, prospective pain and damage were averted by concessions; on the winning side, the capacity for inflicting further harm was traded for concessions. The same is true in a successful kidnapping. It only reminds us that the purpose of pure pain and damage is extortion; it is *latent* violence that can be used to advantage. A well-behaved occupied country is not one in which violence plays no part; it may be one in which latent violence is used so skillfully that it need not be spent in punishment.

This brings us to the third stage in the relation of civilian violence to warfare. If the pain and damage can be inflicted during war itself, they need not wait for the surrender negotiation that succeeds a military decision. If one can coerce people and their governments while war is going on, one does not need to wait until he has achieved victory or risk losing that coercive power by spending it all in a losing war. General Sherman's march through Georgia might have made as much sense, possibly more, had the North been losing the war, just as the German buzz bombs and V–2 rockets can be thought of as coercive instruments to get the war stopped before suffering military defeat.

In the present era, since at least the major East-West powers are capable of massive civilian violence during war itself beyond anything available during the Second World War, the occasion for restraint does not await the achievement of military victory or truce. The principal restraint during the Second World War was a temporal boundary, the date of surrender. In the present era we find the violence dramatically restrained during war itself. The Korean War was furiously "all-out" in the fighting, not only on the peninsular battlefield but in the resources used by both sides. It was "all-out," though, only within some dramatic restraints; no nuclear weapons, no Russians, no Chinese territory, no Japanese territory, no bombing of ships at sea or even airfields on the United Nations side of the line. It was a contest in military strength circumscribed by the threat of unprecedented civilian violence. Korea may or may not be a good model for speculation on limited war in the age of nuclear violence, but it was dramatic evidence that the capacity for violence can be consciously restrained even under the provocation of war that measures its military dead in tens of thousands and that fully preoccupies two of the largest countries in the world.

A consequence of this third stage is that "victory" inadequately expresses what a nation wants from its military forces. Mostly it wants, in these times, the influence that resides in latent force. It wants the bargaining power that comes from its capacity to hurt, not just the direct consequence of successful military action. Even total victory over an enemy provides at best an opportunity for unopposed violence against the enemy population. How to use that opportunity in the national interest, or in some wider interest, can be just as important as the achievement of victory itself; but traditional military science does not tell us how to use that capacity for inflicting pain. And if a nation, victor or potential loser, is going to use its capacity for pure violence to influence the enemy, there may be no need to await the achievement of total victory.

Actually, this third stage can be analyzed into two quite different variants. In one, sheer pain and damage are primary instruments of coercive warfare and may actually be applied, to intimidate or to deter. In the other, pain and destruction *in* war are expected to serve little or no purpose but *prior threats* of sheer violence, even of automatic and uncontrolled violence, are coupled to military force. The difference is in the all-or-none character of deterrence and intimidation. Two acute dilemmas arise. One is the choice of making prospective violence as frightening as possible or hedging with some capacity for reciprocated restraint. The other is the choice of making retaliation as automatic as possible or keeping deliberate control over the fateful decisions. The choices are determined partly by governments, partly by technology. Both variants are characterized by the coercive role of pain and destruction—of threatened (not inflicted) pain and destruction. But in one the threat either succeeds or fails altogether, and any ensuing violence is gratuitous; in the other, progressive pain and damage may actually be used to threaten more. The present era, for countries possessing nuclear weapons, is a complex and uncertain blend of the two. . . .

The power to hurt is nothing new in warfare, but for the United States modern technology has drastically enhanced the strategic importance of pure, unconstructive, unacquisitive pain and damage, whether used against us or in our own defense. This in turn enhances the importance of war and threats of war as techniques of influence, not of destruction; of coercion and deterrence, not of conquest and defense; of bargaining and intimidation. . . .

War no longer looks like just a contest of strength. War and the brink of war are more a contest of nerve and risk-taking, of pain and endurance. Small wars embody the threat of a larger war; they are not just military engagements but "crisis diplomacy." The threat of war has always been somewhere underneath international diplomacy, but for Americans it is now much nearer the surface. Like the threat of a strike in industrial relations, the threat of divorce in a family dispute, or the threat of bolting the party at a political convention, the threat of violence continuously circumscribes international politics. Neither strength nor goodwill procures immunity.

Military strategy can no longer be thought of, as it could for some countries in some eras, as the science of military victory. It is now equally, if not more, the art of coercion, of intimidation and deterrence. The instruments of war are more punitive than acquisitive. Military strategy, whether we like it or not, has become the diplomacy of violence.

Questions for Review

Schelling's title "The Diplomacy of Violence" would seem to be a contradiction. How does he meld the two? What is the significance of the difference between brute force and coercion?

Notes

1 Paul I. Wellman, *Death on the Prairie* (New York: Macmillan, 1934), p. 82.

2 Winston Churchill is often credited with the term, "balance of terror," and the following quotation succinctly expresses the familiar notion of nuclear mutual deterrence. This, though, is from a speech in Commons in November 1934. "The fact remains that when all is said and done as regards defensive methods, pending some new discovery the only direct measure of defense upon a great scale is the certainty of being able to inflict simultaneously upon the enemy as great damage as he can inflict upon ourselves. Do not let us undervalue the efficiency of this procedure. It may well prove in practice—I admit I cannot prove it in theory—capable of giving complete immunity. If two Powers show themselves equally capable of inflicting damage upon each other by some particular process of war, so that neither gains an advantage from its adoption and both sufer the most hideous reciprocal injuries, it is not only possible but it seems probable that neither will employ that means . . . "

3 (Chicago: University of Chicago Press), 1942, p. 296.

What is Terrorism?

BRUCE HOFFMAN

What is terrorism? Few words have so insidiously worked their way into our everyday vocabulary. Like "Internet"—another grossly overused term that has similarly become an indispensable part of the argot of the early twenty-first century—most people have a vague idea or impression of what terrorism is but lack a more precise, concrete, and truly explanatory definition of the word. This imprecision has been abetted partly by the modern media, whose efforts to communicate an often complex and convoluted message in the briefest amount of airtime or print space possible have led to the promiscuous labeling of a range of violent acts as "terrorism." Pick up a newspaper or turn on the television and—even within the same broadcast or on the same page—one can find such disparate acts as the bombing of a building, the assassination of a head of state, the massacre of civilians by a military unit, the poisoning of produce on supermarket shelves, or the deliberate contamination of over-the-counter medication in a drugstore, all described as incidents of terrorism. Indeed, virtually any especially abhorrent act of violence perceived as directed against society—whether it involves the activities of antigovernment dissidents or governments themselves, organized-crime syndicates, common criminals, rioting mobs, people engaged in militant protest, individual psychotics, or lone extortionists—is often labeled "terrorism" . . .

Why Is Terrorism So Difficult to Define?

Not surprisingly, as the meaning and usage of the word have changed over time to accommodate the political vernacular and discourse of each successive era, terrorism has proved increasingly elusive in the face of attempts to construct one consistent definition. At one time, the terrorists themselves were far more cooperative in this endeavor than they are today. The early practitioners didn't mince their words or hide behind the semantic camouflage of more anodyne labels such as "freedom fighter" or "urban guerrilla." The nineteenth-century anarchists, for example, unabashedly proclaimed themselves to be terrorists and frankly proclaimed their tactics to be terrorism. The members of Narodnaya Volya similarly displayed no qualms in using these same words to describe themselves and their deeds. Such frankness did not last, however. Although the Jewish terrorist group of the 1940s known as Lehi (the Hebrew acronym for Lohamei Herut Yisrael, the Freedom Fighters for Israel), but more popularly called the Stern Gang after its founder and first leader, Abraham Stern, would admit to its effective use of terrorist tactics, its members never considered themselves to be terrorists. It is significant, however, that even Lehi, while it may have been far more candid than its latter-day counterparts, chose as the name of the organization not Terrorist Fighters for Israel but the far less pejorative Freedom Fighters for Israel. Similarly, although more than twenty years later the Brazilian revolutionary Carlos Marighela displayed little compunction about openly advocating the use of "terrorist" tactics, he still insisted on depicting himself and his disciples as "urban guerrillas" rather than "urban terrorists." Indeed, it is clear from Marighela's writings that he was well aware of the word's undesirable connotations and strove to displace them with positive resonances. "The words 'aggressor' and 'terrorist,'" Marighela wrote in his famous *Handbook of Urban Guerrilla War* (also known as the "Mini-Manual"), "no longer mean what they did. Instead of arousing fear or censure, they are a call to action. To be called an aggressor or a terrorist in Brazil is now an honour to any citizen, for it means that he is fighting, with a gun in his hand, against the monstrosity of the present dictatorship and the suffering it causes."

This trend toward ever more convoluted semantic obfuscations to sidestep terrorism's pejorative overtones has, if anything, become more entrenched in recent decades. Terrorist organizations almost without exception now regularly select names for themselves that consciously eschew the word "terrorism" in any of its forms. Instead these groups actively seek to evoke images of

- freedom and liberation (e.g., the National Liberation Front, the Popular Front for the Liberation of Palestine, Freedom for the Basque Homeland);
- armies or other military organizational structures (e.g., the National Military Organization, the Popular Liberation Army, the Fifth Battalion of the Liberation Army);
- actual self-defense movements (e.g., the Afrikaner Resistance Movement, the Shankhill Defence Association, the Organization for the Defence of the Free People, the Jewish Defense Organization);
- righteous vengeance (the Organization for the Oppressed on Earth, the Justice Commandos of the Armenian Genocide, the Palestinian Revenge Organization)

—or else deliberately choose names that are decidedly neutral and therefore bereft of all but the most innocuous suggestions or associations (e.g., the Shining Path, Front Line, al-Dawa (the Call), Alfaro Lives—Damn It!, Kach (Thus), al-Gamat al-Islamiya (the Islamic Organization), the Lantaro Youth Movement, and *especially* al Qaeda (the Arabic word for the "base of operation" or "foundation"—meaning the base or foundation from which worldwide Islamic revolution can be waged—or, as other translations have it, the "precept" or "method").

What all these examples suggest is the terrorists clearly do not see or regard themselves as others do. "Above all I am a family man," the archterrorist Carlos, the Jackal, described himself to a French newspaper following his capture in 1994. Similarly, when the infamous KSM—Khalid Sheikh Mohammed, mastermind of the 9/11 attacks whom bin Laden called simply "al Mukhtar" (Arabic for "the brain")—was apprehended in March 2003, a photograph of him with his arms around his two young sons was found next to the bed in which he had been sleeping. Cast perpetually on the defensive and forced to take up arms to protect themselves and their real or imagined constituents only, terrorists perceive themselves as reluctant warriors, driven by desperation—and lacking any viable alternative—to violence against a repressive state, a predatory rival ethnic or nationalist group, or an unresponsive international order. This perceived characteristic of self-denial also distinguishes the terrorist from other types of political extremists as well as from people similarly involved in illegal, violent avocations. A communist or a revolutionary, for example, would likely readily accept and admit that he is in fact a communist or a revolutionary. Indeed, many would doubtless take particular pride in claiming either of those appellations for themselves. Similarly, even a person engaged in illegal, wholly disreputable, or entirely selfish violent activities, such as robbing banks or carrying out contract killings, would probably admit to being a bank robber or a murderer for hire. The terrorist, by contrast, will *never* acknowledge that he is a terrorist and moreover will go to great lengths to evade and obscure any such inference or connection. . . . The terrorist will always argue that it is society or the government or the socioeconomic "system" and its laws that are the *real* "terrorists," and moreover that if it were not for this oppression, he would not have felt the need to defend either himself or the population he claims to represent.

On one point, at least, everyone agrees: "Terrorism" is a pejorative term. It is a word with intrinsically negative connotations that is generally applied to one's enemies and opponents, or to those with whom one disagrees and would otherwise prefer to ignore. "What is called terrorism," Brian Jenkins has written, "thus seems to depend on one's point of view. Use of the term implies a moral judgement; and if one party can successfully attach the label *terrorist* to its opponent, then it has indirectly persuaded others to adopt its moral viewpoint." Hence the decision to call someone or label some organization "terrorist" becomes almost unavoidably subjective, depending largely on whether one sympathizes with or opposes the person/group/cause concerned. If one identifies with the victim of the violence, for example, then the act is terrorism. If, however, one identifies with the perpetrator, the violent act is regarded in a more sympathetic, if not positive (or, at the worst, ambivalent) light, and it is not terrorism. . . .

The opposite approach, in which identification with the victim determines the classification of a violent act as terrorism, is evident in the conclusions of a parliamentary working group of NATO (an organization comprising long-established, status quo Western states). The final report of the 1989 North Atlantic Assembly's Subcommittee on Terrorism states: "Murder, kidnapping, arson and other felonious acts constitute criminal behavior, but many non-Western nations have proved reluctant to condemn as terrorist acts what they consider to be struggles of national liberation." In this reasoning, the defining characteristic of terrorism is the act of violence itself, not the motivations or justification for or reasons behind it. . . .

But this is not an entirely satisfactory solution either, since it fails to differentiate clearly between violence perpetrated by states and by nonstate entities, such as terrorists. Accordingly, it plays into the hands of terrorists and their apologists who would argue that there is no difference between the "low-tech" terrorist pipe bomb placed in the rubbish bin at a crowded market that wantonly and indiscriminately kills or maims everyone within a radius measured in tens of feet and the "high-tech" precision-guided ordnance dropped by air force fighter-bombers from a height of twenty thousand feet or more that achieves the same wanton and indiscriminate effects on the crowded marketplace far below. This rationale thus equates the random violence inflicted on enemy population centers by military forces—such as the Luftwaffe's raids on Warsaw and Coventry, the Allied firebombings of Dresden and Tokyo, and the atomic bombs dropped by the United States on Hiroshima and Nagasaki during the Second World War, and indeed the countervalue strategy of the postwar superpowers' strategic nuclear policy, which deliberately targeted the enemy's civilian population—with the violence committed by substate entities labeled "terrorists," since both involve the infliction of death and injury on noncombatants. . . .

It is a familiar argument. Terrorists, as we have seen, deliberately cloak themselves in the terminology of military jargon. They consciously portray themselves as bona fide (freedom) fighters, if not soldiers, who—though they wear no identifying uniform or insignia—are entitled to treatment as prisoners of war (POWs) if captured and therefore should not be prosecuted as common criminals in ordinary courts of law. Terrorists further argue that, because of their numerical inferiority, far more limited firepower, and paucity of resources compared with an established nation-state's massive defense and national security apparatus, they have no choice but to operate clandestinely, emerging from the shadows to carry out dramatic (in other words, bloody and destructive) acts of hit-and-run violence in order to attract attention to, and ensure publicity for, themselves and their cause. The bomb in the rubbish bin, in their view, is merely a circumstantially imposed "poor man's air force": the only means with which the terrorist can challenge—and get the attention of—the more powerful state. "How else can we bring pressure to bear on the world?" one of Arafat's political aides once inquired. "The deaths are regrettable, but they are a fact of war in which innocents have become involved. They are no more innocent than the Palestinian women and children killed by the Israelis and we are ready to carry the war all over the world."

But rationalizations such as these ignore the fact that, even while national armed forces have been responsible for far more death and destruction than terrorists might ever aspire to bring about, there nonetheless is a fundamental qualitative difference between the two types of violence. Even in war there are rules and accepted norms of behavior that prohibit the use of certain types of weapons (for example, hollow-point or "dum-dum" bullets, CS "tear" gas, chemical and biological warfare agents) and proscribe various tactics and outlaw attacks on specific categories of targets. Accordingly, in theory, if not always in practice, the rules of war—as observed from the early seventeenth century when they were first proposed by the Dutch jurist Hugo Grotius and subsequently codified in the famous Geneva and Hague Conventions on Warfare of the 1860s, 1899, 1907, and 1949—not only grant civilian noncombatants immunity from attack but also

- prohibit taking civilians as hostages;
- impose regulations governing the treatment of captured or surrendered soldiers (POWs);
- outlaw reprisals against either civilians or POWs;
- recognize neutral territory and the rights of citizens of neutral states; and
- uphold the inviolability of diplomats and other accredited representatives.

Even the most cursory review of terrorist tactics and targets over the past quarter century reveals that terrorists have violated all these rules. They not infrequently have

- taken civilians as hostages, and in some instances then brutally executed them (e.g., the former Italian prime minister Aldo Moro and the German industrialist Hans Martin Schleyer, who, respectively, were taken captive and later murdered by the Red Brigades and the Red Army Faction in the 1970s and, more recently, Daniel Pearl, a *Wall Street Journal* reporter, and Nicholas Berg, an American businessmen, who were kidnapped by radical Islamic terrorists in Pakistan and Iraq, respectively, and grotesquely beheaded);
- similarly abused and murdered kidnapped military officers—even when they were serving on UN-sponsored peacekeeping or truce supervisory missions (e.g., the American Marine Lieutenant Colonel William Higgins, the commander of a UN truce-monitoring detachment, who was abducted by Lebanese Shi'a terrorists in 1989 and subsequently hanged);
- undertaken reprisals against wholly innocent civilians, often in countries far removed from the terrorists' ostensible "theater of operation," thus disdaining any concept of neutral states or the rights of citizens of neutral countries (e.g., the brutal 1986 machine-gun and hand-grenade attack on Turkish Jewish worshipers at an Istanbul synagogue carried out by the Palestinian Abu Nidal Organization (ANO) in retaliation for a recent Israeli raid on a guerrilla base in southern Lebanon); and
- repeatedly attacked embassies and other diplomatic installations (e.g., the bombings of the U.S. embassies in Nairobi and Dar es Salaam in 1998 and in Beirut and Kuwait City in 1983 and 1984, and the mass hostage-taking at the Japanese ambassador's residence in Lima, Peru, in 1996–97), as well as deliberately targeting diplomats and other accredited representatives (e.g., the British ambassador to Uruguay, Sir Geoffrey Jackson, who was kidnapped by leftist terrorists in that country in 1971, and the fifty-two American diplomats taken hostage at the Tehran legation in 1979).

Admittedly, the armed forces of established states have also been guilty of violating some of the same rules of war. However, when these transgressions do occur—when civilians are deliberately and wantonly attacked in war or taken hostage and killed by military forces—the term "war crime" is used to describe such acts and, as imperfect and flawed as both international and national judicial remedies may be, steps nonetheless are often taken to hold the perpetrators accountable for the crimes. By comparison, one of the fundamental raisons d'être of international terrorism is a refusal to be bound by such rules of warfare and codes of conduct. International terrorism disdains any concept of delimited areas of combat or demarcated battlefields, much less respect for neutral territory. Accordingly, terrorists have repeatedly taken their often parochial struggles to other, sometimes geographically distant, third-party countries and there deliberately enmeshed people completely unconnected with the terrorists' cause or grievances in violent incidents designed to generate attention and publicity. . . .

If it is impossible to define terrorism, as Laqueur argues, and fruitless to attempt to cobble together a truly comprehensive definition, as Schmid admits, are we to conclude that terrorism is impervious to precise, much less accurate definition? Not entirely. If we cannot define terrorism, then we can at least usefully distinguish it from other types of violence and identify the characteristics that make terrorism the distinct phenomenon of political violence that it is.

Distinctions as a Path to Definition

Guerrilla warfare and insurgency are good places to start. Terrorism is often confused or equated with, or treated as synonymous with, guerrilla warfare and insurgency. This is not entirely surprising, since guerrillas and insurgents often employ the same tactics (assassination, kidnapping, hit-and-run attack, bombings of public gathering places, hostage-taking, etc.) for the same purposes (to intimidate or coerce, thereby affecting behavior through the arousal of fear) as terrorists. In addition, terrorists as well as guerrillas and insurgents wear neither uniform nor identifying insignia and thus are often indistinguishable from noncombatants. However, despite the inclination to lump terrorists, guerrillas, and insurgents into the same catchall category of "irregulars," there are nonetheless fundamental differences among the three. "Guerrilla," for example, in its most widely accepted usage, is taken to refer to a numerically larger group of armed individuals, who operate as a military unit, attack enemy military forces, and seize and hold territory (even if only ephemerally during daylight hours), while also exercising some form of sovereignty or control over a defined geographical area and its population. "Insurgents" share these same characteristics: however, their strategy and operations transcend hit-and-run attacks to embrace what in the past has variously been called "revolutionary guerrilla warfare," "modern revolutionary warfare," or "people's war" but is today commonly termed "insurgency." Thus, in addition to the irregular military tactics that characterize guerrilla operations, insurgencies typically involve coordinated informational (e.g., propaganda) and psychological warfare efforts designed to mobilize popular support in a struggle against an established national government, imperialist power, or foreign occupying force. Terrorists, however, do not function in the open as armed units, generally do not attempt to seize or hold territory, deliberately avoid engaging enemy military forces in combat, are constrained both numerically and logistically from undertaking concerted mass political mobilization efforts, and exercise no direct control or governance over a populace at either the local or the national level.

It should be emphasized that none of these are pure categories and considerable overlap exists. Established terrorist groups like Hezbollah, FARC (Revolutionary Armed Forces of Colombia), and the LTTE (Liberation Tigers of Tamil Eelam, or Tamil Tigers), for example, are also often described as guerrilla movements because of their size, tactics, and control over territory and populace. Indeed, nearly a third of the thirty-seven groups on the U.S. State Department's "Designated Foreign Terrorist Organizations" list could just as easily be categorized as guerrillas. The ongoing insurgency in Iraq has further contributed to this semantic confusion. The 2003 edition of the State Department's *Global Patterns of Terrorism* specifically cited the challenge of making meaningful distinctions between these categories, lamenting how the "line between insurgency and terrorism has become increasingly blurred as attacks on civilian targets have become more common." Generally, the State Department considers attacks against U.S. and coalition military forces as insurgent operations and incidents such as the August 2003 suicide vehicle-borne bombings of the UN headquarters in Baghdad and the Jordanian embassy in that city, the assassinations of Japanese diplomats, and kidnapping and murder of aid workers and civilian contractors as terrorist attacks. The definitional rule of thumb therefore is that secular Ba'athist Party loyalists and other former regime elements who stage guerrillalike hit-and-run assaults or carry out attacks using roadside IEDs (improvised explosive devices) are deemed "insurgents," while foreign jihadists and domestic Islamic extremists who belong to groups like al Qaeda in Mesopotamia, led by Abu Musab Zarqawi, and who are responsible for most of the suicide attacks and the videotaped beheading of hostages, are labeled terrorists.

It is also useful to distinguish terrorists from ordinary criminals. Like terrorists, criminals use violence as a means to attain a specific end. However, while the violent act itself may be similar—kidnapping, shooting, and arson, for example—the purpose or motivation clearly is different. Whether the criminal employs violence as a means to obtain money, to acquire material goods, or to kill or injure a specific victim for pay, he is acting primarily for selfish, personal motivations (usually material gain). Moreover, unlike terrorism, the ordinary criminal's violent act is not designed or intended to have consequences or create psychological repercussions beyond the act itself. The criminal may of course use some short-term act of violence to "terrorize" his victim, such as waving a gun in the face of a bank clerk during a robbery in order to ensure the clerk's expeditious compliance. In these instances, however, the bank robber is conveying no "message" (political or otherwise) through his act of violence beyond facilitating the rapid handing over of his "loot." The criminal's act therefore is not meant to have any effect reaching beyond either the incident itself or the immediate victim. Further, the violence is neither conceived nor intended to convey any message to anyone other than the bank clerk himself, whose rapid cooperation is the robber's only objective. Perhaps most fundamentally, the criminal is not concerned with influencing or affecting public opinion; he simply wants to abscond with his money or accomplish his mercenary task in the quickest and easiest way possible so that he may reap his reward and enjoy the fruits of his labors. By contrast, the fundamental aim of the terrorist's violence is ultimately to change "the system"—about which the ordinary criminal, of course, couldn't care less.

The terrorist is also very different from the lunatic assassin, who may use identical tactics (e.g., shooting, bombing) and perhaps even seeks the same objective (e.g., the death of a political figure). However, while the tactics and targets of terrorists and lone assassins are often identical, their purpose is different. Whereas the terrorist's goal is again ineluctably *political* (to change or fundamentally alter a political system through his violent act), the lunatic assassin's goal is more often intrinsically idiosyncratic, completely egocentric and deeply personal. John Hinckley, who tried to kill President Reagan in 1981 to impress the actress Jodie Foster, is a case in point. He acted not from political motivation or ideological conviction but to fulfill some profound personal quest (killing the president to impress his screen idol). Such entirely *apolitical* motivations can in no way be compared to the rationalizations used by the Narodnaya Volya to justify its campaign of tyrannicide against the czar and his minions, nor even to the Irish Republican Army's efforts to assassinate Prime Minister Margaret Thatcher or her successor, John Major, in hopes of dramatically changing British policy toward Northern Ireland. Further, just as one person cannot credibly claim to be a political party, so a lone individual cannot be considered to constitute a terrorist group. In this respect, even though Sirhan Sirhan's assassination of presidential candidate and U.S. senator Robert Kennedy in 1968 had a political motive (to protest against U.S. support for Israel), it is debatable whether the murder should be defined as a terrorist act since Sirhan belonged to no organized political group and there is no evidence that he was directly influenced or inspired by an identifiable political or terrorist movement. Rather, Sirhan acted entirely on his own, out of deep personal frustration and a profound animus.

Finally, the point should be emphasized that, unlike the ordinary criminal or the lunatic assassin, the terrorist is not pursuing purely egocentric goals; he is not driven by the wish to line his own pocket or satisfy some personal need or grievance. The terrorist is fundamentally an *altruist:* he believes that he is serving a "good" cause designed to achieve a greater good for a wider constituency—whether real or imagined—that the terrorist and his organization purport to represent. The criminal, by comparison, serves no cause at all, just his own personal aggrandizement and material satiation. Indeed, a "terrorist without a cause (at least in his own mind)," Konrad Kellen has argued, "is not a terrorist." Yet the possession or identification of a cause is not a sufficient criterion for labeling someone a terrorist. In this key respect, the difference between terrorists and political extremists is clear. Many people, of course, harbor all sorts of radical and extreme beliefs and opinions, and many of them belong to radical or even illegal or proscribed political organizations. However, if they do not use violence in the pursuit of their beliefs, they cannot be considered terrorists. The terrorist is fundamentally a *violent intellectual,* prepared to use and, indeed, committed to using force in the attainment of his goals.

In the past, terrorism was arguably easier to define than it is today. To qualify as terrorism, violence had to be perpetrated by an individual acting at the behest of or on the behalf of some existent organizational entity or movement with at least some conspiratorial structure and identifiable chain of command. This criterion, however, is no longer sufficient. In recent years, a variety of terrorist movements have increasingly adopted a strategy of "leaderless networks" in order to thwart law enforcement and intelligence agency efforts to penetrate them. Craig Rosebraugh, the publicist for a radical environmentalist group calling itself the Earth Liberation Front (ELF), described the movement in a 2001 interview as a deliberately conceived "series of cells across the country with no chain of command and no membership roll . . . only a shared philosophy." It is designed this way, he continued, so that "there's no central leadership where [the authorities] can go and knock off the top guy and [the movement then] will be defunct." Indeed, an ELF recruitment video narrated by Rosebraugh advises "individuals interested in becoming active in the Earth Liberation Front to . . . form your own close-knit autonomous cells made of trustworthy and sincere people. Remember, the ELF and each cell within it are anonymous not only to one another but to the general public." As a senior FBI official conceded, the ELF is "not a group you can put your fingers on" and thus is extremely difficult to infiltrate.

This type of networked adversary is a new and different breed of terrorist entity to which traditional organizational constructs and definitions do not neatly apply. It is populated by individuals who are ideologically motivated, inspired, and animated by a movement or a leader, but who neither formally belong to a specific, identifiable terrorist group nor directly follow orders issued by its leadership and are therefore outside any established chain of command. It is a structure and approach that al Qaeda has also sought to implement. Ayman al-Zawahiri, bin Laden's deputy and al Qaeda's chief theoretician, extolled this strategy in his seminal clarion call to jihad (Arabic for "striving," but also "holy war"), *Knights Under the Prophet's Banner: Meditations on the Jihadist Movement.* The chapter titled "Small Groups Could Frighten the Americans" explains:

> Tracking down Americans and the Jews is not impossible. Killing them with a single bullet, a stab, or a device made up of a popular mix of explosives or hitting them with an iron rod is not impossible. Burning down their property with Molotov cocktails is not difficult. With the available means, small groups could prove to be a frightening horror for the Americans and the Jews.

Whether termed "leaderless resistance," "phantom cell networks," "autonomous leadership units," "autonomous cells," a "network of networks," or "lone wolves," this new conflict paradigm conforms to what John Arquilla and David Ronfeldt call "netwar":

> an emerging mode of conflict (and crime) at societal levels, short of traditional military warfare, in which the protagonists use network forms of organization and related doctrines, strategies, and technologies attuned to the information age. These protagonists are likely to consist of dispersed organizations, small groups, and individuals who communicate, coordinate, and conduct their campaigns in an internetted manner, often without precise central command.

Unlike the hierarchical, pyramidal structure that typified terrorist groups of the past, this new type of organization is looser, flatter, more linear. Although there is a leadership of sorts, its role may be more titular than actual, with less a direct command and control relationship than a mostly inspirational and motivational one. "The organizational structure," Arquilla and Ronfeldt explain,

> is quite flat. There is no single central leader or commander; the network as a whole (but not necessarily each node) has little to no hierarchy. There may be multiple leaders. Decisionmaking and operations are decentralized and depend on consultative consensus-building that allows for local initiative and autonomy. The design is both acephalous (headless) and polycephalous (Hydra-headed)—it has no precise heart or head, although not all nodes may be "created equal."

As part of this "leaderless" strategy, autonomous local terrorist cells plan and execute attacks independently of one another or of any central command authority, but through their individual terrorist efforts seek the eventual attainment of a terrorist organization or movement's wider goals. Although these ad hoc terrorist cells and lone individuals may be less sophisticated and therefore less capable than their more professional, trained counterparts who are members of actual established terrorist groups, these "amateur" terrorists can be just as bloody-minded. A recent FBI strategic planning document, for instance, describes lone wolves as the "most significant domestic terrorism threat" that the United States faces. "They typically draw ideological inspiration from formal terrorist organizations," the 2004–09 plan states, "but operate on the fringes of those movements. Despite their ad hoc nature and generally limited resources, they can mount high-profile, extremely destructive attacks, and their operational planning is often difficult to detect."

Conclusion

By distinguishing terrorists from other types of criminals and irregular fighters and terrorism from other forms of crime and irregular warfare, we come to appreciate that terrorism is

- ineluctably political in aims and motives;
- violent—or, equally important, threatens violence;

- designed to have far-reaching psychological repercussions beyond the immediate victim or target;
- conducted *either* by an organization with an identifiable chain of command or conspiratorial cell structure (whose members wear no uniform or identifying insignia) or by individuals or a small collection of individuals directly influenced, motivated, or inspired by the ideological aims or example of some existent terrorist movement and/or its leaders; and
- perpetrated by a subnational group or nonstate entity.

We may therefore now attempt to define terrorism as the deliberate creation and exploitation of fear through violence or the threat of violence in the pursuit of political change. All terrorist acts involve violence or the threat of violence. Terrorism is specifically designed to have far-reaching psychological effects beyond the immediate victim(s) or object of the terrorist attack. It is meant to instill fear within, and thereby intimidate, a wider "target audience" that might include a rival ethnic or religious group, an entire country, a national government or political party, or public opinion in general. Terrorism is designed to create power where there is none or to consolidate power where there is very little. Through the publicity generated by their violence, terrorists seek to obtain the leverage, influence, and power they otherwise lack to effect political change on either a local or an international scale.

Questions for Review

Why does it matter how we define terrorism? Can one separate an analysis of terrorism from a moral stance toward it?

Chapter 6
The Utility of Force Today

The Fungibility of Force

Robert J. Art

There are two fundamental reasons why military power remains more essential to statecraft than is commonly thought. First, in an anarchic realm (one without a central government), force is integral to political interaction. Foreign policy cannot be divorced from military power. Second, force is "fungible." It can be used for a wide variety of tasks and across different policy domains; it can be employed for both military and nonmilitary purposes. . . .

Power Assets: Comparisons and Confusions

. . . I have argued that force is integral to statecraft because international politics is anarchic. By itself, that fact makes force fungible to a degree. Exactly how fungible an instrument is military power, however, and how does it compare in this regard to the other power assets a state wields? In this section, I answer these questions. First, I make a rough comparison as to the fungibility of the main instruments of statecraft. Second, I present a counterargument that force has little fungibility and then critique it.

Comparing Power Assets

Comparing the instruments of statecraft according to their fungibility is a difficult task. We do not have a large body of empirical studies that systematically analyze the comparative fungibility of a state's power assets. The few studies we do have, even though they are carefully done, focus on only one or two instruments and are more concerned with looking at assets within specific issue areas than with comparing assets across issue areas. As a consequence, we lack sufficient evidence to compare power assets according to their fungibility. Through a little logic, however, we can provide some ballpark estimates.

Consider what power assets a state owns. They include population—the size, education level, and skills of its citizenry; geography—the size, location, and natural resource endowment of the state; governance—the effectiveness of its political system; values—the norms a state lives by and stands for, the nature of its ideology, and the extent of its appeal to foreigners; wealth—the level, sources, and nature of its productive economy; leadership—the political skill of its leaders and the number of skillful leaders it has; and military power—the nature, size, and composition of its military forces. Of all these assets, wealth and political skill look to be the most versatile, geography and governance the least versatile, because both are more in the nature of givens that set the physical and political context within which the other assets operate; values and population are highly variable, depending, respectively, on the content of the values and on the education and skill of the populace; and military power lies somewhere between wealth and skill on the one hand, and geography and governance on the other hand, but closer to the former than to the latter. In rank order, the three most fungible power assets appear to be wealth, political skill, and military power.

Economic wealth has the highest fungibility. It is the easiest to convert into the most liquid asset of all, namely, money, which in turn can be used to buy many different things—such as a good press, topflight international negotiators, smart lawyers, cutting-edge technology, bargaining power in international organizations, and so on. Wealth is also integral to military power. A rich state can generate more military power than a poor one. A state that is large and rich can, if it so chooses, generate especially large amounts of military power. The old mercantilist insight that wealth generates power (and vice-versa) is still valid.

Political skill is a second power asset that is highly fungible. By definition, skilled political operators are ones who can operate well in different policy realms because they have mastered the techniques of persuasion and influence. They are equally adept at selling free trade agreements, wars, or foreign aid to their citizens. Politically skillful statesmen can roam with ease across different policy realms. Indeed, that is what we commonly mean by a politically skillful leader—one who can lead in many different policy arenas. Thus, wealth and skill are resources that are easily transferable from one policy realm to another and are probably the two most liquid power assets.

Military power is a third fungible asset. It is not as fungible as wealth or skill, but that does not make it illiquid. Military power possesses versatility because force is integral to politics, even when states are at peace. If force is integral to international politics, it must be fungible. It cannot have pervasive effects and yet be severely restricted in its utility. Its pervasive effects, however, can be uniformly strong, uniformly weak, or variable in strength. Which is the case depends on how military power affects the many domains, policy arenas, and disparate issues that come within its field. At the minimum, however, military power is fungible to a degree because its physical use, its threatened use, or simply its mere presence structure expectations and influence the political calculations of actors. The gravitational effects of military power mean that its influence pervades the other policy realms, even if it is not dominant in most of them. Pervasiveness implies fungibility.

In the case of military power, moreover, greater amounts of it increase its fungibility. Up to a reasonable point, more of it is therefore better than less. It is more desirable to be militarily powerful than militarily weak. Militarily powerful states have greater clout in world politics than militarily weak ones. Militarily strong states are less subject to the influence of other states than militarily weak ones. Militarily powerful states can better offer protection to other states, or more seriously threaten them, in order to influence their behavior than can militarily weak ones. Finally, militarily powerful states are more secure than militarily weak ones. To have more clout, to be less subject to the will of others, to be in a stronger position to offer protection or threaten harm, and to be secure in a world where others are insecure—these are political advantages that can be diplomatically exploited, and they can also strengthen the will, resolve, and bargaining stance of the state that has them. Thus, although military power ranks behind wealth and skill in terms of its versatility, it can be a close third behind those two, at least for those great powers that choose to generate large amounts of it and then to exploit it.

Conflating Sufficiency and Fungibility

The view argued here—that military power possesses a relatively high degree of fungibility—is not the conventional wisdom. Rather, the commonly accepted view is that put forward by David Baldwin, who argues that military power is of restricted utility. Baldwin asserts:

> Two of the most important weaknesses in traditional theorizing about international politics have been the tendency to exaggerate the effectiveness of military power resources and the tendency to treat military power as the ultimate measuring rod to which other forms of power should be compared.[1]

Baldwin's view of military power follows from his more general argument that power assets tend to be situationally specific. By that he means: "What functions as a power resource in one policy-contingency framework may be irrelevant in another." If assets are situationally or domain-specific, then they are not easily transferable from one policy realm to another. In fact, as Baldwin argues: "Political power resources . . . tend to be much less liquid than economic resources"; and although power resources vary in their degree of fungibility, "no political power resource begins to approach the degree of fungibility of money."[2]

For Baldwin, two consequences flow from the domain-specific nature of power resources. First, we cannot rely on a gross assessment of a state's overall power assets in order to determine how well it will do in any specific area. Instead, we must assess the strength of the resources that it wields in that specific domain. Second, the generally low fungibility of political power resources explains what Baldwin calls the "paradox of unrealized power": the fact that a strong state can prevail in one policy area and lose in another. The reason for this, he tells us, is simple: The state at issue has strong assets in the domain where it prevails and weak ones where it does not.

On the face of it, Baldwin's argument is reasonable. It makes intuitive sense to argue, for example, that armies are better at defeating armies than they are at promoting stable exchange rates. It also makes good sense to take the position that the more carefully we assess what specific assets a state can bring to bear on a specific issue, the more fine-tuned our feel will be of what the state can realistically accomplish on that issue. To deny that all power assets are domain-specific to a degree is therefore absurd. Equally absurd, however, are the positions that all assets are domain-specific to the same degree, and that a gross inventory of a state's overall power assets is not a reliable, even if only a rough, guide to how well the state is likely to do in any given domain. Assets are not equal in fungibility, and fine-tuning does not mean dramatically altering assessments.

What does all this mean for the fungibility of military power? Should we accept Baldwin's view about it? I argue that we should not. To see why, let us look in greater detail at what else he has to say.

Baldwin adduces four examples that purport to demonstrate the limited versatility of military power.[3] The examples are hypothetical, but are nonetheless useful to analyze because they are equivalent to thought experiments. These are the examples:

> Possession of nuclear weapons is not just irrelevant to securing the election of a U.S. citizen as UN secretary-general; it is a hindrance.
>
> . . . The owner of a political power resource, such as the means to deter atomic attack, is likely to have difficulty converting this resource into another resource that would, for instance, allow his country to become the leader of the Third World.
>
> Planes loaded with nuclear weapons may strengthen a state's ability to deter nuclear attacks but may be irrelevant to rescuing the Pueblo [a U.S. destroyer seized by the North Koreans in early 1968] on short notice.
>
> The ability to get other countries to refrain from attacking one's homeland is not the same as the ability to "win the hearts and minds of the people" in a faraway land [the reference is to the Vietnam War].[4]

Seemingly persuasive at first glance, the examples are, in fact, highly misleading. A little reflection about each will show how Baldwin has committed the cardinal error of conflating the insufficiency of an instrument with its low fungibility, and, therefore, how he has made military power look more domain-specific in each example than it really is.

Consider first the United Nations case. Throughout the United Nations' history, the United States never sought, nor did it ever favor, the election of an American as secretary-general. If it had, money and bribes would have been of as little use as a nuclear threat. The Soviet Union would have vetoed it, just as the United States would have vetoed a Soviet national as secretary-general. Neither state would have countenanced the appointment of a citizen from the other, or from one of its client states. The reason is clear: The Cold War polarized the United

Nations between East and West, and neither superpower was willing to allow the other to gain undue influence in the institution if they could prevent it. Therefore, because neither superpower would have ever agreed on a national from the other camp, both sought a secretary-general from the ranks of the unaligned, neutral nations. This explains why cold war secretaries-general came from the unaligned Scandinavian or Third World nations (Dag Hammarskjold from Sweden; U Thant from Burma, for example), particularly during the heyday of the Cold War. This arrangement, moreover, served both superpowers' interest. At those rare times when they both agreed that the United Nations could be helpful, UN mediation was made more effective because it had a secretary-general that was neutral, not aligned.

Finally, even if America's military power had nothing to do with electing secretaries-general, we should not conclude that it has nothing to do with America's standing within the institution. America's preeminence within the United Nations has been clear. So, too, is the fact that this stems from America's position as the world's strongest nation, a position deriving from both its economic and military strength. Thus, although nuclear weapons cannot buy secretary-general elections, great military power brings great influence in an international organization, one of whose main purposes, after all, is to achieve collective security through the threat or use of force.

The Third World example is equally misleading. To see why, let us perform a simple "thought experiment." Although a Third World leader that had armed his state with nuclear weapons might not rise automatically to the top of the Third World pack, he or she would become a mighty important actor nonetheless. Think of how less weighty China and India, which have nuclear weapons, would appear to other states if they did not possess them; and think of how Iraq, Iran, or Libya, which do not have them, would be viewed if they did. For the former set of states, nuclear weapons add to their global political standing; for the latter set, their mere attempts to acquire them have caused their prominence to rise considerably. By themselves, nuclear weapons cannot buy the top slot in the Third World or elsewhere. Neither economic wealth, nor military power, nor any other power asset alone, can buy top dog. That slot is reserved for the state that surpasses the others in all the key categories of power. Although they do not buy the top position, nuclear weapons nevertheless do significantly enhance the international influence of any state that possesses them, if influence is measured by how seriously a state is taken by others. In this particular case, then, Baldwin is correct to argue that nuclear weapons are not readily convertible into another instrument asset. Although true, the point is irrelevant: They add to the ultimate resource for which all the other assets of a state are mustered—political influence.

The *Pueblo* example is the most complex of the cases, and the one, when reexamined, that provides the strongest support for Baldwin's general argument.[5] Even when reexamined, this strong case falls far short of demonstrating that military power has little fungibility.

The facts of the *Pueblo* case are straightforward. On 23 January 1968, North Korea seized the USS *Pueblo*, an intelligence ship that was fitted with sophisticated electronic eavesdropping capabilities and that was listening in on North Korea, and did not release the ship's crew members until 22 December 1968, almost a year after they had been captured. North Korea claimed the ship was patrolling inside its twelve-mile territorial waters limit; the United States denied the claim because its radio "fix" on the *Pueblo* showed that it was patrolling fifteen and a half nautical miles from the nearest North Korean land point. Immediately after the seizure, the United States beefed up its conventional and nuclear forces in East Asia, sending 14,000 Navy and Air Force reservists and 350 additional aircraft to South Korea, as well as moving the aircraft carrier USS *Enterprise* and its task force within a few minutes' flying time of Wonsan, North Korea. Some of the aircraft sent to South Korean bases and those on the *Enterprise* were nuclear capable. According to President Johnson, several military options were considered but ultimately rejected:

> mining Wonsan harbor; mining other North Korean harbors; interdicting coastal shipping; seizing a North Korean ship; striking selected North Korean targets by air and naval gunfire. In each case we decided that the risk was too great and the possible accomplishment too small. "I do not want to win the argument and lose the sale," I consistently warned my advisers.[6]

The American government's denial, its military measures, and its subsequent diplomatic efforts, were to no avail. North Korea refused to release the crew. In fact, right from the outset of the crisis, the North Korean negotiators made clear that only an American confession that it had spied on North Korea and had intruded into its territorial waters would secure the crew's release. For eleven months the United States continued to insist that the *Pueblo* was not engaged in illegal activity, and that it had not violated North Korea's territorial waters. Only on 22 December, when General Gilbert Woodward, the U.S. representative to the negotiations, signed a statement in which the U.S. government apologized for the espionage and the intrusion, did North Korea release the crew. The American admission of guilt, however, was made under protest: Immediately before signing the statement, the government disavowed what it was about to sign; and immediately after the signing, the government disavowed what it had just admitted.

Although the facts of the *Pueblo* case are straightforward, the interpretation to be put on them is not. This much is clear: Neither nuclear weapons, nor any of America's other military assets, appear to have secured the crew's release. Equally clear, however, is that none of its other assets secured the crew's release either. Should we then conclude from this case that military power, diplomacy, and whatever other assets were employed to secure the crew's release have low fungibility? Clearly, that would be a foolish conclusion to draw. There was only one thing that secured the crew's release: the public humiliation of the United

States. If nothing but humiliation worked, it is reasonable to conclude that humiliation either was, or more likely, quickly became North Korea's goal. When an adversary is firmly fixed on humiliation, military posturing, economic bribes, diplomatic pressure, economic threats, or any other tool used in moderation is not likely to succeed. Only extreme measures, such as waging war or economic blockade, are likely to be successful. At that point, the costs of such actions must be weighed against the benefits. One clear lesson we can draw from the *Pueblo* case is that sometimes there are tasks for which none of the traditional tools of statecraft are sufficient. These situations are rare, but they do on occasion occur. The *Pueblo* was one of them.

There is, however, a second and equally important point to be drawn from this example. Although it is true that America's military power did not secure the crew's release, nevertheless, there were other reasons to undertake the military buildup the United States subsequently engaged in. Neither the United States nor South Korea knew why the North had seized the *Pueblo*. President Johnson and his advisors, however, speculated that the seizure was related to the Tet offensive in Vietnam that began eight days after the *Pueblo*'s capture. They reasoned that the *Pueblo*'s seizure was deliberately timed to distract the United States and to frighten the South Koreans. Adding weight to this reasoning was the fact that the *Pueblo* was not an isolated incident. Two days earlier, thirty-one special North Korean agents infiltrated into Seoul and got within one-half mile of the presidential palace before they were overcome in battle. Their mission was to kill President Park. The United States feared that through these two incidents, and perhaps others to come, North Korea was trying to divert American military resources from Vietnam to Korea and to make the South Koreans sufficiently nervous that they would bring their two divisions fighting in Vietnam back home.[7]

The *Pueblo*'s seizure thus raised three problems for the United States: how to get its crew and ship back; how to deter the North from engaging in further provocative acts; and how to reassure the South Koreans sufficiently so that they would keep their troops in South Vietnam. A strong case could be made that the last two tasks, not the first, were the primary purposes for the subsequent American military buildup in East Asia. After all, the United States did not need additional forces there to pressure the North militarily to release the crew. There were already about 100,000 American troops in East Asia. A military buildup, however, would be a useful signal for deterrence of further provocations and reassurance of its ally. Until (or if) North Korea's archives are opened up, we cannot know whether deterrence of further provocation worked, because we do not know what additional plans the North had. What we do know is that the reassurance function of the buildup did work: South Korea kept its divisions in South Vietnam. Thus, America's military buildup had three purposes. Of those, one was achieved, another was not, and the third we cannot be certain about. In sum, it is wrong to draw the conclusion that the *Pueblo* case shows that force has little fungibility, even though military posturing appears not to have gotten the crew released.

Baldwin's final example is equally problematic if the point is to show that military power has little fungibility. Yes, it is true that preventing an attack on one's homeland is a different task than winning the hearts and minds of a people in a distant land. Presumably, however, the point of the example is to argue that the latter task is not merely different from the former, but also more difficult. If this is the assertion, it is unexceptionable: Compelling another government to change its behavior has always been an inherently more difficult task than deterring a given government from attacking one's homeland. Not only is interstate compellence more difficult than interstate deterrence, but intrastate compellence is more difficult than interstate compellence. Forcing the adversaries in a civil war to lay down their arms and negotiate an end to their dispute is a notoriously difficult task, as the Chinese civil war in the 1940s, the Vietnamese civil war in the 1960s, and the Bosnian civil war in the 1990s all too tragically show. It is an especially difficult task in a situation like Vietnam, where the outside power's internal ally faces an adversary that has the force of nationalism on its side. (Ho Chi Minh was Vietnam's greatest nationalist figure of the twentieth century and was widely recognized as such within Vietnam.) It is hard to prevail in a civil war when the adversary monopolizes the appeal of nationalism. Equally important, however, it is hard to prevail in a civil war without resort to force. The United States could not have won in Vietnam by force alone, but it would have had no chance at all to win without it.

No thoughtful analyst of military power would therefore disagree with the following propositions that can be teased out of the fourth example: (1) military power works better for defense than for conquest; (2) military power alone cannot guarantee pacification once conquest has taken place; (3) military power alone is not sufficient to compel a populace to accept the legitimacy of its government; and (4) compellence is more difficult than deterrence. These are reasonable statements. There is, however, also a fifth that should be drawn from this example: (5) when an outside power arrays itself in a civil war on the wrong side of nationalism, not only will force be insufficient to win, but so, too, will nearly all the other tools of statecraft—money, political skill, propaganda, and so on. In such cases military power suffers from the same insufficiency as the other instruments. That makes it no more, but no less, fungible than they are.

All four of Baldwin's examples demonstrate an important fact about military power: Used alone, it cannot achieve many things. Surely, this is an important point to remember, but is it one that is peculiar to military power alone or that proves that it has little fungibility? Surely not. Indeed, no single instrument of statecraft is ever sufficient to attain any significant foreign policy objective—a fact I shall term "task insufficiency."[8] There are two reasons for this. First, a statesman must anticipate the counteractions that will be undertaken by the states he is trying to influence. They will attempt to counter his stratagems with those of their own; they will use different types of instruments to offset the ones he is using;

and they will attempt to compensate for their weakness in one area with their strength in another. A well-prepared influence attempt therefore requires a multi-instrumental approach to deal with the likely counters to it. Second, any important policy itself has many facets. A multifaceted policy by necessity requires many instruments to implement it. For both reasons, all truly important matters require a statesman to muster several, if not all, the instruments at his disposal, even though he may rely more heavily on some than on others. In sum, in statecraft no tool can stand alone.

For military power, then, as for the other instruments of statecraft, fungibility should not be equated with sufficiency, and insufficiency should not be equated with low fungibility. A given instrument can carry a state part of the way to a given goal, even though it cannot carry the state all the way there. At one and the same time, an instrument of statecraft can usefully contribute to attaining many goals and yet by itself be insufficient to attain any one of them. Thus, careful consideration of Baldwin's examples demonstrates the following: (1) military power was not sufficient to achieve the defined task; (2) none of the other traditional policy instruments were sufficient either; and (3) military power was of some value, either for the defined task or for another task closely connected to it. What the examples did not demonstrate is that states are unable to transfer military power from one policy task to another. Indeed, to the contrary: Each showed that military power can be used for a variety of tasks, even though it may not be sufficient, by itself, to achieve any of them.

How Force Achieves Fungibility

If military power is a versatile instrument of statecraft, then exactly how does it achieve its fungibility? What are the paths through which it can influence events in other domains?

There are two paths. The first is through the spill-over effects that military power has on other policy domains; the second, through the phenomenon of "linkage politics." In the first case, military power encounters military power, but from this military encounter ensues an outcome with significant consequences for nonmilitary matters. In the second case, military power is deliberately linked to a nonmilitary issue, with the purpose of strengthening a state's bargaining leverage on that issue. In the first case, force is used against force; in the second, force is linked with another issue. In both cases, military power becomes fungible because it produces effects outside the strictly military domain. I explain how each path works and illustrate both with examples.

Spill-Over Effects

A military encounter, whether peaceful or forceful, yields a result that can be consequential to the interactions and the outcomes that take place in other domains. This result, which I term the "spill-over effect," is too often forgotten.[9] Military-to-military encounters do not produce only military results—cities laid waste, armies defeated, enemies subdued, attacks prevented, allies protected. They also bring about political effects that significantly influence events in other domains. Military power achieves much of its fungibility through this effect: The political shock waves of a military encounter reverberate beyond the military domain and extend into the other policy domains as well. The exercise of successful deterrence, compellence, or defense affects the overall political framework of relations between two states. Because all policy domains are situated within this overarching framework, what happens in the latter affects what happens in these domains. Spill-over effects define with more precision why force acts akin to a gravitational field.

A spill-over effect can be understood either as a prerequisite or a by-product. As a prerequisite, the result produced by the act of force checking force creates something that is deliberate and viewed as essential in order to reach a given outcome in another domain. As a by-product, the encounter produces something in another domain that may be beneficial but is incidental or even unintended. Of course, what is by-product and what is prerequisite hangs on what outcomes are valued in that other domain. Two examples will illustrate how the spill-over effect works and how it manifests itself either as a prerequisite or a by-product.

Examples: Banking and Cold War Interdependence

The first example has to do with banks; the second with recent history. The banking example demonstrates the role force plays in solvency; the historical example, the role that U.S. military power played in creating today's economic interdependence.

First, the banking example. Begin with this question, Why do we deposit our money in a bank? The answer is we put our money in a bank because we think we can take it out whenever we want. We believe the money is there when we want it. In short, we believe the bank to be solvent.

Solvency is usually thought of solely in economic terms: A bank is solvent because it has enough assets to meet its financial liabilities if they are called.[10] Solvency, however, is a function, not simply of finances, but of physical safety. A bank's solvency depends on the fact both that its assets exceed its liabilities (its balance sheet is in the black) and that its assets are physically secure (not easily stolen). Physical security is therefore as important to a bank's solvency as its liquidity, even though we generally take the former for granted when we reside in a stable domestic order. If the banks within a state could be robbed at will, then its citizens would not put their money in them. A state makes banks physically secure by using its military power to deter and defend against would-be robbers and to compel them to give back the funds if a robbery takes place (assuming they are caught and the funds recovered). Through its use of its legitimate monopoly on the use of force, a state seeks to neutralize the threat of forcible seizure. If the state succeeds in establishing the physical security of its banks, it produces one of the two prerequisites required for a bank's solvency.

In sum, in a well-ordered state, public force suppresses private force. The effect of this suppression is to create a generalized stability that sets the context within which all societal interactions take place. This effect spills over into numerous other domains and produces many manifestations, one of which is confidence about the physical security of banks. This confidence can be viewed as a by-product of the public suppression of private force, as a prerequisite to banking solvency, or, more sensibly, as both.

A good historical example of the spill-over effect of military power is the economic interdependence produced among the free world's economies during the Cold War. In a fundamental sense, this is the banking analogy writ large. The bank is the free world economies, the potential robber is the Soviet Union, and the provider of physical safety is the United States.

During the Cold War era, the United States used its military power to deter a Soviet attack on its major allies, the Western Europeans and the Japanese. American military power checked Soviet military power. This military-to-military encounter yielded a high degree of military security for America's allies, but it also produced several by-products, one of the most important of which was the creation of an open and interdependent economic order among the United States, Western Europe, and Japan. Today's era of economic interdependence is in no small part due to the exercise of American military power during the Cold War. A brief discussion will show how American military power helped create the economic interdependence from which much of today's world benefits.

America's forty-year struggle with the Soviets facilitated economic integration within Western Europe and among Western Europe, North America, and Japan. Obviously, American military power was not the sole factor responsible for today's interdependence among the major industrialized nations. Also crucial were the conversion of governments to Keynesian economics; their overwhelming desire to avoid the catastrophic experience of the Great Depression and the global war it brought in its wake; the lesson they learned from the 1930s about how non-cooperative, beggar-thy-neighbor policies ultimately redound to the disadvantage of all; the willingness of the United States to underwrite the economic costs of setting up the system and of sustaining it for a time; the acceptance by its allies of the legitimacy of American leadership; the hard work of the peoples involved; and so on. Important as all these factors were, however, we must remember where economic openness first began and where it subsequently flourished most: among the great powers that were allied with the United States against the Soviet Union.

How, then, did the Soviet threat and the measures taken to counter it help produce the modern miracle of economic interdependence among America's industrial allies? And how, exactly, did America's military power and its overseas military presence contribute to it? There were four ways.

First, the security provided by the United States created a political stability that was crucial to the orderly development of trading relations. Markets do not exist in political vacuums; rather, they work best when embedded in political frameworks that yield predictable expectations. American military power deployed in the Far East and on the European continent brought these stable expectations, first, by providing the psychological reassurance that the Europeans and the Japanese needed to rebuild themselves and, second, by continuing to provide them thereafter with a sense of safety that enabled their economic energies to work their will. Indeed, we should remember that the prime reason NATO was formed was psychological, not military: to make the Europeans feel secure enough against the Soviets so that they would have the political will to rebuild themselves economically. The initial purpose of NATO is the key to its (and to the U.S.–Japan defense treaty's) long-lasting function: the creation of a politically stable island amidst a turbulent international sea.

Second, America's provision of security to its allies in Europe and in the Far East dampened their respective concerns about German and Japanese military rearmament. The United States presence protected its allies not only from the Soviets, but also from the Germans and the Japanese. Because German and Japanese military power was contained in alliances that the United States dominated, and especially because American troops were visibly present and literally within each nation, Germany's and Japan's neighbors, while they did not forget the horrors they suffered at the hands of these two during the Second World War, nevertheless, were not paralyzed from cooperating with them. The success of the European Common Market owes as much to the presence of American military power on the continent of Europe as it does to the vision of men like Monnet. The same can be said for the Far East. America's military presence has helped "oil the waters" for Japan's economic dominance there.

Third, America's military presence helped to dampen concerns about disparities in relative economic growth and about vulnerabilities inherent in interdependence, both of which are heightened in an open economic order. Freer trade benefits all nations, but not equally. The most efficient benefit the most; and economic efficiencies can be turned to military effect. Interdependence brings dependencies, all the greater the more states specialize economically. Unequal gains from trade and trade dependencies all too often historically have had adverse political and military effects. Through its provision of military protection to its allies, the United States mitigated the security externalities of interdependence and enabled the Germans and the Japanese to bring their neighbors (America's allies) into their economic orbits without those neighbors fearing that German or Japanese military conquest or political domination would follow. With the security issue dealt with, the economic predominance of the Germans and Japanese was easier for their neighbors to swallow.

Finally, America's military presence fostered a solidarity that came by virtue of being partners against a common enemy. That sense of solidarity, in turn, helped develop the determination and the goodwill necessary to overcome the inevitable economic disputes that interdependencies bring. The "spill-over" effects of military cooperation against the Soviets on the political will to sustain economic openness should not be underestimated, though they are difficult to pinpoint and quantify. Surely, however, the sense of solidarity and good will that alliance in a common cause bred must have had these spill-over effects. Finally, the need to preserve a united front against the common enemy put limits on how far the allies, and the United States, would permit their economic disputes to go. The need to maintain a united political-military front bounded the inevitable economic disputes and prevented them from escalating into a downward-spiraling economic nationalism. Political stability, protection from potential German and Japanese military resurgence, the dampening of concerns about relative gains and dependencies, and the sense of solidarity—all of these were aided by the American military presence in Europe and the Far East.

Linkage Politics

The second way force exerts influence on other domains of policy is through the power of linkage politics. In politics, whether domestic or foreign, issues are usually linked to one another. The link can be either functional or artificial. If two issues are linked functionally, then there is a causal connection between them: A change in one produces a change in the other. The price of the dollar (its exchange rate value) and the price of oil imports, for example, are functionally linked, because the global oil market is priced in dollars. (Not only that, oil can only be bought with dollars.) A decline in the value of the dollar will increase the cost of a given amount of oil imported to the United States. Similarly, a rise in the value of the dollar will decrease the cost of a given amount of imported oil. As long as oil remains priced in dollars, the functional tie between exchange rates and energy cannot be delinked. Moreover, as the oil-dollar example illustrates, functional linkages generally have corresponding spill-over effects. That is, weakness on one issue (a weaker dollar) produces more weakness on the other (more money spent on energy imports); and strength on one (a stronger dollar) produces greater strength on the other (cheaper energy imports). Thus, functional linkages produce causal effects that either magnify a state's weakness or add to its strength.

When two issues are linked artificially, there is no causal connection between them. A change in one does not automatically produce a change in the other. Instead, the two issues become linked because a statesman has made a connection where none before existed. Usually, but not always, this will be done to gain bargaining leverage. By making a link between two heretofore unconnected issues, statesmen try to bring about politically what is not produced functionally. They make a link in order to compensate for weakness on a given issue. Their method is to tie an issue where they are weak to an issue where they are strong. Their goal is to produce a more desirable outcome in the weak area either by threatening to do something undesirable in the strong area, or by promising to do something beneficial there. If they can make the connection stick, then the result of an artificial linkage is a strengthening of a state's overall position. Unlike a functional linkage, where weakness begets weakness and strength begets strength, in an artificial linkage, strength offsets weakness. Thus, an artificial linkage is a bargaining connection that is made in the head of a statesman, but it is not any less real or any less effective as a result. I provide an example of a bargaining linkage below.

Whether functional or artificial, issue linkages have a crucial consequence for both the analysis and the exercise of state power. We can put the point more strongly: Because issues are connected, domains cannot be wholly delinked from one another. If they cannot be delinked, then we should not view them in isolation from one another. Therefore, any explanation of an outcome in a given domain that is based only on what goes on in that domain will always be incomplete, if not downright wrong. In sum, issue linkages limit the explanatory power of a domain-restricted analysis.

Bargaining linkages in particular make state assets more fungible than they might otherwise be. Linkage politics is a fact of international political life. We should not expect otherwise. Statesmen are out to make the best deals they can by compensating for weakness in one area with strength in others. Powerful states can better engage in these compensatory linkages than can weak ones. They are stronger in more areas than they are weak; consequently, they can more easily utilize their leverage in the strong areas to make up for their deficit in the weak ones. Great powers are also better able to shift assets among issue areas in order to build positions of bargaining strength when necessary. They can, for example, more easily generate military power when they need to in order to link it to nonmilitary tasks. Therefore, because powerful states can link issues more easily than can weaker ones, can compensate for deficiencies better, can generate more resources and do so more quickly when needed, and can shift assets around with greater ease, how powerful a state is overall remains an essential determinant to how successful it is internationally, irrespective of how weak it may be at any given moment on any specific issue in any particular domain. In sum, linkage politics enhances the advantages of being powerful and boosts the fungibility of force by enabling it to cross domains. . . .

Examples: Deficits, Petrodollars, and Oil Prices

Three . . . brief examples show the range of state goals that can be served by constructing such linkages.

The first involves the relation between America's large and continuing balance of payments deficits and its global alliance system. Throughout most of the Cold War era, the United States ran an annual large balance of payments deficits. Historically, no nation has been able to buy more abroad than it sells abroad (import more than it exports) in as huge a volume and for as long a period as has the United States. There were many reasons why it was able to, ranging from the liquidity that deficit dollars provided, which enabled world trade to grow, to general confidence in the American economy, which caused foreigners to invest their dollar holdings in the United States. Part of the reason that foreigners continued to take America's continuing flow of dollars, however, was an implicit, if not explicit, tradeoff: In return for their acceptance of American IOU's (deficit dollars), the United States provided the largest holders of them (the Germans, the Japanese, and the Saudis) military protection against their enemies. America's military strength compensated for its lack of fiscal discipline.[11]

A second example involves the recycling of petrodollars.[12] After the oil price hikes of the 1970s, the OPEC producers, especially the Persian Gulf members, were accumulating more dollars than they could profitably invest at home. Where to put those dollars was an important financial decision, especially for the Saudis, who were generating the largest dollar surpluses. There is strong circumstantial evidence that the Saudis agreed to park a sizable portion of their petrodollars in U.S. Treasury bills (T-bills) in part because of an explicit American proposal "to provide a security umbrella for the Gulf."[13] As David Spiro notes: "By the fourth quarter of 1977, Saudi Arabia accounted for twenty percent of all holdings of Treasury notes and bonds by foreign central banks."[14] The Saudis also continued to agree to price oil in dollars rather than peg it to a basket of currencies. Although there were clear financial incentives for both Saudi decisions, the incentives are not sufficient to explain Saudi actions. The Kuwaitis, for example, never put as many of their petrodollars in the United States, nor as many in T-bills, as did the Saudis. Moreover, an internal U.S. Treasury study concluded that the Saudis would have done better if oil had been pegged to a basket of currencies than to dollars. Indeed, OPEC had decided in 1975 to price oil in such a basket, but never followed through.[15] America's provision of security to the Saudis was an important, even if not sufficient, ingredient in persuading them both to price oil in dollars and then to park the dollars in the United States. Both decisions were of considerable economic benefit to the United States. Parking Saudi dollars in T-bills gave the American government "access to a huge pool of foreign capital"; pricing oils in dollars meant that the United States "could print money to buy oil."[16] Military power bought economic benefits.

A third example, again involving the Saudis, concerns the link between American military protection and the price of oil. The Saudis have a long-term economic interest that dictates moderation in oil prices. With a relatively small population and with the world's largest proven oil reserves, their strategy lies in maximizing revenue from oil over the long term. It is therefore to their advantage to keep the price of oil high enough to earn sizable profits, but not so high as to encourage investment in alternative energy sources. Periodically, Saudi Arabia has faced considerable pressure from the price hawks within OPEC to push prices higher than its interest dictates. American military protection has strengthened Saudi willingness to resist the hawks.

A specific instance of this interaction between U.S. protection and Saudi moderation, for example, occurred in the fall of 1980, with the onset of the Iran–Iraq war. Iraq attacked Iran in September, and the two countries proceeded to bomb one another's oil facilities. The initial stages of the war removed about four million barrels of oil per day from world markets and drove the price of oil to its highest level ever ($42 per barrel).[17] As part of their balancing strategy in the Gulf, this time the Saudis had allied themselves with Iraq and, fearing Iranian retaliation against their oil fields, asked for American military intervention to deter Iranian attacks on their oil fields and facilities. The United States responded by sending AWACS aircraft to Saudi Arabia and by setting up a joint Saudi-American naval task force to guard against Iranian attacks on oil tankers in the Gulf.[18] In return, the Saudis increased their oil production from 9.7 million barrels per day (mbd) to 10.3, which was the highest level it could sustain, and kept it there for the next ten months. Saudi actions had a considerable effect on oil prices, as Safran argues:

> Physically, the Saudi increase of 0.5 [sic, 0.6] was hardly enough to make up for the shortfall caused by the war . . . . Psychologically, however, the Saudi action was crucial in preventing the development of the kind of panic that had sent oil prices soaring after the fall of the shah and the Saudis' April 1979 decision to cut production by 1 mbd.[19]

As in the other cases, in this instance, American military power alone was not sufficient to cause Saudi actions to lower oil prices, but it was essential because during this turbulent period Saudi decisions on how much oil they would pump were not determined solely by economic factors. True, the Saudis, against the desires of the price hawks, which included the Iranians, had been pumping more oil since 1978 in order to lower oil prices. The Saudis had also violated their long-term strategy in March 1979, however, when they decided to cut oil production by 1 mbd, primarily to appease Iran, a move that triggered a rapid increase in oil prices. This pumping decision followed a political decision to move diplomatically away from the United States. Only a few months later, however, the conflict within the Saudi ruling family between an American-versus an Arab-oriented strategy was resolved in a compromise that led to a political reconciliation with the United States; and this political decision was followed by another to increase oil production by 1 mbd, starting 1 July 1979.[20] Before the Iran-Iraq war, then, Saudi pumping decisions were affected by political calculations about their security, in which the strategic connection with the Americans played a prominent role. If this was true in peacetime, surely it was so in wartime, too. The military protection announced by the Americans on 30 September 1980 was a necessary condition for the Saudi increase in oil production that followed in October. Again, military power had bought an economic benefit.

In sum, these . . . examples . . . America's ability to run deficits, petrodollar recycling, and moderate oil prices—all illustrate just how pervasive bargaining linkages are in international politics and specifically how military power can be linked politically to produce them. In all cases, military power was not sufficient. Without it, however, the United States could not have produced the favorable economic outcomes it achieved.

Question for Review

What examples (other than those mentioned in this selection) can you think of where military power produces political results through spill-over effects and linkage politics?

Notes

1 David Baldwin, *Paradoxes of Power* (New York: Blackwell, 1989), 151–52. Baldwin first developed his argument in his "Power Analysis and World Politics," *World Politics* 31, 1 (January 1979), 161–94, which is reprinted in *Paradoxes of Power*.

2 Quotes from Baldwin, *Paradoxes of Power*, 134–35, 135, and 136, respectively.

3 In fairness to Baldwin, these examples were not fully developed, but consist of only a sentence or two. Nevertheless, they are fair game because Baldwin used them as illustrations of his more general point about the limits to the utility of military power. The fact that he did not develop them further led him astray, in my view. He was trying to show with them that military power is less effective than commonly thought. I reinterpret these examples to show how versatile military power in fact is. Neither Baldwin nor I, however, can put a number on the fungibility of military power, and I certainly agree with him that "no political power resource begins to approach the degree of fungibility of money" (Baldwin, *Paradoxes of Power*, 135).

4 Baldwin, *Paradoxes of Power*, 134, 135, 133.

5 For the facts and interpretation of this case, I have relied on Lyndon Baines Johnson, *The Vantage Point: Perspectives of the Presidency, 1963–1969* (New York: Holt, Rinehart, Winston, 1971), 385, 387, and 532–37; Barry M. Blechman and Stephen S. Kaplan, *Force Without War: U.S. Armed Forces as a Political Instrument* (Washington, D.C.: Brookings, 1978), 48 and 71–72; Richard P. Stebbins and Elaine P. Adam, *Documents on American Foreign Relations, 1968–69* (New York: Simon & Schuster, 1972), 292–302; and the *New York Times Index*, 1968, 732–36.

6 Johnson, 536.

7 Johnson, 535; Blechman and Kaplan, 72.

8 Baldwin, of course, agrees with this point. He has written: "Actually, any technique of statecraft works poorly in isolation from the others." See David A. Baldwin, *Economic Statecraft* (Princeton: Princeton University Press, 1985), 143.

9 I have borrowed this term from Ernst Haas, even though I am using it differently than he does. He used the phrase to describe the effects that cooperation on economic matters among the states of Western Europe could have on their political relations. He argued that cooperation on economic matters would spill over into their political relations, induce greater cooperation there, and lead ultimately to the political integration of Western Europe. See Ernst Haas, *Beyond the Nation State: Functionalism and International Organization* (Stanford: Stanford University Press, 1964), 48. For Haas's later assessment of how effective spill-over effects were, see Ernst Haas, *The Obsolescence of Regional Integration Theory* (Berkeley: Institute of International Studies, University of California, 1974).

10 Solvency is to be distinguished from liquidity. A bank can be solvent but not liquid. Liquidity refers to the ability of a bank to meet all its liabilities upon demand. Most banks are not able to do so if all the demands are called at the same time. The reason is that many assets of any given bank are tied up in investments that cannot be called back on short notice but take time to convert into cash. The function of a central bank is to solve the liquidity problem of a nation's banking system by providing the liquidity in the short term in order to prevent runs on a bank.

11 As Gilpin put it: "Partially for economic reasons, but more importantly for political and strategic ones, Western Europe (primarily West Germany) and Japan agreed to finance the American balance of payments deficit." See Robert Gilpin, *U.S. Power and the Multinational Corporation: The Political Economy of Direct Investment* (New York: Basic Books, 1975), 154.

12 For this example, I have relied exclusively on David Spiro's original and thorough research. See David E. Spiro, *Hegemony Unbound: Petrodollar Recycling and the De-Legitimation of American Power* (Ithaca: Cornell University Press, forthcoming), chap. 4.

13 The quote is from an interview conducted by Spiro in Boston in 1984 with a former American ambassador to the Middle East. See Spiro, 271. (All page references are for the manuscript version.)

14 Spiro, 261.

15 Spiro, 263–66, 281–83.

16 Spiro, 259, 287.

17 Daniel Yergin, *The Prize: The Epic Quest for Oil, Money and Power* (New York: Simon & Schuster, 1992), 711.

18 Nadav Safran, *Saudi Arabia: The Ceaseless Quest for Security* (Ithaca: Cornell University Press, 1988), 322, 410–11.

19 Safran, 411.

20 Safran, 237.

Why Civil Resistance Works

ERICA CHENOWETH AND MARIA STEPHAN

In recent years organized civilian populations have successfully used nonviolent resistance methods, including boycotts, strikes, protests, and organized non-cooperation to exact political concessions and challenge entrenched power. To name a few, sustained and systematic nonviolent sanctions have removed autocratic regimes from power in Serbia (2000), Madagascar (2002), Georgia (2003), and Ukraine (2004–2005), after rigged elections; ended a foreign occupation in Lebanon (2005); and forced Nepal's monarch to make major constitutional concessions (2006). In the first two months of 2011, popular nonviolent uprisings in Tunisia and Egypt removed decades-old regimes from power. As this book goes to press, the prospect of people power transforming the Middle East remains strong.

In our Nonviolent and Violent Campaigns and Outcomes (NAVCO) data set, we analyze 323 violent and nonviolent resistance campaigns between 1900 and 2006. Among them are over one hundred major nonviolent campaigns since 1900, whose frequency has increased over time. In addition to their growing frequency, the success rates of nonviolent campaigns have increased. How does this compare with violent insurgencies? One might assume that the success rates may have increased among both nonviolent and violent insurgencies. But in our data, we find the opposite: although they persist, the success rates of violent insurgencies have declined.

The most striking finding is that between 1900 and 2006, nonviolent resistance campaigns were nearly twice as likely to achieve full or partial success as their violent counterparts. . . . The effects of resistance type on the probability of campaign success are robust even when we take into account potential confounding factors, such as target regime type, repression, and target regime capabilities.

The results begin to differ only when we consider the objectives of the resistance campaigns themselves. Among the 323 campaigns, in the case of antiregime resistance campaigns, the use of a nonviolent strategy has greatly enhanced the likelihood of success. Among campaigns with territorial objectives, like antioccupation or self-determination, nonviolent campaigns also have a slight advantage. Among the few cases of major resistance that do not fall into either category (antiapartheid campaigns, for instance), nonviolent resistance has had the monopoly on success.

The only exception is that nonviolent resistance leads to successful secession less often than violent insurgency. Although no nonviolent secession campaigns have succeeded, only four of the forty-one violent secession campaigns have done so (less than 10 percent), also an unimpressive figure. The implication is that campaigns seeking secession are highly unlikely to succeed regardless of whether they employ nonviolent or violent tactics. . . . The success of these nonviolent campaigns—especially in light of the enduring violent insurgencies occurring in many of the same countries—begs systematic exploration . . .

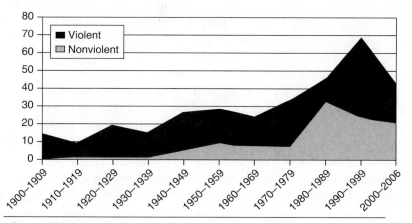

Figure 1 Frequency of Nonviolent and Violent Campaign End Years

The Argument

Our central contention is that nonviolent campaigns have a participation advantage over violent insurgencies, which is an important factor in determining campaign outcomes. The moral, physical, informational, and commitment barriers to participation are much lower for nonviolent resistance than for violent insurgency. Higher levels of participation contribute to a number of mechanisms necessary for success, including enhanced resilience, higher probabilities of tactical innovation, expanded civic disruption (thereby raising the costs to the regime of maintaining the status quo), and loyalty shifts involving the opponent's erstwhile supporters, including members of the security forces. Mobilization among local supporters is a more reliable source of power than the support of external allies, which many violent campaigns must obtain to compensate for their lack of participants.

Physical Barriers

Active participation in a resistance campaign requires variable levels of physical ability. The physical risks and costs of participation in a violent resistance campaign may be prohibitively high for many potential members. . . .

Physical barriers to participation may be lower for nonviolent resistance since the menu of tactics and activities available to nonviolent activists is broad and includes a wide spectrum, ranging from high-risk confrontational tactics to low-risk discreet tactics. Generally, participation in labor strikes, consumer boycotts, lockdowns, and sit-ins does not require strength, agility, or youth. Participation in a nonviolent campaign is open to female and elderly populations, whereas participation in a violent resistance campaign is often, though not always, physically prohibitive. . . .

Informational Difficulties

Scholars have found that individuals are more likely to engage in protest activity when they expect large numbers of people to participate. To successfully recruit members, campaigns must publicize their activities to demonstrate their goals, abilities, and existing numbers to potential recruits. Because of the high risks associated with violent activity, however, movement activists may be limited in how much information they can provide. They may need to remain underground, thereby exacerbating informational problems. Although violent acts, including assassinations, ambushes, bombings, and kidnappings, are public and often attract significant media attention providing signals of the campaign's abilities, the majority of the campaign's operational realities—including information about the numbers of active members—often remain unseen and unknown. The absence of visible signs of opposition strength is, therefore, problematic from the perspective of recruitment. . . . The counterargument, of course, is that dramatic acts of violence achieve a bigger bang for the buck. Whereas nonviolent organization requires communication and coordination involving larger numbers of people, a single suicide bomber can wreak great damage while attracting significant media attention at relatively little cost. . . .

On the other hand, nonviolent, public tactics have important demonstration effects, which help address the informational problem. Nonviolent campaigns sometimes include clandestine activities (e.g., the use of samizdat underground publications during the Polish Solidarity struggle, or the actual planning of non-violent campaigns by the leadership), particularly during the early stages when the resistance is most vulnerable to regime repression and decapitation. Typically, however, nonviolent campaigns rely less on underground activities than do armed struggles. When communities observe open, mass support and collective acts of defiance, their perceptions of risk may decline, reducing constraints on participation. . . . Courage breeds courage, particularly when those engaged in protest activities are ordinary people who would be conformist, law-abiding citizens under typical circumstances. Media coverage amplifies the demonstration effects of their acts of defiance.

Another factor that enhances participation in nonviolent campaigns is the festival-like atmosphere that often accompanies nonviolent rallies and demonstrations—as exemplified by the recent nonviolent campaigns in Serbia, Ukraine, Lebanon, and Egypt—where concerts, singing, and street theater attracted large numbers of people (particularly young people) interested in having fun while fighting for a political cause. Humor and satire, which have featured prominently in nonviolent campaigns (less so in armed campaigns), have helped break down barriers of fear and promote solidarity among victims of state-sponsored oppression. (Kishtainy 2010).

Moral Barriers

Moral barriers may constrain potential recruits to resistance campaigns, but such constraints may inhibit participation in nonviolent resistance far less than participation in violent activities. Although an individual's decision to resist the status quo may follow a certain amount of moral introspection, taking up weapons and killing adds a new moral dimension. Unwillingness to commit violent acts or to support armed groups necessarily disqualifies segments of the population that sympathize with the resistance but are reluctant to translate that sympathy into violence. . . . [Nonviolent] resistant campaigns, however, can potentially mobilize the entire aggrieved population without the need to face moral barriers. . . .

Moreover, we find that the transitions that occur in the wake of successful nonviolent resistance movements create much more durable and internally peaceful democracies than transitions provoked by violent insurgencies. On the whole, nonviolent resistance campaigns are more effective in getting results and, once they have succeeded, more likely to establish democratic regimes with a lower probability of a relapse into civil war. . . .

We explain the relative effectiveness of nonviolent resistance in the following way: nonviolent campaigns facilitate the active participation of many more people than violent campaigns, thereby broadening the base of resistance and raising the costs to opponents of maintaining the status quo. The mass civilian participation in a nonviolent campaign is more likely to backfire in the face of repression, encourage loyalty shifts among regime supporters, and provide resistance leaders with a more diverse menu of tactical and strategic choices. To regime elites, those engaged in civil resistance are more likely to appear as credible negotiating partners than are violent insurgents, thereby increasing the chance of winning concessions.

However, we also know that resistance campaigns are not guaranteed to succeed simply because they are nonviolent. One in four nonviolent campaigns since 1900 was a total failure. In short, we argue that nonviolent campaigns fail to achieve their objectives when they are unable to overcome the challenge of participation, when they fail to recruit a robust, diverse, and broad-based membership that can erode the power base of the adversary and maintain resilience in the face of repression.

Moreover, more than one in four violent campaigns has succeeded. . . . Whereas the success of nonviolent campaigns tends to rely more heavily on local factors, violent insurgencies tend to succeed when they achieve external support or when they feature a central characteristic of successful nonviolent campaigns, which is mass popular support. The presence of an external sponsor combined with a weak or predatory regime adversary may enhance the credibility of violent insurgencies, which may threaten the opponent regime. The credibility gained through external support may also increase the appeal to potential recruits, thereby allowing insurgencies to mobilize more participants against the opponent. . . .

The Evidence

Some readers may be tempted to dismiss our findings as the results of selection effects, arguing that the nonviolent campaigns that appear in our inventory are biased toward success, since it is the large, often mature campaigns that are most commonly reported. Other would-be nonviolent campaigns that are crushed in their infancy (and therefore fail) are not included in this study. This is a potential concern that is difficult to avoid.

We adopted a threefold data-collection strategy to address this concern. First, our selection of campaigns and their beginning and end dates is based on consensus data produced by multiple sources. Second, we have established rigorous standards of inclusion for each campaign. The nonviolent campaigns were initially gathered from an extensive review of the literature on nonviolent conflict and social movements. . . .

Nonetheless, what remains absent from the data set is a way to measure the nonstarters, the nonviolent or violent campaigns that never emerged because of any number of reasons. Despite this concern, we feel confident proceeding with our inquiry for two main reasons. First, this bias applies as much to violent campaigns as to nonviolent ones—many violent campaigns that were defeated early on are also unreported in the data. Second, this study is not concerned primarily with *why* these campaigns emerge but with *how well* they perform relative to their competitors that use different methods of resistance. We focus on the efficacy of campaigns as opposed to their origins, and we argue that we can say something about the effectiveness of nonviolent campaigns *relative to* violent campaigns. We do concede, however, that improved data collection and analysis and finding ways to overcome the selection bias inherent in much scholarship on conflict are vital next steps for the field.

Scholarly Implications

What is perhaps obvious is our voluntaristic approach to the study of resistance. . . . We make the case that voluntaristic features of campaigns, notably those related to the skills of the resistors, are often better predictors of success than structural determinants. On the surface, this argument immediately puts us at odds with structural explanations of outcomes such as political opportunity approaches. Such approaches argue that movements will succeed and fail based on the opening and closing of opportunities created by the structure of the political order. . . .

What we have found, however, is that the political opportunity approach fails to explain why some movements succeed in the direst of political circumstances where chances of success seem grim, whereas other campaigns fail in political circumstances that might seem more favorable. Such explanatory deficiencies leave us wondering how the actions of the groups themselves shape the outcomes of their campaigns.

For instance, a common misperception about nonviolent resistance is that it can succeed only against liberal, democratic regimes espousing universalistic values like respect for human rights. Besides the implicit and false assumption that democracies do not commit mass human rights abuses, the empirical record does not support this argument. . . .

The claim that nonviolent resistance could never work against genocidal foes like Adolph Hitler and Joseph Stalin is the classic straw man put forward to demonstrate the inherent limitations of this form of struggle. While it is possible that nonviolent resistance could not be used effectively once genocide has broken out in full force (or that it is inherently inferior to armed struggle in such circumstances), this claim is not backed by any strong empirical evidence (Summy 1994). Collective nonviolent struggle was not used with any strategic forethought during World War II, nor was it ever contemplated as an overall strategy for resisting the Nazis. Violent resistance, which some groups attempted for ending Nazi occupation, was also an abject failure. . . .

Wider Implications

Beyond scholarly contributions, this research possesses a number of important implications for public policy. Research regarding the successes and failures of nonviolent campaigns can provide insight into the most effective ways for external actors—governmental and nongovernmental—to aid such movements. From the perspective of an outside state, providing support to nonviolent campaigns can sometimes aid the movements but also introduces a new set of dilemmas, including the free-rider problem and the potential loss of local legitimacy. This study strongly supports the view that sanctions and state support for nonviolent campaigns work best when they are coordinated with the support of local opposition groups; but they are never substitutes.

For instance, although there is no evidence that external actors can successfully initiate or sustain mass nonviolent mobilization, targeted forms of external support have been useful in some cases, like the international boycotts targeting the apartheid regime in South Africa. The existence of organized solidarity groups that maintained steady pressure on governments allied with the target regimes proved to be very helpful, suggesting that "extending the battlefield" is sometimes necessary for opposition groups to enhance their leverage over the target. Lending diplomatic support to human rights activists, independent civil society groups, and democratic opposition leaders while penalizing regimes (or threatening penalties) that target unarmed activists with violent repression may be another way that governments can improve the probability of nonviolent campaign success. Coordinated multinational efforts that used a combination of positive and negative sanctions to isolate egregious rights violators supported successful civil resistance movements in South Africa and Eastern Europe.

Questions for Review

How can Chenoweth and Stephan argue that civil resistance can be effective against a ruthless regime? How are we to explain that the power of civil resistance was for so long ignored or denigrated by mainstream scholars?

Shape of Violence Today

THE WORLD BANK

Interstate and Civil Wars Have Declined since Peaking in the Early 1990s

Wars between states are now relatively rare (compared with the large wars of the 20th century). Major civil wars, after peaking in the early 1990s, have since declined (see Box 1). The annual number of battle deaths from civil war fell from more than 160,000 a year in the 1980s to less than 50,000 a year in the 2000s. Homicide rates in most regions have also been declining, except in Latin America and the Caribbean and possibly Sub-Saharan Africa.

The last two decades have also seen progress in developing global and regional standards to check the violent or coercive exercise of power. In Africa, the Lomé Declaration in 2000, which established standards and a regional response mechanism to unconstitutional changes in government, has been associated with a reduction in coups d'état from 15 in the 1990s to 5 from 2000 to mid-2010. And, despite an increase in coups in the last five years, continental action to restore constitutionality has been consistently strong. . . . New norms and associated sanctions to protect human rights have also made it possible to prosecute leaders for using extreme violence and coercion against their citizens: since 1990,

Box 1

Interstate and Civil War—1900 to the Present

Interstate war has declined dramatically since the two world wars of the first half of the 20th century. Major civil conflicts (those with more than 1,000 battle deaths a year) increased during the postcolonial and Cold War era, peaking in the late 1980s and early 1990s (Figure A). Since 1991–92, when there were 21 active major civil wars, the number has steadily fallen to less than 10 each year since 2002. The declines are all the more remarkable given the rising number of sovereign states—from around 50 in 1900 to more than 170 in 2008. Despite a tripling in the number of states and a doubling of popula-

tion in the last 60 years, the percentage of countries involved in major conflicts (interstate or civil) has not increased, and there has been a decline since 1992.

In addition, civil wars have become less violent. Battle deaths have dropped from an average of 164,000 a year in the 1980s and 92,000 a year in the 1990s to 42,000 a year in the 2000s (Figure B). This is consistent with recent evidence of declines in the number of wars, human rights abuses, and fatalities in war—and in the indirect deaths associated with wars.

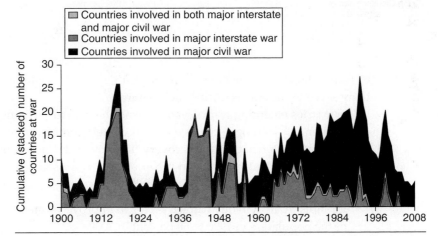

Figure A Civil Wars Peaked in the Early 1990s and Then Declined

Major civil wars increased from 1966 through the late 1980s and have decreased since the early 1990s.

SOURCES: Uppsala/PRIO Armed Conflict dataset (Harbom and Wallensteen 2010; Lacina and Gleditsch 2005).

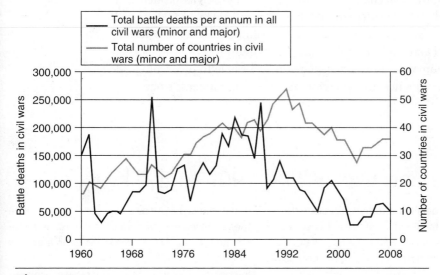

Figure B Deaths from Civil Wars Are Also on the Decline

As the number of civil wars declined, the total annual deaths from these conflicts (battle deaths) fell from more than 200,000 in 1988 to less than 50,000 in 2008.

NOTE: Civil wars are classified by scale and type in the Uppsala/PRIO Armed Conflict database (Harbom and Wallensteen 2010; Lacina and Gleditsch 2005). The minimum threshold for monitoring is a minor civil war with 25 or more battle deaths a year. Low, high, and best estimates of annual battle deaths per conflict are in Lacina and Gleditsch (2005, updated in 2009). Throughout this report, best estimates are used, except when they are not available, in which case averages of the low and high estimates are used.

SOURCES: Uppsala/PRIO Armed Conflict dataset (Harbom and Wallenstein 2010; Lacina and Gleditsch 2005); Gleditsch and others 2002; Sundberg 2008; Gleditsch and Ward 1999; Human Security Report Project 2010.

67 former heads of state have been prosecuted for serious human rights violations or economic crimes during their tenures.

Countries emerging from severe violence have made striking development gains, often with strong assistance from the international community. Conflict-affected states often begin their recovery from lower development levels than is "natural," given their human and physical capital. This makes rapid strides in development possible, as shown in the following examples:

- Ethiopia more than quadrupled access to improved water, from 13 percent of the population in 1990 to 66 percent in 2009–10.
- Mozambique more than tripled its primary school completion rate in just eight years, from 14 percent in 1999 to 46 percent in 2007.
- Rwanda cut the prevalence of undernourishment from 53 percent of the population in 1997 to 34 percent in 2007.
- Bosnia and Herzegovina, between 1995 and 2007, increased measles immunizations from 53 to 96 percent for children aged 12–23 months, and

reduced infant mortality from 16 to 12.6 per 1,000 live births. Telephone
lines per 100 people increased fourfold, from 7 to 28.

. . .

Modern Violence Comes in Various Forms and Repeated Cycles

The tendency to see violence as interstate warfare and major civil war obscures the
variety and prevalence of organized violence—and underestimates its impact on
people's lives. The organized violence that disrupts governance and compromises
development also includes local violence involving militias or between ethnic
groups, gang violence, local resource-related violence and violence linked to
trafficking (particularly drug trafficking), and violence associated with global
ideological struggles. This violence is often recurrent, with many countries now
experiencing repeated cycles of civil conflict and criminal violence.

Violence is Often Interlinked

. . . Many types of violence have direct links to each other, as illustrated in the
following examples:

- Countries rich in oil and other minerals that can be illegally trafficked
  are much more likely to have a civil war, and a longer one, with rebels
  financing their activity through the sale of lootable resources, such as
  diamonds in Sierra Leone and coltan (the mineral columbite-tantalite) in
  the Democratic Republic of Congo. Illegal trafficking has been a source of
  finance for armed groups in Afghanistan, Mindanao, and Northern Ireland.
- In countries as diverse as Côte d'Ivoire, Jamaica, Kenya, and the Solomon
  Islands, militant groups or criminal gangs have been mobilized during past
  political contests and elections.
- In Melanesia, the ritualized community conflicts of previous generations
  have escalated into urban gang violence associated with particular ethnic
  groups.
- In Central America, combatants on both sides of political conflicts between
  the state and rebel movements have migrated into organized crime.

In other cases, violence may be linked through underlying institutional weaknesses. Yemen now faces four separate conflicts: the Houthi rebellion in the North,
the presence of Al-Qaeda in the Arabian Peninsula, grievances in the south, and
the popular protests for change that have swept through the Arab world. There
is little direct evidence of links between these conflicts, other than through the
weakness of national institutions to address them. Similarly, in Nepal, following
a decade-long insurrection, 1996–2006, a Comprehensive Peace Agreement was
signed between the Maoist rebels and the government. But violence between
political rivals, quasi-political extortion, and criminal gang activity have increased
markedly since the civil war.

The modern landscape of violence also includes terrorist attacks by movements that claim ideological motives and recruit internationally. Terrorism—commonly, though not universally, defined as the use of force by nonstate actors against civilians—stretches back at least to the Middle Ages. In modern times, the tactics and organizations have mutated. The dominant forms and groups from the 1960s to the early 1990s were leftist or nationalist groups based in OECD (Organisation for Economic Co-operation and Development) countries (the Baader-Meinhof Group, Red Brigades, the IRA, the Euskadi Ta Askatasuna (ETA), and groups associated with the Israeli-Palestinian struggle). In contrast, the 1990s saw a surge in right-wing nationalism and antigovernment libertarian terrorism in the West, until the center of gravity shifted with 9/11 and the later attacks in, among other places, Jakarta, London, Madrid, and Mumbai. . . . While the preoccupation with terrorism is high in Western countries, some perspective on the global phenomenon is necessary—fatalities have been overwhelmingly concentrated on nonwestern targets in every year except 2001.

Organized Crime and Trafficking Are an Important Part of Current Violent Threats

Trafficking of drugs, people, and commodities has been an international concern for decades. Criminal networks take advantage of communications, transport, and financial services—and overwhelm enforcement mechanisms that are either rooted in national jurisdictions or hampered by low cooperation and weak capacity. Drugs connect some of the wealthiest and poorest areas of the world in mutual violence, showing that many solutions to violence require a global perspective. The annual value of the global trade in cocaine and heroin today is estimated at US$153 billion (heroin US$65 billion and cocaine US$88 billion). Europe and North America consume 53 percent of the heroin and 67 percent of the cocaine; however, the high retail prices in these markets mean that economic share of consumption in Europe and North America is even higher: cocaine consumption in the two regions accounted for an estimated US$72 billion of the US$88 billion in global trade. Drugs provide the money that enables organized criminals to corrupt and manipulate even the most powerful societies—to the ultimate detriment of the urban poor, who provide most of the criminals' foot-soldiers and who find themselves trapped in environments traumatized by criminal violence.

Drug trafficking organizations thus have resources that can dwarf those of the governments attempting to combat them. The value-added of cocaine traveling the length of Central America is equivalent to 5 percent of the region's GDP—and more than 100 times the US$65 million the United States allocates under the Mérida Initiative to assist interdiction efforts by Mexico and Central American nations. Conservative estimates suggest there are 70,000 gang members in Central America, outnumbering military personnel there. In many countries, drug cartels exert a heavy influence over provincial governance and, occasionally, national governance. . . .

Today's Violence Occurs in Repeated Cycles

There has been a tendency in the development community to assume that the progression from violence to sustained security is fairly linear—and that repeated violence is the exception. But recurring civil wars have become a dominant form of armed conflict in the world today. Every civil war that began since 2003 was a resumption of a previous civil war. Of all conflicts initiated in the 1960s, 57 percent were the first conflict in their country (many countries having been newly created after the colonial era). First conflicts fell significantly in each subsequent decade, to the point where 90 percent of conflicts initiated in the 21st century were in countries that had already had a civil war (Table 1). Fighting has also continued after several recent political settlements, as in Afghanistan and the Democratic Republic of Congo. As the previous section showed, successful peace agreements can be followed by high levels of criminal violence.

Several Central American countries that ended civil wars are now experiencing more violent deaths from criminal activity than during their civil wars. Since 1999, homicide rates have increased in El Salvador (+101 percent), Guatemala (+91 percent), and Honduras (+63 percent) as criminal networks linked to drug trafficking have become more active. All these countries suffered civil wars or political instability in the 1980s and 1990s. While El Salvador and Guatemala signed peace accords in the 1990s that avoided a return to civil war, both now face levels of violent organized crime equally disruptive to development.

The Developmental Consequences of Violence Are Severe

The costs of violence for citizens, communities, countries, and the world are enormous, both in terms of human suffering and social and economic consequences. The costs are both direct (loss of life, disability, and destruction) and indirect (prevention, instability, and displacement). While some of these losses

Table 1 Countries Often Relapse into Conflict

Decade	Onsets in countries with no previous conflict (%)	Onsets in countries with a previous conflict (%)	Number of onsets
1960s	57	43	35
1970s	43	57	44
1980s	38	62	39
1990s	33	67	81
2000s	10	90	39

Repeated violence is common in the world today, suggesting that few countries are ever truly "post-conflict." The rate of onset in countries with a previous conflict has been increasing since the 1960s, and every civil war that began since 2003 was in a country that had had a previous civil war.

can be directly measured and quantified in economic terms, others are not easily measured (trauma, loss of social capital and trust, prevention cost, and forgone investment and trade).

Questions for Review

How do you reconcile the claim that violence is decreasing with what you read in the media? Even if violence has been decreasing, what theories lead you to expect this trend to continue?

Chapter 7
The Nuclear Future

Losing Control in Crises

ROBERT JERVIS

Nuclear weapons embody multiple paradoxes. The one I explore here involves the actors' need to keep things under control while simultaneously threatening that things will spiral out of control. On the one hand, the enormous power of nuclear weapons requires the most exquisite control of them since all-out war would be a disaster for both sides. On the other hand, since it is irrational to fight a nuclear war, the most potent threat is not that you will decide that waging it is preferable to not doing so, but that in the course of the confrontation you will lose control of your senses or your forces and that war will occur even though no one wants it to. The ultimate threat, then, depends on the state doing things that could lead to an outcome it regards with horror. On the surface—and perhaps deeper inspection—this does not make much sense. But a lot of things about nuclear weapons and nuclear strategy do not fit with common sense.

To make this clearer, I will look at some arguments and incidents in the Cold War, but the argument can be applied to American relations with China and Russia, relations between those two countries, the conflict between India and Pakistan, and interactions among other countries that might get nuclear weapons.

The fear of events getting out of control was crucial to the resolution of the Cuban missile crisis. At its climax, President John Kennedy told Soviet First Secretary Nikita Khrushchev: "developments [are] approaching a point where events could . . . become unmanageable."[1] Indeed it was this fear—"the smell of scorching in the air"—that probably drove Khrushchev to pull back in October 1962. As he put it at the time:

> If you have not lost command of yourself and realize clearly what this could lead to, then, Mr. President, you and I should not now pull on the ends of the rope in which you have tied a knot of war, because the harder you and I pull, the tighter this knot will become. And a time may come when this knot is tied so tight that the person who tied it is no longer capable of untying it, and then the knot will have to be cut. What that would mean I need not explain to you, because you yourself understand perfectly what dread forces our two countries possess.[2]

It was also this fear—more than expectations of when the missiles would become operational—that led Kennedy to press for a speedy conclusion to the crisis. Especially after the shooting down of the U-2 over Cuba, he felt that the chances of the situation's escaping control were so great that it could not be allowed to continue. Interestingly enough, this dynamic was not anticipated at the start. In his speech announcing the Soviet deployment and the American response, Kennedy said the crisis could last for months, and in the next days American decision makers seemed prepared for prolonged bargaining. But as the pace of events quickened, complexities grew, and the participants became increasingly exhausted, they came to feel that the confrontation simply had to be brought to a head. Those who felt that the United States should have sought additional gains by maintaining if not increasing the pressure believed that people like McNamara who opposed continuing the crisis overestimated these dangers because of their lack of experience. Although I do not think this attribution is correct, it does support the argument that a large part of the difference between the conflicting views about force and nuclear strategy is to be explained by differing beliefs—often implicit—about whether tense situations can readily be kept under control.

We should not believe that the Cuban and later experiences have enabled us to avoid the dangers of the unintended results of putting force into motion. On July 3, 1988, when an American cruiser shot down an Iranian airliner in the Persian Gulf because of a series of errors on the part of the former's crew, including misreading the airline schedule, the radar scope, and transponder signals. Even though the cruiser's equipment apparently was working flawlessly, the crew's tensions, fears, and expectations led them to see an attack when none was under way. It also appears that the Iranians could not believe that the American action was inadvertent. Indeed, one reason why they agreed to a truce with Iraq shortly thereafter was the belief that if the United States was cruel and desperate enough to destroy an airliner, it might stage even bloodier interventions if the war continued. But in other cases the result could be increased violence.

In some cases, creating risk can be the explicit purpose of the behavior. In others, it is simply the by-product of resisting the adversary's moves. But the state that wants to resist has no choice but to enter into a contest of willingness to run risks, even though it will simultaneously seek to keep them under control. Thus there is often a trade-off between the requirements of crisis bargaining and those of crisis management. The former seeks to maximize pressure on the adversary and so needs to create a significant chance that things will get out of control; the latter seeks to keep these risks to a minimum. But even crisis management, if it is not to abandon all goals other than avoiding immediate war, must involve some dangers.

In many cases, merely being willing to engage in a confrontation will meet this requirement, As King Victor Emanuel of Italy put it when the German gunboat *Panther* sailed into the harbor at Agadir in 1911, leading to the second Moroccan Crisis: "on such occasions canons have a way of going off on their own."[3] What Clausewitz said about war can be extended to severe crises in the modern era; "War is the realm of chance. No other human activity gives it greater scope." "Everything in war is very simple, but the simplest thing is difficult."[4] The Cuban missile crisis again provides an illustration. The proponents of an air strike argued that while the blockade could prevent additional missiles from entering the country, it could not remove those that were there. While this is only common sense— the ships could not drive up on dry land—the argument overlooked the fact that the blockade was dangerous and therefore generated pressures that could—and did—persuade the Soviets to withdraw.

The course of the crisis demonstrated the power and the mechanisms of risk. While both sides went to extraordinary efforts to try to keep the situation under control, neither could be completely confident that they would succeed. President Kennedy sought to supervise even the small details of the way his policy was being implemented, but such efforts could not prevent all untoward incidents, such as the U-2 that strayed over the Soviet Union during the height of the crisis, the navy's harassment of Soviet submarines, covert actions by the CIA-trained exiles, or the SAC commander's unauthorized and unreported decision to send an alerting message to his forces not in the normal encoded form, but "in the clear," which could have been much more provocative. Kennedy understood this pattern. As he put it after the U-2 incident: "There is always some so-and-so [carrying out the policy] who doesn't get the word."[5] It is not surprising that Robert McNamara, having witnessed these events, argues that the most important lesson of the crisis is "McNamara's Law": "It is impossible to predict with a high degree of confidence what effects of the use of military force will be because of the risks of accident, miscalculation, misperception, and inadvertence."[6]

The ways by which control could be lost are numerous and it is not likely that either we or decision makers could think of all of them in advance. But we can specify three categories: control can be undermined by the decision makers' emotions, by their inability to understand what the other side (and, indeed, their own side) is doing, and by the loss of control over their own forces.

To start with the first possibility, decision makers might escalate a conflict more quickly and more violently than rational analysis would suggest is appropriate. When under great pressure, individuals do sometimes commit suicide. Less extreme emotionally based behavior is also possible and dangerous. The newspaper carries the following story:

> A pedestrian was stabbed to death on 42nd Street in Manhattan yesterday morning after he accosted a motorist whose van may have grazed him as he tried to cross the intersection, . . . Mr. Louzader was in the middle of the street when a . . . man made a left turn and either grazed him or nearly struck him. Mr. Louzader slapped the van with his hand and yelled at the driver, the police said, and the driver pulled over and got out, Witnesses said the two men exchanged words and the driver punched Mr. Louzader, who punched back. The driver then pulled a knife and stabbed the victim. . . . "It looks like it just got out of hand," [the police captain] said.[7] . . .

Of course states are not individuals, statesmen are socialized to keep control of their emotions, and high emotions do not automatically lead to violence. Fear, in particular, can produce restraint as well as lashing out, Indeed it is probably impossible to identify a single war that was unambiguously caused by this sort of loss of control. But a limited war that could end in the destruction of civilization would put unprecedented strain on people's emotions. In more ordinary crises the pressures are sufficiently great to lower the quality of decision making, and in a crisis a number of psychological mechanisms could lead statesmen to overestimate the inevitability of war or the advantages of going first, thus encouraging a preemptive strike. Furthermore, a statesman can act rationally on the basis of the facts as he believes them, but psychological biases may operate to distort his information processing. For example, people are slow to alter incorrect beliefs in the face of discrepant information; historical analogies are applied promiscuously; subtle—and not so subtle—signals rarely are interpreted as the sender intends; and a person who has become committed to a particular course of action may underestimate its risks and overestimate its chances of success. While these effects do not constitute loss of calculated control in the same way that overpowering emotion does, they are ways in which people's behavior is driven by forces they do not recognize, which do not fit with most conceptions of rationality, and which could produce a war that both sides wanted to avoid.

Even if decision makers remained in full control of their cognitive faculties and emotions, it is far from certain that they would be able to understand what was happening well enough to maintain control of the conflict. The situation inevitably would be very confused and ambiguous and, even if all the command, control, communications and intelligence (C^3I) systems were working adequately, it could be difficult for statesmen to comprehend the course of events. Even before force was used, too much would be happening for the decision maker to be fully informed. Thus only much later was it discovered that, by coincidence, the Jupiter missiles were turned over to Turkey (the warheads remained in American control) on the very day that Kennedy announced the blockade of Cuba. . . . In wartime it would be still more likely that, not knowing what the situation was, decision makers' actions would erode the tacit bargains required to keep the conflict limited. Statesmen do not understand what their state's armed forces do when they go on alert. They have little sense for what the "rules of engagement" authorize their military to do in specific situations, and it is not likely that they would know exactly what had transpired in a limited war. Technical advances may not have reduced, and certainly have not eliminated, the "fog of war." It is crucial but difficult for statesmen to know where their forces are, what they have done, what damage they have sustained, and (important in this context) what restraints they have maintained. Furthermore, decision makers are as likely to be misinformed as to be uninformed, an even more dangerous situation. If they seek to maintain limits, they will usually believe that their forces are being restrained. Any undesired expansion of the violence will be attributed to the other side's actions, and indeed to the other's intentions. . . .

The actions of third parties can further increase the chances of misinterpretation. Each superpower is likely to view local adversaries as the other's clients, if not its puppets. For example, during the Cuban missile crisis the United States underestimated Castro's independent role. In another Arab-Israeli war, the Soviet Union would be likely to view Israel's behavior as reflecting American intentions, and American decision makers would probably see Arab actions as at least having been approved if not ordered by Moscow. The result could be undesired escalation as each superpower matches the provocative behavior of the other's ally in the mistaken belief that it is responding to the other superpower. . . .

The discussion so far has assumed that the key decision makers are a handful of national leaders and that C^3I systems would remain intact in the event of war. But these assumptions are heroic ones. Even if the communication system continues to function well, limited wars require significant delegation to field commanders. This was true even in Korea and Vietnam; it would be true to a greater extent in quicker and more intense combat, which would require greater flexibility to take advantage of opportunities and to parry expected enemy thrusts. . . .

Furthermore, decision makers' anticipation that they would lose the ability to fight a war in a coordinated manner could lead them to escalate while they could still do so effectively. Compounding this, the expectation that the same pressures were operating on the other side could lead them to preempt. These processes could be accelerated if a limited war began to degrade the systems essential for fighting at a higher level of violence. Barry Posen has shown how a conventional war on the northern flank of Europe would have this effect and there is no reason to believe that this geographical area is unique. Limited attacks on strategic C^3 systems would in all likelihood produce even stronger reasons to escalate. The pressures on the state to relax the limits on its endangered systems while they could still be used would be great, especially if, as is likely to be the case, each side sees the other's actions as an attempt to gain unilateral advantage. . . .

Questions for Review

Does it make any sense to talk about countries losing control when the Cuban Missile Crisis clearly shows both sides doing everything they can to maintain control? What is the role, if any, of good government in keeping control?

Notes

1 "Message in Reply to a Broadcast by Chairman Khrushchev on the Cuban Crises," in *Public Papers of the Presidents, John F. Kennedy, 1962* (Washington, D.C.: Government Printing Office, 1963), p. 814.

2 Nikita Khrushchev, "The Present International Situation and the Foreign Policy of the Soviet Union," *Current Digest of the Soviet Press*, 14 (January 16, 1963).

3 Quoted in Holger Herwig, *Germany's Vision of Empire in Venezuela, 1871–1914*, (Princeton: Princeton University Press, 1986), p. 231.

4 Carl von Clausewitz, *On War*, ed. and trans. Michael Howard and Peter Paret (Princeton: Princeton University Press, 1976), pp. 101, 119; also see p. 85.

5 Quoted in Roger Hilsman, *To Move a Nation* (Garden City, N.Y.: Doubleday, 1964), p. 221.

6 Quoted in James Blight, Joseph Nye, Jr., and David Welch, "The Cuban Missile Crisis Revisited," *Foreign Affairs*, 66 (Fall 1987), p. 186, Albert Wohlstetter makes a similar remark: "No substantial conflict, nuclear or non-nuclear, is likely to be neat and perfectly controlled. . . . There will always be a substantial chance that violence would climb disastrously beyond any expected bound" ("Swords without Shields," *National Interest*, no. 8 [Summer 1983], 39). This sensible understanding of crises undercuts many of McNamara's arguments about the lack of utility of nuclear weapons and Wohlstetter's arguments for the utility of nuclear options.

7 Todd Purdum, "Man Slain by Motorist in Midtown," *New York Times*, April 29, 1987.

Our Not So Peaceful Nuclear Future

HENRY D. SOKOLSKI

The Obama Administration is noteworthy among recent presidencies for having consciously tried to integrate U.S. nuclear arms control efforts and its nonproliferation policies. Following President Barack Obama's 2009 appeal to eliminate nuclear weapons presented in Prague, the U.S. government made reducing nuclear arms a prerequisite for preventing their further spread. If we expect other nations to repress their own nuclear weapons aspirations, administration officials now argue that the nuclear superpowers have to demonstrate a greater willingness to disarm themselves. Such disarmament is feasible, they insist, because nuclear weapons are, in their view, only useful to deter other hostile nuclear weapons states. . . .

Hawkish supporters of nuclear weapons have a very different view. They argue that reducing American and Russian nuclear arms has little or no impact on reducing others' nuclear weapons activities or holdings (e.g., North Korea and Iran). In fact, reducing America's nuclear arsenal might only entice China to build up to America's current nuclear numbers and encourage America's key non-nuclear allies and friends—e.g., South Korea, Japan, Saudi Arabia, and Turkey—to hedge their bets against decreasingly credible U.S. nuclear security alliance guarantees by developing nuclear weapons options of their own. . . .

The most radical of academic nuclear skeptics, who identify themselves as neorealists, also question whether nuclear weapons reductions are needed to

Henry D. Sokolski, "What We Think" is excerpted from *Underestimated: Our Not So Peaceful Nuclear Future* (Carlisle, PA: Strategic Studies Institute, 2016).

reduce further proliferation. Although they concede that further nuclear weapons proliferation may be inevitable, they argue that it's unlikely to be destabilizing. They argue that a credible nuclear deterrent force needs only to be able to hold several major cities at risk, and therefore, it need only be a relatively small, "finite" force. . . .

A second, more recent version of such thinking has been made popular by such scholars as John Mueller. Dr. Mueller takes a different tack but reaches similar conclusions. He argues that nuclear weapons actually do a poor job of deterring small or major wars.[1] . . . Also, smaller wars—e.g., the Israeli War of '73, the Korean and Vietnam wars—Mueller notes, clearly were not deterred by anyone's nuclear weapons. Nor were the terrorist attacks of 9/11 in 2001 or the terrorist attacks on Mumbai in 2008: The implication is that nuclear weapons are so ineffective at deterring aggression and their use is so unlikely that their further spread is not all that consequential. . . .

Reservations

These. . . three views on how nuclear weapons reductions and nonproliferation relate are clear, plausible, and popular. They dominate the current debate over nuclear weapons policies. There is only one problem: In practice, none of them make nearly as much sense as their supporters claim. [See Figure 1, p. 269].

One can see this most readily by examining how each school addresses the simplest and most popular of policy questions: Should one be for or against nuclear weapons? Add to this question (for the purposes of this inquiry) the matter of nuclear weapons proliferation, and the query admits to two easy answers—yes (in support of nuclear weapons and additional proliferation) or no against both.

Let's take the against-side first. Those opposed to nuclear weapons and their further proliferation—i.e., those who want to move toward zero nuclear weapons as soon as possible—go to great lengths explaining why a world without nuclear weapons is preferable to our current world. . . . Unfortunately, these same analysts are far less articulate on how one might persuade existing nuclear weapons states to give their weapons up or how exactly one would get to zero. So far, the United States and Russia have reduced their nuclear holdings from over 70,000 nuclear weapons to fewer than 2,000 strategic warheads on each side. This begs the question, though: How easy would it be to reduce further to a few hundred warheads if other states (e.g., China, Israel, France, the United Kingdom (UK), North Korea, Pakistan and India) acquire or deploy as many or more? Would this not encourage increased military competitions, nuclear arms racing that could prompt mutual fears, miscalculation, and unnecessary and potentially disastrous wars?

Securing clear answers to such questions, of course, is difficult. Nonetheless, analysts backing zero nuclear weapons do offer a general picture of how things might work. According to their narrative, the more the U.S. government increases its support for nuclear weapons reductions and reduces its own arsenals with Russia, the more other nuclear-armed states (e.g., China, India, Pakistan) are likely to fall into line. . . . With increasing nuclear restraint by the major nuclear states, states lacking nuclear weapons would become more inclined to eschew nuclear weapons and support nuclear nonproliferation more generally.

This is the upbeat narrative, but there also is a downbeat one. It has us clinging to our bombs. The more we maintain our nuclear stockpiles, we are warned, the more it will undermine our claim we want to rely less on nuclear arms to assure our security. This, in turn, risks encouraging other states to acquire nuclear weapons (i.e., promoting more North Koreas, Irans, and Pakistans), which will only strain existing security relations and tempt America's allies (e.g., South Korea, Japan, Saudi Arabia, Turkey, etc.) to acquire nuclear weapons options of their own. . . .

Bottom line: The possession and spread of nuclear weapons generally undermines security. What, then, are nuclear weapons good for? Only the peculiar task of deterring other states from using their nuclear weapons.

This last reflection, of course, is intended to further demonstrate how little value nuclear weapons have and why their early elimination is desired. This conclusion, however, is triple-edged. Certainly, if nuclear weapons truly are not all that militarily valuable, what is the urgency to eliminate them? . . . On the other hand, if nuclear weapons can effectively deter other nuclear-armed states, wouldn't that make their acquisition by nonweapons states all but irresistible? The refrain of security analysts after the first Gulf War against Iraq was that the United States would never have tried to remove Saddam Hussein if he actually had the bomb. In what way were they wrong? . . .

Finally, is it reasonable to think that no one will ever use their nuclear weapons first? Don't states that believe in nuclear deterrence presume that if they lacked a survivable nuclear deterrent, their nuclear adversaries might strike their or their allies' vulnerable forces in an attempt to gain some clear advantage? . . .

This, then, brings us to those hawks. . . who are "for" nuclear weapons. Their brief essentially is that nuclear weapons have kept the peace. If you push for deeper nuclear reductions, they argue, it will do nothing to slow determined proliferators from acquiring nuclear weapons. More important, it could undermine our security alliance system, which, in turn, would increase the risks that our friends and allies might go nuclear. All of this would only increase the prospects for war and the possible use of nuclear weapons.

This line of argument, like that of the zero nuclear weapons crowd, makes a number of sensible points. Yet, it too is imperfect. First, as has already been noted, we know that nuclear weapons have not deterred all wars. Both North Korea and North Vietnam took the United States on in long-fought wars. Nor did U.S. nuclear weapons deter China and Russia from lending Hanoi and Pyongyang substantial military support. Then there's the Israeli war of 1973. Israeli possession of nuclear arms may have changed the way the war was fought (the United States finally came to Israel's aid at the last moment for fear that the war might go nuclear). But Israeli nuclear weapons did not prevent the war. Finally, it is unclear how, if at all, nuclear weapons might deter nonstate actors from engaging in terrorism—nuclear or nonnuclear.

Perhaps the point is nuclear weapons have prevented "major" (nuclear) wars or "major" defeats rather than all forms of military aggression. Certainly, the number of war casualties as a percentage of the world's population has declined significantly since Hiroshima and Nagasaki. This seems more persuasive.

The first problem, here, though, is that any "proof" of why something didn't happen can never be known with scientific certainty. . . . A good number of security experts question if nuclear deterrence ever really "worked" during the Cold War. . . .

[For Hawks], an unspoken assumption is that nuclear deterrence will work perfectly (as it supposedly did with Russia during the Cold War) and that it can be counted upon to work forever into the future with every other nuclear-armed state. This is presumed no matter how many nuclear-armed states there might be, how rash or reckless these countries' leaders are, or how ill-prepared their forces might be to absorb a first strike. It also presumes, sub silentio, that the lack of truly disastrous nuclear weapons accidents, unauthorized firings, acts of nuclear terrorism, and thefts we have experienced so far is a permanent feature. . . .

Yet another unspoken assumption at play is that smaller nuclear weapons states and states eager to develop a nuclear weapons option are merely "lesser included threats." The notion is that if the United States can deter or constrain Russia, the largest nuclear weapons state, the United States and its allies are safe (or much safer) against any other lesser nuclear-armed state. . . .

This set . . . of questions brings us to the views of radical academic skeptics. As already noted, this group can be split into two groups. The first includes those who think that the further proliferation of nuclear weapons may be beneficial, that upon a state's acquisition of nuclear arms effective nuclear deterrence is automatically assured. The second includes those who question the deterrence value of nuclear arms but who also believe that preventing their proliferation is generally unnecessary and misguided.

What is appealing about the second group is its willingness to take on those who extol the virtues of nuclear deterrence (i.e., of the academic skeptics' first camp and of hawkish supporters of nuclear weapons). . . . Did they deter the Soviet Union's nuclear and conventional forces from invading Europe during the Cold War? *No*, what kept the peace after 1945 was the creation of effective East-West security alliance systems and the very real fears these military alliances fostered of a massive, conventional WWIII breaking out if Cold War diplomacy failed.

This second group of academic skeptics also offers thoughtful rejoinders to the conventional wisdom that nuclear terrorism should be worry number one. Is the threat of nuclear terrorism the most imminent and extreme security threat we face? *Not really.* There are good reasons why no acts of nuclear terrorism have yet taken place and these are likely to apply well into the future. Building or stealing nuclear weapons is too large and complex an operation for most terrorist organizations. A terrorist team tasked to build or seize such weapons would constantly have to worry about being penetrated and betrayed to authorities. Certainly, the high levels of trust and cooperation needed to pull off such operations would be difficult to maintain. Nor is it in the interest of states that possess such weapons to let anyone but the most trusted and loyal gain access to them. . . .

Optimists All

Putting aside the close calls during the various Cold War crises (e.g., the Cuban Missile Crisis), the hair-raising nuclear brinkmanship that has been conducted by India and Pakistan, and the nuclear preemption and dares of the Israeli wars of 1967 and 1973, none of the cases noted above seem to support the idea that nuclear proliferation is "inconsequential," much less stabilizing. Just the opposite. Of course, until and unless there is nuclear use, there is no proof in these matters: We can't predict the future and the causes of wars are always complex. All we know is that the United States fired nuclear weapons in anger on Hiroshima and Nagasaki, that the United States and Russia threatened to use them several times during the Cold War, but that, for some reason, since 1945, they never have been used.

It would be nice to believe that they never will. Unfortunately, they might. Russia and Pakistan are quite explicit about the advantages of using nuclear weapons first against their adversaries. Some analysts also now believe China's no first use policies may be undergoing revision. All of these states, plus Israel, North Korea, and India are increasing or modernizing their nuclear arsenals. If these states are followed by Iran, South Korea, Japan, Turkey, the United Arab Emirates (UAE), or Saudi Arabia, the chances for nuclear miscalculations and war would likely go up, not down. . . .

Each of our current views of nuclear proliferation, then, ends up serving our highest hopes. The question is do they adequately address what we should be most worried about? Do they deal with the possible military diversion of "peaceful" nuclear energy—a dual-use technology sure to spread further? Do they adequately address the perils of making nuclear cuts as other states continue to hold or increase their arsenals? Do they assume that if we maintain our nuclear weapons force capabilities, we will forever deter the worst? Do they fully consider the military risks states run when they acquire their first nuclear weapon or try to ramp up existing arsenals significantly? Can any of them alone serve as a practical guide to reduce the nuclear challenges we face?

Figure 1. Nuclear Proliferation: What We Think

View	Selected Representatives	Favor Relying on Nuclear Weapons for Security	Believe Nuclear Weapons Deter	Willing to Go to Zero	Support Sharing Civil Nuclear Energy	Support Sharing Nuclear Weapons-related Technology
Official/ Arms Control Perspective	Most Western governments (e.g. the U.S., France, the UK, Japan, etc.) International forums (e.g. IAEA, NPT Review Conference)	No	Yes	Yes	Yes	No
Hawkish Supporters of Nuclear Weapons	Nuclear weapons enthusiasts Reagan-era Hawks (e.g., Donald Rumsfeld, Dick Cheney)	Yes	Yes	No	Yes (for friends) No (for enemies)	Yes (to some friends) No (for enemies)
Radical Academic Skeptics/ Finite Deterrence Enthusiasts	French proponents of Force de Frappe & early backers of U.S. SLBM force (e.g., Pierre Gallois, Arleigh Burke) Neorealists (e.g., Ken Waltz)	Yes	Yes	No	Unclear	Yes
Radical Academic Skeptics/ Finite Deterrence Critics	Post-neorealists (e.g., John Mueller)	No	No	Yes	Yes	No

Questions for Review

How does Sokolski relate analysts' stances toward proliferation to their general views about nuclear weapons? Are there overlaps between the views of Hawks and Doves on these issues?

Notes

1 See Mueller, *Atomic Obsession*.

A World without Nuclear Weapons?

THOMAS C. SCHELLING

A new and popular disarmament movement was provoked by a completely unexpected combination of Henry A. Kissinger, William J. Perry, Sam Nunn, and George P. Shultz with their op-ed pieces in *The Wall Street Journal* from January 4,

2007, and January 15, 2008. For the first time since the demise of General and Complete Disarmament (GCD) in the 1960s, there is a serious discussion of the possibility of utterly removing nuclear weapons from the planet Earth. Furthermore, the discussion is taking place among nuclear policy professionals, the people who publish in *Foreign Affairs, International Security,* and other serious journals. . . .

Some of the motivation, among the diverse respondents on the issue, is to fulfill, or appear to fulfill, the "commitment" undertaken by the official nuclear-weapons states in the Non-Proliferation Treaty (NPT) "to pursue negotiations in good faith on effective measures relating to cessation of the nuclear arms race at an early date and to nuclear disarmament, and on a treaty on general and complete disarmament under strict and effective international control." The underlying motive would be to renew and strengthen the Treaty itself, by removing an objection often voiced by non-nuclear governments about unacceptable discrimination. Some of the motivation is evidently to spur an overdue drastic reduction in Russian and American nuclear warheads, especially those on high alert.

But hardly any of the analyses or policy statements that I have come across question overtly the ultimate goal of total nuclear disarmament.[1] Nearly all adduce the unequivocal language of *The Wall Street Journal* quadrumvirate.

None explicitly addresses the question, why should we expect a world without nuclear weapons to be safer than one with (some) nuclear weapons? That drastic reductions make sense, and that some measures to reduce alert status do, too, may require no extensive analysis. But considering how much intellectual effort in the past half-century went into the study of the "stability" of a nuclear-deterrence world, it ought to be worthwhile to examine contingencies in a nuclear-free world to verify that it is superior to a world with (some) nuclear weapons.

I have not come across any mention of what would happen in the event of a major war. One might hope that major war could not happen in a world without nuclear weapons, but it always did. One can propose that another war on the scale of the 1940s is less to worry about than anything nuclear. But it might give pause to reflect that the world of 1939 was utterly free of nuclear weapons, yet they were not only produced, they were invented, during war itself and used with devastating effect. Why not expect that they could be produced—they've already been invented—and possibly used in some fashion?

In 1976, I published an article, "Who Will Have the Bomb?" in which I asked, "Does India have the bomb?"[2] India had exploded a nuclear device a couple of years earlier. I pursued the question, what do we mean by "having the bomb?" I alleged that we didn't mean, or perhaps didn't even care, whether India actually possessed in inventory a nuclear explosive device, or an actual nuclear weapon. We meant, I argued, that India "had" the potential: it had the expertise, the personnel, the laboratories and equipment to produce a weapon if it decided to. (At the time, India pretended that its only interest was in "Peaceful Nuclear Explosives" [PNEs].) I proposed an analogy: does Switzerland have an army? I answered, not really, but it could have one tomorrow if it decided today.

The answer to the relevant question about nuclear weapons must be a schedule showing how many weapons (of what yield) a government could mobilize on what time schedule.

It took the United States about five years to build two weapons. It might take India—now that it has already produced nuclear weapons—a few weeks, or less, depending on how ready it kept its personnel and supplies for mobilization. If a "world without nuclear weapons" means no mobilization bases, there can be no such world. Even starting in 1940 the mobilization base was built. And would minimizing mobilization potential serve the purpose? To answer this requires working through various scenarios involving the expectation of war, the outbreak of war, and the conduct of war. That is the kind of analysis I haven't seen.

A crucial question is whether a government could hide weapons-grade fissile material from any possible inspection-verification. Considering that enough plutonium to make a bomb could be hidden in the freezing compartment of my refrigerator, or to evade radiation detection could be hidden at the bottom of the water in a well, I think only the fear of a whistle-blower could possibly make success at all questionable. I believe that a "responsible" government would make sure that fissile material would be available in an international crisis or war itself. A responsible government must at least assume that other responsible governments will do so.

We are so used to thinking in terms of thousands, or at least hundreds, of nuclear warheads that a few dozen may offer a sense of relief. But if, at the outset of what appears to be a major war, or the imminent possibility of major war, every responsible government must consider that other responsible governments will mobilize their nuclear weapons base as soon as war erupts, or as soon as war appears likely, there will be at least covert frantic efforts, or perhaps purposely conspicuous efforts, to acquire deliverable nuclear weapons as rapidly as possible. And what then?

I see a few possibilities. One is that the first to acquire weapons will use them, as best it knows how, to disrupt its enemy's or enemies' nuclear mobilization bases, while itself continuing its frantic nuclear rearmament, along with a surrender demand backed up by its growing stockpile. Another possibility is to demand, under threat of nuclear attack, abandonment of any nuclear mobilization, with unopposed "inspectors" or "saboteurs" searching out the mobilization base of people, laboratories, fissile material stashes, or anything else threatening. A third possibility would be a "decapitation" nuclear attack along with the surrender demand. And I can think of worse. All of these, of course, would be in the interest of self-defense.

Still another strategy might, just might, be to propose a crash "rearmament agreement," by which both sides (all sides) would develop "minimum deterrent" arsenals, subject to all the inspection-verification procedures that had already been in place for "disarmament."

An interesting question is whether "former nuclear powers"—I use quotation marks because they will still be latent nuclear powers—would seek ways to make it known that, despite "disarmament," they had the potential for a rapid buildup. It has been suggested that Saddam Hussein may have wanted it believed that he had nuclear weapons, and Israel has made its nuclear capability a publicized secret. "Mutual nuclear deterrence" could take the form of letting it be known that any evidence of nuclear rearmament would be promptly reciprocated. Reciprocation could take the form of hastening to have a weapon to use against the nuclear facilities of the "enemy."

But war is what I find most worrisome. In World War II there was some fear in the U.S. nuclear weapons community that Germany might acquire a nuclear capability and use it. There is still speculation whether, if Germany had not already surrendered, one of the bombs should have been used on Berlin, with a demand that inspection teams be admitted to locate and destroy the nuclear establishment. Would a government lose a war without resorting to nuclear weapons? Would a war include a race to produce weapons capable of coercing victory?

Could a major nation maintain "conventional" forces ready for every contingency, without maintaining a nuclear backup? Just as today's intelligence agencies and their clandestine operators are devoted to discovering the location of terrorist organizations and their leaders, in a non-nuclear world the highest priority would attach to knowing the exact locations and readiness of enemy nuclear mobilization bases.

Would a political party, in the United States or anywhere else, be able to campaign for the abandonment of the zero-nuclears treaty, and what would be the response in other nations?

I hope there are favorable answers to these questions. I'm uncertain who in government or academia is working on them.

One can take the position that substantial nuclear disarmament makes sense, and that the abstract goal of a world without nuclear weapons helps motivate reduction as well as presents an appearance of fulfilling the NPT commitment. Maybe some leaders of the movement have no more than that in mind. But even as a purely intellectual enterprise the "role of deterrence in total disarmament," to use the title of an article I published 47 years ago, deserves just as thoughtful analysis as mutual nuclear deterrence ever received.[3]

In summary, a "world without nuclear weapons" would be a world in which the United States, Russia, Israel, China, and half a dozen or a dozen other countries would have hair-trigger mobilization plans to rebuild nuclear weapons and mobilize or commandeer delivery systems, and would have prepared targets to preempt other nations' nuclear facilities, all in a high-alert status, with practice drills and secure emergency communications. Every crisis would be a nuclear crisis, any war could become a nuclear war. The urge to preempt would dominate; whoever gets the first few weapons will coerce or preempt. It would be a nervous world. . . .

We have gone, as I write this, more than 63 years without any use of nuclear weapons in warfare. We have experienced, depending on how you count, some eight wars during that time in which one party to the war possessed nuclear weapons: United States vs. North Korea, United States vs. People's Republic of China, United States vs. Viet Cong, United States vs. North Vietnam, United States vs. Iraq twice, United States vs. Taliban in Afghanistan, Israel vs. Syria and Egypt, United Kingdom vs. Argentina, and USSR vs. Afghanistan. In no case was nuclear weapons introduced, probably not seriously considered.

The "taboo," to use the term of Secretary of State John Foster Dulles in 1963—he deplored the taboo—has apparently been powerful. The ability of the United States and the Soviet Union to collaborate, sometimes tacitly, sometimes explicitly, to "stabilize" mutual deterrence despite crises over Berlin and Cuba, for the entire postwar era prior to the dissolution of the USSR, would not have been countenanced by experts or strategists during the first two decades after 1945.

These are two different phenomena, the taboo and mutual deterrence. We can hope that mutual deterrence will subdue Indian–Pakistani hostility; we can hope that the taboo will continue to caution Israel, and that it will affect other possessors of nuclear weapons, either through their apprehension of the curse on nuclear weapons or their recognition of the universal abhorrence of nuclear use.[4]

There is no sign that any kind of nuclear arms race is in the offing—not, anyway, among the current nuclear powers. Prospects are good for substantial reduction of nuclear arms among the two largest arsenals, Russian and American. That should contribute to nuclear quiescence.

Concern over North Korea, Iran, or possible non-state violent entities is justified, but denuclearization of Russia, the United States, China, France, and the United Kingdom is pretty tangential to those prospects. Except for some "rogue" threats, there is little that could disturb the quiet nuclear relations among the recognized nuclear nations. This nuclear quiet should not be traded away for a world in which a brief race to reacquire nuclear weapons could become every former nuclear state's overriding preoccupation.

Questions for Review

Why does Schelling doubt that a world without nuclear weapons would be a safe one? What evidence would be relevant to assessing the conflicting claims here?

Notes

1 For exceptions, see Harold Brown and John Deutch, "The Nuclear Disarmament Fantasy," *The Wall Street Journal*, November 19, 2007, and Charles L. Glaser, "The Instability of Small Numbers Revisited," in *Rebuilding the NPT*

Consensus, ed. Michael May (Stanford, Calif.: Center for International Security and Cooperation, Stanford University, October 2008), http://iis-db.stanford.edu/pubs/22218/RebuildNPTConsensus.pdf.

2 Thomas C. Schelling, "Who Will Have the Bomb?" *International Security* 1 (Summer 1976): 77–91.

3 Thomas C. Schelling, "The Role of Deterrence in Total Disarmament," *Foreign Affairs* 40 (1962): 392–406.

4 T. V. Paul, *The Tradition of the Non-Use of Nuclear Weapons* (Stanford. Calif.: Stanford University Press, 2008); Nina Tannenwald, *The Nuclear Taboo* (Cambridge: Cambridge University Press, 2007); and Thomas C. Schelling, "The Legacy of Hiroshima," in Schelling, *Strategies of Commitment and Other Essays* (Cambridge, Mass.: Harvard University Press, 2006).

Part III
International Political Economy and Globalization

 ## Learning Objectives

III.1 Discuss the two major views on the relationship of politics and economics.

III.2 Explore the international political economy, globalization and its impact on technology, innovation, services, and poverty today.

III.3 Analyze possible solutions for the problems that exist in the world political economy.

In Part I, we examined the meaning of anarchy and saw the consequences for state behavior that flowed from it. In Part II, we analyzed in more detail one of the primary instruments that states can and must use, namely, military power. In Part III, we are concerned with the other primary instrument of state action—economic power and with the economically globalized world in which we now live.

Disparities in power, as we saw earlier, have important effects on state behavior. Such disparities occur not simply because of the differences in military power that states wield, but also because of the differences in economic resources that they generate. In the first instance, the force that a nation can deploy is dependent in part on the economic wealth that it can muster to support and sustain its military forces. Wealth is therefore a component of state power. But the generation of wealth, unlike the generation of military power, is also an end of state action. Except in the rarest of circumstances, military power is never sought as an end in itself, but rather is acquired as a means to attain security or the other ends that a state pursues. By contrast, wealth is both a component of state power and a good that can be consumed by its citizenry. Force is mustered primarily for the external arena. Wealth is sought for both the external and the domestic arena. Moreover, wealth and power differ in the degree to which states can pursue each without detriment to the positions and interests of other nations. No situation in international politics is ever totally cooperative or conflictual, but the potential for cooperative behavior is greater in the realm of wealth than in the realm of power.

It is the duality of economic power (as a component of state power and an end of state action) and its greater potential for common gains that make the analysis of the role it plays in state behavior and international interactions complex and elusive. The study of international political economy, as it has been traditionally understood, encompasses both these aspects of economic power. More recently, scholars and citizens have become concerned about the costs and benefits of the globalized world that we now inhabit.

Perspectives on Political Economy

III.1 Discuss the two major views on the relationship of politics and economics.

"The science of economics presupposes a given political order, and cannot be profitably studied in isolation from politics." So wrote E. H. Carr in his seminal work, *The Twenty Years' Crisis,* in 1939. Fifty years earlier, in an essay titled "Socialism: Utopian or Scientific," Karl Marx's coauthor, Friedrich Engels, asserted: "The materialist conception of history starts from the proposition that the production of the means to support human life . . . is the basis of all social structure. . . . " These two views—that economic processes are not autonomous but require political structures to support them, and that economic factors determine the social and political structures of states—represent the polar extremes on the relationship of politics and economics.

Which view is correct? To this question there is no simple or single answer. Any reply is as much philosophical as it is empirical. The economic interests of individuals in a state and of states within the international arena do powerfully affect the goals that are sought and the degree of success with which they are attained. But the fundamental political structure of international action is also a constraint. Anarchy makes cooperative actions more difficult to attain than would otherwise be the case and requires that statesmen consider both relative and absolute positions when framing actions in the international economic realm. And often in international politics the imperatives of security and survival override the dictates of economic interests. War, after all, almost never pays in a strict balance-sheet sense, particularly when waged between states of roughly equal power. The economic wealth lost in fighting is usually not recouped in the peace that follows.

The best discussions of the relations between politics and economics in international affairs have been by the classical theorists of international politics. Robert Gilpin examines three schools of thought—liberalism, Marxism, and mercantilism. Unlike the other two, liberal political economists have stressed the cooperative, not the conflictual, nature of international economic relations. They have extended Adam Smith's arguments about the domestic economy to the international economy. Smith argued that the specialization of function by individuals within a state, together with their unfettered pursuit of their own self-interests, would increase the wealth of a nation and thereby benefit all. Collective harmony and national wealth could thus be the product of self-interested behavior, if only the government would provide order with as little restraint on individual action as was necessary. The eighteenth-century Philosophes and the nineteenth- and twentieth-century free traders argued that what was good for individuals within a state would also be good for states in the international arena. By trading freely with one another, states could specialize according to their respective comparative advantages and the wealth of all nations would, as a consequence, increase. "Make trade, not war" has been the slogan of the liberal free traders.

By contrast, both mercantilists and Marxists have seen state relations as inherently conflictual. For Marxists, this is so because capitalists within and among states compete fiercely with one another to maximize their profits. Driven by their greed, they are incapable of cooperating with one another. Because a state's policy is determined by the capitalist ruling class, states will wage wars for profit and, under Lenin's dictum, will wage wars to redivide the world's wealth. Imperialism as the highest stage of capitalism is a classic zero-sum situation. Mercantilists also argue that economic factors make relations among states conflictual. Their analysis, however, rests not on the externalization of class conflict, but on the nature of political and economic power. For eighteenth-century mercantilists, the world's wealth was fixed and could only be redivided. For nineteenth- and twentieth-century mercantilists, wealth could be increased for all, but because wealth contributes to national power and power is relative, not absolute, conflict would continue.

All three schools of thought are motivated by their views on the relation of politics to economics. Mercantilists stress the primacy of politics and the consequent pursuit of national power and relative position in the international arena. Both liberals and Marxists stress the primacy of economics. For the former, the potential for economic harmony can override the forces of nationalism if free trade is pursued. For the latter, economic interests determine political behavior and, because the first is conflictual, the second must be also. Both liberals and Marxists want to banish politics from international relations, the former through free trade, the latter through the universal spread of communism. Mercantilists, like realists, view these prescriptions as naïve and believe that the national interests of every state are only partly determined by their economic interests.

Another important perspective on political economy concerns the relationship between economic interdependence and war. Economic interdependence means that two states have extensive economic relations with one another, whether in the form of trade, direct investments in one another's economies, or the holding of a substantial portion of another state's debt. States that are economically interdependent with one another have an economic stake in each other's health. Take trade, for example. If two states extensively trade with one another—that is, import and export a lot to one another—then clearly each has an interest in the other doing well economically. If my economy is doing poorly, then I am able to buy fewer of your exports. If my economy is booming, I can buy more goods from you. States that are interdependent economically with one another therefore have a vested interest in the other doing well economically.

The question then becomes: What is the political effect of high levels of economic interdependence? Traditionally, there have been two views. Realists and Neorealists tend to argue that high levels of economic interdependence carry no great weight in interstate relations. Security considerations predominate and will override economic interests when security is at stake. Liberals, on the other hand, have argued that high levels of economic interdependence have pacific effects on interstate relations. The bumper sticker for Liberals is: "make trade, not war." If a state can grow economically through trade, why engage in military conquest, especially when it is quite expensive.

Dale Copeland's essay provides a resolution of this debate by offering a theory of trade expectation. States that are economically dependent on one another are more likely to choose peace if they expect future trade levels between them to be high; conversely, they are more likely to choose war if they expect future trade between them to be low. In short, between two states that experience high economic interdependence, expectations about future levels of trade govern the extent to which their relations remain peaceful or turn conflictual.

Although some liberals see free trade as an unalloyed good and believe that opposition springs only from ignorance or narrow self-interest on the part of uncompetitive sectors, Dani Rodrik points out that once barriers to trade have been reduced to a low level, which is true today, the general benefits of further reductions may be much smaller than the redistributive consequences. In other words, there is good reason to expect that additional reductions will meet with strong political opposition and may undercut domestic support for an open world economy.

Globalization Today

III.2 **Explore the international political economy, globalization and its impact on technology, innovation, services, and poverty today.**

At the beginning of the twenty-first century, which way will the international political economy go? Where should it go? Has globalization fundamentally changed the world economy and, if so, will national borders lose even more of their economic significance in the future? Will there be a protectionist backlash? Are new forms of protectionism now more important than tariffs as technology, innovation, and services become more important? Have the poor, in both the United States and abroad, suffered because of globalization? These are difficult questions to answer. How they are answered depends heavily on how economically interdependent one sees the nations of the world today.

Interdependence can be high or low. As stated earlier, many analysts believe that high levels of interdependence should facilitate cooperation among states for their mutual gain. Others argue that interdependence increases conflict by reducing autonomy, and even if this is not correct, myriad disputes are possible about how to divide the gains from high levels of economic intercourse. Interdependence can exist between pairs of countries and can be generated by important but narrow flows of goods. Globalization, as the term indicates, involves most, if not all, countries and a wide range of economic transactions. The potential loss of autonomy is broader because the nature of national economies, the abilities of states to direct their individual economic and even social policies, and the stability of governments are affected by the movement toward a truly worldwide (or global) economy.

After World War II, the United States used its considerable economic and military power to create an open international economic order by working to lower the barriers among nations to the flow of manufactured goods, raw materials other than agriculture, and capital. The result of this international economic openness was a rise in the level of globalization, particularly among the industrialized nations of the world, but also, to a considerable degree, among the industrializing nations in East Asia and Latin America. But globalization has its costs as well as its benefits. High levels of participation in the international economy can bring the benefits of efficiency that flow from specialization, but also the destruction of national industries that can no longer compete internationally. States today must reconcile the imperatives of what Gilpin has called "Keynes at home" with

"Smith abroad": maintenance of full employment domestically and competitive participation in the international economy. Through exports and capital inflows, globalization can help a state increase its wealth, but it also brings vulnerabilities that derive from the need to rely partially on others for one's own prosperity. Balancing the two imperatives is a difficult political act.

The readings in this section pick up on some of these themes and deal with the nature of globalization today. Jeffrey Frankel provides several benchmarks by which to measure the globalization and integration of the current world economy and then presents a tentative balance sheet on the economic and social effects of globalization. Moisés Naím shows that the debates can be clarified by separating the various effects that do and do not flow from globalization. It has not abolished power politics or brought peace to the world, but it has helped lift hundreds of millions out of poverty and create a booming middle class in countries like Brazil, China, and India. Finally, Erik Byrnjolfsson and his co-authors assess the role of technological change in the global economy, especially the changes brought on by the digital revolution, and show why, in their view, people who can create new ideas and innovations will prosper while both capital and cheap labor will see their relative positions suffer.

Fixing the World Political Economy

III.3 **Analyze possible solutions for the problems that exist in the world political economy.**

Politics created today's globalized world. What politics has created politics can rend asunder. Globalization should neither be taken for granted nor viewed as an irresistible force. The world financial crisis that started in 2008 has cast a new and disturbing light on globalization. Although there had been vigorous debates on the pros and cons in the preceding decades, especially in terms of the impact on the Third World, the consensus had been that the Western countries had mastered the use of economic policies to conquer both rampant inflation and persistent depression and had entered the era of the "Great Moderation." Unfortunately, we have now learned that this is incorrect. Although the post-2008 distress was deeper in some countries than in others, all of the developed economies were significantly harmed. As a result, not only did millions of individuals suffered very badly, but political conflicts within and between countries were heightened. The future of the Euro-zone is in doubt, the wisdom of close European integration is being questioned, and for many the fruits of globalization have turned rotten. Right-wing movements have grown in many European countries and frictions between countries have increased roughly in proportion to the extent to which countries depend on each other economically. The mutual recriminations between Greece and Germany are the most obvious and severe example, but the phenomenon is more general, and to be expected because economic deterioration has political consequences.

Scholars and officials of course differ in their diagnoses and their prescriptions. Clearly lax or badly designed financial regulation was part of the problem, but how much and how to remedy it remain a subject of debate both within and between countries. Eric Helleiner presents a pessimistic view of the changes made to the global financial system, argues that no major transformation of global financial governance has taken place, explains why this is so, and explores different scenarios for the future. Joseph E. Stiglitz argues that part of the problem with the global financial system today lies in the dollar's continuing role as the world's reserve currency, and suggests creating a new global reserve system that will supplant the dollar's role and will go part of the way to fixing the global financial architecture. Dani Rodrik calls for "a sane globalization" that would preserve the benefits of a global division of labor by generating the public support that is necessary to sustain widespread openness to trade and investment from abroad. To do this, the "rules of the game" will have to provide a significant role for national regulation, especially in the financial area, permit a more international labor market with significantly higher levels of regulated migration, and negotiate an accommodation with China.

Part III Question for Review

Which of the following do you conclude from the readings in Part 3: (1) political factors dominate economic factors; (2) economic factors dominate political factors; (3) neither of the first two is the case because there are interactive effects between economic and political factors? Give the reasons why you believe which one of these three positions is closest to the truth.

Chapter 8

Perspectives on Political Economy

The Nature of Political Economy

ROBERT GILPIN

> The international corporations have evidently declared ideological war on the "antiquated" nation state. . . . The charge that materialism, modernization and internationalism is the new liberal creed of corporate capitalism is a valid one. The implication is clear: The nation state as a political unit of democratic decision-making must, in the interest of "progress," yield control to the new mercantile mini-powers.[1]

> While the structure of the multinational corporation is a modern concept, designed to meet the requirements of a modern age, the nation state is a very old-fashioned idea and badly adapted to serve the needs of our present complex world.[2]

These two statements—the first by Kari Levitt, a Canadian nationalist, the second by George Ball, a former United States undersecretary of state—express a dominant theme of contemporary writings on international relations. International society, we are told, is increasingly rent between its economic and its political organization. On the one hand, powerful economic and technological forces are creating a highly interdependent world economy, thus diminishing the traditional significance of national boundaries. On the other hand, the nation-state continues to command men's loyalties and to be the basic unit of political decision making. As one writer has put the issue, "The conflict of our era is between ethnocentric nationalism and geocentric technology."[3]

Ball and Levitt represent two contending positions with respect to this conflict. Whereas Ball advocates the diminution of the power of the nation-state in order to give full rein to the productive potentialities of the multinational corporation, Levitt argues for a powerful nationalism which could counterbalance American corporate domination. What appears to one as the logical and desirable consequence of economic rationality seems to the other to be an effort on the part of American imperialism to eliminate all contending centers of power.

Although the advent of the multinational corporation has put the question of the relationship between economics and politics in a new guise, it is an old issue. In the nineteenth century, for example, it was this issue that divided classical liberals like John Stuart Mill from economic nationalists, represented by Georg Friedrich List. Whereas the former gave primacy in the organization of society to economics and the production of wealth, the latter emphasized the political determination of economic relations. As this issue is central both to the contemporary debate on the multinational corporation and to the argument of this study, this chapter analyzes the three major treatments of the relationship between economics and politics—that is, the three major ideologies of political economy.

The Meaning of Political Economy

The argument of this study is that the relationship between economics and politics, at least in the modern world, is a reciprocal one. On the one hand, politics largely determines the framework of economic activity and channels it in directions intended to serve the interests of dominant groups; the exercise of power in all its forms is a major determinant of the nature of an economic system. On the other hand, the economic process itself tends to redistribute power and wealth; it transforms the power relationships among groups. This in turn leads to a transformation of the political system, thereby giving rise to a new structure of economic relationships. Thus, the dynamics of international relations in the modern world is largely a function of the reciprocal interaction between economics and politics.

First of all, what do I mean by "politics" or "economics"? Charles Kindleberger speaks of economics and politics as two different methods of allocating scarce resources: the first through a market mechanism, the latter through a budget.[4] Robert O. Keohane and Joseph Nye, in an excellent analysis of international political economy, define economics and politics in terms of two levels of analysis: those of structure and of process.[5] Politics is the domain "having to do with the establishment of an order of relations, a structure. . . . "[6] Economics deals with "short-term allocative behavior (i.e., holding institutions, fundamental assumptions, and expectations constant). . . . "[7] Like Kindleberger's definition, however, this definition tends to isolate economic and political phenomena except under certain conditions, which Keohane and Nye define as the "politicization" of the economic system. Neither formulation comes to terms adequately with the dynamic and intimate nature of the relationship between the two.

In this study, the issue of the relationship between economics and politics translates into that between wealth and power. According to this statement of the problem, economics takes as its province the creation and distribution of wealth; politics is the realm of power. I shall examine their relationship from several ideological perspectives, including my own. But what is wealth? What is power?

In response to the question, What is wealth?, an economist-colleague responded, "What do you want, my thirty-second or thirty-volume answer?" Basic concepts are elusive in economics, as in any field of inquiry. No unchallengeable definitions are possible. Ask a physicist for his definition of the nature of space, time, and matter, and you will not get a very satisfying response. What you will get is an *operational* definition, one which is usable: It permits the physicist to build an intellectual edifice whose foundations would crumble under the scrutiny of the philosopher.

Similarly, the concept of wealth, upon which the science of economics ultimately rests, cannot be clarified in a definitive way. Paul Samuelson, in his textbook, doesn't even try, though he provides a clue in his definition of economics as "the study of how men and society *choose* . . . to employ *scarce* productive resources . . . to produce various commodities . . . and distribute them for consumption."[8] Following this lead, we can say that wealth is anything (capital, land, or labor) that can generate future income; it is composed of physical assets and human capital (including embodied knowledge).

The basic concept of political science is power. Most political scientists would not stop here; they would include in the definition of political science the purpose for which power is used, whether this be the advancement of the public welfare or the domination of one group over another. In any case, few would dissent from the following statement of Harold Lasswell and Abraham Kaplan:

> The concept of power is perhaps the most fundamental in the whole of political science: The political process is the shaping, distribution, and exercise of power (in a wider sense, of all the deference values, or of influence in general).[9]

Power as such is not the sole or even the principal goal of state behavior. Other goals or values constitute the objectives pursued by nation-states: welfare, security, prestige. But power in its several forms (military, economic, psychological) is ultimately the necessary means to achieve these goals. For this reason, nation-states are intensely jealous of, and sensitive to, their relative power position. The distribution of power is important because it profoundly affects the ability of states to achieve what they perceive to be their interests.

The nature of power, however, is even more elusive than that of wealth. The number and variety of definitions should be an embarrassment to political scientists. Unfortunately, this study cannot bring the intradisciplinary squabble to an end. Rather, it adopts the definition used by Hans J. Morgenthau in his influential *Politics Among Nations:* "man's control over the minds and actions of other men."[10] Thus, power, like wealth, is the capacity to produce certain results.

Unlike wealth, however, power cannot be quantified; indeed, it cannot be overemphasized that power has an important psychological dimension. Perceptions of power relations are of critical importance; as a consequence, a fundamental task of statesmen is to manipulate the perceptions of other statesmen regarding the distribution of power. Moreover, power is relative to a specific situation or set of circumstances; there is no single hierarchy of power in international relations. Power may take many forms—military, economic, or psychological—though, in the final analysis, force is the ultimate form of power. Finally, the inability to predict the behavior of others or the outcome of events is of great significance. Uncertainty regarding the distribution of power and the ability of the statesmen to control events plays an important role in international relations. Ultimately, the determination of the distribution of power can be made only in retrospect as a consequence of war. It is precisely for this reason that war has had, unfortunately, such a central place in the history of international relations. In short, power is an elusive concept indeed upon which to erect a science of politics.

Such mutually exclusive definitions of economics and politics as these run counter to much contemporary scholarship by both economists and political scientists, for both disciplines are invading the formerly exclusive jurisdictions of the other. Economists, in particular, have become intellectual imperialists; they are applying their analytical techniques to traditional issues of political science with great success. These developments, however, really reinforce the basic premise of this study, namely, the inseparability of economics and politics.

The distinction drawn above between economics as the science of wealth and politics as the science of power is essentially an analytical one. In the real world, wealth and power are ultimately joined. This, in fact, is the basic rationale for a political economy of international relations. But in order to develop the argument of this study, wealth and power will be treated, at least for the moment, as analytically distinct.

To provide a perspective on the nature of political economy, the next section will discuss the three prevailing conceptions of political economy: liberalism, Marxism, and mercantilism. Liberalism regards politics and economics as relatively separable and autonomous spheres of activities; I associate most professional economists as well as many other academics, businessmen, and American officials with this outlook. Marxism refers to the radical critique of capitalism identified with Karl Marx and his contemporary disciples; according to this conception, economics determines politics and political structure. Mercantilism is a more questionable term because of its historical association with the desire of nation-states for a trade surplus and for treasure (money). One must distinguish, however, between the specific form mercantilism took in the seventeenth and eighteenth centuries and the general outlook of mercantilistic thought. The essence of the mercantilistic perspective, whether it is labeled economic nationalism, protectionism, or the doctrine of the German Historical School, is the subservience of economy to the state and its interests—interests that range from matters of domestic welfare to those of international security. It is this more general meaning of mercantilism that is implied by the use of the term in this study.

Following the discussion of these three schools of thought, I shall elaborate my own, more eclectic, view of political economy and demonstrate its relevance for understanding the phenomenon of the multinational corporation.

Three Conceptions of Political Economy

The three prevailing conceptions of political economy differ on many points. Several critical differences will be examined in this brief comparison. (See Table 1.)

Table 1 Comparison of the Three Conceptions of Political Economy

	Liberalism	**Marxism**	**Mercantilism**
Nature of economic relations	Harmonious	Conflictual	Conflictual
Nature of the actors	Households and firms	Economic classes	Nation-states
Goal of economic activity	Maximization of global welfare	Maximization of class interests	Maximization of national interest
Relationship between economics and politics	Economics should determine politics	Economics does determine politics	Politics determines economics
Theory of change	Dynamic equilibrium	Tendency toward disequilibrium	Shifts in the distribution of power

The Nature of Economic Relations

The basic assumption of liberalism is that the nature of international economic relations is essentially harmonious. Herein lay the great intellectual innovation of Adam Smith. Disputing his mercantilist predecessors, Smith argued that international economic relations could be made a positive-sum game; that is to say, everyone could gain, and no one need lose, from a proper ordering of economic relations, albeit the distribution of these gains may not be equal. Following Smith, liberalism assumes that there is a basic harmony between true national interest and cosmopolitan economic interest. Thus, a prominent member of this school of thought has written, in response to a radical critique, that the economic efficiency of the sterling standard in the nineteenth century and that of the dollar standard in the twentieth century serve "the cosmopolitan interest in a national form."[11] Although Great Britain and the United States gained the most from the international role of their respective currencies, everyone else gained as well.

Liberals argue that, given this underlying identity of national and cosmopolitan interests in a free market, the state should not interfere with economic transactions across national boundaries. Through free exchange of commodities, removal of restrictions on the flow of investment, and an international division of labor, everyone will benefit in the long run as a result of a more efficient utilization of the world's scarce resources. The national interest is therefore best served, liberals maintain, by a generous and cooperative attitude regarding economic relations with other countries. In essence, the pursuit of self-interest in a free, competitive economy achieves the greatest good for the greatest number in international no less than in the national society.

Both mercantilists and Marxists, on the other hand, begin with the premise that the essence of economic relations is conflictual. There is no underlying harmony; indeed, one group's gain is another's loss. Thus, in the language of game theory, whereas liberals regard economic relations as a non-zero-sum game, Marxists and mercantilists view economic relations as essentially a zero-sum game.

The Goal of Economic Activity

For the liberal, the goal of economic activity is the optimum or efficient use of the world's scarce resources and the maximization of world welfare. While most liberals refuse to make value judgments regarding income distribution, Marxists and mercantilists stress the distributive effects of economic relations. For the Marxist the distribution of wealth among social classes is central; for the mercantilist it is the distribution of employment, industry, and military power among nation-states that is most significant. Thus, the goal of economic (and political) activity for both Marxists and mercantilists is the redistribution of wealth and power.

The State and Public Policy

These three perspectives differ decisively in their view regarding the nature of the economic actors. In Marxist analysis, the basic actors in both domestic and international relations are economic classes; the interests of the dominant class determine the foreign policy of the state. For mercantilists, the real actors in international economic relations are nation-states; national interest determines foreign policy. National interest may at times be influenced by the peculiar economic interests of classes, elites, or other subgroups of the society; but factors of geography, external configurations of power, and the exigencies of national survival are primary in determining foreign policy. Thus, whereas liberals speak of world welfare and Marxists of class interests, mercantilists recognize only the interests of particular nation-states.

Although liberal economists such as David Ricardo and Joseph Schumpeter recognized the importance of class conflict and neoclassical liberals analyze economic growth and policy in terms of national economies, the liberal emphasis is on the individual consumer, firm, or entrepreneur. The liberal ideal is summarized in the view of Harry Johnson that the nation-state has no meaning as an economic entity.[12]

Underlying these contrasting views are differing conceptions of the nature of the state and public policy. For liberals, the state represents an aggregation of private interests: public policy is but the outcome of a pluralistic struggle among interest groups. Marxists, on the other hand, regard the state as simply the "executive committee of the ruling class," and public policy reflects its interests. Mercantilists, however, regard the state as an organic unit in its own right: the whole is greater than the sum of its parts. Public policy, therefore, embodies the national interest or Rousseau's "general will" as conceived by the political elite.

The Relationship between Economics and Politics: Theories of Change

Liberalism, Marxism, and mercantilism also have differing views on the relationship between economics and politics. And their differences on this issue are directly relevant to their contrasting theories of international political change.

Although the liberal ideal is the separation of economics from politics in the interest of maximizing world welfare, the fulfillment of this ideal would have important political implications. The classical statement of these implications was that of Adam Smith in *The Wealth of Nations*.[13] Economic growth, Smith argued, is primarily a function of the extent of the division of labor, which in turn is dependent upon the scale of the market. Thus he attacked the barriers erected by feudal principalities and mercantilistic states against the exchange of goods and the enlargement of markets. If men were to multiply their wealth, Smith argued, the contradiction between political organization and economic rationality had to be resolved in favor of the latter. That is, the pursuit of wealth should determine the nature of the political order.

Subsequently, from nineteenth-century economic liberals to twentieth-century writers on economic integration, there has existed "the dream . . . of a great republic of world commerce, in which national boundaries would cease to have any great economic importance and the web of trade would bind all the people of the world in the prosperity of peace."[14] For liberals the long-term trend is toward world integration, wherein functions, authority, and loyalties will be transferred from "smaller units to larger ones; from states to federalism; from federalism to supranational unions and from these to superstates."[15] The logic of economic and technological development, it is argued, has set mankind on an inexorable course toward global political unification and world peace.

In Marxism, the concept of the contradiction between economic and political relations was enacted into historical law. Whereas classical liberals—although Smith less than others—held that the requirements of economic rationality *ought* to determine political relations, the Marxist position was that the mode of production does in fact determine the superstructure of political relations. Therefore, it is argued, history can be understood as the product of the dialectical process—the contradiction between the evolving techniques of production and the resistant sociopolitical system.

Although Marx and Engels wrote remarkably little on international economics, Engels, in his famous polemic, *Anti-Duhring*, explicitly considers whether economics or politics is primary in determining the structure of international relations.[16] E. K. Duhring, a minor figure in the German Historical School, had argued, in contradiction to Marxism, that property and market relations resulted less from the economic logic of capitalism than from extraeconomic political factors: "The basis of the exploitation of many by man was an historical act of force which created an exploitative economic system for the benefit of the stronger man or class."[17] Since Engels, in his attack on Duhring, used the example of the unification of Germany through the Zollverein or customs union of 1833, his analysis is directly relevant to this discussion of the relationship between economics and political organization.

Engels argued that when contradictions arise between economic and political structures, political power adapts itself to the changes in the balance of economic forces; politics yields to the dictates of economic development. Thus, in the case of nineteenth-century Germany, the requirements of industrial production had become incompatible with its feudal, politically fragmented structure. "Though political reaction was victorious in 1815 and again in 1848," he argued, "it was unable to prevent the growth of large-scale industry in Germany and the growing participation of German commerce in the world market."[18] In summary, Engels wrote, "German unity had become an economic necessity."[19]

In the view of both Smith and Engels, the nation-state represented a progressive stage in human development, because it enlarged the political realm of economic activity. In each successive economic epoch, advances in technology and an increasing scale of production necessitate an enlargement of political organization. Because the city-state and feudalism restricted the scale of production and the division of labor made possible by the Industrial Revolution, they prevented the efficient utilization of resources and were, therefore, superseded by larger political units. Smith considered this to be a desirable objective; for Engels it was an historical necessity. Thus, in the opinion of liberals, the establishment of the Zollverein was a movement toward maximizing world economic welfare;[20] for Marxists it was the unavoidable triumph of the German industrialists over the feudal aristocracy.

Mercantilist writers from Alexander Hamilton to Frederich List to Charles de Gaulle, on the other hand, have emphasized the primacy of politics; politics, in this view, determines economic organization. Whereas Marxists and liberals have pointed to the production of wealth as the basic determinant of social and political organization, the mercantilists of the German Historical School, for example, stressed the primacy of national security, industrial development, and national sentiment in international political and economic dynamics.

In response to Engels's interpretation of the unification of Germany, mercantilists would no doubt agree with Jacob Viner that "Prussia engineered the customs union primarily for political reasons, in order to gain hegemony or at least influence over the lesser German states. It was largely in order to make certain that the hegemony should be Prussian and not Austrian that Prussia continually opposed Austrian entry into the Union, either openly or by pressing for a customs union tariff lower than highly protectionist Austria could stomach."[21] In pursuit of this strategic interest, it was "Prussian might, rather than a common zeal for political unification arising out of economic partnership, [that] . . . played the major role."[22]

In contrast to Marxism, neither liberalism nor mercantilism has a developed theory of dynamics. The basic assumption of orthodox economic analysis (liberalism) is the tendency toward equilibrium; liberalism takes for granted the existing social order and given institutions. Change is assumed to be gradual and adaptive—a continuous process of dynamic equilibrium. There is no necessary connection between such political phenomena as war and revolution and the evolution of the economic system, although they would not deny that misguided statesmen can blunder into war over economic issues or that revolutions are conflicts over the distribution of wealth; but neither is inevitably linked to the evolution of the productive system. As for mercantilism, it sees change as taking place owing to shifts in the balance of power; yet, mercantilist writers such as members of the German Historical School and contemporary political realists have not developed a systematic theory of how this shift occurs.

On the other hand, dynamics is central to Marxism; indeed Marxism is essentially a theory of social *change.* It emphasizes the tendency toward *dis*equilibrium owing to changes in the means of production and the consequent effects on the ever-present class conflict. When these tendencies can no longer be contained, the sociopolitical system breaks down through violent upheaval. Thus war and revolution are seen as an integral part of the economic process. Politics and economics are intimately joined.

Why an International Economy?

From these differences among the three ideologies, one can get a sense of their respective explanations for the existence and functioning of the international economy.

An interdependent world economy constitutes the normal state of affairs for most liberal economists. Responding to technological advances in transportation and communications, the scope of the market mechanism, according to this analysis, continuously expands. Thus, despite temporary setbacks, the long-term trend is toward global economic integration. The functioning of the international economy is determined primarily by considerations of efficiency. The role of the dollar as the basis of the international monetary system, for example, is explained by the preference for it among traders and nations as the vehicle of international commerce.[23] The system is maintained by the mutuality of the benefits provided by trade, monetary arrangements, and investment.

A second view—one shared by Marxists and mercantilists alike—is that every interdependent international economy is essentially an imperial or hierarchical system. The imperial or hegemonic power organizes trade, monetary, and investment relations in order to advance its own economic and political interests. In the absence of the economic and especially the political influence of the hegemonic power, the system would fragment into autarkic economies or regional blocs. Whereas for liberalism maintenance of harmonious international market relations is the norm, for Marxism and mercantilism conflicts of class or national interests are the norm.

Perspective of the Author

My own perspective on political economy rests on what I regard as a fundamental difference in emphasis between economics and politics; namely, the distinction between absolute and relative gains. The emphasis of economic science—or, at least, of liberal economics—is on *absolute* gains; the ultimate defense of liberalism is that over the long run everyone gains, albeit in varying degrees, from a liberal economic regime. Economics, according to this formulation, need not be a zero-sum game. Everyone can gain in wealth through a more efficient division of labor; moreover, everyone can lose, in absolute terms, from economic inefficiency. Herein lies the strength of liberalism.

This economic emphasis on absolute gains is, in fact, embodied in what one can characterize as the ultimate ideal of liberal economics: the achievement of a "Pareto optimum" world. Such a properly ordered world would be one wherein "by improving the position of one individual (by adding to his possessions) no one else's position is deteriorated." As Oskar Morgenstern has observed, "[e]conomic literature is replete with the use of the Pareto optimum thus formulated or in equivalent language."[24] It is a world freed from "interpersonal comparisons of utility," and thus a world freed from what is central to politics, i.e., ethical judgment and conflict regarding the just and relative distribution of utility. That the notion of a Pareto optimum is rife with conceptual problems and is utopian does not detract from its centrality as the implicit objective of liberal economics. And this emphasis of economics on absolute gains for all differs fundamentally from the nature of political phenomena as studied by political scientists: viz., struggles for power as a goal itself or as a means to the achievement of other goals.

The essential fact of politics is that power is always relative; one state's gain in power is by necessity another's loss. Thus, even though two states may be gaining absolutely in wealth, in political terms it is the effect of these gains on relative power positions which is of primary importance. From this *political* perspective, therefore, the mercantilists are correct in emphasizing that in power terms, international relations is a zero-sum game.

In a brilliant analysis of international politics, the relativity of power and its profound implications were set forth by Jean-Jacques Rousseau:

> The state, being an artificial body is not limited in any way. . . . It can always increase; it always feels itself weak if there is another that is stronger. Its security and preservation demand that it make itself more powerful than its neighbors. It can increase, nourish and exercise its power only at their expense . . . while the inequality of man has natural limits that between societies can grow without cease, until one absorbs all the others. . . . Because the grandeur of the state is purely relative it is forced to compare itself with that of the others. . . . It is in vain that it wishes to keep itself to itself; it becomes small or great, weak or strong, according to whether its neighbor expands or contracts, becomes stronger or declines. . . .
>
> The chief thing I notice is a patent contradiction in the condition of the human race. . . . Between man and man we live in the condition of the civil state, subjected to laws; between people and people we enjoy natural liberty, which makes the situation worse. Living at the same time in the social order and in the state of nature, we suffer from the inconveniences of both without finding . . . security in either. . . . We see men united by artificial bonds, but united to destroy each other; and all the horrors of war take birth from the precautions they have taken in order to prevent

them. . . . War is born of peace, or at least of the precautions which men have taken for the purpose of achieving durable peace.[25]

Because of the relativity of power, therefore, nation-states are engaged in a never-ending struggle to improve or preserve their relative power positions.

This rather stark formulation obviously draws too sharp a distinction between economics and politics. Certainly, for example, liberal economists may be interested in questions of distribution; the distributive issue was, in fact, of central concern to Ricardo and other classical writers. However, when economists stop taking the system for granted and start asking questions about distribution, they have really ventured into what I regard as the essence of politics, for distribution is really a political issue. In a world in which power rests on wealth, changes in the relative distribution of wealth imply changes in the distribution of power and in the political system itself. This, in fact, is what is meant by saying that politics is about relative gains. Politics concerns the efforts of groups to redistribute gains to their own advantage.

Similarly, to argue that politics is about relative gains is not to argue that it is a constant-sum game. On the contrary, man's power over nature and his fellow man has grown immensely in absolute terms over the past several centuries. It is certainly the case that everyone's absolute capabilities can increase due to the development of new weaponry, the expansion of productive capabilities, or changes in the political system itself. Obviously such absolute increases in power are important politically. Who can deny, for example, that the advent of nuclear weapons has profoundly altered international politics? Obviously, too, states can negotiate disarmament and other levels of military capability.

Yet recognition of these facts does not alter the prime consideration that changes in the relative distribution of power are of fundamental significance politically. Though all may be gaining or declining in absolute capability, what will concern states principally are the effects of these absolute gains or losses on relative positions. How, for example, do changes in productive capacity or military weaponry affect the ability of one state to impose its will on another? It may very well be that in a particular situation absolute gains will not affect relative positions. But the efforts of groups to cause or prevent such shifts in the relative distribution of power constitute the critical issue of politics.

This formulation of the nature of politics obviously does not deny that nations may cooperate in order to advance their mutual interest. But even cooperative actions may have important consequences for the distribution of power in the system. For example, the Strategic Arms Limitation Talks (SALT) between the United States and the Soviet Union are obviously motivated by a common interest in preventing thermonuclear war. Other states will also benefit if the risk of war between the superpowers is reduced. Yet, SALT may also be seen as an attempt to stabilize the international distribution of power to the disadvantage of China and other third powers. In short, in terms of the system as a whole, political cooperation can have a profound effect on the relative distribution of power among nation-states.

The point may perhaps be clarified by distinguishing between two aspects of power. When one speaks of absolute gains in power, such as advances in economic capabilities or weapons development, one is referring principally to increases in physical or material capabilities. But while such capabilities are an important component of power, power, as we have seen, is more than physical capability. Power is also a psychological relationship: Who can influence whom to do what? From this perspective, what may be of most importance is how changes in capability affect this psychological relationship. Insofar as they do, they alter the relative distribution of power in the system.

In a world in which power rests increasingly on economic and industrial capabilities, one cannot really distinguish between wealth (resources, treasure, and industry) and power as national goals. In the short run there may be conflicts between the pursuit of power and the pursuit of wealth; in the long run the two pursuits are identical. Therefore, the position taken in this study is similar to Viner's interpretation of classical mercantilism:

> What then is the correct interpretation of mercantilist doctrine and practice with respect to the roles of power and plenty as ends of national policy? I believe that practically all mercantilists, whatever the period, country, or status of the particular individual, would have subscribed to all of the following propositions: (1) wealth is an absolutely essential means to power, whether for security or for aggression; (2) power is essential or valuable as a means to the acquisition or retention of wealth; (3) wealth and power are each proper ultimate ends of national policy; (4) there is long-run harmony between these ends, although in particular circumstances it may be necessary for a time to make economic sacrifices in the interest of military security and therefore also of long-run prosperity.[26]

This interpretation of the role of the economic motive in international relations is substantially different from that of Marxism. In the Marxist framework of analysis, the economic factor is reduced to the profit motive, as it affects the behavior of individuals or firms. Accordingly, the foreign policies of capitalist states are determined by the desire of capitalists for profits. This is, in our view, far too narrow a conception of the economic aspect of international relations. Instead, in this study we label "economic" those sources of wealth upon which national power and domestic welfare are dependent.

Understood in these broader terms, the economic motive and economic activities are fundamental to the struggle for power among nation-states. The objects of contention in the struggles of the balance of power include the centers of economic power. As R. G. Hawtrey has expressed it, "the political motives at work can only be expressed in terms of the economic. Every conflict is one of power and power depends on resources."[27] In pursuit of wealth *and* power, therefore, nations (capitalist, socialist, or fascist) contend over the territorial division and exploitation of the globe.

Even at the level of peaceful economic intercourse, one cannot separate out the political element. Contrary to the attitude of liberalism, international economic

relations are in reality political relations. The interdependence of national economies creates economic power, defined as the capacity of one state to damage
another through the interruption of commercial and financial relations.[28] The
attempts to create and to escape from such dependency relationships constitute
an important aspect of international relations in the modern era.

The primary actors in the international system are nation-states in pursuit
of what they define as their national interest. This is not to argue, however, that
nation-states are the only actors, nor do I believe that the "national interest" is
something akin to Rousseau's "general will"—the expression of an organic entity
separable from its component parts. Except in the abstract models of political
scientists, it has never been the case that the international system was composed
solely of nation-states. In an exaggerated acknowledgment of the importance of
nonstate or transnational actors at an earlier time, John A. Hobson asked rhe-
torically whether "a great war could be undertaken by any European state, or
a great state loan subscribed, if the House of Rothschild and its connexions set
their face against it."[29] What has to be explained, however, are the economic and
political circumstances that enable such transnational actors to play their semi-
independent role in international affairs. The argument of this study is that the
primary determinants of the role played by these non-state actors are the larger
configurations of power among nation-states. What is determinant is the interplay
of national interests.

As for the concept of "national interest," the national interest of a given
nation-state is, of course, what its political and economic elite determines it to
be. In part, as Marxists argue, this elite will define it in terms of its own group or
class interests. But the national interest comprehends more than this. More general
influences, such as cultural values and considerations relevant to the security of
the state itself—geographical position, the evolution of military technology, and
the international distribution of power—are of greater importance. There is a
sense, then, in which the factors that determine the national interest are objective. A ruling elite that fails to take these factors into account does so at its peril.
In short, then, there is a basis for considering the nation-state itself as an actor
pursuing its own set of security, welfare, and status concerns in competition or
cooperation with other nation-states.

Lastly, in a world of conflicting nation-states, how does one explain the
existence of an interdependent international economy? Why does a liberal international economy—that is, an economy characterized by relatively free trade, currency convertibility, and freedom of capital movement—remain intact rather than
fragment into autarkic national economies and regional or imperial groupings?
In part, the answer is provided by liberalism: economic cooperation, interdependence, and an international division of labor enhance efficiency and the maximization of aggregate wealth. Nation-states are induced to enter the international
system because of the promise of more rapid growth; greater benefits can be had
than could be obtained by autarky or a fragmentation of the world economy.
The historical record suggests, however, that the existence of mutual economic

benefits is not always enough to induce nations to pay the costs of a market system or to forgo opportunities of advancing their own interests at the expense of others. There is always the danger that a nation may pursue certain short-range policies, such as the imposition of an optimum tariff, in order to maximize its own gains at the expense of the system as a whole.

For this reason, a liberal international economy requires a power to manage and stabilize the system. As Charles Kindleberger has convincingly shown, this governance role was performed by Great Britain throughout the nineteenth century and up to 1931, and by the United States after 1945.[30] The inability of Great Britain in 1929 to continue running the system and the unwillingness of the United States to assume this responsibility led to the collapse of the system in the "Great Depression." The result was the fragmentation of the world economy into rival economic blocs. Both dominant economic powers had failed to overcome the divisive forces of nationalism and regionalism.

The argument of this study is that the modern world economy has evolved through the emergence of great national economies that have successively become dominant. In the words of the distinguished French economist François Perroux, "the economic evolution of the world has resulted from a succession of dominant economies, each in turn taking the lead in international activity and influence. . . . Throughout the nineteenth century the British economy was the dominant economy in the world. From the [eighteen] seventies on, Germany was dominant in respect to certain other Continental countries and in certain specified fields. In the twentieth century, the United States economy has clearly been and still is the internationally dominant economy."[31]

An economic system, then, does not arise spontaneously owing to the operation of an invisible hand and in the absence of the exercise of power. Rather, every economic system rests on a particular political order; its nature cannot be understood aside from politics. This basic point was made some years ago by E. H. Carr when he wrote that "the science of economics presupposes a given political order, and cannot be profitably studied in isolation from politics."[32] Carr sought to convince his fellow Englishmen that an international economy based on free trade was not a natural and inevitable state of affairs but rather one that reflected the economic and political interests of Great Britain. The system based on free trade had come into existence through, and was maintained by, the exercise of British economic and military power. With the rise after 1880 of new industrial and military powers with contrasting economic interests—namely, Germany, Japan, and the United States—an international economy based on free trade and British power became less and less viable. Eventually this shift in the locus of industrial and military power led to the collapse of the system in World War I. Following the interwar period, a liberal international economy was revived through the exercise of power by the world's newly emergent dominant economy—the United States.

Accordingly, the regime of free investment and the preeminence of the multinational corporation in the contemporary world have reflected the economic and political interests of the United States. The multinational corporation has prospered because it has been dependent on the power of, and consistent with the political interests of, the United States. This is not to deny the analyses of economists who argue that the multinational corporation is a response to contemporary technological and economic developments. The argument is rather that these economic and technological factors have been able to exercise their profound effects because the United States—sometimes with the cooperation of other states and sometimes over their opposition—has created the necessary political framework. As former Secretary of the Treasury Henry Fowler stated several years ago, "it is . . . impossible to overestimate the extent to which the efforts and opportunities for American firms abroad depend upon the vast presence and influence and prestige that America holds in the world."[33]

By the mid-1970s, however, the international distribution of power and the world economy resting on it were far different from what they had been when Fowler's words were spoken. The rise of foreign economic competitors, America's growing dependence upon foreign sources of energy and other resources, and the expansion of Soviet military capabilities have greatly diminished America's presence and influence in the world. One must ask if, as a consequence, the reign of the American multinationals over international economic affairs will continue into the future.

In summary, although nation-states, as mercantilists suggest, do seek to control economic and technological forces and channel them to their own advantage, this is impossible over the long run. The spread of economic growth and industrialization cannot be prevented. In time the diffusion of industry and technology undermines the position of the dominant power. As both liberals and Marxists have emphasized, the evolution of economic relations profoundly influences the nature of the international political system. The relationship between economics and politics is a reciprocal one.

Although economic and accompanying political change may well be inevitable, it is not inevitable that the process of economic development and technological advance will produce an increasingly integrated world society. In the 1930s, Eugene Staley posed the issue:

> A conflict rages between technology and politics. Economics, so closely linked to both, has become the major battlefield. Stability and peace will reign in the world economy only when, somehow, the forces on the side of technology and the forces on the side of politics have once more become accommodated to each other.[34]

Staley believed, as do many present-day writers, that politics and technology must ultimately adjust to one another. But he differed with contemporary writers with regard to the inevitability with which politics would adjust to technology. Reflecting the intense economic nationalism of the period in which he wrote, Staley pointed out that the adjustment may very well be the other way around. As he reminds us, in his own time and in earlier periods economics has had to adjust to political realities: "In the 'Dark Ages' following the collapse of the Roman

Empire, technology adjusted itself to politics. The magnificent Roman roads fell into disrepair, the baths and aqueducts and amphitheatres and villas into ruins. Society lapsed back to localism in production and distribution, forgot much of the learning and the technology and the governmental systems of earlier days."[35]

Conclusion

The purpose of this chapter has been to set forth the analytical framework that will be employed in this study. This framework is a statement of what I mean by "political economy." In its eclecticism it has drawn upon, while differing from, the three prevailing perspectives of political economy. It has incorporated their respective strengths and has attempted to overcome their weaknesses. In brief, political economy in this study means the reciprocal and dynamic interaction in international relations of the pursuit of wealth and the pursuit of power. In the short run, the distribution of power and the nature of the political system are major determinants of the framework within which wealth is produced and distributed. In the long run, however, shifts in economic efficiency and in the location of economic activity tend to undermine and transform the existing political system. This political transformation in turn gives rise to changes in economic relations that reflect the interests of the politically ascendant state in the system.

Questions for Review

How do Gilpin's preconceptions of political economy track with other schools of thought about international politics in general? Do you agree with Gilpin's argument that the fundamental difference between economics and politics lies in the fact that the former stresses absolute gains whereas and the latter stresses relative gains?

Notes

1 Kari Levitt, "The Hinterland Economy," *Canadian Forum* 50 (July–August 1970): p. 163.

2 George W. Ball, "The Promise of the Multinational Corporation," *Fortune*, June 1, 1967, p. 80.

3 Sidney Rolfe, "Updating Adam Smith," *Interplay* (November 1968): p. 15.

4 Charles Kindleberger, *Power and Money: The Economics of International Politics and the Politics of International Economics* (New York: Basic Books, 1970), p. 5.

5 Robert Keohane and Joseph Nye, "World Politics and the International Economic System," in C. Fred Bergsten, ed., *The Future of the International Economic Order: An Agenda for Research* (Lexington, Mass.: D.C. Heath, 1973), p. 116.

6 Ibid.

7 Ibid., p. 117.

 8 Paul Samuelson, *Economics: An Introductory Analysis* (New York: McGraw-Hill, 1967), p. 5.

 9 Harold Lasswell and Abraham Kaplan, *Power and Society: A Framework for Political Inquiry* (New Haven, Conn.: Yale University Press, 1950), p. 75.

10 Hans Morgenthau, *Politics Among Nations* (New York: Alfred A. Knopf), p. 26. For a more complex but essentially identical view, see Robert Dahl, *Modern Political Analysis* (Englewood Cliffs, N.J.: Prentice-Hall, 1963).

11 Kindleberger, *Power and Money*, p. 227.

12 For Johnson's critique of economic nationalism, see Harry Johnson, ed., *Economic Nationalism in Old and New States* (Chicago: University of Chicago Press, 1967).

13 Adam Smith, *The Wealth of Nations* (New York: Modern Library, 1937).

14 J. B. Condliffe, *The Commerce of Nations* (New York: W. W. Norton, 1950), p. 136.

15 Amitai Etzioni, "The Dialectics of Supernational Unification" in *International Political Communities* (New York: Doubleday, 1966), p. 147.

16 The relevant sections appear in Ernst Wangerman, ed., *The Role of Force in History: A Study of Bismarck's Policy of Blood and Iron,* trans. Jack Cohen (New York: International Publishers, 1968).

17 Ibid., p. 12.

18 Ibid., p. 13.

19 Ibid., p. 14.

20 Gustav Stopler, *The German Economy* (New York: Harcourt, Brace and World, 1967), p. 11.

21 Jacob Viner, *The Customs Union Issue,* Studies in the Administration of International Law and Organization, No. 10 (New York: Carnegie Endowment for International Peace, 1950), pp. 98–99.

22 Ibid., p. 101.

23 Richard Cooper, "Eurodollars, Reserve Dollars, and Asymmetrics in the International Monetary System," *Journal of International Economics* 2 (September 1972): pp. 325–44.

24 Oskar Morgenstern, "Thirteen Critical Points in Contemporary Economic Theory: An Interpretation," *Journal of Economic Literature* 10 (December 1972): p. 1169.

25 Quoted in F. H. Hinsley, *Power and the Pursuit of Peace* (Cambridge: Cambridge University Press, 1963), pp. 50–51.

26 Jacob Viner, "Power versus Plenty as Objectives of Foreign Policy in the Seventeenth and Eighteenth Centuries," in *The Long View and the Short: Studies in Economic Theory and Practice* (Glencoe, Ill.: The Free Press, 1958), p. 286.

27 R. G. Hawtrey, *Economic Aspects of Sovereignty* (London: Longmans, Green, 1952), p. 120.

28 Albert Hirshman, *National Power and the Structure of Foreign Trade* (Berkeley: University of California Press, 1969), p. 16.

29 John A. Hobson, *Imperialism: A Study* (1902; 3rd ed., rev., London: G. Allen and Unwin, 1938), p. 57.

30 Charles Kindleberger, *The World in Depression 1929–1939* (Berkeley: University of California Press, 1973), p. 293.

31 François Perroux, "The Domination Effect and Modern Economic Theory," in *Power in Economics*, ed. K. W. Rothschild (London: Penguin, 1971), p. 67.

32 E. H. Carr, *The Twenty Years' Crisis, 1919–1939* (New York: Macmillan, 1951), p. 117.

33 Quoted in Kari Levitt, *Silent Surrender: The American Economic Empire in Canada* (New York: Liveright Press, 1970), p. 100.

34 Eugene Staley, *World Economy in Transition: Technology vs. Politics, Laissez Faire vs. Planning, Power vs. Welfare* (New York: Council on Foreign Relations [under the auspices of the American Coordinating Committee for International Studies], 1939), pp. 51–52.

35 Ibid., p. 52.

Economic Interdependence and War

Dale C. Copeland

Does economic interdependence increase or decrease the probability of war among states?. . . . In this article, I provide a new dynamic theory to help overcome some of the theoretical and empirical problems with current liberal and realist views on the question.

The prolonged debate between realists and liberals on the causes of war has been largely a debate about the relative salience of different causal variables. Realists stress such factors as relative power, while liberals focus on the absence or presence of collective security regimes and the pervasiveness of democratic communities. Economic interdependence is the only factor that plays an important causal role in the thinking of both camps, and their perspectives are diametrically opposed.

Liberals argue that economic interdependence lowers the likelihood of war by increasing the value of trading over the alternative of aggression: interdependent states would rather trade than invade. As long as high levels of interdependence can be maintained, liberals assert, we have reason for optimism. Realists dismiss the liberal argument, arguing that high interdependence increases rather than decreases the probability of war. In anarchy, states must constantly worry about their security. Accordingly, interdependence—meaning mutual dependence and thus vulnerability—gives states an incentive to initiate war, if only to ensure continued access to necessary materials and goods.

The unsatisfactory nature of both liberal and realist theories is shown by their difficulties in explaining the run-ups to the two World Wars. The period up to World War I exposes a glaring anomaly for liberal theory: the European powers had reached unprecedented levels of trade, yet that did not prevent them from going to war. Realists certainly have the correlation right—the war was preceded by high interdependence—but trade levels had been high for the previous thirty years; hence, even if interdependence was a necessary condition for the war, it was not sufficient.

At first glance, the period from 1920 to 1940 seems to support liberalism over realism. In the 1920s, interdependence was high, and the world was essentially peaceful; in the 1930s, as entrenched protectionism caused interdependence to fall, international tension rose to the point of world war. Yet the two most aggressive states in the system during the 1930s, Germany and Japan, were also the most highly dependent despite their efforts towards autarchy, relying on other states, including other great powers, for critical raw materials. Realism thus seems correct in arguing that high dependence may lead to conflict, as states use war to ensure access to vital goods. Realism's problem with the interwar era, however, is that Germany and Japan had been even more dependent in the 1920s, yet they sought war only in the late 1930s when their dependence, although still significant, had fallen.

The theory presented in this article—the theory of trade expectations—helps to resolve these problems. The theory starts by clarifying the notion of economic interdependence, fusing the liberal insight that the benefits of trade give states an incentive to avoid war with the realist view that the potential costs of being cut off can push states to war to secure vital goods. The total of the benefits and potential costs of trade versus autarchy reveals the true level of dependence a state faces, for if trade is completely severed, the state not only loses the gains from trade but also suffers the costs of adjusting its economy to the new situation.

Trade expectations theory introduces a new causal variable, the expectations of future trade, examining its impact on the overall expected value of the trading option if a state decides to forgo war. This supplements the static consideration in liberalism and realism of the levels of interdependence at any point in time, with the importance of leaders' dynamic expectations into the future.

Levels of interdependence and expectations of future trade, considered simultaneously, lead to new predictions. Interdependence can foster peace, as liberals argue, but this will only be so when states expect that trade levels will be high into the foreseeable future. If highly interdependent states expect that trade will be severely restricted—that is, if their expectations for future trade are low—realists are likely to be right: the most highly dependent states will be the ones most likely to initiate war, for fear of losing the economic wealth that supports their long-term security. In short, high interdependence can be either peace-inducing or war-inducing, depending on the expectations of future trade.

This dynamic perspective helps bridge the gaps within and between current approaches. Separating levels of interdependence from expectations of future trade indicates that states may be pushed into war even if current trade levels are high, if leaders have good reason to suspect that others will cut them off in the future. In such a situation, the expected value of trade will likely be negative, and hence the value of continued peace is also negative, making war an attractive alternative. This insight helps resolve the liberal problem with World War I: despite high trade levels in 1913–14, declining expectations for future trade pushed German leaders to attack, to ensure long-term access to markets and raw materials.

Even when current trade is low or non-existent, positive expectations for future trade will produce a positive expected value for trade, and therefore an incentive for continued peace. This helps explain the two main periods of détente between the Cold War superpowers, from 1971 to 1973 and in the late 1980s: positive signs from U.S. leaders that trade would soon be significantly increased coaxed the Soviets into a more cooperative relationship, reducing the probability of war. But in situations of low trade where there is no prospect that high trade levels will be restored in the future, highly dependent states may be pushed into conflict. This was the German and Japanese dilemma before World War II. . . .

The Liberal and Realist Debate on Economic Interdependence and War

The core liberal position is straightforward. Trade provides valuable benefits, or "gains from trade," to any particular state. A dependent state should therefore seek to avoid war, since peaceful trading gives it all the benefits of close ties without any of the costs and risks of war. Trade pays more than war, so dependent states should prefer to trade not invade. This argument is often supported by the auxiliary proposition that modern technology greatly increases the costs and risks of aggression, making the trading option even more rational.

The argument was first made popular in the 1850s by Richard Cobden, who asserted that free trade "unites" states, "making each equally anxious for the prosperity and happiness of both."[1] This view was restated in *The Great Illusion* by Norman Angell just prior to World War I and again in 1933. Angell saw states having to choose between new ways of thinking, namely peaceful trade, and the "old method" of power politics. Even if war was once profitable, modernization now makes it impossible to "enrich" oneself through force; indeed, by destroying trading bonds, war is "commercially suicidal."[2]

Why do wars nevertheless occur? While the start of World War I just after *The Great Illusion*'s initial publication might seem to refute his thesis, Angell in the 1933 edition argued that the debacle simply confirmed the unprofitability of modern wars. He thus upheld the common liberal view that wars, especially major wars, result from the misperceptions of leaders caught up in the outmoded belief that war still pays. Accordingly, his is "not a plea for the impossibility of war . . . but for its futility," since "our ignorance on this matter makes war not only possible, but extremely likely."[3] In short, if leaders fail to see how unprofitable war is compared to the benefits of trade, they may still erroneously choose the former.

Richard Rosecrance provides the most extensive update of the Cobden-Angell thesis to the nuclear era. States must choose between being "trading states," concerned with promoting wealth through commerce, and "territorial states," obsessed with military expansion. Modern conditions push states towards a predominantly trading mode: wars are not only too costly, but with the peaceful trading option, "the benefits that one nation gains from trade can also be realized by others." When the system is highly interdependent, therefore, the "incentive to wage war is absent," since "trading states recognize that they can do *better* through internal economic development sustained by a worldwide market for their goods and services than by trying to conquer and assimilate large tracts of land."[4] Rosecrance thus neatly summarizes the liberal view that high interdependence fosters peace by making trading more profitable than invading.

Realists turn the liberal argument on its head, arguing that economic interdependence not only fails to promote peace, but in fact heightens the likelihood of war States concerned about security will dislike dependence, since it means that crucial imported goods could be cut off during a crisis. This problem is particularly acute for imports like oil and raw materials; while they may be only a small percentage of the total import bill, without them most modern economies would collapse. Consequently, states dependent on others for vital goods have an increased incentive to go to war to assure themselves of continued access of supply.

Neorealist Kenneth Waltz puts the argument as follows: actors within a domestic polity have little reason to fear the dependence that goes with specialization. The anarchic structure of international politics, however, makes states worry about their vulnerability, thus compelling them "to control what they depend on or to lessen the extent of their dependency." For Waltz, it is this "simple thought" that explains, among other things, "their imperial thrusts to widen the scope of their control."[5] For John Mearsheimer, nations that "depend on others for critical economic supplies will fear cutoff or blackmail in time of crisis or war." Consequently, "they may try to extend political control to the source of supply, giving rise to conflict with the source or with its other customers." Interdependence, therefore, "will probably lead to greater security competition."[6]. . . .

In sum, realists seek to emphasize one main point: political concerns driven by anarchy must be injected into the liberal calculus. Since states must be primarily concerned with security and therefore with control over resources and markets, one must discount the liberal optimism that great trading partners will always continue to be great trading partners simply because both states benefit absolutely. Accordingly, a state vulnerable to another's policies because of dependence will tend to use force to overcome that vulnerability.

Trade or Invade? A Theory of Trade Expectations

This section introduces the theory of trade expectations. This theory extends liberal and realist views regarding interdependence and war, by synthesizing their strengths while formulating a dynamic perspective on state decision-making that is at best only implicit in current approaches. The strength of liberalism lies in its consideration of how the benefits or gains from trade give states a material incentive to avoid war, even when they have unit-level predispositions to favor it. The strength of realism is its recognition that states may be vulnerable to the potential costs of being cut off from trade on which they depend for wealth and ultimately security. Current theories, however, lack a way to fuse the benefits of trade and the costs of severed trade into one theoretical framework.

More significantly, these theories lack an understanding of how rational decision-makers incorporate the future trading environment into their choice between peace and war. Both liberalism and realism often refer to the future trading environment, particularly in empirical analyses. But in constructing a theoretical logic, the two camps consider the future only within their own ideological presuppositions. Liberals, assuming that states seek to maximize absolute welfare, maintain that situations of high trade should continue into the foreseeable future as long as states are rational; such actors have no reason to forsake the benefits from trade, especially if defection from the trading arrangement will only lead to retaliation. Given this presupposition, liberals can argue that interdependence—as reflected in high trade at any particular moment in time—will foster peace, given the benefits of trade over war. Realists, assuming states seek to maximize security, argue that concerns for relative power and autonomy will eventually push some states to sever trade ties (at least in the absence of a hegemon). Hence, realists can insist that interdependence, again manifest as high trade at any moment in time, drives dependent states to initiate war now to escape potential vulnerability later.

For the purposes of forging strong theories, however, trading patterns cannot be simply assumed *a priori* to match the stipulations of either liberalism or of realism. Trade levels fluctuate significantly over time, both for the system as a whole and particularly between specific trading partners, as the last two centuries demonstrate. Accordingly, we need a theory that incorporates how a state's expectations of its trading environment—either optimistic or pessimistic—affect its decision-calculus for war or peace. This is where the new theory makes its most significant departure. Liberalism and realism are theories of "comparative statics," drawing predictions from a snapshot of the level of interdependence at a single point in time. The new theory, on the other hand, is dynamic in its internal structure: it provides a new variable, the "expectations of future trade," that incorporates in the theoretical logic an actor's sense of the future trends and possibilities. This variable is essential to any leader's determination not just of the immediate value of peace versus war at a particular moment in time, but of the overall expected value of peace and war over the foreseeable future.

From consideration of the expectations-of-future-trade variable along with a state's level of dependence, one can derive a consistent deductive theory of state decision-making showing the conditions under which high interdependence will lead to peace or to war. High interdependence can be peace-inducing, as liberals maintain, as long as states expect future trade levels to be high in the future: positive expectations for future trade will lead dependent states to assign a high expected value to a continuation of peaceful trade, making war the less appealing option. If, however, a highly dependent state expects future trade to be low due to the policy decisions of the other side, then realists are likely to be correct: the state will attach a low or even negative expected value to continued peace without trade, making war an attractive alternative if its expected value is greater than peace, Moreover, since a negative expected value of trade implies a long-term decline in power, even if war is not profitable *per se*, it may be chosen as the lesser of two evils.

The deductive logic of the alternative theory, as with liberalism and realism, centers on an individual state's efforts to manage its own situation of dependence. Consider a two-actor scenario, where one state "A" may trade with another state "B." If state A moves away from the initial position of autarchy to begin trading, and trade is free and open, it will expect to receive the benefits of trade stressed by liberals, namely, the incremental increase in A's total welfare due to trade. Note that a state can still be aware of the "benefits of trade" even if present trade is non-existent, since they represent the potential gains from trade that would accrue to the state should trade levels become high in the future. It is a state's ability to foresee future potential benefits that allows it to attach a high expected value to the peaceful trading option even when current trade levels are low (as long as it expects current restrictions to be relaxed).

When a state trades, it specializes in and exports goods in which it enjoys a comparative advantage, while forgoing the production of other goods, which it then imports. This process of specialization, however, entails potentially large costs of adjustment if trade is subsequently cut off. This is especially so in the modern world if the state becomes dependent on foreign oil and certain raw materials. With the economy's capital infrastructure (machines, factories, transportation systems, etc.) geared to function only with such vital goods, a severing of trade would impose huge costs as the economy struggles to cope with the new no-trade situation. In short, the severing of trade, as realists would argue, would put the state in a situation far worse than if it had never specialized in the first place.

This analysis leads to a clearer understanding of any particular state's total level of "dependence." On a bilateral basis, that level is represented by the sum of the benefits that the state would receive from free and open trade with another state (versus autarchy), and the costs to the state of being cut off from that trade after having specialized (versus autarchy). If state A started with an economy of 100 units of GNP before any trade with B (the autarchic position), and open trade with B would mean economic expansion to a level of 110 units of GNP on an ongoing basis, then the "benefits of trade" could be considered as 10 units. If the specialization that trade entails, however, would mean the economy would fall to 85 units should B sever trade ties, then the "costs of severed trade" would be 15 units versus autarchy. State A's total dependence level would thus be the benefits of trade plus the costs of severed trade after specialization, or 25 units.

The dependence level will itself be a function of such parameters as the overall compatibilities of the two economies for trade, the degree of A's need for vital goods such as oil and raw materials, and the availability of alternative suppliers and markets. Thus if A's need for trade with B is great because the economies are highly compatible (say, in terms of mutual comparative advantages), B has valuable natural resources that A lacks, and A has few other countries to turn to, then A's dependence can be considered high.

In deciding between peace and war, however, a state can not refer simply to its dependence level. Rather, it must determine the overall expected value of trade and therefore the value of continued peace into the foreseeable future. The benefits of trade and the costs of severed trade on their own say nothing about this expected value. Dynamic expectations of future trade must be brought in. If the state has positive expectations that the other will maintain free and open trade over the long term, then the expected value of trade will be close to the value of the benefits of trade. On the other hand, if the state, after having specialized, comes to expect that trade will be severed by the trading partner, then the expected value of trade may be highly negative, that is, close to the value of the costs of severed trade. In essence, the expected value of trade may be anywhere between the two extremes, depending on a state's estimate of the expected probability of securing open trade, or of being cut off.

This leads to a crucial hypothesis. For any given expected value of war, we can predict that the lower the expectations of future trade, the lower the expected value of trade, and therefore the more likely it is that war will be chosen.

It is important to note that the expected value of trade will not be based on the level of trade at a particular moment in time, but upon the stream of expected trade levels into the future. It really does not matter that trade is high today: if state A knows that B will cut all trade tomorrow and shows no signs of being willing to restore it later, the expected value of trade would be negative. Similarly, it does not matter if there is little or no trade at present: if state A is confident that B is committed to freer trade in the future, the expected value of trade would be positive.

The fact that the expected value of trade can be negative even if present trade is high, due to low expectations for future trade, goes a long way towards resolving such manifest anomalies for liberal theory as German aggression in World War I. Despite high levels of trade up to 1914, German leaders had good reason to believe that the other great powers would undermine this trade into the future; hence, a war to secure control over raw materials and markets was required for the long-term security of the German nation. Since the expected value of trade can be positive even though present trade is low, due to high expectations for future trade, we can also understand such phenomena as the periods of détente in U.S.–Soviet relations during the Cold War (1971–73 and after 1985). While East–West trade was still relatively low during these times, the Soviet need for Western technology, combined with a growing belief that large increases in trade with the West would be forthcoming, gave the Soviets a high enough expected value of trade to convince them to be more accommodating in superpower relations.

In making the final decision between peace and war, however, a rational state will have to compare the expected value of trade to the expected value of going to war with the other state.

The expected value of war, as a realist would emphasize, cannot be ascertained without considering the relative power balance. As one state moves from a position of relative inferiority in economic and military power to relative superiority, the expected value of war will move from negative to positive or even highly positive. This proposition follows directly from the insights of deterrence theory: the larger the state in relative size, the higher the probability of winning a victory, while the lower the costs of fighting the war. Hence, if victory entails occupying the other state and absorbing its economy, war can take on a very positive expected value when a large power attacks a small state. For example, if Iraq had been allowed to hold on to Kuwait after its August 1990 invasion, war for Iraq would certainly have "paid." Similarly, Czechoslovakia was an easy and attractive target for Germany by 1938–39, as were the other smaller states of Europe, and evidence suggests that war against these nations was indeed profitable for the Nazis. On the other hand, war between more equal great powers is likely to have a much lower or even negative expected value. The Spartan leadership took Sparta into war against Athens in 431 BC, for example, under no illusions that war would be a profitable venture. While the Athenian economy presented a large prize should victory be attained, war with a near-equal adversary could be expected to be very costly, with a low likelihood of victory.

Where we would anticipate a low or negative expected value to the option of war, the expectations-of-future-trade variable should have a determinant effect on the likelihood of war. If state A has positive expectations for future trade with B, and A and B are roughly equal in relative power, then state A will assign a high expected value to continued peaceful trade, will compare this to the low or negative expected value for invasion, and will choose peace as the rational strategy. The higher A's dependence and the higher the expectations for future trade, the higher the expected value for peaceful trade, and therefore the more likely A is to avoid war. But if state A is dependent and has negative expectations for future trade with B, then the expected value of trade will be very low or negative. If the expected value for trade is lower than the expected value for invasion, war becomes the rational choice, and this is so even when the expected value of invasion is itself negative: war becomes the lesser of two evils.

Questions for Review

How does Copeland meld the Realist and Liberal perspectives? If expectations about future trade are so important, how do states go about assessing these prospects?

Notes

1 Richard Cobden, *The Political Writings of Richard Cobden* (London: T. Fischer Unwin, 1903), p. 225.

2 Norman Angell, *The Great Illusion*, 2d ed. (New York: G.P. Putnam's Sons, 1933), pp. 33, 59–60, 87–89.

3 Ibid., pp. 59–62, 256.

4 Richard Rosecrance, *The Rise of the Trading State: Commerce and Conquest in the Modern World* (New York: Basic Books, 1986), pp. 13–14; 24–25 (emphasis added); see also Rosecrance, "War, Trade and Interdependence," in James N. Rosenau and Hylke Tromp, eds., *Interdependence and Conflict in World Politics* (Aldershot, U.K.: Avebury, 1989), pp. 48–57; Rosecrance, "A New Concert of Powers," *Foreign Affairs*, Vol. 71, No. 2 (Spring 1992), pp. 64–82.

5 Kenneth Waltz, *Theory of International Politics* (New York: Random House, 1979), p. 106.

6 John J. Mearsheimer, "Disorder Restored," in Graham Allison and Gregory E. Treverton, eds., *Rethinking America's Security* (New York: W.W. Norton, 1992), p. 223.

Why Doesn't Everyone Get the Case for Free Trade?

DANI RODRIK

Free trade is not the natural order of things. We get free trade—or something approximating it—only when the stars are lined up just right and the interests behind free trade have the upper hand both politically and intellectually. But why should this be so? Doesn't free trade make us all better off—over the long run? If free trade is so difficult to achieve, is that because of narrow self-interest, obscurantism, political failure, or all of these combined?

It would be easy to associate free trade always with economic and political progress and protectionism with backwardness and decline. It would also be misleading. . . . The real case for trade is subtle and therefore depends heavily on context. We need to understand not just the economics of free trade, but also its implications for distributive justice and social norms.

Trade and Income Distribution

College students learn about the gains from trade not from Martyn, Smith, or even Ricardo, but from a diagram which is the staple of every introductory economics textbook. The professor draws a couple of demand and supply curves, points to where the market prices are with and without tariffs, and then asks how much the economy would gain from removing the tariff. He carefully labels areas representing income gain and loss to different groups in society: area A captures the loss to competing producers at home, area B the gain to domestic consumers, and area C the loss in tariff revenue for the government. And the "net" gain to the economy? He adds and subtracts all these areas as appropriate, and voilà! We are left with two triangles that represent the gains from trade to the economy—or equivalently the "deadweight loss" of the tariff. Here is why tariffs are a bad idea, and here is how much we gain by removing them.

It is a handy demonstration, and I must admit that I too take a certain pleasure whenever I go through these motions—the joy of bringing the uninitiated into the fold. No need to confuse the students at this point by pointing out that the supply and demand curves we used to calculate the "net" gains are not necessarily the appropriate ones. The demand and supply schedules represent, respectively, "willingness to pay" and "marginal cost"—of the individual consumers and producers in that specific market. When private and social valuations diverge, neither of these will be a good guide to how much society is willing to pay or the costs society incurs. Even without that complication, however, the blackboard demonstration makes two important points obvious.

First, income redistribution is the other side of the gains from trade. If trade causes some activities to contract and others to expand—as it must if the full gains from trade are to be reaped—those groups whose economic fortunes are tied to shrinking sectors will necessarily take a hit. These losses are not transitory. If I have skills specific to garment production, I will suffer a permanent fall in my earnings even if I manage to avoid unemployment and find a job doing something else. Such income losses are estimated to lie between 8 and 25 percent of pre-displacement earnings in the United States. Any temporary adjustment costs—such as transitional unemployment or a dip in earnings below their long-run level—would be additional to these losses.

Here lies a common misunderstanding in the public debate on trade. Free trade advocates will often grant that some people may get hurt in the short run, but will continue to argue that in the long run everyone (or at least most people) will be better off. In fact there is nothing in economics that guarantees this, and much that suggests otherwise. A famous result due to Wolfgang Stolper and Paul Samuelson states that some groups will *necessarily* suffer long-term losses in income from free trade. In a wealthy country such as the United States, these are likely to be unskilled workers such as high school dropouts. This renders the whole notion of "gains from trade" suspect, since it is not at all clear how we can decide whether a country *as a whole* is better off when some people gain and others lose.

Nor are these ongoing distributional effects specific to the simplified textbook exposition. The trade economist's toolkit encompasses a wide variety of complicated and advanced models of trade, most of which generate sharp distributional conflict from trade. All of these approaches share a fundamental intuition: since economic restructuring generates efficiency gains, and sectors with comparative advantage will expand while others contract, redistribution is often the necessary handmaiden of the gains from trade. Advocates who claim that trade has huge benefits but only modest distributional impacts either do not understand how trade really works, or have to jump through all kinds of hoops to make their arguments halfway coherent. The reality is more simple: no pain, no gain.

The second implication of the classroom exposition is a bit more subtle, and the professor is not likely to dwell on it. But the more attentive among the students will notice that the gains from trade look rather paltry compared to the redistribution of income. It is not just that some win and others lose when tariffs are removed. It is also that the size of the redistribution swamps the "net" gain. This is a generic consequence of trade policy under realistic circumstances.

To drive the point home, I once quantified the ratio of redistribution-to-efficiency gains following the standard assumptions economists make when we present the case for free trade. The numbers I got were huge—so large in fact that I was compelled to redo the calculations several times to make sure I wasn't making a mistake: For example, in an economy like the United States, where average tariffs are below 5 percent, a move to complete free trade would reshuffle more than $50 of income among different groups for each dollar of efficiency or "net" gain created! Read the last sentence again in case you went through it quickly: we are talking about $50 of redistribution for every $1 of aggregate gain. It's as if we give $51 to Adam, only to leave David $50 poorer.

A major reason the redistribution-to-efficiency-gains ratio is so high is that tariffs are so low to begin with in today's economy. If tariffs had stood at, say, 40 percent, this ratio would have been around 6 instead. But even in this second case, the redistribution from David to Adam is enormous. It is unlikely that we would countenance so much redistribution in other policy domains without at least some assurance that the process conforms with our conceptions of distributive justice.

When confronted with such situations, most of us would want to know more. Who exactly are David and Adam and what did they do to bring this change about? Is David poorer or richer than Adam, and by how much? How will the proposed move affect them and their families? Does David have access to safety nets and other governmental transfer programs that provide compensation? Some cases will be easy in light of the answers to those questions. If David turns out to be rich, lazy, or otherwise undeserving, and fully responsible for the lousy decisions that result in the loss, we are likely to look kindly on the change. But what if none of these things is true, and Adam has acted in ways that many would consider unethical?

We must ask the same questions when we consider the case of large distributional changes caused by trade. Two questions are of particular importance. Are the gains too small relative to the potential losses to low-income or other disadvantaged groups that may have little recourse to safety nets? And does the trade involve actions that would violate widely shared norms or the social contract if carried out at home—such as employing child labor, repressing labor rights, or using environmentally harmful practices? When the answers to both these questions are yes, the legitimacy of trade will be in question, and appropriately so. There will need to be public debate about the right course of action, which will sometimes result in more rather than less intervention in trade. . . .

The gains from removing restrictions on trade run into diminishing returns as trade becomes freer and freer, with the consequence that the distributional effects begin to loom larger and larger. Most recent estimates put the "overall" gains to the United States from a global move to free trade in tenths of 1 percent of U.S. gross domestic product. No doubt certain export interests would benefit considerably more; but the losses to others would be commensurately large as well. The more open an economy is, the worse the redistribution-to-efficiency ratio gets. The political and social-cost-benefit ratio of trade liberalization looks very different when tariffs are 5 percent instead of 50 percent. It is inherent in the economics of trade that going the last few steps to free trade will be particularly difficult because it generates lots of dislocation but little overall gain. There is nothing similarly self-exhausting in the case of technical progress.

So the economist's triangles and technical progress analogy are conversation starters, not conversation enders. Considerations of justice and procedural fairness may complicate the simple (simplistic?) case for gains from trade, but they help us understand why trade is often so contentious. Resistance to free trade is not just a matter of narrow self-interest or ignorance—at least not always.

Importantly, this broader perspective also helps us distinguish pure protectionism from legitimate and well-grounded opposition to free trade. A deserving argument against free trade must overcome at least one of the two hurdles mentioned above: the economic gains from freer trade must remain small compared to the distributional "costs"; and trade must entail practices that violate prevailing norms and social contracts at home. Redistributions that provide large net gains and do not infringe on accepted ways of doing business may be okay; redistributions that fail these tests are open to greater scrutiny. Remember these principles, as we will use them as building blocks for the reform of the global economic system.

What Economists Will Not Tell You

Here is an interesting experiment I wish a news reporter would undertake. Let him call an economist on the phone, identifying himself as a reporter, and ask the economist whether she thinks free trade with country X or Y is a good idea. We can be fairly certain about the kind of response he will get: "Oh yes, free trade is a great idea," the economist will immediately say, possibly adding: "And those who are opposed to it either do not understand the principle of comparative advantage, or they represent the selfish interests of certain lobbies (such as labor unions)."

Now let the reporter dress in the casual and rumpled clothes of the typical graduate student in economics and walk into an advanced seminar on international trade theory in any one of the leading universities of the nation. Let him pose the same question to the instructor: Is free trade good? I doubt that the question will be answered as quickly and succinctly this time around. The professor is in fact likely to be stymied and confused by the question. "What do you mean by 'good'?" she may ask. "Good for whom?" If the reporter/student looks puzzled, she will add: "As we will see later in this course, in most of our models free trade makes some groups better off and others worse off." If this gets disappointed looks, she will then expand: "But under certain conditions, and assuming we can tax the beneficiaries and compensate the losers, freer trade has the *potential* to increase everyone's well-being."

Now the economist has begun to warm up to the subject. She will continue: "Notice how I said, 'under some conditions.' Asking you to list those conditions would make a good exam question, so pay attention as I run through them." Unless your lifelong dream was to become a PhD economist, it is unlikely that you will derive any pleasure from what is about to come (or any illumination, for that matter). But I must provide a full account of the economics professor's answer, so I will put it all into really small font. Here is what her list of preconditions will look like:

> The import liberalization must be complete, covering all goods and trade partners, or else the reduction in import restrictions must take into account the potentially quite complicated structure of substitutability and complementarity across restricted commodities. (So in fact a preferential trade agreement with one or a few trade partners is unlikely to satisfy the requirement.) There must be no microeconomic market imperfections other than the trade restrictions in question, or if there are some, the second-best interactions that are entailed must not be too adverse. The home economy must be "small" in world markets, or else the liberalization must not put the economy on the wrong side of the "optimum tariff." The economy must be in reasonably full employment, or if not, the monetary and fiscal authorities must have effective tools of demand management at their disposal. The income redistributive effects of the liberalization should not be judged undesirable by society at large, or if they are, there must be compensatory tax-transfer schemes with low enough excess burden. There must be no adverse effects on the fiscal balance, or if there are, there must be alternative and expedient ways of making up for the lost fiscal revenues. The liberalization must be politically sustainable and hence credible so that economic agents do not fear or anticipate a reversal.

By now the professor is looking really smug, because she has just shown her students not only how complicated even seemingly simple economics questions are, but also how economic science can shed light (if that is what this jargon can be called!) on the answers.

The journalist/graduate student will not have understood much of this, but at least he has gotten an answer. "So, provided these conditions are satisfied, we can be sure that freer trade will improve our economy's performance and raise its rate of growth?" he may ask hopefully. "Oh, no!" the professor will reply. "Who said anything about growth? These were only the requirements for an increase in the *level of aggregate* real income. Saying something definite about growth is much, much harder." With a self-satisfied smile on her face, she may then provide the following explanation:

> In our standard models with exogenous technological change and diminishing returns to reproducible factors of production (e.g., the neoclassical model of growth), a trade restriction has no effect on the

long-run (steady-state) rate of growth of output. This is true regardless of the existence of market imperfections. However, there may be growth effects during the transition to the steady state. (These transitional effects could be positive or negative depending on how the long-run level of output is affected by the trade restriction.) In models of endogenous growth generated by non-diminishing returns to reproducible factors of production or by learning-by-doing and other forms of endogenous technological change, the presumption is that lower trade restrictions boost output growth in the world economy as a whole. But a subset of countries may experience diminished growth depending on their initial factor endowments and levels of technological development. It all depends on whether the forces of comparative advantage pull resources into growth-generating sectors and activities, or away from them.

Noticing the student's expression, the professor may helpfully add, "I think you really have to come to me during office hours for all this."

You don't have to read the fine print above, but if you have deduced that the answer in the seminar room differs greatly from the answer on the phone, you are quite correct. A direct, unqualified assertion about the unquestionable benefits of trade has now been transformed into a statement adorned by all kinds of ifs and buts. Yet somehow the knowledge that the professor willingly imparts with great pride to her advanced students is deemed to be too dangerous for the general public. The qualifications of the seminar room are forgotten lest they lead the public "astray." . . .

Confronted by the gap between what they teach and what they preach, economists will take refuge in a number of arm-waving arguments. Here is a fairly complete list of what you might hear:

1. In practice free trade will make most people better off in the long run, just as technological progress does.

2. Even if trade creates complications, the best way to deal with those is through other policies and not trade restrictions.

3. Even if some people lose out, it should be possible to compensate them and still have everyone come out ahead.

4. The case for free trade goes beyond economics: it is a moral one that has to do with people's freedom to choose who they do business with.

5. Anti-trade views are prevalent enough; our job is to present the other side.

6. The caveats will be hijacked by protectionists who will use them for their own purposes.

7. And besides, the nuances will simply confuse people.

Yet none of these arguments is thought through with anything approaching the level of rigor that goes into demonstrating the standard theorems of trade. None is particularly convincing. . . .

Why do economists' analytical minds turn into mush when they talk about trade policy in the real world? Some of it has to do with the idea of comparative advantage being the crown jewel of the profession. . . . .It is too painful to let go of. Some boils down to what I call the "barbarians at the gate" syndrome. Economists worry that any doubts they express in public on the benefits of free trade will serve to empower those "barbarians" who are interested not in nuanced views but in pushing for their *dirigiste* agendas. No doubt some has to do with ideology. Even if many economists don't think of themselves as politically conservative, their views tend to be aligned with free market enthusiasts rather than interventionists.

The unanimity that economists exhibit over free trade does not apply to other areas of economic policy. Economists speak with many voices when it comes to important areas of domestic policy such as health, education, or taxes. But on globalization one would have had to look really hard until recently to locate a scholar in any of the top universities who would depart from the boilerplate response. . . .

[The] points . . . about the ambiguities of the case for trade are well known within the professional economics community. The problem is that economists guard them like state secrets and look on those who would share them with ordinary folk as apostates.

When economists oversell globalization by presenting an incomplete case for it, they not only lose an opportunity to educate the public, they also lose credibility. They become viewed as advocates or as hired guns for the "stateless elites" whose only interest is to remove impediments to their international operations. This wouldn't be all that bad if economics didn't have a lot to offer. Applied with a good dose of common sense, economics would have prepared us for the flaws we have experienced in globalization. And used appropriately, economic analysis can point us in the right direction for the fixes. Designing a better balance between states and markets—a better globalization—does not mean that we jettison conventional economics. It requires that we actually pay more attention to it. The economics we need is of the "seminar room" variety, not the "rule-of-thumb" kind. It is an economics that recognizes its limitations and caveats and knows that the right message depends on the context. The fine print *is* what economists have to contribute.

Question for Review

If the income redistributive effects of free trade overwhelm the gains from trade, does that mean free trade is not in a state's overall interest, or does it mean that the state can capture the gains from trade if it acts in ways to mitigate those redistributive effects?

Chapter 9
Globalization Today

Globalization of the Economy

JEFFREY FRANKEL

Economic globalization is one of the most powerful forces to have shaped the post-war world. In particular, international trade in goods and services has become increasingly important over the past fifty years, and international financial flows over the past thirty years. This chapter documents quantitatively the process of globalization for trade and finance. It then briefly goes beyond the causes of international economic integration to consider its effects, concluding that globalization is overall a good thing, not just for economic growth but also when noneconomic goals are taken into account.

The two major drivers of economic globalization are reduced costs to transportation and communication in the private sector and reduced policy barriers to trade and investment on the part of the public sector. Technological progress and innovation have long been driving the costs of transportation and communication steadily lower. In the postwar period we have seen major further cost-saving advances, even within ocean shipping: supertankers, roll-on-roll-off ships, and containerized cargo. Between 1920 and 1990 the average ocean freight and port charges per short ton of U.S. import and export cargo fell from $95.00 to $29.00 (in 1990 dollars). An increasing share of cargo goes by air. Between 1930 and 1990, average air transport revenue per passenger mile fell from $0.68 to $0.11. Jet air shipping and refrigeration have changed the status of goods that had previously been classified altogether as not tradable internationally. Now fresh-cut flowers, perishable broccoli and strawberries, live lobsters, and even ice cream are sent between continents. Communications costs have fallen even more rapidly. Over this period the cost of a three-minute telephone call from New York to London fell from $244.65 to $3.32. Recent inventions such as faxes and the Internet require no touting.

It is easy to exaggerate the extent of globalization. Much excited discussion of the topic makes it sound as though the rapid increase in economic integration across national borders is unprecedented. Some commentators imply that it has now gone so far that it is complete; one hears that distance and national borders no longer matter, that the nation-state and geography are themselves no longer relevant for economic purposes, and that it is now as easy to do business with a customer across the globe as across town. After all, has not the World Wide Web reduced cross-border barriers to zero?

It would be a mistake for policymakers or private citizens to base decisions on the notion that globalization is so new that the experience of the past is not relevant, or that the phenomenon is now irreversible, or that national monetary authorities are now powerless in the face of the global marketplace, or that the quality of life of Americans—either economic or noneconomic aspects—is determined more by developments abroad than by American actions at home.

It is best to recognize that at any point in history many powerful forces are working to drive countries apart, at the same time as other powerful forces are working to shrink the world. In the 1990s, for example, at the same time that forces such as the Internet and dollarization have led some to proclaim the decline of the nation-state, more new nations have been created (out of the ruins of the former Soviet bloc) than in any decade other than the decolonizing 1960s, each with its own currencies and trade policies. The forces of shrinkage have dominated in recent decades, but the centrifugal forces are important as well.

Two Benchmarks for Measuring Economic Integration

The overall post–World War II record of economic integration across national borders, powerful as it has been, is, in two respects, not as striking as widely believed. The first perspective is to judge by the standard of 100 years ago. The second is to judge by the standard of what it would mean to have truly perfect global integration.

Judging Globalization 2000 by the Standard of 1900

The globalization that took place in the nineteenth century was at least as impressive as the current episode. The most revolutionary breakthroughs in transportation and communication had already happened by 1900—for example, the railroad, steamship, telegraph, and refrigeration. Freight rates had fallen sharply throughout the century. An environment of political stability was provided by the Pax Britannica, and an environment of monetary stability was provided by the gold standard. Kevin O'Rourke and Jeffrey Williamson show that, as a result of rapidly growing trade, international differences in commodity prices narrowed dramatically.

It is inescapable to invoke a particularly famous quote from John Maynard Keynes: "What an extraordinary episode in the progress of man that age was which came to an end in August 1914! . . . The inhabitant of London could order by telephone, sipping his morning tea in bed, the various products of the whole earth . . . he could at the same time and by the same means adventure his wealth in the natural resources and new enterprise of any quarter of the world."[1]

The world took a giant step back from economic globalization during the period 1914–1944. Some of the causes of this retrogression were isolationist sentiments in the West that followed World War I, the monetary instability and economic depression that plagued the interwar period, increases in tariffs and other trade barriers including most saliently the adoption by the U.S. Congress of the Smoot-Hawley tariff of 1930, the rise of the fascist bloc in the 1930s, and the rise of the communist bloc in the 1940s. All of these factors pertain to barriers that were created by governments, in contrast to the forces of technology and the private marketplace, which tend to reduce barriers. As a result, the world that emerged in 1945 was far more fragmented economically than the world that had turned to war in 1914.

The victors, however, were determined not to repeat the mistakes they had made at the time of the first world war. This time, they would work to promote economic integration in large part to advance long-term political goals. To govern international money, investment, and trade, they established multilateral institutions—the International Monetary Fund, World Bank, and General Agreement on Tariffs and Trade. The United States initially led the way by reducing trade barriers and making available gold-convertible dollars.

By one basic measure of trade, exports or imports of merchandise as a fraction of total output, it took more than twenty-five years after the end of World War II before the United States around 1970 reached the same level of globalization that it had experienced on the eve of World War I. This fraction continued to increase rapidly between 1971 and 1997—reaching about 9 percent [in 2000], still far lower than that in Britain throughout the late and early twentieth centuries. By other measures, some pertaining to the freedom of factor movements, the world even by the turn of the millennium was no more integrated than that of the preceding turn of the century.

Most people find it surprising that trade did not reattain its pre–World War I importance until the early 1970s. The significance of the comparison with 100 years ago goes well beyond factoids that economic historians enjoy springing on the uninitiated. Because technological know-how is irreversible—or was irreversible over the second millennium, if not entirely over the first—there is a tendency to see globalization as irreversible. But the political forces that fragmented the world for thirty years (1914–44) were evidently far more powerful than the accretion of technological progress in transport that went on during that period. The lesson is that nothing is inevitable about the process of globalization. For it to continue, world leaders must make choices of the sort made in the aftermath of World War II, instead of those made in the aftermath of World War I.

Judging by the Globalization 2000 Standard of Perfect International Integration

Perhaps perfect economic integration across national borders is a straw man. . . . But straw men have their purposes, and in this case ample rhetoric exists to justify the interest. A good straw man needs to be substantial enough to impress the crows and yet not so substantial that he can't be knocked flat. On both scores the proposition of complete international integration qualifies admirably.

Consider again the basic statistics of trade integration—a country's total exports of goods and services, or total imports, as a fraction of GDP. With the rapid increase in services included, these ratios now average 12 percent for the United States. The current level of trade likely represents a doubling from 100 years ago. As remarkable as is this evidence of declining transportation costs, tariffs, and other barriers to trade, it is still very far from the condition that would prevail if these costs and barriers were zero. More sophisticated statistics below will document this claim. But a very simple calculation is sufficient to make the point. U.S. output is about one-fourth of gross world product. The output of producers in other countries is thus about three-fourths of gross world product. If Americans were prone to buy goods and services from foreign producers as easily as from domestic producers, then foreign products would constitute a share of U.S. spending equal to that of the spending of the average resident of the planet. The U.S. import-GDP ratio would equal .75. The same would be true of the U.S. export-GDP ratio. And yet these ratios are only about one-sixth of this hypothetical level (12 percent/75 percent = one-sixth). In other words, globalization would have to increase another sixfold, as measured by the trade ratio, before it would literally be true that Americans did business as easily across the globe as across the country.

Other countries are also a long way from perfect openness in this sense. The overall ratio of merchandise trade to output worldwide is about twice the U.S. ratio. This is to be expected, as other countries are smaller. For the other two large economies—Japan and the European Union considered as a whole—the ratio is closer to the U.S. level. In almost all cases, the ratio falls far short of the level that would prevail in a perfectly integrated world. In Figure 1, the vertical dimension represents the share of a country's output that is sold to its fellow citizens, rather than exported. The downward movement for most countries illustrates that they have become more open over the past 130 years. (One can also see that the integration trend was interrupted during the interwar period.) The United States is still far from perfect openness: the share of output sold at home is disproportionate to the share of world output. Other countries have a higher ratio of trade to GDP than the United States as a result of being smaller and less self-sufficient. Nonetheless, they are similarly far from perfect openness.

Why is globalization still so far from complete? To get an idea of the combination of transportation costs, trade barriers, and other frictions that remains yet to be dismantled, we must delve more deeply into the statistics.

Share of output sold at home

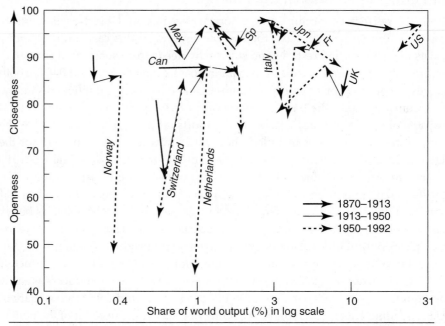

Figure 1

Country Size (Share of World Output) versus Closedness (Sales at Home/Total Output)
NOTE: Closedness = (1 – (x/GDP))*100.

SOURCE: Author's calculations and data from Angus Maddison, Monitoring the World Economy (Paris: Development Center of the Organization for Economic Cooperation and Development, 1995).

Statistical Measures of Economic Integration

It can be instructive to look at direct measures of how some of the barriers to transborder integration have changed during the twentieth century—the level of tariffs on manufactures as an illustration of trade policy, or the price of a trans-Atlantic telephone call as an illustration of technological change in communications and transportation. Nevertheless, the political and physical determinants are too numerous and varied to be aggregated into a few key statistics that are capable of measuring the overall extent of integration in trade or finance. Tariff rates, for example, differ tremendously across commodities, and there is no single sensible way to aggregate them. The situation is even worse for nontariff barriers. Alternative possible measures of the importance of tariffs and other trade barriers have very low correlation with each other. . . .

It is more rewarding to look at summary measures of the *effects* of cross-border barriers on the patterns of trade and investment than to look at measures of the barriers themselves. Two sorts of measures are in use: those pertaining to quantities and those pertaining to prices.

Measures of quantities might appear more direct: "just how big are international flows?" But economists often prefer to look at price measures. In the first place, the quality of the data is often higher for prices than quantities. (This is particularly true of data on international financial markets—the data on the prices of foreign securities are extremely good, the data on aggregate international trade in securities are extremely bad.) In the second place, even at a conceptual level, international differentials in the prices of specific goods or specific assets, which measure the ability of international arbitrage to hold these prices in line, are more useful indicators of the extent of integration in a causal sense. Consider the example of U.S. trade in petroleum products. It is not especially large as a percentage of total U.S. output or consumption of petroleum products. And yet arbitrage ties the price of oil within the United States closely to the price in the world market. Even a pair of countries that records no bilateral oil trade whatsoever will find that their prices move closely together. It is the absence of barriers and the *potential* for large-scale trade that keeps prices in line and makes the markets integrated in the most meaningful sense, not the magnitude of trade that takes place.

The Ability of Arbitrage to Eliminate International Differentials in Goods Prices

According to basic economic theory, arbitrage, defined as the activity of buying an item in a place where it is cheap and simultaneously selling the same item where it is expensive, should drive prices into equality. Its failure to do so perfectly is a source of repeated surprise to economists (though perhaps to nobody else). Often the explanation is that the commodities in question are not in fact identical. Brand names matter, if for no other reason than matters of retailing, warranty, and customer service. A BMW is certainly not the same automobile as a Lexus, and even a BMW sold in Germany is not the same as a BMW sold in the United States (different air pollution control equipment, for example). When the comparison across countries uses aggregate price indexes, as in standard tests of "purchasing power parity," it is no surprise to find only weak evidence of arbitrage. The finding of international price differentials is more surprising in the case of nondifferentiated non-brand-name commodities such as standardized ball bearings. Tests find that price differentials for specific goods are far larger across national borders than they are within countries. Exchange rate variability is a likely culprit.

Even more surprising is the paucity of evidence of a tendency for price differentials to diminish over the long sweep of history. Kenneth Froot, Michael Kim, and Kenneth Rogoff have obtained data on prices in England and Holland since the year 1273 for eight commodities (barley, butter, cheese, eggs, oats, peas, silver, and wheat).[2] Deviations from the so-called Law of One Price across the English Channel are no smaller or less persistent now than they were in the past, even though technological progress has certainly reduced the cost of shipping these products dramatically. Evidently other forces have counteracted the fall in transport costs; candidates are trade barriers under Europe's Common Agricultural Policy and volatility in the exchange rate between the guilder and the pound.

Factors Contributing to Home-Country Bias in Trade

Geography in general—and distance in particular—remain far more important inhibitions to trade than widely believed.

DISTANCE   Distance is still an important barrier to trade and not solely because of physical shipping costs. The effects of informational barriers are observed to decrease with proximity and with linguistic, cultural, historical, and political links. We might call it social distance. Hans Linnemann called it "psychic distance," and Peter Drysdale and Ross Garnaut named it "subjective resistance."[3]

Among many possible proofs that distance is still important, one of the simplest is the observed tendency toward geographical agglomeration of industries. The tendency for industry to concentrate regionally is evidence both of costs to transportation and communication and of increasing returns to scale in production.

The agglomeration occurs even in sectors where physical transport costs are negligible, as in financial services or computer software. Financial firms concentrate in Manhattan and information technology firms concentrate in Silicon Valley. The reason they choose to locate near each other is not because they are trading physical commodities with each other and wish to save on shipping costs. Rather, face-to-face contact is important for exchanging information and negotiating deals.

The importance of distance is also revealed by analysis of data on prices of goods in different locations. If transport costs and other costs of doing business at a distance are important, then arbitrage should do a better job of keeping prices of similar goods in line when they are sold at locations close together rather than far apart. Charles Engel and John Rogers study prices in fourteen consumption categories for twenty-three Canadian and U.S. cities. They find that the distance between two North American cities significantly affects the variability of their relative prices. . . .

Statistical estimates find highly significant effects of distance on bilateral trade. When the distance between two countries is increased by 1 percent, trade between them falls by 0.7 to 1.0 percent. This statistic, like the others that follow, pertains to the effect in isolation, holding constant other effects on trade, such as the size of the trading partners. . . .

OTHER GEOGRAPHICAL VARIABLES   Other physical attributes of location also have statistically significant effects. Land-locked countries engage in less trade by a factor of about one-third, holding other factors equal. Two countries that are adjacent to each other trade about 80 percent more than two otherwise similar countries.

LINGUISTIC AND COLONIAL FACTORS   Linguistic barriers remain an impediment to trade. Two countries that speak the same language trade about 50 percent more than two otherwise similar countries. The multitude of languages is one of the reasons why economic integration remains far from complete in the European Union.

Colonial links have also been important historically. In 1960, the year when the break-up of the largest colonial empires began in earnest, trade between colonies and the colonial power was on average two to four times greater than for otherwise similar pairs of countries. This effect, already reduced from an earlier peak in the colonial era, has continued to decline in the 1970s and 1980s. But it has not disappeared. Indeed, if small dependencies are included in the sample, then two units that share the same colonizer still trade on average an estimated 80 percent more with each other than two otherwise similar countries (as recently as 1990). In addition, if one of the pair is the colonial mother country, trade is five to nine times greater than it would otherwise be.

MILITARY FACTORS   The effects on bilateral trade of politico-military alliances, wars, have also been examined. Theoretically and empirically (in the gravity framework) trade is generally higher among countries that are allies and lower among countries that are actual or potential adversaries. Understandably, if two countries are currently at war, there is usually a negative effect on trade. It runs as high as a 99 percent reduction in 1965. More typical is an 82 percent reduction in 1990.[4]

FREE TRADE AREAS   Regional trading arrangements reduce tariffs and other trade barriers within a group of countries, though there is a range from mild preferential trading arrangements to full-fledged economic unions. Often the members of such groups are already tightly linked through proximity, common language, or other ties. But even holding constant for such factors, in the gravity model, the formation of a free trade area is estimated on average to raise trade by 70 to 170 percent. A serious common market, such as the European Union, can have a bigger effect. Nevertheless, in each of the EU member countries, a large bias toward trade within that country remains.

POLITICAL LINKS   A naïve economist's view would be that once tariffs and other explicit trade barriers between countries are removed, and geographic determinants of transportation costs are held constant, trade should move as easily across national boundaries as within them. But this is far from the case in reality. If two geographic units belong to the same sovereign nation, such as France and its overseas departments, trade is roughly tripled. Thus political relationships among geographic units have larger effects on trade than such factors as explicit trade policies or linguistic barriers.

COMMON COUNTRY   Even after adjusting for distance (including noncontiguity) and linguistic barriers, all countries still exhibit a substantial bias toward buying domestic goods rather than foreign. . . .

There would be some great advantages of having data at the level of states or provinces within countries. We would be able to ascertain how trade between two geographical entities is affected by their common membership in a political union. We have learned that when two geographical units share such links as speaking a common language, their bilateral trade is clearly boosted. It stands to reason that when two units share a common cultural heritage or legal system, their trade will be enhanced by even more. Data are not generally available on trade among U.S. states, Japanese prefectures, German länder, British counties, or French departments. But there do exist data on trade undertaken by Canadian provinces, among one another and with major American states. They show a strong intranational bias to trade. Ontario exports three times as much to British Columbia as to California, even though the latter has ten times as many people. (The figures are for 1988.) . . .

CURRENCIES There has long been reason to suspect that the existence of different currencies, and especially the large fluctuation in the exchange rates between currencies since the break-up of the Bretton Woods monetary system in 1971, has been a barrier to international trade and investment. Exchange rate fluctuations are clearly related to the failures of the law of one price observed in goods markets. When it is observed that, for example, Canadians and Americans trade far more with their countrymen than with each other, in a context where trade barriers, geography, and linguistic barriers have been eliminated, the currency difference is one of the prime suspects. . . .

Promoting trade and finance is one of several motivations for the recent adoption of common currencies or currency boards by roughly twenty countries over the past decade (including the eleven members of the European Economic and Monetary Union in 1999). At the same time, however, approximately the same number of new currencies have come into existence, as a result of the breakup of the former Soviet bloc.

Measures of Financial Market Integration

The delegates who met at Bretton Woods in 1944 had a design for the world monetary system that explicitly did not accord financial markets the presumption that was accorded trade in goods, the presumption that international integration was unambiguously good and that barriers should be liberalized as rapidly as possible. Although economic theory can make as elegant a case in favor of free trade in assets as for free trade in goods and services, the delegates had been persuaded by the experience of the 1930s that some degree of controls on international capital movements was desirable. It was not until the final 1973 breakdown of the system of fixed exchange rates that Germany and the United States removed their capital controls. Japan and the United Kingdom kept theirs until the end of the 1970s, and most other European countries did not liberalize until the end of the 1980s. Many emerging-market countries also opened up to large-scale international capital movements in the 1990s (though the subsequent crises have convinced some observers that those delegates at Bretton Woods might have had it right in the first place).

Tests regarding financial markets show international integration that has increased tremendously over the past thirty years but that is less complete than often supposed. This generalization applies to quantity-based tests as well as to price-based tests.

It is true that the gross volume of cross-border capital flows has grown very large. Perhaps the most impressive and widely cited statistic is the gross volume of turnover in foreign exchange markets: $1.5 trillion per day worldwide, by April 1998, which is on the order of a hundred times greater than the volume of trade in goods and services. *Net* capital flows are for most purposes more interesting than gross flows, however. Net capital flows today are far smaller as a share of GDP than were pre-World War I net flows out of Great Britain and into such land-abundant countries as Argentina, Australia, and Canada. Furthermore, Martin Feldstein and Charles Horioka argued in a very influential paper that net capital flows are far smaller than one would expect them to be in a world of perfect international capital mobility: a country that suffers a shortfall in national saving tends to experience an almost commensurate fall in investment, rather than making up the difference by borrowing from abroad. Similarly, investors in every country hold far lower proportions of their portfolios in the form of other countries' securities than they would in a well-diversified portfolio, a puzzle known as home country bias. Evidently, imperfect information and transactions costs are still important barriers to cross-country investment.

The ability of arbitrage to equate asset prices or rates of return across countries has been widely tested. One would expect in the absence of barriers to cross-border financial flows, arbitrage would bring interest rates into equality. But the answer depends on the precise condition tested. Interest rates that have had the element of exchange risk removed by forward market cover are indeed virtually equated across national borders among industrialized countries, showing that they have few controls on international capital movements. But interest rates seem not to be equalized across countries when they are adjusted for expectations of exchange rate changes rather than for forward exchange rates, and interest rates are definitely not equalized when adjusted for expected inflation rates. Evidently, currency differences are important enough to drive a wedge between expected rates of return. Furthermore, residual transactions costs or imperfect information apparently affects cross-border investment in equities. They discourage investors altogether from investing in some information-intensive assets, such as mortgages, across national borders. Furthermore, country risk still adds a substantial penalty wedge to all investments in developing countries.

In short, though international financial markets, much like goods markets, have become far more integrated in recent decades, they have traversed less of the distance to perfect integration than is widely believed. Globalization is neither new, nor complete, nor irreversible.

The Impact of Economic Globalization

What are the effects of globalization and its merits? We must acknowledge a lower degree of certainty in our answers. It becomes harder to isolate cause and effect. Moreover, once we extend the list of objectives beyond maximizing national incomes, value judgments come into play. Nevertheless, economic theory and empirical research still have much to contribute.

The Effect of Trade on the Level and Growth of Real Income

Why do economists consider economic integration so important? What are the benefits of free trade for the economy?

THE THEORETICAL CASE FOR TRADE   Classical economic theory tells us that there are national gains from trade, associated with the phrase "comparative advantage." Over the past two decades, scholars have developed a "new trade theory." It suggests the existence of additional benefits from trade, which are termed dynamic. We consider each theory in turn.

The classical theory goes back to Adam Smith and David Ricardo. Adam Smith argued that specialization—the division of labor—enhances productivity. David Ricardo extended this concept to trade between countries. The notion is that trade allows each country to specialize in what it does best, thus maximizing the value of its output. If a government restricts trade, resources are wasted in the production of goods that could be imported more cheaply than they can be produced domestically.

What if one country is better than anyone else at producing *every* good? The argument in favor of free trade still carries the day. All that is required is for a country to be *relatively* less skilled than another in the production of some good in order for it to benefit from trade. This is the doctrine of comparative advantage— the fundamental (if perhaps counterintuitive) principle that underlies the theory of international trade. It makes sense for Michael Jordan to pay someone else to mow his lawn, even if Jordan could do it better himself, because he has a comparative advantage at basketball over lawn mowing. Similarly, it makes sense for the United States to pay to import certain goods that can be produced more efficiently abroad (apparel, shoes, tropical agriculture, consumer electronics), because the United States has a comparative advantage in other goods (aircraft, financial services, wheat, and computer software).

This is the classical view of the benefits of free trade in a nutshell. Two key attributes of the classical theory are worth flagging. First, it assumes perfect competition, constant returns to scale, and fixed technology, assumptions that are not very realistic. Second, the gains from trade are primarily static in nature—that is, they affect the *level* of real income. The elimination of trade barriers raises income, but this is more along the lines of a one-time increase.

What of the "new trade theory"? It is more realistic than the classical theory, in that it takes into account imperfect competition, increasing returns to scale, and changing technology. It can be viewed as providing equally strong, or stronger, support for the sort of free trade policies that the United States has followed throughout the postwar period, that is, multilateral and bilateral negotiations to reduce trade barriers, than did the classical theory.

To be sure, these theories say that, under certain very special conditions, one country can get ahead by interventions (for example, subsidies to strategic sectors), provided the government gets it exactly right and provided the actions of other countries are taken as given. But these theories also tend to have the property that a world in which everyone is subsidizing at once is a world in which everyone is worse off, and that we are all better off if we can agree to limit subsidies or other interventions.

Bilateral or multilateral agreements where other sides make concessions to U.S. products, in return for whatever concessions the United States makes, are virtually the only sorts of trade agreements the United States has made. Indeed, most recent trade agreements (like the North American Free Trade Agreement and China's accession to the WTO) have required much larger reductions in import barriers by U.S. trading partners than by the United States. The reason is that their barriers were higher than those of the United States to start with. But the natural implication is that such agreements raise foreign demand for U.S. products by more than they raise U.S. demand for imports. Hence the United States is likely to benefit from a positive "terms of trade effect." This just adds to the usual benefits of increased efficiency of production and gains to consumers from international trade.

Furthermore, even when a government does not fear retaliation from abroad for trade barriers, intervention in practice is usually based on inadequate knowledge and is corrupted by interest groups. Seeking to rule out all sector-specific intervention is the most effective way of discouraging rent-seeking behavior. Globalization increases the number of competitors operating in the economy. Not only does this work to reduce distortionary monopoly power in the marketplace (which is otherwise exercised by raising prices), it can also reduce distortionary corporate power in the political arena (which is exercised by lobbying).

Most important, new trade theory offers reason to believe that openness can have a permanent effect on a country's rate of growth, not just the level of real GDP. A high rate of economic interaction with the rest of the world speeds the absorption of frontier technologies and global management best practices, spurs innovation and cost-cutting, and competes away monopoly.

These dynamic gains come from a number of sources. They include the benefits of greater market size and enhanced competition. Other sources include technological improvements through increased contact with foreigners and their alternative production styles. Such contact can come, for example, from direct investment by foreign firms with proprietary knowledge or by the exposure to imported goods that embody technologies developed abroad. Each of these elements of international trade and interactions has the effect of promoting growth in the domestic economy. When combined with the static effects, there is no question that the efforts to open markets, when successful, can yield significant dividends.

THE EMPIRICAL CASE FOR TRADE   Citing theory is not a complete answer to the question, "how do we know that trade is good?" We need empirical evidence. Economists have undertaken statistical tests of the determinants of countries' growth rates. Investment in physical capital and investment in human capital are the two factors that emerge the most strongly. But other factors matter. Estimates of growth equations have found a role for openness, measured, for example, as the sum of exports and imports as a share of GDP. David Romer and I look at a cross-section of 100 countries during the period since 1960. The study sought to address a major concern about simultaneous causality between growth and trade: does openness lead to growth, or does growth lead to openness? We found that the effect of openness on growth is even stronger when we correct for the simultaneity compared with standard estimates.

The estimate of the effect of openness on income per capita ranges from 0.3 to 3.0. Consider a round middle number such as 1.0. The increase in U.S. openness since the 1950s is 0.12. Multiplying the two numbers together implies that the increased integration has had an effect of 12 percent on U.S. income. More dramatically, compare a stylized Burma, with a ratio close to zero, versus a stylized Singapore, with a ratio close to 100 percent. Our ballpark estimate, the coefficient of 1.0, implies that Singapore's income is 100 percent higher than Burma's as a result of its openness. The fact that trade can affect a country's growth rate—as opposed to affecting the level of its GDP in a "one-shot" fashion—makes the case for trade liberalization even more compelling. . . .

MACROECONOMIC INTERDEPENDENCE   Trade and financial integration generally increase the transmission of business cycle fluctuations among countries. Floating exchange rates give countries some insulation against one another's fluctuations. When capital markets are highly integrated, floating rates do not give complete insulation, as the post-1973 correlation among major industrialized economies shows. But international transmission can be good for a country as easily as bad, as happens when adverse domestic developments are in part passed off to the rest of the world. The trade balance can act as an important automatic stabilizer for output and employment, improving in recessions and worsening in booms.

Contagion of financial crises is more worrying. The decade of the 1990s alone abounds with examples: the 1992–93 crises in the European exchange rate mechanism, the "tequila crisis" that began with the December 1994 devaluation of the Mexican peso, and the crises in East Asia and emerging markets worldwide from July 1997 to January 1999. Evidently when one country has a crisis it affects others. There is now a greater consensus among economists than before that not all of the observed volatility, or its cross-country correlation, can be attributed to efficient capital markets punishing or rewarding countries based on a rational evaluation of the economic fundamentals. It is difficult to do justice in one paragraph to a discussion that is as voluminous and vigorous as the debate over the welfare implications of the swelling international capital flows. Still, the majority view remains that countries are overall better off with modern globalized financial markets than without them.

The Effect of Trade on Other Social Goals

Many who fear globalization concede that trade has a positive effect on aggregate national income but suspect that it has adverse effects on other highly valued goals such as labor rights, food safety, culture, and so forth. Here we consider only two major values—equality and the environment—and briefly at that.

INCOME DISTRIBUTION   International trade and investment can be a powerful source of growth in poor countries, helping them catch up with those who are ahead in endowments of capital and technology. This was an important component of the spectacular growth of East Asian countries between the 1960s and the 1990s, which remains a miracle even in the aftermath of the 1997–98 currency crises. By promoting convergence, trade can help reduce the enormous worldwide inequality in income. Most of those who are concerned about income distribution, however, seem more motivated by within-country equality than global equality.

A standard textbook theory of international trade, the Heckscher-Ohlin-Samuelson model, has a striking prediction to make regarding within-country income distribution. It is that the scarce factors of production will lose from trade, and the abundant factors will benefit. This means that in rich countries, those who have capital and skills will benefit at the expense of unskilled labor, whereas in poor countries it will be the other way around. The same prediction holds for international capital mobility (or, for that matter, for international labor mobility). It has been very difficult, however, to find substantial direct evidence of the predictions of the model during the postwar period, including distribution effects within either rich or poor countries. Most likely the phenomena of changing technology, intraindustry trade, and worker ties to specific industries are more important today than the factor endowments at the heart of the Heckscher-Ohlin-Samuelson model.

In the United States, the gap between wages paid to skilled workers and wages paid to unskilled workers rose by 18 percentage points between 1973 and 1995 and then leveled off. The fear is that trade is responsible for some of the gap, by benefiting skilled workers more than unskilled workers. Common statistical estimates—which typically impose the theoretical framework rather than testing it—are that between 5 and 30 percent of the increase is attributable to trade. Technology, raising the demand for skilled workers faster than the supply, is the major factor responsible for the rest. One of the higher estimates is that trade contributes one-third of the net increase in the wage gap.

On a sample of seventy-three countries, Chakrabarti finds that trade actually reduces inequality, as measured by the Gini coefficient. This relationship also holds for each income class.

Clearly, income distribution is determined by many factors beyond trade. One is redistribution policies undertaken by the government. In some cases such policies are initiated in an effort to compensate or "buy off" groups thought to be adversely affected by trade. But a far more important phenomenon is the tendency for countries to implement greater redistribution as they grow richer.

A long-established empirical regularity is the tendency for income inequality to worsen at early stages of growth and then to improve at later stages. The original explanation for this phenomenon, known as the Kuznets curve, had to do with rural-urban migration. But a common modern interpretation is that income redistribution is a "superior good"—something that societies choose to purchase more of, even though at some cost to aggregate income, as they grow rich enough to be able to afford to do so. If this is right, then trade can be expected eventually to raise equality, by raising aggregate income.

ENVIRONMENT   Similar logic holds that trade and growth can also be good for the environment, once the country gets past a certain level of per capita income. Gene Grossman and Alan Krueger found what is called the environmental Kuznets curve: growth is bad for air and water pollution at the initial stages of industrialization but later on reduces pollution as countries become rich enough to pay to clean up their environments. . . . A key point is that popular desires need not translate automatically into environmental quality; rather government intervention is usually required to address externalities.

The idea that trade can be good for the environment is surprising to many. The pollution-haven hypothesis instead holds that trade encourages firms to locate production of highly polluting sectors in low-regulation countries in order to stay competitive. But economists' research suggests that environmental regulation is not a major determinant of firms' ability to compete internationally. Furthermore, running counter to fears of a "race to the bottom," is the Pareto-improvement point: trade allows countries to attain more of whatever their goals are, including higher market-measured income for a given level of environmental quality or a better environment for a given level of income. . . .

The econometric studies of the effects of trade and growth on the environment get different results depending on what specific measures of pollution they use. There is a need to look at other environmental criteria as well. It is difficult to imagine, for example, that trade is anything but bad for the survival of tropical hardwood forests or endangered species, without substantial efforts by governments to protect them.

The argument that richer countries will take steps to clean up their environments holds only for issues when the effects are felt domestically—where the primary "bads," such as smog or water pollution, are external to the firm or household but internal to the country. Some environmental externalities that have received increased attention in recent decades, however, are global. Biodiversity, overfishing, ozone depletion, and greenhouse gas emissions are four good examples. A ton of carbon dioxide has the same global warming effect regardless of where in the world it is emitted. In these cases, individual nations can do little to improve the environment on their own, no matter how concerned their populations or how effective their governments. For each of the four examples, governments have negotiated international treaties in an attempt to deal with the problem. But only the attempt to address ozone depletion, the Montreal Protocol, can be said as yet to have met with much success.

Is the popular impression then correct, that international trade and finance exacerbates these global environmental externalities? Yes, but only in the sense that trade and finance promote economic growth. Clearly if mankind were still a population of a few million people living in preindustrial poverty, greenhouse gas emissions would not be a big issue. Industrialization leads to environmental degradation, and trade is part of industrialization. But virtually everyone wants industrialization, at least for themselves. Deliberate self-impoverishment is not a promising option. Once this point is recognized, there is nothing special about trade compared with the other sources of economic growth: capital accumulation, rural-urban migration, and technological progress. . . .

Summary of Conclusions

This chapter gives confident answers to questions about the extent and sources of economic globalization and moderately confident answers to some questions about its effects.

The world has become increasingly integrated with respect to trade and finance since the end of World War II, owing to declining costs to transportation and communication and declining government barriers. The phenomenon is neither new nor complete, however. Globalization was more dramatic in the half-century preceding World War I, and much of the progress during the last half-century has merely reversed the closing off that came in between. In the second regard, globalization is far from complete. Contrary to popular impressions, national borders and geography still impede trade and investment substantially. A simple calculation suggests that the ratio of trade to output would have to increase at least another sixfold before it would be true that Americans trade across the globe as readily as across the country. Such barriers as differences in currencies, languages, and political systems each have their own statistically estimated trade-impeding influences, besides the remaining significant effects of distance, borders, and other geographical and trade policy variables.

The chapter's discussion of the impacts of economic globalization has necessarily been exceedingly brief. Both theory and evidence are read as clearly supportive of the proposition that trade has a positive effect on real incomes. This is why economists believe it is important that the process of international integration be allowed to continue, especially for the sake of those countries that are still poor.

Effects on social values other than aggregate incomes can be positive or negative, depending on the details, and the statistical evidence does not always give clear-cut answers about the bottom line. In the two most studied cases, income distribution and environmental pollution, there seems to be a pattern whereby things get worse in the early stages of industrialization but then start to get better at higher levels of income. Societies that become rich in terms of market-measured output choose to improve their quality of life in other ways as well. It is possible that the same principle extends to noneconomic values such as safety, human rights, and democracy. In short, there is reason to hope that, aside from the various more direct effects of trade on noneconomic values, there is a general indirect beneficial effect that comes through the positive effect of trade on income. . . .

Question for Review

How do we measure the extent of economic globalization in the world today and what are its presumed benefits?

Notes

1 John Maynard Keynes, *The Economic Consequences of the Peace* (Harcourt Brace, and Howe, 1920).

2 Kenneth Froot, Michael Kim, and Kenneth Rogoff, "The Law of One Price over 700 Years," Working Paper 5132 (Cambridge, Mass.: National Bureau of Economic Research, May 1995).

3 Hans Linnemann, *An Econometric Study of International Trade Flows* (Amsterdam: North-Holland, 1960); and Peter Drysdale and Ross Garnaut, "Trade Intensities and the Analysis of Bilateral Trade Flows in a Many-Country World," *Hitotsubashi Journal of Economics,* Vol. 22 (1982), pp. 62–84.

4 Edward Mansfield, "Effects of International Politics on Regionalism in International Trade," in Kym Anderson and Richard Blackhurst, eds., *Regional Integration and the Global Trading System* (Harvester Wheatsheaf, 1993); Edward Mansfield and Rachel Bronson, "The Political Economy of Major-Power Trade Flows," in Edward Mansfield and Helen Milner, eds., *The Political Economy of Regionalism* (Columbia University Press 1997); and Joanne Gowa and Edward Mansfield, "Power Politics and International Trade," *American Political Science Review,* Vol. 87 (June 1993), pp. 408–20.

What Globalization Is and Is Not

MOISÉS NAÍM

"Globalization Is a Casualty of the Economic Crisis."

No. That is, not unless you believe that globalization is mainly about international trade and investment. But it is much more than that, and rumors of its demise—such as Princeton economic historian Harold James's recent obituary for "The Late, Great Globalization"—have been greatly exaggerated.

Jihadists in Indonesia, after all, can still share their operational plans with like-minded extremists in the Middle East, while Vietnamese artists can now more easily sell their wares in European markets, and Spanish magistrates can team up with their peers in Latin America to bring torturers to justice. Globalization, as political scientist David Held and his coauthors put it, is nothing less than the "widening, deepening and speeding up of worldwide interconnectedness in all aspects of contemporary social life"—and not just from one Bloomberg terminal to another.

Around the world, all kinds of groups are still connecting, and the economic crisis will not slow their international activities. In some cases, it might even bolster them. Global charities, for instance, will face soaring demand for their services as the economic crisis greatly expands the number of those in need. Religions, too, will benefit, as widespread hardship heightens interest in the hereafter. At a time when cash is king and jobs are scarce, globalized criminals will be one of the few, if not the only, sources of credit, investment, and employment in some places. And transnational terrorists will not be deterred by a bad economy. The collapse of the credit-default swap market didn't prevent 10 Pakistani militants from wreaking havoc in Mumbai in November [2008].

It's true that private flows of credit and investment across borders have temporarily plummeted. . . . but as private economic activity falls, the international movement of public funds is booming. In the fall of 2008, the U.S. Federal Reserve and the central banks of Brazil, Mexico, Singapore, and South Korea launched $30 billion worth of currency arrangements for each country designed to stabilize their financial markets. Similar reciprocal deals now tie together central banks throughout Asia, Europe, and the Middle East.

Yes, some governments might be tempted to respond to the crisis by adopting trade-impairing policies, imposing rules that inhibit global financial integration, or taking measures to curb immigration. The costs of doing so, however, are enormous and hard to sustain in the long run. What's more, the ability of any government to shield its economy and society from outside influences and dangers has steadily evaporated in the past two decades. There is no indication that this trend will be reversed.

Globalization is such a diverse, broad-based, and potent force that not even today's massive economic crash will dramatically slow it down or permanently reverse it. Love it or hate it, globalization is here to stay.

"Globalization Is Nothing New."

Yes it is. Historians . . . have argued in recent years that the wave of globalization that surged in the 1990s is just a continuation of a long-term process that started as far back as when migrating premodern human communities first encountered each other. They also note that the steamship revolutionized transportation as much or more than the advent of containerized cargo shipping and that the printing press, the telegraph, and the telephone were technologies as disruptive in their day as the Internet. In short, there is nothing new under the sun.

Still, the current wave of globalization has many unprecedented characteristics. As Internet access penetrates the most remote corners of the globe, it is transforming the lives of more people, in more places, more cheaply than ever before—and the pace of change is accelerating faster than we can hope to chronicle it.

Today's globalization is also more individualized than ever. The telegraph was most intensively used by institutions, but the Internet is a truly personal tool that allows Spanish women to find marriage prospects in Argentina, and South African teenagers to share music files with peers in Scotland. Contemporary globalization is also different in that the speed at which it is integrating human activities is often instantaneous and almost costless. Moreover, the quantitative change in each of globalization's components—economic, cultural, military, etc.—is so enormous that it creates a qualitative change. This alone has opened possibilities that are completely new—and also consequences that humanity has never seen before.

"Globalization No Longer Means Americanization."

It never did. For some critics, globalization has been little more than an American project aimed at expanding U.S. economic, military, and cultural dominance. Yet, since the 1980s, Japanese sushi has gone as global as Latin American *telenovelas* or fundamentalist Islam, while massive inflows of Hispanic immigrants have had a huge impact on U.S. society.

Indeed, it is hard to defend the proposition that globalization is a one-way street designed to spread American values and interests around the world. The changes wrought by globalization have enabled new and improbable rivals to dispute America's hegemony in a wide variety of sectors. Al Qaeda and the Taliban have proven to be resilient adversaries for the mighty U.S. military. Their international mobility, funding sources, and recruiting prowess are greatly enhanced by the forces that drive globalization: ease of travel, transportation, and communication; economic liberalization; and porous borders. The sovereign wealth funds from Asia and the Middle East that have displaced American banks, the successful challenge that Indian filmmakers and Latin TV producers have mounted against Hollywood's leadership in the global entertainment markets, and the success of Chinese manufacturers are also rooted in a world shaped by two decades of rapid economic growth and globalization.

The United States has greatly benefited from globalization. But it has hardly been alone in doing so.

"Great Power Politics Are Back."

They never went away. We only thought they did.

Back in the 1990s, the dominant view of globalization held that booming business ties between countries were the best antidote to war. International commerce was seen as a strong countervailing force against nationalistic impulses. Thanks to revolutionary innovations in information technology, communication, and transportation, distance and geography were perceived to be less important in shaping international politics and economics. Power, it was thought, would inevitably shift from governments to the private sector and nongovernmental organizations. . . .

Then came the attacks of Sept. 11, 2001. Minimalist government went out of fashion and demands mounted for the state to provide security at any cost. The financial crisis has amplified this trend. Laissez-faire is out and activist governments are in; deregulation has become a four-letter word and the cry for more government control of the financial sector is universal.

Now that the world economy has tanked, globalization skeptics say the value of commercial ties as a prophylactic against conflict has weakened along with it. And with the return of stronger governments, they say, traditional power plays between rival countries are bound to intensify. Evidence for this view abounds, from resurgent nationalism in Russia, Asia, and Latin America to the obvious role of history and geography in fueling the conflicts in the Middle East and South Asia. Such examples, they argue, show that the stabilizing effects of economic globalization are vastly overstated.

But claims about the return of strong governments and nationalism are equally overstated. Yes, China might team up with Russia to counterbalance the United States in relation to Iran, but meanwhile, the Chinese and U.S. economies will be joined at the hip (China holds more than a trillion dollars of U.S. debt and the United States is the main destination for its exports). Russian Prime Minister Vladimir Putin's tough talk about restoring his country's international standing and challenging America's leadership will be hard to sustain given that Russia's economy is one of the most damaged by the financial crisis, and the oil revenues that enabled its newfound influence are dwindling. Venezuelan President Hugo Chávez is inviting foreign oil companies back.

The bottom line: Nationalism never disappeared. Globalization did not lessen national identities; it just rendered them more complex. Even in a Bill Gates era, today's Otto von Bismarcks still wield great power. Globalization and geopolitics coexist, and neither is going anywhere.

"Globalization Is by and for Rich People."

Go tell the Indians. Or, for that matter, the Chinese, or the emerging middle classes in Brazil, Turkey, Vietnam, and countless other countries that owe their recent success to trade and investment booms facilitated by globalization. Until the financial crisis broke out in 2008, the middle class in poor countries was the fastest-growing segment of the world's population.

This trend will undoubtedly slow, and in some countries it will be tragically reversed as the crisis pushes back large numbers of people into the ranks of the poor. But the fact is that in the past two decades, a significant number of poor countries succeeded in lifting tens of millions out of poverty thanks to globalization. In China, for example, the poverty rate fell 68 percent between 1981 and 2005.

China and India are the paradigmatic examples. Unfortunately, they are also paradigmatic examples of countries where abject poverty coexists with obscene wealth. In poor and rich countries alike, economic inequality has become a major concern and globalization, especially the freer trade it produces, often gets blamed as the source of widening income disparities. It's maddeningly hard, though, to prove that globalization actually produces inequality. We don't even know whether inequality in the world is going up or down. . . . On the other hand, the evidence that absolute poverty has sharply declined during the same time frame is overwhelming.

"Globalization Has Made the World a Safer Place."

Not really. It's true that in the past 20 years, the number of armed conflicts between countries has plummeted. Even accounting for the wars in Iraq and Afghanistan, the amount of armed conflict in the world is at an ebb not seen since the 1970s. One study found that between 1989 and 2003, only seven wars between nation-states broke out. The likelihood that any given country was embroiled in a conflict was at its lowest point since the 1950s.

The problem is that other forms of conflict and violence have soared. The number of people killed or injured by terrorists has gone from about 7,000 in 1995 to more than 25,000 in 2006. Very often, these terrorist attacks are either directly carried out by foreigners or planned, funded, and coordinated by networks that operate internationally. Violent crimes are also going up in many countries, especially the poorest ones. Often, these high crime rates result from the activities of international criminals, mainly narcotraffickers. These days, more beheadings are taking place in Mexico than in Iraq or Afghanistan. Many European countries are reporting higher crime rates as a result of the expanded presence of international criminal gangs in their midst. One could also add the spread of contagious diseases and nuclear proliferation to the list.

Today's world may be at a lower risk for total annihilation than it was when rival superpowers armed with large nuclear arsenals threatened each other with mutual assured destruction, but we now live in an age where a large and growing number of actors empowered by globalization have the potential to cause large-scale damage and substantial loss of human lives. . . . As the economic crisis deepens, desperation might lead to heightened violence, and some governments might be more tempted to exploit international conflicts to distract their impoverished populations from their dire situations at home.

"The Financial Crisis Is a Symptom of Globalization Run Amok."

No, you just think it is. Longtime anti-globalization activists . . . may feel vindicated by the present state of affairs, faulting villains on Wall Street and in world capitals for promoting a form of "disaster capitalism" that has spiraled out of control. Yes, globalization has multiplied the number of problems that no organization or country can solve on its own: not just international economic crises, but also nuclear proliferation, illegal migration, transnational crime, pandemics, and more. The need to collaborate in solving collective problems is as obvious as the difficulties in achieving solutions. The world's multilateral institutions are Cold War holdovers more often described as "dysfunctional" than "indispensable."

But they *are* indispensable, and with the world in crisis mode, demands to shore up global governance have increased. But no matter how many high-level commissions, think-tank reports, books, and articles on the subject, these efforts have not yielded urgently needed drastic changes in multilateral institutions, international law, rules, and coordinating mechanisms.

One reason for the lack of progress: There's still no clarity on how to overcome the obstacles that have long blocked any major reforms. Most proposals for a global governance structure built for the globalization era rest on the assumption that what has been missing is the political will of the world's most powerful countries, notably the United States. This approach fails to address the obvious fact that collaborating with others often means relinquishing power, a concession that does not come easily to sovereign nations.

This does not mean that countries ought to cede power to a world government or to an all-powerful, supranational entity that will rule over world affairs. It is precisely because such an institution is not possible that governments must collaborate with one another more effectively. Yet that is a goal that has proved very elusive.

Unfortunately, it is highly likely that the efforts to minimize the costs of globalization, steer international integration, solve international crises, and better manage the global commons will continue to fall short. Whether the issue is climate change or terrorism, loose nukes or avian flu, the gap between the need for effective collective action at the global level and the ability of the international community to satisfy that need is the most dangerous deficit facing humanity.

Question for Review

On balance, does Naim think globalization is a beneficial or a deleterious force in world politics?

Labor, Capital, and Ideas in the Power Law Economy

ERIK BRYNJOLFSSON, ANDREW MCAFEE, AND MICHAEL SPENCE

Recent advances in technology have created an increasingly unified global marketplace for labor and capital. The ability of both to flow to their highest-value uses, regardless of their location, is equalizing their prices across the globe. In recent years, this broad factor-price equalization has benefited nations with abundant low-cost labor and those with access to cheap capital. Some have argued that the current era of rapid technological progress serves labor, and some have argued that it serves capital. What both camps have slighted is the fact that technology is not only integrating existing sources of labor and capital but also creating new ones.

Machines are substituting for more types of human labor than ever before. As they replicate themselves, they are also creating more capital. This means that the real winners of the future will not be the providers of cheap labor or the owners of ordinary capital, both of whom will be increasingly squeezed by automation. Fortune will instead favor a third group: those who can innovate and create new products, services, and business models.

The distribution of income for this creative class typically takes the form of a power law, with a small number of winners capturing most of the rewards and a long tail consisting of the rest of the participants. So in the future, ideas will be the real scarce inputs in the world—scarcer than both labor and capital—and the few who provide good ideas will reap huge rewards. Assuring an acceptable standard of living for the rest and building inclusive economies and societies will become increasingly important challenges in the years to come.

Labor Pains

Turn over your iPhone and you can read an eight-word business plan that has served Apple well: "Designed by Apple in California. Assembled in China." With a market capitalization of over $500 billion, Apple has become the most valuable company in the world. Variants of this strategy have worked not only for Apple and other large global enterprises but also for medium-sized firms and even "micro-multinationals." More and more companies have been riding the two great forces of our era—technology and globalization—to profits.

Technology has sped globalization forward, dramatically lowering communication and transaction costs and moving the world much closer to a single, large global market for labor, capital, and other inputs to production. Even though labor is not fully mobile, the other factors increasingly are. As a result, the various components of global supply chains can move to labor's location with little friction or cost. About one-third of the goods and services in advanced economies are tradable, and the figure is rising. And the effect of global competition spills over to the nontradable part of the economy, in both advanced and developing economies.

All of this creates opportunities for not only greater efficiencies and profits but also enormous dislocations. If a worker in China or India can do the same work as one in the United States, then the laws of economics dictate that they will end up earning similar wages (adjusted for some other differences in national productivity). That's good news for overall economic efficiency, for consumers, and for workers in developing countries—but not for workers in developed countries who now face low-cost competition. Research indicates that the tradable sectors of advanced industrial countries have not been net employment generators for two decades. That means job creation now takes place almost exclusively within the large nontradable sector, whose wages are held down by increasing competition from workers displaced from the tradable sector.

Even as the globalization story continues, however, an even bigger one is starting to unfold: the story of automation, including artificial intelligence, robotics, 3-D printing, and so on. And this second story is surpassing the first, with some of its greatest effects destined to hit relatively unskilled workers in developing nations.

Visit a factory in China's Guangdong Province, for example, and you will see thousands of young people working day in and day out on routine, repetitive tasks, such as connecting two parts of a keyboard. Such jobs are rarely, if ever, seen anymore in the United States or the rest of the rich world. But they may not exist for long in China and the rest of the developing world either, for they involve exactly the type of tasks that are easy for robots to do. As intelligent machines become cheaper and more capable, they will increasingly replace human labor, especially in relatively structured environments such as factories and especially for the most routine and repetitive tasks. To put it another way, offshoring is often only a way station on the road to automation.

This will happen even where labor costs are low. Indeed, Foxconn, the Chinese company that assembles iPhones and iPads, employs more than a million low-income workers—but now, it is supplementing and replacing them with a growing army of robots. So after many manufacturing jobs moved from the United States to China, they appear to be vanishing from China as well. (Reliable data on this transition are hard to come by. Official Chinese figures report a decline of 30 million manufacturing jobs since 1996, or 25 percent of the total, even as manufacturing output has soared by over 70 percent, but part of that drop may reflect revisions in the methods of gathering data.) As work stops chasing cheap labor, moreover, it will gravitate toward wherever the final market is, since that will add value by shortening delivery times, reducing inventory costs, and the like.

The growing capabilities of automation threaten one of the most reliable strategies that poor countries have used to attract outside investment: offering low wages to compensate for low productivity and skill levels. And the trend will extend beyond manufacturing. Interactive voice response systems, for example, are reducing the requirement for direct person-to-person interaction, spelling trouble for call centers in the developing world. Similarly, increasingly reliable computer programs will cut into transcription work now often done in the developing world. In more and more domains, the most cost-effective source of "labor" is becoming intelligent and flexible machines as opposed to low-wage humans in other countries.

Capital Punishment

If cheap, abundant labor is no longer a clear path to economic progress, then what is? One school of thought points to the growing contributions of capital: the physical and intangible assets that combine with labor to produce the goods and services in an economy (think of equipment, buildings, patents, brands, and so on). As the economist Thomas Piketty argues in his best-selling book *Capital in the Twenty-first Century*, capital's share of the economy tends to grow when the rate of return on it is greater than the general rate of economic growth, a condition he predicts for the future. The "capital deepening" of economies that Piketty forecasts will be accelerated further as robots, computers, and software (all of which are forms of capital) increasingly substitute for human workers. Evidence indicates that just such a form of capital-based technological change is taking place in the United States and around the world.

In the past decade, the historically consistent division in the United States between the share of total national income going to labor and that going to physical capital seems to have changed significantly. As the economists Susan Fleck, John Glaser, and Shawn Sprague noted in the U.S. Bureau of Labor Statistics' *Monthly Labor Review* in 2011, "Labor share averaged 64.3 percent from 1947 to 2000. Labor share has declined over the past decade, falling to its lowest point in the third quarter of 2010, 57.8 percent." Recent moves to "re-shore" production from overseas, including Apple's decision to produce its new Mac Pro computer in Texas, will do little to reverse this trend. For in order to be economically viable, these new domestic manufacturing facilities will need to be highly automated.

Other countries are witnessing similar trends. The economists Loukas Karabarbounis and Brent Neiman have documented significant declines in labor's share of GDP in 42 of the 59 countries they studied, including China, India, and Mexico. In describing their findings, Karabarbounis and Neiman are explicit that progress in digital technologies is an important driver of this phenomenon: "The decrease in the relative price of investment goods, often attributed to advances in information technology and the computer age, induced firms to shift away from labor and toward capital. The lower price of investment goods explains roughly half of the observed decline in the labor share."

But if capital's share of national income has been growing, the continuation of such a trend into the future may be in jeopardy as a new challenge to capital emerges—not from a revived labor sector but from an increasingly important unit within its own ranks: digital capital.

In a free market, the biggest premiums go to the scarcest inputs needed for production. In a world where capital such as software and robots can be replicated cheaply, its marginal value will tend to fall, even if more of it is used in the aggregate. And as more capital is added cheaply at the margin, the value of existing capital will actually be driven down. Unlike, say, traditional factories, many types of digital capital can be added extremely cheaply. Software can be duplicated and distributed at almost zero incremental cost. And many elements of computer hardware, governed by variants of Moore's law, get quickly and consistently cheaper over time. Digital capital, in short, is abundant, has low marginal costs, and is increasingly important in almost every industry.

Even as production becomes more capital-intensive, therefore, the rewards earned by capitalists as a group may not necessarily continue to grow relative to labor. The shares will depend on the exact details of the production, distribution, and governance systems.

Most of all, the payoff will depend on which inputs to production are scarcest. If digital technologies create cheap substitutes for a growing set of jobs, then it is not a good time to be a laborer. But if digital technologies also increasingly substitute for capital, then all owners of capital should not expect to earn outsized returns, either.

Techcrunch Disrupt

What will be the scarcest, and hence the most valuable, resource in what two of us (Erik Brynjolfsson and Andrew McAfee) have called "the second machine age," an era driven by digital technologies and their associated economic characteristics? It will be neither ordinary labor nor ordinary capital but people who can create new ideas and innovations.

Such people have always been economically valuable, of course, and have often profited handsomely from their innovations as a result. But they had to share the returns on their ideas with the labor and capital that were necessary for bringing them into the marketplace. Digital technologies increasingly make both ordinary labor and ordinary capital commodities, and so a greater share of the rewards from ideas will go to the creators, innovators, and entrepreneurs. People with ideas, not workers or investors, will be the scarcest resource.

The most basic model economists use to explain technology's impact treats it as a simple multiplier for everything else, increasing overall productivity evenly for everyone. This model is used in most introductory economics classes and provides the foundation for the common—and, until recently, very sensible— intuition that a rising tide of technological progress will lift all boats equally, making all workers more productive and hence more valuable.

A slightly more complex and realistic model, however, allows for the possibility that technology may not affect all inputs equally but instead favor some more than others. Skill-based technical change, for example, plays to the advantage of more skilled workers relative to less skilled ones, and capital-based technical change favors capital relative to labor. Both of those types of technical change have been important in the past, but increasingly, a third type—what we call superstar-based technical change—is upending the global economy.

Today, it is possible to take many important goods, services, and processes and codify them. Once codified, they can be digitized, and once digitized, they can be replicated. Digital copies can be made at virtually zero cost and transmitted anywhere in the world almost instantaneously, each an exact replica of the original. The combination of these three characteristics—extremely low cost, rapid ubiquity, and perfect fidelity—leads to some weird and wonderful economics. It can create abundance where there had been scarcity, not only for consumer goods, such as music videos, but also for economic inputs, such as certain types of labor and capital.

The returns in such markets typically follow a distinct pattern—a power law, or Pareto curve, in which a small number of players reap a disproportionate share of the rewards. Network effects, whereby a product becomes more valuable the more users it has, can also generate these kinds of winner-take-all or winner-take-most markets. Consider Instagram, the photo-sharing platform, as an example of the economics of the digital, networked economy. The 14 people who created the company didn't need a lot of unskilled human helpers to do so, nor did they need much physical capital. They built a digital product that benefited from network effects, and when it caught on quickly, they were able to sell it after only a year and a half for nearly three-quarters of a billion dollars—ironically, months after the bankruptcy of another photography company, Kodak, that at its peak had employed some 145,000 people and held billions of dollars in capital assets.

Instagram is an extreme example of a more general rule. More often than not, when improvements in digital technologies make it more attractive to digitize a product or process, superstars see a boost in their incomes, whereas second bests, second movers, and latecomers have a harder time competing. The top performers in music, sports, and other areas have also seen their reach and incomes grow since the 1980s, directly or indirectly riding the same trends upward.

But it is not only software and media that are being transformed. Digitization and networks are becoming more pervasive in every industry and function across the economy, from retail and financial services to manufacturing and marketing. That means superstar economics are affecting more goods, services, and people than ever before.

Even top executives have started earning rock-star compensation. In 1990, CEO pay in the United States was, on average, 70 times as large as the salaries of other workers; in 2005, it was 300 times as large. Executive compensation more generally has been going in the same direction globally, albeit with considerable variation from country to country. Many forces are at work here, including tax and policy changes, evolving cultural and organizational norms, and plain luck. But as research by one of us (Brynjolfsson) and Heekyung Kim has shown, a portion of the growth is linked to the greater use of information technology. Technology expands the potential reach, scale, and monitoring capacity of a decision-maker, increasing the value of a good decision-maker by magnifying the potential consequences of his or her choices. Direct management via digital technologies makes a good manager more valuable than in earlier times, when executives had to share control with long chains of subordinates and could affect only a smaller range of activities. Today, the larger the market value of a company, the more compelling the argument for trying to get the very best executives to lead it.

When income is distributed according to a power law, most people will be below the average, and as national economies writ large are increasingly subject to such dynamics, that pattern will play itself out on the national level. And sure enough, the United States today features one of the world's highest levels of real GDP per capita—even as its median income has essentially stagnated for two decades.

Preparing for the Permanent Revolution

The forces at work in the second machine age are powerful, interactive, and complex. It is impossible to look far into the future and predict with any precision what their ultimate impact will be. If individuals, businesses, and governments understand what is going on, however, they can at least try to adjust and adapt.

The United States, for example, stands to win back some business as the second sentence of Apple's eight-word business plan is overturned because its technology and manufacturing operations are once again performed inside U.S. borders. But the first sentence of the plan will become more important than ever, and here, concern, rather than complacency, is in order. For unfortunately, the dynamism and creativity that have made the United States the most innovative nation in the world may be faltering.

Thanks to the ever-onrushing digital revolution, design and innovation have now become part of the tradable sector of the global economy and will face the same sort of competition that has already transformed manufacturing. Leadership in design depends on an educated work force and an entrepreneurial culture, and the traditional American advantage in these areas is declining. Although the United States once led the world in the share of graduates in the work force with at least an associate's degree, it has now fallen to 12th place. And despite the buzz about entrepreneurship in places such as Silicon Valley, data show that since 1996, the number of U.S. start-ups employing more than one person has declined by over 20 percent.

If the trends under discussion are global, their local effects will be shaped, in part, by the social policies and investments that countries choose to make, both in the education sector specifically and in fostering innovation and economic dynamism more generally. For over a century, the U.S. educational system was the envy of the world, with universal K–12 schooling and world-class universities propelling sustained economic growth. But in recent decades, U.S. primary and secondary schooling have become increasingly uneven, with their quality based on neighborhood income levels and often a continued emphasis on rote learning.

Fortunately, the same digital revolution that is transforming product and labor markets can help transform education as well. Online learning can provide students with access to the best teachers, content, and methods regardless of their location, and new data-driven approaches to the field can make it easier to measure students' strengths, weaknesses, and progress. This should create opportunities for personalized learning programs and continuous improvement, using some of the feedback techniques that have already transformed scientific discovery, retail, and manufacturing.

Globalization and technological change may increase the wealth and economic efficiency of nations and the world at large, but they will not work to everybody's advantage, at least in the short to medium term. Ordinary workers, in particular, will continue to bear the brunt of the changes, benefiting as consumers but not necessarily as producers. This means that without further intervention, economic inequality is likely to continue to increase, posing a variety of problems. Unequal incomes can lead to unequal opportunities, depriving nations of access to talent and undermining the social contract. Political power, meanwhile, often follows economic power, in this case undermining democracy.

These challenges can and need to be addressed through the public provision of high-quality basic services, including education, health care, and retirement security. Such services will be crucial for creating genuine equality of opportunity in a rapidly changing economic environment and increasing intergenerational mobility in income, wealth, and future prospects.

As for spurring economic growth in general, there is a near consensus among serious economists about many of the policies that are necessary. The basic strategy is intellectually simple, if politically difficult: boost public-sector investment over the short and medium term while making such investment more efficient and putting in place a fiscal consolidation plan over the longer term. Public investments are known to yield high returns in basic research in health, science, and technology; in education; and in infrastructure spending on roads, airports, public water and sanitation systems, and energy and communications grids. Increased government spending in these areas would boost economic growth now even as it created real wealth for subsequent generations later.

Should the digital revolution continue to be as powerful in the future as it has been in recent years, the structure of the modern economy and the role of work itself may need to be rethought. As a group, our descendants may work fewer hours and live better—but both the work and the rewards could be spread even more unequally, with a variety of unpleasant consequences. Creating sustainable, equitable, and inclusive growth will require more than business as usual. The place to start is with a proper understanding of just how fast and far things are evolving.

Question for Review

What is the "power law economy," and why is education so critical for competing in this new economy?

Chapter 10

Fixing the World Political Economy

The Status Quo Crisis

Eric Helleiner

1

The financial crisis of 2008 was the worst global financial meltdown experienced since the early 1930s. Major financial institutions collapsed or were nationalized, and many others stayed afloat only because of extensive public support. Global industrial production, world trade, and the value of world equity markets all fell more rapidly in the first ten months after April 2008 than they had during the same period after the start of the Great Depression. Although the impact of the crisis was felt differently across the world, all regions were affected by it in some way.

Because of the severity of the crisis, many analysts immediately predicted that it would be very transformative for global financial governance. Four developments in 2008–09 reinforced these expectations. The first was the decision in November 2008 by the heads of state of the world's most important economies to create a new body—the G20 leaders' forum—to help manage the crisis. The future of the dollar's role as the world's key currency also quickly became a topic of widespread debate in public policy circles. In addition, the G20 leaders committed quickly to an extensive agenda for international regulatory reforms, reinforcing the widespread view that the crisis would provoke a major backlash against the market-friendly nature of pre-crisis international financial standards. Finally, a new international institution was created in April 2009—the Financial Stability Board (FSB)—that top policymakers described as a novel "fourth pillar" of the global economic architecture, alongside the International Monetary Fund, World Bank, and World Trade Organization.

From the vantage point of five years after the crisis, this book argues that none of these developments looks as significant as it initially appeared. The G20's contribution to the financial management of the crisis ended up being much less significant than advertised. The US dollar remained unchallenged as the world's dominant international currency. The market-friendly character of international financial standards was not overturned in a significant way. And the FSB's capacity to act as a kind of fourth pillar of global economic governance turned out to be very limited.

In these respects, the crisis of 2008 has been—at least so far—more of a status quo event than a transformative one. The crisis may, of course, have unleashed developments that could generate important change in the spheres of global financial governance over the medium to long term. . . . The main focus of . . . , is on what was witnessed across these four issue areas in the first half decade since the peak of the crisis in the fall of 2008. From this vantage point, the crisis was a strangely conservative event.

Why were the expectations of transformation in global financial governance not borne out? The book attributes this outcome largely to a specific configuration of power and politics among and within influential states. Particularly important were the structural power and active policy choices of the country at the center of the crisis: the United States. In many key instances, status quo outcomes also reflected the unexpected weakness of Europe and conservatism of governments in China and other large emerging market countries. This explanation of the status quo nature of the crisis calls attention to the enduring state-centric foundations of global financial governance in contrast to analyses that focus more on the growing significance of international institutions or of transnational elites and ideologies. If global financial governance is to be transformed in more substantial ways in the coming years, the argument suggests that power and politics among and within these key states will play the central role.

The Crisis

The sequence of events involved in the unfolding of the 2008 global financial crisis is by now very well known and can be recounted quickly. The first signs appeared when US real estate prices began to decline in 2006 and defaults on US subprime mortgages started increasing. By the summer of 2007, financial institutions that had invested heavily in securities linked to those mortgages—particularly in the United States and Europe—faced huge losses. As concerns grew about the extent of the exposure of various financial firms, some international financial markets began to freeze up in August 2007. This phenomenon only compounded the difficulties many financial institutions faced, particularly those that were highly leveraged and dependent on short-term funding. Confidence was eroded further in September 2007 when one such institution in Britain—Northern Rock—experienced the first serious bank run in that country since the mid-19th century.

The crisis then intensified in March 2008 when the large US investment bank Bear Stearns ran into deep trouble and was rescued only by a takeover by J.P. Morgan Chase, assisted by the Federal Reserve Bank of New York. The most acute phase of the crisis then came in September 2008. Early in the month, the US government effectively nationalized the giant US mortgage lending institutions Fannie Mae and Freddie Mac by placing them under a public "conservatorship."

In mid-September, the US investment bank Lehman Brothers collapsed, triggering massive panic in global financial markets because of its size and the extent of its connections with other financial institutions. Fear among investors only intensified when it became clear that the American International Group (AIG)—the world's largest insurance company—was on the verge of bankruptcy as well. It was quickly rescued by a massive initial $85 billion bailout from the US government.

This combination of events generated severe downward pressure on asset values in major world financial markets in the fall of 2008. As financial institutions struggled to cope with their losses and reduce their exposure to the financial instability, enormous deleveraging took place, generating a vicious downward spiral of selling, further price declines, and more deleveraging. Many financial institutions did not survive, while others were saved only with extensive public support.

Although the 2008 crisis was centered in US and European markets, it had worldwide repercussions. Indeed, economic historians show that the 2008 meltdown was the first truly global-scale financial crisis of the post-1945 period because it affected all regions and major financial centers. Its impact was also felt well outside of the financial sector. International trade and financial flows declined rapidly as the crisis intensified, and by the fall of 2008, the entire world economy had entered a severe recession.

Given its scale, it is not surprising that many anticipated that the crisis would quickly usher in major transformations in global financial governance. By November 2008, prominent figures such as Nobel Prize winning economist Joseph Stiglitz were arguing that that it was a "Bretton Woods moment." The phrase invoked the 1944 conference at where an entirely new international financial order was created for the postwar world. . . . This book details how and why these expectations of major transformation in global financial governance did not pan out. . . .

Did the G20 Save the Day?

The first set of arguments . . . concerns the significance of the G20 as a financial crisis manager. Immediately after its creation, the G20 leaders' forum was seen as a major institutional innovation in global financial governance that would help manage the financial crisis. Unlike the G7, the G20 included all the large emerging market countries, many of which could make an important contribution to addressing the financial turmoil. The G20 had already met regularly since 1999 as a grouping of finance ministry and central bank officials. By creating a G20 leaders' forum, heads of state of the most important economies seemed to be signaling the seriousness of their intention to develop cooperative solutions to the crisis.

The expectations for the G20's crisis management role were only reinforced by the results of its first two summits in November 2008 and April 2009. At both meetings, the G20 leaders signaled their determination to fight the crisis collectively through what appeared to be bold initiatives. In the financial realm, they committed to coordinate national macroeconomic stimulus programs and even backed an ambitious $1.1 trillion support program for the world economy, the centerpiece of which was a massive increase in the lending capacity of the International Monetary Fund (IMF). When the crisis began to subside in the summer of 2009, the G20 leaders' forum was widely heralded—including by the leaders themselves—as an innovative institution that had helped prevent a repetition of the 1930s dilemma. . . .

Chapter 2 argues that this narrative seriously overstates the significance of the G20's creation for the financial dimensions of the management of the crisis. Though there is little doubt that the expansionary monetary and fiscal policies of G20 countries helped avert a second Great Depression, the role of the G20 leaders' forum in coordinating these policies is questionable. Governments were responding more to domestic political pressures in the context of a common global economic shock than to the G20 summits. The economic significance of the headline-grabbing $1.1 trillion support program announced at the London summit should also not be exaggerated. Particularly important was the fact that many poorer countries were reluctant in 2008–09 to borrow from the international institution—the IMF—whose resources had been so dramatically boosted by the G20. Those countries had become extremely wary of the Fund because of its role in the East Asian financial crisis of 1997–98, a wariness that had encouraged them to build up foreign exchange reserves before the 2008 crisis in ways that helped buffer them from the shock without IMF assistance.

Even more striking was the fact that the G20 leaders' forum was completely uninvolved in organizing the most important cooperative dimension of the financial management of the crisis: large-scale lending by the US Federal Reserve to foreign central banks. The Fed's loans came in the form of a series of ad hoc bilateral swaps created between December 2007 and October 2008, all in advance of the first G20 leaders' meeting. Foreign drawing on these Fed swap lines was very large, peaking at almost $600 billion in late 2008—a figure far higher than IMF lending during the crisis. In addition to supporting the balance of payments position of some countries, the Fed's loans were critically important in enabling many foreign central banks to provide much-needed dollar liquidity to troubled firms and markets in their respective jurisdictions. With its extensive swap program, the Fed acted as a crucial international lender-of-last-resort during the crisis. To some extent, this role was also played by the Fed through the unilateral provision of dollar liquidity directly to distressed foreign financial institutions, as well as the US Treasury whose assistance to troubled domestic institutions also supported the foreign counterparties of those firms.

The fact that the United States acted as a key international lender-of-last-resort in the crisis signaled a continuity in global financial governance rather than change. During previous post–World War II international financial crisis, US authorities had often played this critical role. During the 2008 crisis (as in the past), they had a unique capacity to produce unlimited sums of dollars, the currency that many foreigners needed because of the greenback's dominant role in the global financial system. As in the past, the enduring centrality of the United States in global finance also helped motivate its authorities to act as international lender-of-last-resort: internationally oriented US financial firms, US financial markets, and the dollar were all vulnerable to financial instability abroad. The financial dimensions of the successful cooperative management of the crisis thus had much more to do with this ongoing US ability and willingness to act as international-lender-of-last-resort than with the establishment of the new G20 leaders' forum.

When the G20 subsequently explored initiatives to reform global financial governance to prevent future crises, it continued to refrain from taking a leadership role in this area. After the Fed swaps expired in early 2010, the G20 leaders considered proposals to expand and institutionalize a new swap regime, but ultimately rejected them. US officials were particularly concerned about the burdens and risks that this initiative might generate for the Fed. They were also reluctant to back IMF reforms that might allow that institution to assume a greater role in this field in the future. The consequence was that, five years after the financial meltdown, the crisis-management dimensions of global financial governance remained heavily dependent on ad hoc US international lender-of-last-resort activities, just as they had throughout the postwar era. Rather than demonstrating the effectiveness of a new global financial crisis manager, the crisis and its aftermath highlighted the importance of the old.

Was the Dollar's Global Role Undermined?

The crisis also did little to change the dollar's dominant role as the world's key currency. When the crisis first broke out, there were widespread predictions that this role would be seriously challenged by a major collapse in the value of the dollar. . . . These fears were understandable. Not only was the United States at the center of the crisis, but it had also become very dependent on foreign capital to fund large current account deficits at the time. For the first time in the postwar period, the dollar also faced a serious rival in international currency use, the euro, which had been created in 1999 and whose international role was expanding at the time the crisis began. In these circumstances, the United States looked extremely vulnerable to a serious currency crisis, a development that seemed very likely to undermine the dollar's international standing.

But no dollar crisis unfolded. Indeed . . . the dollar's value appreciated as the global financial crisis intensified in the summer of 2008. What explains this result? One explanation is that there was strong international private demand for the US currency as the crisis intensified. Some of this demand reflected the fact that foreign financial institutions needed dollars to cover their deteriorating positions in dollar-dominated global financial markets. As the global crisis intensified, investors also perceived the dollar to be a safe haven currency because it was backed by the world's dominant power and the unique liquidity and depth of the US Treasury bill market. The dollar also benefited from eroding investor confidence in its main competitor, the euro, in the face of the uncoordinated manner by which national authorities in the Eurozone responded to distressed financial institutions at the time.

The dollar also benefitted from the support of a number of foreign governments—particularly China—that did not dump their large reserve holdings of the US currency during the crisis. This foreign official support emerged more from the unilateral decisions of these governments than from any explicit negotiations with US officials. Many governments with large reserves saw dollar holdings—particularly US Treasury bills—as a relatively more attractive asset in the crisis for the same reasons that private investors did. The crisis also reinforced, rather than undermined, some of the broader political reasons for why they had held large dollar reserves before it began. One was that reserves served as a form of "self-insurance" to protect their country against external instability—a goal that became even more significant in the crisis. In export-oriented economies, dollar reserves also helped to support their major export market and to keep their exchange rate competitive during the crisis. The risk of a dollar crisis also highlighted starkly to Chinese authorities the extent to which they now had a very large financial stake in the dollar's stability, given the enormous reserves they had already accumulated. In countries that were close geopolitical allies of the United States, support for the dollar may also have been linked to broader strategic concerns.

Rather than undermining the dollar's global role, the crisis thus provided new insights about the sources of its dominance. The decisions of private investors and foreign governments to support the dollar were shaped by the euro's governance weaknesses and broader "structural power" of the United States in the global political economy stemming from the its financial markets, centrality in world trade, geopolitical dominance, and the prominence global financial role of the US dollar itself during the pre-crisis years. The dollar also benefitted from the strength of the commitments among many emerging market countries—particularly China—to self-insurance and export-oriented development strategies. Foreign support was reinforced by US policy choices such as the maintenance of open markets and decisions to bail out troubled domestic financial firms in which foreigners had heavy stakes.

In the wake of the crisis, the dollar quickly faced new challenges, as many foreign governments expressed frustrations about the dollar's global dominance and pressed for international monetary reform. One initiative was to bolster the international role of a supranational reserve asset that had first been created in the late 1960s: the IMF's Special Drawing Rights (SDRs). While the G20 leaders agreed at their second summit to the first new issue of SDRs in three decades, the SDR posed little challenge to the dollar's global role in the absence of more substantial efforts to strengthen its significance. This latter goal did have supporters in China, France, and some other countries, but it encountered a number of opponents, notably the US government, whose voting share within the IMF gave it the power to veto reforms of this kind. The reluctance of the United States to embrace major reform reflected a number of factors, including its dependence on foreign capital and the fact that various US private and public interests benefitted from the dollar's international role and the pre-crisis growth model with which it was associated.

Other foreign critics of the dollar's international role after the crisis urged the internationalization of their own countries' currencies in order to create a more multipolar currency order. Many Europeans hoped that the euro could serve as one such pole. But the European currency's ability to challenge the dollar was constrained by the outbreak of European debt crises after early 2010. These crises revealed serious weaknesses in the currency's governance and even called into question the euro's survival. Because of these troubles, the euro's international role was undermined, rather than strengthened, in the wake of the crisis.

From 2009 onward, the Chinese government expressed heightened interest in backing the greater internationalization of its currency, the renminbi (RMB), through various initiatives. The RMB's international role had previously been negligible and these initiatives encouraged some growth. But its international use remained extremely limited in comparison to that of the dollar because the Chinese government refused to embrace more far-reaching reforms that would make the RMB fully convertible and enhance the attractiveness of Chinese financial markets to foreigners. These kinds of reforms were resisted largely because they would undermine the government's tight control over finance that was at the core of the Chinese investment-led, export-oriented development model. . . . The result was that the dollar's status as the world's dominant currency emerged remarkably unscathed not just from the crisis experience but also from post-crisis challenges. Five years after the crisis, its international role was almost identical to what it had been just before the financial upheaval had begun. Despite widespread dissatisfaction with the dollar's international role, it was clear that the task of dislodging the greenback from its preeminent global position faced difficult political obstacles.

Was the Market-Friendly Nature of International Financial Standards Overturned?

The third aspect of global financial governance . . . is the content of international financial standards. Throughout 2008, there were widespread expectations that the crisis would provoke a major backlash against the market-friendly nature of international financial standards that had been developed since the 1990s. Expectations were raised further by the final communiqué from the first G20 leaders' summit in November 2008 which outlined a detailed agenda for international regulatory reforms. Working closely with international standard setting bodies and other international institutions, the G20 subsequently endorsed many reforms to existing international financial standards as well as the development of a number of new standards.

. . . despite the various international regulatory reforms, the market-friendly nature of pre-crisis international financial standards was not overturned in a significant way. To be sure, some existing regulations . . . have been tightened. Public oversight was also extended to sectors where private international financial standards or voluntary rules had dominated before the crisis, such as accounting, hedge funds, credit rating agencies, and over-the-counter (OTC) derivatives. In addition, G20 financial officials endorsed the use of restrictions on cross-border financial transactions in late 2011, a move echoed by the IMF in a formal statement in late 2012. But these changes were less significant than they appeared. . . .

Five years after the crisis, the content of post-crisis international financial regulatory reforms thus looked remarkably tame in comparison to the predictions made in 2008. Rather than overturning the market-friendly nature of pre-crisis international financial standards, the G20 leaders tweaked its content. . . . In the end, the content of international regulatory reforms was shaped heavily by US priorities, as it had often been in the past. US influence stemmed from the global importance of its financial markets as well as the fact that US officials were "first-movers" in initiating domestic reforms which often then acted as focal points for international standards. US interest in international regulatory reform was shaped directly by those domestic reforms: internationally coordinated regulatory tightening would help minimize competitive disadvantages for US markets and firms that could result from unilateral US reforms. But the limitations of subsequent US domestic regulatory initiatives then set limits on what the US was willing to endorse at the international level. The weak nature of the challenge to pre-crisis market-friendly international financial standards often simply reflected this constraint imposed by the US domestic context.

A second assumption was that the crisis would weaken the political influence of private financial interests that had often promoted market-friendly regulation before 2008. In fact, however, those interests remained powerful in many contexts, particularly in the United States, where the generosity and success of the government's rescue operations ensured that many private interests rebounded from the crisis quickly and retained enormous influence in post-crisis regulatory debates. Those interests watered down many US domestic regulatory reforms, a result that helped to explain the weak content of a number of international regulatory initiatives.

One final assumption was that the credibility of market-friendly or "neoliberal" thinking in finance would be severely undermined by the crisis. Many of the post-crisis reforms were indeed driven by a newly influential "macroprudential" philosophy that highlighted how previous thinking had downplayed the prevalence of systemic risk in financial markets. But macroprudential thinking had somewhat ambiguous policy implications. Although it could justify anti-market regulation, many officials—particularly in the US—embraced a more minimalist version of macroprudential ideas that supported enhanced public oversight without actually constraining private financial activity in significant ways. This limitation provided a further explanation for why the market-friendly nature of international financial standards was not significantly overturned.

Was a Fourth Pillar of Global Economic Architecture Created?

The fourth and final issue. . . . is the significance of the creation of the FSB by the G20 leaders in April 2009. The FSB was the only new international institution—aside from the G20 leaders' forum itself—to emerge from the crisis and it was touted as a very important innovation in strengthening the governance of international financial standards. In a widely quoted comment, US Treasury Secretary Tim Geithner described the FSB just after its creation as a new "fourth pillar" of global economic architecture that would help to ensure that post-crisis international financial regulatory reforms were implemented in a harmonized fashion.

If it could perform this role effectively, the FSB would indeed have been an important innovation. International financial standards had long been developed by international standard setting bodies with little power and few staff. In contrast to international trade rules, these standards were "soft law" with which compliance was entirely voluntary. Not surprisingly, implementation of international financial standards by national authorities had often been inconsistent in the pre-crisis period. The FSB was promoted as a body that could address this weakness in the international financial standards regime. . . . Rather than being an entirely new institution, the FSB was simply a reformed version of an ineffectual body that the G7 had created a decade earlier: the Financial Stability Forum (FSF). The latter's membership had initially included the G7 countries, international standard setting bodies, and various international financial institutions, and it had attempted to encourage implementation of international financial standards. But it had been given no charter, no formal power of any kind, and only a tiny staff. Indeed, the FSF had represented a kind of pinnacle of the loose, soft-law, network-based governance that characterized the international financial standards regime before the 2008 crisis.

When the FSB was created, it was given a formal charter, more staff, more specific mandates than the FSF, and a wider country membership that included all G20 countries. But the FSB inherited the basic weaknesses of its predecessor: it had no formal power. Although the FSB's charter committed member countries to implement international standards, the commitment had little formal meaning because membership in the body created no legal obligations of any kind. The FSB's capacity to foster implementation was restricted entirely to "soft" mechanisms such as peer review, transparency, and monitoring.

In 2010, FSB members did announce an initiative that initially appeared to signal a more serious effort to encourage implementation by threatening sanctions against noncomplying jurisdictions. But the limitations of the initiative quickly became clear. Sanctions could be applied only with the consensus of all FSB members, thereby ensuring that no member would be targeted because each could exercise a veto. Even for nonmembers, the initiative focused only on some very basic pre-crisis principles relating to international cooperation and information exchange rather than the post-crisis international regulatory reforms. Efforts to encourage compliance with the latter continued to focus entirely on voluntary mechanisms for both FSB members and nonmembers.

The establishment of the FSB thus did little to alter the soft-law character of the international financial standards regime. Despite the rhetoric touting a new fourth pillar of global economic architecture, the FSB remained—like the FSF—a remarkably toothless organization. . . .

The failure of the G20 to create a stronger international institution to address these challenges largely reflected widespread resistance to the idea of accepting infringements on sovereignty in the realm of financial regulatory policymaking. While some French and British policymakers pushed ambitious plans for a strong global institution in the regulatory arena, many others were much more wary, including US authorities who had long been reluctant to accept international constraints on their policy autonomy in this sphere. Concerns about delegating regulatory authority to an international body were only reinforced by the failures of cooperation during the crisis to resolve failing institutions or share the burden of bailouts. If the costs of distressed financial institutions were going to fall on host countries (as they had during the crisis), national authorities had good reason for wanting to keep regulatory powers in their own hands. . . . These post-crisis initiatives signaled that nation-states—rather than the FSB—remained the key pillars of global economic governance in the financial regulatory realm.

Explaining the Status Quo Outcomes

. . . . What accounts for absence of a significant transformation of global financial governance in the wake of the worst global financial crisis since the early 1930s? Although each case had its own dynamics, there were some common themes across the four issues areas that can be briefly summarized.

The first was the structural power of the country at the center of the crisis: the United States. In a number of instances, the absence of significant change reflected the fact that private actors and other states responded to the crisis in a global financial environment shaped by factors such as the dollar's global role, the relative attractiveness of US financial markets, the US role as an export market, US geopolitical strength, and US influence in institutions such as the IMF. In the early 1980s, Susan Strange noted that the US was "still an extraordinary power" in this structural sense in international financial affairs. The crisis and post-crisis period revealed starkly that it retained this position of unparalleled structural power three decades later. This power helped—often with little direct agency by US officials—to inhibit major transformation of global financial governance in this period.

But US officials also made active policy choices that shaped outcomes in important ways. Some of these choices involved initiatives whereby the US government helped to preserve the status quo by performing classic global economic leadership functions such as lender-of-last-resort activities and the maintenance of open markets. In other cases, they blocked, or diluted the ambition of, post-crisis reforms, such as those relating to the IMF governance, the creation of a multilateral swap regime, SDR reform, as well as the strengthening of international regulation and the FSB's role. These various choices reflected a number of factors, including the country's dependence on foreign capital, the enduring influence of domestic groups that favored the status quo, as well as policymakers' commitments to policy autonomy, domestic financial stability, neoliberal ideas, the country's pre-crisis growth model, and the international competitiveness of US financial markets and institutions. For all these reasons, US policymakers acted as a particularly significant conservative force during and in the wake of the crisis.

The power and agency of some other leading states was also significant in explaining the limited post-crisis change in global financial governance. A number of the outcomes reflected the unexpected weakness of Europe. At the start of the crisis, European policymakers were often among the most enthusiastic in calling for more radical change in global financial governance. This ambition—and the European capacity to realize it—quickly faded in the context of the serious problems in the Eurozone and difficulties of coordinating Europe-wide positions on international reforms.

The choices of policymakers from some emerging market countries, particularly China, were also important. They contributed to status quo outcomes through their enduring preferences for self-insurance and export-oriented growth strategies as well as through their caution about internationalizing local currencies or challenging the content of international regulatory reforms. The conservatism of these policymakers across these various areas reflected the influence of entrenched policy frameworks and domestic interests as well as their risk aversion in the context of domestic political and economic challenges.

These factors help to explain the status quo results across the four cases, but it is worth noting that the respective outcomes also reinforced each other in important ways. For example, if the dollar had experienced a serious crisis in 2008 or if the Fed had not acted as international lender-of-last-resort, the crisis would have been much worse—a development that might have generated much greater political pressures for more radical regulatory responses. There was also a strong complementarity between state priorities and powerful domestic interests in the United States and China favoring the continuation of pre-crisis growth models. If the domestic political context in either country had changed more significantly, reactions might have been triggered in the other with results that generated more dramatic changes in global financial governance. . . .

From a more institutionalist standpoint, some scholars have argued that the strength of the contemporary international institutional landscape helped to foster cooperation and prevent a collapse of the global economy similar to that of the early 1930s. International economic institutions are seen to have been significant in providing focal points for coordination, rules that constrained behavior and reduced uncertainty, and expertise that helped to promote shared understandings. The analysis in this book differs by highlighting the relative weaknesses and lack of influence of key international bodies such as the G20, IMF, and FSB in global financial governance. Indeed, this book even downplays the significance of international cooperation more generally in explaining key developments that helped to prevent a global economic collapse, such as the macroeconomic stimulus programs of 2008–09 and the absence of a dollar crisis. Where cooperation was key to explaining outcomes—as in the case of the Fed swaps—it often took a bilateral and ad hoc form rather than a multilateral institutionalized one. . . .

In sum . . . the status quo outcome had a number of causes, of which the power and agency of dominant states, especially the United States, were particularly important. Their importance provides a useful lesson for analytical understandings of the political economy of global finance. In the years leading up to the crisis, there was much scholarly analysis of the growing significance of transnational non-state actors, private regimes, and international institutions in global financial governance. Post-2008 developments highlight more than ever the fact that global financial governance continues to rest on very state-centric foundations.

What Next?

What is in store for the future of global financial governance? . . . Although . . . the crisis has been a status quo event to date, the crisis could certainly have more transformative effects over the longer term. The final chapter explores in a more speculative manner four scenarios of how the crisis might influence the evolution of global financial governance in the coming years.

Under the first scenario, the longer term legacy of the crisis would involve a strengthening of liberal multilateral features of global financial governance. As we have seen, the crisis generated new multilateral institutions such as the G20 leaders' forum and the FSB, as well as reforms to the IMF. This book highlights the limitations of these institutional innovations in the realms of crisis management (in the cases of the G20 and IMF), international currency issuance (the IMF's SDR), and the international regulatory regime (the FSB). But over time and with the support of cooperation among the major powers, these limitations may be overcome in ways that allow these international bodies to play a more central role in global financial governance. In that event, the crisis might be seen in future years as an important event that laid the groundwork for a strengthened liberal multilateral global financial order.

The second scenario anticipates an opposite outcome in which global financial governance was characterized by growing fragmentation and conflict between the major powers. Under this scenario, international financial crises would be increasingly addressed by governments through competing regional, bilateral, and unilateral mechanisms. Currency rivalries between the dollar and emerging challengers such as the euro and RMB would intensify. Global regulatory cooperation would break down as countries and regions introduced various unilateral controls to insulate themselves from instability abroad and to defend their regulatory autonomy, particularly to tighten controls over financial markets. The crisis of 2008 already encouraged some of these tendencies, which could easily intensify in the coming years if cooperation between the major powers were to break down.

A third scenario of "cooperative decentralization" sits between the first and second. In this future world, multilateralism would remain an important feature of global financial governance but it would serve a more decentralized order. Crisis management would be increasingly handled through regional, bilateral, and national mechanisms but with the IMF and G20 supplementing and/or supporting these mechanisms in a number of ways. A more multipolar currency order would emerge but one characterized more by cooperation between the world's major currency zones than by conflict and rivalry. In the regulatory realm, national and regional authorities would carve out greater policy space through initiatives that created a more fragmented global financial system but in a cooperative manner that was supported and overseen by the FSB and IMF. In each of these contexts, this scenario would reconcile divergent legacies of the 2008 crisis in ways that would require cooperation between the major powers but of a much less ambitious kind than the first scenario.

A final scenario is one that would build on the initial post-crisis experience examined in this book: enduring status quo. International crisis management would remain heavily dependent on ad hoc US international lender-of-last-resort activities. The dollar would endure as the world's dominant currency. International financial standards would continue to be developed and refined with largely market-friendly content. The FSB would survive as a weak and fragile body trying, with uneven success, to encourage implementation of those standards through voluntary mechanisms. It may seem unlikely that this kind of status quo could persist over the longer term, but the experience of the crisis of 2008 highlights how plausible this scenario may be, particularly if there are no major shifts in the power and interests of dominant states in the coming years. . . .

Questions for Review

What caused the financial crisis of 2008, and which country played the greatest role in preventing the "Great Recession" from becoming another great depression? Has the crisis produced a fundamental reform of the global financial system?

A New Global Reserve System

JOSEPH E. STIGLITZ

Concerned about its holdings of dollars, in March 2009 the head of China's central bank lent support to a long-standing idea: creation of a global reserve currency. Keynes pushed the idea some seventy-five years ago, and it was part of his original conception for the IMF. Additionally, support for this idea has come from another quarter—a UN commission of experts on the restructuring of the global financial and economic system, which I chaired.

Developing countries, *China foremost*, today hold trillions of dollars in reserves—money they can draw upon in the event of a crisis, such as the Great Recession. In chapter 1, I emphasized that this crisis exposed the problem of a global insufficiency of aggregate demand. Sadly, *so far*, neither the U.S. administration nor the G-20 has even begun to discuss this underlying problem—let alone take action. Annual emissions of a new global reserve currency would mean that countries would no longer have to set aside part of their current income as protection against global volatility—instead, they could set aside the newly issued "money." This would thereby increase global aggregate demand and strengthen the global economy.

There are two other important reasons for this initiative. The first is that the present system is unstable. Currently, countries hold dollars to provide confidence to their currency and country as a kind of insurance against the vicissitudes of the global marketplace. As more and more dollars are held by foreigners in their reserves, there is greater and greater anxiety about America's increasing indebtedness abroad.

There is another reason why the current system contributes to instability. If some countries insist on having a trade surplus (exporting more than they import) in order to build up reserves, other countries have to have trade deficits; the sum of the surpluses must equal the sum of the deficits. But trade deficits can be a problem—countries with persistent trade deficits are more likely to face an economic crisis—and countries have worked hard to get rid of them. If one country gets rid of its trade deficit, then some other country's deficit must rise (if the surplus countries don't change their behavior), so trade deficits are like a hot potato. In recent years, most countries have learned how to avoid deficits, with the result that the United States has become the "deficit of last resort." In the long run, America's position is clearly untenable. Creating a global reserve currency with annual emissions would provide a buffer. A country could run a small trade deficit and still build up its reserves, because of the allocation of new global reserve currency that it receives. As investors see reserves build up, they would gain confidence.

Poor countries are lending to the United States hundreds of billions, indeed trillions, of dollars at a low . . . interest rate. That they do it even when there are so many high-return investment projects within their own countries is testament to the importance of reserves and the magnitude of global instability. While the costs of maintaining reserves are very high, the benefits still exceed the costs. The value of the implicit foreign aid that the United States receives, in being able to borrow at a lower interest rate than it otherwise would be able to, exceeds by some calculations the total value of the foreign aid that the country gives.

A good reserve currency needs to be a good store of value—a stable currency—but the dollar has been highly volatile and is likely to remain so. Already, many smaller countries have moved much of their reserves out of dollars, and even China is reported to have a quarter or more of its reserves in other currencies. The question is not whether the world will move away from the dollar reserve system altogether, but whether it does it thoughtfully and carefully. Without a clear plan the global financial system would become even more unstable.

Some within the United States will resist the move to create a global reserve system. They see the benefit in being able to borrow at a low cost, but they don't see the costs, which are huge. Producing and exporting T-bills to be held in foreign reserves creates no jobs, whereas exporting goods most certainly would. The flip side of the demand for U.S. T-bills and money to hold in reserves is the U.S. trade deficit, and the trade deficit weakens America's aggregate demand. To offset this, government runs a fiscal deficit. It is all part of an "equilibrium": to finance the deficit the government sells T-bills abroad (another way of saying it borrows money), and many of these T-bills are then put into reserves.

With the new global reserve currency, countries wouldn't need to buy U.S. T-bills to hold in their reserves. Of course, that would mean that the value of the dollar would decrease, U.S. exports would increase, U.S. imports would decrease, aggregate demand would be stronger, and there would be less need for the government to run a big deficit to maintain the economy at full employment. Knowing that it would be more difficult to borrow might curb America's profligacy, which would enhance global stability. America, and the world, would benefit from this new system.

Already, there are initiatives to create regional reserve arrangements. The Chiang Mai Initiative in East Asia allows countries to exchange their reserves; in response to the crisis, they increased the size of the program by 50 percent. The world may move to a two- (or three-) currency system, with both the dollar and euro in use. But such a system could be even more unstable than the current one. For the world, it might mean that if the euro is expected to gain relative to the dollar, countries would start to shift their holdings into euros. As they do this, the euro strengthens, reinforcing their beliefs—until some event, a political or economic disturbance, starts the reverse process. For Europe, it would pose a special problem, since countries in the European Union have constraints on their ability to run fiscal deficits to offset weak demand.

The dollar-based global reserve system is fraying, but efforts to create an alternative are only just beginning. Central bankers have at last learned the basic lesson of wealth management—diversification—and for years many have been moving reserves out of the dollar. In 2009, the G-20 agreed to a large ($250 billion) issuance of special drawing rights (SDRs), which are a kind of global reserve currency created by the IMF. But the SDRs have strong limitations. They are allocated to countries on the basis of their IMF "quotas" (their effective share holdings)—with the United States getting the largest piece. But the United States obviously has no need to hold reserves, since it can simply print dollar bills. The system would work far better if the reserve emissions were allocated to countries that otherwise would be expanding their reserves; alternatively, new global reserve emissions could go to poor countries needing assistance.

It would be even better if the new system was designed to discourage trade surpluses. The United States hectors China about its surplus, but in current arrangements there are strong incentives for countries to maintain reserves, and to run surpluses to add to reserves. Those countries that had large reserves fared far better in this crisis than those without adequate reserves. In a well-designed global reserve system, countries with persistent surpluses would have their reserve currency allocation diminished, and this, in turn, would encourage them to maintain a better balance. A well-designed global reserve system could go further in stabilizing the global economy, for if more of the global reserve currency were issued when global growth was weak, it would encourage spending—with a concomitant increase in growth and employment. . . . The world will be moving away from the dollar-based reserve system. Without an agreement on the creation of a new global reserve system, the world is likely to move out of the dollar and into a multiple-currency reserve system, producing global financial instability in the short term and a regime more unstable than the current system in the long term. . . .

Questions for Review

Why will the creation of a new global reserve system stabilize the global economy? Can you think of reasons why such a system will not come into existence?

A Sane Globalization

DANI RODRIK

Reforming the International Trade Regime

Our current trade strategy, centered on trade agreements to open markets, wastes a lot of political and negotiating capital for the prospect of meager economic gains. Worse still, it neglects the system's major defect, which is its lack of widespread support among ordinary people.

Today's challenge is no longer to open up the trade regime; that battle was fought in the 1960s and 1970s and has been decisively won. The infamous Smoot-Hawley Tariff of the 1930s has turned into a symbol of everything that can go wrong when nations turn their back on the world economy. "Protectionism" has become a dirty word. Import tariffs and other restrictions that governments impose on international trade have been reduced to the lowest levels the world has ever seen. . . . As a result, the gains that we stand to reap from removing the remaining vestiges of protectionism are puny—much smaller than what the pundits and the financial press presume. One recent study estimates those benefits to rise to no more than one third of 1 percent of world GDP (and this at the end of a full decade).[1] Most other credible estimates are also in the same ball park. . . .

Our challenge today is to render the existing openness sustainable and consistent with broader social goals. This requires a decisive shift in the focus of multilateral negotiations. When trade ministers get together, they should talk about expanding the maneuvering room for individual nations rather than narrowing it further through cuts in tariffs and subsidies. They should create the domestic space needed to protect social programs and regulations, renew domestic social contracts, and pursue locally tailored growth policies. They should be bargaining about policy space rather than market access. Such a reorientation would benefit rich and poor nations alike. Expanding policy space to accomplish domestic objectives does not negate an open, multilateral trade regime; it is a precondition for it.

The world's trade rules already allow nations to resort to "safeguards" in the form of higher import tariffs when a sudden surge in imports puts domestic firms in difficulty. I would like to see the WTO's Agreement on Safeguards . . . rewritten to expand policy space under a broader set of circumstances. A wider interpretation of safeguards would acknowledge that countries may wish to restrict trade or suspend WTO obligations—exercise "opt-outs"—for reasons other than a competitive threat to their industries. Distributional concerns, conflicts with domestic norms and social arrangements, prevention of the erosion of domestic regulations, or developmental priorities would be among such legitimate grounds.

Specifically, countries would be able to "violate" WTO rules when those rules threaten to undermine domestic labor and environmental standards or when they hamper the pursuit of sound development policies. In effect, the agreement would be recast into an expanded Agreement on *Developmental and Social Safeguards.* A country that applies such a safeguard would have to satisfy a key procedural requirement: it would need to demonstrate that it followed democratic procedures in reaching the determination that the safeguard measure is in the public interest. The specific criteria might include transparency, accountability, inclusiveness, and evidence-based deliberation. This hurdle would replace the current agreement's "serious injury" test, which focuses largely on domestic firms' financial profitability. . . .

An extension of safeguards to cover environmental, labor, and consumer safety standards or developmental priorities at home—with appropriate procedural restraints against abuse—would increase the legitimacy and resilience of the world trading system and render it more development-friendly. It would breathe life into the principle that countries have the right to uphold national standards when trade undermines broadly popular domestic practices, by withholding market access or suspending WTO obligations if necessary. Advanced countries could seek temporary protection against imports originating from countries with weak enforcement of labor rights when these imports worsen working conditions at home. Poor nations might be allowed to subsidize industrial activities (and indirectly their exports) when those subsidies contribute to a broadly supported development strategy aimed at stimulating technological capabilities. . . .

Consider what happens if we continue on our current path. The Doha Round of trade negotiations, with which the world's trade officialdom remains preoccupied, focuses on reducing the remaining barriers at the borders, especially in agriculture. The round was launched in 2001 and has experienced one collapse after another. Despite all the hoopla that accompanies these negotiations, it is safe to say that the prospective gains from a successful completion of the Doha Round are quite small—even paltrier than the one third of 1 percent of world income that a movement to full liberalization would entail.

Of course, there may still be some big winners from the Doha agenda. In particular, cotton growers in West Africa would benefit substantially from the removal of subsidies in the United States, their incomes rising by up to 6 percent—not a small amount for farmers so close to the subsistence level. On the other hand, poor urban consumers who do not grow their food and low-income food-importing countries would be hurt by the increase in the world price of agricultural commodities as rich country subsidies are phased out.

Taken as a whole, Doha should be considered small potatoes. After the kind of progress achieved by export-oriented East Asian economies in recent decades, facing barriers even higher than those of today, no serious economist would argue that the existing restrictions on market access limit seriously the growth prospects of poor countries (or anyone else, for that matter). Indeed, the lack of political momentum behind Doha can be explained at least in part by the weak prospects of significant economic gains.

National borders *do* impose significant transaction costs on trade. However, these costs derive less from protectionism at the border than from differences in standards, currencies, legal systems, social networks, and so on. Squeezing large gains from the world trade regime would require extensive institutional surgery, going beyond conventional trade liberalization and reaching behind borders to harmonize national standards and regulations. Those gains would be quite ephemeral, as they would come at the expense of the benefits of institutional diversity and policy space. . . .

The Doha Round's troubles are indicative of the impasse in which the trade regime finds itself. They exemplify the problems of the prevailing low-return, high-cost strategy, which leaves the world economy straddling a choice between two unappetizing options. One possibility is that popular pressure will force governments to resort to unilateral protectionism outside existing rules, inviting retaliation from others. Nations will refuse to sign on to substantive trade agreements for fear that the commitments will severely undermine policy space. International cooperation will gradually erode. Another possibility is that the spirit of "deep integration" will ultimately prevail and governments will sign ever-constraining trade agreements. The room for institutional diversity will then shrink and the legitimacy of the trade regime and prospects for economic development will both suffer.

Either way, the "business as usual" approach poses a greater risk to globalization's health than the reforms I have outlined here. It may seem like a paradox, but it isn't: reempowering national democracies is a precondition for an open world economy, not an obstacle to it.

Regulating Global Finance

The subprime mortgage meltdown has laid bare the inadequacies of the prevailing approach to regulation—both nationally and internationally. Loopholes in the rules allowed financial entities to take on risks that endangered not only themselves but society at large. The fallout has unleashed a flurry of efforts to improve the stringency and soundness of financial regulation. The measures under discussion include tighter capital-adequacy standards, restrictions on leverage, caps on executive pay, rules that facilitate bank closures, broader disclosure requirements, greater regulatory oversight, and limits on bank size.

These efforts are marred by a big fudge. Policy makers pay lip service to regulatory diversity and the push and pull of domestic politics that lead major players like the United States and the European Union to design their own regulations. Yet these same policy makers press for regulatory harmonization, fearful that diverse regulations will raise transaction costs and impede financial globalization. . . . No one has articulated how to steer a sensible path between these competing objectives. The attempt to have one's cake and eat it too is not just misguided; it leaves the world economy exposed to exactly the kind of mishaps that almost brought it down.

For global governance enthusiasts, international cooperation has produced a few successes since the crisis. These fall far short of a real shift in authority away from national policy makers. A global regulator, say, or a world central bank remains as much a fantasy as ever. The changes are minor and somewhat cosmetic. Most notably, the Group of Seven, the rich country club which serves as the global economy's talking shop, has been effectively supplanted by the Group of Twenty, which includes in addition a number of major developing nations. The International Monetary Fund has received additional financial resources. The Financial Stability Board (previously Forum), an association of two dozen nations' regulators and central banks, has been given new monitoring responsibilities. The Basel Committee on Banking Supervision has been put to work on a new set of global principles for bank regulation, its third in barely more than two decades.

The real story of financial regulation is one of international discord rather than harmony. Domestic pressure is forcing national politicians to act quickly on financial reforms rather than wait for bankers to come up with globally harmonized rules.

The fault lines among industrial countries fall along expected lines. With some important exceptions, continental Europeans tend to favor a more stringent approach, while the Americans and the British are wary of regulatory overreach that would cripple their financial industries. . . .

We have to think of these differences not as aberrations from the norm of international harmonization, but as the natural consequences of varying national circumstances. In a world where national interests, perceived or real, differ, the desire to coordinate regulations can do more harm than good. Even when successful, it produces either weak agreements based on the lowest common denominator or tougher standards that may not be appropriate to all. It is far better to recognize these differences than to presume that they can be papered over given sufficient time, negotiation, and political pressure.

The principle we should apply here is the same one that we apply in the case of consumer safety. If another country wants to export us toys, it has to make sure that those toys pass our lead-content and other safety standards. Similarly, when a financial firm does business in our economy, it has to comply with our financial regulations, regardless of where it is based. That means it has to hold the same level of capital reserves as domestic firms, face the same disclosure requirements, and abide by the same trading rules. It's a simple principle: if you want to be part of our game, you have to play by our rules. . . . The fly in the ointment is that maintaining regulatory differences when finance can freely cross national boundaries is quite difficult. Banks and investment houses can simply move to jurisdictions with less onerous restrictions. Financial globalization in effect neutralizes differences in national regulations. This is what is known in the trade as "regulatory arbitrage," a race to the bottom in finance.

For this reason, a commitment to regulatory diversity has a very important corollary: the need for restrictions on global finance. The rules of the game have to allow for restrictions on cross-border finance designed to counter regulatory arbitrage and protect the integrity of national regulations. Governments should be able to keep banks and financial flows out—not for financial protectionism but to prevent the erosion of national regulations. None of the leading governments has acknowledged this need explicitly to date, yet without such restrictions domestic regulations would have little effect and domestic firms would stand little chance to compete with financial services exported from lax jurisdictions. The domestic economy would remain hostage to the risks emanating from those transactions.

Hence a new global financial order must be constructed on the back of a minimal set of international guidelines and with limited international coordination. The new arrangements would certainly involve an improved IMF with increased resources and a larger voice for developing nations. It might require an international financial charter with limited aims, focused on encouraging financial transparency, promoting consultation and information sharing among national regulators, and placing limits on jurisdictions (such as financial safe havens) that export financial instability. A small global tax on financial transactions (say on the order of one tenth of 1 percent) would generate tens of billions of dollars to address global challenges such as climate change or health pandemics at little economic cost. But the responsibility for regulating leverage, setting capital standards, and supervising financial markets more broadly would rest squarely at the national level. Most important, the rules would explicitly recognize governments' right to limit cross-border financial transactions, insofar as the intent and effect are to prevent foreign competition from less strict jurisdictions from undermining domestic regulatory standards. . . . For developing countries, these rules would have additional benefits. They would open up the policy space for them to manage international capital flows and prevent sudden stops and overvalued currencies. Excessive focus on international harmonization has sidelined the specific interests of emerging nations. . . .

Short-term capital flows wreak havoc with domestic macroeconomic management and aggravate adverse currency movements. "Hot money" can make it difficult for financially open economies like Brazil, South Africa, or Turkey to maintain a competitive currency, depriving them of a potent form of industrial policy. Prudent controls, managed in a counter-cyclical manner so as to deter excessive financial inflows in good times, are part and parcel of good economic policy. Their importance only grows in a world where the mood in global finance can swing from euphoria to gloom in short order. International bodies such as the IMF and the Group of Twenty must look sympathetically, rather than frown, on such controls.

Of course, groups of like-minded countries that desire deeper financial integration would be free to harmonize their regulations, provided they do not use this as a cover for financial protectionism. One can imagine Europe taking this route and opting for a common regulator. East and Southeast Asian nations may eventually produce a regional zone of deep integration around an Asian monetary fund.

The rest of the world would have to live with a certain amount of financial segmentation—the necessary counterpart to regulatory diversity. That is as it should be. In a diverse world with divided sovereignty, it is the prospect of the deepening of financial globalization that should cause us to lose sleep.

Reaping the Benefits of Global Labor Flows

The problems in international trade and finance arise from too much globalization, not properly managed. By contrast, one large segment of the world economy is not globalized nearly enough. Further economic openness in the world's labor markets could potentially provide huge benefits, especially to the world's poor. Even a minor liberalization of the advanced countries' restrictions on the use of foreign workers would produce a large impact on global incomes. In fact, the gains would outstrip comfortably any other proposal currently on the table, including the entire package of trade measures being considered under the Doha Round of negotiations! Labor markets are the unexploited frontier of globalization. . . .

If the leaders of the advanced nations were serious about boosting incomes around the world and in doing so equitably, they would focus single-mindedly on reforming the rules that govern international labor mobility. Nothing else on their agenda—not Doha, not global financial regulation, not even expanding foreign aid—comes even close in terms of potential impact on enlarging the global pie. I am not talking about total liberalization. A complete, or even significant, reduction in visa restrictions in the advanced countries would be too disruptive. It would set off a mass migration that would throw labor markets and social policies in the advanced nations into disarray. But a small-scale program of expanded labor mobility would be manageable, and still generate very large economic gains for the migrant workers and their home economies.

Here is what I have in mind. Rich nations would commit to a *temporary* work visa scheme that would expand their total labor force by no more than 3 percent. Under the scheme, a mix of skilled and unskilled workers from poor nations would be allowed to fill jobs in the rich countries for a period of up to five years. To ensure that the workers return home at the end of their contracts, the programs would be supported by a range of carrots and sticks applied by both home and host countries. As the original migrants return home, a new wave of workers from the same countries would replace them.

Such a system would produce an estimated gain of $360 billion annually for the world economy, a sum considerably greater than what an agreement to remove *all* remaining tariffs and subsidies in global trade in goods could deliver. The bulk of this increase in income would accrue directly to citizens of developing nations—the poorest workers in the world. We wouldn't have to wait for the benefits to trickle down to them as is the case for trade and financial liberalization. Equally important, these numbers underestimate the overall gains since they do not account for the additional economic benefits that returnees would generate for their home countries. Workers who have accumulated know-how, skills, networks, and savings in rich countries could be true agents of change for their societies upon return. Their experience and investments would spark positive economic and social dynamics. The powerful contribution that former émigrés have made in getting software and other skill-intensive industries off the ground in India and Taiwan indicates the potential benefits of this plan. . . .

Today, the global labor regime looks like the international trade regime in 1950—full of high barriers that prevent the world's economies from reaping substantial benefits. The transformation that the trade regime has undergone since that time gives hope that something similar might happen in the area of immigration as well. . . .

Accommodating China in the World Economy

China was globalization's greatest success story during the last quarter century. Yet it may prove to be the reason for its downfall during the next.

China embodies all the major challenges that the global economy must overcome. How do we reconcile an open economy with the distributional and adjustment difficulties that trade with low-cost countries raises? How do we address the adverse effects that such trade can have on the welfare states, labor markets, tax regimes, and other social arrangements of advanced nations? How do we help developing countries restructure their economies while retaining an open, rules-based world economy? How do we integrate a large authoritarian regime into a global economy where the major players are all democratic?

These difficulties are all rooted in the enormous institutional diversity that exists around the globe. There are few nations whose institutions are as idiosyncratic as China's or leave as large a footprint on the world's marketplace. The appropriate way to respond to these challenges is not through tighter international rules or coordination, as we so often hear. It is possible to provide all countries, *including* China, with greater room to run their economic and social policies, and do so in ways that reduce adverse effects across national borders. . . . 1.3 billion and rapidly growing wealth ensure that it projects a very large image on the global screen.

China's economic rise has been a boon for the world economy for the most part. . . . But the picture is not all pretty. China and its trade partners have become embroiled in a growing number of trade disputes in recent years on product safety, patent and copyright infringement, government subsidies, dumping, currency manipulation, and market-access restrictions of various kinds. Imports from China have become a leading scapegoat for the stagnant median wages in the United States. . . .

And China is widely blamed for running roughshod over human rights and good governance in Africa in its quest for natural resources.

The conflict that poses the greatest threat in the near term concerns China's trade imbalance. The country's current account surplus (a broad measure of the excess of export receipts over imports) has risen to great heights in recent years, reaching an astounding 11 percent of GDP on the eve of the financial crisis in 2007 (from low single digits a decade ago). This imbalance increases global demand for goods produced in China at the cost of reducing it elsewhere, greatly complicating the economic recovery in the rest of the world. It has adverse effects on the health of manufacturing sectors everywhere but China. But the problem is not just an economic one. Historically, large trade imbalances have created fertile ground for protectionism. If China's trade surplus does not shrink, the United States likely will resort to trade barriers directed at Chinese exports, inviting retaliation from China and similar tactics from other countries. A major political backlash against China's trade and globalization in general will become a real possibility.

Has China's dependence on exports put the world economy on a collision course? Do we face a fundamental, irremovable conflict between China's development strategy, on the one hand, and economic and social stability in the rest of the world, on the other?

Not necessarily. A trade surplus is only an *incidental* consequence of China's growth strategy, more the result of our present global rules than of the inherent logic of that strategy. To see why, we must return briefly to the story of Chinese growth. The Chinese strategy relies on rapid structural change, which the government accomplishes by promoting industrialization together with continuous upgrading of the country's productive structure. Most of the economic activities that the government encourages are tradable, mainly manufactures. This strategy is perfectly compatible with balance on the external trade accounts as long as the increased supply of electronic products, steel, autos, and other manufactured goods that China's factories turn out is matched by increased demand in China for such goods—not necessarily product by product but in total.

Until very recently, the Chinese model worked this way. Even though the Chinese government has promoted manufacturing heavily since the 1980s, it did so through industrial policies—trade restrictions, investment incentives, subsidies, and domestic-processing requirements—that did not spill over into a trade imbalance.

Things began to change in the second half of the 1990s as the government prepared for membership in the World Trade Organization. It brought tariffs down sharply and phased out many of the subsidies and domestic-processing requirements to bring policies in line with WTO requirements. But the Chinese government wasn't about to give up on its growth strategy. To compensate for the decline in protection and direct support to manufacturing, it allowed the renminbi to become increasingly undervalued.

A cheap domestic currency has the same economic effects as a subsidy on exports *combined with a tax on imports.* Unlike conventional industrial policy, it necessarily generates a trade surplus. So China's membership in the WTO in December 2001 produced an unwelcome side effect: a precipitous rise in its trade surplus followed at just around the same time.

We can now better understand why the Chinese government resists so vehemently external pressure for the renminbi's appreciation. Such a policy would help reduce global imbalances, but it would also threaten China's economic growth. My own research suggests that China's growth might be reduced by 2 percentage points or more if the renminbi is allowed to appreciate sufficiently to eliminate its undervaluation. A reduction of this magnitude would in turn bring growth below the 8 percent threshold that the Chinese leadership believes is necessary for the economy to generate sufficient employment and avoid social strife. Given the size and geopolitical importance of the country, anything that undermines China's political stability should be of great concern to the rest of the world as well.

Unlike the picture that the typical commentary in the Western press suggests, this is not a simple morality play, with the Chinese as the "bad guys." China's trade surplus threatens the world economy, but so does a significant slowdown in its growth.

Such is the conundrum that our present rules have produced. Many consider the WTO's ability to constrain the use of subsidies and other industrial policies a great achievement for the world economy. It was a Pyrrhic victory. Restricting industrial policies has forced China to resort to what is, for the rest of the world, a much inferior tool: currency undervaluation. Since the Chinese government has to buy dollars to prevent its currency from appreciating, it has also required China to accumulate more than $2 trillion in reserves—low-return U.S. Treasury bills and other assets for which the country has no conceivable use. The paradox—more apparent than real—is that tighter global rules have led to worse global problems.

The right approach would be to leave China, and indeed all emerging nations, free to pursue their own growth policies. WTO restrictions on subsidies and other industrial policies should be suspended or subsumed under a general exception for developing nations. It would then be reasonable to expect that China and other emerging nations will pursue currency, financial, and macroeconomic policies that do not generate large trade imbalances. The quid pro quo would be this: you are entitled to your own growth strategy, but you also need to ensure that you do not produce large negative effects for the rest of the world in the form of trade surpluses. This would enable China to employ smart industrial policies in support of its employment and growth objectives without fear of WTO sanction. It would also allow China to let the renminbi appreciate without fear of adverse effects on growth. At the very least, it would eliminate the only sound justification for China's refusal to shrink its trade surplus. . . .

Ultimately, the world economy must reconcile the big differences in China's cultural, social, and political system with the Western values and institutions that have dominated it to date. Americans and Europeans might assume that economic growth will make China more Western: liberal, capitalist, and democratic. But as the British scholar and journalist Martin Jacques reminds us, there is little reason to believe in such convergence.[2] China has distinctive views, rooted in its long history, on the organization of the economy, society, and government, and on the proper relationships among them. As China gains economic power, it will advocate for a world order that better reflects these views.

The resulting tensions will not be easy to manage. But the challenge will be considerably easier to handle under global rules that respect diversity and minimize the need for international fetters than under rules that maximize reliance on coordination and common standards. These rules need not be underpinned by a single hegemon (whether the United States or China) and they will provide for greater stability in the world economy as the U.S. role inevitably wanes. That emphasis should suit China as well. The humiliations the country suffered during the nineteenth century at the hands of Britain and other imperialist powers have made the Chinese leaders great believers in national sovereignty and non-interference in domestic affairs. A light global touch would be consistent with those values.

Question for Review

What are the fixes necessary to make the world political economy run more smoothly?

Notes

1 Antoine Bouët, "The Expected Benefits of Trade Liberalization for World Income and Development," Food Policy Review No. 8, International Food Policy Research Institute, Washington, DC, 2008. These estimates refer to the standard gains from freeing up trade, and neglect the second-best considerations we encountered earlier that might make trade restrictions economically beneficial in certain products for low-income countries.

2 Martin Jacques, When China Rules the World: The End of the Western World and the Birth of a New Global Order (New York: Penguin, 2009).

Part IV
Contemporary Issues in World Politics

 LEARNING OBJECTIVES

IV.1 Answer questions related to war and terrorism, including the actors involved in waging war, the magnitude and frequency of war in the future, and the existence of terrorism and its possible end in the future.

IV.2 Discuss the proliferation of civil wars in the post-Cold War era, human rights, regime change, and humanitarian intervention.

IV.3 Explore the state system and the state's role in world politics.

IV.4 Analyze issues related to the global commons and global governance.

IV.5 Discuss the future of world politics by exploring additional factors such as the power distribution among states, the frequency of war, climate change, and the continuing rise of China.

With the Cold War having ended a little over 25 years ago, we have entered a new era of international politics. In Part IV we have picked five features of this era that we believe are the most important for understanding its major contours and that constitute challenges for more systematic analysis. They are: the future of interstate war and terrorism; the challenges of domestic collapse, regime change, civil wars, humanitarian intervention, and the international community's commitment to the protection of human rights and the rule of international law; the effects on world politics wrought by the rise of nonstate and transnational actors; the necessity of, and difficulties in, dealing with global commons problems, especially global warming, together with the search for new modes of global governance to deal with these global problems; and, finally, future developments that might give us clues to the shape of international politics a decade or two from now.

Interstate War and Terrorism

IV.1 **Answer questions related to war and terrorism, including the actors involved in waging war, the magnitude and frequency of war in the future, and the existence of terrorism and its possible end in the future.**

War is as old as the time when human beings first organized themselves into groups. It has been the great powers that have fought most, and that have always conducted their policies with the possibility of war in mind. Will the world be as ravaged by war in the decades to come as it has been since the dawn of civilization? Or are we now entering a new era when interstate war will disappear or be transformed? If war continues, will it still be waged between the kinds of actors who were most prominent in the past? Finally, will terrorism at its current magnitude and frequency remain with us for the indefinite future? How does terrorism end?

Robert Jervis, Robert J. Art, and Audrey Kurth Cronin address these questions. Jervis argues that war among the rich democracies of North America, Western Europe, and Japan is not only a thing of the past but is no longer even contemplated. War among the leading powers has been the motor of traditional international politics, and so the coming era will be radically different. The rest of the world is not likely to remain at peace, however, and the United States may continue to intervene abroad. In much of the Third World, conflicts between, but especially within, states rage and disputes over borders and natural resources provide proximate reasons for conflict. Art argues that the future of U.S.–China relations is not as bleak as many would have us believe. Compared to other conflicts between a dominant great power and a rapidly rising challenger, the Sino–American relationship has several features that should make us more optimistic that a great power war will not result between the two. Cronin surveys the demise of terrorist groups and demonstrates that there are six distinct paths through which terrorist groups die.

Civil Wars, Human Rights, Regime Change, and Humanitarian Intervention

IV.2 **Discuss the proliferation of civil wars in the post-Cold War era, human rights, regime change, and humanitarian intervention.**

Although civil strife and domestic collapse are as old as history, they have become more prominent after the Cold War and have become even more important recently through the perceived links to terrorism. State failures and civil wars are fed by both internal and external causes, which make them particularly hard to understand and deal with. Because of the growth in the number of states—and the heightened consequences of disturbance in one area for regions, if not for the entire world—these subjects are now high on the agenda of both scholars and policymakers. Because we live in a well-established country with a high degree of public order, most of us forget that this situation is not a natural one, but rather the hard-won result of a broad concatenation of political, economic, and social forces. Under some circumstances, central authority can be subject not only to violent dispute, but also can be so torn apart that it simply disappears, resulting in the national government being replaced by local warlords, roving bands of thugs, and chaos.

In the absence of effective international government, there is no choice but to rely on states for the enforcement of human rights. Human rights, Rhoda E. Howard and Jack Donnelly argue, are fundamental to human existence. Even though cultures and systems of governance differ among states, each individual human being has a set of rights by virtue of being human. Civil wars grossly violate these rights because of the cruelties inflicted on innocent civilians. To protect these human rights, it has been outside states that have acted, and when he was Secretary General of the UN, Kofi Annan argued that states not only have the right but also the duty to intervene in extreme and limited conditions to protect human rights by intervening in the affairs of the transgressor state.

How has this worked out in practice? Jon Western and Joshua S. Goldstein argue that after a good deal of trial and error, the international community has learned how to do humanitarian intervention quite well.

The West has intervened, not only to save lives, but also to change regimes. Is this a good idea? Alexander B. Downes expresses a deep skepticism about the beneficial consequences of military intervention to make governments democratic. Perhaps there is an alternative. Caroline A. Hartzell and Mathew Hoddie look to internal solutions for civil wars, especially to arrangements in which the two (or more) sides share power. Uncomfortable as this is, it is often the best if not the only way to bring these conflicts to an end.

Transnational Actors and New Forces

IV.3 Explore the state system and the state's role in world politics, compared to non-state actors' role

The state system we live in today dates roughly from the Peace of Westphalia, which ended the Thirty Years' War, one of the bloodiest in human history. Consequently, the modern international system of states has just celebrated its 368th anniversary. Will the state system itself continue, and will the state remain the *most* important, although not the only important, actor in world politics, or are there new actors and new forces that are challenging the primacy of the state?

Part of the answer to this question lies in assessing how strong non-state and transnational actors have become vis-à-vis the state. Clearly, these actors have become increasingly important. Margaret E. Keck and Kathryn Sikkink provide a more systematic analysis of NGOs and show how transnational networks operate and affect state action. In addition to new actors, we are also witnessing the rise of new forces that can potentially challenge the ability of states to control events within their borders. Cyberwar is one such new force. It not only enhances the ability of one state to control what happens in another state, short of war, but it also potentially empowers individuals and small groups to challenge state control. Herbert Lin assesses the potential challenge of cyber conflict to undermine state control. Equally important are the potential effects of the internet and the social media to undermine state control, especially by authoritarian governments over their people. Steven R. Ratner argues that international law is having a greater effect on state action and, by implication, that international politics is becoming more regulated and domestic-like. More international law is being written and enforcement is being improved.

The Global Commons and Global Governance

IV.4 Analyze issues related to the global commons and global governance.

Protection of the global environment is not a new issue, but its political salience has greatly increased over the last 15 years because of factors such as the depletion of the world's fisheries, the degradation of the ozone layer, and the threats to the quality of human life posed by global warming and climate change. The United Nations Conference on the Environment held in Rio in 1992 marked a watershed in international awareness of the increasing threat to the global environment.

Truly global environmental threats, as opposed to strictly national ones, are especially difficult to deal with because they are a "commons" problem. In such cases, joint state action does not come easily because the situation looks as follows: No single state owns the resource being consumed (or abused), but all use it (or abuse it), and none can be prevented from using and abusing it. A commons (or public) good is therefore one that no single individual or entity owns, but that all need and can use. For such goods, no individual or state has an incentive to minimize its exploitation unless it is persuaded that all others will act in a similar fashion. This represents a collective action problem: Uncoordinated individual action produces collective disaster. This is the "tragedy of the commons" and the message of Garrett Hardin's article. Solving commons problems is therefore not easy.

Climate change is the biggest and most challenging commons problem of them all. Widespread and growing use of fossil fuels to develop and sustain modern economies has added enough carbon dioxide to the world's atmosphere to cause the average global temperature to increase by approximately 0.75 degrees centigrade since the onset of the Industrial Revolution in 1750. This may sound insignificant, but it is not. The overall change in global temperature from the depths of the last Ice Age until now can be measured within the range of four to nine degrees centigrade. The best published estimates of climatologists predict that if carbon dioxide levels in the atmosphere double, then an increase in average global temperature of more than 5 degrees Fahrenheit is likely, adding a huge amount of energy to the planet's climate system. Climate change raises dangers not only of widespread dislocations but also of catastrophic climate change if warming feeds on itself—a situation climatologists call "positive feedback" in which warming produces more warming. How can the nations of the earth deal with commons problems like global warming? Pope Francis in his *Papal Encyclical on the Environment* raises serious questions about the adverse effects of the capitalist system on the environment, as exemplified by the effects of global warming and strongly suggests that a major cultural revolution regarding our values and goals is necessary if we are to preserve "Spaceship Earth."

In addition, old modes of global government may no longer be appropriate for the new and complex world in which we live. The uncoordinated decisions of individual states cannot provide the sort of order that is needed. Too many issues spill over national borders; too many problems require joint efforts by a range of actors; in too many cases, one state's policies will have adverse impacts around the globe. The need for states to come together led to the formation of the League of Nations after World War I and to a stronger United Nations after World War II. Adam Roberts and Dominik Zaum assess the contributions to world peace made by the United Nations Security Council and the likelihood of changes in its structure to make it more effective. While its role has expanded after the Cold War, the center of decision will remain with the individual states. This leads Kenneth N. Waltz to argue that international organizations, globalization, and transnational forces have not removed states from their central role: if there is to be world governance, it will come through the decisions and actions of states. Under certain circumstances, the array of international organizations has been strongly influenced by the leading role of the United States. Stewart Patrick assesses the nature of global governance in a world order that lacks a central government. He finds a multitude of multilateral organizations that deal with specific problems and finds that the governance they provide is "good enough." A central question about the current international order is how it will accommodate rising powers, especially China. G. John Ikenberry argues that these arrangements are open and flexible enough to accommodate newcomers, thereby greatly contributing to prospects for world peace. In his view the rising nations of the developing world, such as China, Brazil, and India, will not subvert the liberal international order the United States created after World War II and has sustained ever since. Instead, they will merely seek a greater role and power within that liberal system.

The Shape of the Future

IV.5 **Discuss the future of world politics by exploring additional factors such as the power distribution among states, the frequency of war, climate change, and the continuing rise of China.**

Whether the new forces and actors described above will eventually subvert the state system or instead remain subservient to it, whether some new patterns now difficult to imagine will emerge, and whether current and future modes of international governance will be adequate for the challenges ahead is something we will be able to answer definitively only several decades from now. Although these factors will significantly influence what the future of international politics looks like, so, too, will the power distribution among states, the frequency of war, both civil and international, climate change, the effects wrought by demographic factors that have now been set in motion, and the continuing rise of China.

This last section provides six selections that touch upon these additional factors. First, the distribution of power among countries is likely to change, and Barry R. Posen argues that while power will diffuse, the international system will not necessarily become less stable, but it will be more complex and in flux than was the bipolar world of the Cold War era. Alan Dupont assesses the strategic implications of climate change: How will changes in rainfall patterns, rising sea levels, and more severe droughts affect the fault lines of international politics?

Everyone agrees that political and economic factors will be crucial for the future, but the agreement ends there. Jonathan Kirshner looks at one aspect of economic power—the role of the dollar as the key international currency—and lays out the geopolitical consequences of the dollar's position weakening both for the United States and for the world. Michael Cox believes that the decline of the West in general and the U.S. in particular is greatly exaggerated. Stephen Walt assesses the current cohesion of the European Union and lays out three possible futures for it, suggesting that the Union's best days are behind it. Most likely, the world will develop in ways that surprise us. Almost never have people been able to foresee the future; indeed, if they could they might act in ways that would make events turn out differently. In 1800 it appeared that the coming century would be a very grim one; in 1900 the future of humankind looked bright. For better or for worse—or perhaps for better and for worse—human beings move in odd ways, collective outcomes diverge from individual preferences, and technological and ideological changes appear unbidden. But for students and scholars as well as for policymakers, thinking about the future can sharpen ideas and raise questions as well as induce an appropriate sense of humility.

Part IV Question for Review

How do the various theories presented in Parts 1-3 help you better understand the contemporary issues covered in Part 4?

Chapter 11

Interstate War and Terrorism

The Era of Leading Power Peace

ROBERT JERVIS

War and the possibility of war among the great powers has been the motor of international politics, not only strongly influencing the boundaries and distribution of values among them, but deeply affecting their internal arrangements and shaping the fates of the smaller ones. Being seen as an ever-present possibility produced by deeply-rooted factors such as human nature and the lack of world government, this force was expected to continue indefinitely. But I would argue that war among the leading great powers—the most developed states of the United States, West Europe, and Japan—will not occur in the future, and indeed is no longer a source of concern for them (Mueller 1989).

Now, however, the leading states form what Karl Deutsch called a pluralistic security community, a group among whom war is literally unthinkable—i.e., neither the publics nor the political elites nor even the military establishments expect war with each other (Deutsch et al. 1957). No official in the Community would advocate a policy on the grounds that it would improve the state's position in the event of war with other members or allow the state to more effectively threaten them.

Although no one state can move away from the reliance on war by itself lest it become a victim, they can collectively do so if each forsakes the resort to force. This development challenges many of our theories and raises the question of what international politics will be like in the future.

Security communities are not unprecedented. But what is unprecedented is that the states that constitute this one are the leading members of the international system and so are natural rivals who in the past were central to the violent struggle for security, power, and contested values. Winston Churchill exaggerated only slightly when he declared that "people talked a lot of nonsense when they said nothing was ever settled by war. Nothing in history was ever settled *except* by wars" (quoted in Gilbert 1983, 860–61). Even cases of major change without war, such as Britain yielding hegemony in the Western hemisphere to the United States at the turn of the twentieth century, were strongly influenced by security calculations. Threatening war, preparing for it, and trying to avoid it have permeated all aspects of politics, and so a world in which war among the most developed states is unthinkable will be very different from the history with which we are familiar. To paraphrase and extend a claim made by Evan Luard (1986, 77), given the scale and frequency of war among the great powers in the preceding millennia, this is a change of spectacular proportions, perhaps the single most striking discontinuity that the history of international politics has anywhere provided.

Two major states, Russia and China, might fight each other or a member of the Community. But, as I will discuss below, such a conflict would be different from traditional wars between great powers. Furthermore, these countries lack many of the attributes of great powers: their internal regimes are shaky, they are not at the forefront of any advanced forms of technology or economic organization, they can pose challenges only regionally, and they have no attraction as models for others. They are not among the most developed states and I think it would be fair to put them outside the ranks of the great powers as well. But their military potential, their status as nuclear powers, and the size of their economies renders that judgment easily debatable and so I will not press it but rather will argue that the set of states that form the Community are not all the great powers, but all the most developed ones.

Central Questions

Five questions arise. First, does the existence of the Community mean the end of security threats to its members, and more specifically to the United States? Second, will the Community endure? Third, what are the causes of its construction and maintenance? Fourth, what are the implications of this transformation for the conduct of international affairs? Finally, what does this say about theories of the causes of war?

Continued Threats

The fact that the United States is not menaced by the most developed countries does not mean that it does not face any military threats at all. Indeed, some see the United States as no more secure than it was during the Cold War, being imperiled by terrorists and "rogue" states, in addition to Russia and China. But even if I am wrong to believe that these claims are greatly exaggerated, these conflicts do not have the potential to drive world politics the way that clashes among the leading powers did in the past. They do not permeate all facets of international politics and structure state–society relations; they do not represent a struggle for dominance in the international system or a direct challenge to American vital interests.

Recent terrorist attacks are of unprecedented magnitude and will have a significant impact on domestic and international politics, but I do not think they have the potential to be a functional substitute for great power war—i.e., to be the driving force of politics. Despite rhetoric to the contrary, there is little chance that all the countries will unite to combat terrorism; the forms of this scourge are too varied and indeed often are a useful tool for states, and states have many other interests that are at least as important as combating terrorism. Similarly, although the events of September 11 have triggered significant changes in American foreign policy and international alignments, I believe that in a fairly short period of time previous outlooks and conflicts of interest will reassert themselves. Even if this is not the case and if combating terrorism becomes the most important goal for most or all states, the move away from leading power war is still both important and puzzling.

Will the Security Community Last?

Predictions about the maintenance of the Community are obviously disputable (indeed, limitations on people's ability to predict could undermine it), but nothing in the short period since the end of the Cold War points to an unraveling. We could make a long list of disputes, but there were at least as many in the earlier period. The Europeans' effort to establish an independent security force is aimed at permitting them to intervene when the United States chooses not to (or perhaps by threatening such action, to trigger American intervention), not at fighting the United States. Even if Europe were to unite either to balance against the United States or because of its own internal dynamics and the world were to become bipolar again, it is very unlikely that suspicions, fears for the future, and conflicts of interest would be severe enough to break the Community.

A greater threat would be the failure of Europe to unite coupled with an American withdrawal of forces, which could lead to "security competition" within Europe (Art 1996; Mearsheimer 2001, 385–96). Partly general, the fears would focus on Germany. Their magnitude is hard to gauge and it is difficult to estimate what external shocks or kinds of German behavior would activate them. The fact that Thatcher and Mitterrand opposed German unification is surely not forgotten in Germany and is an indication that concerns remain. But this danger is likely to constitute a self-denying prophecy in two ways. First, many Germans are aware of the need not only to reassure others by tying themselves closely to Europe, but also to seek to make it unlikely that future generations of Germans would want to break these bonds even if they could. Second, Americans who worry about the residual danger will favor keeping some troops in Europe as the ultimate intra-European security guarantee.

Expectations of peace close off important routes to war. The main reason for Japanese aggression in the 1930s was the desire for a self-sufficient sphere that would permit Japan to fight the war with the Western powers that was seen as inevitable, not because of particular conflicts, but because it was believed that great powers always fight each other. By contrast, if states believe that a security community will last they will not be hypersensitive to threats from within it and will not feel the need to undertake precautionary measures that could undermine the security of other members. Thus the United States is not disturbed that British and French nuclear missiles could destroy American cities and while those two countries object to American plans for missile defense, they do not feel the need to increase their forces in response. As long as peace is believed to be very likely, the chance of inadvertent spirals of tension and threat is low.

Nevertheless, the point with which I began this section is unavoidable. World politics can change rapidly and saying that nothing foreseeable will dissolve the Community is not the same as saying that it will not dissolve (Betts 1992). To the extent that it rests on democracy and prosperity (see below), anything that would undermine these would also undermine the Community. Drastic climate change could also shake the foundations of much that we have come to take for granted. But it is hard to see how dynamics at the international level (i.e., the normal trajectory of fears, disputes, and rivalries) could produce war among the leading states. In other words, the Community does not have within it the seeds of its own destruction.

Our faith in the continuation of this peace is increased to the extent that we think we understand its causes and have reason to believe that they will continue. This is our next topic.

Explanations for the Security Community

There are social constructivist, liberal, and realist explanations for the Community which, although proceeding from different assumptions and often using different terms, invoke overlapping factors.

Social Constructivism

Social constructivist accounts stress the role of norms of non-violence and shared identities that, through an interactive process of reciprocal behaviors and expectations, have led the advanced democracies to assume the role of each other's friend. In contradistinction to the liberal and realist explanations, this downplays the importance of material factors and elevates ideas, images of oneself and others, and conceptions of appropriate conduct. The roots of the changes that have produced this enormous shift in international politics among some countries but not others is not specified in detail, but the process is a self-reinforcing one—a benign cycle of behavior, beliefs, and expectations.

People become socialized into attitudes, beliefs, and values that are conducive to peace. Individuals in the Community may see their own country as strong and good—and even better than others—but they rarely espouse the virulent nationalism that was common in the past. Before World War I, one German figure could proclaim that the Germans were "the greatest civilized people known to history" while another declared that the Germans were "the chosen people of this century," which explains "why other people hate us.

They do not understand us but they fear our tremendous spiritual superiority." Thomas Macaulay similarly wrote that the British were "the greatest and most highly civilized people that ever the world saw" and were "the acknowledged leaders of the human race in the causes of political improvement," while Senator Albert Beveridge proclaimed that "God has made us the master organizers of the world" (quoted in Van Evera 1984, 27). These sentiments are shocking today because they are so at variance from what we have been taught to think about others and ourselves. We could not adopt these views without rejecting a broad set of beliefs and values. An understanding of the effects of such conceptions led the Europeans, and to an unfortunately lesser extent the Japanese, to de-nationalize and harmonize their textbooks after World War II and has similarly led countries with remaining enemies to follow a different path: The goals for the education of a 12-year-old child in Pakistan include the "ability to know all about India's evil designs about Pakistan; acknowledge and identify forces that may be working against Pakistan; understand the Kashmir problem" (quoted in Kumar 2001, 29).

The central objection to constructionism is that it mistakes effect for cause: its description is correct, but the identities, images, and self-images are superstructure, being the product of peace and of the material incentives discussed below. What is crucial is not people's thinking, but the factors that drive it. The validity of this claim is beyond the reach of current evidence, but it points to a critique of the constructivist argument that the Community will last, which places great faith in the power of socialization and the ability of ideas to replicate and sustain themselves. This conception may betray an excessive faith in the validity of ideas that seem self-evident today, but that our successors might reject. Constructivism may present us with actors who are "over-socialized" (Wrong 1976, ch. 2) and leave too little role for agency in the form of people who think differently, perhaps because their material conditions are different.

Liberalism

The liberal explanation has received the most attention. Although it comes in several variants, the central strands are the pacifying effects of democracy and economic interdependence.

DEMOCRACY The members of the Community are democracies, and many scholars argue that democracies rarely if ever fight each other. Although the statistical evidence is, as usual, subject to debate, Jack Levy is correct to claim that it is "as close as anything we have to an empirical law in international politics" (Levy 1989, 88).

Less secure, however, is our understanding of why this is the case. We have numerous explanations, which can be seen as competing or complementary. Democracies are systems of dispersed power, and dispersed power means multiple veto points and groups that could block war. (This seems true almost by definition, but if the accounts of former Soviet leaders are to be trusted, Brezhnev was more constrained by his colleagues than was Nixon, at least where arms control was concerned.) Related are the norms of these regimes: democracies function through compromise, non-violence, and respect for law. To the extent that these values and habits govern foreign policy, they are conducive to peace, especially in relations with other democracies who reciprocate.

Other scholars have argued that the key element lies in the realm of information. By having a relatively free flow of intelligence and encouraging debate, democracies are less likely to make egregious errors in estimating what courses of action will maintain the peace. The other side of the informational coin is that democracies can more effectively telegraph their own intentions, and so avoid both unnecessary spirals of conflict and wars that stem from others' incorrect beliefs that the democracy is bluffing (although an obvious cost is an inability to bluff).

Finally, in a recasting of the traditional argument that democracies are less likely to go to war because those who hold ultimate authority (i.e., the general public) will pay the price for conflict, some argue that the institutional and coalitional nature of democratic regimes requires their leaders to pursue successful policies if they are to stay in office. Thus democracies will put greater efforts into winning wars and be careful to choose to fight only wars they can win. Autocracies have a much narrower base and so can stay in power by buying off their supporters even if their foreign policies are unnecessarily costly. These arguments, while highly suggestive, share with earlier liberal thinking quite stylized assumptions about the preferences of societal actors and pay little attention to how each country anticipates the behavior of others and assesses how others expect it to behave.

These explanations for the democratic peace are thoughtful and often ingenious, but not conclusive. Many of them lead us to expect not only dyadic effects, but monadic ones as well—i.e., democracies should be generally peaceful, not only peaceful toward each other, a finding that most scholars deny. They would also lead us to expect that one democracy would not seek to overthrow another, a proposition that is contradicted by American behavior during the Cold War. Furthermore, most of the arguments are built around dyads but it is not entirely clear that the posited causes would apply as well to multilateral groupings like the Community.

The causal role of democracy is hard to establish because these regimes have been relatively rare until recently, much of the democratic peace can be explained by the Soviet threat, and the same factors that lead countries to become democratic (e.g., being relatively rich and secure) are conducive to peace between them. It is particularly important and difficult to control for the role of common interest, which loomed so large during the Cold War. But interests are not objective and may be strongly influenced by the country's internal regime. Thus the democracies may have made common cause during the Cold War in part because they were democracies; common interest may be a mechanism by which the democratic peace is sustained as much as it is a competing explanation for it (for this and related issues, see Farber and Gowa 1995, 1997; Gartzke 1998, 2000; Maoz 1997; Oneal and Russett 1999; Schweller 2000). Moreover, if democracies are more likely to become economically interdependent with one another, additional common interest will be created. But to bring up the importance of interest is to highlight an ambiguity and raise a question. The ambiguity is whether the theory leads us to expect democracies *never* to fight each other or "merely" to fight *less* than do other dyads. (Most scholars take the latter view, but this does not mean that this is what most versions of the theory actually imply.) The related hypothetical question is: Is it impossible for two democracies to have a conflict of interest so severe that it leads to war? This troubles the stronger version of the argument because it is hard to answer in the affirmative.

But would democracies let such a potent conflict of interest develop? At least as striking as the statistical data is the fact—or rather, the judgment—that the regimes that most disturbed the international order in the twentieth century also devastated their own peoples—the USSR, Germany under the Nazis and, perhaps, under Kaiser Wilhelm. One reason for this connection may be the desire to remake the world (but because the international order was established by countries that were advanced democracies, it may not be surprising that those who opposed it were not). Not all murderous regimes are as ambitious (e.g., Idi Amin's Uganda), and others with both power and grand designs may remain restrained (e.g., Mao's China), but it is hard to understand the disruptive German and Soviet foreign policy without reference to their domestic regimes.

INTERDEPENDENCE   The second leg of the liberal explanation for the Community is the high level of economic interdependence. The basic argument was developed by Cobden, Bright, and the other nineteenth-century British liberals. As the former put it: "Free Trade is God's diplomacy and there is no other certain way of uniting people in bonds of peace." (Quoted in Bourne 1970, 85. For a general treatment of Cobden's views, see Cain 1979. For the most recent evidence, see McMillan 1997; Russett and Oneal 2001, ch. 4; for arguments that interdependence has been exaggerated and misunderstood, see Waltz 1970, 1979 ch. 7, 1999. Most traditional liberal thinking and the rest of my brief discussion assumes symmetry; as Hirschman 1945 showed, asymmetric dependence can provide the basis for exploitative bargaining.) Although the evidence for this proposition remains in dispute, the causal argument is relatively straightforward. "If goods cannot cross borders, armies will" is the central claim, in the words of the nineteenth-century French economist Frederick Bastiat which were often repeated by Secretary of State Cordell Hull (perhaps excessively influenced by the experience of the 1930s). Extensive economic intercourse allows states to gain by trade the wealth that they would otherwise seek through fighting. Relatedly, individuals and groups who conduct these economic relations develop a powerful stake in keeping the peace and maintaining good relations. Thus it is particularly significant that in the contemporary world many firms have important ties abroad and that direct foreign investment holds the fates of important actors hostage to continued good relations. There can be a benign cycle here as increasing levels of trade strengthen the political power of actors who have a stake in deepening these ties.

The liberal view assumes that actors place a high priority on wealth, that trade is a better route to it than conquest, and that actors who gain economically from the exchange are politically powerful. These assumptions are often true, especially in the modern world, but are not without their vulnerabilities. At times honor and glory, in addition to more traditional forms of individual and national interest, can be more salient than economic gain. Thus as the Moroccan crisis of 1911 came to its climax, General von Moltke wrote to his wife: "If we again slip away from this affair with our tail between our legs . . . I shall despair of the future of the German Empire. I shall then retire. But before handing in my resignation I shall move to abolish the Army and to place ourselves under Japanese protectorate; we shall then be in a position to make money without interference and to develop into ninnies" (quoted in Berghahn 1973, 97). Traditional liberal thought understood this well and stressed that economic activity was so potent not only because it gave people an interest in maintaining peace, but because it reconstructed social values to downgrade status and glory and elevate material well-being. It follows that the stability of the Community rests in part upon people giving priority to consumption. Critics decry modern society's embodiment of individualistic, material values, but one can easily imagine that others could generate greater international conflict.

There are four general arguments against the pacific influence of interdependence. First, if it is hard to go from the magnitude of economic flows to the costs that would be incurred if they were disrupted, it is even more difficult to estimate how much political impact these costs will have, which depends on the other considerations in play and the political context. This means that we do not have a theory that tells us the expected magnitude of the effect. Second, even the sign of the effect can be disputed: interdependence can increase conflict as states gain bargaining leverage over each other, fear that others will exploit them, and face additional sources of disputes. These effects might not arise if states expect to remain at peace with each other, however. Third, it is clear that interdependence does not guarantee peace. High levels of economic integration did not prevent World War I, and nations that were much more unified than any security community have peacefully dissolved or fought civil wars. But this does not mean that interdependence is not conducive to peace. Fourth, interdependence may be more an effect than a cause, more the product than a generator of expectations of peace and cooperation.

Realist Explanations

The crudest realist explanation for the Community would focus on the rise of the common threat from Russia and China. While not entirely implausible, this argument does not fit the views espoused by most elites in Japan and Europe, who are relatively unconcerned about these countries and believe that whatever dangers emanate from them would be magnified rather than decreased by a confrontational policy.

AMERICAN HEGEMONY   Two other realist accounts are stronger. The first argues that the Community is largely caused by the other enormous change in world politics—the American dominance of world politics. U.S. defense spending, to take the most easily quantifiable indicator, is now greater than that of the next 8 countries combined (O'Hanlon 2001, 4–5). Furthermore, thanks to the Japanese constitution and the integration of armed forces within NATO, America's allies do not have to fear attacks from each other: their militaries (especially Germany's) are so truncated that they could not fight a major war without American assistance or attack each other without undertaking a military buildup that would give others a great deal of warning. American dominance also leads us to expect that key outcomes, from the expansion of NATO, to the American-led wars in Kosovo and the Persian Gulf, to the IMF bailouts of Turkey and Argentina in the spring of 2001, will conform to American preferences.

But closer examination reveals differences between current and past hegemonies. The United States usually gives considerable weight to its partners' views and indeed its own preferences are often influenced by theirs, as was true in Kosovo. For their parts, the other members of the Community seek to harness and constrain American power, not displace it. The American hegemony will surely eventually decay but increased European and Japanese strength need not lead to war, contrary to the expectations of standard theories of hegemony and great power rivalry. Unlike previous eras of hegemony, the current peace seems uncoerced and accepted by most states, which does not fit entirely well with realism.

NUCLEAR WEAPONS   The second realist argument was familiar during the Cold War but receives less attention now. This is the pacifying effect of nuclear weapons, which, if possessed in sufficient numbers and invulnerable configurations, make victory impossible and war a feckless option. An immediate objection is that not all the major states in the Community have nuclear weapons. But this is only technically correct: Germany and Japan could produce nuclear weapons if a threat loomed, as their partners fully understand. The other factors discussed in the previous pages may or may not be important; nuclear weapons by themselves would be sufficient to keep the great powers at peace.

While there is a great deal to this argument, it is not without its problems. First, because this kind of deterrence rests on the perceived possibility of war, it may explain peace, but not a security community. Second, mutual deterrence can be used as a platform for hostility, coercion, and even limited wars. In what Glenn Snyder (1965; also see Jervis 1989, 19–23, 74–106) calls the stability-instability paradox, the common realization that all-out war would be irrational provides a license for threats and the use of lower levels of violence. Under some circumstances a state could use the shared fear of nuclear war to exploit others. If the state thinks that the other is preoccupied with the possibility of war and does not anticipate that the state will make the concessions needed to reduce this danger, it will expect the other to retreat and so can stand firm. In other words, the fact that war would be the worst possible outcome for both sides does not automatically lead to uncoerced peace, let alone to a security community.

A Synthetic Interactive Explanation

I think the development and maintenance of the Community is best explained by a combination and reformulation of several factors discussed previously. Even with the qualifications just discussed, a necessary condition is the belief that conquest is difficult and war is terribly costly. When conquest is easy, aggression is encouraged and the security dilemma operates with particular viciousness as even defensive states need to prepare to attack (Van Evera 1999). But when states have modern armies with extensive firepower and, even more, nuclear weapons, it is hard for anyone to believe that war could make sense.

Statesmen must consider the gains that war might bring as well as the costs. Were they to be very high, they might outweigh great expected costs. But, if anything, the expected benefits of war within the Community have declined, in part because the developed countries, including those that lost World War II, are generally satisfied with the status quo. Even in the case that shows the greatest strain—U.S.–Japanese relations—no one has explained how a war could provide either side much gross, let alone net, benefit. It is then hard to locate a problem for which war among the Community members would provide a solution. Furthermore, as liberals have stressed, peace within the Community brings many gains, especially economic.

Of course costs and benefits are subjective, depending as they do on what the actors value, and changes in values are the third leg of my explanation. Most political analysis takes the actors' values for granted because they tend to be widely shared and to change slowly. Their importance and variability becomes clear only when we confront a case like Nazi Germany which, contrary to standard realist conceptions of national interest and security, put everything at risk in order to seek the domination of the Aryan race.

The changes over the last 50–75 years in what the leaders and publics in the developed states value drive some of the calculations of costs and benefits. To start with, war is no longer seen as good in itself; no great power leader today would agree with Theodore Roosevelt that "no triumph of peace is quite so great as the supreme triumph of war" (quoted in Harbaugh 1961, 99). In earlier eras it was commonly believed that war brought out the best in individuals and nations and that the virtues of discipline, risk-taking, and self-sacrifice that war required were central to civilization. Relatedly, honor and glory used to be central values. In a world so constituted, the material benefits of peace would be much less important; high levels of trade, the difficulty of making conquest pay, and even nuclear weapons might not produce peace.

Democracy and identity also operate through what actors value, and may in part be responsible for the decline in militarism just noted. Compromise, consideration for the interests of others, respect for law, and a shunning of violence outside this context all are values that underpin democracy and are reciprocally cultivated by it. The Community also is relatively homogeneous in that its members are all democracies and have values that are compatibly similar. One impulse to war is the desire to change the other country, and this disappears if values are shared. The United States could conquer Canada, for example, but what would be the point when so much of what it wants to see there is already in place?

Central to the rise of the Community is the decline in territorial disputes among its members. Territory has been the most common cause and object of conflicts in the past, and we have become so accustomed to their absence that it is easy to lose sight of how drastic and consequential this change is. Germans no longer care that Alsace and Lorraine are French; the French are not disturbed by the high level of German presence in these provinces. The French furthermore permitted the Saar to return to Germany and are not bothered by this loss, and indeed do not feel it as a loss at all. Although for years the Germans refused to renounce their claims to the "lost territories" to the east, they did so upon unification and few voices were raised in protest.

The causes of these changes in values in general and nationalism and concern with territory in particular are subject to dispute, as are the developments that could reverse them. In particular, it is unclear how much they are rooted in material changes, most obviously the increased destructiveness of war and the unprecedented prosperity that is seen as linked to good political relations, and to what extent they are more autonomous, following out perhaps a natural progression and building on each other. They may be linked (inextricably?) to high levels of consumption, faith in rationality, and the expectation of progress, although it is not unreasonable to argue that this describes Europe in 1914 as well. The decreased salience of territory and decline of territorial disputes is almost surely produced in part by the decoupling of territorial control and national prosperity, and most of the other relationships between material structures and ideational patterns are complex and reciprocal. Just as capitalism is built and sustained by pre-capitalist values and post-materialism may grow from prosperity so the values that sustain the Community can neither be separated nor simply deduced from changes in the means and levels of production and potential destruction.

The increased destructiveness of war, the benefits of peace, and the changes in values interact and reinforce each other. If war were not so dreadful, it could be considered as an instrument for national enrichment; if peace did not seem to bring prosperity and national well-being, violence would at least be contemplated; that military victory is no longer seen as a positive value both contributes to and is in part explained by, the high perceived costs of war. Similarly, expectations of peace allow states to value each other's economic and political successes. Although these may incite envy, they no longer produce strong security fears, as they did in the past. The Community may then contain within it the seeds of its own growth through the feedbacks among its elements.

Another dynamic element is crucial as well: the progress of the Community is path-dependent in that without the Cold War it is unlikely that the factors we have discussed could have overcome prevalent fears and rivalries. The conflict with the Soviet Union produced American security guarantees and an unprecedented sense of common purpose among the states that now form the Community. Since the coalition could be undermined by social unrest or political instability, each country sought to see that the others were well off and resisted the temptation to solve its own problems by exporting them to its neighbors. Since the coalition would have been disrupted had any country developed strong grievances against other members, each had reason to moderate its demands and mediate when conflicts developed between others. To cultivate better relations in the future, leaders consciously portrayed the others as partners and sponsored the socialization practices discussed above. The American willingness to engage in extensive cooperation abroad, the European willingness to go far down the road of integration, the Japanese willingness to tie itself closely to the United States were improbable without the Cold War. But having been established, these forms of cooperation set off positive feedback and are now self-sustaining.

Implications

What are the implications of the existence of the security community for how these states will carry out relations among themselves and for general theories of war and peace?

International Politics within the Community

In previous eras, no aspect of international politics and few aspects of domestic politics were untouched by the anticipation of future wars among the leading powers. Much will then change in the Community. In the absence of these states amalgamating—a development that is out of the question outside of Europe and unlikely within it—they will neither consider using force against one another nor lose their sovereignty. There will then be significant conflicts of interest without clear means of resolving them. They will continue to be rivals in some respects, and to bargain with each other. Indeed, the stability-instability paradox implies that the shared expectation that disputes will remain peaceful will remove some restraints on vituperation and competitive tactics. The dense network of institutions within the Community should serve to provide multiple means for resolving conflicts, but will also provide multiple ways for a dissatisfied country to show its displeasure and threaten disruption.

The fact that the situation is a new one poses challenges and opportunities for states. What goals will have highest priority? How important will considerations of status be? Will non-military alliances form? Bargaining will continue, and this means that varieties of power, including the ability to help and hurt others, will remain relevant. Threats, bluffs, warnings, the mobilization of resources for future conflicts, intense diplomatic negotiations, and shifting patterns of working with and against others all will remain. But the content of these forms will differ from those of traditional international politics.

Politics within the Community may come to resemble the relations between the United States and Canada and Australia that Keohane and Nye (1977) described as complex interdependence: extensive transnational and transgovernmental relations, bargains carried out across different issue areas, and bargaining power gained through asymmetric dependence but limited by overall common interests. Despite this path-breaking study, however, we know little about how this kind of politics will be conducted. As numerous commentators have noted, economic issues and economic resources will play large roles, but the changed context will matter. Relative economic advantage was sought in the past in part because it contributed to military security. This no longer being the case, the possibilities for cooperation are increased.

Even though force will not be threatened within the Community, it will remain important in relations among its members. During the Cold War the protection the United States afforded to its allies gave it an important moral claim and significant bargaining leverage. Despite the decreased level of threat, this will be true for the indefinite future because militarily Japan and Europe need the United States much more than the United States needs them. While the unique American ability to lead military operations like those in the Persian Gulf and Kosovo causes resentments and frictions with its allies, it also gives it a resource that is potent even—or especially—if it is never explicitly brought to the table.

FOUR POSSIBLE FUTURES   Even within the contours of a Community, there is a significant range of patterns of relations that are possible, four of which can be briefly sketched.

The greatest change would be a world in which national autonomy would be further diminished and the distinctions between domestic and foreign policy would continue to erode. Medieval Europe, with its overlapping forms of sovereignty rather than compartmentalized nation-states, which might dissolve because they are no longer needed to provide security and can no longer control their economies, is one model here. Although most scholars see the reduction of sovereignty and the growth of the power of non-governmental organizations as conducive to peace and harmony, one can readily imagine sharp conflicts, for example among business interests, labor, and environmentalists (many Marxists see class conflicts as increasingly important); between those with different views of the good life; between those calling for greater centralization to solve common problems and those advocating increased local control. But state power and interest would in any case be greatly decreased. The notion of "national interest," always contested, would become even more problematic.

A second world, not completely incompatible with the first, would be one in which states in the Community play a large role, but with more extensive and intensive cooperation. Relations would be increasingly governed by principles and laws, a change that could benignly spill over into relations outside the Community. Although bargaining would not disappear, there would be more joint efforts to solve common problems and the line between "high" and "low" politics would become even more blurred.

In this world, the United States would share more power and responsibility with the rest of the Community than is true today. While popular with scholars at least as likely is a continuation of the present trajectory in which the United States maintains hegemony and rejects significant limitations on its freedom of action. National interests would remain distinct and the United States would follow the familiar pattern in which ambitions and perceived interests expand as power does. Both conflicts of interest and the belief that hegemony best produces collective goods would lead the United States to oppose the efforts of others to become a counterweight if not a rival to it. In effect, the United States would lead an empire, but probably a relatively benign one. Doing so would be rendered more difficult by the fact that the American self-image precludes seeing its role for what it is, in part because of the popularity of values of equality and supranationalism. Other members of the Community would resent seeing their interests overridden by the United States on some occasions, but the exploitation would be limited by their bargaining power and the American realization that excessive discontent would have serious long-term consequences. Others might accept these costs in return for the U.S. security guarantee and the ability to keep their own defense spending very low, especially because the alternative to American-dominated stability might be worse.

The fourth model also starts with the American attempt to maintain hegemony, but this time the costs and dangers of American unilateralism become sufficient to lead others to form a counter-balancing coalition, one that might include Russia and China as well. Europe and Japan might also become more assertive because they fear that the United States will eventually withdraw its security guarantee, thereby accelerating if not creating a rift within the Community. Much that realism stresses—the clash of national interests, the weakness of international institutions, maneuvering for advantage, and the use of power and threats—would come to the fore, but with the vital difference that force would not be contemplated and the military balance would enter in only indirectly, as discussed above. This would be a strange mixture of the new and the familiar, and the central question is what *ultima ratio* will replace cannons. What will be the final arbiter of disputes? What kinds of threats will be most potent? How fungible will the relevant forms of power be?

Outlining these possibilities raises two broad questions that I cannot answer. First, is the future essentially determined, as many structural theories would imply, or does it depend on national choices strongly influenced by variable domestic politics, leaders, and accidents? Second, if the future is not determined, how much depends on choices the United States has yet to make, and what will most influence these choices?

Implications for Theories of the Causes of War

Whatever its explanation, the very existence of a security community among the leading powers refutes many theories of the causes of war, or at least indicates they are not universally valid. Thus human nature and the drive for dominance, honor, and glory may exist and contribute to a wide variety of human behaviors but they are not fated to lead to war.

The obvious rebuttal is that war still exists outside the Community and that civil wars continue unabated. But only wars fought by members of the Community have the potential to undermine the argument that, under some conditions, attributes of humans and societies that were seen as inevitably producing wars in fact do not do so. The cases that could be marshalled are the Gulf War and the operation in Kosovo, but they do not help these theories. These wars were provoked by others, gained little honor and glory for the Community, and were fought in a manner that minimized the loss of life on the other side. It would be hard to portray them as manifestations of brutal or evil human nature. Indeed, it is more plausible to see the Community's behavior as consistent with a general trend toward its becoming less violent generally: the abolition of official torture and the decreased appeal of capital punishment, to take the most salient examples (Mueller 1989).

The existence of the Community also casts doubt on theories that argue that the leading powers always struggle for dominance for gain, status, or security, and are willing to use force to this end. Traditional Marxist theories claim that capitalists could never cooperate; proponents of the law of uneven growth see changes in the relative power of major states as producing cycles of domination, stability, challenge, and war. Similarly, "power transitions" in which rising powers catch up with dominant ones are seen to be very difficult to manage peacefully. These theories, like the version of hegemonic stability discussed above, have yet to be tested because the United States has not yet declined. But if the arguments made here are correct, transitions will not have the same violent outcome that they had in the past, leading us to pay greater attention to the conditions under which these theories do and do not hold.

For most scholars, the fundamental cause of war is international anarchy, compounded by the security dilemma. These forces press hardest on the leading powers because while they may be able to guarantee the security of others, no one can provide this escape from the state of nature for them. As we have seen, different schools of thought propose different explanations for the rise of the Community and so lead to somewhat different propositions about the conditions under which anarchy can be compatible with peace. Constructivism stresses the importance of identities and ideas; liberalism argues for the power of material incentives for peace; realism looks at the costs of war and the details of the payoff structure; my composite explanation stresses the interaction among several factors of costs, benefits, values, and path-dependence. But what is most important is that the Community constitutes a proof by existence of uncoerced peace without central authority. Because these countries are the most powerful ones and particularly war-prone, the Community poses a fundamental challenge to our understanding of world politics and our expectations of future possibilities.

Questions for Review

How does the existence of a Security Community among what Jervis calls the leading powers effect the rest of world politics? If this is such a big change for the better, why is the United States not more secure?

References

Art, Robert J. 1996. "Why Western Europe Needs the United States and NATO." *Political Science Quarterly* 111 (Spring): 1–39.

Berghahn, V. R. 1973. *Germany and the Approach of War in 1914.* New York: St. Martin's Press.

Betts, Richard. 1992. "Systems of Peace or Causes of War? Collective Security, Arms Control, and the New Europe." *International Security* 17 (Summer): 5–43.

Bourne, Kenneth. 1970. *The Foreign Policy of Victorian England: 1830–1902.* Oxford: Clarendon Press.

Cain, Peter. 1979. "Capitalism, War and Internationalism in the Thought of Richard Cobden." *British Journal of International Studies* 5 (October): 229–47.

Deutsch, Karl W., et al. 1957. *Political Community and the North Atlantic Area: International Organizations in the Light of Historical Experience.* Princeton, NJ: Princeton University Press.

Farber, Henry, and Joanne Gowa. 1995. "Polities and Peace." *International Security* 20 (Fall): 393–417.

Farber, Henry and Joanne Gowa. 1997. "Common Interests or Common Polities?" *Journal of Politics* 59 (May): 123–46.

Gartzke, Erik. 1998. "Kant We All Get Along? Motive, Opportunity, and the Origins of the Democratic Peace." *American Journal of Political Science* 42 (1): 1–27.

Gartzke, Erik. 2000. "Preferences and Democratic Peace." *International Studies Quarterly* 44 (June): 191–212.

Gilbert, Martin. 1983. *Winston S. Churchill*, Volume VI, *Finest Hour 1939–1941.* London: Heinemann.

Harbaugh, William Henry. 1961. *The Life and Times of Theodore Roosevelt.* New York: Collier Books.

Hirschman, Albert O. 1945. *National Power and the Structure of Foreign Trade.* Berkeley and Los Angeles: University of California Press.

Jervis, Robert. 1989. *The Meaning of Nuclear Revolution: Statecraft and the Prospect of Armageddon.* Ithaca, NY: Cornell University Press.

Keohane, Robert O., and Joseph Nye, eds. 1977. *Power and Interdependence: World Politics in Transition.* Boston, MA: Little Brown.

Kumar, Amitava. 2001. "Bristling on the Subcontinent." *The Nation.* April 23, 2001, 29–30.

Levy, Jack S. 1989. "Domestic Politics and War." In *The Origins and Prevention of Major Wars,* eds. Robert I. Rotberg and Theodore K. Rabb. Cambridge: Cambridge University Press. pp. 79–100.

Luard, Evan. 1986. *War in International Society: A Study in International Sociology.* London: I.B. Tauris.

Maoz, Zeev. 1997. "The Controversy Over the Democratic Peace: Rearguard Action or Cracks in the Wall?" *International Security* 22 (Summer): 162–98.

McMillan, Susan M. 1997. "Interdependence and Conflict." *Mershon International Studies Review* 41, supplement 1 (May): 33–58.

Mearsheimer, John J. 2001. *The Tragedy of Great Power Politics.* New York: Norton.

Mueller, John. 1989. *Retreat from Doomsday: The Obsolescence of Major War.* New York: Basic Books.

O'Hanlon, Michael E. 2001. *Defense Policy Choices for the Bush Administration.* Washington, DC: Brookings Institution Press.

Oneal, John R., and Bruce Russett. 1999. "Is the Liberal Peace Just an Artifact of Cold War Interests? Assessing Recent Critiques." *International Interactions* 25 (3): 213–41.

Russett, Bruce, and John R. Oneal. 2001. *Triangulating Peace: Democracy, Interdependence, and International Organizations.* New York: Norton.

Schweller, Randall L. 2000. "Democracy and the Post–Cold War Era." In *The New World Order,* eds. Birthe Hansen and Bertel Heurlin. New York: St. Martin's Press. pp. 46–80.

Snyder, Glenn. 1965. "The Balance of Power and the Balance of Terror." In *The Balance of Power,* ed. Paul Seabury. San Francisco: Chandler. pp. 184–201.

Van Evera, Stephen. 1984. "The Cult of the Offensive and the Origins of the First World War." *International Security* 9 (Summer): 58–107.

Van Evera, Stephen. 1999. *Causes of War: Power and the Roots of Conflict.* Ithaca, NY: Cornell University Press.

Waltz, Kenneth N. 1970. "The Myth of National Interdependence." In *The International Corporation,* ed. Charles P. Kindleberger. Cambridge, MA: MIT Press. pp. 205–23.

Waltz, Kenneth N. 1979. *Theory of International Politics.* Reading, MA: Addison-Wesley Publishing.

Waltz, Kenneth N. 1999. "Globalization and Governance." *PS: Political Science & Politics* 32 (December): 693–700.

Wrong, Dennis H. 1976. *Skeptical Sociology.* New York: Columbia University Press.

The United States and the Rise of China

ROBERT J. ART

Today, the United States stands at the pinnacle of its power when power is measured in terms of hard economic and military assets. Although its economy will continue to grow and although it will remain the most powerful military nation on earth for some time to come, America's economic and military edge *relative* to the world's other great powers will inevitably diminish over the next several decades.

The country best positioned to challenge America's preeminence, first in East Asia, and then perhaps later globally, is China. If China's economy continues to grow for two more decades at anything close to the rate of the last two decades, then it will eventually rival and even surpass the United States in the size of its gross domestic product (measured in purchasing power parity terms, not in constant dollar terms), although not in per capital GDP.[1] Even if its economy never catches up to America's, China's remarkable economic growth has already given it significant political influence in East Asia, and that influence will only grow as China's economy continues to grow. Moreover, having emerged as the low-cost manufacturing platform of the world, China's economic influence extends well beyond East Asia and affects not only the rich great powers but also the struggling smaller developing ones, because of both its competitive prices for low cost goods and its voracious appetite for raw materials. China is already the dominant military land power on the East Asian mainland, and it has made significant strides in creating pockets of excellence in its armed forces. If it continues to channel a healthy portion of its GDP into its military forces over several more decades and if it makes a determined naval and air power projection effort, China might be able to deploy a maritime force that could contest America's supremacy at sea in East Asia, much as the German fleet built by Tirpitz in the decade before World War I posed a severe threat to the British fleet in the North Sea.

Historically, the rise of one great power at the expense of the dominant one has nearly always led to conflictual relations between the two, and, more often than not, eventually to a war between them that has dragged in other great powers.[2] Is the history of dominant-rising great power dyads the future for U.S.–China relations?

Clearly, there will be political and economic conflicts and friction between the United States and China as its economic and military power in East Asia, and its global economic and political reach, continue to expand. Clearly, there will also be some arms racing between China and the United States as each jockeys for advantage over the other, and as each is driven by their respective military necessities of intimidating and defending Taiwan, and as the United States responds to China's growing power projection capabilities. Historically, dominant powers have not readily given up their position of number one to rising challengers, and rising challengers have always demanded the fruits that they believe their growing power entitles them to. There is no reason to expect that things will be different in this regard with China and the United States. Thus, they will not be able to avoid a certain level of conflictual relations and political friction over the next several decades.

Are mostly political friction and conflictual relations, and even war, the main things that these two powers have to look forward to, or are there also some significant shared interests and hence bases for cooperation in both the medium and the longer term such that the peace-inducing aspects of the U.S.-China relationship could come to overshadow the conflict-producing ones? No one can say for certain which is the case. However, if we believe that there are distinct elements in the Sino-American relationship that differ from past dominant power-rising power dyads, then the dismal history of such dyads need not be the future of this one. If this is so, then the right policy choices by both countries can keep the two on a path that has more cooperative than conflictual elements to it, thereby avoiding the doom-and-gloom scenario that too many of today's analysts portray.

Power Transitions and Security Dilemma Dynamics

A third benchmark for U.S. policy toward a rising China is this: do not assume that Sino-American relations will follow the course of recent cases where a rising power has challenged a dominant one. There are too many significant differences between these cases and the current one to draw such a firm conclusion.

To defend this assertion, in Table 1 I compare the current Sino-American competition with the three most important rising-power-versus-dominant-power competitions of the last one hundred years—those that resulted in either a great power hegemonic war or a sustained and intense political-military competition for hegemonic dominance between two great powers. (Hegemonic wars and hegemonic political-military competitions are conducted to determine which power will be number one and be able to set the rules of the international system.) The first two competitions—Britain versus Germany in the decade before World War I and Britain versus Germany from 1933–1939—resulted in war; the third— the United States versus the Soviet Union during the Cold War—resulted in an uneasy peace between the two powers, punctuated by numerous proxy wars.[3]

I focus on three variables in order to explain the outcome of these cases: the level of security that both powers enjoyed, or believed they enjoyed, in general and vis-à-vis one another, with security defined as protection of the state's homeland from physical attack and its political sovereignty from severe infringement; the extent of economic interdependence between them, with interdependence defined in terms of the level of economic interactions—especially trade—between the two states; and the degree and intensity of ideological competition that they experienced. I do not present these three variables as a full-blown deductive theory about war and peace between rising and dominant great powers; such theories have been presented by others, although with somewhat contradictory results.[4] Instead, I argue that these three factors—and especially the first, as made clear

---

Table1 Dominant Power versus Rising Power Competitions

Dominant-Rising Power Dyad	Security Enjoyed by Both Powers Vis-à-Vis One Another	Level of Economic Interdependence	Ideological Competition	Outcome
United Kingdom-Germany pre 1914	In 1914 security thought to be low for the future if corrective action (war) not taken	High	Low	War
United Kingdom-Germany pre 1939	Low in the 1930s due to presumed airpower threat	Low to medium	Medium to high	War
U.S.-Soviet Union during the Cold War	Initially believed to be low; turned out later to be high	Low	High and intense	Cold War; serious crises at first; then an uneasy peace
U.S.-China today	High for U.S., but problematical for China because Chinese nuclear forces at present are potentially vulnerable to a U.S. first strike	High	As yet, low to nonexistent	To be determined

below—are the most important ones to look at in order to determine the level and intensity of hostility and conflict, and hence the likelihood of war, between two great powers that believe they are experiencing, or may soon experience, a fundamental power shift between them.

All other things being equal, the intensity of competition and the likelihood of war between a dominant power and a rising challenger should vary as follows. First, the lower the level of security each enjoys or believes it enjoys vis-à-vis the other or in general, the more likely are serious security dilemma dynamics, intense arms racing, and war between the two. Conversely, if these states feel that they are relatively secure from attack and that their political sovereignty is not being compromised (or will not be compromised) by the actions of the other, then they can experience a greater level of hostility that may arise from conflicts over nonsecurity issues without war being the result. There are many reasons why two states can wage war with one another; however, if each believes it is relatively safe from attack by the other, then one of the most powerful historic incentives for war—security—is removed.

Second, under the right conditions, the higher the level of economic interdependence between two states, the less likely will security competitions and war between them take place. The three conditions under which high levels of economic interdependence can be peace-inducing are: (1) when two states believe that they can more profitably resort to economic rather than military means in order to prosper; (2) when they believe that the economic vulnerabilities that result from economic interdependence cannot be quickly and easily turned to their military disadvantage; and (3) when they believe that should the first two conditions change, they can readily protect themselves or find allies who will.[5]

Finally, the greater the ideological differences between the two states, the more intense will be their competition and the more likely they are to experience arms races, intense security dilemmas, and war. Security concerns have been powerful factors for war, but they are not the only factors. Ideological hostilities—conflicts over how social power should be organized within states—have also contributed to hostility and war between states. The Cold War, for example, was not simply about U.S.-Soviet security, it was also about values—democratic market capitalism versus communism—and which would prevail globally.

Close inspection of Table 1 reveals that neither economic interdependence nor ideological competition is a good predictor of whether a dominant and rising power will go to war or remain at peace. In 1914, for example, Germany was England's second best customer for its exports, and England was Germany's best customer for its exports.[6] Before the war, they did not experience intense ideological competition, and in fact shared many political similarities. Yet, the two ended up at war. Throughout the 1930s, England and Germany did not have as high a level of economic interdependence with one another as they had before World War I, and they did experience some ideological competition.[7] At the outset of, and during the course of, the Cold War, the United States and the Soviet Union experienced a low level of economic interdependence with one another, and their ideological competition was high and intense.[8] Yet they remained in an uneasy peace, although one that was much more fragile during the first part of the Cold War than during the second. Thus, the relationship between levels of economic interdependence and intensity of ideological competition, on the one hand, and war or peace, on the other, is indeterminate. High and low levels of interdependence are correlated with war, and high and low levels of ideological competition are correlated with both war and peace.

Therefore, it is the degree of security enjoyed by these pairs of states vis-à-vis one another, and especially the severity of the threat to its security that the dominant state perceives emanating from the rising state, that constitutes the most important variable to predict whether a hegemonic struggle will result in war.[9] When security was low or believed to be low, intense crises and war were more likely; when security was high or believed to be high, better relations and peace tended to prevail. Economic interdependence and ideological competition are not irrelevant to producing peace and war, but they are only "helper variables." They can reinforce peaceful trends when the security enjoyed by both states vis-à-vis one another is high, but they cannot override the deleterious effects produced when the security enjoyed by both states vis-à-vis one another is low.

In 1914, Germany needed England to stand aside so that it could shore up its failing great power ally Austria-Hungary and deal with the growing power of Russia. Diplomatic isolation for Germany (the dissolution of Austria-Hungary) meant the political encirclement and eventual strangulation of Germany in the eyes of Germany's leaders. If Britain stood aside while Germany attained continental hegemony, however, then Britain's security would be at risk if a hegemonic Germany deployed the resources of the European continent against it. So, in classic security dilemma terms, Britain's security would be at risk by the continental hegemony that Germany believed it needed for its security, and, similarly, Germany's leaders believed that Germany's security would be at risk if Britain denied it continental hegemony. The same logic applies to the British-German struggle during the 1930s. A Nazi Germany that had defeated Russia and vanquished the continent could aggregate its resources and turn them into an invasion force to crush England's defenses. The threat that German hegemony posed to Britain brought on the two World Wars.

Security factors were also central in explaining why the Cold War stayed "cold." The United States and the Soviet Union experienced an intense ideological competition for most of the Cold War, but that competition never turned into a direct war between the two primarily because of the restraining effects of nuclear deterrence. True, the stability-instability paradox did not work to prevent all serious crises between the two, and true, two of these crises—the Berlin Blockade crisis of 1948 and the Cuban Missile crisis of 1962—brought the United States and the Soviet Union closer to war than either would have liked.[10] However, the workings of the stability-instability paradox were ultimately beneficial: it worked to prevent those crises that did occur from escalating to war, and it worked, ultimately, to reduce dramatically the frequency and the severity of crises after the Cuban Missile Crisis. In fact, one could make a strong argument that with one exception serious security crises between the United States and the Soviet Union disappeared after 1973.[11]

China does not present the type of security threat to the United States that Germany did to Britain, or Britain to Germany. America's nuclear forces make it secure from any Chinese attack on the homeland. Moreover, China clearly presents a potentially different type of threat to the United States than the Soviet Union did during the Cold War because the geopolitics of the two situations are different. The Soviet geopolitical (as opposed to the nuclear) threat was twofold: to conquer and dominate the economic-industrial resources of western Eurasia and to control the oil reserves of the Persian Gulf. Europe and the Persian Gulf constituted two of the five power centers of the world during the Cold War—Japan, the Soviet Union, and the United States being the other three. If the Soviets had succeeded in dominating Europe and the Persian Gulf through either conquest or political-military intimidation, then it would have controlled three of the five power centers of the world. That would have been a significant power transition.

China's rise does not constitute the same type of geopolitical threat to the United States that the Soviet Union did. If China ends up dominating the Korean peninsula and a significant part of continental Southeast Asia, so what? As long as Japan remains outside the Chinese sphere of influence and allied with the United States, and as long as the United States retains some naval footholds in Southeast Asia, such as in Singapore, the Philippines, or Indonesia, China's domination of these two areas would not present the same type of geopolitical threat that the Soviet Union did. As long as Europe, the Persian Gulf, Japan, India, and Russia (once it reconstitutes itself as a serious great power) remain either as independent power centers or under U.S. influence, Chinese hegemony on land in East and Southeast Asia will not tip the world balance of power. The vast size and central position of the Soviet Union in Eurasia constituted a geopolitical threat to American influence that China cannot hope to emulate.

If judged by the standards of the last three dominant power-rising power competitions of the last one hundred years, then, the U.S.-China competition appears well placed to be much safer. Certainly, war between the two is not impossible because either or both governments could make a serious misstep over the Taiwan issue. War by miscalculation is always possible, but the possession of nuclear weapons by both sides has to have a restraining effect on both by dramatically raising the costs of miscalculation, thereby increasing the incentives not to miscalculate. Nuclear deterrence should work to lower dramatically the possibility of war by either miscalculation or deliberate decision (or if somehow such a war broke out, then nuclear deterrence should work against its escalation into a large and fearsome one). Apart from the Taiwan issue, it is hard to figure out how to start a war between the United States and China. There are no other territorial disputes of any significance between the two, and there are no foreseeable economic contingencies that could bring on a war between them. Finally, the high economic interdependence and the lack of intense ideological competition between them help to reinforce the pacific effects induced by the condition of mutual assured destruction.

The workings of these three factors should make us cautiously optimistic about keeping Sino-American relations on the peaceful rather than the warlike track. The peaceful track does not, by any means, imply the absence of political and economic conflicts in Sino-American relations, nor does it foreclose coercive diplomatic gambits by each against the other. What it does mean is that the conditions are in place for war to be a low probability event, if policymakers are smart in both states (see below), and that an all-out war is nearly impossible to imagine. By the historical standards of recent dominant-rising state dyads, this is no mean feat.

In sum, there will be some security dilemma dynamics at work in the U.S.-China relationship, both over Taiwan and over maritime supremacy in East Asia should China decide eventually to contest America's maritime hegemony, and there will certainly be economic and political conflicts, but nuclear weapons should work to mute their severity because the security of each state's homeland will never be in doubt as long as each maintains a second-strike capability vis-à-vis the other. If two states cannot conquer one another, then the character of their relation and their competition changes more dramatically than would be the case if they could.

Questions for Review

Why is Art optimistic that a Sino-American war will not result from the rise of China, and why does he believe that a Cold War between the two is not likely either? What common interests do the two states share?

Notes

1 For a skeptical view of this happening anytime soon, see Lester Thurow, "A Chinese Century: Maybe It's the Next One," *New York Times,* August 19, 2007, p. 4 (business section).

2 See Dale C. Copeland, *The Origins of Major War* (Ithaca, NY: Cornell University Press, 2000); and Robert Gilpin, *War and Change in International Politics* (Cambridge: Cambridge University Press, 1981).

3 These three cases do not include all the great power cases of rising-versus-dominant power dyads of the last one hundred years. Most prominently and deliberately excluded is the U.S.-British case of the late nineteenth/early twentieth centuries. In this table, I am focusing on two types of competitions: those that resulted in a great power hegemonic war or those that entailed a hostile, intense, and sustained political competition for hegemony and that involved heavy reliance on military force to fight proxy wars or to engage in arms races so as to achieve political hegemony. The U.S.-British case does not fall into either category, although the United States did threaten the British with a naval arms race after World War I if they did not renounce the Anglo-Japanese Treaty of 1902. By focusing on the three cases I have chosen, I have selected on the dependent variable—on those cases in which the outcome is either war or a sustained political-military rivalry rather than peace or peaceful accommodation, with the result that the conclusions of this analysis are to a degree biased. Nonetheless, there is still analytical merit in focusing on these two types of hegemonic competitions to see what conclusions we can draw. For a slightly different list of important power transitions, see Jacek Kugler and A. F. K. Organski, *The War Ledger* (Chicago: University of Chicago Press, 1980), p. 49. For an analysis of why the U.S.-British case ended in peace, not war, see Stephen R. Rock, *When Peace Breaks Out: Great Power Historical Rapprochement in Historical Perspective* (Chapel Hill: The University of North Carolina Press, 1989), chap. 2. For a more general treatment of the strategies that dominant powers employ to cope with rising powers, see Randell L. Schweller, "Managing the Rise of Great Powers: History and Theory," in Robert S. Ross and Alastair Iain Johnston, eds., *Engaging China: The Management of an Emerging Power* (London: Routledge, 1999), pp. 1–32.

4 There are four distinct theories as to why wars occur between rising and dominant great powers, but in one way or another, all four revolve around perceptions of, or actual manifestations of, fundamental power shifts between the two states. The first three theories argue that the dominant power launches the hegemonic war; the fourth, that the rising power launches the hegemonic war. Dale Copeland argues that the dominant power will launch a preventive war against a rising power when it believes that its own decline is both inevitable and steep and at a time when it believes it is still more powerful than the rising challenger. (See Dale C. Copeland, *The Origins of Major Wars,* chap. 2.) Robert Gilpin argues that hegemonic wars occur between a dominant and rising power when the governance of the system and its power distribution are in disequilibrium, in other words, when the rising power does not benefit from the system as much as its power entitles or enables it to, and although he is a little vague about which state starts the war, it is generally the declining but still dominant power that does. (See Robert Gilpin, *War and Change in World*

Politics, chap. 5.) Stephen Van Evera argues that windows of vulnerability and opportunity produce war between a declining dominant and a rising power when the former attacks the latter. (See Stephen Van Evera, *The Causes of War: Power and the Roots of Conflict* [Ithaca, NY: Cornell University Press, 1999], chap. 4.) Finally, the power transition school, founded by A. F. K. Organski, argues that peace obtains when the dominant state has a huge preponderance of power over any potential challenger, but that wars occur as the power disparity between the dominant and rising power narrows and occurs just before the rising power achieves parity with the dominant power, or at the moment when it has achieved parity, or just after it has overtaken the dominant power—the time when war is initiated depending on which version of the power transition theory is used. (See A. F. K. Organski, *World Politics,* 1st ed. [New York: Alfred A. Knopf, 1958] chap. 12, esp. p. 333 Jacek Kugler and A. F. K. Organski, *The War Ledger,* pp. 19–22 and 49–61; Jacek Kugler and Douglas Lemke, eds., *Parity and War: Evaluations and Extensions of the War Ledger* [Ann Arbor: University of Michigan Press, 1996], chap. 1 and Ronald L. Tammen et al., *Power Transitions: Strategies for the 21st Century* [New York: Chatham House Publishers, 2000], chap. 1.)

5 See Robert J. Art, *A Grand Strategy for America* [Ithaca, NY: Cornell University Press, 2003], pp. 66–67.

6 In 1913, 10 percent of Britain's total trade (imports and exports) was with Germany, and 12 percent of Germany's total trade was with Britain. These percentages are derived from the Correlates of War data. The data was prepared by Katherine Barbieri for her doctoral dissertation *Economic Interdependence and Militarized Interstate Conflict, 1870–1985* (Binghamton University, Binghamton, NY, 1996). The dataset is at http://cow2.la.psu.edu/. I am indebted to Loren Cass for arranging the data for easy use.

7 In 1938, 4 percent of Britain's total trade (imports and exports) was with Germany, and 6 percent of Germany's total trade was with Britain.

8 In 1977, for example, during the height of détente between the United States and the Soviet Union, when one would expect trade to be the highest, the United States sent 1.4 percent of its total exports to the Soviet Union and received 0.3 percent of its total imports from the Soviet Union. By 1983, when détente had ended and U.S.-Soviet relations were hostile, the United States sent 0.1 percent of its exports to, and received 0.1 percent of its imports from, the Soviet Union. In 1977, the Soviets exported 2.5 percent of its exports to the United States and took 8 percent of its imports from the United States. By 1983, these Soviet figures had fallen to 1 percent and 5.7 percent, respectively. See International Monetary Fund, *Direction of Trade Statistics Yearbook, 1984* (Washington, DC: International Monetary Fund, 1984), pp. 378 and 385.

9 This is close to the argument that Dale Copeland makes about the causes of hegemonic great power wars. See Dale C. Copeland, *The Origins of Major War,* chaps. 1 and 2.

10 The stability-instabilty paradox says either that two nuclear-armed and hostile states will start a conventional war with each other because they feel confident that it will not escalate to all-out nuclear war, or that they will not start such a war because they fear that it might escalate to all-out nuclear war. During the Cold War, the paradox produced the second, not the first, effect. Glenn Snyder was the first to formulate the paradox. See Glenn H. Snyder, "The Balance of Power and the Balance of Terror," in Paul Seabury, ed., *The Balance of Power* (San

Francisco: Chandler, 1965), pp. 198–199. Also see Robert Jervis, *The Illogic of American Nuclear Strategy* (Ithaca, NY: Cornell University Press, 1984), pp. 31–33 and 148–157.

11 The exception came in November 1983 with the NATO exercise "Able Archer." This was a serious crisis from the Soviets' point of view, and they briefly believed a nuclear from the West was imminent. At the time, however, neither the United States nor NATO was aware of the Soviet concerns, making this crisis hard to classify. See John Lewis Gaddis, *The Cold War: A New History* (New York: Penguin Press, 2005), pp. 227–228.

Ending Terrorism

AUDREY KURTH CRONIN

Examining How Terrorist Campaigns Have Ended

Although there are natural variations in the way specific [terrorist] groups end, demise generally follows six pathways, usually characterised by watershed events that lead to a diminution in the rate or lethality of attacks. . . . Some of the processes of decline are set in motion by the state, some by the group itself and some mainly by the audience. . . .

Catching or Killing the Leaders

First among the range of actions a government may take in pushing a group towards its end is to capture or kill its leader. Terrorist groups do sometimes meet their demise as a result of decapitation. . . . Terrorist groups often feature an individual who exploits a sense of hope and a feeling of grievance or frustration, thereby streamlining the frustrating complexities of life and presenting terrorist attacks as a way of nudging history forwards to a new, more desirable future. Little wonder that governments like to target the top.

The effects of decapitation have varied, especially according to whether a group was hierarchically organised and oriented towards a charismatic leader. Cases of groups that were badly damaged by the capture of their leader include Shining Path in Peru, the Real IRA and Aum Shinrikyo. . . . There is considerable evidence to indicate that capturing leaders has been more effective than killing them in ending a group. . . . That said, it is important how leaders are handled after they are apprehended. High-profile arrests sometimes backfire if jailed leaders are allowed to communicate with followers from prison, or when group members still on the outside attempt to free them. Examples include Sheikh Omar Abd al-Rahman (the so-called Blind Sheikh). Convicted for conspiracy in the bombing of the World Trade Center in 1993, he continued to communicate and radicalise followers from his cell. . . .

Cases where a group has ended following the *killing* of the leader are less common. The two states most active in carrying out assassinations of terrorist leaders (apart from the United States in its campaign against al-Qaeda) are Israel and Russia . . . . Killings target not just the top leadership but also mid-level military and political leaders who are believed to be involved in planning operations. . . . The question of whether or not the policy is justified is highly contentious. Many point to evidence of a drop-off in the frequency and lethality of terrorist attacks against Israeli civilians, although determining the degree to which this outcome reflects "targeted killings" as opposed to other factors (such as the security fence) is impossible. Others argue that targeted killings have attracted recruits to terrorist organisations, undercut Palestinian moderates and indirectly led to the election of a Hamas government in 2006. This debate is beyond the scope of this paper: whatever the benefits or drawbacks of targeted killings, they have not ended terrorism.

Before targeting a leader, it is best to think through the question of who the successor is likely to be. In 1973, Israeli agents killed Mohamed Boudia, an Algerian who had orchestrated Palestinian terrorist operations in Western Europe. He was replaced by Carlos ("the jackal"), an even more ruthless and cunning man. . . .

Crushing Terrorism with Force

The second way that states often try to end terrorism is through the use of brute force. This approach may involve aggressive military campaigns abroad (as with Israel's intervention in Lebanon in 1982) or domestic crackdowns at home (as with Turkey and the PKK), or some combination of the two (as in Colombia). Law enforcement is vital to any counter terrorism strategy. Steady, law-abiding police work, particularly surveillance and prevention, can hold domestic campaigns in check and reassure the populace that legal norms persist; however, normal police work rarely *ends* campaigns, especially when they cross borders. Most governments faced by major terrorist campaigns have been compelled to institute some type of emergency measures to answer the threat . . . Whether held to be desirable or regrettable, there is nothing historically *unusual* in the exertion of overwhelming state force, which is after all nothing more than the modern nation-state responding to a threat in exactly the way it is designed to do. But does it work in ending terrorism? At times, domestic and international repression has indeed been effective in pushing groups towards their decline and demise. Historical cases include the Russian government's campaign against Narodnaya Volya, the Peruvian government's repression of Shining Path between 1980 and 1992 and the Turkish government's crushing of the PKK between 1984 and 1999. If the only goal is to end violence against noncombatants for a time within a given territory, then the use of force can be said to have achieved this repeatedly throughout history. . . .

Repression also regularly proves to be only a temporary solution, resulting in the export of the problem to another country or region, as in the spreading of violence from Chechnya to other parts of the Caucasus. It is especially difficult for democracies to engage successfully in repression over time, since such measures require distinguishing targets from the rest of the population, often undermine civil liberties and change the very nature of the state. Keeping a domestic population anxious about the threat of further terrorist attacks and uninformed of the costs of repression appears to be crucial. . . . The use of repression against terrorism can undermine liberal or liberalising regimes, as with Uruguay's crackdown on the Tupamaros and its takeover by a military government in 1973. Massive state repression often kills many more people than the initial terrorist attacks. . . .

Achieving the Strategic Objective

Although in the current climate it may be anathema to say so, the third way in which terrorism has ended has been as a result of success. A few terrorist groups have triumphed—that is, they have achieved their long-term strategic or "outcome" goals and then either disbanded or adopted a more legitimate political form and stopped engaging in attacks against non-combatants. Given the nature of the tactic used, it is difficult to discuss this kind of ending dispassionately. . . .

National self-determination was the most important goal of terrorism in the twentieth century. In other cases, groups such as the Tamil Tigers, the PKK and the Basque separatists have sought independence or autonomy within an established state. Groups also sometimes aim to bring about a new social organisation as a successor to the nation-state. The Russian anarchists fit this description, although their specific aims evolved and are not easy to summarise. Indeed, long-term aims may be difficult to visualise: the goal may be to bring on the apocalypse (as with Aum Shinrikyo) or to merely act as a catalyst to the forces of history (as with the Russian social revolutionaries).

Very few terror groups achieve their stated strategic aims. . . . In killing non-combatants, terrorism can attract people's attention, provoke tactical responses, lead a state to undermine itself and create a *cause célèbre*, but it almost never installs new rulers, inspires ideological change, takes over territory or constructs new institutions of governance (as terrorist leaders typically claim). Historically, by virtually any standard of measurement, terrorist successes, by which is meant campaigns that achieve long-term objectives and are then ended, are the rare exceptions.

There are, however, some well-known, even legendary, examples of groups that succeeded in achieving major political change and then either disbanded or moved on to more legitimate political behaviour. These are regularly cited, rightly or wrongly, by successors who hope to duplicate the outcome. The best known is Irgun Zvai Leumi, the Jewish organization that fought to protect Jews in the Palestinian Mandate and to advance the cause of an independent Jewish state. Irgun attacks such as the 1946 bombing of the King David Hotel in Jerusalem hastened Britain's withdrawal from Palestine. Irgun was never a strong organization, lacking both widespread popular support and resources; at no point did it pose a serious military threat to the British. But at the heart of its power was a sophisticated propaganda war, what one prominent member labelled its "campaign of enlightenment," directed especially toward a sympathetic international audience in the wake of horrifying evidence of the plight of the Jewish people during the Second World War. The British were economically crippled in the early postwar years and withdrawing from other commitments elsewhere. The decision to quit Palestine was ripe for implementation and, within the highly politicised international context, Irgun's attacks were an effective catalyst. The group disbanded with the creation of the state of Israel in 1948.

The African National Congress (ANC) is another example of a successful group that used terror tactics. The ANC created a military wing, Umkhonto (MK), and, after nearly five decades of nonviolent resistance, turned to terrorist attacks in 1961. It fought to end apartheid and establish a multiracial state in South Africa. The MK's last attack occurred in 1989, and the ANC became a legitimate political party in 1990, with its leader, Nelson Mandela, elected first president of post-apartheid South Africa. But the question of cause and effect in these two examples (as in others) is complex: there is a great deal of evidence to indicate that both strategic outcomes were achieved at least as much *despite* the use of terrorism as because of it. In the ANC case, for example, the extensive pressures that led to the end of apartheid, including economic, cultural and sporting sanctions by the international community, a revolt among white English- and Afrikaner-speaking youth, a political revolt among members of the South African National Party and widespread, grassroots frustration and organisation on the part of the black community all undermined the legitimacy of the policy of apartheid and were more important than terrorist attacks in ending it.

These and other oft-cited cases lead to the conclusion that the keys to strategic success for terrorist groups are fourfold. Firstly (and most obviously), groups must have well defined and realizable aims; i.e., it is impossible to succeed if no one knows what your aims are. . . . Secondly, groups are best able to succeed when they can convince major powers of the legitimacy of their cause and gain their backing, morally or materially or both. As is the case with insurgencies, terrorist campaigns benefit tremendously from outside support. Thirdly, groups that use terrorism can only succeed when their actions comport with broader historical, economic and political changes that are occurring anyway in the international system. It is no coincidence that the most successful cases in the twentieth century are those where a colonial power found itself unable to hold onto its territories—as in Vietnam, Cyprus, Algeria and Ireland. . . . Finally, terrorism succeeds best when it is part of a broader campaign and the tactic is replaced by more legitimate means, especially popular uprisings, guerrilla warfare and insurgency. A weak and illegitimate tactic, terrorism *alone* has never succeeded in achieving strategic ends.

Moving Toward a Legitimate Political Process

The fourth means by which terrorism can be said to have ended revolves around the concept of a negotiated settlement. . . . Clichés about talking to terrorists do not hold up: after groups survive past the five- or six-year mark, it is not at all clear that refusing to negotiate with them shortens their violent campaigns any more than entering into negotiations prolongs them. Negotiations can facilitate a process of decline, but they have rarely been the single factor driving an outcome.

Looking at the recent history of terrorist campaigns, there are a number of interesting patterns with respect to negotiations. Firstly, there is a direct correlation between the age of the group and the probability of talks. The longer a group exists, the greater the likelihood that a peace process will begin, as groups become desperate for a resolution and governments come to realise that these non-state actors cannot be avoided or crushed. But this does not mean that most groups that engage in terrorist attacks negotiate: only about one in five groups of *any* age have entered into talks on strategic issues. Talks with groups that use terrorism are the exception, not the rule. Secondly, the vast majority of negotiations that do occur yield neither a clear resolution nor a cessation of the conflict.

A common scenario has been for negotiations to drag on, occupying an uncertain middle ground between a stable ceasefire and high levels of violence. About half of the groups that have negotiated in recent years have continued violent actions as the talks have unfolded, usually at a lower level of intensity and frequency. Negotiations seem to be more effective in gradually driving a group towards decline than single-handedly occasioning its abrupt end. . . .

Groups often splinter as a result of talks, and this can be either a good or a bad thing depending on the circumstances. Examples of this pattern include the Provisional IRA and the PLO. Dividing terrorist groups into factions has either isolated the most radical elements, which has the advantage of making them easier to target, or increased the violence against civilians in the short term, as radical factions try to demonstrate their viability by carrying out new attacks. . . .

Spoilers receive a great deal of attention in the context of negotiations, as terrorist attacks by splinter groups or disgruntled factions aim to derail or destroy talks. Clearly, talks that are not marred by spoiler attacks promise better outcomes. . . .

Judging the efficacy of negotiations is thus not simply a matter of whether or not they result in the end of violence in the short term. The most likely result for a government that chooses to negotiate and can withstand domestic pressure is long-term management of the threat over a lengthy period of gradual decline. Unlike civil wars and inter-state conflicts, where fighting normally stops while talks proceed, negotiations during terrorist campaigns redirect the contest into a less violent channel as the campaign winds down for other reasons. Talks carry risks and can pose a serious challenge for a democratic state that enters into them without a firm domestic mandate to do so, managed expectations and a back-up plan for when terrorism recurs. From the state's perspective, while negotiations are not a promising tactical means to end terrorist campaigns by themselves, if well handled they are nonetheless a wise and durable strategic tool for managing violence, splintering the opposition and facilitating its longer-term decline.

Implosion and Loss of Popular Support

The fifth way terrorist groups die is because they become cut off from their source of sustenance, or implode. Firstly, and arguably most importantly, groups regularly fail to move beyond the first generation, for reasons that are both internal and external to them. . . .

Some grievances have been easier to translate from one generation to another; in the twentieth century, those connected either to territory or to the identity of a group's supporters or constituents conveyed well. Leftwing ideologies have had less staying power than ethno-nationalist causes. . . .

A second cause of self-destruction is infighting and factionalization. The pressures of continuing a campaign have regularly led to counterproductive and dysfunctional behavior among a group's members, including struggles over doctrine, operations, leadership and tactics. Individuals may struggle for predominance within a group (as with the GIA in Algeria in 1994–95) or over the nature or pace of operations (as with the Provisional IRA or the Red Army Faction). When groups break up into factions, internecine competition may make them more concerned with stamping out competitors than furthering a common cause. . . .

A third reason for self-destruction is the tendency of terrorist groups to lose control over operations. This is a classic problem, especially when groups are faced with police or military pressure that makes it difficult to maintain both personal security and operational efficiency. Groups seeking to evade detection often adopt more horizontal structures so as to limit the damage to a hierarchy if a member is caught. . . . Uncoordinated, poorly planned or badly targeted operations increase the likelihood of a popular backlash against a group. Without some level of popular support, a group quickly dies. . . .

Moving to Other Malignant Forms

The sixth and final way terrorism can "end" is when the violence continues, but assumes another form. Groups that use terrorism at times reorient their behaviour, moving away from politically motivated attacks on civilians or noncombatants towards criminality (as with Abu Sayyaf or the Revolutionary Armed Forces of Colombia (FARC)) or toward full insurgency and even conventional war (as with the Algerian FLN or the Kashmiri groups Lashkar-e-Tayiba and Jaish-e-Mohammed). . . .

Criminal behaviour is by no means good news, but when a group moves away from terrorism and towards criminality the challenge it presents can at least potentially be managed within existing legal frameworks. Moreover, criminal activities often harm the reputation of a revolutionary group within its actual or potential constituency, making its commitment to an ideology or cause seem shallow.

Terrorist campaigns may also develop in the direction of more conventional types of violence. Terrorism and insurgency overlap and are cousins, and the same organizations can use both methods, but they are different phenomena.

Reviewing the twentieth-century record, the success rate for insurgencies (which attack military targets and typically shore up a constituency's support) has been higher than the success rate for terrorist organizations (which attack civilian or noncombatant targets and often undermine their own support). Terrorism is the *weak* tactic of the weak: used alone it rarely proves to be a winning approach over the long term. Being seen as an insurgency gives a campaign a degree of legitimacy: "terrorist" is a pejorative term in a way that "insurgent" is not. From the perspective of strategic counter terrorism, a group gaining enough strength to move into an insurgency is a bad outcome. . . .

Implications for Counterterrorism

The relevant question for policymakers in the midst of the current campaign is not "how are we doing?" but rather "how will it end?" Believing that a conflict never ends is psychologically self-defeating: war is prolonged because we have no firm idea how to avoid classic mistakes and bring it to a close, and thus we do not put in place policies that are designed with an end in mind. But there is a great deal of experience with terrorist campaigns ending, either because of actions taken against them or because of dynamics of their own, frequently related to the vulnerable connection between groups and their constituents or audiences. . . .

Policymakers who become caught up in the short-term goals and spectacle of terrorist attacks relinquish the broader historical perspective and phlegmatic approach that is crucial to the reassertion of state power. Their goal must be to think strategically and avoid falling into the trap of reacting narrowly and directly to the violent initiatives taken by these groups. Consciously driving a terrorist campaign toward its end is preferable to answering the tactical elements of a movement as it unfolds, and is also far more likely to result in success.

Questions for Review

What are the pathways by which terrorist campaigns have ended? Which one(s) appear most relevant to the eventual demise of ISIS?

Chapter 12

Civil Wars, Human Rights, Regime Change, and Humanitarian Intervention

Reflections on Intervention

KOFI ANNAN

The United Nations is . . . an association of sovereign States, and sovereign States do tend to be extremely jealous of their sovereignty. Small States, especially, are fearful of intervention in their affairs by great Powers. And indeed, our century has seen many examples of the strong "intervening"—or interfering—in the affairs of the weak, from the Allied intervention in the Russian civil war in 1918 to the Soviet "interventions" in Hungary, Czechoslovakia and Afghanistan. Others might refer to the American intervention in Viet Nam, or even the Turkish intervention in Cyprus in 1974. The motives, and the legal justification, may be better in some cases than others, but the word "intervention" has come to be used almost as a synonym for "invasion."

The Charter of the United Nations gives great responsibilities to great Powers, in their capacity as permanent members of the Security Council. But as a safe-guard against abuse of those powers, Article 2.7 of the Charter protects national sovereignty even from intervention by the United Nations itself. I'm sure every-one in this audience knows it by heart. But, let me remind you—just in case—that Article forbids the United Nations to intervene "in matters which are essentially within the domestic jurisdiction of any State."

That prohibition is just as relevant today as it was in 1945: violations of sov-ereignty remain violations of the global order. Yet, in other contexts the word "intervention" has a more benign meaning. We all applaud the policeman who intervenes to stop a fight, or the teacher who prevents big boys from bullying a smaller one. And medicine uses the word "intervention" to describe the act of the surgeon, who saves life by "intervening" to remove malignant growth, or to repair damaged organs. Of course, the most intrusive methods of treatment are not always to be recommended. A wise doctor knows when to let nature take its course. But a doctor who never intervened would have few admirers, and probably even fewer patients.

So it is in international affairs. Why was the United Nations established, if not to act as a benign policeman or doctor? Our job is to intervene: to prevent conflict where we can, to put a stop to it when it has broken out, or—when neither of those things is possible—at least to contain it and prevent it from spreading. That is what the world expects of us, even though—alas—the United Nations by no means always lives up to such expectations. It is also what the Charter requires of us, particularly in Chapter VI, which deals with the peaceful settlement of disputes, and Chapter VII, which describes the action the United Nations must take when peace comes under threat, or is actually broken.

The purpose of Article 2.7, which I quoted just now, was to confine such interventions to cases where the international peace is threatened or broken, and to keep the United Nations from interfering in purely domestic disputes. Yet even that article carries the important rider that "this principle shall not prejudice the application of enforcement measures under Chapter VII." In other words, even national sovereignty can be set aside if it stands in the way of the Security Council's overriding duty to preserve international peace and security. On the face of it, there is a simple distinction between international conflict, which is clearly the United Nations business, and domestic disputes, which are not. The very phrase "domestic dispute" sounds reassuring. It suggests a little local difficulty which the State in question can easily settle, if only it is left alone to do so.

We all know that in recent years it has not been like that. Most wars nowadays are civil wars. Or at least that is how they start. And these civil wars are anything but benign. In fact they are "civil" only in the sense that civilians—that is, non-combatants—have become the main victims.

In the First World War, roughly 90 per cent of those killed were soldiers, and only 10 per cent civilians. In the Second World War, even if we count all the victims of Nazi death camps as war casualties, civilians made up only half, or just over half, of all those killed. But in many of today's conflicts, civilians have become the main targets of violence. It is now conventional to put the proportion of civilian casualties somewhere in the region of 75 per cent.

I say "conventional" because the truth is that no one really knows. Relief agencies such as the Office of the United Nations High Commissioner for Refugees (UNHCR) and the Red Cross rightly devote their resources to helping the living rather than counting the dead. Armies count their own losses, and sometimes make boasts about the number of enemies they have killed. But there is no agency whose job is to keep a tally of civilians killed. The victims of today's brutal conflicts are not merely anonymous, but literally countless.

Yet so long as the conflict rages within the borders of a single State, the old orthodoxy would require us to let it rage. We should leave it to "burn itself out," or perhaps to "fester." (You can choose your own euphemism.) We should leave it even to escalate, regardless of human consequences, at least until the point when its effects begin to spill over into neighbouring States so that it becomes, in the words of so many Security Council resolutions, "a threat to international peace and security."

In reality, this "old orthodoxy" was never absolute. The Charter, after all, was issued in the name of "the peoples," not the governments, of the United Nations. Its aim is not only to preserve international peace—vitally important though that is—but also "to reaffirm faith in fundamental human rights, in the dignity and worth of the human person." The Charter protects the sovereignty of peoples. It was never meant as a licence for governments to trample on human rights and human dignity. Sovereignty implies responsibility, not just power.

This year we celebrate the fiftieth anniversary of the Universal Declaration of Human Rights. That declaration was not meant as a purely rhetorical statement. The General Assembly which adopted it also decided, in the same month, that it had the right to express its concern about the apartheid system in South Africa. The principle of international concern for human rights took precedence over the claim of non-interference in internal affairs.

And the day before it adopted the Universal Declaration, the General Assembly had adopted the Convention on the Prevention and Punishment of the Crime of Genocide, which puts all States under an obligation to "prevent and punish" this most heinous of crimes. It also allows them to "call upon the competent organs of the United Nations" to take action for this purpose.

Since genocide is almost always committed with the connivance, if not the direct participation, of the State authorities, it is hard to see how the United Nations could prevent it without intervening in a State's internal affairs. . . .

State frontiers, ladies and gentlemen, should no longer be seen as a watertight protection for war criminals or mass murderers. The fact that a conflict is "internal" does not give the parties any right to disregard the most basic rules of human conduct. Besides, most "internal" conflicts do not stay internal for very long. They soon "spill over" into neighbouring countries.

The most obvious and tragic way this happens is through the flow of refugees. But there are others, one of which is the spread of knowledge. News today travels around the world more rapidly than we could imagine even a few years ago. Human suffering on a large scale has become impossible to keep quiet. People in far-off countries not only hear about it, but often see it on their TV screens.

That in turn leads to public outrage, and pressure on governments to "do something," in other words, to intervene. Moreover, today's conflicts do not only spread across existing frontiers. Sometimes they actually give birth to new States, which of course means new frontiers. In such cases, what started as an internal conflict becomes an international one. That happens when peoples who formerly lived together in one State find each other's behaviour so threatening, or so offensive, that they can no longer do so. Such separations are seldom as smooth and trouble-free as the famous "velvet divorce" between Czechs and Slovaks. All too often they happen in the midst of, or at the end of, a long and bitter conflict, as was the case with Pakistan and Bangladesh, with the former Yugoslav republics, and with Ethiopia and Eritrea. In other cases, such as the former Soviet Union, the initial separation may be largely non-violent, and yet it soon gives rise to new conflicts, which pose new problems to the international community. In many cases, the conflict eventually becomes so dangerous that the international community finds itself obliged to intervene. By then it can only do so in the most intrusive and expensive way, which is military intervention.

And yet the most effective interventions are not military. It is much better, from every point of view, if action can be taken to resolve or manage a conflict before it reaches the military stage.

Sometimes this action may take the form of economic advice and assistance. In so many cases, ethnic tensions are exacerbated by poverty and famine, or by uneven economic development which brings wealth to one section of a community while destroying the homes and livelihood of another. If outsiders can help avert this by suitably targeted aid and investment, by giving information and training to local entrepreneurs, or by suggesting more appropriate State policies, their "intervention" should surely be welcomed by all concerned. That is why I see the work of the United Nations Development Programme, and of our sister Bretton Woods institutions in Washington, as organically linked to the United Nations work on peace and security.

In other cases what is most needed is skillful and timely diplomacy. . . . [but] if diplomacy is to succeed, it must be backed both by force and by fairness. The agreement was also a reminder to the entire world of why this Organization was established in the first place: to prevent the outbreak of unnecessary conflict; to seek to find international solutions to international problems; to obtain respect for international law and agreements from a recalcitrant party without destroying forever that party's dignity and willingness to cooperate. . . .

We must assume . . . that there will always be some tragic cases where peaceful means have failed: where extreme violence is being used, and only forceful intervention can stop it. Even during the cold war, when the United Nations' own enforcement capacity was largely paralysed by divisions in the Security Council, there were cases where extreme violations of human rights in one country led to military intervention by one of its neighbours. In 1971 Indian intervention ended the civil war in East Pakistan, allowing Bangladesh to achieve independence. In 1978 Viet Nam intervened in Cambodia, putting an end to the genocidal rule of the Khmer Rouge. In 1979 Tanzania intervened to overthrow Idi Amin's erratic dictatorship in Uganda.

In all three of those cases the intervening States gave refugee flows across the border as the reason why they had to act. But what justified their action in the eyes of the world was the internal character of the regimes they acted against. And history has by and large ratified that verdict. Few would now deny that in those cases intervention was a lesser evil than allowing massacre and extreme oppression to continue. Yet at the time, in all three cases, the international community was divided and disturbed. Why? Because these interventions were unilateral. The States in question had no mandate from anyone else to act as they did. And that sets an uncomfortable precedent.

Can we really afford to let each State be the judge of its own right, or duty, to intervene in another State's internal conflict? If we do, will we not be forced to legitimize Hitler's championship of the Sudeten Germans, or Soviet intervention in Afghanistan?

Most of us would prefer, I think—especially now that the cold war is over—to see such decisions taken collectively, by an international institution whose authority is generally respected. And surely the only institution competent to assume that role is the Security Council of the United Nations. The Charter clearly assigns responsibility to the Council for maintaining international peace and security. I would argue, therefore, that only the Council has the authority to decide that the internal situation in any State is so grave as to justify forceful intervention.

As you know, many Member States feel that the Council's authority now needs to be strengthened by an increase in its membership, bringing in new permanent members or possibly adding a new category of member. Unfortunately a consensus on the details of such a reform has yet to be reached.

This is a matter for the Member States. As Secretary-General I would make only three points. First, the Security Council must become more representative in order to reflect current realities, rather than the realities of 1945. Secondly, the Council's authority depends not only on the representative character of its membership but also on the quality and speed of its decisions. Humanity is ill served when the Council is unable to react quickly and decisively in a crisis. Thirdly, the delay in reaching agreement on reform, however regrettable, must not be allowed to detract from the Council's authority and responsibility in the meanwhile.

The Council in its present form derives its authority from the Charter. That gives it a unique legitimacy as the linch-pin of world order, which all Member States should value and respect. It also places a unique responsibility on Council members, both permanent and non-permanent—a responsibility of which their governments and indeed their citizens should be fully conscious.

Of course the fact that the Council has this unique responsibility does not mean that the intervention itself should always be undertaken directly by the United Nations, in the sense of forces wearing blue helmets and controlled by the United Nations Secretariat. No one knows better than I do, as a former Under-Secretary-General in charge of peacekeeping, that the United Nations lacks the capacity for directing large-scale military enforcement operations.

At least for the foreseeable future, such operations will have to be undertaken by Member States, or by regional organizations. But they need to have the authority of the Security Council behind them, expressed in an authorizing resolution. That formula, developed in 1990 to deal with the Iraqi aggression against Kuwait, has proved its usefulness and will no doubt be used again in future crises.

But we should not assume that intervention always needs to be on a massive scale. There are cases where the speed of the action may be far more crucial than the size of the force. Personally, I am haunted by the experience of Rwanda in 1994: a terrible demonstration of what can happen when there is no intervention, or at least none in the crucial early weeks of a crisis. General Dallaire, the commander of the United Nations mission, has indicated that with a force of even modest size and means he could have prevented much of the killing. Indeed he has said that 5,000 peacekeepers could have saved 500,000 lives. How tragic it is that at the crucial moment the opposite course was chosen, and the size of the force reduced.

Surely things would have been different if the Security Council had at its disposal a small rapid reaction force, ready to move at a few days' notice. I believe that if we are to avert further such disasters in the future we need such a capacity; that Member States must have appropriately trained stand-by forces immediately available, and must be willing to send them quickly when the Security Council requests it. . . .

In any case, let me stress that I am not asking for a standing army at the beck and call of the Secretary-General. The decision to intervene, I repeat, can only be taken by the Security Council. But at present the Council's authority is diminished, because it lacks the means to intervene effectively even when it wishes to do so.

Let me conclude by coming back to where I started. The United Nations is an association of sovereign States, but the rights it exists to uphold belong to peoples, not governments. By the same token, it is wrong to think the obligations of United Nations membership fall only on States. Each one of us—whether as workers in government, in intergovernmental or non-governmental organizations, in business, in the media, or simply as human beings—has an obligation to do whatever he or she can to correct injustice. Each of us has a duty to halt—or, better, to prevent—the infliction of suffering. . . .

When People are in danger, everyone has a duty to speak out. No one has a right to pass by on the other side. If we are tempted to do so, we should call to mind the unforgettable warning of Martin Niemöller, the German Protestant theologian who lived through the Nazi persecution:

"In Germany they came first for the Communists. And I did not speak up because I was not a Communist. Then they came for the Jews. And I did not speak up, because I was not a Jew. Then they came for the trade unionists. And I did not speak up, because I was not a trade unionist. Then they came for the Catholics. And I did not speak up, because I was a Protestant. Then they came for me. And by that time there was no one left to speak up."

Questions for Review

How does the former UN Secretary General square the need for humanitarian intervention with the well-established principles of state sovereignty? Does—and should—the Security Council have a privileged role to play here?

Human Rights in World Politics

Rhoda E. Howard and Jack Donnelly

The International Human Rights Covenants[1] note that human rights "derive from the inherent dignity of the human person." But while the struggle to assure a life of dignity is probably as old as human society itself, reliance on human rights as a mechanism to realize that dignity is a relatively recent development.

Human rights are, by definition, the rights one has simply because one is a human being. This simple and relatively uncontroversial definition, though, is more complicated than it may appear on the surface. It identifies human rights as *rights,* in the strict and strong sense of that term, and it establishes that they are held simply by virtue of being human. . . .

What Rights Do We Have?

The definition of human or natural rights as the rights of each person simply as a human being specifies their character; they are rights. The definition also specifies their source: (human) nature. . . .

What is it in human nature that gives rise to human rights? There are two basic answers to this question. On the one hand, many people argue that human rights arise from human needs, from the naturally given requisites for physical and mental health and well-being. On the other hand, many argue that human rights reflect the minimum requirements for human dignity or *moral* personality. These latter arguments derive from essentially philosophical theories of human "nature," dignity, or moral personality.

Needs theories of human rights run into the problem of empirical confirmations; the simple fact is that there is sound scientific evidence only for a very narrow list of human needs. But if we use "needs" in a broader, in part nonscientific, sense, then the two theories overlap. We can thus say that people have human rights to those things "needed" for a life of dignity, for the full development of their moral personality. The "nature" that gives rise to human rights is thus *moral* nature.

This moral nature is, in part, a social creation. Human nature, in the relevant sense, is an amalgam consisting both of psycho-biological facts (constraints and possibilities) and of the social structures and experiences that are no less a part of the essential nature of men and women. Human beings are not isolated individuals, but rather individuals who are essentially social creatures, in part even social creations. Therefore, a theory of human rights must recognize both the essential universality of human nature and the no less essential particularity arising from cultural and socioeconomic traditions and institutions.

Human rights are, by their nature, universal; it is not coincidental that we have a *Universal* Declaration of Human Rights, for human rights are the rights of all men and women. Therefore, in its basic outlines a list of human rights must apply at least more or less "across the board." But the nature of human beings is also shaped by the particular societies in which they live. Thus the universality of human rights must be qualified in at least two important ways.

First, the forms in which universal rights are institutionalized are subject to some legitimate cultural and political variation. For example, what counts as popular participation in government may vary, within a certain range, from society to society. Both multiparty and single-party regimes may reflect legitimate notions of political participation. Although the ruling party cannot be removed from power, in some one-party states individual representatives can be changed and electoral pressure may result in significant policy changes.

Second, and no less important, the universality (in principle) of human rights is qualified by the obvious fact that any particular list, no matter how broad its cross-cultural and international acceptance, reflects the necessarily contingent understandings of a particular era. For example, in the seventeenth and eighteenth centuries, the rights of man were indeed the rights of men, not women, and social and economic rights (other than the right to private property) were unheard of. Thus we must expect a gradual evolution of even a consensual list of human rights, as collective understandings of the essential elements of human dignity, the conditions of moral personality, evolve in response to changing ideas and material circumstances.

In other words, human rights are by their essential nature universal in form. They are, by definition, the rights held by each (and every) person simply as a human being. But any universal list of human rights is subject to a variety of justifiable implementations.

In our time, the Universal Declaration of Human Rights (1948) is a minimum list that is nearly universally accepted, although additional rights have been added (e.g., self-determination) and further new rights (e.g., the right to nondiscrimination on the grounds of sexual orientation or the right to peace) may be added in the future. We are in no position to offer a philosophical defense of the list of rights in the Universal Declaration. To do so would require an account of the source of human rights—human nature—that would certainly exceed the space available to us. Nonetheless, the Universal Declaration is nearly universally accepted by states. For practical political purposes we can treat it as authoritative. . . .

International Human Rights Institutions

The international context of national practices deserves some attention. There are, as we have already noted, international human rights standards that are widely accepted—in principle at least—by states. Thus the discussion and evaluation of national practices take place within an overarching set of international standards to which virtually all states have explicitly committed themselves. Whatever the force of claims of national sovereignty, with its attendant legal immunity from international action, the evaluation of national human rights practices from the perspective of the international standards of the Universal Declaration thus is certainly appropriate, even if one is uncomfortable with the moral claim sketched above that such universalistic scrutiny is demanded by the very idea of human rights.

In the literature on international relations it has recently become fashionable to talk of "international regimes," that is, norms and decision-making procedures accepted by states in a given issue area. National human rights practices do take place within the broader context of an international human rights regime centered on the United Nations.

We have already sketched the principal norms of this regime—the list of rights in the Universal Declaration. These norms/rights are further elaborated in two major treaties, the International Covenant on Economic, Social and Cultural Rights and the International Covenant on Civil and Political Rights, which were opened for signature and ratification in 1966 and came into force in 1976. Almost all of the countries studied in this volume have ratified (become a party to) both the Covenant on Civil and Political Rights and the Covenant on Economic, Social and Cultural Rights. . . . Even the countries that are not parties to the Covenants often accept the principles of the Universal Declaration. In addition, there are a variety of single-issue treaties that have been formulated under UN auspices on topics such as racial discrimination, the rights of women, and torture. These later Covenants and Conventions go into much greater detail than the Universal Declaration and include a few important changes. For example, the Covenants prominently include a right to national self-determination, which is absent in the Universal Declaration, but do not include a right to private property. Nevertheless, for the most part they can be seen simply as elaborations on the Universal Declaration, which remains the central normative document in the international human rights regime.

What is the legal and political force of these norms? The Universal Declaration of Human Rights was proclaimed in 1948 by the United Nations General Assembly. As such, it has no force of law. Resolutions of the General Assembly, even solemn declarations, are merely recommendations to states; the General Assembly has no international legislative powers. Over the years, however, the Universal Declaration has come to be something more than a mere recommendation.

There are two principal sources of international law, namely, treaty and custom. Although today we tend to think first of treaty, historically custom is at least as important. A rule or principle attains the force of customary international law when it can meet two tests. First, the principle or rule must reflect the general practice of the overwhelming majority of states. Second, what lawyers call *opinio juris*, the sense of obligation, must be taken into account. Is the customary practice seen by states as an obligation, rather than a mere convenience or courtesy? Today it is a common view of international lawyers that the Universal Declaration has attained something of the status of customary international law, so that the rights it contains are in some important sense binding on states.

Furthermore, the International Human Rights Covenants are treaties and as such do have the force of international law, but only for the parties to the treaties, that is, those states that have (voluntarily) ratified or acceded to the treaties. The same is true of the single-issue treaties that round out the regime's norms. It is perhaps possible that the norms of the Covenants are coming to acquire the force of customary international law even for states that are not parties. But in either case, the fundamental weakness of international law is underscored: Virtually all international legal obligations are voluntarily accepted.

This is obviously the case for treaties: states are free to become parties or not, entirely as they choose. It is no less true, though, of custom, where the tests of state practice and *opinio juris* likewise assure that international legal obligation is only voluntarily acquired. In fact, a state that explicitly rejects a practice during the process of custom formation is exempt even from customary international legal obligations. For example, Saudi Arabia's objection to the provisions on the equal rights of women during the drafting of the Universal Declaration might be held to exempt it from such a norm, even if the norm is accepted internationally as customarily binding. Such considerations are particularly important when we ask what force there is to international law and what mechanisms exist to implement and enforce the rights specified in the Universal Declaration and the Covenants.

Acceptance of an obligation by states does not carry with it acceptance of any method of international enforcement. Quite the contrary. Unless there is an explicit enforcement mechanism attached to the obligation, its enforcement rests simply on the good faith of the parties. The Universal Declaration contains no enforcement mechanisms of any sort. Even if we accept it as having the force of international law, its implementation is left entirely in the hands of individual states. The Covenants do have some implementation machinery, but the machinery's practical weakness is perhaps its most striking feature. . . .

The one other major locus of activity in the international human rights regime is the UN Commission on Human Rights. In addition to being the body that played the principal role in the formulation of the Universal Declaration, the Covenants and most of the major single-issue human rights treaties, it has some weak implementation powers. Its public discussion of human rights situations in various countries can help to mobilize international public opinion, which is not always utterly useless in helping to reform national practice. For example, in the 1970s the Commission played a major role in publicizing the human rights conditions in Chile, Israel, and South Africa. Furthermore, it is empowered by ECOSOC resolution 1503 (1970) to investigate communications (complaints) from individuals and groups that "appear to reveal a consistent pattern of gross and reliably attested violations of human rights."

The 1503 procedure, however, is at least as thoroughly hemmed in by constraints as are the other enforcement mechanisms that we have considered.[2] Although individuals may communicate grievances, the 1503 procedure deals only with *"situations"* of gross and systematic violations, not the particular cases of individuals. Individuals cannot even obtain an international judgment in their particular case, let alone international enforcement of the human rights obligations of their government. Furthermore, the entire procedure remains confidential until a case is concluded, although the Commission does publicly announce a "blacklist" of countries being studied. In only four cases (Equatorial Guinea, Haiti, Malawi, and Uruguay) has the Commission gone public with a 1503 case. Its most forceful conclusion was a 1980 resolution provoked by the plight of Jehovah's Witnesses in Malawi, which merely expressed the hope that all human rights were being respected in Malawi.

In addition to this global human rights regime, there are regional regimes. The 1981 African Charter of Human and Peoples' Rights, drawn up by the Organization of African Unity, provides for a Human Rights Commission, but it is not yet functioning. In Europe and the Americas there are highly developed systems involving both commissions with very strong investigatory powers and regional human rights courts with the authority to make legally binding decisions on complaints by individuals (although only eight states have accepted the jurisdiction of the Inter-American Court of Human Rights).

Even in Europe and the Americas, however, implementation and enforcement remain primarily national. In nearly thirty years the European Commission of Human Rights has considered only about 350 cases, while the European Court of Human Rights has handled only one-fifth that number. Such regional powers certainly should not be ignored or denigrated. They provide authoritative interpretations in cases of genuine disagreements and a powerful check on backsliding and occasional deviations by states. But the real force of even the European regime lies in the voluntary acceptance of human rights by the states in question, which has infinitely more to do with domestic politics than with international procedures.

In sum, at the international level there are comprehensive, authoritative human rights norms that are widely accepted as binding on all states. Implementation and enforcement of these norms, however, both in theory and in practice, are left to states. The international context of national human rights practices certainly cannot be ignored. Furthermore, international norms may have an important socializing effect on national leaders and be useful to national advocates of improved domestic human rights practices. But the real work of implementing and enforcing human rights takes place at the national level. . . . Before the level of the nation-state is discussed, however, one final element of the international context needs to be considered, namely, human rights as an issue in national foreign policies.

Human Rights and Foreign Policy

Beyond the human rights related activities of states in international institutions such as those discussed in the preceding section, many states have chosen to make human rights a concern in their bilateral foreign relations.[3] In fact, much of the surge of interest in human rights in the last decade can be traced to the catalyzing effect of President Jimmy Carter's (1977–1981) efforts to make international human rights an objective of U.S. foreign policy.

In a discussion of human rights as an issue in national foreign policy, at least three problems need to be considered. First, a nation must select a particular set of rights to pursue. Second, the legal and moral issues raised by intervention on behalf of human rights abroad need to be explored. Third, human rights concerns must be integrated into the nation's broader foreign policy, since human rights are at best only one of several foreign policy objectives.

The international normative consensus on human rights noted above largely solves the problem of the choice of a set of rights to pursue, for unless a state chooses a list very similar to that of the Universal Declaration, its efforts are almost certain to be dismissed as fatally flawed by partisan or ideological bias. Thus, for example, claims by officials of the Reagan administration that economic and social rights are not really true human rights are almost universally denounced. By the same token, the Carter administration's serious attention to economic and social rights, even if it was ultimately subordinate to a concern for civil and political rights, greatly contributed to the international perception of its policy as genuinely concerned with human rights, not just a new rhetoric for the Cold War or neo-colonialism. Such an international perception is almost a necessary condition—although by no means a sufficient condition—for an effective international human rights policy.

A state is, of course, free to pursue any objectives it wishes in its foreign policy. If it wishes its human rights policy to be taken seriously, however, the policy must at least be enunciated in terms consistent with the international consensus that has been forged around the Universal Declaration. In practice, some rights must be given particular prominence in a nation's foreign policy, given the limited material resources and international political capital of even the most powerful state, but the basic contours of policy must be set by the Universal Declaration.

After the rights to be pursued have been selected, the second problem, that of intervention on behalf of human rights, arises. When state A pursues human rights in its relations with state B, A usually will be seeking to alter the way that B treats its own citizens. This is, by definition, a matter essentially within the domestic jurisdiction of B and thus outside the legitimate jurisdiction of A. A's action, therefore, is vulnerable to the charge of intervention, a charge that carries considerable legal, moral, and political force in a world, such as ours, that is structured at the international level around sovereign nation-states.

The legal problems raised by foreign policy action on behalf of human rights abroad are probably the most troubling. Sovereignty entails the principle of non-intervention; to say that A has sovereign jurisdiction over X is essentially equivalent to saying that no one else may intervene in A with respect to X. Because sovereignty is the foundation of international law, any foreign policy action that amounts to intervention is prohibited by international law. On the face of it at least, this prohibition applies to action on behalf of human rights as much as any other activity.

It might be suggested that we can circumvent the legal proscription of intervention in the case of human rights by reference to particular treaties or even the general international normative consensus discussed above. International norms per se, however, do not authorize even international organizations, let alone individual states acting independently, to enforce those norms. Even if all states are legally bound to implement the rights enumerated in the Universal Declaration, it simply does not follow, in logic or in law, that any particular state or group of states is entitled to enforce that obligation. States are perfectly free to accept international legal obligations that have no enforcement mechanisms attached.

Scrupulously avoiding intervention (coercive interference) thus still leaves considerable room for international action at improving the human rights performance of a foreign country. Quiet diplomacy, public protests or condemnations, downgrading or breaking diplomatic relations, reducing or halting foreign aid, and selective or comprehensive restrictions of trade and other forms of interaction are all actions that fall short of intervention. Thus in most circumstances they will be legally permissible actions on behalf of human rights abroad.

An international legal perspective on humanitarian intervention, however, does not exhaust the subject. Recently, several authors have argued, strongly and we believe convincingly, that moral considerations in at least some circumstances justify humanitarian intervention on behalf of human rights.[4] Michael Walzer, whose book *Just and Unjust Wars* has provoked much of the recent moral discussion of humanitarian intervention, can be taken as illustrative of such arguments.

Walzer presents a strong defense of the morality of the general international principle of nonintervention, arguing that it gives force to the basic right of peoples to self-determination, which in turn rests on the rights of individuals, acting in concert as a community, to choose their own government. Walzer has been criticized for interpreting this principle in a way that is excessively favorable to states by arguing that the presumption of legitimacy (and thus against intervention) should hold in all but the most extreme circumstances. Nonetheless, even Walzer allows that intervention must be permitted "when the violation of human rights is so terrible that it makes talk of community or self-determination . . . seem cynical and irrelevant,"[5] when gross, persistent, and systematic violations of human rights shock the moral conscience of mankind.

The idea underlying such arguments is that human rights are of such paramount moral importance that gross and systematic violations present a moral justification for remedial international action. If the international community as a whole cannot or will not act—and above we have shown that an effective collective international response will usually be impossible—then one or more states may be morally justified in acting ad hoc on behalf of the international community.

International law and morality thus lead to different and conflicting conclusions in at least some cases. One of the functions of international politics is to help to resolve such a conflict; political considerations will play a substantial role in determining how a state will respond in its foreign policy to the competing moral and legal demands placed on it. But the political dimensions of such decisions point to the practical dangers by moral arguments in favor of humanitarian intervention. . . .

Human rights may be moral concerns, but often they are not *merely* moral concerns. Morality and realism are not necessarily incompatible, and to treat them as if they always were can harm not only a state's human rights policy but its broader foreign policy as well.

Sometimes a country can afford to act on its human rights concerns; other times it cannot. Politics involves compromise, as a result of multiple and not always compatible goals that are pursued and the resistance of a world that more often than not is unsupportive of the particular objectives being sought. Human rights, like other goals of foreign policy, must at times be compromised. In some instances there is little that a country can afford to do even in the face of major human rights violations. . . .

If such variations in the treatment of human rights violators are to be part of a consistent policy, human rights concerns need to be explicitly and coherently integrated into the broader framework of foreign policy. A human rights policy must be an integral part of, not just something tacked on to, a country's overall foreign policy.

Difficult decisions have to be made about the relative weights to be given to human rights, as well as other foreign policy goals, and at least rough rules for making trade-offs need to be formulated. Furthermore, such decisions need to be made early in the process of working out a policy, and as a matter of principle. Ad hoc responses to immediate problems and crises, which have been the rule in the human rights policies of countries such as Canada and the United States, are almost sure to lead to inconsistencies and incoherence, both in appearance and in fact. Without such efforts to integrate human rights into the structure of national foreign policy, any trade-offs that are made will remain, literally, unprincipled.

Standards will be undeniably difficult to formulate, and their application will raise no less severe problems. Hard cases and exceptions are unavoidable. So are gray areas and fuzzy boundaries. Unless such efforts are seriously undertaken, however, the resulting policy is likely to appear baseless or inconsistent, and probably will be so in fact as well.

There are many opportunities for foreign policy action on behalf of human rights in foreign countries, but effective action requires the same sort of care and attention required for success in any area of foreign policy. . . .

Culture and Human Rights

This view of the creation of the individual, with individual needs for human rights is criticized by many advocates of the "cultural relativist" school of human rights. They present the argument that human rights are a "Western construct with limited [universal] applicability."[6] But cultural relativism, as applied to human rights, fails to grasp the nature of culture. A number of erroneous assumptions underlies this viewpoint.

Criticism of the universality of human rights often stems from erroneous perceptions of the persistence of traditional societies, societies in which principles of social justice are based not on rights but on status and on the intermixture of privilege and responsibility. Often anthropologically anachronistic pictures are presented of premodern societies, taking no account whatsoever of the social change we have described above. It is assumed that culture is a static entity. But culture—like the individual—is adaptive. One can accept the principle that customs, values, and norms do indeed glue society together, and that they will endure, without assuming cultural stasis. Even though elements of culture have a strong hold of people's individual psyches, cultures can and do change. Individuals are actors who can influence their own fate, even if their range of choice is circumscribed by the prevalent social structure, culture, or ideology.

Cultural relativist arguments also often assume that culture is a unitary and unique whole; that is, that one is born into, and will always be, a part of a distinctive, comprehensive, and integrated set of cultural values and institutions that cannot be changed incrementally or only in part. Since in each culture the social norms and roles vary, so, it is argued, human rights must vary. The norms of each society are held to be both valuable in and of their own right, and so firmly rooted as to be impervious to challenge. Therefore, such arguments are applicable only to certain Western societies; to impose them on other societies from which they did not originally arise would do serious and irreparable damage to those cultures. In fact, though, people are quite adept cultural accommodationists; they are able to choose which aspects of a "new" culture they wish to adopt and which aspects of the "old" they wish to retain. For example, the marabouts (priests), who lead Senegal's traditional Muslim brotherhoods, have become leading political figures and have acquired considerable wealth and power through the peanut trade.

Still another assumption of the cultural relativism school is that culture is unaffected by social structure. But structure does affect culture. To a significant extent cultures and values reflect the basic economic and political organization of a society. For example, a society such as Tokugawa Japan that moves from a feudal structure to an organized bureaucratic state is bound to experience changes in values. Or the amalgamation of many different ethnic groups into one nation-state inevitably changes the way that individuals view themselves: For example, state-sponsored retention of ethnic customs, as under Canada's multicultural policy of preserving ethnic communities, cannot mask the fact that most of those communities are merging into the larger Canadian society.

A final assumption of the cultural relativist view of human rights is that cultural practices are neutral in their impact on different individuals and groups. Yet very few social practices, whether cultural or otherwise, distribute the same benefits to each member of a group. In considering any cultural practice it is useful to ask, who benefits from its retention? Those who speak for the group are usually those most capable of articulating the group's values to the outside world. But such spokesmen are likely to stress, in their articulation of "group" values, those particular values that are most to their own advantage. Both those who choose to adopt "new" ideals, such as political democracy or atheism, and those who choose to retain "old" ideals, such as a God-fearing political consensus, may be doing so in their own interests. Culture is both influenced by, and an instrument of, conflict among individuals or social groups. Just as those who attempt to modify or change customs may have personal interests in so doing, so also do those who attempt to preserve them. Quite often, relativist arguments are adopted principally to protect the interests of those in power.

Thus the notion that human rights cannot be applied across cultures violates both the principle of human rights and its practice. Human rights mean precisely that: rights held by virtue of being human. Human rights do not mean human dignity, nor do they represent the sum of personal resources (material, moral, or spiritual) that an individual might hold. Cultural variances that do not violate basic human rights undoubtedly enrich the world. But to permit the interests of the powerful to masquerade behind spurious defenses of cultural relativity is merely to lessen the chance that the victims of their policies will be able to complain. In the modern world, concepts such as cultural relativity, which deny to individuals the moral right to make comparisons and to insist on universal standards of right and wrong, are happily adopted by those who control the state.

Third World Criticisms

In recent years a number of commentators from the Third World have criticized the concept of universal human rights. Frequently, the intention of the criticisms appears to be to exempt some Third World governments from the standard of judgment generated by the concept of universal human rights. Much of the criticism in fact serves to cover abuses of human rights by state corporatist, developmental dictatorship, or allegedly "socialist" regimes.

A common criticism of the concept of universal human rights is that since it is Western in origin, it must be limited in its applicability to the Western world. Both logically and empirically, this criticism is invalid. Knowledge is not limited in its applicability to its place or people of origin—one does not assume, for example, that medicines discovered in the developed Western world will cure only people of European origin. Nor is it reasonable to state that knowledge or thought of a certain kind—about social arrangements instead of about human biology or natural science—is limited to its place of origin. Those same Third World critics who reject universal concepts of human rights often happily accept Marxist socialism, which also originated in the Western world, in the mind of a German Jew.

The fact that human rights is originally a liberal notion, rooted in the rise of a class of bourgeois citizens in Europe who demanded individual rights against the power of kings and nobility, does not make human rights inapplicable to the rest of the world. As we argue above, all over the world there are now formal states, whose citizens are increasingly individualized. All over the world, therefore, there are people who need protections against the depradations of class-ruled governments.

Moreover, whatever the liberal origins of human rights, the list now accepted as universal includes a wide range of economic and social rights that were first advocated by socialist and social-democratic critics of liberalism. Although eighteenth-century liberals stressed the right to private property, the 1966 International Human Rights Covenants do not mention it, substituting instead the right to sovereignty over national resources. . . . To attribute the idea of universal human rights to an outdated liberalism, unaffected by later notions of welfare democracy and uninfluenced by socialist concerns with economic rights, is simply incorrect.

The absence of a right to private property in the Covenants indicates a sensitivity to the legitimate preoccupations of socialist and postcolonial Third World governments. Conservative critics of recent trends in international human rights in fact deplore the right to national sovereignty over resources, as some of them also deplore any attention to the economic rights of the individual. We certainly do not share this view of rights; we believe that the economic rights of the individual are as important as civil and political rights. But it is the individual we are concerned with. We would like to see a world in which *every individual* has enough to eat, not merely a world in which every *state* has the right to economic sovereignty.

We are skeptical, therefore, of the radical Third Worldist assertion that "group" rights ought to be more important than individual rights. Too often, the "group" in question proves to be the state. Why allocate rights to a social institution that is already the chief violator of individuals' rights? Similarly, we fear the expression "peoples' rights." The communal rights of individuals to practice their own religion, speak their own language, and indulge in their own ancestral customs are protected in the Covenant on Civil and Political Rights. Individuals are free to come together in groups to engage in those cultural practices which are meaningful to them. On the other hand, often a "group" right can simply mean that the individual is subordinate to the group—for example, that the individual Christian fundamentalist in the Soviet Union risks arrest because of the desire of the larger "group" to enforce official atheism.

The one compelling use that we can envisage for the term "group rights" is in protection of native peoples, usually hunter-gatherers, pastoralists, or subsistence agriculturalists, whose property rights as collectivities are being violated by the larger state societies that encroach upon them. Such groups are fighting a battle against the forces of modernization and the state's accumulative tendencies. For example, native peoples in Canada began in the 1970s to object to state development projects, such as the James Bay Hydroelectric project in Quebec, which deprived them of their traditional lands. At the moment, there is no international human rights protection for such groups or their "way of life."

One way to protect such group rights would be to incorporate the group as a legal entity in order to preserve their land claims. However, even if the law protects such group rights, individual members of the group may prefer to move into the larger society in response to the processes of modernization discussed above. Both opinions must be protected.

If the purpose of group rights is to protect large, established groups of people who share the same territory, customs, language, religion, and ancestry, then such protection could only occur at the expense of states' rights. These groups, under international human rights law, do not have the right to withdraw from the states that enfold them. Moreover, it is clearly not the intention of Third World defenders of group rights to allow such a right to secession. A first principle of the Organization of African Unity, for example, is to preserve the sovereignty of all its member states not only against outside attack but also against internal attempts at secession. Group rights appear to mean, in practice, states' rights. But the rights of states are the rights of the individuals and classes who control the state.

Many Third World and socialist regimes also argue that rights ought to be tied to duties. A citizen's rights, it is argued, ought to be contingent upon his duties toward the society at large—privilege is contingent on responsibility. Such a view of rights made sense in nonstate societies in which each "person" fulfilled his roles along with others, all of the roles together creating a close-knit, tradition-bound group. But in modern state societies, to tie rights to duties is to risk the former's complete disappearance. All duties will be aimed toward the preservation of the state and of the interests of those who control it.

It is true that no human rights are absolute; even in societies that adhere in principle to the liberal ethos, individuals are frequently deprived of rights, especially in wartime or if they are convicted of criminal acts. However, such deprivations can legitimately be made only after the most scrupulous protection of civil and political rights under the rule of law. The difficulty with tying rights to duties without the intermediate step of scrutiny by a genuinely independent judiciary is the likelihood of wholesale cancellation of rights by the ruling class. But if one has rights merely because one is human, and for no other reason, then it is much more difficult, in principle, for the state to cancel them. It cannot legitimate the denial of rights by saying that only certain types of human beings, exhibiting certain kinds of behavior, are entitled to them.

One final criticism of the view of universal human rights embedded in the International Covenants is that an undue stress is laid on civil and political rights, whereas the overriding rights priority in the Third World is economic rights. In this view, the state as the agent of economic development—and hence, presumably, of eventual distribution of economic goods or "rights" to the masses—should not be bothered with problems of guaranteeing political participation in decision making, or of protecting people's basic civil rights. These rights, it is argued, come "after" development is completed. The empirical basis for this argument is weak. . . . Economic development per se will not guarantee future human rights, whether of an economic or any other kind. Often, development means economic growth, but without equitable distributive measures. Moreover, development strategies often fail because of insufficient attention to citizens' needs and views. Finally, development plans are often a cover for the continued violations of citizens' rights by the ruling class.

Thus we return to where we started: the rights of all men and women against all governments to treatment as free, equal, materially and physically secure persons. This is what human dignity means and requires in our era. And the individual human rights of the Universal Declaration and the Covenants are the means by which individuals today carry out the struggle to achieve their dignity. . . .

Questions for Review

What rights do human beings have as humans? How assertive should the international community be in enforcing human rights within states that grossly violate them?

Notes

1 The International Bill of Human Rights includes the Universal Declaration of Human Rights (1948), the International Covenant on Economic, Social and Cultural Rights (1966), the International Covenant on Civil and Political Rights (1966), and the Optional Protocol to the latter Covenant.

2 Howard Tolley, "The Concealed Crack in the Citadel: The United Nations Commission on Human Rights' Response to Confidential Communications," *Human Rights Quarterly* 6 (November 1984): 420–62.

3 This section draws heavily on Jack Donnelly, "Human Rights and Foreign Policy," *World Politics* 34 (July 1982): 574–95, and "Human Rights, Humanitarian Intervention and American Foreign Policy: Law, Morality and Politics," *Journal of International Affairs* 37 (Winter 1984): 311–28.

4 See, for example, Jerome Slater and Terry Nardin, "Nonintervention and Human Rights," *Journal of Politics* 48 (February 1986): 86–96; Charles R. Beitz, "Nonintervention and Communal Integrity," *Philosophy and Public Affairs* 9 (Summer 1980): 385–91; and Robert Matthews and Cranford Pratt, "Human Rights and Foreign Policy: Principles and Canadian Practice," *Human Rights Quarterly* 7 (May 1985): 159–88.

5 Michael Walzer, *Just and Unjust Wars* (New York: Basic Books, 1977), p. 90. For criticisms of Walzer see Jerome Slater and Terry Nardin, "Nonintervention and Human Rights," *Journal of Politics* 48 (February 1986); 86–9; and Charles R. Beitz, "Nonintervention and Communal Integrity," *Philosophy and Public Affairs* 9 (Summer 1980); 385–91.

6 Adamantia Pollis and Peter Schwab, "Human Rights: A Western Concept with Limited Applicability," in *Human Rights: Cultural and Ideological Perspectives*, Pollis and Schwab, ed. (New York: Praeger, 1979), pp. 1–18.

Humanitarian Intervention Comes of Age

Jon Western and Joshua S. Goldstein

. . . [I]t is important to examine the big picture of humanitarian intervention—and the big picture is decidedly positive. Over the last 20 years, the international community has grown increasingly adept at using military force to stop or prevent mass atrocities.

Humanitarian intervention has also benefited from the evolution of international norms about violence, especially the emergence of "the responsibility to protect," which holds that the international community has a special set of responsibilities to protect civilians—by force, if necessary–from war crimes, crimes against humanity, ethnic cleansing, and genocide when national governments fail to do so. The doctrine has become integrated into a growing tool kit of conflict management strategies that includes today's more robust peacekeeping operations and increasingly effective international criminal justice mechanisms. Collectively, these strategies have helped foster an era of declining armed conflict, with wars occurring less frequently and producing far fewer civilian casualties than in previous periods.

A Turbulent Decade

Modern humanitarian intervention was first conceived in the years following the end of the Cold War. The triumph of liberal democracy over communism made Western leaders optimistic that they could solve the world's problems as never before. Military force that had long been held in check by superpower rivalry could now be unleashed to protect poor countries from aggression, repression, and hunger. At the same time, the shifting global landscape created new problems that cried out for action. Nationalist and ethnic conflicts in former communist countries surged, and recurrent famines and instability hit much of Africa. A new and unsettled world order took shape, one seemingly distinguished by the frequency and brutality of wars and the deliberate targeting of civilians. The emotional impact of these crises was heightened by new communications technologies that transmitted graphic images of human suffering across the world. For the first time in decades, terms such as "genocide" and "ethnic cleansing" appeared regularly in public discussions.

Western political elites struggled to respond to these new realities. When U.S. marines arrived in Somalia in December 1992 to secure famine assistance that had been jeopardized by civil war, there were few norms or rules of engagement to govern such an intervention and no serious plans for the kinds of forces and tactics that would be needed to establish long-term stability. Indeed, the marines' very arrival highlighted the gap between military theory and practice: the heavily armed troops stormed ashore on a beach occupied by only dozens of camera-wielding journalists.

Although the Somalia mission did succeed in saving civilians, the intervention was less successful in coping with the political and strategic realities of Somali society and addressing the underlying sources of conflict. U.S. forces were drawn into a shooting war with one militia group, and in the October 1993 "Black Hawk down" incident, 18 U.S. soldiers were killed, and one of their bodies was dragged through the streets of Mogadishu while television cameras rolled. Facing domestic pressures and lacking a strategic objective, President Bill Clinton quickly withdrew U.S. troops. The UN soon followed, and Somalia was left to suffer in a civil war that continues to this day.

Meanwhile, two days after the "Black Hawk down" fiasco, the UN Security Council authorized a peacekeeping mission for Rwanda, where a peace agreement held the promise of ending a civil war. The international force was notable for its small size and paltry resources. Hutu extremists there drew lessons from the faint-hearted international response in Somalia, and when the conflict reignited in April 1994, they killed ten Belgian peacekeepers to induce the Belgian-led UN force to pull out. Sure enough, most of the peacekeepers withdrew, and as more than half a million civilians were killed in a matter of months, the international community failed to act.

Around the same time, a vicious war erupted throughout the former Yugoslavia, drawing a confused and ineffective response from the West. At first, in 1992, U.S. Secretary of State James Baker declared that the United States did not "have a dog in that fight." Even after the world learned of tens of thousands of civilian deaths, in May 1993, Clinton's secretary of state, Warren Christopher, described the so-called ancient hatreds of ethnic groups there as a presumably unsolvable "problem from hell." Unwilling to risk their soldiers' lives or to use the word "genocide," with all of its political, legal, and moral ramifications, the United States and European powers opted against a full-scale intervention and instead supported a UN peacekeeping force that found little peace to keep. At times, the UN force actually made things worse, promising protection that it could not provide or giving fuel and money to aggressors in exchange for the right to send humanitarian supplies to besieged victims.

The UN and Western powers were humiliated in Somalia, Rwanda, and the former Yugoslavia. War criminals elsewhere appeared to conclude that the international community could be intimidated by a few casualties. And in the United States, a number of prominent critics came to feel that humanitarian intervention was an ill-conceived enterprise. . . .

Other critics concluded that applying military force to protect people often prolonged civil wars and intensified the violence, killing more civilians than otherwise might have been the case. And still others argued that intervention fundamentally altered intrastate political contests, creating long-term instability or protracted dependence on the international community.

Nonetheless, international actors did not abandon intervention or their efforts to protect civilians. Rather, amid the violence, major intervening powers and the UN undertook systematic reviews of their earlier failures, updated their intervention strategies, and helped foster a new set of norms for civilian protection.

A key turning point came in 1995, when Bosnian Serb forces executed more than 7,000 prisoners in the UN-designated safe area of Srebrenica. The Clinton administration quickly abandoned its hesitancy and led a forceful diplomatic and military effort to end the war. The persistent diplomacy of Anthony Lake, the U.S. national security adviser, persuaded the reluctant Europeans and UN peacekeeping commanders to support Operation Deliberate Force, NATO's aggressive air campaign targeting the Bosnian Serb army. That effort brought Serbia to the negotiating table, where U.S. Assistant Secretary of State Richard Holbrooke crafted the Dayton agreement, which ended the war. In place of the hapless UN force, NATO sent 60,000 heavily armed troops into the "zone of separation" between the warring parties, staving off renewed fighting.

The "problem from hell" stopped immediately, and the ensuing decade of U.S.-led peacekeeping saw not a single U.S. combat-related casualty in Bosnia. Unlike previous interventions, the post-Dayton international peacekeeping presence was unified, vigorous, and sustained, and it has kept a lid on ethnic violence for more than 15 years. A related innovation was the International Criminal Tribunal for the Former Yugoslavia (ICTY), a court that has indicted 161 war criminals, including all the principal Serbian wartime leaders. Despite extensive criticism for ostensibly putting justice ahead of peace, the tribunal has produced dramatic results. Every suspected war criminal, once indicted, quickly lost political influence in postwar Bosnia, and not one of the 161 indictees remains at large today.

Buoyed by these successes, NATO responded to an imminent Serbian attack on Kosovo in 1999 by launching a major air war. Despite initial setbacks (the operation failed to stop a Serbian ground attack that created more than a million Kosovar Albanian refugees), the international community signaled that it would not back down. Under U.S. leadership, NATO escalated the air campaign, and the ICTY indicted Serbian President Slobodan Milosevic for crimes against humanity. Within three months, the combined military and diplomatic pressure compelled Serbia to withdraw its forces from Kosovo. And even though many observers, including several senior Clinton administration officials, feared that the ICTY's indictment of Milosevic in the middle of the military campaign would make it even less likely that he would capitulate in Kosovo or ever relinquish power, he was removed from office 18 months later by nonviolent civil protest and turned over to The Hague.

Outside the Balkans, the international community continued to adapt its approach to conflicts with similar success. In 1999, after a referendum on East Timor's secession from Indonesia led to Indonesian atrocities against Timorese civilians, the UN quickly authorized an 11,000-strong Australian-led military force to end the violence. The intervention eventually produced an independent East Timor at peace with Indonesia. Later missions in Sierra Leone, Liberia, and Côte d'Ivoire used a similar model of deploying a regional military force in coordination with the UN and, on occasion, European powers.

Correcting the Record

Despite the international community's impressive record of recent humanitarian missions, many of the criticisms formulated in response to the botched campaigns of 1992–95 still guide the conversation about intervention today. The charges are outdated. Contrary to the claims that interventions prolong civil wars and lead to greater humanitarian suffering and civilian casualties, the most violent and protracted cases in recent history—Somalia, Rwanda, the Democratic Republic of the Congo, Bosnia before Srebrenica, and Darfur—have been cases in which the international community was unwilling either to intervene or to sustain a commitment with credible force. Conversely, a comprehensive study conducted by the political scientist Taylor Seybolt has found that aggressive operations legitimized by firm UN Security Council resolutions, as in Bosnia in 1995 and East Timor in 1999, were the most successful at ending conflicts.

Even when civil wars do not stop right away, external interventions often mitigate violence against civilians. This is because, as the political scientist Matthew Krain and others have found, interventions aimed at preventing mass atrocities often force would-be killers to divert resources away from slaughtering civilians and toward defending themselves. This phenomenon, witnessed in the recent Libya campaign, means that even when interventions fail to end civil wars or resolve factional differences immediately, they can still protect civilians.

Another critique of humanitarian interventions is that they create perverse incentives for rebel groups to deliberately provoke states to commit violence against civilians in order to generate an international response. By this logic, the prospect of military intervention would generate more rebel provocations and thus more mass atrocities. Yet the statistical record shows exactly the opposite. Since the modern era of humanitarian intervention began, both the frequency and the intensity of attacks on civilians have declined. During the Arab Spring protests this year, there was no evidence that opposition figures in Tunisia, Egypt, Syria, or Yemen sought to trigger outside intervention. In fact, the protesters clearly stated that they would oppose such action. Even the Libyan rebels, who faced long odds against Qaddafi's forces, refused what would have been the most effective outside help: foreign boots on the ground.

Recent efforts to perfect humanitarian intervention have been fueled by deep changes in public norms about violence against civilians and advances in conflict management. Two decades of media exposure to mass atrocities, ethnic cleansing, and genocide have altered global—not simply Western—attitudes about intervention. The previously sacrosanct concept of state sovereignty has been made conditional on a state's responsible behavior, and in 2005, the UN General Assembly unanimously endorsed the doctrine of the responsibility to protect at the UN's World Summit. NATO's intervention in Libya reflects how the world has become more committed to the protection of civilians. Both UN Security Council resolutions on Libya this year passed with unprecedented speed and without a single dissenting vote.

In the wake of conflicts as well, the international community has shown that it can and will play a role in maintaining order and restoring justice. Peacekeeping missions now enjoy widespread legitimacy and have been remarkably successful in preventing the recurrence of violence once deployed. And because of successful postconflict tribunals and the International Criminal Court, individuals, including national leaders, can now be held liable for egregious crimes against civilians.

Collectively, these new conflict management and civilian protection tools have contributed to a marked decline in violence resulting from civil war. According to the most recent Human Security Report, between 1992 and 2003 the number of conflicts worldwide declined by more than 40 percent, and between 1988 and 2008 the number of conflicts that produced 1,000 or more battle deaths per year fell by 78 percent. Most notably, the incidence of lethal attacks against civilians was found to be lower in 2008 than at any point since the collection of such data began in 1989.

Still, although international norms now enshrine civilian protection and levels of violence are down, humanitarian interventions remain constrained by political and military realities. . . . neither the UN nor any major power is willing or prepared to intervene when abusive leaders firmly control the state's territory and the state's security forces and are backed by influential allies. Furthermore, the concept of civilian protection still competes with deeply held norms of sovereignty, especially in former colonies. Although humanitarian intervention can succeed in many cases, given these constraints, it is not always feasible.

Getting Better All the Time

It is against this backdrop that the international community should evaluate the two most recent interventions, in Côte d'Ivoire and Libya. In Côte d'Ivoire, a civil war that began in 2002 led to the partition of the country, with a large UN force interposed between the two sides. After years of peacekeeping, the UN oversaw long-delayed elections in 2010 and declared the opposition leader victorious. The incumbent, President Laurent Gbagbo, refused to leave, causing a months-long standoff during which Gbagbo's forces killed nearly 3,000 people. As another civil war loomed, France sent in a powerful military force that, in tandem with the UN peacekeepers, deposed Gbagbo and put the legitimate winner in the presidential palace.

Two decades ago, a similar situation in Angola led to disaster. After the UN sent a mere 500 military observers to monitor elections in 1992, the losing candidate resorted to war and the international community walked away. The crisis in Côte d'Ivoire ended much differently, partly because the mission was broadly seen as legitimate. Supporters of the action included not just the UN Security Council and Western governments but also the African Union, neighboring West African countries, and leading human rights groups. Moreover, the intervention in Côte d'Ivoire applied escalating military force over the course of several months that culminated in overwhelming firepower. The operation's planners allowed for, but did not count on, diplomacy and negotiation to dislodge Gbagbo. When those paths proved fruitless, the international community hardened its resolve.

Although the final chapter of the Libya mission has yet to be written and serious challenges remain, it has enjoyed several of the same advantages. The international response began in February when, as Qaddafi's security forces intensified their efforts to crush the protests, the UN Security Council unanimously passed Resolution 1970, which condemned the violence, imposed sanctions on the regime, and referred the case to the International Criminal Court. Three weeks later, Qaddafi's forces moved toward the rebel capital of Benghazi, a city of more than 700,000, and all signs pointed to an imminent slaughter. The Arab League demanded quick UN action to halt the impending bloodshed, as did major human rights organizations, such as the International Crisis Group and Human Rights Watch. In response, the Security Council passed Resolution 1973, which demanded a suspension of hostilities and authorized NATO to enforce a no-fly zone to protect civilians. Although five members of the Security Council—Brazil, China, Germany, India, and Russia—expressed reservations, none of them ultimately opposed the resolution. The subsequent intervention has been a genuinely multinational operation in which the United States at first played a central combat role and then stepped back, providing mostly support and logistics.

The intervention has accomplished the primary objective of Resolution 1973. It saved civilian lives by halting an imminent slaughter in Benghazi, breaking the siege of Misratah, and forcing Qaddafi's tank and artillery units to take cover rather than commit atrocities. And despite the initial military setbacks and some frustration over the length and cost of the operation, the intervention contributed to the end of the civil war between Qaddafi and the rebels, which otherwise might have been much longer and more violent.

Lessons Learned

Ever since U.S. marines stormed the Somali coast in 1992, the international community has grappled with the recurring challenges of modern humanitarian intervention: establishing legitimacy, sharing burdens across nations, acting with proportionality and discrimination, avoiding "mission creep," and developing exit strategies. These challenges have not changed, but the ways the international community responds to them have. Today's successful interventions share a number of elements absent in earlier, failed missions.

First, the interventions that respond the most quickly to unfolding events protect the most lives. Ethnic cleansing and mass atrocities often occur in the early phases of conflicts, as in Rwanda and Bosnia. This highlights the necessity of early warning indicators and a capacity for immediate action. The UN still lacks standby capabilities to dispatch peacekeepers instantly to a conflict area, but national or multinational military forces have responded promptly under

UN authority, and then after a number of months, they have handed off control to a UN peacekeeping force that may include soldiers from the original mission. This model worked in East Timor, Chad, and the Central African Republic, and it guided the international community's response to the impending massacre in Benghazi.

Second, the international community has learned from Somalia, Rwanda, and Bosnia that it needs access to enough military power and diplomatic muscle to back up a credible commitment to protecting civilians and to prevail even if things go wrong along the way. Lighter deployments may also succeed if members of the international community have additional forces close at hand that can be accessed if needed. When UN peacekeepers ran into trouble in Sierra Leone in 2000, for example, the United Kingdom rushed in with 4,500 troops to save the government and the peacekeeping mission from collapse.

Third, intervening governments must be sensitive to inevitable opposition from domestic constituencies and must design interventions that can withstand pressure for early exits. As Libya has demonstrated, protecting civilians from intransigent regimes often requires persistent and sustained action. In all likelihood, seemingly straightforward operations will turn out to be much less so. In past, failed missions, the international community was unwilling to accept coalition casualties and responded by withdrawing. Successful interventions, by contrast, have been designed to limit the threat to the intervening forces, thus allowing them to add resources and broaden the dimensions of the military operations in the face of difficulties.

Fourth, legitimate humanitarian interventions must be supported by a broad coalition of international, regional, and local actors. Multilateral interventions convey consensus about the appropriateness of the operations, distribute costs, and establish stronger commitments for the post-intervention transitions. But multilateralism cannot come at the expense of synchronized leadership. War criminals usually look to exploit divisions between outside powers opposing them. Interventions need to avoid having multiple states and organizations dispatch their own representatives to the conflict, sending mixed signals to the target states.

Finally, perhaps the most daunting challenge of a humanitarian intervention is the exit. Because violence against civilians is often rooted in deeper crises of political order, critics note that once in, intervenors confront the dilemma of either staying indefinitely and assuming the burdens of governance, as in Bosnia, or withdrawing and allowing the country to fall back into chaos, as in Somalia.

Some observers, then, have demanded that any intervention be carried out with a clearly defined exit strategy. Yet more important than an exit strategy is a comprehensive transition strategy, whereby foreign combat forces can exit as peacekeepers take over, and peacekeepers can exit when local governing institutions are in place and an indigenous security force stands ready to respond quickly if violence resumes. The earliest phases of an intervention must include planning for a transition strategy with clearly delineated political and economic benchmarks, so that international and local authorities can focus on the broader, long-term challenges of reconstruction, political reconciliation, and economic development.

Successful transition strategies include several crucial elements. For starters, negotiations that end humanitarian interventions must avoid laying the groundwork for protracted international presences. The Dayton peace accords, for example, created a duel-entity structure in Bosnia that has privileged nationalist and ethnic voices, and Kosovo's final status was left unresolved. Both of these outcomes unwittingly created long-term international commitments.

Intervening powers must also proceed with the understanding that they cannot bring about liberal democratic states overnight. Objectives need to be tempered to match both local and international political constraints. Recent scholarship on postconflict state building suggests that the best approach may be a hybrid one in which outsiders and domestic leaders rely on local customs, politics, and practices to establish new institutions that can move over time toward international norms of accountable, legitimate, and democratic governance.

Humanitarian interventions involve an inherent contradiction: they use violence in order to control violence. Setbacks are almost inevitable, and so it is no surprise that the operations often attract criticism. Yet when carried out thoughtfully, legitimately, and as part of a broader set of mechanisms designed to protect civilians, the use of military force for humanitarian purposes saves lives. Mass atrocities, ethnic cleansing, and genocide are truly problems from hell, but their solutions—honed over the course of two decades of experience from Mogadishu to Tripoli—are very much of this world. . . .

Questions for Review

What are the costs of military interventions by outside powers in civil wars to save lives? Do these interventions effectively deal with the underlying political problems that gave rise to the civil war?

To the Shores of Tripoli? Regime Change and Its Consequences

ALEXANDER B. DOWNES

Still knee-deep in the quagmires of Iraq and Afghanistan, in the spring of 2011, the United States entered the regime change business in Libya.

After Libyan leader Moammar Qaddafi sent his thugs into the streets to suppress a popular uprising, the United Nations Security Council—believing a humanitarian disaster was in the offing—authorized a no-fly zone to protect civilians. President Barack Obama made it clear from the beginning that half-measures would not suffice, asserting in March that Qaddafi had "lost the legitimacy to lead" and demanding that the Libyan leader "step down from power and leave." Although the president later backtracked somewhat from his hawkish stance, in April he reaffirmed that regime change was the U.S. objective. . . .

The Libyan operation is the third post-9/11 U.S. military intervention whose explicit goal is regime change. (The United States also played a role in a fourth case, the removal of Haitian President Jean-Bertrand Aristide in 2004.)

As a presidential candidate, George W. Bush criticized Clinton-era intervention in conflicts and humanitarian crises of questionable relevance to the national interest and promised to focus instead on great power politics. The 9/11 attacks, however, triggered a reversal in priorities, prompting Bush to launch wars for regime change in Afghanistan and Iraq and engage in massive nation-building efforts in those countries. . . .

Obama's reasons for confronting Qaddafi are more reminiscent of those that motivated Clinton in Bosnia and Kosovo than those that compelled Bush-era regime change, but several enduring factors trump changes in administration and provide a powerful impetus for continuing efforts at regime change spearheaded by the U.S. military.

First, there are few external constraints on the exercise of American power: the United States spends nearly as much on defense as the rest of the world combined and dwarfs most potential adversaries in military capability. . . . As long as the United States is committed to providing stability in most of the world, rooting out terrorism, stopping the spread of WMD, curbing human rights abuses, spreading democracy, and generally pursuing global primacy, frequent intervention is unavoidable.

Second, there are also few domestic hurdles for U.S. leaders to surmount when they want to take military action abroad. Even though regime changes are costly and can result in prolonged occupations and insurgencies, U.S. leaders can successfully downplay or lie about the potential costs of interventions in order to obtain public approval. . . .

Finally, Americans tend to personalize their conflicts. Almost every target of U.S. intervention in the post–Cold War world has been labeled "another Hitler." It is enticing to believe that removing one person from power will fix a problem. This "evil leader" syndrome is one reason why it is so difficult for the United States to fight wars for limited objectives; the temptation to "go to Baghdad" rather than make peace with a dictator is strong. . . .

Beyond the question of whether it is wise for the United States to seek regime change in yet another country while it continues to clean up the mess from the last two, the possibility of toppling another foreign dictator begs a reconsideration of the consequences of regime change. Focusing on consequences, I will steer clear of issues about the legality of regime change and whether it can be justified in moral terms. Rather, I ask what the historical record tells us about whether externally imposed regime change results in peace, stability, and democracy in target countries. Is the bloody aftermath of regime change in Afghanistan and Iraq the exception or the rule? Does regime change work?

The short answer is: rarely. The reasons for consistent failure are straightforward. Regime change often produces violence because it inevitably privileges some individuals or groups and alienates others. Intervening forces seek to install their preferred leadership but tend to have little knowledge of domestic politics in the target country or of the backlash their choice is likely to engender there. Moreover, interveners often lack the will or commitment to remain indefinitely in the face of violent resistance, which encourages regime change opponents to keep fighting. Regime change generally fails to promote democracy because installing pliable dictators is in the intervener's interest and because many targets lack the necessary preconditions for democracy.

Before proceeding, a point about terminology. "Foreign-imposed regime change" refers to instances where a state (or group of states) removes the effective political leader of another state by the threat or use of force and brings a different leader to power. About one-fifth of regime changes are undertaken to restore a previously governing ruler who was recently deposed in a coup, revolution, or by another foreign power. A good example is the U.S. intervention in Haiti that returned Aristide to office in 1994. The vast majority of regime changes, however, like those in Afghanistan and Iraq, empower new leaders who have not held power before. In this article, I focus on this more common type of regime change.

History

Regime change is nothing new to the United States. Since the defeat of Napoleon in 1815, the United States has been the world's foremost practitioner of regime change. Of the roughly one hundred cases of externally imposed regime change in that period, the United States has been responsible for more than twenty. These are only the "successful" attempts. Regime change is so common in part because it enjoys bipartisan support. Historically, many Democrats have been regime change enthusiasts. Woodrow Wilson overthrew leaders in Mexico (1914), the Dominican Republic (1914, 1916), and Haiti (1915) and demanded that German militarists leave power during World War I. Wilson's Democratic successors Franklin Roosevelt and Harry Truman presided over the most ambitious regime changes in history—the remaking of West Germany and Japan after World War II—and Truman sought to unify Korea under democratic governance during the early stages of the Korean War. President Kennedy tried on multiple occasions to oust (or kill) Castro—most ignominiously at the Bay of Pigs in 1961—and approved the coup against Diem in South Vietnam. And Bill Clinton intervened in Haiti in 1994 to return Aristide to power.

Republican presidents have not shied away from regime change as a policy instrument, either. William Howard Taft sent Marines to help oust Presidents José Santos Zelaya and José Madriz of Nicaragua, and Miguel Dávila of Honduras. On Eisenhower's watch, the CIA helped depose Mohammad Mossadeq in Iran and Jacobo Arbenz in Guatemala. Eisenhower also ordered the overthrow of

Indonesia's Sukarno and Congo's Patrice Lumumba, although Belgium was actually responsible for the latter's ouster and subsequent murder. In 1970, following Salvador Allende's election in Chile, Richard Nixon ordered the CIA to "prevent Allende from coming to power or to unseat him." The United States played a supporting role in the coup that ultimately felled Allende. Ronald Reagan went after Grenada and supported the Contras' effort to topple the Sandinista government in Nicaragua, and George H. W. Bush brought down Manuel Noriega in Panama.

The neoconservatives of the George W. Bush administration are thus not alone in pushing regime change. Liberal internationalists such as President Obama share many of the same goals as neoconservatives (such as maintaining U.S. primacy and spreading democracy), differing mainly in their greater trepidation about using force. And liberal internationalists have additional goals, such as preventing massive human rights abuses, that make regime change an attractive policy.

The United States has not been the sole practitioner of regime change. The Soviet Union installed communist governments in Eastern Europe after World War II and interfered regularly to keep friendly rulers in power. Nazi Germany overthrew multiple leaders in Western Europe and the Balkans in World War II. France has intervened on numerous occasions in its former African colonies to depose leaders it viewed as hostile. Great Britain twice tried, with little success, to place puppets on the Afghan throne in the nineteenth century.

Minor powers have also played the regime change game. Of the eight Honduran leaders who have been overthrown by outside actors, seven were removed by neighboring Guatemala, El Salvador, and Nicaragua. Other minor powers that have engaged in regime change include Brazil and Argentina in Paraguay (1869), Chile in Peru (1881–82), Tanzania in Uganda (1979), Vietnam in Cambodia (1979), and Rwanda and Uganda in Congo (1997).

The Logic of Regime Change

The circumstances behind instances of regime change vary, but the underlying commonality is that the target state is engaged in some behavior that the intervener finds objectionable or threatening, and the intervener believes that installing new leadership will correct that behavior. In certain cases the growing power of a rival state or the erratic behavior of a particular leader prompts a state to intervene. For example, during both World Wars, Allied leaders decided that it would serve little purpose to make peace with Germany because the potential military power of the country would remain a latent threat. Their solution was to impose a benign democratic regime. In the case of Iraq in 2003, Bush administration officials and their supporters became convinced that Saddam Hussein was a reckless gambler—"unintentionally suicidal," in the memorable phrase of Kenneth Pollack—who was bent on obtaining nuclear weapons that he would share with terrorists. To prevent this nightmare scenario, the United States again chose regime change.

In another scenario, the target itself is not a threat, but is simply a weak state that looks as if it may fall under the influence of a more powerful, threatening, one. Under these circumstances, interveners seek to install leaders more disposed to their own interests. British fears that Afghanistan was in danger of falling into Russia's orbit, for example, which would put Tsarist troops directly across the border from India, prompted both British incursions into Afghanistan to remove Afghan leaders in the nineteenth century. A similar logic applied in Nicaragua and Honduras in the early twentieth century when the United States deposed their leaders after they sought loans from Europe.

Leaders may also want to replace rulers who subscribe to a competing ideology, the spread of which they view as dangerous in its own right or as extending the influence of a rival state. For instance, the adoption of communism—or even populist leftism—by governments outside of the Soviet Union's immediate sphere of influence in Eastern Europe during the Cold War was often sufficient to incite a U.S. military response to topple such regimes. The communist—and by extension Soviet—threat led the United States to make common cause with right-wing dictators and work to overthrow leftist regimes (or regimes viewed as susceptible to leftist influence) in Iran, Indonesia, Guatemala, Congo, Cuba, Ecuador, Brazil, Guyana, Chile, and Nicaragua.

Whatever the individual circumstances, when states install new rulers in other states, they empower leaders they believe will be friendly and reliable allies; the intervening state doesn't want to take responsibility for governing. In the case of imposed dictatorships, the new leaders are beholden to the interveners—not to their constituency. The newly empowered leaders may share the intervening power's ideology, further cementing ties, and the intervener may install institutions that help maintain the new alliance. Democratic interveners who impose democracy often believe that democratic systems generate elites with compatible views on the illegitimacy of using force against other democracies, respect for human rights, and the need for democracies to band together to oppose autocracies.

Foreign-imposed regime change, in sum, is a method whereby countries can neutralize threats and spread their own influence by empowering leaders who share their own preferences. And all this is supposed to come on the cheap, avoiding the costs of outright conquest in blood, treasure, and reputation.

Internal War

Despite what interveners hope, regime change implemented by outsiders is not a force for stability in target states. More than 40 percent of states that experience foreign-imposed regime change have a civil war within the next ten years. Regime change can generate civil wars in three distinct ways. First, civil war can be part of the process of removing the old regime from power and suppressing its remnants. . . .

Second, regime change fosters civil war because it results in an abrupt status reversal for formerly advantaged groups. On many occasions, remnants of the old regime's leadership or army wage an insurgency against the new rulers rather than accept a subordinate position. This happened in Cambodia following the Vietnamese invasion in December 1978. The Vietnamese army quickly defeated the Khmer Rouge in conventional battles, but Pol Pot, other top leaders, and many fighters escaped to remote jungle hide-outs along the Thai and Laotian borders. Determined to regain power, the Khmer Rouge waged a decade-long insurgency against Vietnam's puppet, Heng Samrin, and occupying forces. Similarly, after the U.S. invasion of Iraq, Sunni Baathist ex-soldiers took up arms to eject U.S. occupiers and restore Sunni rule.

Finally, regime change can contribute to the outbreak of entirely new civil wars by reversing popular policies or instituting unpopular ones. Guatemala is an apt case. Arbenz's U.S.-supported successors rolled back the signal achievement of his administration: land reform that had redistributed property from large land-holders such as United Fruit to peasants. . . . Civil war continued in Guatemala in one form or another for more than thirty years, killing approximately 200,000 people. . . .

So externally imposed regime change can generate grievances that drive segments of the population to war against the intervener and the new government. Regime change also tends to sap the capabilities of the state to maintain order, reducing its ability to respond to internal opposition. In many cases, including Afghanistan and Iraq, the central government completely collapses and the security forces disintegrate. Foreign occupiers, meanwhile, don't necessarily want to get involved in providing law and order, and often lack the local knowledge required to differentiate friend from foe. These conditions create an opening that makes rebellion possible. Regime change therefore provides two of the key ingredients—motive and opportunity—for civil war.

Leadership Instability

In order for the intervener to succeed, its chosen leader usually must remain in office. An examination of the historical record shows this is a risky bet. Most foreign-installed leaders don't stick around long enough to secure peace or do their foreign benefactor's bidding.

Leaders leave office in one of two ways: regularly or irregularly. Regular exits follow the established norms and procedures of a country's political system, such as elections. Leaders removed in a regular fashion rarely suffer punishment beyond removal. Irregular forms of removal, on the other hand, involve the threat or use of force, and leaders ousted in this way are likely to suffer imprisonment, exile, or death. The degree to which foreign-imposed leaders are removed irregularly should, therefore, tell us something about regime change's capacity to create new and lasting allies.

Research by political scientists Hein Goemans, Giacomo Chiozza, and Kristian Skrede Gleditsch shows that roughly 65 percent of political leaders leave office via regular procedures. By contrast, less than 20 percent lose power in irregular fashion. Natural deaths and other mechanisms account for the remainder. Leaders that come to power after a foreign-imposed regime change, however, are overthrown by domestic opponents at a much higher rate. Indeed, 65 percent of them are ousted violently, most within five years of taking power and almost all within ten years. Compared to other leaders removed by violent means, leaders put in power by outsiders remain in office almost a year less. . . .

Exceptions do exist. In countries that are successfully democratized after regime change—such as West Germany, Japan, and Panama—leaders have fared much better, serving out their terms and leaving office via regular procedures. Such examples, however, are few and far between. Those leaders, such as Augusto Pinochet in Chile and Mohammad Reza Pahlavi in Iran, who maintain power usually do so by repression with the assistance of the intervener.

Democratic Potential

Can regime change bring about democratic transition? This was certainly the expectation in Iraq, where the Bush administration argued that removing Saddam Hussein would not only bring democracy to Iraq, but would prompt a wave of liberalization across the Middle East. This is not always the intention—with the exception of Grenada in 1983, no Cold-War era attempt at regime change saw a democratic intervener try to foster democracy. Anti-communism rather than adherence to democratic principles was the primary quality sought in leaders brought to power by the United States. These days, however, democratization is thought to be the default goal among democratic interveners.

There are two circumstances in which democratic interveners have succeeded in promoting democracy when they have tried to do so. The first is when democracies have restored to power democratic governments that were previously overthrown, such as in Belgium in 1918, France in 1944, Norway in 1945, and Haiti in 1994. These cases are not strong evidence of the democratizing power of regime change because these countries were all previously democratic; they were merely experiencing autocratic interregna at the hands of foreign occupiers or domestic coup-makers. The second circumstance consists of countries that have favorable preconditions for democracy, such as high income, homogeneous populations, strong bureaucratic institutions, and some previous experience with constitutional rule. West Germany and Japan remain the principal examples, joined by tiny Grenada and Panama. Most targets of regime change lack these preconditions; hence few successes are to be found.

Conclusion

The record of foreign-imposed regime change over the last two centuries is not a happy one. The promise of a quick, all-in-one solution is an illusion. U.S. leaders must face up to this illusion and begin treating regime change with serious skepticism. The United States can easily use force given its great power and ineffective domestic opposition: just think of the Obama administration's rationalization before Congress in June that the United States was not engaged in hostilities in Libya even while dropping bombs on the country. However, just because one can take action does not mean that one should. Reality is far different from illusion: regime change is highly destabilizing, and outcomes depend less on the good intentions or strategy of the intervener and more on conditions in the target country that are out of the intervener's control.

Not only is regime change difficult and unpredictable, but it is usually strategically unnecessary for the United States because so few countries pose any threat. It has fallen out of fashion to say so after 9/11, but the United States enjoys a high level of security. It dominates its hemisphere, possesses the world's best conventional military and a robust nuclear arsenal to deter the North Koreas and Irans of the world. Few terrorist groups want to attack the United States—most have local goals, and only a handful have publicly pledged allegiance to Al Qaeda—and few countries want to host such groups because it would put them in the U.S.'s gunsights. The United States should continue to take prudent measures against terrorism, including vigorous homeland defense, but regime change is unlikely to be useful in the fight against terrorists because of its potential to make the problem worse. Indeed, in most of the places where U.S. leaders will contemplate future regime changes—such as Iran, Syria, Pakistan, Sudan, or Myanmar—intervention is more likely to produce chaos than calm.

Furthermore, removing individual leaders is unlikely to cure what ails most countries. There is no doubt that men such as Saddam Hussein and Moammar Qaddafi have brought misery to their societies. Repairing the damage they have done, however, is far more complicated than simply driving them from power. And anointing average thugs such as Mahmoud Ahmadinejad or Bashar Assad the next Hitler merely makes it harder *not* to take action. Most of the time, regime change is best left to domestic forces, as it was in Serbia in 2000. External involvement should be limited to diplomatic pressure in support of legitimate domestic demands, as was the case with the ouster of Ferdinand Marcos in the Philippines. Weakening U.S. cover during the Carter and Reagan years forced Marcos to reckon with a domestic nonviolent revolution and eventually submit to elections that he would lose in 1986.

What circumstances, if any, might justify regime change? The likely costs need to be weighed against the good that can be done. Because the costs can be high, it is important to reserve the extreme option of regime change—as opposed to less intrusive forms of intervention—only to stop real disasters. For the United States, as noted above, the case for regime change on strategic grounds is weak. The most compelling scenario—the possibility that a state might develop nuclear weapons and give one to a terrorist organization—is highly unlikely. Preventing loose nukes might warrant inspections, sanctions, embargoes, sabotage, and a host of other counter-proliferation and counterterrorist measures, but not regime change.

There is a stronger argument to be made for regime change on humanitarian grounds, but even here the case is not clear-cut. Where to draw the line is the first problem. Repression in dictatorships is business as usual; a desire to halt all state-led violence cannot be the trigger. The second problem is that this is truly uncharted territory. None of the handful of genocidal leaders—Hitler, Pol Pot, and Idi Amin—who have been overthrown by foreign invaders were ousted on humanitarian grounds: ending mass killing was a byproduct of regime change undertaken for strategic reasons. In the most egregious cases, therefore, the key question is what is the advantage of changing the regime beyond stopping the violence? Experience has shown that getting the international community to intervene for humanitarian reasons is difficult enough. Regime change, in most cases, is probably a bridge too far.

Questions for Review

Obama criticizes George W. Bush for invading Iraq, yet he himself helped use force to change the regime in Libya. Is there a contradiction here? When does forcible regime change by external actors produce good results?

Crafting Peace through Power Sharing

CAROLINE A. HARTZELL AND MATTHEW HODDIE

Power Sharing as a Means of Managing Conflict in Post–Civil War States

Key Findings

The statistical analyses that form the heart of this study each seek to illustrate the role that power-sharing and power-dividing institutions play during the process of peacefully ending civil war. Collectively, these findings indicate that the chances for an enduring peace are greatly enhanced when competing parties include power-sharing or power-dividing provisions for multiple dimensions of state power as part of their negotiated agreement to end civil war.

Factors Associated with Creating Power-Sharing and Power-Dividing Institutions

Taking into account all civil wars ending between 1945 and 1999, we conclude that the odds that a war would terminate with a power-sharing settlement is largely determined by factors related to both the nature of the conflict and the international conflict environment. In terms of conditions defining the nature of the conflict, civil wars with the strongest potential to end with a power-sharing or power-dividing arrangement are those in which the dispute has proved enduring and included relatively few casualties. Long-lasting wars encourage compromise based on power-sharing and power-dividing principles as each side realizes that it lacks the capacity to prevail on the battlefield; at the same time, lower levels of bloodshed facilitate bargaining success among adversaries by minimizing the mutual distrust and animosity that define civil war.

The only factor related to the international conflict environment that has demonstrated a capacity to increase the odds of reaching a power-sharing or power-dividing arrangement is the promised introduction of foreign peacekeepers into the state emerging from civil war. We do not interpret this statistical association as indicating that peacekeepers themselves encourage the adoption of these institutions. Instead, we view the commitment to introduce peacekeepers as influencing the bargaining process by sufficiently reassuring parties to the dispute about their security to enable them to contemplate potential compromises with their adversaries. Bargains to share or divide power with an enemy appear less risky when third-party troops are present to assist in developing new governing institutions and potentially protecting those left vulnerable through their participation in the peace process.

Linking these disparate influences together is their effect on the perceptions of those at the bargaining table. Only when outright victory seems beyond reach (as indicated by the duration of the conflict) and parties to the dispute feel that the potential remains for relatively low-risk compromise with their enemies (as reflected in low levels of conflict and the promised introduction of peacekeepers) does a heightened possibility exist for a bargained resolution to emerge based on the principles of sharing and dividing state power.

Power-Sharing and Power-Dividing Institutions as a Means of Institutionalizing Peace

Holding all other potential influences constant, we find that the prospects for peace remaining intact are enhanced with each additional power-sharing aspect included as part of the settlement to end the war. Agreements that include requirements for sharing or dividing the political, military, territorial, and economic dimensions of state power are far more likely to foster an enduring peace as compared to those agreements that fail to include these provisions among the settlement's terms.

We interpret the value of these arrangements to the peace process as being based on both the substantive and symbolic importance attributed to them by former adversaries. Substantively, agreeing to establish these mechanisms guarantees that no single group will monopolize state power and use this position of dominance to threaten the security of others. Each additional power-sharing and power-dividing dimension specified in a settlement increases confidence that abandoning a wartime posture will not place a collectivity's membership at the mercy of its former adversaries. Through these provisions, each group's leadership also receives a commitment that it will have its influence felt in some aspects of governance of the postwar state and that it can use this power to protect its membership's interests. In short, the substantive value of power-sharing and power-dividing institutions is that they provide each contending group with a level of state power, which, while inhibiting their ability to establish dominance, guarantees them a capacity to check the predatory actions of their rivals.

The symbolic significance of these power-sharing and power-dividing mechanisms is the costly indication of conciliatory intent embodied in the agreement to create institutions based on the principles of cooperation. Signing on to the establishment of power-sharing and power-dividing institutions requires that adversaries abandon the typical wartime aim of monopoly control of the government and instead work together in the context of the institutional arrangements of the new state. In this sense, adversaries that commit themselves to the idea of sharing and dividing power have indicated to one another an interest in peace by virtue of their willingness to forgo priorities that seemed nonnegotiable at the initiation of hostilities.

The Significance of Implementing Power-Sharing and Power-Dividing Arrangements

In recognition of the limited information available concerning the postwar implementation process, we chose to focus solely on those states emerging from civil war between 1980 and 1996 that had committed to establishing military power-sharing and power-dividing institutions as part of their negotiated peace settlement. Our findings indicate that faithfully and completely implementing this aspect of a settlement's provisions substantially reduced the potential for a return to war in comparison to those cases in which combatants failed to fulfill these obligations. Only one of ten states returned to war following the full implementation of its military power-sharing arrangement; conversely, half of those agreements in which implementation was incomplete or failed led to the renewal of hostilities.

We account for the relationship between complete implementation and the maintenance of peace by again referring to the costly signals former enemies send to one another during the peace process. Group leaders that are successful at implementing military power-sharing and power-dividing provisions have demonstrated their genuine interest in peace by virtue of their willingness to absorb two categories of unavoidable costs. First, they have gone through with the commitments outlined in the original agreement and have participated in creating institutions that, by virtue of their existence, limit their own political power. Second, they have endured, and in many instances overcome, militant critics within their groups who emerge during the implementation of an agreement and charge the leadership with "selling out" the interests of the collectivity. By absorbing these costs inextricably linked to the implementation process, former adversaries indicate to one another their sincere commitment to maintaining the nascent peace. The new sense of security engendered through this process substantially reduces the risk of a return to war.

In summary, the findings . . . suggest that power-sharing and power-dividing institutions, when included as part of a negotiated settlement to end civil war, can play an important and positive role in fostering an enduring peace. Through their own efforts at developing these institutions, wartime adversaries foster a new sense of confidence that the postwar state will not be dominated by a single party with the intention of attacking the interests of its rivals.

Alternatives to Power-Sharing and Power-Dividing Institutions in Resolving Civil Wars

While this book has focused on the adoption of power-sharing and power-dividing institutions as a means to peacefully resolve civil wars, this is far from the only policy prescription that has been offered with the intent of definitively ending these conflicts. Below we offer a critical discussion of three alternative mechanisms that have been considered as a means to bring peace to states experiencing civil war; we suggest that these paths to peace have inherent limitations that make them less desirable as mechanisms for securing stability when compared to the adoption of a negotiated settlement based on the principles of sharing and dividing state power.

Military Victory

The most common means by which civil wars are brought to an end is when one party to the dispute establishes its dominance on the battlefield and forces its enemies to surrender. While people rarely advocate this outcome openly, members of the policy-making community have often tolerated such an approach through their well-documented reluctance to commit troops and resources toward efforts that might end ongoing civil violence. There is often a preference for allowing these conflicts to burn themselves out even when no immediate end to the war is in sight.

The death and destruction that come with waiting for a definitive military victory are thought to be a price worth paying because wars decided on the battlefield unambiguously establish one collectivity's hegemony over the society as a whole. With victory, it has been argued, the organizational identities of any competing groups are effectively erased along with their capacity to compete for the reins of power in the context of the postwar state. Achieving peace does not require engaging in the often frustrating process of bargaining and compromise but is instead asserted by the only party that has demonstrated having sufficient power to impose its will on others.

Although a military victory can secure peace, reasons still exist to question whether such an outcome is desirable in most circumstances. . . . some of the costs associated with achieving a military victory are much greater than would have been the case if competitors had proved capable of reaching a mutually acceptable settlement. In addition, the perceived need to destroy the present and future capacity of defeated enemies to compete for political power encourages the continuation of mass violence even when the final outcome of the war is no longer in doubt. If civil wars resolved through negotiations provide a means for groups to live together within the context of a single state, wars ended through a military victory give the winning side the often employed capacity simply to eliminate their competitors.

Members of the defeated groups surviving the initial stages of defeat have little reason to expect that governance of the postwar state will favor their interests. While isolated instances may exist in which an especially magnanimous victor has prioritized accommodating the concerns of the losing sides, in most cases the defeated become marginalized politically and in other ways. This was the case in Rwanda, for example, where the Tutsi army that proved victorious in 1994 has since made little or no effort to incorporate the majority Hutu into the new government.

In short, while military victories in civil war establish peace, they also foster an environment in which the grievances that formed the original basis for the conflict remain salient. The absence of violence within the state is solely a function of the continuing coercion of weaker parties. In this sense, military victories may ensure stability, but they also tend to create a set of governing institutions unresponsive to the concerns of those on the losing end of the civil war.

Partition

A second prescription for resolving civil wars that has garnered a great deal of attention in recent years is the suggestion that these countries be partitioned so that each competing group holds its own sovereign state. While a traditional emphasis on state sovereignty has meant that the international community has been reluctant to favor partition as a means of conflict management, the tactic has been employed for exactly this purpose both explicitly (e.g., East Timor's independence from Indonesia) and implicitly (e.g., the de facto partition of Cyprus).

Advocates of this method of ending civil wars suggest that the risks of a renewal of hostilities following partition are minimal given that each side holds its own territory and the ability to protect its own borders. By dividing groups into defensible states, partition establishes a sense that enemies can be kept at bay. . . .

While at first impression the partition solution to civil wars might appear less costly in comparison to ending conflict through military victory, the historical record indicates that partitioning states has rarely been achieved without producing substantial numbers of casualties and refugees. The partition of India and Pakistan is just one example of an effort at conflict management using this mechanism that produced enormous human costs. This partition resulted in an estimated hundreds of thousands of deaths and millions of refugees.

Evidence also calls into question whether partitioning provides an enduring solution to civil conflict. The recurrence of conflict between communities in the partitioned states of India/Pakistan and Ethiopia/Eritrea reflects the failings of this strategy. These examples do not appear to be the exception to the more general trend of stability following a state's division. . . .

As with the prescription to allow civil wars to end in military victory, the costs associated with employing the partition solution often seem unacceptably high in comparison to the negotiated resolution of these conflicts. While less pronounced than a battlefield solution, partitioning imposes substantial population losses as the process of dividing the state takes hold; partitioning also does little to encourage these groups to establish institutional mechanisms for peacefully managing the differences that formed the basis for war beyond demarcating a border between enemies.

Creating Incentives for Moderation

A third and final prescription for resolving civil wars we consider suggests that the interests of peace would best be served by establishing a set of postwar institutions that reward moderate behavior by a country's politicians. This category of policy recommendations was initially developed as a critique of Arend Lijphart's advocacy of power sharing for managing conflict in multiethnic states. It also sought to outline a viable alternative to Lijphart's emphasis on guaranteeing each group a share of state power as the most assured means of facilitating their continued loyalty to the national government.

The central criticism of Lijphart's position voiced as part of this perspective is that power-sharing institutions encourage people to cling to those identities that are the original basis for conflict within the state. Because the legitimacy of a claim to government power is dependent on meeting the criteria defined within the context of the peace agreement or constitution, people have a strong incentive to continue defining themselves and their interests along those lines. Individuals will thus find it difficult to develop new solidarities that cross-cut those linked to the war given that the state neither recognizes nor privileges these alternative forms of identity. In a state governed by a power-sharing arrangement in which ethnicity is the sole criterion for distributing influence and resources, competing sources of loyalty that might bring wartime adversaries together, such as class, gender, or regional identities, have little prospect of gaining saliency. . . .

With this critique of power sharing in mind, the alternative favored by those categorized within this perspective is to structure incentives in such a way that they encourage people to move beyond identities inextricably linked to the initial conflict. Most prominently, Donald Horowitz identifies a set of government institutions with the potential to encourage cooperative behavior among different groups by rewarding those politicians capable of reaching beyond their own base and incorporating former enemies as part of their coalition of supporters. He suggests, among other things, that states divided by ethnic differences would best be served by using an electoral system in which candidates could only gain office if they proved capable of garnering a degree of electoral support from those outside their own community. He also advocates adopting a federal system in which each of the country's states include multiple ethnic groups with the expectation that this would often force local politicians to seek support from the diverse collectivities that form their constituency.

In a similar vein, Philip Roeder has advanced the claim that postwar institutions should be engineered toward the goal of encouraging individuals to move beyond wartime identities. He focuses on two sets of policies consistent with this goal. First, he suggests that issues particularly likely to be a source of identity-based conflicts should be placed beyond the authority of government. Second, he advocates constructing an institutional structure of checks and balances intended to prevent any single group from monopolizing the political system. Roeder identifies the United States as the prime example of this conflict-management system in practice. The constitution's separation of church and state ensures that the contentious issue of religion is kept outside the reach of government authorities who might seek to impose the views of the majority on religious minorities. At the same time, constructing a presidential system, bicameral legislature, and independent judiciary provides multiple points in the political system to challenge, and potentially stop, the passage or implementation of laws that do not have a substantial level of support (or at least acquiescence from) interested parties.

Could the institutions described by either Horowitz or Roeder facilitate an enduring peace in states emerging from civil war? Answering this question is simply impossible given the rarity with which the structures advocated by these scholars have been adopted in the aftermath of war. While this does not serve as an indictment of this approach's value to conflict management, it does suggest its lack of appeal to former combatants as they transition from war to peaceful cooperation. In a situation in which individuals are emerging from sustained violence, it is clear that there is a preference for strong security guarantees that go beyond encouraging moderation or providing promises of institutional checks and balances. Power-sharing and power-dividing mechanisms, by ensuring access to different dimensions of state power, provide a straightforward and intuitive means of protecting collectivities' interests during a period of intense uncertainty and transition. For this reason, power-sharing and power-dividing mechanisms have become a common feature of negotiated settlements to end civil wars.

Power-sharing and power-dividing institutions can reinforce wartime identities. In the immediate aftermath of conflict, however, anticipating that new identities and sources of cleavages would emerge in the short term seems premature. Identities that formed the basis for conflict in this environment are inescapable, and only after political institutions have demonstrated a capacity for providing security on the basis of those identities may people reach beyond them to a new set of loyalties.

The Limitations of Power-Sharing and Power-Dividing Institutions

Power sharing does not resolve all of the dilemmas facing a post-civil war society. Below we describe some of the pathologies that come with adopting a power-sharing or power-dividing regime. We suggest that these costs are worth absorbing, at least in the immediate aftermath of civil war, in the interest of creating a sense of security among former enemies.

Power Sharing and Inefficient Governance

A problem that is almost always apparent immediately following the establishment of a power-sharing or power-dividing arrangement is the creation of a system in which government gridlock becomes unavoidable. By providing each wartime adversary a guaranteed share of political power, legislation is often blocked unless it meets with the approval of all interested parties. While this fosters a level of confidence that no group will be threatened by state actions that might compromise their security, it also makes responding quickly to the many challenges facing a state emerging from civil war exceedingly difficult for the government.

Bosnia's postwar experience demonstrates this problematic aspect of power-sharing and power-dividing arrangements. With a parliament divided among three collectivities, passing new legislation and autonomously moving the peace process forward have proved challenging for the government. Recognizing the difficulties inherent in reaching agreement among the contending groups, this task instead has been carried out by Bosnia's International High Representative, who has often opted to impose laws after they failed to receive sufficient support from elected officials.

Power Sharing and Uncompetitive Democracy

A second dilemma confronting regimes based on the principles of sharing and dividing state power is that they typically offer very limited opportunities for a genuinely open and competitive democratic political system. For most power-sharing and power-dividing systems to operate as intended, a group's leaders must have a relatively free hand to bargain and compromise with the representatives of competing interests within the society. Gaining this enhanced capacity for compromise, however, often means that leaders must act in ways that are decidedly out of step with common expectations of politicians' behavior in the context of a democracy.

While not initially considered in this light, we described exactly this type of antidemocratic behavior in our discussion of the costly signals that take place while implementing a peace agreement. Group leaders who ignore or suppress militant members of their own constituency in order to fulfill the obligations outlined in a settlement are indicating to their former adversaries that they have a genuine interest in peace. At the same time, however, this behavior silences and marginalizes those who would be most likely to articulate concerns with the direction in which leaders are taking the postwar state. This tendency to ignore the interests of their own constituencies in favor of focusing on the bargaining process with former adversaries suggests that the system tends toward an often elitist and antidemocratic orientation.

The Inflexibility of Power-Sharing Arrangements

Finally, power-sharing and power-dividing arrangements are sometimes criticized for proving inflexible and unable to adapt to changing times. When established at the conclusion of the conflict, these arrangements distribute power among groups on the basis of their interests and relative power as they appear at that point in time. Yet if circumstances change within the state in the aftermath of the war, the existing settlement may come under attack as being inadequate to address current conditions. Conflict could reignite as parties maneuver to enhance or protect the role assigned to them in the original peace deal.

Lebanon's National Pact of 1943 is one example of the dangers inherent in the inability of power-sharing arrangements to evolve with changing times. Reached during a period when the country's Christian population was obviously in the majority, the provisions of the pact became progressively less acceptable to Muslims as the demographic balance of power shifted in their favor. This disjuncture between the provisions of an antiquated settlement and the realities within the state eventually led to a return to civil war.

Addressing the Limitations Associated with Power-Sharing and Power-Dividing Arrangements

Problems that may affect states that use power-sharing and power-dividing institutions to manage intrastate conflict take the form of the potential for inefficient governance, limited prospects for open political competition, and arrangements that lack a capacity to evolve with changing times. With all of these inherent limitations, however, the fact remains that power-sharing and power-dividing institutions have a unique and demonstrated capacity to fulfill the one task that is essential to ensuring the successful transition from war to peace—guaranteeing that former combatants feel sufficiently secure to participate in establishing new governing institutions with the capacity to peacefully manage intrastate disputes.

It is perhaps expecting too much that these countries would prove able to establish governing institutions capable of addressing such diverse goals as promoting open political competition and ensuring efficient governance in the immediate aftermath of civil war. The reality facing groups in a postwar state is that they place their highest priority on providing for their security. It thus makes perfect sense that the institutions that are most commonly employed are those with the demonstrated capacity to perform this task.

Because states with negotiated civil war settlements are most likely to have their institutional architecture characterized by power sharing for a number of years, it seems reasonable to ask whether any means of minimizing some of the limitations typically associated with these arrangements exist. Turning first to the problem of inefficient governance, little can probably be done with respect to this issue in a post-civil war environment. To a very real extent, institutional arrangements involve trade-offs between policy efficiency and the credibility of policy commitments. Institutions that disperse power, as is the case with power-sharing and power-dividing institutions, reduce the risk of unpredictable government action. By doing so, these institutions facilitate the emergence of a stable policy environment in which governments can make policy commitments that are credible into the future. As civil war adversaries who negotiate an end to a civil war place a premium on credible commitments of this nature, of less importance to them is that politically fragmented institutions of the type they have designed do not generally make for responsive and adaptable govern-ments. Faced with this trade-off, former rivals will tend to opt for inefficiency even if they are aware that this may produce other problems in the future Under these circumstances, rivals may, at best, be aware of the trade-off they face and attempt, with the passage of time, to give greater emphasis to policy efficiency as a goal.

Along the same lines, groups may be able to do little regarding the lim-ited prospects for open political competition that power-sharing and power-dividing institutions can produce beyond cultivating an awareness of this fact and attempting to address it at the margins. Particularly noteworthy in this respect has been the recent emergence of civil society in countries that have experienced civil war. As groups emerge that are beyond the control of the leadership of the parties that have negotiated a settlement, the political land-scape may slowly start to expand beyond the contours agreed to in the initial negotiated settlement.

Ultimately, if power-sharing and power-dividing arrangements have met the goal of fostering a sense of security among former adversaries, and new priorities have emerged that cannot be addressed under the current arrangements, the pos-sibility remains that these institutions may be amended or discarded altogether. Because institutions are "sticky," they are likely to leave behind traces. In the case of power-sharing and power-dividing arrangements, the institutional legacy one hopes these measures will produce includes an increased sense of security and the emergence of new norms of nonviolent conflict management. With these in place, alternative institutional futures are possible. . . .

Once the international community promises to send peacekeepers into the conflict arena, it must be aware that the effect of their presence extends beyond helping to stop the killing by separating the belligerent parties. Settlements negotiated in an environment into which peacekeeping troops are expected to be deployed are more likely to be highly institutionalized than settlements designed in the absence of such promises. Although it is unlikely the peacekeepers themselves are encouraging the creation of these institutions, by sending in these troops third parties may provide a sense of security that gives adversaries the courage to design institutions that involve compromising over future control of the state. The international community may well want to factor in the effect the presence of peacekeepers has on levels of settlement institutionalization as it makes future choices about where to deploy these troops.

Somewhat less-complicated measures third parties can take to encourage the adoption of highly institutionalized settlements include increasing awareness of the relationship between such settlements and the stability of peace and providing incentives to encourage groups to design power-sharing institutions. Neither of these policy suggestions should be seen as encouraging the international community to take the lead role in designing the conflict-management institutions for a state attempting to emerge from civil war . . . the institutional choices adversaries make as well as the efforts they make to implement them are important signals of the groups' commitment to peace. Third parties that impose institutions on a postwar society run the risk of interfering with this process of signaling intentions among former adversaries. However, third parties can play a productive role by educating antagonists who are considering the adoption of power-sharing and power-dividing measures as part of a negotiated settlement about the relationship between high levels of institutionalization and the durability of peace.

The international community can also facilitate the adoption of a diverse range of power-sharing and power-dividing institutions by helping to provide resources the belligerents consider necessary to design or implement the institutions. In cases such as El Salvador, for example, financial commitments by outside actors appear to have played a key role in enabling the antagonists to agree to include economic power sharing as part of the settlement.

Summary

With wars now more common within states than among them, a pressing need exists to identify means of resolving these conflicts. By focusing on civil wars ended though a process of negotiation, the research we have presented in this book indicates that power-sharing and power-dividing institutions enhance the prospects of establishing a lasting postwar peace. Institutions that require former enemies to share or divide power have this demonstrated capacity to encourage peace because they go beyond simply requiring an end to the killing—they also establish a new set of rules and expectations intended to ensure that former antagonists can engage one another in political competition without threatening any collectivity's sense of safety. This unique capacity of power-sharing and power-dividing institutions to foster a sense of security, and sometimes trust, among former rivals allows them to serve as the foundations for an enduring peace.

Question for Review

Hartzell and Hoddie argue that power-sharing has been a more effective mechanism to stop civil wars than other mechanisms, but that power-sharing has its own problems. What are those problems, and do they make you less confident about the "healing powers" of power-sharing?

Chapter 13

Transnational Actors and New Forces

Transnational Activist Networks

MARGARET E. KECK AND KATHRYN SIKKINK

Networks are forms of organization characterized by voluntary, reciprocal, and horizontal patterns of communication and exchange. . . . Major actors in advocacy networks may include the following: (1) international and domestic nongovernmental research and advocacy organizations; (2) local social movements; (3) foundations; (4) the media; (5) churches, trade unions, consumer organizations, and intellectuals; (6) parts of regional and international intergovernmental organizations; and (7) parts of the executive and/or parliamentary branches of governments. Not all these will be present in each advocacy network. Initial research suggests, however, that international and domestic NGOs [non-governmental organizations] play a central role in all advocacy networks, usually initiating actions and pressuring more powerful actors to take positions. NGOs introduce new ideas, provide information, and lobby for policy changes.

Groups in a network share values and frequently exchange information and services. The flow of information among actors in the network reveals a dense web of connections among these groups, both formal and informal. The movement of funds and services is especially notable between foundations and NGOs, and some NGOs provide services such as training for other NGOs in the same and sometimes other advocacy networks. Personnel also circulate within and among networks, as relevant players move from one to another in a version of the "revolving door." . . .

Advocacy networks are not new. We can find examples as far back as the nineteenth-century campaign for the abolition of slavery. But their number, size, and professionalism, and the speed, density, and complexity of international linkages among them has grown dramatically in the last three decades. . . .

Transnational advocacy networks appear most likely to emerge around those issues where (1) channels between domestic groups and their governments are blocked or hampered or where such channels are ineffective for resolving a conflict, setting into motion the "boomerang" pattern of influence characteristic of these networks; (2) activists or "political entrepreneurs" believe that networking will further their missions and campaigns, and actively promote networks; and (3) conferences and other forms of international contact create arenas for forming and strengthening networks. Where channels of participation are blocked, the international arena may be the only means that domestic activists have to gain attention to their issues. Boomerang strategies are most common in campaigns where the target is a state's domestic policies or behavior; where a campaign seeks broad procedural change involving dispersed actors, strategies are more diffuse.

It is no accident that so many advocacy networks address claims about rights in their campaigns. Governments are the primary "guarantors" of rights, but also their primary violators. When a government violates or refuses to recognize rights, individuals and domestic groups often have no recourse within domestic political or judicial arenas. They may seek international connections finally to express their concerns and even to protect their lives.

When channels between the state and its domestic actors are blocked, the boomerang pattern of influence characteristic of transnational networks may occur: Domestic NGOs bypass their state and directly search out international allies to try to bring pressure on their states from outside. This is most obviously the case in human rights campaigns. Similarly, indigenous rights campaigns and environmental campaigns that support the demands of local peoples for participation in development projects that would affect them frequently involve this kind of triangulation. Linkages are important for both sides: For the less powerful Third World actors, networks provide access, leverage, and information (and often money) they could not expect to have on their own; for northern groups, they make credible the assertion that they are struggling with, and not only for, their southern partners. Not surprisingly, such relationships can produce considerable tensions. . . .

Just as oppression and injustice do not themselves produce movements or revolutions, claims around issues amenable to international action do not produce transnational networks. Activists—"people who care enough about some issue that they are prepared to incur significant costs and act to achieve their goals"[1]— do. They create them when they believe that transnational networking will further their organizational missions—by sharing information, attaining greater visibility, gaining access to wider publics, multiplying channels of institutional access, and so forth. For example, in the campaign to stop the promotion of infant formula to poor women in developing countries, organizers settled on a boycott of Nestlé, the largest producer, as its main tactic. Because Nestlé was a transnational actor, activists believed a transnational network was necessary to bring pressure on corporations and governments.[2] Over time, in such issue areas, participation in transnational networks has become an essential component of the collective identities of the activists involved, and networking a part of their common repertoire. The political entrepreneurs who become the core networkers for a new campaign have often gained experience in earlier ones.

Opportunities for network activities have increased over the last two decades. In addition to the efforts of pioneers, a proliferation of international organizations and conferences has provided foci for connections. Cheaper air travel and new electronic communication technologies speed information flows and simplify personal contact among activists. Underlying these trends is a broader cultural shift. The new networks have depended on the creation of a new kind of global public (or civil society), which grew as a cultural legacy of the 1960s. . . .

How Do Transnational Advocacy Networks Work?

Transnational advocacy networks seek influence in many of the same ways that other political groups or social movements do. Since they are not powerful in a traditional sense of the word, they must use the power of their information, ideas, and strategies to alter the information and value contexts within which states make policies. The bulk of what networks do might be termed persuasion or socialization, but neither process is devoid of conflict. Persuasion and socialization often involve not just reasoning with opponents, but also bringing pressure, arm-twisting, encouraging sanctions, and shaming. . . .

Our typology of tactics that networks use in their efforts at persuasion, socialization, and pressure includes (1) *information politics*, or the ability to quickly and credibly generate politically usable information and move it to where it will have the most impact; (2) *symbolic politics*, or the ability to call upon symbols, actions, or stories that make sense of a situation for an audience that is frequently far away; (3) *leverage politics*, or the ability to call upon powerful actors to affect a situation where weaker members of a network are unlikely to have influence; and (4) *accountability politics*, or the effort to hold powerful actors to their previously stated policies or principles. . . .

Network members actively seek ways to bring issues to the public agenda by framing them in innovative ways and by seeking hospitable venues. Sometimes they create issues by framing old problems in new ways; occasionally they help transform other actors' understanding of their identities and their interests. Land use rights in the Amazon, for example, took on an entirely different character and gained quite different allies viewed in a deforestation frame than they did in either social justice or regional development frames. In the 1970s and 1980s many states decided for the first time that promotion of human rights in other countries was a legitimate foreign policy goal and an authentic expression of national interest. This decision came in part from interaction with an emerging global human rights network. We argue that this represents not the victory of morality over self-interest, but a transformed understanding of national interest, possible in part because of structured interactions between state components and networks. This changed understanding cannot be derived solely from changing global and economic conditions, although these are relevant. . . .

Information Politics

Information binds network members together and is essential for network effectiveness. Many information exchanges are informal—telephone calls, e-mail and fax communications, and the circulation of newsletters, pamphlets, and bulletins. They provide information that would not otherwise be available, from sources that might not otherwise be heard, and they must make this information comprehensible and useful to activists and publics who may be geographically and/ or socially distant.

Nonstate actors gain influence by serving as alternate sources of information. Information flows in advocacy networks provide not only facts but testimony— stories told by people whose lives have been affected. Moreover, activists interpret facts and testimony, usually framing issues simply, in terms of right and wrong, because their purpose is to persuade people and stimulate them to act. How does this process of persuasion occur? An effective frame must show that a given state of affairs is neither natural nor accidental, identify the responsible party or parties, and propose credible solutions. These aims require clear, powerful messages that appeal to shared principles, which often have more impact on state policy than advice of technical experts. An important part of the political struggle over information is precisely whether an issue is defined primarily as technical—and thus subject to consideration by "qualified" experts—or as something that concerns a broader global constituency. . . .

Networks strive to uncover and investigate problems, and alert the press and policymakers. One activist described this as the "human rights methodology"— "promoting change by reporting facts."[3] To be credible, the information produced by networks must be reliable and well documented. To gain attention, the information must be timely and dramatic. Sometimes these multiple goals of information politics conflict, but both credibility and drama seem to be essential components of a strategy aimed at persuading publics and policymakers to change their minds.

The notion of "reporting facts" does not fully express the way networks strategically use information to frame issues. Networks call attention to issues, or even create issues by using language that dramatizes and draws attention to their concerns. A good example is the recent campaign against the practice of female genital mutilation. Before 1976 the widespread practice of female circumcision in many African and a few Asian and Middle Eastern countries was known outside these regions mainly among medical experts and anthropologists.[4] A controversial campaign, initiated in 1974 by a network of women's and human rights organizations, began to draw wider attention to the issues by renaming the problem. Previously the practice was referred to by technically "neutral" terms such as female circumcision, clitoridectomy, or infibulation. The campaign around female genital "mutilation" raised its salience, literally creating the issue as a matter of public international concern. By renaming the practice the network broke the linkage with male circumcision (seen as a personal medical or cultural decision), implied a linkage with the more feared procedure of castration, and reframed the issue as one of violence against women. It thus resituated the practice as a human rights violation. . . .

Human rights activists, baby food campaigners, and women's groups . . . dramatize the situations of the victims and turn the cold facts into human stories, intended to move people to action. The baby food campaign, for example, relied heavily on public health studies that proved that improper bottle feeding contributed to infant malnutrition and mortality, and that corporate sales promotion was leading to a decline in breast feeding. Network activists repackaged and interpreted this information in dramatic ways designed to promote action: The British development organization War on Want published a pamphlet entitled "The Baby Killers," which the Swiss Third World Action Group translated into German and retitled "Nestlé Kills Babies." Nestlé inadvertently gave activists a prominent public forum when it sued the Third World Action Group for defamation and libel. . . .

A dense web of north-south exchange, aided by computer and fax communication, means that governments can no longer monopolize information flows as they could a mere half-decade ago. These technologies have had an enormous impact on moving information to and from Third World countries, where mail service has often been slow and precarious; they also give special advantages, of course, to organizations that have access to them. A good example of the new informational role of networks occurred when U.S. environmentalists pressured President George Bush to raise the issue of gold miners' ongoing invasions of the Yanomami indigenous reserve when Brazilian president Fernando Collor de Mello was in Washington in 1991. Collor believed that he had squelched protest over the Yanomami question by creating major media events out of the dynamiting of airstrips used by gold miners, but network members had current information faxed from Brazil, and they countered his claims with evidence that miners had rebuilt the airstrips and were still invading the Yanomami area. . . .

The media is an essential partner in network information politics. To reach a broader audience, networks strive to attract press attention. Sympathetic journalists may become part of the network, but more often network activists cultivate a reputation for credibility with the press, and package their information in a timely and dramatic way to draw press attention.

Symbolic Politics

Activists frame issues by identifying and providing convincing explanations for powerful symbolic events, which in turn become catalysts for the growth of networks. Symbolic interpretation is part of the process of persuasion by which networks create awareness and expand their constituencies. Awarding the 1992 Nobel Peace Prize to Maya activist Rigoberta Menchú and the UN's designation of 1993 as the Year of Indigenous Peoples heightened public awareness of the situation of indigenous peoples in the Americas. Indigenous peoples' use of 1992, the 500th anniversary of the voyage of Columbus to the Americas, to raise a host of issues well illustrates the use of symbolic events to reshape understandings. . . .

Leverage Politics

Activists in advocacy networks are concerned with political effectiveness. Their definition of effectiveness often includes some policy change by "target actors" such as governments, international financial institutions like the World Bank, or private actors like transnational corporations. In order to bring about policy change, networks need to pressure and persuade more powerful actors. To gain influence the networks seek leverage (the word appears often in the discourse of advocacy organizations) over more powerful actors. By leveraging more powerful institutions, weak groups gain influence far beyond their ability to influence state practices directly. The identification of material or moral leverage is a crucial strategic step in network campaigns.

Material leverage usually links the issue to money or goods (but potentially also to votes in international organizations, prestigious offices, or other benefits). The human rights issue became negotiable because governments or financial institutions connected human rights practices to military and economic aid, or to bilateral diplomatic relations. In the United States, human rights groups got leverage by providing policymakers with information that convinced them to cut off military and economic aid. To make the issue negotiable, NGOs first had to raise its profile or salience, using information and symbolic politics. Then more powerful members of the network had to link cooperation to something else of value: money, trade, or prestige. Similarly, in the environmentalists' multilateral development bank campaign, linkage of environmental protection with access to loans was very powerful.

Although NGO influence often depends on securing powerful allies, their credibility still depends in part on their ability to mobilize their own members and affect public opinion via the media. In democracies the potential to influence votes gives large membership organizations an advantage over nonmembership organizations in lobbying for policy change; environmental organizations, several of whose memberships number in the millions, are more likely to have this added clout than are human rights organizations.

Moral leverage involves what some commentators have called the "*mobilization of shame*," where the behavior of target actors is held up to the light of international scrutiny. Network activists exert moral leverage on the assumption that governments value the good opinion of others; insofar as networks can demonstrate that a state is violating international obligations or is not living up to its own claims, they hope to jeopardize its credit enough to motivate a change in policy or behavior. The degree to which states are vulnerable to this kind of pressure varies, and will be discussed further below.

Accountability Politics

Networks devote considerable energy to convincing governments and other actors to publicly change their positions on issues. This is often dismissed as inconsequential change, since talk is cheap and governments sometimes change discursive positions hoping to divert network and public attention. Network activists, however, try to make such statements into opportunities for accountability politics. Once a government has publicly committed itself to a principle—for example, in favor of human rights or democracy—networks can use those positions, and their command of information, to expose the distance between discourse and practice. This is embarrassing to many governments, which may try to save face by closing that distance.

Perhaps the best example of network accountability politics was the ability of the human rights network to use the human rights provisions of the 1975 Helsinki Accords to pressure the Soviet Union and the governments of Eastern Europe for change. The Helsinki Accords helped revive the human rights movement in the Soviet Union, spawned new organizations like the Moscow Helsinki Group and the Helsinki Watch Committee in the United States, and helped protect activists from repression.[5] The human rights network referred to Moscow's obligations under the Helsinki Final Act and juxtaposed these with examples of abuses. . . .

Question for Review

International transnational advocacy networks (TANs) are akin to lobbying groups within a state. What contemporary examples of TANs can you think of, and have they significantly influenced the actions of the states they have targeted?

Notes

1 Pamela E. Oliver and Gerald Marwell, "Mobilizing Technologies for Collective Action," in *Frontiers in Social Movement Theory*, ed. Aldon D. Morris and Carol McClurg Mueller (New Haven: Yale University Press, 1992), p. 252.

2 See Kathryn Sikkink, "Codes of Conduct for Transnational Corporations: The Case of the WHO/UNICEF Code," *International Organization* 40 (Autumn 1986): 815–40.

3 Dorothy Q. Thomas, "Holding Governments Accountable by Public Pressure," in *Ours by Right: Women's Rights as Human Rights*, ed. Joanna Kerr (London: Zed Books, 1993), p. 83.

4 Female genital mutilation is most widely practiced in Africa, where it is reported to occur in at least twenty-six countries. Between 85 and 114 million women in the world today are estimated to have experienced genital mutilation. *World Bank Development Report 1993: Investing in Health* (New York: Oxford University Press, 1993), p. 50.

5 Discussion of the Helsinki Accords is based on Daniel Thomas, "Norms and Change in World Politics: Human Rights, the Helsinki Accords, and the Demise of Communism, 1975–1990," Ph.D. diss., Cornell University, 1997.

Cyber Conflict and National Security[1]

Herbert Lin

What Is Cyberspace and Why Is It Important?

In the 21st century, information is the key coin of the realm, and thus entities from nation-states to individuals are increasingly dependent on information and information technology (to include both computer and communications technologies). Businesses rely on information technology (IT) to conduct operations (e.g., payroll and accounting, recording inventory and sales, research and development (R&D)). Distribution networks for food, water, and energy rely in IT at every stage, as do transportation, health care, and financial services. Factories use computer-controlled machinery to manufacture products more rapidly and more efficiently than ever before.

Military forces are no exception. IT is used to manage military forces (e.g., for command and control and for logistics). The use of IT embedded in modern weapons systems increases the lethality and reduces the collateral damage associated with the use of such weapons. Movements and actions of military forces can be coordinated through networks that allow information and common pictures of the battlefield to be shared widely.

Terrorists also use IT. Although the kinetic weapons of terrorists are generally low-tech, terrorist use of IT for recruitment, training, and communications is often highly sophisticated.

What Is Conflict in Cyberspace?

Given the increasing importance of information and IT, it is not surprising that parties might seek to gain advantage over their adversaries by using various tools and techniques for taking advantage of certain aspects of cyberspace—what this paper will call "conflict in cyberspace" or "cyber conflict."[2]

Tools/Techniques

The tools and techniques of conflict in cyberspace can be usefully separated into tools based on technology and techniques that focus on the human being. Offensive tools and techniques allow a hostile party to do something undesirable. Defensive tools and techniques seek to prevent a hostile party from doing so.

TECHNOLOGY-BASED TOOLS An offensive tool requires three components:

1. Access refers to how the hostile party gets at the IT of interest. Access may be remote (e.g., through the Internet, through a dial-up modem attached to it, through penetration of the wireless network to which it is connected). Alternatively, access may require close physical proximity (e.g., spies acting or serving as operators, service technicians, or vendors). Close access is a

possibility anywhere in the supply chain (e.g., during chip fabrication, assembly, loading of system software, during shipping to the customer, during operation).

2. A vulnerability is an aspect of the IT that can be used to compromise it. Vulnerabilities may be accidentally introduced through a design or implementation flaw, or introduced intentionally (see close-access above). An unintentionally introduced defect ("bug") may open the door for opportunistic use of the vulnerability by an adversary.

3. Payload is the term used to describe the mechanism for affecting the IT after access has been used to take advantage of a vulnerability. For example, once a software agent (such as a virus) has entered a computer, its payload can be programmed to do many things—reproducing and retransmitting itself, destroying files on the system, altering files. Payloads can be designed to do more than one thing, or to act at different times. If a communications channel is available, payloads can be remotely updated.

Defensive tools address one or more of these elements. For example, some tools (e.g., firewalls) close off routes of access that might be inadvertently left open. Other tools identify programming errors (vulnerabilities) that can be fixed before a hostile party can use them. Still others serve to prevent a hostile party from doing bad things with any given payload (e.g., a confidential file may be encrypted so that even if a copy is removed from the system, it is useless to the hostile party).

PEOPLE-BASED TECHNIQUES People interact with information technology, and it is often easier to trick, bribe, or blackmail an insider into doing the bidding of a hostile party. For example, close access to a system may be obtained by bribing a janitor to insert a USB flash drive into a computer. A vulnerability may be installed by blackmailing a programmer into writing defective code. Note that in such cases, technical tools and people-based techniques can be combined.

Defensive people-based techniques essentially involve inducing people to not behave in ways that compromise security. Education teaches (some) people not to fall for scams that are intended to obtain log-in names and passwords. Audits of activity persuade (some) people not to use IT in ways that are suspicious. Rewards for reporting persuade (some) people to report questionable or suspicious activity to the proper authorities.

Possible Offensive Operations in Cyberspace

Offensive activity in cyberspace can be described as cyberattack or cyber exploitation.

1. Cyberattack refers to the use of deliberate activities to alter, disrupt, deceive, degrade, or destroy computer systems or networks used by an adversary

or the information and/or programs resident in or transiting these systems or networks. The activities may also affect entities connected to these systems and networks. A cyberattack might be conducted to prevent authorized users from accessing a computer or information service (a denial of service attack), to destroy computer controlled machinery (the alleged purpose of the Stuxnet cyberattack[3]), or to destroy or alter critical data (e.g., timetables for the deployment of military logistics). Note that the direct effects of a cyberattack (damage to a computer) may be less significant than the indirect effects (damage to a system connected to the computer).

2. Cyber exploitation refers to deliberate activities to penetrate computer systems or networks used by an adversary for obtaining information resident on or transiting through these systems or networks. Cyberexploitations do not seek to disturb the normal functioning of a computer system or network from the user's point of view—indeed, the best cyberexploitation is one that such a user never notices. The information sought is generally information that the adversary wishes not to be disclosed. A nation might conduct cyber exploitations to gather for valuable intelligence information, just as it might deploy human spies to do so. It might seek information on an adversary's R&D program for producing nuclear weapons, or on the adversary's order of battle, its military operational plans, and so on. Or it might seek information from a company's network in another country in order to benefit a domestic competitor of that company. Of particular interest is information that will allow it to conduct further penetrations on other systems and networks to gather additional information.

Note that press accounts often refer to cyberattacks when the activity conducted is a cyber exploitation.

Actors/Participants and Their Motivations

What actors might conduct such operations? The nature of information technology is such that the range of actors who can conduct operations of national-level significance is potentially large. Certain nation states, such as the United States, China, Russia, and Israel, are widely regarded as having potent offensive cyber capabilities, although smaller nation states can also conduct offensive operations in cyberspace.

To date, the known actors who have perpetrated acts of cyber exploitation and cyberattack are subnational parties—mostly individuals and mostly for profit. It is often alleged that Russia was behind the cyberattacks against Estonia in 2007 and Georgia in 2008, that China is behind a number of high-profile cyber exploitations against entities in many nations, and that the United States and/or Israel were responsible for the cyberattack on Iranian nuclear facilities (Stuxnet); however, none of these nations have officially acknowledged undertaking any of these activities, and conclusive proof, if any, that the political leadership of any nation ordered or directed any of these activities has not been made public.

A variety of subnational actors—including individuals, organized crime, and terrorists—might conduct cyberattacks and/or cyber exploitations. Indeed, some (but only some) such operations can be conducted with information and software found on the Internet and hardware available at Best Buy or Amazon.

Motivations for conducting such operations also span a wide range. One of the most common reasons today is financial. Because a great deal of commerce is enabled through the Internet or using IT, some parties are cyber criminals who seek illicit financial gain through their offensive actions. Cyber exploitations can yield valuable information, such as credit card numbers or bank log-in credentials; trade secrets; business development plans; or contract negotiation strategies. Cyberattacks can disrupt the production schedules of competitors, destroy valuable data belonging to a competitor, or be used as a tool to extort money from a victim. Perpetrators might conduct a cyberattack for hire (it is widely believed that the cyberattack on Estonia was conducted using a rented cyber weapon).

Another possible reason for such operations is political—the perpetrator might conduct the operation to advance some political purpose. A cyberattack or exploitation may be conducted to send a political message to a nation, to gather intelligence for national purposes, to persuade or influence another party to behave in a certain manner, or to dissuade another party from taking certain actions.

Still another reason for conducting such operations is personal—the perpetrator might conduct the operation to obtain "bragging rights," to demonstrate mastery of certain technical skills, or to satisfy personal curiosities.

Lastly, such operations may be conducted for military reasons, in the same way that traditional military operations involving kinetic weapons are used. This point is discussed below.

How Conflict in Cyberspace Compares to Conflict in Physical Space

Much about cyber conflict upends our understanding of how conflict might unfold. Although most observers would acknowledge clear differences between the cyber domain and physical domains, it is easy to underestimate just how far-reaching these differences are. Consider, for example, the impact of:

1. Venue for conflict. In traditional kinetic conflict (TKC), military activities occur in a space that is largely separate from the space in which large numbers of civilians are found. In cyber conflict, the space in which many military activities occur is one in which civilians are ubiquitous.

2. The offense-defense balance. In TKC, offensive technologies and defensive technologies are often in rough balance. In cyber conflict (at least prior to the

outbreak of overt hostilities), the offense is inherently superior to the defense, because the offense needs to be successful only once, whereas the defense needs to succeed every time.

3. Attribution. TKC is conducted by military forces that are presumed to be under the control of national governments. No such presumptions govern the actors participating in cyber conflict, and definitive attribution of acts in cyberspace to national governments is very difficult or impossible (see discussion below).

4. Capabilities of non-state actors. In TKC, the effects that non-state actors can produce are relatively small compared to those that can be produced by state actors. In cyber conflict, non-state actors can produce some of the large-scale effects that large-scale actors can produce.

5. The importance of distance and national borders. In TKC, distance looms large, and violations of national borders are significant. In cyber conflict, distance is more or less irrelevant, and penetrations of national boundaries for both attack and exploitation occur routinely and without notice.

These differences have pervasive effects on how to conceptualize conflict. The laws of armed conflict (LOAC) and the UN Charter were developed to cope with TKC, but although the fundamental principles underlying these laws remain valid, how they apply to cyber conflict in any specific instance is at best uncertain today. The intuitions of commanders (and their legal advisors) have been honed in environments of TKC. And apart from a few specialists, an understanding of cyber conflict does not exist broadly within the personnel of today's armed forces.

Conduct of Cyber Conflict (and its Connection to Kinetic Conflict)

It is helpful to discuss cyber conflict in two different contexts—when overt hostilities have not broken out, and when they have broken out. These contexts are fundamentally different, because in the first as compared to the second, there is a great deal of time to prepare for the onset of conflict. That time can be used to gather intelligence and prepare the cyber "battlefield."

1. Intelligence gathering. Although reliable and relevant intelligence information about an adversary has always been important in traditional kinetic conflict, it is superlatively important for cyber conflict. Because the successful penetration of an adversary's system depends on knowing its vulnerabilities and having access, intelligence is required to obtain such knowledge and access. Some such knowledge may be available from public sources; in other instances, automated means may be capable of gathering some relevant information; in still other instances, necessary knowledge may be available only through traditional spycraft. And other intelligence information is needed to develop an appropriate payload that will perform the required functions.

2. Preparation of the cyber battlefield entails the identification and/or deliberate insertion of vulnerabilities into access paths to an adversary's computer systems and networks. No deliberately hostile acts are undertaken—only pre-installation of the capability to take such acts when necessary. Preparation of the cyber battlefield can be regarded as analogous to clandestinely digging a tunnel under an adversary's defensive lines. Digging a tunnel under such circumstances is a hostile action, but it is not the equivalent of initiating armed hostilities.

In the absence of intelligence information or proper battlefield preparation, cyberattacks can only be "broad-spectrum" and relatively indiscriminate or blunt. Precisely targeted cyberattacks have substantial intelligence requirements.

When overt conflict breaks out, there is less time available to collect intelligence on new cyber targets that may be identified. Thus, offensive cyber operations may have their greatest value before overt conflict breaks out or in the early stages of a conflict. (Previously identified cyber targets are vulnerable at any point in time, as long as the intelligence information remains valid and cyber-battlefield preparations remain in place. An adversary knowing that conflict is imminent or ongoing may well take measures to invalidate intelligence previously collected and/or to eliminate pre-positioned vulnerabilities or access paths.)

In addition, if TKC is involved in overt conflict, cyber operations become—in principle—just one additional tool in the arsenal of the operational commander. Assuming that legal and policy issues can be resolved (see below), cyber operations that are coordinated with kinetic operations can have powerfully synergistic effects. For example, it is common practice for operational commanders to suppress adversary air defenses to protect follow-on air strikes. Suppression can use traditional kinetic means, but cyber suppression of air defenses may be possible as well if the attacker has properly prepared the battlefield (e.g., implanted vulnerabilities in the computers controlling the air defense radars) and if adequate intelligence information is available.

Some Important Issues

Cyber conflict raises many complex issues for national security. The issues described below are intended as a sampling of the most salient, but this description is not intended to be comprehensive.

Attribution

As noted above, a key technical attribute of cyber operations is the difficulty of attributing any given cyber operation to its perpetrator. In this context, the definition of "perpetrator" can have many meanings:

1. The attacking machine that is directly connected to the target. Of course, this machine—the one most proximate to the target—may well belong to an innocent third party who has no knowledge of the operation being conducted.

2. The machine that launched or initiated the operation.

3. The geographical location of the machine that launched or initiated the operation.

4. The individual sitting at the keyboard of the initiating machine.

5. The nation under whose jurisdiction the named individual falls (e.g., by virtue of his physical location when he typed the initiating commands).

6. The entity under whose auspices the individual acted, if any.

In practice, a judgment of attribution is based on all available sources of information, which could include technical signatures and forensics collected regarding the act in question, intelligence information (e.g., intercepted phone calls monitoring conversations of senior leaders), prior history (e.g., similarity to previous cyber operations), and knowledge of those with incentives to conduct such operations.

It is commonly said that attribution of hostile cyber operations is impossible. The statement does have an essential kernel of truth: if the perpetrator makes no mistakes, uses techniques that have never been seen before, leaves behind no clues that point to himself, does not discuss the operation in any public or monitored forum, and does not conduct his actions during a period in which his incentives to conduct such operations are known publicly, then identification of the perpetrator may well be impossible.

Indeed, sometimes all of these conditions are met, and policy makers rightly despair of their ability to act appropriately under such circumstances. But in other cases, the problem of attribution is not so dire, because one or more of these conditions are not met, and it may be possible to make some useful (if incomplete) judgments about attribution.

For example, even if one does not know the location of the machine that launched a given attack, signals or human intelligence might provide the identity of the entity under whose auspices the attack was launched. The latter might be all that is necessary to take further action against the perpetrator.

Deterrence and Defense in Cyberspace

A great deal of policy attention today is given to protecting information and IT that is important to the nation. There are two ways (not mutually exclusive) of providing such protection—defending one's assets against offensive actions and dissuading a hostile party from taking such actions.

Defense involves measures that decrease the likelihood that an offensive action will succeed. Such measures include those that prevent a perpetrator from gaining access, that eliminate vulnerabilities, or that enable the victim of an operation to recover quickly from a successful offensive action.

Dissuasion involves persuading an adversary not to launch the offensive action in the first place. Deterrence is an approach to dissuasion that involves the certain imposition of high costs on an adversary that is unwise enough to initiate offensive action.

Such costs may be imposed on an identified adversary in the cyber domain in response to some hostile action in cyberspace. But there is no logical necessity for restricting a response to this domain, and decision makers have a wide choice of response options that include changes in defensive postures, law enforcement actions, economic actions, diplomacy, and military operations involving traditional forces, as well as cyber operations.

Traditionally, the U.S. national security posture has been based on a robust mix of defense and deterrence. But cyberspace turns this mix on its head. The inherent superiority of offensive cyber operations over defensive operations has led many to consider a strategy of deterrence to dissuade adversaries from conducting such operations against us. But senior policy makers have concluded that because deterrence in cyberspace is such a difficult strategy to implement, we must do a more effective job of defense.[4] If the reader finds this intellectual state of affairs unsatisfactory, s/he is not alone.

Laws of War as They Apply to Cyber Conflict

Armed conflict between nations is today governed by two bodies of international law: jus ad bellum, the body of law that governs when a nation may engage in armed conflict, and jus in bello, the body of law that regulates how a nation engaged in armed conflict must behave. (Such law refers to treaties (written agreements among nations) and customary international law (general and consistent practices of nations followed from a sense of legal obligation).)

Today, the primary instrument of jus ad bellum is the United Nations Charter, which explicitly forbids all signatories from using force except in two instances—when authorized by the Security Council and when a signatory is exercising its inherent right of self-defense when it has been the target of an armed attack. Complications and uncertainty regarding how the UN Charter should be interpreted when cyberattacks occur result from three fundamental facts.

First, the UN Charter was written in 1945, long before the notion of cyberattacks was even imagined. The underlying experiential base for the formulation of the Charter involved TKC among nations, and thus the framers of the Charter could not have imagined how it might apply to cyber conflict.

Second, the UN Charter itself contains no definitions for certain key terms, such as "use of force," "threat of force," or "armed attack." Thus, what these terms mean cannot be understood by reference to the Charter. Definitions and meanings can only be inferred from historical precedent and practice—how individual nations, the UN itself, and international tribunals have defined these terms in particular instances. Given a lack of clarity for what these terms might mean in the context of TKC, it is not surprising that there is even less clarity for what they might mean in the context of cyber conflict.

Third, the Charter is in some ways internally inconsistent. It bans certain acts (uses of force) that could damage persons or property, but allows other acts (economic sanctions) that could damage persons or property. The use of operations not contemplated by the framers of the UN Charter—that is, cyber operations—may well magnify such inconsistencies.

An example will help to illustrate some of the complications that may arise. An offensive operation involving a number of cyberattacks conducted over time against a variety of different financial targets in an adversary nation could cause extensive economic loss, panic in the streets, and shake public confidence in the incumbent regime—but without directly causing physical damage or any loss of life. Assuming the perpetrator of this operation can be identified, on what basis, if any, would such an operation be construed under the UN Charter as a use of force or an armed attack?

Answers to such questions under various circumstances involving cyberattack matter both to the attacked party and the attacking party.

1. Answers matter to **attacked** party, because they influence when and under what authority law enforcement (vis-á-vis military) takes the lead in responding, and what rights the victim might have in responding.

2. Answers matter to **attacking** party, because they set a threshold that policy makers may not wish to cross in taking assertive/aggressive actions to further its interests.

Jus in bello is based in large part on the Geneva Conventions. Some of the important principles underlying *jus in bello* are the principle of non-perfidy (military forces cannot pretend to be legally protected entities, such as hospitals); the principle of proportionality (the military advantage gained by a military operation must not be disproportionate to the collateral damage on civilian targets); and the principle of distinction (military operations may be conducted only against "military objectives" and not against civilian targets).

As with the UN Charter, the Geneva Conventions are silent on cyberattack as a modality of conflict, and how to apply the principles mentioned above in any instance involving cyber conflict may be uncertain in some cases. Some interesting hypothetical cases include the following:

1. Under the principle of distinction, nations have some affirmative obligations to enable an adversary to distinguish between civilian and military entities. (For example, the use of human shields around military targets is regarded as a violation of the laws of armed conflict.) Today, a large fraction of U.S. military communications are routed over communications facilities that are primarily used for civilian purposes. Similarly, military bases in the United States depend on the commercial power grid. Do these facts suggest that U.S. communications facilities and its power grid would be valid military targets for a nation engaged in armed hostilities with the United States?

2. Under the principle of proportionality, some degree of collateral damage is allowable, but not if the foreseeable collateral damage is disproportionate compared to the military advantage likely to be gained from the attack. If, for example, a power plant is the target of a cyberattack, a judgment must

be made that the harm to the civilian population from disrupting electrical service was not disproportionate to the military advantage that might ensue from attacking the plant. Before such a judgment could be made, the commander would have to have adequate intelligence about the plant (and what was dependent on the plant) on which to base the judgment.

3. Under the principle of non-perfidy, an attack cannot be launched from a legally protected facility (no mortars from hospital roofs). What if Nation A uses the information systems in a hospital located in Nation C as a launching point for its cyberattacks against Nation B? Does Nation B have the right to neutralize the systems in Nation C?

Such examples suggest that there may be considerable uncertainty about how a serious LOAC analysis of any given operational scenario might proceed if cyberattacks are involved.

Potential Human Rights Implications

Human rights restrain governmental action with respect to those under the jurisdiction of the government in question. Such rights can originate nationally (e.g., the rights granted to Americans under the U.S. Constitution), in international treaties (e.g., the Convention on the Elimination of All Forms of Discrimination Against Women), or in customary international law.

The International Covenant on Civil and Political Rights (ICCPR) was ratified by the United States in September 1992 and by a number of other states. Although a variety of human rights organizations strongly disagree, the United States has argued that the Convention does not apply extraterritorially, so it would not regulate the behavior of any signatory acting in any other country, whether or not it had signed the treaty.

If the contrary position is adopted, two of the rights enumerated in the ICCPR may be relevant to the cyber domain. Article 17 (protecting privacy and reputation) might be relevant to cyber operations intended to harm the reputation of an individual, e.g., by falsifying computer-based records about transactions in which he or she had engaged, or to uncover private information about an individual. Article 19 (protecting rights to seek information) might be relevant to cyberattacks intended to prevent individuals from obtaining service from the Internet or other media. A number of other rights, such as the right to life, may be implicated as well. Respecting these other rights could suggest, for example, that a cyberattack intended to enforce economic sanctions would still have to allow transactions related to the acquisition of food and medicine.

A number of nations have declared that access to the Internet is a fundamental right of their societies. (As of August 2011, these nations include Estonia, France, Spain, Finland, and Greece.) Thus, if access to the Internet is a human right, then actions curtailing or preventing Internet access violate that right.

In addition, an important and contested point in human rights law is the extent of its applicability during acknowledged armed conflict or hostilities. The position of the U.S. government is the imperatives of minimizing unnecessary human suffering are met by the requirements of the laws of armed conflict (specifically *jus in bello*), and thus that human rights law should not place additional constraints on the actions of its armed forces. By contrast, many human rights observers argue that human rights law can and should apply as well as LOAC during hostilities.

Role of Private Sector as Target and as Conductor of Offensive Cyber Operations

The private sector is deeply involved in matters related to cyber conflict in many ways—and much more so than it is involved in traditional kinetic conflict. The most obvious connection is that private sector entities are quite often the targets of hostile cyber operations. The perpetrators of most such operations against private sector entities are generally believed to be criminals (e.g., those seeking credit card numbers), but nation states may conduct cyber operations against them for a variety of purposes as well (as discussed in Section 2.3).

In addition and especially in the United States, military and civilian actors share infrastructure to a very large degree. A very large fraction of U.S. military communications pass over networks owned by the private sector and operated largely for the benefit of civilian users. The same is true for electric power—U.S. military bases depend on the civilian power grid for day to day operations. Under many interpretations of the laws of armed conflict, military dependence on civilian infrastructure makes that civilian infrastructure a legitimate target for adversary military operations.

Another important connection is that the artifacts of cyberspace are largely developed, built, operated, and owned by private sector entities—companies that provide IT-related goods and services. In some cases, the cooperation of these entities may be needed to provide adequate defensive measures. For example, some analysts argue that an adequate defensive posture in cyberspace will require the private sector to authenticate users in such a way that anonymous behavior is no longer possible). In other cases, private sector cooperation may be needed to enable offensive cyber operations against adversaries. For example, the cooperation of a friendly Internet service provider may be needed to launch a cyberattack over the Internet.

Many questions arise regarding the private sector connection to cyber conflict. For example:

1. What actions beyond changes in defense posture and calling law enforcement should private sector be allowed to take in response to hostile cyber operations? Specifically, how aggressive should private sector entities be permitted to be in their responses?

2. How, and to what extent and under what circumstances, if any, should the U.S. government conduct offensive operations to respond to cyberattacks on private sector entities (or authorize an aggressive private sector response)?

3. How might private sector actions interfere with U.S. government cyber operations?

4. What is the U.S. government responsibility for private sector actions that rise to "use of force" (in the UN Charter sense of the term)?

Preventing Escalation and Terminating Conflict in Cyberspace

Small conflicts can sometimes grow into larger ones. Of particular concern to decision makers is the possibility that the level of violence could increase to a level not initially contemplated or desired by any party to the conflict.

In considering TKC, analysts have often thought about escalation dynamics and terminating conflict. In a cyber context, escalation dynamics refers to the possibility that initial conflict in cyberspace may grow. Much of the thinking regarding cyber conflict is focused on the first (initial) stages of conflict—what do we do if X conducts a serious cyberattack on the United States?—with the implicit assumption that such an attack is the first such cyberattack.

But what if it is not? How would escalation unfold? How could it be prevented (or deterred)? There are theories of escalation dynamics, especially in the nuclear domain, but because of the profound differences between the nuclear and cyber domains, there is every reason to expect a theory of escalation dynamics in cyberspace would be very different from a theory of escalation dynamics in the nuclear domain. Some of the significant differences include the fact that attribution is much more uncertain, the ability of nonstate actors to interfere in the management of a conflict, and the existence of a multitude of states that have nontrivial capabilities to conduct cyber operations.

Conflict termination in cyberspace poses many difficulties as well. Conflict termination is the task faced by decision makers on both sides when they have agreed to cease hostilities. A key issue in implementing such agreements is knowing that the other side is abiding by the negotiated terms. How would one side know that the other side is honoring a cease-fire in cyberspace, given that one or both sides are likely to be targets of hostile cyber operations from other parties that do not cease just because there is cyber conflict between the two principal actors? (That is, there is a constant background of hostile cyberoperations going on all the time.) And might one side have to inform the other of all of the battlefield preparations it had undertaken prior to the conflict? Such an act, analogous to demining operations, would require each side to keep careful track of its various preparations.

Escalation can occur through a number of mechanisms (which may or may not simultaneously be operative in any instance).[5] One party to a conflict may deliberately escalate a conflict, with a specific purpose in mind. It might inadvertently escalate a conflict by taking an action that it does not believe is escalatory but that its opponent perceives as escalatory. It might accidentally escalate a conflict if its forces take some unintended action (e.g., they strike the wrong target). Lastly, catalytic escalation occurs when some third party succeeds in provoking two parties to engage in conflict ("let's you and him fight"). Catalytic provocation is facilitated by the possibility of anonymous or unattributable action.

Conclusion

Conflict can and does occur in cyberspace. How and to what extent does recent history about conflict in cyberspace presage the future?

Two things are clear today. First, only a small fraction of the possibilities for cyber conflict have been experienced to date, and actual experience with cyber conflict has been limited. Indeed, nearly all of the adversarial actions known to have been taken in cyberspace against the United States or any other nation, including both cyberattack and cyberexploitation, have fallen short of any plausible threshold for defining "armed conflict," "use of force," or "armed attack." This fact has two consequences: many possibilities for serious cyber conflict have not yet been seen,[6] and how to respond to hostile actions in cyberspace that do not rise to these thresholds is the most pressing concern of policy makers today.

Second, many of our assumptions and understandings about conflict— developed in the context of traditional kinetic conflict—either are not valid in cyberspace or are applicable only with difficulty. Thus, decision makers are proceeding into largely unknown territory—a fact that decreases the predictability of the outcome of any actions they might take.

These conclusions suggest that the need to develop new knowledge and insight into technical and legal instruments to support informed policy making in this area will provide full employment for many analysts for a long time to come.

Questions for Review

What if anything makes conflict in cyberspace distinctive? Can we draw lines between offense and defense and between espionage and attack in this realm?

Notes

1 The intellectual content of this report is drawn primarily from National Research Council, *Technology, Policy, Law, and Ethics Regarding U.S. Acquisition and Use of Cyberattack Capabilities* (William Owens, Kenneth Dam, Herbert Lin, editors), National Academies Press, 2009, available at http://www.nap.edu/catalog.php?record_id=12651.

2 This definition implies that "armed conflict" or "military conflict" are subsets— and only subsets—of the broader term "conflict," which may entail a conflict over economic, cultural, diplomatic, and other interests as well as conflict involving military matters or the use of arms.

3 A primer on Stuxnet can be found at http://topics.nytimes.com/top/reference/timestopics/subjects/c/computer_malware/stuxnet/index.htm | ?scp=1-spot&sq=stuxnet&st=cse.

4 William Lynn, "Defending a New Domain: the Pentagon's Cyberstrategy," *Foreign Affairs*, September/October 2010.

5 RAND, *Dangerous Thresholds: Managing Escalation in the 21st Century*, 2008, available at www.rand.org/pubs/monographs/2008/RAND_MG614.pdf.

6 Gregory Rattray and Jason Healey, "Categorizing and Understanding Offensive Cyber Capabilities and Their Use," in National Research Council, *Proceedings of a Workshop on Deterring Cyber Attacks: Informing Strategies and Developing Options for U.S. Policy*, National Academies Press, 2010, pp. 77–98, available at http://www.nap.edu/catalog/12997.html.

International Law: The Trials of Global Norms

Steven R. Ratner

The move from describing the world to prescribing for it forms the core of international law. Can those committing human rights atrocities—war criminals from Bosnia or political leaders from Cambodia—be tried in foreign courts or before international tribunals? How can members of the United Nations ensure respect for the decisions of its Security Council? What is the best way to regulate transnational environmental hazards such as greenhouse gas emissions or ocean dumping? Can the United States allow its citizens to sue European companies for their use of land and factories confiscated by the Cuban government from Americans more than a generation ago?

All these questions turn on political decisions by states—but what international lawyers see and seek in such scenarios is a process whose actions are informed and influenced by principles of law, not just raw power. For international lawyers, devising and enforcing universal rules of conduct for states means overcoming two cardinal challenges: how to make such precepts legitimate in a diverse community of nations; and how to make them stick in the absence of any one sovereign authority or supranational enforcement mechanism. . . .

Today, the end of the Cold War has loosened many of the blockages to international lawmaking and implementation. Although legal scholars still ask what states can do on their own—pass extraterritorial laws, use force, or prosecute war criminals—they do so assuming that coordinated action is now more feasible than in the past. Global and regional treaties such as the Chemical Weapons Convention, the Convention on the Prohibition of Anti-Personnel Mines, the Maastrict Treaty, and the North American Free Trade Agreement now serve as the starting point for scrutinizing state behavior according to some objective standard.

The ground seems ready then for an acceleration of this century's great trend in international law: the increasing international regulation of more and more issues once typically seen as part of state domestic jurisdiction. But any attempt to create the lofty, supranational legal edifice idealized by some of the field's practitioners and scholars promises to be problematic at best. Once paralyzed by the deadlock between East and West, and between North and South, the international legal system must now contend not just with the challenge of persuading new states such as Belarus or Croatia to comply with established norms but of coping with Somalia and other failed states, whose circumstances make a mockery of international rules. International law must seek to embrace a growing range of forms, topics, and technologies, as well as a host of new actors. And as it moves further away from strictly "foreign" concerns—the treatment of diplomats or ships on the seas—to traditionally domestic areas—environmental or labor standards—its proponents must increasingly confront new obstacles head-on.

New Realities, New Ideas

This new global context surrounding the field has led to at least four fundamental shifts in the kinds of issues that legal scholars now talk about and study.

New Forms, New Players

Traditionally, most rules of international law could be found in one of two places: treaties—binding, written agreements between states; or customary law—uncodified, but equally binding rules based on longstanding behavior that states accept as compulsory. The strategic arms reduction treaties requiring the United States and Russia to cut their nuclear weapons arsenals offer examples of the former; the rule that governments cannot be sued in the courts of another state for most of their public acts provides an example of the latter. Historically, treaties have gradually displaced much customary law, as international rules have become increasingly codified.

But as new domains from the environment to the Internet come to be seen as appropriate for international regulation, states are sometimes reluctant to embrace any sort of binding rule. In the past, many legal scholars and international courts simply accepted the notion that no law governed a particular subject until a new treaty was concluded or states signaled their consent to a new customary-law rule (witness the reluctance with which human rights norms were considered law prior to the UN's two key treaties in 1966) or, alternatively, struggled to find customary law where none existed. However, today all but the most doctrinaire of scholars see a role for so-called soft law—precepts emanating from international bodies that conform in some sense to expectations of required behavior but that are not binding on states.

For example, in 1992 the World Bank completed a set of Guidelines on the Treatment of Foreign Direct Investment. Though these are not binding on any bank member, states and corporations invoke them as the standard for how developing nations should treat foreign capital to encourage investment. This soft law enables states to adjust to the regulation of many new areas of international concern without fearing a violation (and possible legal countermeasures) if they fail to comply. Normative expectations are built more quickly than they would through the evolution of a customary-law rule, and more gently than if a new treaty rule were foisted on states. Soft law principles also represent a starting point for new hard law, which attaches a penalty to noncompliance. In this case, the bank's guidelines have served as the basis for the negotiation of a new treaty—the Multilateral Agreement on Investment (MAI)—by the Organization for Economic Cooperation and Development (OECD). The MAI gives foreign investors the right to take any government to international arbitration for compensation when a law or state practice limits their freedom to invest or divest.

Whether in the case of hard or soft law, new participants are making increased demands for representation in international bodies, conferences, and other legal groupings and processes. They include substate entities, both those recognized in some way by the international community (Chechnya, Hong Kong) and those not (Tibet, Kashmir); nongovernmental organizations (NGOs); and corporations. Claiming that the states to which they belong do not always adequately represent their interests, these nonstate actors demand a say in the content of new norms. Some have faced staunch opposition to their participation in decision making: In 1995, China's government relegated NGOs to a distant venue during the UN's Fourth World Conference on Women in Beijing.

But other groups may succeed even as far as effectively taking over an official delegation. For example, U.S. telecommunications companies such as Motorola have seemed almost to dictate U.S. positions in the International Telecommunication Union (ITU), the UN agency responsible for setting global telecommunications standards. At the ITU's 1992 conference on allocating the radio spectrum for new technologies, Motorola's stake in protecting its plans for new satellites became a paramount U.S. interest, resulting in a sizeable Motorola team attending as part of the U.S. delegation. Other corporations have acted outside government channels entirely by promulgating private codes: in response to public pressure, Nike issued a set of self-imposed rules to protect worker rights in the developing world. It is not that states are no longer the primary makers of international law. But . . . these other actors have independent views—and the resources to push them—that do not fit neatly into traditional theories of how law is made and enforced.

New Enforcement Strategies

Most states comply with much, even most, international law almost continually—whether the law of the sea, diplomatic immunity, or civil aviation rules. But without mechanisms to bring transgressors into line, international law will be "law" in name only. This state of affairs, when it occurs, is ignored by too many lawyers, who delight in large bodies of rules but often discount patterns of noncompliance. For example, Western governments, and many scholars, insisted throughout the 1960s and 1970s that when nationalizing foreign property, developing states were legally bound to compensate former owners for the full economic value, despite those states' repeated refusals to pay such huge sums.

The traditional toolbox to secure compliance with the law of nations consists of negotiations, mediation, countermeasures (reciprocal action against the violator), or, in rare cases, recourse to supranational judicial bodies such as the International Court of Justice. (The last of these was the linchpin of the world of law that Americans such as Andrew Carnegie and Elihu Root sought to bring into being.) For many years, these tools have been supplemented by the work of international institutions, whose reports and resolutions often help "mobilize shame" against violators. But today, states, NGOs, and private entities, aided by their lawyers, have striven for sanctions with more teeth. They have galvanized the UN Security Council to issue economic sanctions against Iraq, Haiti, Libya, Serbia, Sudan, and other nations refusing to comply with UN resolutions.

On the free-trade front, the dispute settlement panels in the World Trade Organization (WTO) now have the legal authority to issue binding rulings that allow the victor in a trade dispute to impose specific tariffs on the loser. . . . And the UN's ad hoc criminal tribunals for the former Yugoslavia and Rwanda show that it is at least possible to devise institutions to punish individuals for human rights atrocities. Nonetheless, as the impunity to date of former Bosnian Serb president Radovan Karadzic and General Ratko Mladic reveals, the success of these enforcement mechanisms depends on the willingness of states to support them: legalism meets realism. . . .

Increasingly, domestic courts provide an additional venue to enforce international law. In Spain, for example, Judge Manuel García Castellóni of the National Court has agreed to hear a controversial human rights case involving charges against Chile's former dictator, General Augusto Pinochet. Meanwhile, Castellóni's colleague, Judge Baltasar Garzón, hears testimony against those responsible for the "Dirty War" of the 1970s in Argentina. (Spain is asserting jurisdiction in both cases because its nationals were among the thousands of victims tortured and killed.) And though Karadzic remains at large, he has been sued in U.S. federal court under the Alien Tort Claims Act, which allows foreign nationals recovery against Karadzic for the rape and torture of civilians during his "ethnic cleansing" campaign in the former Yugoslavia. At a minimum, this provides a symbolic measure of solace for his victims.

The Legitimacy Problem

Even as scholars seek to devise better enforcement mechanisms, a serious debate is brewing about the legitimacy of such measures. As international organizations are freed up to take more actions by the end of the East-West conflict and the tempering of North-South tensions, the United States and its like-minded allies seem well positioned to impose their agenda on all. Legal scholars question whether Western dominance of the Organization for Security and Cooperation in Europe, UN, WTO, and other international institutions is not merely raw power asserting its muscle again, albeit through multilateral bodies, to the detriment of a genuine rule of law. That this debate is more than academic can be seen vividly in the ongoing discussion about reforming the Security Council. Many Americans may laud the council's new muscle—during the last five years, it has slapped a debilitating embargo and weapons inspection regime on Iraq, prohibited air traffic with Libya due to its sanctuary for those accused of the Pan Am 103 bombing, and approved a U.S.-led occupation of Haiti. But smaller states feel threatened by a Security Council in which the West is often able to convince enough states to approve such council actions, and only a Chinese veto (which was used only once in the last 25 years) seems to protect them. . . .

Focusing on enforcement and legitimacy also provides a useful lens through which to evaluate U.S. reactions to international norms: Even as the United States seeks to strengthen the enforcement of international law for its own ends, it has often recoiled at the prospect that these norms might be enforced against it. In the WTO, the very dispute resolution panels that the United States hopes to use to force open closed markets could order it to choose between environmental protection laws (such as those banning imports of tuna caught in nets that kill dolphins) and the prospects of retaliatory sanctions if those laws have incidental discriminatory effects on trade. In such a scenario, international law, as interpreted by the WTO, becomes the friend of business and bugaboo of environmentalists. But when the UN seeks to promulgate environmental law, as it has with the proposed greenhouse gas convention just concluded at Kyoto, then the tables are turned.

Similarly, the United States wants to use the Security Council to keep in place a comprehensive sanctions regime on Iraq that has the diplomatic appeal of being "international" rather than "U.S.-imposed," all the while holding back on paying its dues because not all UN programs conform to Washington's wishes. As the world's sole superpower, the United States can defy international standards with little fear of immediate sanction; but other states will begin to question its motives in trying to strengthen important legal regimes such as those covering nuclear and chemical nonproliferation.

New Linkages

The notion of hermetically sealed areas of international law—each a nice chapter in a treatise—is increasingly anachronistic. Environmental and trade law can no longer be discussed separately as the tuna–dolphin example shows; and when private investors have to reckon with serious abuses by local governments, foreign investment law cannot be examined without some consideration of human rights and labor law. The result is a new breed of scholarship linking previously distinct subjects and the realization among some practitioners that overspecialization leads to myopic lawyering.

Moreover, beyond the legal field, international lawyers must address the two-way interaction between international law and broader sociological and cultural trends in society. In one notable example, the debate on a clash of cultures involving so-called Asian values has forced students of human rights to stand back and consider whether rights granted in human rights treaties mean the same thing in all states. Can Singapore suppress free speech for the goal of national unity and development, especially if it claims that its culture sees uninhibited political speech as less than a birthright? Of course, cultural assertions tend to be overly broad, and many human rights activists interpret these claims as excuses for authoritarianism; the arguments, however, can no longer be ignored, and black and white rules of treaty interpretation will not help much.

In the other direction, the proliferation of new norms has direct effects on debates over globalization—the "Jihad versus McWorld" controversy. A global treaty on ozone or greenhouse gases, for instance, will clearly accommodate different perspectives on the priority of environmental protection versus development, but once adopted it cannot tolerate violations in the name of "diversity." Indeed, almost by definition, the decision by states to subject a once strictly domestic conceit to international regulation means that cultural, value-based, or "sovereignty" arguments no longer enjoy the upper hand. If a state elects not to sign a major treaty, or ignores one it has signed—as with the United States and the agreement on the elimination of landmines or Iraq and the one on nuclear nonproliferation—it is more likely to be condemned as a pariah than admired for its rugged individualism.

Questions for Review

Is it the case that international law is becoming more and more intrusive in the domestic affairs of states? If so, how and why is this happening? Is Ratner's view of the role of international law in international politics significantly different from Hoffman's selection in Part I?

Chapter 14
The Global Commons and Global Governance

The Tragedy of the Commons

GARRETT HARDIN

We can make little progress in working toward optimum population size until we explicitly exorcize the spirit of Adam Smith in the field of practical demography. In economic affairs, *The Wealth of Nations* (1776) popularized the "invisible hand," the idea that an individual who "intends only his own gain," is, as it were, "led by an invisible hand to promote . . . the public interest." Adam Smith did not assert that this was invariably true, and perhaps neither did any of his followers. But he contributed to a dominant tendency of thought that has ever since interfered with positive action based on rational analysis, namely, the tendency to assume that decisions reached individually will, in fact, be the best decisions for an entire society. If this assumption is correct it justifies the continuance of our present policy of laissez-faire in reproduction. If it is correct we can assume that men will control their individual fecundity so as to produce the optimum population. If the assumption is not correct, we need to reexamine our individual freedoms to see which ones are defensible.

Tragedy of Freedom in a Commons

The rebuttal to the invisible hand in population control is to be found in a scenario first sketched in a little-known pamphlet in 1833 by a mathematical amateur named William Foster Lloyd (1794–1852). We may well call it "the tragedy of the commons," using the word "tragedy" as the philosopher Whitehead used it: "The essence of dramatic tragedy is not unhappiness. It resides in the solemnity of the remorseless working of things." He then goes on to say, "This inevitableness of destiny can only be illustrated in terms of human life by incidents which in fact involve unhappiness. For it is only by them that the futility of escape can be made evident in the drama."

The tragedy of the commons develops in this way. Picture a pasture open to all. It is to be expected that each herdsman will try to keep as many cattle as possible on the commons. Such an arrangement may work reasonably satisfactorily for centuries because tribal wars, poaching, and disease keep the numbers of both man and beast well below the carrying capacity of the land. Finally, however, comes the day of reckoning, that is, the day when the long-desired goal of social stability becomes a reality. At this point, the inherent logic of the commons remorselessly generates tragedy.

As a rational being, each herdsman seeks to maximize his gain. Explicitly or implicitly, more or less consciously, he asks, "What is the utility *to me* of adding one more animal to my herd?" This utility has one negative and one positive component.

The positive component is a function of the increment of one animal. Since the herdsman receives all the proceeds from the sale of the additional animal, the positive utility is nearly +1.

The negative component is a function of the additional overgrazing created by one more animal. Since, however, the effects of overgrazing are shared by all the herdsmen, the negative utility for any particular decision-making herdsman is only a fraction of –1.

Adding together the component partial utilities, the rational herdsman concludes that the only sensible course for him to pursue is to add another animal to his herd. And another; and another. . . . But this is the conclusion reached by each and every rational herdsman sharing a commons. Therein is the tragedy. Each man is locked into a system that compels him to increase his herd without limit—in a world that is limited. Ruin is the destination toward which all men rush, each pursuing his own best interest in a society that believes in the freedom of the commons. Freedom in a commons brings ruin to all. . . .

In an approximate way, the logic of the commons has been understood for a long time, perhaps since the discovery of agriculture or the invention of private property in real estate. But it is understood mostly only in special cases which are not sufficiently generalized. Even at this late date, cattlemen leasing national land on the western ranges demonstrate no more than an ambivalent understanding, in constantly pressuring federal authorities to increase the head count to the point where overgrazing produces erosion and weed-dominance. Likewise, the oceans of the world continue to suffer from the survival of the philosophy of the commons. Maritime nations will respond automatically to the shibboleth of the "freedom of the seas." Professing to believe in the "inexhaustible resources of the oceans," they bring species after species of fish and whales closer to extinction. . . .

Pollution

In a reverse way, the tragedy of the commons reappears in problems of pollution. Here it is not a question of taking something out of the commons, but of putting something in—sewage, or chemical, radioactive, and heat wastes into water; noxious and dangerous fumes into the air; and distracting and unpleasant advertising signs into the line of sight. The calculations of utility are much the same as before. The rational man finds that his share of the cost of the wastes he discharges into the commons is less than the cost of purifying his wastes before releasing them. Since this is true for everyone, we are locked into a system of "fouling our own nest," so long as we behave only as independent, rational, free-enterprisers.

The tragedy of the commons as a food basket is averted by private property, or something formally like it. But the air and waters surrounding us cannot readily be fenced, and so the tragedy of the commons as a cesspool must be prevented by different means, by coercive laws or taxing devices that make it cheaper for the polluter to treat his pollutant than to discharge them untreated. We have not progressed as far with the solution of this problem as we have with the first. Indeed, our particular concept of private property, which deters us from exhausting the positive resources of the earth, favors pollution. The owner of a factory on the bank of a stream—whose property extends to the middle of the stream—often has difficulty seeing why it is not his natural right to muddy the waters flowing past his door. The law, always behind the times, requires elaborate stitching and fitting to adapt to it this newly perceived aspect of the commons.

The pollution problem is a consequence of populations. It did not much matter how a lonely American frontiersman disposed of his waste. "Flowing water purifies itself every 10 miles," my grandfather used to say, and the myth was near enough to the truth when he was a boy, for there were not too many people. But as population became denser, the natural chemical and biological recycling processes became overloaded, calling for a redefinition of property rights.

How to Legislate Temperance?

Analysis of the pollution problem as a function of population density uncovers a not generally recognized principle of morality, namely: *The morality of an act is a function of the state of the system at the time it is performed.* Using the commons as a cesspool does not harm the general public under frontier conditions, because there is no public; the same behavior in a metropolis is unbearable. A hundred and fifty years ago a plainsman could kill an American bison, cut out only the tongue for his dinner, and discard the rest of the animal. He was not in any important sense being wasteful. Today, with only a few thousand bison left, we would be appalled by such behavior. . . .

That morality is system-sensitive escaped the attention of most codifiers of ethics in the past. "Thou shalt not . . . " is the form of traditional ethical directives which make no allowance for particular circumstances. The laws of our society follow the pattern of ancient ethics, and therefore are poorly suited to governing a complex, crowded, changeable world. Our epicyclic solution is to augment statutory law with administrative law. Since it is practically impossible to spell out all the conditions under which it is safe to burn trash in the backyard or to run an automobile without smog-control, by law we delegate the details to bureaus. The result is administrative law, which is rightly feared for an ancient reason—*Quis custodiet ipsos custodes?*—"Who shall watch the watchers themselves?" John Adams said that we must have "a government of laws and not men." Bureau administrators, trying to evaluate the morality of acts in the total system, are singularly liable to corruption, producing a government by men, not laws.

Prohibition is easy to legislate (though not necessarily to enforce); but how do we legislate temperance? Experience indicates that it can be accomplished best through the mediation of administrative law. We limit possibilities unnecessarily if we suppose that the sentiment of *Quis custodiet* denies us the use of administrative law. We should rather retain the phrase as a perpetual reminder of fearful dangers we cannot avoid. The great challenge facing us now is to invent the corrective feedbacks that are needed to keep custodians honest. We must find ways to legitimate the needed authority of both the custodians and the corrective feedbacks.

Freedom to Breed Is Intolerable

The tragedy of the commons is involved in population problems in another way. In a world governed solely by the principle of "dog eat dog"—if indeed there ever was such a world—how many children a family had would not be a matter of public concern. Parents who bred too exuberantly would leave fewer descendants, not more, because they would be unable to care adequately for their children. . . .

If each human family were dependent only on its own resources; *if* the children of improvident parents starved to death; *if*, thus, overbreeding brought its own "punishment" to the germ line—*then* there would be no public interest in controlling the breeding of families. But our society is deeply committed to the welfare state and hence is confronted with another aspect of the tragedy of the commons.

In a welfare state, how shall we deal with the family, the religion, the race, or the class (or indeed any distinguishable and cohesive group) that adopts overbreeding as a policy to secure its own aggrandizement? To couple the concept of freedom to breed with the belief that everyone born has an equal right to the commons is to lock the world into a tragic course of action. . . .

Conscience Is Self-Eliminating

It is a mistake to think that we can control the breeding of mankind in the long run by an appeal to conscience. Charles Galton Darwin made this point when he spoke on the centennial of the publication of his grandfather's great book. The argument is straightforward and Darwinian.

People vary. Confronted with appeals to limit breeding, some people will undoubtedly respond to the plea more than others. Those who have more children

will produce a larger fraction of the next generation than those with more susceptible consciences. The difference will be accentuated, generation by generation.

In C. G. Darwin's words: "It may well be that it would take hundreds of
generations for the progenitive instinct to develop in this way, but if it should
do so, nature would have taken her revenge, and the variety *Homo contracipiens*
would become extinct and would be replaced by the variety *Homo progenitivus*."

The argument assumes that conscience or the desire for children (no matter
which) is hereditary—but hereditary only in the most general formal sense. The
result will be the same whether the attitude is transmitted through germ cells,
or exosomatically. . . . The argument has here been stated in the context of the
population problem, but it applies equally well to any instance in which society
appeals to an individual exploiting a commons to restrain himself for the general
good—by means of his conscience. To make such an appeal is to set up a selective
system that works toward the elimination of conscience from the race. . . .

Mutual Coercion Mutually Agreed Upon

The social arrangements that produce responsibility are arrangements that created coercion, of some sort. Consider bank-robbing. The man who takes money
from a bank acts as if the bank were a commons. How do we prevent such action?
Certainly not by trying to control his behavior solely by a verbal appeal to his
sense of responsibility. Rather than rely on propaganda we follow Frankel's lead
and insist that a bank is not a commons; we seek the definite social arrangements
that will keep it from becoming a commons. That we thereby infringe on the
freedom of would-be robbers we neither deny nor regret.

The morality of bank-robbing is particularly easy to understand because we
accept complete prohibition of this activity. We are willing to say "Thou shalt not
rob banks," without providing for exceptions. But temperance also can be created by coercion. Taxing is a good coercive device. To keep downtown shoppers
temperate in their use of parking space we introduce parking meters for short
periods, and traffic fines for longer ones. We need not actually forbid a citizen to
park as long as he wants to; we need merely make it increasingly expensive for
him to do so. Not prohibition, but carefully biased options are what we offer him.
A Madison Avenue man might call this persuasion; I prefer the greater candor of
the word coercion. . . .

To many, the word coercion implies arbitrary decisions of distant and irresponsible bureaucrats; but this is not a necessary part of its meaning. The only
kind of coercion I recommend is mutual coercion, mutually agreed upon by the
majority of the people affected.

To say that we mutually agree to coercion is not to say that we are required to
enjoy it, or even to pretend we enjoy it. Who enjoys taxes? We all grumble about
them. But we accept compulsory taxes because we recognize that voluntary taxes
would favor the conscienceless. We institute and (grumblingly) support taxes and
other coercive devices to escape the horror of the commons. . . .

Recognition of Necessity

Perhaps the simplest summary of this analysis of man's population problems is this: The commons, if justifiable at all, is justifiable only under conditions of low population density. As the human population has increased, the commons has had to be abandoned in one aspect after another.

First we abandoned the commons in food gathering, enclosing farm land and restricting pastures and hunting and fishing areas. These restrictions are still not complete throughout the world.

Somewhat later we saw that the commons as a place for waste disposal would also have to be abandoned. Restrictions on the disposal of domestic sewage are widely accepted in the Western world; we are still struggling to close the commons to pollution by automobiles, factories, insecticide sprayers, fertilizing operations, and atomic energy installations. . . .

Every new enclosure of the commons involves the infringement of somebody's personal liberty. Infringements made in the distant past are accepted because no contemporary complains of a loss. It is the newly proposed infringements that we vigorously oppose; cries of "rights" and "freedom" fill the air. But what does "freedom" mean? When men mutually agreed to pass laws against robbing, mankind became more free, not less so. Individuals locked into the logic of the commons are free only to bring on universal ruin; once they see the necessity of mutual coercion, they become free to pursue other goals. I believe it was Hegel who said, "Freedom is the recognition of necessity."

The most important aspect of necessity that we must now recognize is the necessity of abandoning the commons in breeding. No technical solution can rescue us from the misery of overpopulation. Freedom to breed will bring ruin to all. At the moment, to avoid hard decisions many of us are tempted to propagandize for conscience and responsible parenthood. The temptation must be resisted, because an appeal to independently acting consciences selects for the disappearance of all conscience in the long run, and an increase in anxiety in the short.

The only way we can preserve and nurture other and more precious freedoms is by relinquishing the freedom to breed, and that very soon. "Freedom is the recognition of necessity"—and it is the role of education to reveal to all the necessity of abandoning the freedom to breed. Only so can we put an end to this aspect of the tragedy of the commons.

The variable geometry of the L20 (or a reformed G8) can play a large role in overcoming the pessimism of Underdal's law. At the same time, a concerted effort to focus on more effective ways to slow climate change can offer a model that is useful for many other troubling issues in international cooperation.

Questions for Review

What characteristics, if any, make tragedies of the commons particularly hard to deal with? What distinguishes cases in which the world community has dealt with them successfully from those in which it has not?

The Papal Encyclical on the Environment
POPE FRANCIS

I. Technology: Creativity and Power

Humanity has entered a new era in which our technical prowess has brought us to a crossroads. We are the beneficiaries of two centuries of enormous waves of change: steam engines, railways, the telegraph, electricity, automobiles, aeroplanes, chemical industries, modern medicine, information technology and, more recently, the digital revolution, robotics, biotechnologies and nanotechnologies. It is right to rejoice in these advances and to be excited by the immense possibilities which they continue to open up before us, for "science and technology are wonderful products of a God-given human creativity".[1] The modification of nature for useful purposes has distinguished the human family from the beginning; technology itself "expresses the inner tension that impels man gradually to overcome material limitations".[2] Technology has remedied countless evils which used to harm and limit human beings. How can we not feel gratitude and appreciation for this progress, especially in the fields of medicine, engineering and communications? How could we not acknowledge the work of many scientists and engineers who have provided alternatives to make development sustainable? . . .

Yet it must also be recognized that nuclear energy, biotechnology, information technology, knowledge of our DNA, and many other abilities which we have acquired, have given us tremendous power. More precisely, they have given those with the knowledge, and especially the economic resources to use them, an impressive dominance over the whole of humanity and the entire world. Never has humanity had such power over itself, yet nothing ensures that it will be used wisely, particularly when we consider how it is currently being used. We need but think of the nuclear bombs dropped in the middle of the twentieth century, or the array of technology which Nazism, Communism and other totalitarian regimes have employed to kill millions of people, to say nothing of the increasingly deadly arsenal of weapons available for modern warfare. In whose hands does all this power lie, or will it eventually end up? It is extremely risky for a small part of humanity to have it.

There is a tendency to believe that every increase in power means "an increase of 'progress' itself", an advance in "security, usefulness, welfare and vigour, . . . an assimilation of new values into the stream of culture",[3] as if reality, goodness and truth automatically flow from technological and economic power as such. The fact is that "contemporary man has not been trained to use power well",[4] because our immense technological development has not been accompanied by a development in human responsibility, values and conscience. Each age tends to have only a meagre awareness of its own limitations. It is possible that we do not grasp the gravity of the challenges now before us. . . . Our freedom fades when it is handed over to the blind forces of the unconscious, of immediate needs, of self-interest, and of violence. In this sense, we stand naked and exposed in the face of our ever-increasing power, lacking the wherewithal to control it. We have certain superficial mechanisms, but we cannot claim to have a sound ethics, a culture and spirituality genuinely capable of setting limits and teaching clear-minded self-restraint.

II. The Globalization of the Technocratic Paradigm

The basic problem goes even deeper: it is the way that humanity has taken up technology and its development *according to an undifferentiated and one-dimensional paradigm*. This paradigm exalts the concept of a subject who, using logical and rational procedures, progressively approaches and gains control over an external object. This subject makes every effort to establish the scientific and experimental method, which in itself is already a technique of possession, mastery and transformation. It is as if the subject were to find itself in the presence of something formless, completely open to manipulation. Men and women have constantly intervened in nature, but for a long time this meant being in tune with and respecting the possibilities offered by the things themselves, It was a matter of receiving what nature itself allowed, as if from its own hand. Now, by contrast, we are the ones to lay our hands on things, attempting to extract everything possible from them while frequently ignoring or forgetting the reality in front of us. Human beings and material objects no longer extend a friendly hand to one another; the relationship has become confrontational. This has made it easy to accept the idea of infinite or unlimited growth, which proves so attractive to economists, financiers and experts in technology. It is based on the lie that there is an infinite supply of the earth's goods, and this leads to the planet being squeezed dry beyond every limit. It is the false notion that "an infinite quantity of energy and resources are available, that it is possible to renew them quickly, and that the negative effects of the exploitation of the natural order can be easily absorbed".[5]

It can be said that many problems of today's world stem from the tendency, at times unconscious, to make the method and aims of science and technology an epistemological paradigm which shapes the lives of individuals and the workings of society. The effects of imposing this model on reality as a whole, human and social, are seen in the deterioration of the environment, but this is just one sign of a reductionism which affects every aspect of human and social life. We have to accept that technological products are not neutral, for they create a framework which ends up conditioning lifestyles and shaping social possibilities along the lines dictated by the interests of certain powerful groups. Decisions which may seem purely instrumental are in reality decisions about the kind of society we want to build. . . .

The technocratic paradigm also tends to dominate economic and political life. The economy accepts every advance in technology with a view to profit, without concern for its potentially negative impact on human beings. Finance overwhelms the real economy. The lessons of the global financial crisis have not been assimilated, and we are learning all too slowly the lessons of environmental deterioration. Some circles maintain that current economics and technology will solve all environmental problems, and argue, in popular and non-technical terms, that the problems of global hunger and poverty will be resolved simply by market growth. . . . Yet by itself the market cannot guarantee integral human development and social inclusion.[6] At the same time, we have "a sort of 'superdevelopment' of a wasteful and consumerist kind which forms an unacceptable contrast with the ongoing situations of dehumanizing deprivation",[7] while we are all too slow in developing economic institutions and social initiatives which can give the poor regular access to basic resources. We fail to see the deepest roots of our present failures, which have to do with the direction, goals, meaning and social implications of technological and economic growth. . . .

Ecological culture cannot be reduced to a series of urgent and partial responses to the immediate problems of pollution, environmental decay and the depletion of natural resources. There needs to be a distinctive way of looking at things, a way of thinking, policies, an educational programme, a lifestyle and a spirituality which together generate resistance to the assault of the technocratic paradigm. Otherwise, even the best ecological initiatives can find themselves caught up in the same globalized logic. To seek only a technical remedy to each environmental problem which comes up is to separate what is in reality interconnected and to mask the true and deepest problems of the global system.

Yet we can once more broaden our vision. We have the freedom needed to limit and direct technology; we can put it at the service of another type of progress, one which is healthier, more human, more social, more integral. Liberation from the dominant technocratic paradigm does in fact happen sometimes, for example, when cooperatives of small producers adopt less polluting means of production, and opt for a non-consumerist model of life, recreation and community, Or when technology is directed primarily to resolving people's concrete problems, truly helping them live with more dignity and less suffering. Or indeed when the desire to create and contemplate beauty manages to overcome reductionism through a kind of salvation which occurs in beauty and in those who behold it. An authentic humanity, calling for a new synthesis, seems to dwell in the midst of our technological culture, almost unnoticed, like a mist seeping gently beneath a closed door. Will the promise last, in spite of everything, with all that is authentic rising up in stubborn resistance? . . .

All of this shows the urgent need for us to move forward in a bold cultural revolution. Science and technology are not neutral; from the beginning to the end of a process, various intentions and possibilities are in play and can take on distinct shapes. Nobody is suggesting a return to the Stone Age, but we do need to slow down and look at reality in a different way, to appropriate the positive and sustainable progress which has been made, but also to recover the values and the great goals swept away by our unrestrained delusions of grandeur. . . .

III. Cultural Ecology

Many intensive forms of environmental exploitation and degradation not only exhaust the resources which provide local communities with their livelihood, but also undo the social structures which, for a long time, shaped cultural identity and their sense of the meaning of life and community. The disappearance of a culture can be just as serious, or even more serious, than the disappearance of a species of plant or animal. The imposition of a dominant lifestyle linked to a single form of production can be just as harmful as the altering of ecosystems.

In this sense, it is essential to show special care for indigenous communities and their cultural traditions. They are not merely one minority among others, but should be the principal dialogue partners, especially when large projects affecting their land are proposed. For them, land is not a commodity but rather a gift from God and from their ancestors who rest there, a sacred space with which they need to interact if they are to maintain their identity and values. When they remain on their land, they themselves care for it best. Nevertheless, in various parts of the world, pressure is being put on them to abandon their homelands to make room for agricultural or mining projects which are undertaken without regard for the degradation of nature and culture. . . .

IV. The Principle of the Common Good

An integral ecology is inseparable from the notion of the common good, a central and unifying principle of social ethics. The common good is "the sum of those conditions of social life which allow social groups and their individual members relatively thorough and ready access to their own fulfillment".[8]

Underlying the principle of the common good is respect for the human person as such, endowed with basic and inalienable rights ordered to his or her integral development. It has also to do with the overall welfare of society and the development of a variety of intermediate groups, applying the principle of subsidiarity. Outstanding among those groups is the family, as the basic cell of society. Finally, the common good calls for social peace, the stability and security provided by a certain order which cannot be achieved without particular concern for distributive justice; whenever this is violated, violence always ensues. Society as a whole, and the state in particular, are obliged to defend and promote the common good.

In the present condition of global society, where injustices abound and growing numbers of people are deprived of basic human rights and considered expendable, the principle of the common good immediately becomes, logically and inevitably, a summons to solidarity and a preferential option for the poorest of our brothers and sisters. This option entails recognizing the implications of the universal destination of the world's goods, but, as I mentioned in the Apostolic Exhortation *Evangelii Gaudium*,[9] It demands before all else an appreciation of the immense dignity of the poor in the light of our deepest convictions as believers. We need only look around us to see that, today, this option is in fact an ethical imperative essential for effectively attaining the common good.

V. Justice between the Generations

The notion of the common good also extends to future generations. The global economic crises have made painfully obvious the detrimental effects of disregarding our common destiny, which cannot exclude those who come after us. We can no longer speak of sustainable development apart from intergenerational solidarity. Once we start to think about the kind of world we are leaving to future generations, we look at things differently; we realize that the world is a gift which we have freely received and must share with others. Since the world has been given to us, we can no longer view reality in a purely utilitarian way, in which efficiency and productivity are entirely geared to our individual benefit, Intergenerational solidarity is not optional, but rather a basic question of justice, since the world we have received also belongs to those who will follow us. . . .

What kind of world do we want to leave to those who come after us, to children who are now growing up? This question not only concerns the environment in isolation; the issue cannot be approached piecemeal. When we ask ourselves what kind of world we want to leave behind, we think in the first place of its general direction, its meaning and its values. Unless we struggle with these deeper issues, I do not believe that our concern for ecology will produce significant results. But if those issues are courageously faced, we are led inexorably to ask other pointed questions: What is the purpose of our life in this world? Why are we here? What is the goal of our work and all our efforts? What need does the earth have of us? It is no longer enough, then, simply to state that we should be concerned for future generations. We need to see that what is at stake is our own dignity. Leaving an inhabitable planet to future generations is, first and foremost, up to us. The issue is one which dramatically affects us, for it has to do with the ultimate meaning of our earthly sojourn.

Doomsday predictions can no longer be met with irony or disdain. We may well be leaving to coming generations debris, desolation and filth. The pace of consumption, waste and environmental change has so stretched the planet's capacity that our contemporary lifestyle, unsustainable as it is, can only precipitate catastrophes, such as those which even now periodically occur in different areas of the world. The effects of the present imbalance can only be reduced by our decisive action, here and now. We need to reflect on our accountability before those who will have to endure the dire consequences.

Our difficulty in taking up this challenge seriously has much to do with an ethical and cultural decline which has accompanied the deterioration of the environment. Men and women of our postmodern world run the risk of rampant individualism, and many problems of society are connected with today's self-centred culture of instant gratification. We see this in the crisis of family and social ties and the difficulties of recognizing the other. Parents can be prone to impulsive and wasteful consumption, which then affects their children who find it increasingly difficult to acquire a home of their own and build a family. Furthermore, our inability to think seriously about future generations is linked to our inability to broaden the scope of our present interests and to give consideration to those who remain excluded from development. Let us not only keep the poor of the future in mind, but also today's poor, whose life on this earth is brief and who cannot keep on waiting. Hence, "in addition to a fairer sense of intergenerational solidarity there is also an urgent moral need for a renewed sense of intragenerational solidarity".[10]

Questions for Review

How does Francis distinguish between the benign and the malign effects of technology? Does he think—and do you think—that the world can cope with the challenge of climate change without fundamental changes in politics and indeed in values?

Notes

1 JOHN PAUL II, *Address to Scientists and Representatives of the United Nations University,* Hiroshima (25 February 1981), 3: *AAS* 73 (1981), 422.

2 BENEDICT XVI, Encyclical Letter *Caritas in Veritate* (29 June 2009), 69: *AAS* 101 (2009), 702.

3 ROMANO GUARDINI, *Das Ende der Neuzeil,* 9th ed., Würzburg, 1965, 87 (English: *The End of the Modern World,* Wilmington, 1998, 82).

4 *Ibid.*

5 PONTIFICAL COUNCIL FOR JUSTICE AND PEACE, *Compendium of the Social Doctrine of the Church,* 462.

6 Cf. BENEDICT XVI, Encyclical Letter *Caritas in Veritale* (29 June 2009), 35: *AAS* 101 (2009), 671.

7 *Ibid.,* 22: p. 657.

8 SECOND VATICAN ECUMENICAL COUNCIL, Pastoral Constitution on the Church in the Modern World *Gandium et Spes,* 26.

9 Cf. Nos. 186-201: *AAS* 105 (2013), 1098–1105.

10 BENEDICT XVI, *Message for the 2010 World Day of Peace,* 8: *AAS* 102 (2010), 45.

The U.N. Security Council

ADAMS ROBERTS AND DOMINIK ZAUM

Formal Change: Proposals for Structural Reform of the Security Council

The problems of accountability, the sometimes stifling effect of the veto and the failure of the Council to act in certain crises have led to frequent calls for reform of the composition and procedures of the Council. The demand for reform is also driven by the simple fact that there have been fundamental changes in the realities of power in the world since 1945, in particular the rise of major new powers, of which India and Japan are only the most obvious examples. If the Security Council were being formed afresh today, it would hardly be assigned the exact composition that it currently has. There are obvious dangers in having a Security Council that does not fully reflect today's power realities. Yet structural reform has proven elusive, and continues to face serious obstacles.

Three core reform issues have repeatedly emerged for discussion: the appropriate number of permanent and non-permanent members; the existence and scope of the veto power; and the number of votes required to pass resolutions. The main attempt at reform took place in 2005. Before that there were two other major initiatives: negotiations in 1963–5, which led to an increase in the number of non-permanent members from six to 10 (and with it an increase in the number of votes required to pass a resolution, from seven to nine); and negotiations from 1993 to 1997, which, while failing to achieve any substantial amendments to the composition of the Council to address the developing world's concern about its under-representation, did bring about important changes in the Council's procedures relating to the transparency of its deliberations and its communications with non-Council members. . . .

In March 2005, ongoing debates on reform culminated in the recommendations of Secretary-General Kofi Annan to the member states in advance of the 60th anniversary meeting of the General Assembly in September that year. Following the recommendations of the High-level Panel Report of December 2004, Annan presented member states with two reform options, under both of which the Security Council would increase in size from 15 to 24 members. Neither option involved any change to the number of veto-wielding powers – an aspect of the proposals that was contested by states seeking permanent membership.

Model A envisaged six new permanent members: two from Asia (where the leading candidates were India and Japan); two from Africa (where the main contenders were Nigeria, South Africa and Egypt); one from Europe (Germany); and one from the Americas (Brazil). In addition, there would be three new non-permanent members on a non-renewable two-year term.

Model B envisaged no new permanent members, but instead a new category of eight 'semi-permanent' members, elected on a regional basis for a renewable four-year term; plus one new non-permanent member on a non-renewable two-year term. Model B was fiercely opposed by those countries (particularly Japan and Germany) that had been lobbying for a number of years for a permanent seat. In the end, the negotiations over both models broke down, and the outcome document of the 2005 World Summit said little on Council reform.

It is questionable whether the two proposed solutions were the right ones for the UN in the current context of global politics. Both models took a narrow view in their diagnosis of the problem, and their prescription for addressing it.

Firstly, the reform proposals and the surrounding debate appeared to assume that the weaknesses of the Council were due, not to the complexity of the problems it faces and the inherent limitations within which its members must operate to tackle them, but rather to the Council's composition and the veto. The Council's record over the past three decades does not necessarily support this assumption. The fact is that since the end of the Cold War the Council has been much more active in its management role, and the veto has been employed much less frequently. The breakdown of consensus over Iraq in 2002–3, which sparked the renewed calls for reform, was regrettable, but it is not clear that a larger Council would have been any more likely to agree on a particular course to address the crisis.

Secondly, as many observers have noted, the desire for inclusiveness needs to be balanced against the objective that preoccupied the UN's founders: to avoid replicating the mistakes of the League of Nations. While the General Assembly was to represent the views of the entire membership of international society, when it came to the design of the Security Council, the body primarily responsible for managing threats to peace and security, equal representation and consensus decision-making had to be balanced against the practical need for responsiveness and effectiveness.

Thirdly, the proposed mechanism for enhanced representation – regional groupings – raises a key question: would the new members actually represent their regions (and if so, through what mechanism?), or would they simply be from those regions? These are two very different propositions, and divisions within regions remain significant. It is noteworthy that some of the loudest opposition to aspiring candidates in 2005 was voiced by their neighbours (for example by Pakistan in the case of India's candidacy, and China in the case of Japan's). Moreover, without explicit means for consulting with other member states or nongovernmental organisations, the addition of new members will not automatically enhance representativeness.

The 2005 reform proposals largely made representativeness, as signalled by more seats for the developing world, a proxy for legitimacy. But if the goal is greater legitimacy, then it could be argued that less attention needs to be paid to questions of size, and more to the tricky question of how to enhance the accountability and transparency of the Council.

It is sometimes said that greater representativeness would reduce the selectivity of the Council, and might help to prevent situations such as that regarding Rwanda in 1994, where intervention was not in the national interest of any of the major Security Council members, and the Council thus failed for a long time to address the genocide. However, the link between regional representation and Council activity in that region is not clear. While African states are underrepresented on the Council, Africa has been a key Council concern over the last ten years. . . . It is also unclear whether greater African representation would lead to more forceful UN activity in the continent to address humanitarian emergencies and large-scale human-rights violations – to more peace enforcement, rather than merely consent-based peacekeeping. The fact that African Council members have generally taken a more conciliatory approach towards Khartoum on Darfur than have Western states suggests that it might not. . . .

Informal Change: Reforms to Working Methods

No Charter reform, and therefore no change in the Council's composition, can happen without the consent of each of the P5. As a result, a certain structural immobility is built into the very fabric of the UN, especially the Security Council. Although the failure of reform proposals over the decades has been often blamed on the P5 and their unwillingness to give up or share power, differences among regional groups of states and the broader UN membership have been no less important. The 'North–South divide' between developed and developing countries has made agreement on possible changes very difficult to achieve. This was particularly the case in 2005, with divisions manifesting themselves in bitter debates at the World Summit over the budget, the Peacebuilding Commission and the Human Rights Council.

However, while formal, structural change might be difficult to realise, the Council has changed some of its working methods to increase its effectiveness and address some of the criticisms about participation and accountability. When tackling conflicts and crises, in recent years the Council has frequently complemented its formal decision-making structures with informal, more flexible mechanisms – in particular, so-called 'informal groups' (contact groups and 'groups of friends'), which include non-Council member states that have a special stake or interest in a conflict. While the use of such informal groups goes back to the 1950s, their number increased dramatically in the 1990s, as the Council tried to adapt to the new realities of the post-Cold War world. Such groups allow greater flexibility and privacy, unconstrained by the procedures of formal Council meetings, as well as greater voice and involvement for important interested actors who are not Council members, such as key regional powers, major donors and countries trusted by the conflict parties. This involvement enables the mobilisation of extra diplomatic and other resources for conflict resolution.

Since the early 1990s, there has been a range of other changes designed to increase transparency and participation in Council decision-making (the so-called 'Cluster II' reforms). These include:

1. Fuller and quicker publication of Council draft resolutions and other documents, including its monthly programme;

2. Increased involvement of troop-contributing countries in debates on the mandates of peacekeeping operations. Since 2001, the Council has held mandatory closed sessions with troop contributors before deciding on new mandates or mandate changes;

3. Greater dissemination of information about the work of sanctions committees and other subsidiary bodies to non-Council members, e.g., through regular briefings after meetings;

4. Increased involvement of non-members in Council sessions.

Most of these reforms came about as a result of pressure from the General Assembly or non-permanent members. The P5 have at times been resistant, but they have generally embraced and promoted particular reforms. However, while the changes are important, their impact should not be overstated. Troop-contributing countries, for example, regularly complain about the lack of opportunity for real input at the closed Council meetings, arguing that mandates are effectively written before they are consulted. Similarly, increased opportunities for the participation of non-Council members in Council sessions have been undermined by the growth of informal (and non-public) consultations between Council members, in which it appears that most decisions are taken. In the absence of agreement on structural reform of the Security Council at the 2005 World Summit, the outcome document called for further efforts to enhance transparency and wider participation in Council decision-making. . . .

Our summary of the weaknesses and strengths in the Council's record is necessarily imperfect. It is not always easy to distinguish the effects of Council action and inaction from the role played by other factors in world politics, or indeed from the effects of other UN agencies, particularly the General Assembly. Moreover, aspects of the Council's record are deeply ambiguous and hard to categorise as either strengths or weaknesses. . . .

Weaknesses in the Council's Record

The Security Council's legitimacy and effectiveness in addressing the problem of war and authorising the use of force have been called into question on many occasions. The Council has been criticised both when it has acted, and when it has not. Major controversies about the Council's role have revolved round the following ten issues:

Inaction. This has been a persistent theme throughout the Council's history. The Council's relevance to international crises is undermined by the fact that there have been numerous occasions on which it has been unable to reach decisions about particular wars and threats of war, whether because of lack of interest among the major powers, the resistance of those involved in a conflict, or a threat or use of the veto. The inaction of the Council or of forces operating under it was particularly notable in various crises connected to the Cold War, as well as the Iran–Iraq War, the mass killings in Rwanda in 1994 and the massacre at Srebrenica in Bosnia in 1995.

A particularly disturbing aspect of UN inaction is seen in the fact that states that enjoy a close relationship with a veto-wielding member of the Council can escape criticism or action from the Council. The most highly publicised case is Israel, which has been regularly let off the hook by a US threat or use of the veto. Similarly, though not so frequently, China has used its power in the Council to protect regimes, such as those in Sudan and Myanmar, from UN-authorised action.

Intelligence failures. In many conflicts and crises it has been painfully evident that the UN lacks its own reliable intelligence capacity, with the result that it does not have an independent capability for responding quickly to fast-moving events, and is at risk of acting on unreliable information. While it may not be feasible for the UN to develop an independent capacity to collect secret intelligence, it does need to develop an effective system for sharing and evaluating intelligence in certain issue areas.

Weak assessment of situations. Operating as it does with imperfect information at its disposal, the Council has on occasion approached conflicts in questionable ways: for instance, when it has maintained a neutral stance in circumstances in which there is substantial doubt that a neutral position is appropriate; or when it has shown unnecessary haste in making a judgement about a crisis, most strikingly in its resolution blaming ETA for the Madrid train bombing of 2004.

Difficulty in agreeing on military action. The Council is generally better at agreeing on ends than on means. Even when its directives have been openly flouted, its members have often differed sharply about follow-up action, including the use of force, and have in the end been unable to agree on it. In some cases, such disagreement on the Council may be positive. However, two serious consequences can flow from failure to agree on specific military action. Firstly, to the extent that indecision becomes a pattern, it risks creating a perception of the Council as an organisation whose bark is worse than its bite, or as one that stands by while terrible crimes are committed. Secondly, in cases where there has been an initial authorisation to use force but then there is disagreement on how this should be followed up, the net effect may be that uncontrollable leeway is handed to the authorisee. This was part of the problem regarding Iraq in 2003, when a key question raised was the extent to which pre-existing authorisations to states or coalitions continued when the Council was unable to agree on new ones.

Reliance on the lowest common denominator. There has been a tendency for the Council to focus on 'lowest common denominator' policies – that is, those on which agreement is easy to reach. Such policies often relate to crisis points and short-term problems, and do not tackle the underlying issues at stake in a given conflict. Thus, in many conflict situations, the Council has justifiably called for immediate ceasefires, arms embargoes and urgent humanitarian action, but has been less effective in agreeing policies and actions to address the issues that gave rise to the resort to arms.

Uneasy relations with the US. The relationship of the Council with its most powerful member, the US, has proved perennially difficult. At least since the time of the Korean War, there has been a strand of thought among member states and observers that views the Council as essentially dominated by the US, and therefore a mere instrument of power politics, rather than a cure for it. This view, which is so corrosive of the UN's legitimacy, has become more widespread in the post-Cold War era because of the increased significance of the role of the US, both in the Council and in interventions around the world. At the same time, within the US, there is frequent criticism of the UN, including complaints that the UN framework entangles the US in a complex and unsatisfactory decision-making system, and places disproportionate burdens on it. Since 1945, the US has tended to see itself, rightly or wrongly, as a major provider of security outside a UN framework, for example through its network of alliances: against this background, the obligations arising from Council membership are sometimes presented as unnecessary additions to an already heavy burden.

Violations of the Council's resolutions by its members. On some occasions Council members, including members of the P5, have violated the terms of a Council resolution for which they voted, possibly because they had come to see its provisions as ineffective or damaging. For example, during the arms embargo on the former Yugoslavia from 1991–5, the US and other states connived in the illicit acquisition of weapons by several governments affected by the embargo, including Bosnia and Croatia. Other violations, arguably more damaging in their effects, include various breaches of the sanctions on Iraq between 1991 and 2003: these included Council members trading with Iraq, and the toleration of large-scale smuggling between Iraq and neighbouring states. Some of these developments helped to precipitate the Iraq crisis of 2003.

Poor management of force. The UN has at times proved ineffective in managing the use of force. While the Council has not been directly involved in force management, this problem has primarily been a consequence of the poor quality of certain Council mandates. For example, during UNPROFOR's involvement in the former Yugoslavia, there was strong criticism from military specialists that the Council had set over-elaborate procedures and over-precise rules for the use of military force in protecting the 'safe areas', so that, for example, force could only be used under a 'dual-key' arrangement, and even then, only with smoking-gun evidence against those directly responsible for violations of ceasefire agreements and the protected areas. It could not be used more generally against the forces that had instigated such violations.

Corruption and weak control of operations. Actions initiated by the Council have in some instances been marred by corruption scandals, such as that connected with the Oil-for-Food Programme, which operated from 1995 to 2003 as part of the Council's sanctions regime against Iraq. There have also been instances of corruption in connection with contracts to supply certain UN peacekeeping operations, and of unethical sexual conduct by UN peacekeeping personnel. These cases have raised the question of whether the Council's members have involved themselves sufficiently in the detailed framing and subsequent implementation of its policies.

'Dustbin' and 'punchbag' roles. The UN in general, and the Security Council in particular, continues to play the role of a convenient dustbin into which states can throw issues on which they do not have the will or capacity to act; it also functions as a punchbag for states to hit when other possible targets of their wrath are more difficult to attack. Both these roles reinforce the Council's other weaknesses. . . .

Yet even if there is truth in all the criticisms levelled at it, the Council is not necessarily a failure. When people assert that the Council has failed, it is worth enquiring by what standard they are judging it, and what precisely their judgement means. If the Council's performance is judged against a high standard – for example, if it is viewed as a means of replacing war with law, as a presumed alternative to national defence efforts, or as a provider of the ambitious collective security scheme that the UN Charter is widely perceived as representing – then it is obviously a failure. If, alternatively, it is judged according to the benchmark of whether it has contributed to the management of certain crises in international relations and to a modest degree of stability, then it is at least a partial success.

Strengths in the Council's Record

One of the key strengths of the Security Council in international society lies in its role as a 'collective legitimiser' of the use of force by member states. While collective legitimation is not the exclusive preserve of the UN – other inter-governmental organisations (particularly regional ones) can also play a legitimising role – the UN has been the main focus of states' multilateral efforts to win approval for their policies. In some cases, the Council's endorsement can make a direct material difference, by enabling those leading a military action to obtain troops and financial support from other member states. More commonly, however, the UN stamp of approval has more intangible benefits: it enhances both the lawfulness and the political acceptability of the proposed military campaign. The so-called Just War tradition, which invokes a series of precautionary principles to help to determine the justifiability of a use of force, gives prominent place to the notion of 'proper authority'. In the present era, the UN Security Council is widely seen as constituting that 'proper authority'. As a result, states have invested significant diplomatic capital in garnering Council authorisation for their actions. . . .

A large array of claims can be made for the effectiveness of the Security Council. The eight most important are:

It has assisted in the reduction of the incidence of international war. While it does not amount to the removal of the scourge of war at which the Charter aimed, the reduction in the number and human cost of inter-state wars over the past decades is significant. Many other events, institutions and processes have contributed to this outcome, but the role of the Council in it is not negligible.

It has effectively opposed major invasions aimed at taking over states. A classic issue that any international organisation in the security field must tackle is a major attack by one state upon another. The Council's prompt responses to certain attacks – on South Korea in 1950, on Kuwait in 1990 – reinforced the message, which also came from other quarters, that aggression does not pay. The fact that the Council failed to respond to certain other major attacks, such as Iraq's invasion of Iran in 1980, weakens this message but does not invalidate it.

It has usefully deployed peacekeeping forces. In many cases, UN peace-keepers have helped to stabilise a volatile situation; in particular, some operations have prevented local conflicts from becoming arenas for great-power confrontation. There is also evidence that in some cases, the deployment of peace operations to a territory has helped to prevent the recurrence of civil war.

It has provided a framework for assisting major changes in international relations. Perhaps the two most important changes in the structure of international relations in the UN era have been decolonisation and the end of the Cold War. While both developments have multiple causes, the UN in general and the Security Council in particular can be seen as having assisted them, by providing a forum for discussion between states and a framework through which post-colonial and post-Soviet states could assert their independence and develop relations with other countries.

It has adapted to new developments. The Council's activities have expanded to take account of new developments in the sphere of international peace and security, particularly in international humanitarian law; international criminal law; international efforts to assist the emergence and consolidation of democratic practices in states; and international efforts to combat nuclear-weapons proliferation and global terrorism.

It has assisted in the diffusion of norms. The Council has played a key role in the articulation and diffusion of norms, both new and existing. One long-standing example is the principle of self-determination, which over time both permanent and non-permanent members induced the Council to promote in its resolutions. More recently, the Council's statements and actions have contributed to the development of ideas of human security and the 'responsibility to protect'.

It has provided governance and institution-building capacities to war-torn and failed states. The Council has gradually developed a capacity for providing interim governance and assisting the re-establishment of the functions of government, including democratic processes, in states that have undergone civil war or external domination. . . .

It has assisted great-power cooperation. Engaging in continual interaction and negotiation, the Council has helped to maintain a degree of understanding and cooperation between the great powers both during and after the Cold War, securing agreement on basic norms and helping to settle certain regional conflicts, for example in Central America. Even when agreement has been elusive, the Council has provided a forum where major powers can signal their intentions and the 'red lines' beyond which they should not be pressed.

Many other claims could be made for the Council's uses. Several relate to undramatic but important activities, such as the deployment of missions to conflict zones to gather facts and sketch the basis for peace agreements. The Council has made good use of panels of experts to assess the implementation and impact of sanctions. . . . It appears to have learned from the ineffectiveness and shocking side-effects of some past applications of sanctions, and is moving towards better-targeted measures. As for the future, in an era in which it is sometimes argued that there is a need for the preventive use of force to ward off threats to international peace and security, the UN Security Council is the one body in the world that has the explicit and undisputed legal right to take preventive action against such threats. . . .

Questions for Review

What have been the political impediments to altering the membership on the United Nations Security Council? On balance, has the Security Council been a net plus?

Globalization and Governance

KENNETH N. WALTZ

In 1979 I described the interdependence of states as low but increasing. It has increased, but only to about the 1910 level if measured by trade or capital flows as a percentage of GNP; lower if measured by the mobility of labor, and lower still if measured by the mutual military dependence of states. Yet one feels that the world has become a smaller one. International travel has become faster, easier, and cheaper; music, art, cuisines, and cinema have all become cosmopolitan in the world's major centers and beyond. The *Peony Pavilion* was produced in its entirety for the first time in 400 years, and it was presented not in Shanghai or Beijing, but in New York. Communication is almost instantaneous, and more than words can be transmitted, which makes the reduced mobility of labor of less consequence. High-technology jobs can be brought to the workers instead of the workers to the jobs; foreigners can become part of American design teams without leaving their homelands. Before World War I, the close interdependence of states was thought of as heralding an era of peace among nations and democracy and prosperity within them. Associating interdependence, peace, democracy, and prosperity is nothing new. In his much translated and widely read book, *The Great Illusion* (1933), Norman Angell summed up the texts of generations of classical and neoclassical economists and drew from them the dramatic conclusion that wars would no longer be fought because they would not pay. World War I instead produced the great disillusion, which reduced political optimism to a level that remained low almost until the end of the Cold War. I say "almost" because beginning in the 1970s a new optimism, strikingly similar in content to the old, began to resurface. Interdependence was again associated with peace and peace increasingly with democracy, which began to spread wonderfully to Latin America, to Asia, and with the Soviet Union's collapse, to Eastern Europe. Francis Fukuyama (1992) foresaw a time when all states would be liberal democracies and, more recently, Michael Doyle (1997) projected the year for it to happen as lying between 2050 and 2100. John Mueller (1989), heralding the disappearance of war among the world's advanced countries, argued that Norman Angell's premises were right all along, but that he had published his book prematurely.

Robert Keohane and Joseph Nye in their 1977 book, *Power and Interdependence,* strengthened the notion that interdependence promotes peace and limits the use of force by arguing that simple interdependence had become complex interdependence, binding the economic and hence the political interests of states ever more tightly together. Now, we hear from many sides that interdependence has reached yet another height, transcending states and making *The Borderless World,* which is the title and theme of Kenichi Ohmae's 1990 book. People, firms, markets matter more; states matter less. Each tightening of the economic screw raises the benefits of economic exchange and makes war among

the more advanced states increasingly costly. The simple and plausible propositions are that as the benefits of peace rise, so do the costs of war. When states
perceive wars to be immensely costly, they will be disinclined to fight them.
War becomes rare, but is not abolished because even the strongest economic
forces cannot conquer fear or eliminate concern for national honor (Friedman
1999, 196–97).

Economic interests become so strong that markets begin to replace politics
at home and abroad. That economics depresses politics and limits its significance is taken to be a happy thought. The first section of this paper examines its
application domestically; the second, internationally.

The State of the State

Globalization is the fad of the 1990s, and globalization is made in America.
Thomas Friedman's *The Lexus and the Olive Tree* is a celebration of the American
way, of market capitalism and liberal democracy. Free markets, transparency,
and flexibility are the watchwords. The "electronic herd" moves vast amounts of
capital in and out of countries according to their political and economic merits.
Capital moves almost instantaneously into countries with stable governments,
progressive economies, open accounting, and honest dealing, and out of countries lacking those qualities. States can defy the "herd," but they will pay a price,
usually a steep one, as did Thailand, Malaysia, Indonesia, and South Korea in
the 1990s. Some countries may defy the herd inadvertently (the countries just
mentioned); others, out of ideological conviction (Cuba and North Korea); some,
because they can afford to (oil-rich countries); others, because history has passed
them by (many African countries).

Countries wishing to attract capital and to gain the benefits of today's and
tomorrow's technology have to don the "golden straitjacket," a package of policies including balanced budgets, economic deregulation, openness to investment
and trade, and a stable currency. The herd decides which countries to reward and
which to punish, and nothing can be done about its decisions. In September 1997,
at a World Bank meeting, Malaysia's prime minister, Dr. Mahathir Mohammad,
complained bitterly that great powers and international speculators had forced
Asian countries to open their markets and had manipulated their currencies in
order to destroy them. Friedman (1999, 93) wonders what Robert Rubin, then-
U.S. treasury secretary, might have said in response. He imagines it would have
been something like this: "What planet are you living on? . . . Globalization isn't
a choice, it's a reality, . . . and the only way you can grow at the speed that your
people want to grow is by tapping into the global stock and bond markets, by
seeking out multinationals to invest in your country, and by selling into the global
trading system what your factories produce. And the most basic truth about globalization is this: *No one is in charge.*"

The herd has no telephone number. When the herd decides to withdraw capital from a country, there is no one to complain to or to petition for relief. Decisions

of the herd are collective ones. They are not made; they happen, and they happen because many investors individually make decisions simultaneously and on similar grounds to invest or to withdraw their funds. Do what displeases the herd, and it will trample you into the ground. Globalization is shaped by markets, not by governments.

Globalization means homogenization. Prices, products, wages, wealth, and rates of interest and profit tend to become the same all over the world. Like any powerful movement for change, globalization encounters resistance—in America, from religious fundamentalists; abroad, from anti-Americanists; everywhere from cultural traditionalists. And the resisters become bitter because consciously or not they know they are doomed. Driven by technology, international finance sweeps all before it. Under the protection of American military power, globalization proceeds relentlessly. As Friedman proclaims: "America truly is the ultimate benign hegemony" (375).

The "end of the Cold War and the collapse of communism have discredited all models other than liberal democracy." The statement is by Larry Diamond, and Friedman repeats it with approval. There is one best way, and America has found it. "It's a post-industrial world, and America today is good at everything that is post-industrial" (145, 303). The herd does not care about forms of government as such, but it values and rewards "stability, predictability, transparency, and the ability to transfer and protect its private property." Liberal democracies represent the one best way. The message to all governments is clear: Conform or suffer.

There is much in what Friedman says, and he says it very well. But how much? And, specifically, what is the effect of closer interdependence on the conduct of the internal and external affairs of nations?

First, we should ask how far globalization has proceeded? As everyone knows, much of the world has been left aside: most of Africa and Latin America, Russia, all of the Middle East except Israel, and large parts of Asia. Moreover, for many countries, the degree of participation in the global economy varies by region. Northern Italy, for example, is in; southern Italy is out. In fact, globalization is not global but is mainly limited to northern latitudes. Linda Weiss points out that, as of 1991, 81% of the world stock of foreign direct investment was in high-wage countries of the north: mainly the United States, followed by the United Kingdom, Germany, and Canada. She adds that the extent of concentration has grown by 12 points since 1967 (Weiss 1998; cf., Hirst and Thompson 1996, 72).

Second, we should compare the interdependence of nations now with interdependence earlier. The first paragraph of this paper suggests that in most ways we have not exceeded levels reached in 1910. The rapid growth of international trade and investment from the middle 1850s into the 1910s preceded a prolonged period of war, internal revolution, and national insularity. After World War II, protectionist policies lingered as the United States opened its borders to trade while taking a relaxed attitude toward countries that protected their markets during the years of recovery from war's devastation. One might say that from 1914 into the 1960s an interdependence deficit developed, which helps to explain the steady growth of interdependence thereafter. Among the richest 24 industrial economies (the OECD countries), exports grew at about twice the rate of GDP after 1960. In 1960, exports were 9.5% of their GDPs; in 1900, 20.5% (Wade 1996, 62; cf., Weiss 1998, 171). Finding that 1999 approximately equals 1910 in extent of interdependence is hardly surprising. What is true of trade also holds for capital flows, again as a percentage of GDP (Hirst and Thompson 1996, 36).

Third, money markets may be the only economic sector one can say has become truly global. Finance capital moves freely across the frontiers of OECD countries and quite freely elsewhere (Weiss 1998, xii). Robert Wade notes that real interest rates within northern countries and between northern and southern countries vary by no more than 5%. This seems quite large until one notices variations across countries of 10 to 50 times in real wages, years of schooling, and numbers of working scientists. Still, with the movement of financial assets as with commodities, the present remains like the past. Despite today's ease of communication, financial markets at the turn of the previous century were at least as integrated as they are now (Wade 1996, 73–75).

Obviously, the world is not one. Sadly, the disparities of the North and South remain wide. Perhaps surprisingly, among the countries that are thought of as being in the zone of globalization, differences are considerable and persistent. To take just one example, financial patterns differ markedly across countries. The United States depends on capital imports, Western Europe does not, and Japan is a major capital exporter. The more closely one looks, the more one finds variations. That is hardly surprising. What looks smooth, uniform, and simple from a distance, on closer inspection proves to be pockmarked, variegated, and complex. Yet here, the variations are large enough to sustain the conclusion that globalization, even within its zone, is not a statement about the present, but a prediction about the future.

Many globalizers underestimate the extent to which the new looks like the old. In any competitive system the winners are imitated by the losers, or they continue to lose. In political as in economic development, latecomers imitate the practices and adopt the institution of the countries who have shown the way. Occasionally, someone finds a way to outflank, to invent a new way, or to ingeniously modify an old way to gain an advantage; and then the process of imitation begins anew. That competitors begin to look like one another if the competition is close and continuous is a familiar story. Competition among states has always led some of them to imitate others politically, militarily, and economically; but the apostles of globalization argue that the process has now sped up immensely and that the straitjacket allows little room to wiggle. In the old political era, the strong vanquished the weak; in the new economic era, "the fast eat the slow" (Klaus Schwab quoted in Friedman 1999, 171). No longer is it "Do what the strong party says or risk physical punishment"; but instead "Do what the electronic herd requires or remain impoverished." But then, in a competitive system there are always winners and losers. A few do exceptionally well, some get along, and many bring up the rear.

States have to conform to the ways of the more successful among them or pay a stiff price for not doing so. We then have to ask what is the state of the state? What becomes of politics within the coils of encompassing economic processes? The message of globalizers is that economic and technological forces impose near uniformity of political and economic forms and functions on states. They do so because the herd is attracted only to countries with reliable, stable, and open governments—that is, to liberal democratic ones.

Yet a glance at just the past 75 years reveals that a variety of political-economic systems have produced impressive results and were admired in their day for doing so. In the 1930s and again in the 1950s, the Soviet Union's economic growth rates were among the world's highest, so impressive in the '50s that America feared being overtaken and passed by. In the 1960s President Kennedy got "the country moving again," and America's radically different system gained world respect. In the '70s, Western European welfare states with managed and directed economics were highly regarded. In the late '70s and through much of the '80s, the Japanese brand of neomercantilism was thought to be the wave of the future; and Western Europe and the United States worried about being able to keep up. Imitate or perish was the counsel of some; pry the Japanese economy open and make it compete on our grounds was the message of others. America did not succeed in doing much of either. Yet in the 1990s, its economy has flourished. Globalizers offer it as the ultimate political-economic model—and so history again comes to an end. Yet it is odd to conclude from a decade's experience that the one best model has at last appeared. Globalization, if it were realized, would mean a near uniformity of conditions across countries. Even in the 1990s, one finds little evidence of globalization. The advanced countries of the world have enjoyed or suffered quite different fates. Major Western European countries were plagued by high and persistent unemployment; Northeast and Southeast Asian countries experienced economic stagnation or collapse while China continued to do quite well; and we know about the United States.

Variation in the fortunes of nations underlines the point: The country that has done best, at least lately, is the United States. Those who have fared poorly have supposedly done so because they have failed to conform to the American Way. Globalizers do not claim that globalization is complete, but only that it is in process and that the process is irreversible. Some evidence supports the conclusion; some does not. Looking at the big picture, one notices that nations whose economies have faltered or failed have been more fully controlled, directed, and supported governmentally than the American economy. Soviet-style economies failed miserably; in China, only the free-market sector flourishes; the once much-favored Swedish model has proved wanting. One can easily add more examples. From them it is tempting to leap to the conclusion that America has indeed found, or stumbled onto, the one best way.

Obviously, Thomas Friedman thinks so. Tip O'Neill, when he was a congressman from Massachusetts, declared that all politics are local. Wrong, Friedman says, all politics have become global. "The electronic herd," he writes, "turns the whole world into a parliamentary system, in which every government lives under the fear of a no-confidence vote from the herd" (1999, 62, 115).

I find it hard to believe that economic processes direct or determine a nation's policies, that spontaneously arrived-at decisions about where to place resources reward or punish a national economy so strongly that a government either does what pleases the "herd" or its economy fails to prosper or even risks collapse. We all recall recent cases, some of them mentioned above, that seem to support Friedman's thesis. Mentioning them both makes a point and raises doubts.

First, within advanced countries at similar levels of development that are closely interrelated, one expects uniformities of form and function to be most fully displayed. Yet Stephen Woolcock, looking at forms of corporate governance within the European community, finds a "spectrum of approaches" and expects it to persist for the foreseeable future (1996, 196). Since the 1950s, the economies of Germany and France have grown more closely together as each became the principal trading partner of the other. Yet a study of the two countries concludes that France has copied German policies but has been unwilling or unable to copy institutions (Boltho 1996). GDP per work hour among seven of the most prosperous countries came close together between the 1950s and the 1980s (Boyer 1996, 37). Countries at a high level of development do tend to converge in productivity, but that is something of a tautology.

Second, even if all politics have become global, economies remain local perhaps to a surprising extent. Countries with large economies continue to do most of their business at home. Americans produce 88% of the goods they buy. Sectors that are scarcely involved in international trade, such as government, construction, nonprofit organizations, utilities, and wholesale and retail trade employ 82% of Americans (Lawrence 1997, 21). As Paul Krugman says, "The United States is still almost 90% an economy that produces goods and services for its own use" (1997, 166). For the world's three largest economies—the United States, Japan, and the European Union—taken as a unit, exports are 12% or less of GDP (Weiss 1998, 176). What I found to be true in 1970 remains true today: The world is less interdependent than is usually supposed (Waltz 1970). Moreover, developed countries, oil imports aside, do the bulk of their external business with one another, and that means that the extent of their dependence on commodities that they could not produce for themselves is further reduced.

Reinforcing the parochial pattern of productivity, the famous footloose corporations in fact turn out to be firmly anchored in their home bases. One study of the world's 100 largest corporations concludes that not one of them could be called truly "global" or "footloose." Another study found one multinational corporation that seemed to be leaving its home base: Britain's chemical company, ICI (Weiss 1998, 18, 22; cf., Hirst and Thompson 1996, 82–93, 90, 95ff.). On all the important counts—location of most assets, site of research and development, ownership, and management—the importance of a corporation's home base is marked. And the technological prowess of corporations corresponds closely to that of the countries in which they are located.

Third, the *"transformative capacity"* of states, as Linda Weiss emphasizes, is the key to their success in the world economy (Weiss 1998, xii). Because technological innovation is rapid, and because economic conditions at home and abroad change often, states that adapt easily have considerable advantages. International politics remains inter-national. As the title of a review by William H. McNeill (1997) puts it, "Territorial States Buried Too Soon." Global or world politics has not taken over from national politics. The twentieth century was the century of the nation-state. The twenty-first will be too. Trade and technology do not determine a single best way to organize a polity and its economy. National systems display a great deal of resilience. States still have a wide range of choice. Most states survive, and the units that survive in competitive systems are those with the ability to adapt. Some do it well, and they grow and prosper. Others just manage to get along. That's the way it is in competitive systems. In this spirit, Ezra Taft Benson, when he was President Eisenhower's secretary of agriculture, gave this kindly advice to America's small farmers: "Get big or get out." Success in competitive systems requires the units of the system to adopt ways they would prefer to avoid.

States adapt to their environment. Some are light afoot, and others are heavy. The United States looked to be heavy afoot in the 1980s when Japan's economy was booming. Sometimes it seemed that MITI (Ministry of International Trade and Industry) was manned by geniuses who guided Japan's economy effortlessly to its impressive accomplishments. Now it is the United States that appears light afoot, lighter than any other country. Its government is open: Accurate financial information flows freely, most economic decisions are made by private firms. These are the characteristics that make for flexibility and for quick adaptation to changing conditions.

Competitive systems select for success. Over time, the qualities that make for success vary. Students of American government point out that one of the advantages of a federal system is that the separate states can act as laboratories for social-economic experimentation. When some states succeed, others may imitate them. The same thought applies to nations. One must wonder who the next winner will be.

States adapt; they also protect themselves. Different nations, with distinct institutions and traditions, protect themselves in different ways. Japan fosters industries, defends them, and manages its trade. The United States uses its political, economic, and military leverage to protect itself and manipulate international events to promote its interests. Thus, as David E. Spiro elaborately shows, international markets and institutions did not recycle petrodollars after 1974. The United States did. Despite many statements to the contrary, the United States worked effectively through different administrations and under different cabinet secretaries to undermine markets and thwart international institutions. Its leverage enabled it to manipulate the oil crisis to serve its own interests (1999, chap. 6).

Many of the interdependers of the 1970s expected the state to wither and fade away. Charles Kindleberger wrote in 1969 that "the nation-state is just about through as an economic unit" (207). Globalizers of the 1990s believe that this time it really is happening. The state has lost its "monopoly over internal sovereignty," Wolfgang H. Reinecke writes, and as "an externally sovereign actor" it "will become a thing of the past" (1997, 137; cf., Thurow 1999). Internally, the state's monopoly has never been complete, but it seems more nearly so now than earlier, at least in well-established states. The range of governmental functions and the extent of state control over society and economy has seldom been fuller than it is now. In many parts of the world the concern has been not with the state's diminished internal powers but with their increase. And although state control has lessened somewhat recently, does anyone believe that the United States and Britain, for example, are back to a 1930s level, let alone to a nineteenth-century level of governmental regulation?

States perform essential political social-economic functions, and no other organization appears as a possible competitor to them. They foster the institutions that make internal peace and prosperity possible. In the state of nature, as Kant put it, there is "no mine and thine." States turn possession into property and thus make saving, production, and prosperity possible. The sovereign state with fixed borders has proved to be the best organization for keeping peace and fostering the conditions for economic well being. We do not have to wonder what happens to society and economy when a state begins to fade away. We have all too many examples. A few obvious ones are China in the 1920s and '30s and again in the 1960s and '70s, post-Soviet Russia, and many African states since their independence. The less competent a state, the likelier it is to dissolve into component parts or to be unable to adapt to transnational developments. Challenges at home and abroad test the mettle of states. Some states fail, and other states pass the tests nicely. In modern times, enough states always make it to keep the international system going as a system of states. The challenges vary; states endure. They have proved to be hardy survivors.

Having asked how international conditions affect states, I now reverse the question and ask how states affect the conduct of international political affairs.

The State in International Politics

Economic globalization would mean that the world economy, or at least the globalized portion of it, would be integrated and not merely interdependent. The difference between an interdependent and an integrated world is a qualitative one and not a mere matter of proportionately more trade and a greater and more rapid flow of capital. With integration, the world would look like one big state. Economic markets and economic interests cannot perform the functions of government. Integration requires or presumes a government to protect, direct, and control. Interdependence, in contrast to integration, is "the mere mutualism" of states, as Émile Durkheim put it. It is not only less close than usually thought but also politically less consequential. Interdependence did not produce the world-shaking events of 1989–91. A political event, the failure of one of the world's two great powers, did that. Had the configuration of international politics not fundamentally changed, neither the unification of Germany nor the war against Saddam Hussein would have been possible. The most important events in international politics are explained by differences in the capabilities of states, not by economic forces operating across states or transcending them. Interdependers, and globalizers even more so, argue that the international economic interests of states work against their going to war. True, they do. Yet if one asks whether economic interests or nuclear weapons inhibit war more strongly, the answer obviously is nuclear weapons. European great powers prior to World War I were tightly tied together economically. They nevertheless fought a long and bloody war. The United States and the Soviet Union were not even loosely connected economically. They co-existed peacefully through the four-and-a-half decades of the Cold War. The most important causes of peace, as of war, are found in international-political conditions, including the weaponry available to states. Events following the Cold War dramatically demonstrate the political weakness of economic forces. The integration (not just the interdependence) of the parts of the Soviet Union and of Yugoslavia, with all of their entangling economic interests, did not prevent their disintegration. Governments and people sacrifice welfare and even security to nationalism, ethnicity, and religion.

Political explanations weigh heavily in accounting for international-political events. National *politics*, not international markets, account for many international *economic* developments. A number of students of politics and of economics believe that blocs are becoming more common internationally. Economic interests and market forces do not create blocs; governments do. Without governmental decisions, the Coal and Steel Community, the European Economic Community, and the European Union would not have emerged. The representatives of states negotiate regulations in the European Commission. The Single-Market Act of 1985 provided that some types of directives would require less than a unanimous vote in the Council of Ministers. This political act cleared the way for passage of most of the harmonization standards for Europe (Dumez and Jeunemaître 1996, 229). American governments forged NAFTA; Japan fashioned an East and Southeast Asian producing and trading area. The decisions and acts of a country, or a set of countries arriving at political agreements, shape international political and economic institutions. Governments now intervene much more in international economic matters than they did in the earlier era of interdependence. Before World War I, foreign-ministry officials were famed for their lack of knowledge of, or interest in, economic affairs. Because governments have become much more active in economic affairs at home and abroad, interdependence has become less of an autonomous force in international politics.

The many commentators who exaggerate the closeness of interdependence, and even more so those who write of globalization, think in unit rather than in systemic terms. Many small states import and export large shares of their gross domestic products. States with large GDPs do not. They are little dependent on others, while a number of other states heavily depend on them. The terms of political, economic, and military competition are set by the larger units of the international-political system. Through centuries of multipolarity, with five or so great powers of comparable size competing with one another, the international system was quite closely interdependent. Under bi- and unipolarity the degree of interdependence declined markedly.

States are differentiated from one another not by function but primarily by capability. For two reasons, inequalities across states have greater political impact than inequalities across income groups within states. First, the inequalities of states are larger and have been growing more rapidly. Rich countries have become richer while poor countries have remained poor. Second, in a system without central governance, the influence of the units of greater capability is disproportionately large because there are no effective laws and institutions to direct and constrain them. They are able to work the system to their advantage, as the petrodollar example showed. I argued in 1970 that what counts are states' capacity to adjust to external conditions and their ability to use their economic leverage for political advantage. The United States was then and is still doubly blessed. It remains highly important in the international economy, serving as a principal market for a number of countries and as a major supplier of goods and services, yet its dependence on others is quite low. Precisely because the United States is relatively little dependent on others, it has a wide range of policy choices and the ability both to bring pressure on others and to assist them. The "herd" with its capital may flee from countries when it collectively decides that they are politically and economically unworthy, but some countries abroad, like some firms at home, are so important that they cannot be allowed to fail. National governments and international agencies then come to the rescue. The United States is the country that most often has the ability and the will to step in. The agency that most often acts is the IMF, and most countries think of the IMF as the enforcement arm of the U.S. Treasury (Strange 1996, 192). Thomas Friedman believes that when the "herd" makes its decisions, there is no appeal; but often there is an appeal, and it is for a bail out organized by the United States.

The international economy, like national economies, operates within a set of rules and institutions. Rules and institutions have to be made and sustained. Britain, to a large extent, provided this service prior to World War I; no one did between the wars, and the United States has done so since. More than any other state, the United States makes the rules and maintains the institutions that shape the international political economy.

Economically, the United States is the world's most important country; militarily, it is not only the most important country, it is the decisive one. Thomas Friedman puts the point simply: The world is sustained by "the presence of American power and America's willingness to use that power against those who would threaten the system of globalization. . . . The hidden hand of the market will never work without a hidden fist" (1999, 373). But the hidden fist is in full view. On its military forces, the United States outspends the next six or seven big spenders combined. When force is needed to keep or to restore the peace, either the United States leads the way or the peace is not kept. The Cold War militarized international politics. Relations between the United States and the Soviet Union, and among some other countries as well, came to be defined largely in a single dimension, the military one. As the German sociologist Erich Weede has remarked, "National security decision making in some . . . democracies (most notably in West Germany) is actually penetrated by the United States" (1989, 225). . . .

Many globalizers believe that the world is increasingly ruled by markets. Looking at the state among states leads to a different conclusion. The main difference between international politics now and earlier is not found in the increased interdependence of states but in their growing inequality. With the end of bipolarity, the distribution of capabilities across states has become extremely lopsided. Rather than elevating economic forces and depressing political ones, the inequalities of international politics enhance the political role of one country. Politics, as usual, prevails over economics.[1]

Questions for Review

Why is Waltz sceptical about the argument that globalization has decreased state power? How do you think Thomas Friedman and others would reply to Waltz?

References

Angell, Norman. 1933. *The Great Illusion*. New York: G.P. Putnam's Sons.

Boltho, Andrea. 1996. "Has France Converged on Germany?" In National Diversity and Global Capitalism, ed. Suzanne Berger and Ronald Dore. Ithaca: Cornell University Press.

Boyer, Robert. 1996. "The Convergence Hypothesis Revisited: Globalization But Still the Century of Nations." In *National Diversity and Global Capitalism*, ed. Suzanne Berger and Ronald Dore. Ithaca: Cornell University Press.

Doyle, Michael W. 1997. *Ways of War and Peace: Realism, Liberalism, and Socialism*. New York: W.W. Norton.

Dumez, Hervé, and Alain Jeunemaître. 1996. "The Convergence of Competition Policies in Europe: Internal Dynamics and External Imposition." In *National Diversity and Global Capitalism*, ed. Suzanne Berger and Ronald Dore. Ithaca: Cornell University Press.

Fukuyama, Francis. 1992. *The End of History and the Last Man*. New York: Free Press.

Friedman, Thomas L. 1999. *The Lexus and the Olive Tree*. New York: Farrar, Straus, Giroux.

Hirst, Paul, and Grahame Thompson. 1996. *Globalization in Question: The International Economy and the Possibilities of Governance*. Cambridge, UK: Polity Press.

Keohane, Robert O., and Joseph S. Nye. 1977. *Power and Interdependence: World Politics in Transition*. Boston: Little, Brown.

Kindleberger, Charles P. 1969. *American Business Abroad*. New Haven: Yale University Press.

Krugman, Paul. 1997. "Competitiveness: A Dangerous Obsession." In *The New Shape of World Politics*. New York: W.W. Norton and *Foreign Affairs* 73 (March/April, 1994).

Lawrence, Robert Z. 1997. "Workers and Economists II: Resist the Binge." In The New Shape of Politics. New York: W.W. Norton and *Foreign Affairs* 75 (July/August, 1996).

Mueller, John. 1989. *Retreat from Doomsday: The Obsolescence of Major War*. New York: Basic Books.

McNeill, William H. 1997. "Territorial States Buried Too Soon." *Mershon International Studies Review*.

Ohmae, Kenichi. 1990. *The Borderless World: Power and Strategy in the Interlinked Economy*. New York: HarperBusiness.

Reinecke, Wolfgang H. 1997. "Global Public Policy." *Foreign Affairs* 76 (November/December).

Spiro, David E. 1999. *The Hidden Hand of American Hegemony: Petrodollar Recycling and International Markets*. Ithaca: Cornell University Press.

Strange, Susan. 1996. *The Retreat of the State: The Diffusion of Power in the World Economy*. Cambridge: Cambridge University Press.

Thomson, Janice E., and Stephen D. Krasner. 1989. "Global Transactions and the Consolidation of Sovereignty." In *Global Changes and Theoretical Challenges: Approaches to World Politics for the 1990s*, ed. Ernst-Otto Czempiel and James N. Rosenau. Lexington, MA: Lexington Books.

Thurow, Lester C. 1999. *Building Wealth: The New Rules for Individuals, Companies, and Nations in a Knowledge-Based Economy*. New York: HarperCollins.

Wade, Robert. 1996. "Globalization and Its Limits: Reports of the Death of the National Economy Are Grossly Exaggerated." In *National Diversity and Global Capitalism*, ed. Suzanne Berger and Ronald Dore. Ithaca: Cornell University Press.

Waltz, Kenneth N. 1970. "The Myth of National Interdependence." In *The International Corporation*, ed. Charles P. Kindleberger. Cambridge, MA: MIT Press.

Weede, Erich. 1989. "Collective Goods in an Interdependent World: Authority and Order as Determinants of Peace and Prosperity." In *Global Changes and Theoretical Challenges: Approaches to World Politics for the 1990s*, ed. Ernst-Otto Czempiel and James N. Rosenau. Lexington, MA: Lexington Books.

Weiss, Linda. 1998. *The Myth of the Powerless State: Governing the Economy in a Global Era*. Cambridge, UK: Polity Press.

Woolcock, Stephen. 1996. "Competition among Forms of Corporate Governance in the European Community: The Case of Britain." In *National Diversity and Global Capitalism*, ed. Suzanne Berger and Ronald Dore. Ithaca: Cornell University Press.

Notes

1 Susan Strange, "Finance, Information and Power," *Review of International Studies* 16, no. 3 (July 1990): 259–74.

Good Enough Global Governance

STEWART PATRICK

. . . .The demand for international cooperation has not diminished. In fact, it is greater than ever, thanks to deepening economic interdependence, worsening environmental degradation, proliferating transnational threats, and accelerating technological change. But effective multilateral responses are increasingly occurring outside formal institutions, as frustrated actors turn to more convenient, ad hoc venues. The relative importance of legal treaties and universal bodies such as the UN is declining, as the United States and other states rely more on regional organizations, "minilateral" cooperation among relevant states, codes of conduct, and partnerships with nongovernmental actors. And these trends are only going to continue. The future will see not the renovation or the construction of a glistening new international architecture but rather the continued spread of an unattractive but adaptable multilateral sprawl that delivers a partial measure of international cooperation through a welter of informal arrangements and piecemeal approaches.

"Global governance" is a slippery term. It refers not to world government (which nobody expects or wants anymore) but to something more practical: the collective effort by sovereign states, international organizations, and other non-state actors to address common challenges and seize opportunities that transcend national frontiers. In domestic politics, governance is straightforward. It is provided by actual governments—formal, hierarchical institutions with the authority to establish and enforce binding rules. Governance in the international or transnational sphere, however, is more complex and ambiguous. There is some hierarchy—such as the special powers vested in the permanent members of the UN Security Council—but international politics remain anarchic, with the system composed of independent sovereign units that recognize no higher authority.

Cooperation under such anarchy is certainly possible. National governments often work together to establish common standards of behavior in spheres such as trade or security, embedding norms and rules in international institutions charged with providing global goods or mitigating global bads. But most cooperative multilateral bodies, even those binding under international law, lack real power to enforce compliance with collective decisions. What passes for governance is thus an ungainly patchwork of formal and informal institutions.

Alongside long-standing universal membership bodies, there are various regional institutions, multilateral alliances and security groups, standing consultative mechanisms, self-selecting clubs, ad hoc coalitions, issue-specific arrangements, transnational professional networks, technical standard-setting bodies, global action networks, and more. States are still the dominant actors, but nonstate actors increasingly help shape the global agenda, define new rules, and monitor compliance with international obligations.

The clutter is unsightly and unwieldy, but it has some advantages, as well. No single multilateral body could handle all the world's complex transnational problems, let alone do so effectively or nimbly. And the plurality of institutions and forums is not always dysfunctional, because it can offer states the chance to act relatively deftly and flexibly in responding to new challenges. But regardless of what one thinks of the current global disorder, it is clearly here to stay, and so the challenge is to make it work as well as possible.

Big Game

The centerpiece of contemporary global governance remains the UN, and the core of the UN system remains the Security Council—a standing committee including the most powerful countries in the world. In theory, the Security Council could serve as a venue for coordinating international responses to the world's most important threats to global order. In practice, however, it regularly disappoints—because the five permanent members (the United States, the United Kingdom, France, Russia, and China) often disagree and because their veto power allows the disagreements to block action. This has been true since the UN's inception, of course, but the Security Council's significance has diminished in recent decades as its composition has failed to track shifts in global power.

The Obama administration, like its predecessors, has flirted with the idea of pushing a charter amendment to update the Security Council's membership but has remained wary due to concerns that an enlarged Security Council, with new and more empowered members, might decrease U.S. influence and leverage. But even if Washington were to push hard for change, the status quo would be incredibly hard to overturn. Any expansion plan would require approval by two-thirds of the 193 members of the UN General Assembly, as well as domestic ratification by the five permanent members of the Security Council. And even those countries that favor expansion are deeply divided over which countries should benefit. So in practice, everyone pays lip service to enlargement while allowing the negotiations to drag on endlessly without any result.

This situation seems likely to persist, but at the cost of a deepening crisis of legitimacy, effectiveness, and compliance, as the Security Council's composition diverges ever further from the distribution of global power. Dissatisfied players could conceivably launch an all-out political assault on the institution, but they are much more likely to simply bypass the council, seeking alternative frameworks in which to address their concerns.

The dysfunction of the UN extends well beyond the Security Council, of course. Despite modest management reforms, the UN Secretariat and many UN agencies remain opaque, and their budgeting and operations are hamstrung by outdated personnel policies that encourage cronyism. Within the UN General Assembly, meanwhile, irresponsible actors who play to the galleries often dominate debates, and too many resolutions reflect encrusted regional and ideological blocs that somehow persist long after their sell-by date.

With the Security Council dominated by the old guard, rising powers have begun eyeing possible alternative venues for achieving influence and expressing their concerns. Shifts in global power have always ultimately produced shifts in the institutional superstructure, but what is distinctive today is the simultaneous emergence of multiple power centers with regional and potentially global aspirations. As the United States courts relative decline and Europe and Japan stagnate, China, India, Brazil, Russia, Turkey, Indonesia, and Others are flexing their muscles, expanding their regional influence and insisting on greater voice within multilateral institutions.

Despite these geopolitical shifts, however, no coherent alternative to today's Western order has emerged. This is true even among the much-hyped BRICS: Brazil, Russia, India, China, and, since 2012, South Africa. These countries have always lacked a common vision, but at least initially, they shared a confidence born of economic dynamism and resentment over a global economy they perceived as stacked to favor the West. In recent years, the BRICS have staked out a few common positions. They all embrace traditional conceptions of state sovereignty and resist heavy-handed Western intervention. Their summit communiqués condemn the dollar's privileges as the world's main reserve currency and insist on accelerated governance reforms within the international financial institutions. The BRICS have also agreed to create a full-fledged BRICS bank to provide development aid to countries and for issues the bloc defines as priorities, without the conditionality imposed by Western donors.

Some observers anticipate the BRICS' emerging as an independent caucus and center of gravity within the G-20, rivaling the G-7 nations. But any such bifurcation of the world order between developed and major developing powers seems a distant prospect, for as much divides the BRICS as binds them. China and Russia have no interest in seeing any of their putative partners join them as permanent Security Council members; China and India are emerging strategic competitors with frontier disputes and divergent maritime interests; and China and Russia have their own tensions along the Siberian border. Differences in their internal regimes may also constrain their collaboration. India, Brazil, and South Africa—boisterous multiparty democracies all—have formed a coalition of their own (the India–Brazil–South Africa Dialogue Forum, or IBSA), as have China and Russia (the Shanghai Cooperation Organization). Conflicting economic interests also complicate intra-BRICS relations, something that might increase as the countries' growth slows. . . .

Welcome to the G-X World

But what really marks the contemporary era is not the absence of multilateralism but its astonishing diversity. Collective action is no longer focused solely, or even primarily, on the UN and other universal, treaty-based institutions, nor even on a single apex forum such as the G-20. Rather, governments have taken to operating in many venues simultaneously, participating in a bewildering array of issue-specific networks and partnerships whose membership varies based on situational interests, shared values, and relevant capabilities.

A hallmark of this "G-X" world is the temporary coalition of strange bedfellows. Consider the multinational antipiracy armada that has emerged in the Indian Ocean. This loosely coordinated flotilla involves naval vessels from not only the United States and its NATO allies but also China, India, Indonesia, Iran, Japan, Malaysia, Russia, Saudi Arabia, South Korea, and Yemen. These countries might disagree on many issues, but they have found common cause in securing sea-lanes off the African coast. . . .

In global governance, as elsewhere, necessity is the mother of invention, and the global credit crisis that struck with full force in 2008 led to the rise to prominence of a relatively new international grouping, the G-20. Facing the potential meltdown of the international financial system, leaders of the world's major economies—both developed and developing—shared an overriding interest in avoiding a second Great Depression. Stuck in the same lifeboat, they assented to a slew of institutional innovations, including elevating the G-20 finance ministers' group to the leaders' level, creating an exclusive global crisis-response committee.

The G-20 quickly racked up some notable achievements. It injected unprecedented liquidity into the world economy through coordinated national actions, including some $5 trillion in stimulus at the London summit of April 2009. It created the Financial Stability Board, charged with developing new regulatory standards for systemically important financial institutions, and insisted on new bank capital account requirements under the Basel III agreement. It revitalized and augmented the coffers of the once-moribund International Monetary Fund and negotiated governance reforms within the World Bank and the IMF to give greater voice to emerging economies. And its members adopted "standstill" provisions to avoid a recurrence of the ruinous tit-for-tat trade protectionism of the 1930s. . . .

Governance in Pieces

For much of the past two decades, UN mega-conferences dominated multilateral diplomacy. But when it comes to multilateralism, bigger is rarely better, and the era of the mega-conference is ending as major powers recognize the futility of negotiating comprehensive international agreements among 193 UN member states, in the full glare of the media and alongside tens of thousands of activists, interest groups, and hangers-on. Countries will continue to assemble for annual confabs, such as the Conference of the Parties to the UN Framework Convention on Climate Change (UNFCCC), in the Sisyphean quest to secure "binding" commitments from developed and developing countries. But that circus will increasingly become a sideshow, as the action shifts to less formal settings and narrower groupings of the relevant and capable. Already, the 17 largest greenhouse gas emitters have created the Major Economies Forum on Energy and Climate, seeking breakthroughs outside the lumbering UNFCCC. To date, the forum has underdelivered. But more tangible progress has occurred through parallel national efforts, as states pledge to undertake a menu of domestic actions, which they subsequently submit to the forum for collective review.

There is a more general lesson here. Faced with fiendishly complex issues, such as climate change, transnational networks of government officials now seek incremental progress by disaggregating those issues into manageable chunks and agreeing to coordinate action on specific agenda items. Call it "global governance in pieces." For climate change, this means abandoning the quest for an elusive soup-to-nuts agreement to mitigate and adapt to global warming. Instead, negotiators pursue separate initiatives, such as phasing out wasteful fossil fuel subsidies, launching minilateral clean technology partnerships, and expanding the UN Collaborative Program on Reducing Emissions from Deforestation and Forest Degradation in Developing Countries, among other worthwhile schemes. The result is not a unitary international regime grounded in a single institution or treaty but a cluster of complementary activities that political scientists call a "regime complex."

Something similar is happening in global health, where the once-premier World Health Organization now shares policy space and a division of labor with other major organizations, such as the World Bank; specialized UN agencies, such as UNAIDS; public-private partnerships, such as the GAVI Alliance (formerly called the Global Alliance for Vaccines and Immunization); philanthropic organizations, such as the Bill and Melinda Gates Foundation; consultative bodies, such as the eight-nation (plus the EU) Global Health Security Initiative; and multi-stakeholder bodies, such as the Global Fund to Fight AIDS, Tuberculosis and Malaria. The upshot is a disaggregated system of global health governance.

Sometimes, the piecemeal approach maybe able to achieve more than its stagnant universalist alternative. Given the failure of the WTO's Doha Round, for example, the United States and other nations have turned to preferential trade agreements in order to spur further liberalization of commerce. Some are bilateral, such as the U.S.–South Korean pact. But others involve multiple countries. These include two initiatives that constitute the centerpiece of Obama's second-term trade agenda: the Trans-Pacific Partnership and the Transatlantic Trade and Investment Partnership. The administration describes each as a steppingstone toward global liberalization. And yet future WTO negotiations will likely take a disaggregated form, as subsets of WTO members move forward on more manageable specific issues (such as public procurement or investment) while avoiding those lightning-rod topics (such as trade in agriculture) that have repeatedly stymied comprehensive trade negotiations.

The Rise of the Regions

Ad hoc coalitions and minilateral networks are not the only global governance innovations worthy of mention. Regional organizations are also giving universal membership bodies a run for their money, raising the question of how to make sure they harmonize and complement the UN system rather than undermine it.

This dilemma is older than often assumed. In the months leading up to the San Francisco conference of 1945, at which the UN was established, U.S. and British postwar planners debated whether regional bodies ought to be given formal, even independent, standing within the UN (something British Prime Minister Winston Churchill, among others, had proposed). Most U.S. negotiators were adamantly opposed, fearing that an overtly regional thrust would detract from the UN's coherence or even fracture it into rival blocs. In the end, the Americans' universal vision prevailed. Still, Chapter 8 of the UN Charter acknowledges a legitimate subordinate role for regional organizations.

What few in San Francisco could have envisioned was the dramatic proliferation and increasingly sophisticated capabilities of regional and subregional arrangements, which today number in the hundreds. These bodies play an ever more important role in managing cross-border challenges, facilitating trade, and promoting regional security, often in partnership with the UN and other universal organizations. . . .

Given how overstretched the UN and other global bodies can become, rising regionalism has distinct benefits. Regional bodies are often more familiar with the underlying sources of local conflicts, and they may be more sensitive to and invested in potential solutions. But they are in no position to replace the UN entirely. To begin with, regional organizations vary widely in their aspirations, mandates, capabilities, and activities. They are also vulnerable to the same collective-action problems that bedevil the UN. Their members are often tempted to adopt bland, lowest-common-denominator positions or to try to free-ride on the contributions of others. Local hegemons may seek to hijack them for narrow purposes. The ambitions of regional organizations can also outstrip their ability to deliver. Although the African Union has created the Peace and Security Council, for instance, the organization's capacity to conduct peacekeeping operations remains hamstrung by institutional, professional, technical, material, and logistical shortcomings. Accordingly, burden sharing between the UN and regional organizations can easily devolve into burden shifting, as the world invests unprepared regional bodies with unrealistic expectations.

Governing the Contested Commons

If one major problem in contemporary global governance is the floundering of existing institutions when dealing with traditional challenges, another and equally worrisome problem is the lack of any serious institutional mechanism for dealing with untraditional challenges. The gap between the demand for and the supply of global governance is greatest when it comes to the global commons, those spaces no nation controls but on which all rely for security and prosperity. The most important of these are the maritime, outer space, and cyberspace domains, which carry the flows of goods, data, capital, people, and ideas on which globalization rests. Ensuring free and unencumbered access to these realms is therefore a core interest not only of the United States but of most other nations as well.

For almost seven decades, the United States has provided security for the global commons and, in so doing, has bolstered world order. Supremacy at sea—and, more recently, in outer space and online—has also conferred strategic advantages on the United States, allowing it to project power globally. But as the commons become crowded and cutthroat, that supremacy is fading. Rising powers, as well as nonstate actors from corporations to criminals, are challenging long-standing behavioral norms and deploying asymmetric capabilities to undercut U.S. advantages. Preserving the openness, stability, and resilience of the global commons will require the United States to forge agreement among like-minded nations, rising powers, and private stakeholders on new rules of the road.

From China to Iran, for example, rising powers are seeking blue-water capabilities or employing asymmetric strategies to deny the United States and other countries access to their regional waters, jeopardizing the freedom of the seas. The greatest flashpoint today is in the South China Sea, through which more than $5 trillion worth of commerce passes each year. There, China is locked in dangerous sovereignty disputes with Brunei, Malaysia, the Philippines, Taiwan, and Vietnam over some 1.3 million square miles of ocean, the contested islands therein, and the exploitation of undersea oil and gas reserves. Beijing's assertiveness poses grave risks for regional stability. Most dangerous would be a direct U.S.-Chinese naval clash, perhaps in response to U.S. freedom-of-navigation exercises in China's littoral waters or the reckless actions of a U.S. treaty ally or strategic partner.

Geopolitical and economic competition has also heated up in the warming Arctic, as nations wrangle over rights to extended continental shelves, new sea routes over Asia and North America, and the exploitation of fossil fuel and mineral deposits. . . . Some experts contend that the Arctic needs a comprehensive multilateral treaty to reconcile competing sovereignty claims, handle navigational issues, facilitate collective energy development, manage fisheries, and address environmental concerns. A more productive strategy would be to bolster the role of the Arctic Council, composed of the five Arctic nations plus Finland, Iceland, Sweden, and several indigenous peoples' organizations. Although this forum has historically avoided contentious boundary and legal disputes, it could help codify guidelines on oil and gas development, sponsor collaborative mapping of the continental shelf, create a regional monitoring network, and modernize systems for navigation, traffic management, and environmental protection.

The single most important step the United States could take to strengthen ocean governance, including in the Arctic, would be to finally accede to the UN Convention on the Law of the Sea, as recommended by the last four U.S. presidents, U.S. military leaders, industry, and environmental groups. Beyond defining states' rights and responsibilities in territorial seas and exclusive economic zones and clarifying the rules for transit through international straits, UNCLOS provides a forum for dispute resolution on ocean-related issues, including claims to extended continental shelves. As a nonmember, the United States forfeits its chance to participate in the last great partitioning of sovereign space on earth, which would grant it jurisdiction over vast areas along its Arctic, Atlantic, Gulf, and Pacific coasts. Nor can it serve on the International Seabed Authority, where it would enjoy a permanent seat with an effective veto. By remaining apart, the United States not only undercuts its national interests but also undermines its perceived commitment to a rule-based international order and emboldens revisionist regional powers. Both China in East Asia and Russia in the Arctic have taken advantage of the United States' absence to advance outrageous sovereignty claims. . . .

The Final Frontier

The international rules governing the uses of outer space have also become outdated, as that domain becomes, in the words of former U.S. Deputy Secretary of Defense William Lynn, more "congested, contested, and competitive." As nations and private corporations vie for scarce orbital slots for their satellites and for slices of a finite radio-frequency spectrum, the number of actors operating in space has skyrocketed. Already, nine countries and the European Space Agency have orbital launch capabilities, and nearly 60 nations or government consortiums regulate civil, commercial, and military satellites. The proliferation of vehicles and space debris—including more than 22,000 orbiting objects larger than a softball—has increased the risk of catastrophic collisions. More worrisome, geopolitical competition among spacefaring nations, both established and emerging, raises the specter of an arms race in space.

Yet so far at least, there is little global consensus on what kind of regulatory regime would best ensure the stability and sustainable use of earth's final frontier. The basic convention governing national conduct in outer space remains the Outer Space Treaty of 1967. Although it establishes useful principles (such as a prohibition on sovereignty claims in space), that treaty lacks a dispute-resolution mechanism, is silent on space debris and how to avoid collisions, and inadequately addresses interference with the space assets of other countries.

To address these shortcomings, various parties have suggested options ranging from a binding multilateral treaty banning space weapons to an informal agreement on standards of behavior. Given the problems with a treaty-based approach, . . . a nonbinding international code of conduct for outer space activities that . . . would establish broad principles and parameters for responsible behavior in space [is needed]. Such a voluntary code would carry a lesser obligation than a legally binding multilateral treaty, but it offers the best chance to establish new behavioral norms in the short term. Washington should also consider sponsoring a standing minilateral consultative forum of spacefaring nations.

Lost in Cyberspace

Cyberspace differs from the oceans or outer space in that its physical infrastructure is located primarily in sovereign states and in private hands—creating obvious risks of interference by parties pursuing their own interests. Since the dawn of the digital age, the United States has been the premier champion of an open, decentralized, and secure cyberspace that remains largely private. This posture is consistent with the long-standing U.S. belief that the free flow of information and ideas is a core component of a free, just, and open world and an essential bulwark against authoritarianism. But this vision of global governance in cyberspace is now under threat from three directions.

The first is the demand by many developing and authoritarian countries that regulation of the Internet be transferred from ICANN, the Internet Corporation for Assigned Names and Numbers—an independent, non-profit corporation based in Los Angeles, loosely supervised by the U.S. Department of Commerce—to the UN's ITU (International Telecommunication Union). The second is a growing epidemic of cybercrime, consisting mostly of attempts to steal proprietary information from private-sector actors. Thanks to sophisticated computer viruses, worms, and botnets, what might be termed "cyber public health" has deteriorated dramatically. And there is no cyberspace equivalent to the World Health Organization for dealing with such dangers.

The third major flashpoint is the growing specter of cyberwar among sovereign states. Dozens of nations have begun to develop doctrines and capabilities for conducting so-called information operations, not only to infiltrate but if necessary to disrupt and destroy the critical digital infrastructure (both military and civilian) of their adversaries. Yet there is no broadly accepted definition of a cyberattack, much less consensus on the range of permissible responses; the normative and legal framework governing cyberwar has lagged behind cyberweapons' development and use. Traditional forms of deterrence and retaliation are also complicated, given the difficulty of attributing attacks to particular perpetrators.

No single UN treaty could simultaneously regulate cyberwarfare, counter cybercrime, and protect the civil liberties of Internet users. Liberal and authoritarian regimes disagree on the definition of "cyber-security" and how to achieve it, with the latter generally seeing the free exchange of ideas and information not as a core value but as a potential threat to their stability, and there are various practical hurdles to including cyberweapons in traditional arms control and nonproliferation negotiations. So a piecemeal approach to governance in cyberspace seems more realistic. States will need to negotiate norms of responsibility for cyberattacks and criteria for retaliation. They should also develop transparency and confidence-building measures and agree to preserve humanitarian fundamentals in the event of a cyberwar, avoiding attacks on "root" servers, which constitute the backbone of the Internet, and prohibiting all denial-of-service attacks, which can cripple the Internet infrastructure of the targeted countries. . . .

Technology and the Frontiers of Global Governance

The history of global governance is the story of adaptation to new technologies. As breakthroughs have been made, sovereign governments have sought common standards and rules to facilitate cooperation and mitigate conflict. For example, we now take for granted the world's division into 24 separate time zones, with Greenwich Mean Time as the base line, but in the middle of the nineteenth century, the United States alone had 144 local time zones. It was only the need to standardize train and shipping schedules in the late nineteenth century that convinced major countries to synchronize their time.

Today, the furious pace of technological change risks leaving global governance in the dust. The growing gap between what technological advances permit and what the international system is prepared to regulate can be seen in multiple areas, from drones and synthetic biology to nanotechnology and geoengineering.

When it comes to drones, the United States has struggled mightily to develop its own legal rationale for targeted assassinations. Initial foreign objections to U.S. drone strikes were concentrated within the target countries, but increasingly, their use has been challenged both domestically and internationally, and the rapid spread of drone technology to both state and nonstate actors makes it imperative to create clear rules for their use—and soon.

Rapid advances in biotechnology could pose even greater long-term threats. Scientists today are in a position to create new biological systems by manipulating genetic material. Such "synthetic biology" has tremendous therapeutic and public health potential but could also cause great harm, with rogue states or rogue scientists fabricating deadly pathogens or other bioweapons. At present, only an incomplete patchwork of regulations exist to prevent such risks. Nor are there any international regulatory arrangements to govern research on and uses of nanotechnology: the process of manipulating materials at the atomic or molecular level. Where regulation exists, it is performed primarily on a national basis; in the United States, for example, this function is carried out jointly by the Environmental Protection Agency, the Food and Drug Administration, and the National Institute of Standards and Technology. To make things even more complicated, most research and investment in this area is currently carried out by the private sector, which has little incentive to consider potential threats to public safety.

Finally, the threat of uncoordinated efforts at geoengineering—the attempt to slow or reverse global warming through large-scale tinkering with the planet's climate system—also demands regulation. Such schemes include seeding the world's oceans with iron filings (as one freelancing U.S. scientist attempted in 2012), deflecting solar radiation through a system of space-based mirrors, and preventing the release of methane held in tundras and the ocean. Long dismissed as fanciful, such attempts to reengineer the earth's atmosphere are suddenly being taken seriously by at least some mainstream experts. As warming proceeds, countries and private actors will be increasingly tempted to take matters into their own hands. Only proper regulation has a chance of ensuring that these uncoordinated efforts do not go badly awry, with potentially disastrous consequences.

"Good Enough" Global Governance

As all these examples highlight, demand for effective global governance continues to outstrip supply, and the gap is growing. Absent dramatic crises, multilateral institutions have been painfully slow and lumbering in their response. So even as they try to revitalize the existing international order, diplomats and other interested parties need to turn to other, complementary frameworks for collective action, including ad hoc coalitions of the willing, regional and subregional institutions, public-private arrangements, and informal codes of conduct. The resulting jerry-rigged structure for global cooperation will not be aesthetically pleasing, but it might at least get some useful things done. . . .

Question for Review

Global governance through a central global government is not in the cards for the foreseeable future, but the need for states to cooperate with one another is pressing. Are you persuaded that "good enough global governance" outlined by Stewart is up to the task?

The Future of the Liberal World Order

G. JOHN IKENBERRY

Internationalism after America

There is no longer any question: wealth and power are moving from the North and the West to the East and the South, and the old order dominated by the United States and Europe is giving way to one increasingly shared with non-Western rising states. But if the great wheel of power is turning, what kind of global political order will emerge in the aftermath?

Some anxious observers argue that the world will not just look less American—it will also look less liberal. Not only is the United States' preeminence passing away, they say, but so, too, is the open and rule-based international order that the country has championed since the 1940s. In this view, newly powerful states are beginning to advance their own ideas and agendas for global order, and a weakened United States will find it harder to defend the old system. The hallmarks of liberal internationalism—openness and rule-based relations enshrined in institutions such as the United Nations and norms such as multilateralism—could give way to a more contested and fragmented system of blocs, spheres of influence, mercantilist networks, and regional rivalries.

The fact that today's rising states are mostly large non-Western developing countries gives force to this narrative. The old liberal international order was designed and built in the West. Brazil, China, India, and other fast-emerging states have a different set of cultural, political, and economic experiences, and they see the world through their anti-imperial and anticolonial pasts. Still grappling with basic problems of development, they do not share the concerns of the advanced capitalist societies. The recent global economic slowdown has also bolstered this narrative of liberal international decline. Beginning in the United States, the crisis has tarnished the American model of liberal capitalism and raised new doubts about the ability of the United States to act as the global economic leader.

For all these reasons, many observers have concluded that world politics is experiencing not just a changing of the guard but also a transition in the ideas and principles that underlie the global order. The journalist Gideon Rachman, for example, says that a cluster of liberal internationalist ideas—such as faith in democratization, confidence in free markets, and the acceptability of U.S. military power—are all being called into question. According to this worldview, the future of international order will be shaped above all by China, which will use its growing power and wealth to push world politics in an illiberal direc- tion. Pointing out that China and other non-Western states have weathered the recent financial crisis better than their Western counterparts, pessimists argue that an authoritarian capitalist alternative to Western neoliberal ideas has already emerged. According to the scholar Stefan Halper, emerging-market states "are learning to combine market economics with traditional autocratic or semiau- tocratic politics in a process that signals an intellectual rejection of the Western economic model."

But this panicked narrative misses a deeper reality: although the United States' position in the global system is changing, the liberal international order is alive and well. The struggle over international order today is not about funda- mental principles. China and other emerging great powers do not want to contest the basic rules and principles of the liberal international order; they wish to gain more authority and leadership within it.

Indeed, today's power transition represents not the defeat of the liberal order but its ultimate ascendance. Brazil, China, and India have all become more prosperous and capable by operating inside the existing international order— benefiting from its rules, practices, and institutions, including the World Trade Organization (WTO) and the newly organized G-20. Their economic success and growing influence are tied to the liberal internationalist organization of world politics, and they have deep interests in preserving that system.

In the meantime, alternatives to an open and rule-based order have yet to crystallize. Even though the last decade has brought remarkable upheavals in the global system—the emergence of new powers, bitter disputes among West- ern allies over the United States' unipolar ambitions, and a global financial crisis and recession—the liberal international order has no competitors. On the con- trary, the rise of non-Western powers and the growth of economic and security interdependence are creating new constituencies for it.

To be sure, as wealth and power become less concentrated in the United States' hands, the country will be less able to shape world politics. But the underlying foundations of the liberal international order will survive and thrive. Indeed. now may be the best time for the United States and its democratic partners to update the liberal order for a new era, ensuring that it continues to provide the benefits of security and prosperity that it has provided since the middle of the twentieth century.

The Liberal Ascendancy

China and the other emerging powers do not face simply an American-led order or a Western system. They face a broader international order that is the product of centuries of struggle and innovation. It is highly developed, expansive, integrated, institutionalized, and deeply rooted in the societies and economies of both advanced capitalist states and developing states. And over the last half century, this order has been unusually capable of assimilating rising powers and reconciling political and cultural diversity.

Today's international order is the product of two order-building projects that began centuries ago. One is the creation and expansion of the modern state system, a project dating back to the Peace of Westphalia in 1648. In the years since then, the project has promulgated rules and principles associated with state sovereignty and norms of great-power conduct. The other project is the construction of the liberal order, which over the last two centuries was led by the United Kingdom and the United States and which in the twentieth century was aided by the rise of liberal democratic states. The two projects have worked together. The Westphalian project has focused on solving the "realist" problems of creating stable and cooperative interstate relations under conditions of anarchy, and the liberal-order-building project has been possible only when relations between the great powers have been stabilized. The "problems of Hobbes," that is, anarchy and power insecurities, have had to be solved in order to take advantage of the "opportunities of Locke," that is, the construction of open and rule-based relations.

At the heart of the Westphalian project is the notion of state sovereignty and great-power relations. The original principles of the Westphalian system—sovereignty, territorial integrity, and nonintervention—reflected an emerging consensus that states were the rightful political units for the establishment of legitimate rule. Founded in western Europe, the Westphalian system has expanded outward to encompass the entire globe. New norms and principles—such as self-determination and mutual recognition among sovereign states—have evolved within it, further reinforcing the primacy of states and state authority. Under the banners of sovereignty and self-determination, political movements for decolonization and independence were set in motion in the non-Western developing world, coming to fruition in the decades after World War II. Westphalian norms have been violated and ignored, but they have, nonetheless, been the most salient and agreed-on parts of the international order.

A succession of postwar settlements—Vienna in 1815, Versailles in 1919, Yalta and Potsdam in 1945, and the U.S., Soviet, and European negotiations that ended the Cold War and reunified Germany in the early 1990s—allowed the great powers to update the principles and practices of their relations. Through war and settlement, the great powers learned how to operate within a multipolar balance-of-power system. Over time, the order has remained a decentralized system in which major states compete and balance against one another. But it has also evolved. The great powers have developed principles and practices of restraint and accommodation that have served their interests. The Congress of Vienna in 1815, where post-Napoleonic France was returned to the great-power club and a congress system was established to manage conflicts, and the UN Security Council today, which has provided a site for great-power consultations, are emblematic of these efforts to create rules and mechanisms that reinforce restraint and accommodation.

The project of constructing a liberal order built on this evolving system of Westphalian relations. In the nineteenth century, liberal internationalism was manifest in the United Kingdom's championing of free trade and the freedom of the seas, but it was limited and coexisted with imperialism and colonialism. In the twentieth century, the United States advanced the liberal order in several phases. After World War I, President Woodrow Wilson and other liberals pushed for an international order organized around a global collective-security body, the League of Nations, in which states would act together to uphold a system of territorial peace. Open trade, national self-determination, and a belief in progressive global change also undergirded the Wilsonian worldview—a "one world" vision of nation-states that would trade and interact in a multilateral system of laws. But in the interwar period of closed economic systems and imperial blocs, this experiment in liberal order collapsed.

After World War II, President Franklin Roosevelt's administration tried to construct a liberal order again, embracing a vision of an open trading system and a global organization in which the great powers would cooperate to keep the peace—the United Nations. Drawing lessons from Wilson's failure and incorporating ideas from the New Deal, American architects of the postwar order also advanced more ambitious ideas about economic and political cooperation, which were embodied in the Bretton Woods institutions. This vision was originally global in spirit and scope, but it evolved into a more American-led and Western-centered system as a result of the weakness of postwar Europe and rising tensions with the Soviet Union. As the Cold War unfolded, the United States took command of the system, adopting new commitments and functional roles in both security and economics. Its own economic and political system became, in effect, the central component of the larger liberal hegemonic order.

Another development of liberal internationalism was quietly launched after World War II, although it took root more slowly and competed with aspects of the Westphalian system. This was the elaboration of the universal rights of man, enshrined in the UN and its Universal Declaration of Human Rights. A steady stream of conventions and treaties followed that together constitute an extraordinary vision of rights, individuals, sovereignty, and global order. In the decades since the end of the Cold War, notions of "the responsibility to protect" have given the international community legal rights and obligations to intervene in the affairs of sovereign states.

Seen in this light, the modern international order is not really American or Western—even if, for historical reasons, it initially appeared that way. It is something much wider. In the decades after World War II, the United States stepped forward as the hegemonic leader, taking on the privileges and responsibilities of organizing and running the system. It presided over a far-flung international order organized around multilateral institutions, alliances, special relationships, and client states—a hierarchical order with liberal characteristics.

But now, as this hegemonic organization of the liberal international order starts to change, the hierarchical aspects are fading while the liberal aspects persist. So even as China and other rising states try to contest U.S. leadership—and there is indeed a struggle over the rights, privileges, and responsibilities of the leading states within the system—the deeper international order remains intact. Rising powers are finding incentives and opportunities to engage and integrate into this order, doing so to advance their own interests. For these states, the road to modernity runs through—not away from—the existing international order.

Joining the Club

The liberal international order is not just a collection of liberal democratic states but an international mutual-aid society—a sort of global political club that provides members with tools for economic and political advancement. Participants in the order gain trading opportunities, dispute-resolution mechanisms, frameworks for collective action, regulatory agreements, allied security guarantees, and resources in times of crisis. And just as there are a variety of reasons why rising states will embrace the liberal international order, there are powerful obstacles to opponents who would seek to overturn it.

To begin with, rising states have deep interests in an open and rule-based system. Openness gives them access to other societies—for trade, investment, and knowledge sharing. Without the unrestricted investment from the United States and Europe of the past several decades, for instance, China and the other rising states would be on a much slower developmental path. As these countries grow, they will encounter protectionist and discriminatory reactions from slower-growing countries threatened with the loss of jobs and markets. As a result, the rising states will find the rules and institutions that uphold nondiscrimination and equal access to be critical. The World Trade Organization—the most formal and developed institution of the liberal international order—enshrines these rules and norms, and rising states have been eager to join the WTO and gain the rights and protections it affords. China is already deeply enmeshed in the global trading system, with a remarkable 40 percent of its GNP composed of exports—25 percent of which go to the United States.

China could be drawn further into the liberal order through its desire to have the yuan become an international currency rivaling the U.S. dollar. Aside from conferring prestige, this feat could also stabilize China's exchange rate and grant Chinese leaders autonomy in setting macroeconomic policy. But if China wants to make the yuan a global currency, it will need to loosen its currency controls and strengthen its domestic financial rules and institutions. As Barry Eichengreen and other economic historians have noted, the U.S. dollar assumed its international role after World War II not only because the U.S. economy was large but also because the United States had highly developed financial markets and domestic institutions—economic and political—that were stable, open, and grounded in the rule of law. China will feel pressures to establish these same institutional preconditions if it wants the benefits of a global currency.

Internationalist-oriented elites in Brazil, China, India, and elsewhere are growing in influence within their societies, creating an expanding global constituency for an open and rule-based international order. These elites were not party to the grand bargains that lay behind the founding of the liberal order in the early postwar decades, and they are seeking to renegotiate their countries' positions within the system. But they are nonetheless embracing the rules and institutions of the old order. They want the protections and rights that come from the international order's Westphalian defense of sovereignty. They care about great-power authority. They want the protections and rights relating to trade and investment. And they want to use the rules and institutions of liberal internationalism as platforms to project their influence and acquire legitimacy at home and abroad. The UN Security Council, the G-20, the governing bodies of the Bretton Woods institutions—these are all stages on which rising non-Western states can acquire great-power authority and exercise global leadership.

No Other Order

Meanwhile, there is no competing global organizing logic to liberal internationalism. An alternative, illiberal order—a "Beijing model"—would presumably be organized around exclusive blocs, spheres of influence, and mercantilist networks. It would be less open and rule-based, and it would be dominated by an array of state-to-state ties. But on a global scale, such a system would not advance the interests of any of the major states, including China. The Beijing model only works when one or a few states opportunistically exploit an open system of markets. But if everyone does, it is no longer an open system but a fragmented, mercantilist, and protectionist complex—and everyone suffers.

It is possible that China could nonetheless move in this direction. This is a future in which China is not a full-blown illiberal hegemon that reorganizes the global rules and institutions. It is simply a spoiler. It attempts to operate both inside and outside the liberal international order. In this case, China would be successful enough with its authoritarian model of development to resist the pressures to liberalize and democratize. But if the rest of the world does not gravitate toward this model, China will find itself subjected to pressure to play by the rules. This dynamic was on display in February 2011, when Brazilian President Dilma Rousseff joined U.S. Treasury Secretary Timothy Geithner in expressing concern over China's currency policy. China can free-ride on the liberal international order, but it will pay the costs of doing so—and it will still not be able to impose its illiberal vision on the world.

In the background, meanwhile, democracy and the rule of law are still the hallmarks of modernity and the global standard for legitimate governance. Although it is true that the spread of democracy has stalled in recent years and that authoritarian China has performed well in the recent economic crisis, there is little evidence that authoritarian states can become truly advanced societies without moving in a liberal democratic direction. The legitimacy of one-party rule within China rests more on the state's ability to deliver economic growth and full employment than on authoritarian—let alone communist—political principles. Kishore Mahbubani, a Singaporean intellectual who has championed China's rise, admits that "China cannot succeed in its goal of becoming a modern developed society until it can take the leap and allow the Chinese people to choose their own rulers." No one knows how far or fast democratic reforms will unfold in China, but a growing middle class, business elites, and human rights groups will exert pressure for them. The Chinese government certainly appears to worry about the long-term preservation of one-party rule, and in the wake of the ongoing revolts against Arab authoritarian regimes, it has tried harder to prevent student gatherings and control foreign journalists.

Outside China, democracy has become a near-universal ideal. As the economist Amartya Sen has noted, "While democracy is not yet universally practiced, nor indeed universally accepted, in the general climate of world opinion democratic governance has achieved the status of being taken to be generally right." All the leading institutions of the global system enshrine democracy as the proper and just form of governance—and no competing political ideals even lurk on the sidelines.

The recent global economic downturn was the first great postwar economic upheaval that emerged from the United States, raising doubts about an American-led world economy and Washington's particular brand of economics. The doctrines of neoliberalism and market fundamentalism have been discredited, particularly among the emerging economies. But liberal internationalism is not the same as neoliberalism or market fundamentalism. The liberal internationalism that the United States articulated in the 1940s entailed a more holistic set of ideas about markets, openness, and social stability. It was an attempt to construct an open world economy and reconcile it with social welfare and employment stability. Sustained domestic support for openness, postwar leaders knew, would be possible only if countries also established social protections and regulations that safeguarded economic stability.

Indeed, the notions of national security and economic security emerged together in the 1940s, reflecting New Deal and World War II thinking about how liberal democracies would be rendered safe and stable. The Atlantic Charter, announced by Roosevelt and Winston Churchill in 1941, and the Bretton Woods agreements of 1944 were early efforts to articulate a vision of economic openness and social stability. The United States would do well to try to reach back and rearticulate this view. The world is not rejecting openness and markets; it is asking for a more expansive notion of stability and economic security.

Reason for Reassurance

Rising powers will discover another reason to embrace the existing global rules and institutions: doing so will reassure their neighbors as they grow more powerful. A stronger China will make neighboring states potentially less secure, especially if it acts aggressively and exhibits revisionist ambitions. Since this will trigger a balancing backlash, Beijing has incentives to signal restraint. It will find ways to do so by participating in various regional and global institutions. If China hopes to convince its neighbors that it has embarked on a "peaceful rise," it will need to become more integrated into the international order. . . .

As China's economic and military power grow, its neighbors will only become more worried about Chinese aggressiveness, and so Beijing will have reason to allay their fears. Of course, it might be that some elites in China are not interested in practicing restraint. But to the extent that China is interested in doing so, it will find itself needing to signal peaceful intentions—redoubling its participation in existing institutions, such as the ASEAN Regional Forum and the East Asia Summit, or working with the other great powers in the region to build new ones. This is, of course, precisely what the United States did in the decades after World War II. The country operated within layers of regional and global economic, political, and security institutions and constructed new ones—thereby making itself more predictable and approachable and reducing the incentives for other states to undermine it by building countervailing coalitions.

More generally, given the emerging problems of the twenty-first century, there will be growing incentives among all the great powers to embrace an open, rule-based international system. In a world of rising economic and security interdependence, the costs of not following multilateral rules and not forging cooperative ties go up. As the global economic system becomes more interdependent, all states—even large, powerful ones—will find it harder to ensure prosperity on their own.

Growing interdependence in the realm of security is also creating a demand for multilateral rules and institutions. Both the established and the rising great powers are threatened less by mass armies marching across borders than by transnational dangers. such as terrorism, climate change, and pandemic disease. What goes on in one country—radicalism, carbon emissions, or public health failures—can increasingly harm another country.

Intensifying economic and security interdependence are giving the United States and other powerful countries reason to seek new and more extensive forms of multilateral cooperation. Even now, as the United States engages China and other rising states, the agenda includes expanded cooperation in areas such as clean energy, environmental protection, nonproliferation, and global economic governance. The old and rising powers may disagree on how exactly this cooperation should proceed, but they all have reasons to avoid a breakdown in the multilateral order itself. So they will increasingly experiment with new and more extensive forms of liberal internationalism.

Time for Renewal

Pronouncements of American decline miss the real transformation under way today. What is occurring is not American decline but a dynamic process in which other states are catching up and growing more connected. In an open and rule-based international order, this is what happens. If the architects of the postwar liberal order were alive to see today's system, they would think that their vision had succeeded beyond their wildest dreams. Markets and democracy have spread. Societies outside the West are trading and growing. The United States has more alliance partners today than it did during the Cold War. Rival hegemonic states with revisionist and illiberal agendas have been pushed off the global stage. It is difficult to read these world-historical developments as a story of American decline and liberal unraveling.

In a way, however, the liberal international order has sown the seeds of its own discontent, since, paradoxically, the challenges facing it now—the rise of non-Western states and new transnational threats—are artifacts of its success. But the solutions to these problems—integrating rising powers and tackling problems cooperatively—will lead the order's old guardians and new stakeholders to an agenda of renewal. The coming divide in world politics will not be between the United States (and the West) and the non-Western rising states. Rather, the struggle will be between those who want to renew and expand today's system of multilateral governance arrangements and those who want to move to a less cooperative order built on spheres of influence. These fault lines do not map onto geography, nor do they split the West and the non-West. There are passionate champions of the UN, the WTO, and a rule-based international order in Asia, and there are isolationist, protectionist, and anti-internationalist factions in the West. . . .

As the hegemonic organization of the liberal international order slowly gives way, more states will have authority and status. But this will still be a world that the United States wants to inhabit. A wider array of states will share the burdens of global economic and political governance, and with its worldwide system of alliances, the United States will remain at the center of the global system. Rising states do not just grow more powerful on the global stage; they grow more powerful within their regions, and this creates its own set of worries and insecurities—which is why states will continue to look to Washington for security and partnership. In this new age of international order, the United States will not be able to rule. But it can still lead.

Questions for Review

Ikenberry believes that the liberal international order that the United States created after World War II is alive and well because rising powers, most especially China, have benefitted from that liberal order and continue to do so. Why would they seek to overturn an order from which they benefit, he asks? How do you interpret China's recent actions in the South China Sea and its plans for the Asian infrastructure and investment bank, as well as the relentless growth of its military power, especially maritime power?

Chapter 15

The Shape of the Future

Emerging Multipolarity: Why Should We Care?

Barry R. Posen

A report titled *Global Trends 2025: A Tranformed World*, issued last year by the US National Intelligence Council, advises us that a multipolar world—that is, a world characterized by multiple centers of power—is gradually emerging. The report attributes this to "the rise of emerging powers, a globalizing economy, an historic transfer of relative wealth and economic power from west to east, and the growing influence of non-state actors." Given these trends, it seems appropriate to ask whether a diffusion of power is indeed occurring, why we should care if it is, and what the implications may be for international politics.

The description of the present structure of world power as "unipolar"—a characterization that emerged quickly after the collapse of the Soviet Union and that has gained wide currency since—remains difficult to dispute, even now. The United States still enjoys a very comfortable margin of superiority over other nations in both military power and the economic underpinnings that make those capabilities possible. Additionally, America has the global diplomatic and military presence—and the diplomatic and military skills—necessary to manage and sustain a truly global foreign policy, if not always successfully. No other nation-state can do so at this time. It is difficult for the moment to envision a plausible combination of nation-states that could truly stand against the United States in a hot war (whatever that would look like under present conditions), or even sustain the costs of a cold war.

The *Global Trends 2025* finding that unipolarity is on the wane, to be slowly replaced by multipolarity, is premised on the notion that polarity matters. The notion of polarity as an important causal variable emerges from the realist school of international relations. Realist theory depicts international politics as a self-help system. With no sovereign to adjudicate disputes and impose settlements, each actor must look to its own interests relative to those of others. Each state can, if it has the power, despoil or conquer others. Thus each looks to its own capabilities relative to the others in order to defend itself.

Realists observe that the structure of world power has followed various patterns at various times and believe that these patterns naturally have consequences: Since security is the preeminent issue in an anarchic world, the distribution of capabilities to attack and defend should matter. Some base this belief on observation, others on deduction. Regardless, it is important to remember that structural realism is a theory of environmental constraints and incentives. Structures constrain. They push and they pull. The combination of global anarchy and the distribution of capabilities creates fields of force that *affect* all the states in the system but do not *determine* anything.

Different international structures do appear, however, to encourage different patterns of behavior. Modern international politics has mainly been a multipolar affair, featuring a handful of states with significant capabilities, all of them warily watching one another. During the cold war, we saw for the first time in modern history a bipolar structure of power, which lasted perhaps four decades.

The post-cold war world has seen an equally rare unipolar structure of power, which now seems unlikely to last longer than the cold war's bipolar order lasted. Current discourse seems to expect that the structure of power will, if anything, revert quickly to bipolarity with the rise of China. It seems plausible, however, that a prolonged period of multipolarity will occur before bipolarity reemerges, if indeed it ever does.

Measuring Power

Although political science strives for objective measures of power, they are elusive. In international politics it is the powerful who measure relative power, and their assessments, though not fully auditable, are the ones that matter. This is not to say that statesmen spend their days speculating on the polarity of the international system they inhabit. Rather, they respond to the constraints and possibilities they perceive. Over time their behaviors tell us which powers they believe matter, and why.

Two examples serve to demonstrate the disjunction between seemingly objective measures of polarity and statesmen's behaviors. The Soviet Union was only barely in the league of the United States for most of the cold war in terms of economic capacity, yet we think of the era as a bipolar order. Likewise, the United States was far and away the most economically capable state in the international system on the eve of World War II, yet we view that period as one of multipolarity.

Analysts typically measure polarity by the distribution of states' capabilities, but capabilities can be imminent or latent, and patterns of political behavior can deviate from seemingly objective measures. And polarity is not synonymous with equality. In any given historical period there seems to be a murky threshold that separates most nation-states from the handful that constitute the great powers. The great powers themselves vary in their capabilities.

Since the industrial revolution, military power has depended on the economic power from which it is distilled. Yet most states typically do not distill as much as, in extremis, they could. The Second World War showed what industrial powers can do when they really care, with the United States spending roughly 40 percent of gross domestic product (GDP) on the war effort at its peak, and other combatants spending an even greater share. Peacetime expenditures seldom rise to this level. The United States, the most powerful war machine of World War II, had distilled very little before the war.

Today the United States uses 4 to 5 percent of its GDP for military purposes. None of the other major powers allocates this much, though some could. America's high propensity to distill, compared to that of the rest of the world, contributes substantially to the current pattern of politics that we describe as unipolar. Yet it is plausible that fiscal imbalances will over the next 10 or 15 years require a significant reduction in the share of GDP that the United States devotes to military spending.

The existence of a bipolar world during the cold war was seldom questioned, but in retrospect one marvels a bit that the Soviet Union stayed in the game as long as it did. Its latent power—its GDP—only briefly surpassed half that of the United States. The Soviets simply distilled a greater percentage of their economic capacity into military power. This effort probably helped drive the Soviet economy into its ultimate downward spiral. By the early 1980s even Japan's economic output surpassed that of the Soviet Union. The world was bipolar, but the Soviet grip on its position was not very firm.

The last multipolar world also looks quite unequal when economic power, which translates into latent war potential, is examined. Various measures of economic capability and war potential in the late 1930s show the United States to be wildly superior to other great powers. This world was multipolar because the United States spent a tiny percentage of its wealth on military power, and involved itself only haltingly and episodically in relations among the great powers in Europe and Asia. (We should also note that once the United States did mobilize for war, the capabilities of the "balancing" coalition—America, the United Kingdom, and the Soviet Union—dwarfed those of the Axis powers; yet the reversal of German and Japanese gains proved a difficult, costly, bloody, and time-consuming business.)

So history tells us that equal capabilities are not required for states and statesmen to treat each other as important strategic actors. Nor can we easily predict what ratios of material power will induce them to do so. All we can suggest is that the cold war, when it ended, left the world with a very skewed distribution of capabilities—unipolarity, which does seem to have led to a distinct pattern of international politics. That distribution of power seems destined to change over the next several decades, and I suspect at some point we will begin to see a different, distinct pattern of international politics.

Bipolar and Unipolar

Putting aside real-world strategic factors such as geography and military technology, different systems of polarity should produce different patterns of behavior. Kenneth Waltz famously argued for the stability of the bipolar world, though some of that stability probably arose from matters beyond his abstract depiction of the system. The two major powers in a bipolar system face no security threats remotely as significant as each other. They can find no allies in the world that can consequentially alter the balance of power with the other. The prediction then is that they are obsessed with one another's behavior, internally and externally. Because allies do not add much, the superpowers focus on "internal balancing." They are obsessed with their relative economic and technical prowess, but more specifically they focus on the military balance.

Despite the arithmetical fact that, for the two powers in a bipolar system, allies do not add much capacity relative to the other major power, each power carefully watches the other's external behavior just in case an external move produces an improvement in the other's overall power position. Even gains that are not very cumulative are presumed to be cumulative, unless and until proven otherwise. Thus peripheries disappear.

Finally, because the two watch each other so carefully, one expects their understanding of the power balance, and of the costs of war, to be quite good at any given time. Since they do not depend much on allies for their power, miscalculations about relative power associated with the possible defection of allies are minimized. Although Waltz contended that all this made the bipolar world stable, its short duration suggests otherwise. In fact, bipolarity is a system of chronic overreaction, internal and external. In retrospect it seems that such a structure was destined to exhaust one or both of the players. That it did not erupt in war may be attributable to the fact that the structure of power provided limited scope for miscalculation of power and interest; or it may be a function of the nuclear balance, or a combination.

Although some predicted the demise of one or the other superpower, theorists did not anticipate the unipolar world. Scholars had to figure it out as it unfolded. The United States is the only "unipole" we have ever seen, and it is difficult when evaluating predictions regarding the unipolar world to distinguish between deductions from realist theory and observations of what has actually occurred.

Different schools of realism would offer different predictions for unipolarity. "Offensive realists" would expect the single pole to try to take advantage of its moment of superiority to consolidate that moment: In an anarchical world, permanent top-dog status provides as much security as one can reasonably expect. "Defensive realists" expected the United States to lose its interest in international politics, and simply do less. The structure of power offers no imminent threat, so why divert significant resources from consumption to foreign affairs, including war?

What has actually transpired deviates somewhat from the predictions of both schools. The unipole has thrown its weight around as the offensive realists would expect, and has tried to shape the system according to its perceived interests. On the other hand, lacking the discipline provided by an imminent threat, the United States has engaged abroad capriciously, and with limited energy, which the defensive realists might expect.

Other powers could not make heads or tails of the American orientation. Close and capable cold war allies—NATO, Europe, and Japan—feared that Washington would do too little or do too much, abandon them or drag them into adventures. Broadly speaking, they hugged the United States close and simultaneously hedged against its exit, even as they tried, however haltingly and unsuccessfully, to discipline US behavior. Other middle powers worried more about an excess of US energy, and have done what they could to throw monkey wrenches in the works. Their weakness, however, has constrained their efforts and induced caution.

These patterns of behavior make sense from a realist perspective. They are consistent with a unipole that finds many opportunities in the international system, but little necessity. Other powers are forced to focus on the unipole's real and potential behavior, but they have few options to address either. Nevertheless, they try.

The Multipolar Moment

Theorists and historians know multipolarity better than they do the other two structures of power, but there are no active statesmen today with experience of a multipolar system. The relatively equal distribution of capabilities in a multipolar world, with three or more consequential powers, produces one basic pattern of behavior: The arithmetic of coalitions influences matters great and small. The overall balance of capabilities, and the military balance in particular, are easily altered in a significant way depending on who sides with whom. Internal efforts cannot accomplish nearly as much change, at such a low cost, in such a short time.

Thus states are slower to react to others' internal military developments, because allies can be had to redress the balance. In a multipolar system, states should lack confidence that significant military buildups can help them much, because other states can combine against them. Autonomous military power does remain important, and states will look to their own military capabilities, but diminishing returns should set in sooner than they would in other structures of power.

Diplomacy becomes a respected career again under multipolarity. Hans Morgenthau, a great admirer of multipolarity, was also a great admirer of diplomacy. Isolation is perhaps the most dangerous situation in multipolarity, so states will pay close and constant attention to the game of coalition building. They will try to find and secure allies for themselves, and will eye warily the efforts of others to do the same. All will try to improve their own coalitions and erode those of others.

If indeed the distribution of capabilities among great powers is slowly evolving toward multipolarity, what behaviors might we predict? As we try to say something about real matters in a real world, a problem quickly emerges: Other facts of the case begin to complicate our analysis, even if we stick largely to security matters. The United States is buffered by oceans from much of the world's traditional security competition and remains well endowed with the human and material resources to go it alone. Indeed, many of the world's consequential powers are buffered by geography from one another. All but two of the consequential powers possess significant nuclear forces, which makes them difficult to conquer or even coerce. Japan and Germany are excluded from the nuclear club, but could enter it quickly.

Arguably, even among great powers, a close examination of conventional capabilities might show an emerging "defense dominant" world. It seems plausible that, among proximate technological, economic, and social equals, an ongoing revolution in military information technology—including surveillance and precision targeting—will make it harder to attack than to defend. It should be more difficult to take ground than to hold it, and more challenging to cross oceans with men and materiel and land them on a hostile shore than to prevent amphibious attack. All of these factors, added to a somewhat more equitable distribution of military power, should tend to mute great power military competition.

Some competition for power is to be expected, however. The experience of the United States as the unipole should be a cautionary one—an extremely secure state nevertheless reached out to expand its power and influence. A great deal of American behavior overseas was elicited by some combination of fear about the future and temptation presented by a power vacuum. We can expect national security establishments to worry about the future: So long as anarchy permits predation, they will ensure against the possibility.

Uncertainty about power relationships also will remain. States in normal times may distill economic power into military power at only a fraction of the level they could achieve under other conditions, and none can truly know the others' possible energy or efficiency to distill in the future. Thus, they will seek some comfort margin in the military capabilities that matter most to them, which will in turn discomfit others.

Moreover, some natural resources will seem scarce. Even if market-oriented states eschew direct control of foreign production, they will wish to maintain privileged influence over these producers, as we have seen in the case of energy supplies. States also will continue to worry about the strategic value of key geographic features, locally and globally. All members of the system likely will continue to compete, therefore, to improve their position and simultaneously undermine that of their brothers and sisters.

The Diffusion of Power

The emerging era's great powers, beyond their direct concerns with one another, are likely to face a phenomenon that some are calling "the diffusion of power." This concept remains a bit airy but it encompasses several trends that appear to be real and meaningful. First, despite Western military-technological prowess, the gap appears to be narrowing between the great powers' military capabilities and those of middle powers, small states, and non-state groups that choose to oppose them—at least when it comes to military forces pertinent to conquest and occupation.

One reason for this was the collapse of the Soviet Union and Warsaw Pact, which permitted a vast outflow of infantry weapons. At the same time, some of the former Soviet republics and East European Warsaw Pact states inherited arms production capabilities in search of markets. China will soon begin to produce and export moderately sophisticated military equipment. In addition, some new producers have entered the market, with Iran perhaps the most noteworthy. More states are able to make medium-quality military equipment than has previously been the case. This has the effect of making small states and non-state actors more independent of great power influence than they once were, and more able to inflict costs on great powers that attack them.

Military skill also seems to have diffused. The spread of literacy and the freer flow of people, goods, and information associated with globalization may permit states and non-state groups that are willing to fight larger powers to share lessons and improve their overall military expertise. Moreover, across the developing world, weapons and expertise can be combined with significant numbers of motivated young men. The upshot is that great powers may have to pay a higher premium to push the smaller ones around than has been true in the recent past.

Although comparison is tricky, it is striking that the Americans' effort in Iraq has been about as time-consuming and costly in dollar terms as their effort in Vietnam, and the adversary in Iraq did not have a superpower patron, or even a particularly good cross-border sanctuary. The United States did deploy many fewer people for the Iraq operation than it did in Vietnam, and suffered fewer deaths. A comparison of overall casualties, however, awaits clearer information about the range and duration of less visible physical and psychological injuries that US forces have suffered. The less visible human costs appear to be significant.

The diffusion of power has another meaning. Across much of the developing world, central governments weakened more or less as the cold war ended. Pakistan is only the scariest example. Weakening central governments may find themselves at war with domestic political factions, or as willing or unwilling hosts to violent non-state actors. Even before the Al Qaeda attacks on New York and Washington on September 11, 2001, the great powers were uneasy about these weak or failing states. They loathed the human rights violations that are a hallmark of civil war. And they feared the negative externalities of refugee flows and criminal enterprises. The 9/11 attacks added a concern that these poorly governed spaces would prove hospitable to terrorist groups. Most great power military intervention since the end of the cold war has been driven by the problem of weakened central governments.

Finally, there is particularly great concern about states that are capable enough to build advanced weapons, especially nuclear weapons, but nevertheless weak enough to risk collapse and the loss of control over said weapons. Pakistan is again the most troubling example. The diffusion of power in this case thus creates a strange combination—major threats to the safety of the strong emanating from the weak.

In such an environment, we can expect that the great powers will continue to view the developing world as a source of security threats, meriting intervention. But not all great powers in a multipolar system will agree on any given project, so some will view the "defensive" projects of others as having ulterior motives. Some states will have an incentive to hinder the efforts of their peers to pacify ungoverned spaces. Their direct interest may be engaged, or the intervention may prove a tempting opportunity to "bleed" other great powers. Their capabilities to do so will improve, particularly given the growing military skill of the indigenous peoples they can assist. States organizing interventions will therefore be very concerned about costs. They will seek allies to spread the costs around, and will attempt to dissuade others from helping the locals.

Persistent Competition

What general patterns of great power behavior could emerge in a multipolar environment, based on the situation discussed above? First, the competition for power is likely to persist, though this is more a statement of general realist religious conviction than an inference from the multipolar structure of power. Second, because of "defense dominance," the pattern of competition will look much like an endless series of games played for small stakes. States will want more, but will not wish to court disaster.

Third, and consequently, states will look for ways to "measure power" without war. The diplomacy of making and breaking coalitions, and counting allies, will present itself as an attractive, if complex, alternative. Fourth, competitors likely will believe that the safe way to improve one's relative position is to pursue policies that weaken others. Increasing others' costs when they undertake initiatives will seem wiser than undertaking one's own adventures. John Mearsheimer's "bait and bleed" strategies may become more common.

Fifth, the diffusion of power will continue to seduce great power adventures. Yet the capabilities of local actors, and the potential intervention, even if indirect, of other great powers, will raise the potential costs of those adventures. Therefore, these projects too will increase the importance of other powers. Diplomacy will be required to discourage opposition, encourage alliance, or at least elicit neutrality. Sixth, in general, geography may matter more. If capabilities are more equal, states will have to make harder choices about the kinds of military power they generate. Land powers will be land powers, and sea powers will be sea powers, and thus to tilt with each other they will require allies of the other type.

The Question of Stability

The transition from bipolarity to unipolarity was marked by dramatic events. Perhaps the intense nature of the bipolar competition naturally led to a stark finish of one kind or another: a preventive war, or a national collapse. Unipolarity seems destined for a different kind of transition. The United States has many attributes that contribute to its power advantage and its security, and that have made the world unipolar. It seems unlikely that all of these advantages would suddenly disappear. Direct competition with the United States will appear daunting for quite some time to come.

The costs of U.S. efforts to make the world over in its image, relative to the benefits of such efforts, will ultimately begin to tell, however. America will gradually be inclined to do less. At the same time, uneven growth will alter the basic balance of capabilities among the principal powers. The American capability advantage in economic power will diminish, and concomitantly its advantage in military power will likely narrow. As this occurs, the other principal powers will find themselves better able to tilt with the United States, but also more dependent on themselves. A multipolar order may gradually creep up on us, rather than emerge with a crash.

Many theorists have debated whether one kind of power structure is more "stable" than another. But definitions of stability are fluid. Some mean peace, others mean only the absence of great war, and still others merely mean persistence. Some believe multipolarity is more stable, while others assert the stability of bipolar worlds.

We have experienced long periods of relative peace in multipolar systems. Some scholars refer to the period between the end of the Napoleonic Wars and the outbreak of the First World War as the "hundred years' peace." In that time crises erupted and major powers fought limited wars, but no truly great war took place. That period was, of course, followed by a bloodbath.

The bipolar era lasted a little less than half a century, and no superpower war occurred. But the cold war was characterized by vast military spending, numerous dangerous crises, horrendous proxy wars, and a nuclear arms race that left tens of thousands of warheads on both sides, an absurd accumulation of destructive power. It also probably exhausted the Soviet Union.

The National Intelligence Council's *Global Trends 2025* report warns that multipolar systems are "more unstable than bipolar or unipolar systems." This sentence is difficult to decode. I find it more accurate to speak simply of the differences among these systems. Bipolarity is a tightly coupled, simple, and intensely competitive system. Opportunities for creative expansionists are few, but life is very tense. Multipolarity is complex, flexible, and full of options, and these very qualities seduce the creative expansionist into a search for opportunities, which occasionally exist.

Unipolarity is still the least understood structure of power. Leadership by a single very great power with an incentive to manage the system limits competition among the others through a combination of deterrence and reassurance, but we do not have a good sense of just how superior that power needs to be to sustain this happy outcome. If multipolarity is indeed on the horizon, all I can suggest is that the pattern of international politics ahead will likely be quite different from that of the past 65 years.

Question for Review

Posen argues that international politics is slowly moving from unipolarity to bipolarity and as a consequence, international politics will become more competitive and unpredictable. If that is indeed the case, will international relations also become more dangerous, or will states compete more intensely over smaller stakes?

The Strategic Implications of Climate Change

ALAN DUPONT

Climate change has always been linked to security. There are many historical examples of climatic shifts or extremes of weather triggering conflict and even contributing to the rise and fall of civilisations and nations. Growing aridity and frigid temperatures from a prolonged cold snap caused Huns and German tribes to surge across the Volga and Rhine into the Roman Empire during the fourth and fifth centuries CE, eventually leading to the sack of Rome by Visigoths. Muslim expansion into the Mediterranean and southern Europe in the eighth century was to some extent driven by persistent drought in the Middle East. The Viking community in Greenland died out in the fifteenth century partly because of a sudden cooling of temperatures across northern Europe known as the 'Little Ice Age.' And a changing climate may have been responsible for the collapse of China's Tang dynasty and the disappearance of the Mayan world in Central America a thousand years ago. For the most part, however, these climatic shifts were relatively short lived and far less significant than those in prospect. In a world already populated by 6.5 billion people, a figure projected to reach 9bn by 2050, large deviations from global or regional weather norms, particularly if they occur within the span of a single human generation, would be far more dangerous.

Food and Water Scarcity

Weather extremes and greater fluctuations in rainfall and temperatures have the capacity to refashion the world's productive landscape, especially at a time of rising populations in the developing world and concerns that the green revolution of the twentieth century may have largely run its course. Crop yield increases have levelled off since the 1990s and increases in the frequency of extreme weather events, such as cyclones, riverine flooding, hail and drought will disrupt agriculture and put pressure on prices.

If the gap between global supply and demand for a range of primary foods narrows, price volatility on world markets is likely to increase and will be exacerbated by the reduction in food stockpiles mandated by the implementation of the 1994 World Trade Organisation's Uruguay Round agreement. The world's food stocks are already at historical lows due to a combination of rising demand and crop substitution. Much corn is now converted to ethanol for biofuels, rather than being used for human and animal consumption, and productive farmland is being lost due to environmental degradation and urbanisation. Without the moderating influence of substantial grain stocks, a confluence of unfavourable political and economic influences, aggravated by climate change, could create local scarcities, sparking food riots and domestic unrest. If sustained, reduced crop yields could seriously undermine political and economic stability, especially in the developing world.

Of course, doomsayers have long warned of an approaching food deficit and been proved wrong. Most food economists believe that global supply will be able to keep ahead of rising demand. But their assumptions have not adequately factored in the impact of climate change, especially the shift in rainfall distribution, rising temperatures and the probable increase in extreme weather events. Nor have they accounted for the fact that agricultural yields are heavily dependent on high fertiliser use, which links food production to climate change through the energy cycle. The need to achieve greenhouse-gas reductions will increase energy costs, making it more difficult to maintain the per capita food yield gains of the previous century.

Rising sea levels will inundate and make unusable fertile coastal land, and potential changes in the strength and seasonality of ocean currents will cause fish species to migrate and disrupt breeding grounds. Noncommercial fisheries are likely to decline as coral bleaching takes hold, and the movement of deep-water fish may become more unpredictable, compounding the problem of over-fishing and diminishing global supplies of wild fish. Oceans have already absorbed about half the 800bn tonnes of carbon dioxide humans have pumped into the atmosphere since industrialisation, which over time has increased ocean acidity and further degraded the marine ecosystem. As carbonate ions in the seas disappear because of increased acidity, tiny marine snails and krill at the bottom of the food chain that are the primary source of food for whales and fish could be decimated, possibly within decades. . . .

With less fresh water available to slake the thirst of its booming population and economy, China has redoubled its efforts to redirect the southward flow of rivers from the water-rich Tibetan plateau to water-deficient areas of northern China. The problem is that rivers like the Mekong, Ganges, Brahmaputra and Salween flow through multiple states. China's efforts to rectify its own emergin water and energy problems indirectly threaten the livelihoods of many millions people in downstream, riparian states. Chinese dams on the Mekong are alrea reducing flows to Myanmar, Thailand, Laos, Cambodia and Vietnam. India is cerned about Chinese plans to channel the waters of the Brahmaputra to the used and increasingly desiccated Yellow River. Should China go ahead wi ambitious plan, tensions with India and Bangladesh are likely to rise, as e political and territorial disputes are aggravated by concerns over water s

Heightened Energy Insecurity

In addition to its negative impact on food and water, climate change is heightening concerns about future supplies of energy, complicating energy choices by adding to the costs of production and usage. Coal, for example, is relatively abundant but also highly polluting. Fossil fuels are responsible for nearly 80% of the anthropogenic greenhouse gases that are the major cause of planetary warming. Even if emissions from fossil fuels are stabilised at 1990 levels, as required by the Kyoto Protocol, greenhouse gases will continue to rise for the rest of this century, further heating up the planet. We know this because the increase in greenhouse gases can be extrapolated from current fossil-fuel usage and rates of deforestation.

In 1990, global emissions of carbon dioxide, the main greenhouse gas, totalled 5.8bn tonnes of carbon equivalent, which in a business-as-usual scenario will rise 34% to 7.8bn tonnes by 2010. If every signatory to the Kyoto Protocol reaches its pledged target, an unlikely eventuality since only two countries, the United Kingdom and Sweden, are within their agreed targets, the increase would still be the equivalent of 7.3bn tonnes. This small reduction would be more than offset by the rise in emissions from developing countries, notably China and India, which are exempt from emissions targets under Kyoto but have been reluctant to endorse a successor agreement for fear that signing up to mandatory targets would set back their economic growth. Almost all nations anticipate growth in energy usage in the coming decades. The International Energy Agency forecasts that the world's primary energy needs will grow by 55% between 2005 and 2030 with fossil fuels accounting for 84% of the increase, which will dramatically push up greenhouse-gas emissions in the absence of mitigating strategies. Thus, at the very time the world's appetite for energy is growing exponentially, the environmental cost of using fossil fuels may be a greater, long-term constraint than their availability.

Climate change is also forcing a major reassessment of the utility of nuclear power, once seen as the energy choice of last resort because of its tarnished public image as a dangerous and dirty fuel. Since nuclear power only emits about 25 grams of carbon dioxide equivalent per kilowatt hour, compared with around 450–1,250g for fossil fuels, it is the one source of virtual carbon-free energy that can make a substantial difference to energy supply in the short to medium term. Critics maintain that switching to nuclear power in order to reduce greenhouse-gas emissions is misguided and merely replaces one problem with an even more serious one: the proliferation of plutonium and enriched uranium which can be used for manufacturing nuclear weapons. They contend that safely storing and protecting this material from terrorists and criminal groups intent on acquiring weapons-grade material for use or profit is problematic, and the political and security risks too high.

But the security consequences of unmitigated climate change outweigh the risk of terrorists or rogue states acquiring nuclear material from expanded global stockpiles. The world is already awash in nuclear material, much of it stored in unsafe temporary storage sites located near nuclear reactors. Even if all the nuclear power plants in the world were to be shut down tomorrow and every nuclear weapon dismantled, the accumulated waste of half a century would still have to be isolated, safeguarded and eventually disposed of, either in underground repositories or, less desirably, by reprocessing. Arguing against nuclear power on the grounds of safety does little to address existing problems of waste disposal or proliferation, and even less the issue of climate change.

One aspect of the interrelationship between climate change and energy security that has received scant attention is the impact the submergence of small atolls, rocks and low-lying islands due to sea-level rise could have on the Exclusive Economic Zones (EEZs) of maritime states and disputed seabed resources, including oil and gas. This is a critically important issue since small rocks and islets are commonly used to delineate maritime boundaries and to claim vast tracts of ocean which would otherwise fall outside the EEZs of contiguous states or be designated high seas, opening them up to exploration and exploitation by other nations. International law currently provides no answer to the question of what would happen to sovereignty and EEZ claims should an island, or even a country, be submerged. In the event of significant sea-level rise, the low-water marks from which EEZs are measured would shift, raising the real possibility of serious, new maritime disputes as states argued about the criteria for resetting base lines and redesignating EEZs as high seas. . . .

Warming seas, as a consequence of climate change, are also making it possible to exploit previously inaccessible energy resources under the polar ice caps, threatening what has been characterised as a new 'gold rush,' with claimant states jostling for the rights to exploit potentially rich deposits of oil, gas and minerals on the seabed. The potential for conflict was dramatically brought home by Russia's successful and highly publicised planting of its national flag on the Arctic seabed on 2 August 2007 by two small submersibles, an act that was lauded as 'heroic' by Moscow but condemned by other claimants, notably Canada, which compared the Russian action to a fifteenth-century land grab. Many climate scientists believe that late-summer Arctic ice could disappear entirely by 2060, which would make the exploitation of Arctic resources technically feasible and therefore more likely, unless the five claimant states—Russia, the United States, Canada, Denmark and Norway—can reach an accommodation.

Infectious Disease

Climate change will have a number of serious health-related impacts, including illness and death directly attributable to temperature increases, extreme weather, air pollution, water diseases, vector- and rodent-borne diseases and food and water shortages. 1.7m people die prematurely every year because they do not have access to safe drinking water, and the situation will worsen if waterborne pathogens multiply as a result of rising temperatures. But the greatest security risk is from infectious disease. Temperature is the key factor in the spread of some infectious diseases, especially where mosquitoes are a vector, as with Ross River fever, malaria and dengue fever. As the planet heats up, mosquitoes will move into previously inhospitable areas and higher altitudes, while disease transmission seasons may last longer. A study by the World Health Organisation has estimated that 154,000 deaths annually are attributable to the ancillary effects of global warming due mainly to malaria and malnutrition. This number could nearly double by 2020. Currently, some 40% of the world's population lives in areas affected by endemic malaria.

Extreme weather events and climate-related disasters could lead to short-term disease spikes because of the damage to food production, population displacement and reductions in the availability of fresh water. Poorer nations with limited public health services will be especially vulnerable. Health problems can quickly metamorphose into a national-security crisis if sufficient numbers of people are affected and there are serious economic and social consequences, as occurred during the devastating flu pandemic of 1918–19 which killed from 40–100m people. Climate change does not automatically or always provide a more favourable environment for the spread of infectious diseases, since transmission rates and lethality are a function of many interrelated social, environmental, demographic and political factors, including the level of public health, population density, housing conditions, access to clean water and the state of sewage and waste-management systems, as well as human behaviour. All these factors affect the transmission dynamics of a disease and determine whether or not it becomes an epidemic. But where climate is a consideration, temperature, relative humidity and precipitation will affect the intensity of transmission. Temperature can influence the maturation, reproductive rate and survivability of the disease agent within a vector, or carrier. So climate change will alter the distribution of the animals and insects which are host to dangerous pathogens, increasing or decreasing the range of their habitats and breeding places.

More Frequent Severe Natural Disasters

Natural disasters seem set to climb in line with the warming of the planet. To be sure, the impact of natural disasters may rise for reasons other than climate change: population growth, higher levels of capital investment and migration to more disaster-prone areas. But the insurance industry is adamant that the rise in the number of extreme and damaging climatic events is a significant driver of the upward trend. Around 188m people were adversely affected by natural disasters in the 1990s, six times more than the 31m directly or indirectly affected by war. While such statistics must be treated with caution since they are not yet sufficiently robust to enable definitive judgements about cause and effect, they do suggest an upward trend in extreme weather events. Scientists are divided about whether this change is due to natural fluctuations or global warming, although the differences are partly explicable by the rigorous scientific tradition which requires a higher level of certainty than do intelligence and national-security analysis when considering risk. However, there is clearly a strong correlation between the steady rise in ocean temperatures attributable to anthropogenic greenhouse-gas emissions and the demonstrable increase in storm frequency and intensity.

Hurricanes feed off warm water as trade winds blow over the ocean surface, pulling heat from the water as energy. Typically, large storms require ocean temperatures of 27°C, conditions which are now occurring much more regularly as tropical waters heat up. The strength of category 4 and 5 storms is a direct consequence of these warmer ocean temperatures. Storms of this magnitude have a clear security dimension because of the death and destruction they bring in their wake and the political, economic and social stresses they place on even the most developed states. . . .

Natural disasters linked to climate change may prove an even greater security challenge for developing states, displacing affected populations, calling into question the legitimacy or competence of national governments and feeding into existing ethnic or inter-communal conflicts. In extreme cases, the survival of the nation itself may be in question. For example, the 1998 monsoon season brought with it the worst flood in living memory to Bangladesh, inundating some 65% of the country, devastating its infrastructure and agricultural base and raising fears about Bangladesh's long-term future in a world of higher ocean levels and more intense cyclones. In the absence of effective mitigation strategies, a 1m rise in sea level would flood about 17.5% of Bangladesh and much of the Ganges river delta which is the country's food basket. . . .

Environmental Refugees

The possibility that climate change might cause mass migrations of environmental refugees and displaced persons, with serious consequences for international security, is certainly plausible and should not be dismissed as a figment of Hollywood's imagination.

We already know that refugee flows and unregulated population movements can destabilise states internally, aggravate trans-border conflicts, create political tensions between sending and receiving states and jeopardise human security. One of the defining features of the post-Cold War security environment has been the rapid rise in unregulated population movements around the globe. The causes of these movements are complex and interconnected, but there is growing evidence to suggest that environmental decline is a contributing cause and that, in future, climate change may play a significant ancillary role. Some contend that climate or environmental refugees are now the fastest-growing proportion of refugees globally and that by 2050 up to 150m people may be displaced by the impact of global warming.

Climate-induced migration is set to play out in three distinct ways. First, people will move in response to a deteriorating environment, creating new or repetitive patterns of migration, especially in developing states. Secondly, there will be increasing short-term population dislocations due to particular climate stimuli such as severe cyclones or major flooding. Thirdly, larger-scale population movements that build more slowly but gain momentum as adverse shifts in climate interact with other migration drivers such as political disturbances, military conflict, ecological stress and socio-economic change are possible. Even the beneficial effects of climate change could lead to conflict. In China's Xingiang province, for example, a projected increase in rainfall is likely to attract an influx of Han migrants into the Muslim Uighur ancestral lands, further inflaming ethnic tensions between the two communities where a low-level insurgency is already festering.

Wild Cards

These are some of the security consequences we can reasonably anticipate based on the available scientific data. But what if the speed and extent of temperature increases is greater than projected? Could it be that we have underestimated the threat? After all, climate researchers have identified several episodes of large-scale, abrupt climate change over the past 100,000 years both prior to, and after, the last ice age. In some instances rapid warming (as great as 16°c) took place over spans as short as a decade, although there is still substantial debate over how global these changes were. So what could trigger abrupt, accelerated or runaway climate change, and what strategic consequences might we expect?. . . .

Peter Schwartz and Doug Randall, authors of the Pentagon report commissioned by Andrew Marshall, identified a sudden collapse of the thermohaline circulation as the climate-change event most likely to endanger international security. In their scenario, the warm Gulf Stream cools or shuts down altogether, perhaps irreversibly, creating winters of great severity in the northern hemisphere and triggering catastrophic weather. Rather than causing a gradual heating of the atmosphere over the span of a century, the global warming which has already taken place may suddenly push the climate to a decisive tipping point in which the system that controls the planet's ocean—atmosphere system suddenly flips to an alternative state. North America would then become much colder and the European hinterland might have a climate more like Siberia, precipitating crop losses and population movements.

Schwartz and Randall postulate that as water, food and energy shortages develop, age-old patterns of conflict quickly re-emerge as nations fight for control over diminishing natural resources. Initially, countries attempt to deal diplomatically and collegially with the food, water and energy shortages that develop, along with an upsurge of environmental refugees. But as the decade progresses, international order breaks down because the scale and speed of climate change overwhelms the coping capacities of even the most wealthy and technologically advanced states. Drawing on the findings of Harvard archaeologist

Steven LeBlanc, Schwartz and Randall observe that 'humans fight when they outstrip the carrying capacity of their natural environment. Every time there is a choice between starving and raiding, humans raid.'

With these pessimistic assumptions informing their security scenarios, Schwartz and Randall imagine refugees from the Caribbean flooding into the United States and Mexico and struggles over diminishing supplies of oil as demand skyrockets, bringing the US and Chinese navies into confrontation in the Persian Gulf. With fossil fuels unable to meet demand, nuclear power becomes the alternative energy of choice and further nuclear proliferation becomes inevitable as energy-deficient countries develop enrichment and reprocessing capabilities. Japan, South Korea and Germany develop nuclear weapons, as do Iran, Egypt and North Korea. In Asia, energy-hungry Japan, already suffering from coastal flooding and contamination of its water supply, contemplates seizing Russian oil and gas reserves on nearby Sakhalin Island to power desalination plants and energy-intensive agriculture. Pakistan, India and China skirmish on their borders over refugees and access to shared rivers and arable land. States suffering from famine, pestilence, water and energy shortfalls strike out with 'offensive aggression in order to reclaim balance,' thereby jeopardising their neighbours' security in pursuit of their own.

Many of these projections are highly speculative or simply misleading. . . .

Nevertheless, Schwartz and Randall should be given credit for thinking the unthinkable and identifying how an abrupt-climate-change scenario might impact on international security. Even if the probability is low, it is far from zero and, as the potential impact could be very high indeed, policymakers ought to factor them into their security calculations and alternative-futures planning. . . .

Another risk factor is the stability of high-latitude permafrost. There is clear evidence that ground which was once frozen all year round is melting at higher and higher latitudes. Although there are no definitive estimates of the volume of gases trapped under the permafrost, their carbon content is thought to be considerable—perhaps as much as 500bn tonnes, the equivalent of 70% of all carbon currently present in the atmosphere. Its release could be quite rapid and widespread, as warming progresses, and would include a significant amount of methane gas, which is one of the most damaging of the main greenhouse gases. Should this occur, the authoritative Intergovernmental Panel on Climate Change (IPCC) predictions of future global warming would have to be revised upward by a substantial margin, since IPCC calculations only take account of emissions from fossil-fuel combustion.

Of all the potential climate wild cards, perhaps the greatest strategic risk is from a larger and more rapid than expected reduction of polar ice, which could dramatically increase sea levels, especially if parts of the Greenland and West Antarctic ice caps disappear. If the Greenland ice cap were to melt entirely it would contribute about 7.3m to sea-level rise, which would flood many coastal cities and low-lying areas, causing enormous economic damage, forced population displacements and loss of agricultural land. While this seems unlikely, scientists are concerned by new evidence of ice loss. The US National Snow and Ice Data Centre has concluded that human-induced warming is at least partially responsible for the shrinking of the Arctic ice cap. We know from a variety of independent studies that sea levels have risen by around 10cm globally over the past 55 years, essentially because of the thermal expansion of water and the melting of terrestrial snow and ice. Satellite data released in January 2008 indicate that West Antarctica is losing more ice that previously thought, with ice-sheet loss along the Bellingshausen and Amundsen seas increasing by 59% over the past decade. If this trend continues, then Antarctic melt may also contribute to the expansion of our seas and the inundation of coastal and low-lying areas.

Sea-level rise may have particularly dire consequences for low-lying atoll countries in the Pacific such as Kiribati, the Marshall Islands, Tokelau and Tuvalu. Ultimately, human habitation may not be possible on them even with moderate climate change. If temperature and sea-level rises are at the high end of those projected, then the sea will either eventually submerge the coral atolls or ground water will become so contaminated by salt-water intrusion that agricultural activities will cease. Most of Asia's densest aggregations of people and productive lands are on, or near, the coast, as are many large cities in Europe, the Americas and Africa, so if sea-level rise is at the upper end of the projections, flooding, loss of agricultural land and population displacements will become a serious global problem.

War has customarily been considered the main threat to international security because of the large number of deaths it causes and the threat it poses to the functioning and survival of the state. Judged by these criteria, it is clear that climate change is potentially as detrimental to human life and economic and political order as traditional military threats. Environmental dangers, such as climate change, stem not from competition between states or shifts in the balance of power; rather, they are human-induced disturbances to the fragile balance of nature. But the consequences of these disturbances may be just as injurious to the integrity and functioning of the state and its people as those resulting from military conflict. They may also be more difficult to reverse or repair.

Protecting and stabilising our climate is a legitimate long-term objective of security policy, since human survival is dependent on the health of the biosphere and the coupled ocean-atmosphere. Climate change of the magnitude and time frames projected by climate scientists poses fundamental questions of human security, survival and the stability of nation-states which necessitate judgements about political and strategic risk as well as economic and environmental cost. Based on the evidence to date, it is difficult to see climate change alone compelling a major reconfiguration of the global balance of power in the foreseeable future. Shifts of this order presuppose substantial redistributions of the relative productive capacities of nation-states, but current climate models are still not accurate enough to describe in detail how most individual states will be affected.

While state weakness and destabilising internal conflicts are a more likely outcome than inter-state war, climate change acts as a stress multiplier on all societies and states. In assessing the long-term consequences of climate change for international security we should be mindful of Jared Diamond's warning that in many historical cases a society that was depleting its environmental stocks could absorb losses as long as the climate was benign, but when it became more variable or harsh these societies were pushed over the edge and even collapsed. It was the combination of environmental impact and climate change that proved fatal. Whether or not Diamond's observations are germane to our milieu remains to be seen, but can we afford to ignore the risk? It is sobering that on four out of five previous occasions of mass extinction in the Earth's history, at least half of all animal and plant species are estimated to have been wiped out during periods of warming that are comparable to those in prospect. . . .

In the security domain, strategic doctrines and defence budgets are frequently justified on the basis of far less observable evidence than we have about the climate future which awaits us. Yet very little has been done to research, address or even conceptualise the potential security implications of climate change internationally. Prudence and sensible risk management suggest that policymakers need to take this issue far more seriously. And our strategic planners ought to include worst-case climate-change scenarios in their contingency planning as they do for terrorism, infectious diseases and conventional military challenges to national security. For climate change may well be the threshold event that pushes our already stressed planet past an environmental tipping point from which there will be no return.

Questions for Review

Climate change will not affect all states equally. Some will be hit harder than others. Which states are most likely to be hit hard and which not so hard? What are the consequences for the differential impact of climate change on getting all states to cooperate to reduce their fossil fuel emissions?

Dollar Diminution and U.S. Power

JONATHAN KIRSHNER

U.S. power is facing new macroeconomic constraints. They derive from a basic and generally underappreciated shift in U.S. engagement with the global macroeconomic order, which also complicates international politics. Since before WWII, the international monetary and financial system had served to enhance U.S. power and capabilities in its relations with other states. From the turn of the twenty-first century, however, underlying economic problems threatened to turn this traditional (if implicit) source of strength into a chronic weakness.

The 2007–08 global financial crisis has increased this risk. The United States will likely face new constraints on its power from the crisis and from new complications managing the dollar as a global currency. Moreover, the unfamiliarity of U.S. elites and citizens in facing such constraints will play a crucial role in determining how severe they will be in practice. . . .

The End of the Second U.S. Financial Order

The 2007–08 global financial crisis, the worst economic catastrophe since the Great Depression, was a fundamental disturbance of what I call the "Second Post-War U.S. International Economic Order." The first order forged by the United States, the Bretton Woods system of 1948–1973, was based on an ideology that political scientist John Ruggie dubbed "embedded liberalism"— a market-oriented, internationalist philosophy, but one that was chastened by the failures of the Depression and therefore skeptical of unmediated market forces. The second order, however—the "globalization project" of 1994–2007— had as its touchstone the liberation of finance, both at home and abroad. This new order was based on a very different economic philosophy, one of "market fundamentalism." It was based on the idea that free and unsupervised markets, even financial markets, always know best and naturally provide the most efficient outcomes.

Encouraged by industry and reflecting a new consensus among academic economists, the Clinton administration led a bipartisan charge to dismantle the Depression-era firewalls which had been designed to contain instability in the domestic financial sector. Key players in this effort were Treasury Secretary (and former Goldman Sachs co-chair) Robert Rubin, his deputy (and successor) Lawrence Summers, Senate Banking Committee Chair Phil Gramm (who would join the financial giant UBS immediately upon leaving the Senate), and Federal Reserve Board Chair Alan Greenspan. The efforts to withdraw both regulation and supervision of the financial sector were, if anything, accelerated by the transition to the Bush administration (coupled with continuity at Greenspan's Federal Reserve). The 1999 Gramm–Leach–Bliley Act codified many of these changes, including repealing the 1933 Glass–Steagall Banking Act that regulated and compartmentalized the reckless financial order which contributed so fundamentally to the Depression.

Dismantling existing regulations was only half of the great 1990s financial liberalization project. The other half was the fight *not* to supervise and regulate new and fantastically expanding sectors of the financial economy, which produced massive wealth and fueled the rapid growth of industry—but were inherent carriers of systemic risk. The interrelated phenomena of securitization (the repackaging, blending, and resale of bundles of financial assets such as mortgages) and the astonishing growth of trading in derivatives (any asset whose value "derived" from another asset, from simple futures and options to extremely complex risk and insurance dispersal exotica) forged the financialization of the

U.S. economy. These activities were largely unsupervised by an oversight and regulatory apparatus that was designed long before such products came on the scene. . . .

Not surprisingly in this environment, the U.S. financial sector became larger, more concentrated, and riskier. From 1980–2002, U.S. manufacturing fell from 21 percent of GDP to 14 percent, but finance (the biggest and fastest growing sector in the U.S. economy) increased its share from 14 percent to 21 percent. This was a remarkable transformation, especially when one pauses to remember that finance—like, for example, advertising—is supposed to serve the economy; it is not supposed to *be* the economy. But in 2007, finance accounted for 47 percent of U.S. corporate profits. And from 1981–2008, financial sector debt increased from 22 to 117 percent of GDP, the tip of an iceberg of risk that metastasized in the wake of deregulation.

The Changing Balance of Power

The crisis is producing both material *and* ideational consequences. As a material phenomenon, it is creating new U.S. vulnerabilities and accelerating two preexisting trends: reduced U.S international political capacity and the continuing emergence of China. What was novel about the 2007–08 crisis was not that it occurred—international financial crises are very common phenomena—but that for the U.S. economy, it "hit home." During the age of regulation in the 1940s—1970s, the United States experienced no major financial crisis. They only occurred (with regularity) in the unregulated 19th and early 20th centuries, and reemerged in the 1980s in the age of deregulation. This crisis, then, is distinguished mostly by the fact that the United States was at its epicenter, and that it has borne many of its costs. This is suggestive more generally of a new and unfamiliar level of U.S. economic exposure to external financial pressures. . . .

One challenge to U.S. power concerns the trajectory of the dollar as an international currency. Although the dollar has served as a safe haven during this crisis, the longer-run prospects are more alarming. Because it has served as the world's "key currency," there are an enormous amount of dollars held abroad. Thus if a spark, somewhere, touched off a financial crisis which implicated the dollar, a tidal wave of dollars could flood the market, given the state of underlying expectations about its future value. In sum, the United States has emerged from the crisis with sluggish economic growth, exposed economic weaknesses, and a more suspect dollar.

> If a future financial crisis implicated the dollar, a tidal wave of dollars could flood the market.

All this contrasts with China's relatively rapid recovery from the crisis, to date, which will eventually translate into greater military might as its defense spending will rise commensurately. (China's continued economic growth is however by no means guaranteed, raising a host of other important questions.) Differential rates of recovery from the current crisis have accelerated China's relative economic rise. If sustained, this will have profound *political* consequences. China is now the world's second-largest importer, taking on over $1 trillion worth of other countries' goods each year. As a result, China's status and influence have been enhanced. States which trade with China will consider how their foreign policy decisions might affect their relations with Beijing.

Beyond these changes to the balance of power and relative political influence, ideational consequences of the crisis will also affect world politics. Venerable old banks were not the only things that came crashing down in 2007–08—the legitimacy of the Second Post-War U.S. Order also collapsed. Even if one is inclined to reject the view that the U.S. model of uninhibited finance was flawed, the following three propositions are uncontroversial and consequential: (1) for much of the world, the global financial crisis was the second major financial crisis within the last ten years (most notably, for many, following the 1997 Asian financial crisis); (2) the United States was the epicenter of the crisis; and (3) important international actors do not share the interpretation of the crisis implied by U.S. policy.

In particular, the U.S. response to the crisis suggests that the "market fundamentalist" approach still holds sway. From this perspective, the global financial crisis was a "black swan"—a rare and unpredictable event. Lightning sometimes strikes, at times causing great destruction, but the financial system is about as safe as we can practically expect it to be. Modest tweaks or reforms could make the system even safer, but the underlying philosophy remains that finance is essentially efficient and self-regulating.

This interpretation contrasts with what I would dub a "KKM" perspective, named after John Maynard Keynes, Charles Kindleberger, and Hyman Minsky: these economists argued that financial markets, especially ones left to themselves, were prone to crisis. This view holds that financial crises are common throughout history, and invited by unregulated, unsupervised financial systems. This interpretation implies that the U.S. financial-economic model of the 1990s is flawed and in need of fundamental reform. I would note that KKM clearly has history on its side, but it does not matter who is right for this discussion; it matters that now, after the crisis, a disagreement exists—with different actors holding pointedly different ideas about how to organize the financial economy. Prior to the crisis, the U.S. financial model was broadly accepted as the only game in town; that is no longer the case. . . .

The current crisis, then, has delegitimized the culture of U.S. capitalism, especially as it applies to finance. This will affect both state choices and international politics. . . . The coming years will witness. . . . the likely *erosion* of that influence, as others come to reject the ideas which they once embraced or at least tolerated. With this legitimacy reversal, continuity in the United States and change elsewhere will contribute to a "new heterogeneity" of ideas about finance. States will commonly have divergent preferences about the global financial order, reducing U.S. influence and making cooperation on the governance of money and finance more problematic. In particular, many states will search for ways to insulate themselves from the dangers of unmediated global finance.

> The global financial crisis has delegitimized the culture of U.S. capitalism.

New Thinking in China

Prior to the global financial crisis, elites in China anticipated future RMB (Yuan) internationalization. But the dominant position of the dollar, the emergence of the Euro, and the fragility of China's sheltered domestic financial sector tempered expectations about how quickly the RMB might take its place as an important international currency. In fact on the eve of the 2008 crisis, observers agreed that "China's power in the international financial system, certainly growing, should not be overestimated." Nevertheless, China's continued economic growth and massive holdings of dollar assets assured that, at the very least, discussions of the country's role as a potential monetary powerhouse would take place. As a long-term project, Beijing could envision the day when the Yuan would be the currency of choice in East Asia, a prospect that would further enhance China's political leadership and influence in the region. In the wake of the crisis, that timetable has been accelerated. A new and important motivation has also emerged—to establish some distance from the dollar, and to present a model of economic governance that offers some alternative to radically unmediated global finance.

China has always been wary of exposing itself to international capital markets, and understands that its controls spared it from the Asian financial crisis as well as other tumult since the mid- 1990s. From the early 2000s, China embarked on a cautious path that accommodated controlled RMB appreciation and modest movements toward financial liberalization. But the global financial crisis provided a new impetus to promote the Yuan, while also, crucially, altering visions of the ultimate path. By exposing profound flaws in the U.S. model, the crisis elicited what might be called "buyer's remorse" in Beijing—China regretted its development model that had bound it so tightly to the U.S. economy and made it such a stakeholder in the dollar.

Buyer's remorse also reflects greater disenchantment with the way Washington has managed the dollar and its role in the international financial system more generally, two things about which Chinese observers are increasingly critical. These reassessments have contributed to a desire, in China and elsewhere, to find some insulation from anticipated future instability caused by U.S. mismanagement, and a desire to reform the global macroeconomic order. . . .

> The consensus Chinese view is that a multi-reserve currency era is coming to replace the dollar.

Barriers remain to the emergence of the RMB, in particular the extent of the weakness and discomforting opacity of Chinese banks as well as of its domestic financial sector more generally, which raise doubts about the extent to which the Yuan is ready to step into the role of a major international currency. Nevertheless, after the crisis, Chinese leaders decided to step up the pace of RMB international-ization, promote regional monetary cooperation, and encourage reform of global monetary management. Notably, there is both an increase on the *supply side*, China's willingness to have the RMB deployed in a greater role internationally, and at the same time a clearly increased *demand*, a desire by states to find ways to transact business that do not bind them tightly to (or at least provide some diver-sification away from) the dollar, the U.S. financial model, and the U.S. economy.

The signature move in China's new promotion of the use of the Yuan has been the bilateral currency swap. Such agreements allow China and its trading partners to settle their trading accounts without moving in and out of dollars. China's trading partners, of which there are many, welcome such pacts—the People's Republic is the world's second-largest importer and the most important trading partner for an increasing number of major economies, who share most if not all of China's motives in diversifying away from the dollar. . . . In sum, actions taken by both China and its economic partners suggest the pre-positioning of an apparatus which would support the emergence of the Yuan as the key currency in Asia.

Encroachments on the Dollar

It should be remembered that it is not just the RMB that will be encroaching on the dollar, nor is it solely actors in Asia that will seek greater insulation from potential U.S. financial instability. Europe is certainly down, but not out, and in the longer run the Euro—possibly with China's quiet support—will resume its encroachment on the dollar's international role. Europe's own troubles have cer-tainly exposed the weaknesses of the Euro as a potential peer competitor to the dollar, a status that the European currency seemed close to achieving before the global financial crisis exposed its own problems. And to a considerable extent, Europe's crisis has handed another get-out-of-jail-free card to the profligate dollar, left again as the only game in town.

But dollar-watchers ought to keep three troubling factors in mind: first, the economies of United States and the EU are deeply enmeshed—Europe's struggles are bad for the U.S. economy, which is bad for the dollar. Second, should Europe's sovereign debt crisis worsen, the exposure of U.S. financial institutions should not be underestimated. Third, the crisis will almost certainly force the EU into a "corner solution"—forward or backward—and in either case, the Euro is likely to emerge as an even stronger player on world markets. Again, in a relative sense, this can only come about at the expense of the dollar's reach.

Geopolitical Consequences of Relative Dollar Decline

What does it matter if the international role of the dollar comes under pressure? There are two distinct types of challenges faced by states managing international currencies in *relative* decline: (1) the loss of benefits associated with issuing inter-national money, and (2) the difficulties associated with supervising a currency experiencing a contraction in its global use. As a practical matter, the principal consequences of international currency diminution include pressure on defense spending, reduced macroeconomic autonomy (and thus the ability to finance ambitious foreign policies), vulnerability to currency manipulation, and greater exposure to debilitating financial distress especially during times of international political crisis. In contemporary politics, these difficulties are likely to be exacerbated by increased disagreement and contestation among states over the politics of international monetary relations and global financial governance.

Eroding Global Power

The main perks of issuing a "key" international currency are (1) autonomy and flexibility of balance of payments and (2) structural power. With regard to the former, the United States generally underappreciates how much the special place of the dollar has allowed Washington to shake off the (often costly) burdens of macroeconomic adjustment, and essentially dump them on others. (For example, in 1971, when pressure on the dollar might have led to painful deflationary measures at home, the United States instead changed the rules of the game, ending the Bretton Woods system and forcing others to adjust their policies.) The United States has also been able to sustain deficits on its international accounts that other states could not have, and to adopt economic policies that, attempted elsewhere, would have been overwhelmed by a "disciplinary" response from international financial markets. The erosion of these perks will circumscribe U.S. power and autonomy, and fights over the burdens of adjustment—the normal stuffing of international monetary politics—will become a more common and salient feature of U.S. foreign policy.

The dollar-centric international system has also rewarded the United States with structural power. Structural power is not easily measured, nor obviously "coercive," but reflects, in the words of international relations scholar Susan Strange, "the power to decide how things shall be done, the power to shape frameworks within which states relate to each other." Structural power also affects the pattern of economic relations between states and their calculations of political interest. States that use the dollar (and especially those that hold their reserves in dollars) develop a vested interest in the value and stability of the currency. Once in widespread use, the fate of the dollar becomes more than just a U.S. problem—it becomes the problem of all dollar holders.

A relative contraction of the dollar's international role, then, would reduce both the "hard" and "soft" power the United States previously enjoyed—its coercive power enhanced by greater autonomy and its structural power implicitly shaping the preferences of others. It would also present new challenges and constraints.

Challenges of Relative Decline: Prestige and the Overhang

Were some dollar diminution to take place, the United States will face additional burdens in the costs associated with managing a currency in relative decline. For issuers of once-dominant international money, those new difficulties arise from what can be called the "overhang" problem, and from a loss of prestige.

The overhang problem arises as a function of a currency's one-time greatness. At the height of its attraction, numerous actors are eager to hold international money—governments for reserves, and private actors as a store of value (and often as a medium of exchange). But once the key currency is perceived to be in decline, it becomes suspect, and these actors will, over time, look to get out—to exchange it for some other asset. The need to "mop up" all this excess currency creates chronic monetary pressure on the once great currency; and macroeconomic policy will take place under the shadow of the past excess.

The loss of prestige is also a crucial consequence of managing a currency in decline. Prestige is a very slippery concept, but it finds a home in monetary analysis under the rubric of credibility, which is generally acknowledged to play a crucial role in monetary affairs (even if it, too, is not easily measured). The unparalleled reputation and bedrock credibility of the key currency during its glory days is a key source of the power it provides. The willingness of markets to implicitly tolerate imbalances in accounts and impertinent macroeconomic politics which would not be tolerated in other states rests on these foundations.

The loss of prestige and reduced credibility (which the challenge of the overhang exacerbates) imposes new costs on the issuer of a currency in relative decline. Whereas in the past, the key currency country was exempted from the rules of the game—that is, placed on a much longer leash by international financial markets than other states—the opposite becomes true. With eroding prestige and shared expectations of monetary distress, market vigilance is heightened and discipline imposed more swiftly by the collective expectations of more skeptical market actors. A presumption of confidence is replaced with a more jaundiced reading of the same indicators, and the long leash is replaced by an exceptionally tight choker.

Some of these problems can be illustrated by historical analogies. The experience of the British pound in the decades following World War II offers one, demonstrating the challenges faced by an international currency under pressure. In the 19th and early 20th centuries, sterling served as the international currency of choice, and the pound's key currency status enhanced British power. But eventually, the management of sterling-in-decline became a vexing problem for British authorities, complicating economic management and exacerbating its chronic financial crises in the 1960s. The 1956 Suez Crisis truly showed the constraints of financial fragility: Britain and France invaded Egypt in order to seize the Suez Canal (and, hopefully, bring about the overthrow of President Gamel Abdel Nasser), but Britain was forced to abort the operation-in-progress. A run on the pound had become overwhelming, and the country did not have adequate reserves to save currency on its own. In exchange for assistance from the United States and the IMF, the British agreed to an immediate cease-fire and prompt withdrawal from the Suez Canal zone.

> The 1956 Suez Crisis truly showed the constraints of financial
> fragility.

Suez was a flashpoint, but the crisis also underscored a fundamental new economic inhibition on the exercise of British power. Its suspect and vulnerable currency was routinely rocked by crises throughout the 1960s, which each time required spending cuts to shore up confidence in the economy, cuts that inevitably affected the military. Crisis-induced defense cuts in 1966 and 1967 eventually forced the country to reluctantly abandon its military role "East of Suez." This yielded phased withdrawals from Singapore, Malaysia, and the Persian Gulf. Neither devaluation (in November 1967) nor even the shift to floating exchange rates in the 1970s eliminated these chronic pressures. In 1976, a financial crisis forced Britain to seek help from the IMF, which insisted on still further cuts to domestic spending—including, of course, defense spending—enacted over the strong objections of the armed forces.

There are, of course, fundamental differences between post-war sterling and the contemporary dollar. But as a more extreme case, the British experience helps to expose and magnify the mechanisms by which currency diminution can affect national security. The politics of austerity—everywhere—will not spare military budgets, especially in peacetime and especially if such budgets appear large. Generally, a currency in decline faces increased and more skeptical market scrutiny, especially during moments of international crisis and wartime. Markets tend to react negatively to the prospects for a country's currency as it enters crisis and war, anticipating increased prospects for government spending, borrowing, inflation, and hedging against general uncertainty. In that sense, the Suez analogy is not inappropriate. Nor was this an isolated incident—weak currencies make for timid states. . . .

Reduced autonomy, eroding structural power, vanishing prestige, and a growing overhang problem all suggest a challenging general macroeconomic context for U.S. power in the coming years.

> The overextended dollar might also leave the U.S. vulnerable to economic coercion by other states.

New Vulnerabilities

The overextended dollar might also leave the United States vulnerable to economic coercion by other states. There is a real threat here, though one less apocalyptic than the suggestion that China might threaten to dump its enormous dollar holdings as an act of political coercion against the United States. This possibility is severely circumscribed by the fact that it is not in China's interest to do so, leaving this as a mostly empty threat. China now has, as I have argued above, "buyer's remorse" with regard to its vast dollar holdings. But it did not accumulate those dollar assets as an act of philanthropy, and it currently finds itself as a major stakeholder in the future of the dollar and the health of the U.S. economy.

China would be a big loser in a confrontation that undermined either the greenback or U.S. consumer demand. Despite its remarkable record of economic growth, China's economy has visible fragilities. Significant dollar depreciation would be a blow to its economy; a collapse in the dollar that reduced U.S. demand for imported goods would be a disaster. Thus China could conceivably dump its dollars, but this would be the economic equivalent of the nuclear option. It is possible to imagine scenarios, especially regarding confrontations over Taiwan, where China might try and engage in dollar brinksmanship or even pull the currency trigger—but short of that, China's vested interest in the dollar undercuts the potential political advantages of such a gambit.

This does not, however, leave the dollar in the clear. China has a more subtle lever of monetary power at its disposal—it has the capacity to modulate the rate at which it acquires dollar assets, as well as the ability to manipulate the timing and publicity associated with rebalancing its reserve portfolio (an effort already underway). This channel of influence is more of a one-way street than threats of dumping. A more confident—or more aggrieved—China might use this more subtle technique of monetary power to get the attention of the United States during moments of political conflict. . . .

New Heterogeneity Abroad: Paralysis at Home?

Before the 2007–08 financial crisis, trends at home and abroad suggested new macroeconomic constraints on U.S. power. Assuming continuity in these underlying factors, that crisis has accelerated those underlying trends and left the United States more vulnerable to the possibility that macroeconomic factors will inhibit, rather than enhance, its capabilities on the world stage—a reversal of the experiences of the past seventy years.

The global financial crisis has presented (like the Great Depression and the inflation of the 1970s) a "learning moment" in world politics, but much of that learning is currently taking place *outside* of the United States. That lesson is that completely unbound finance is dangerous, and does not work, and that the U.S. model is disreputable. The emergence of a new heterogeneity of thinking about money and finance will mark the end of the Second Post-War U.S. Order. States will increase their demand for autonomy and insulation from global financial instability, and due to ideological shifts and the acceleration of underlying material trends, U.S. power and influence will be relatively diminished in this new environment.

In addition to changes to the balance of power and political influence, these developments will also contribute to more acrimonious and chronic macroeconomic squabbling between states, which will place additional pressure on the management of the dollar. The underlying problem is that, in general, monetary cooperation is inherently difficult. The natural functioning of the international economy routinely generates pressures on states that require policy responses which affect interest rates, exchange rates, and government spending—involving costs that can be quite high and politically unwelcome. Not surprisingly, states invariably seek to shift the burdens of these adjustments abroad. (Much of Europe's current crisis is a fight over how to distribute the burdens of macroeconomic adjustment.)

Typically, it takes a confluence of exceptional factors for monetary cooperation to be sustained, each of which mitigates the costs of those burdens. A concentration of monetary power can help foster cooperation, because a hegemon can take on a disproportionate share of the costs of adjustment, or it can supervise, police, and enforce arrangements about the nature of adjustment. Ideological homogeneity can also foster cooperation by giving a cloak of economic legitimacy to the economic distress associated with adjustment. And shared, salient security concerns can increase the willingness of partners to bear the costs of adjustment, because they care more about the security situation.

Note that in contemporary international politics all of these variables are moving in the "wrong" direction. U.S. relative power (and monetary power) is in relative decline. There is a new heterogeneity of ideas about money and finance. And the security interests of key players at the monetary table have not been this divergent (if not necessarily oppositional) in over a century. This last change is particularly stark. Every major effort to reconstitute the international monetary order in the second half of the twentieth century was undertaken by the United States and its political allies and military dependencies. That is no longer the case. The United States will find it difficult to simply shrug off the burdens of macroeconomic adjustment (which will inevitably present themselves) onto others. This will compound the new U.S. sensitivity to external constraints. . . .

Questions for Review

What are the two key benefits that the United States derives from having the dollar the world's reserve currency? If the United States loses these, can it still afford to undergird the international financial and political-military order? Can it undergird the latter if it is no longer economically powerful?

Power Shifts, Economic Change, and the Decline of the West?

Michael Cox

Introduction

. . . It is often said that before every great fall there is a period of grace. So it was perhaps with the last hubristic decade of the twentieth century. But the fall when it came was profound nonetheless. . . . It all began with 9/11 and the strategically inept response to this by the Bush administration. It continued with the gradual erosion of economic certainty that finally culminated with the great geopolitical setback of the Western financial crisis. And it went from bad to worse in some eyes when it became increasingly clear that the West itself was facing a massive challenge from other non-Western players in the world capitalist economy. . . .

Unsurprisingly, these seismic alterations generated much intense debate around the world: nowhere more so than in the West itself. Here, opinion veered between the deeply pessimistic—all power transitions it was assumed could only lead to intensified global conflict—through to those who insisted that the new emerging economies could only add to the stock of the world's wealth by bringing more states within the fold of the world market. It was the rise of China, however, that occasioned the greatest discussion of all. . . . In fact, almost overnight, it seemed as if everybody had something significant to say about China. Opinion differed sharply with one or two writers claiming that China was fast becoming a responsible stakeholder in international society, a few that its rapid economic expansion was the only thing standing between the West and a global depression, others that it constituted a real threat to US hegemony and many more that if it continued to grow while the West lurched from low growth to no growth at all, it might soon be running Asia, or possibly even the world. But however one assessed China, one thing looked startlingly obvious. . . . A gravity shift was taking place—or so it was argued—and whether or not one viewed China's economic rise as a foregone conclusion, a necessary corrective to its nineteenth century period of humiliation, worried about its impact on the global economic and political order, or assumed that its rise was bound to lead to increased 'intense security competition', one thing was certain: the international system was undergoing what even Western governments now believed was a transformation that would alter the world forever.

In what follows, I want to address the issues raised by what many are now assuming to be irreversible changes in the world order.

I make several arguments. . . . One is that this modern story, exciting and interesting though it is, tends to focus almost entirely on what is rapidly changing but says little about what is not—and what is changing much less than some are now suggesting is America's position in the world. There has also been a confusion about terms. Nobody serious would want to deny that there have been measurable changes in the shape of the world economy over the past few years. However, too many writers have either assumed that a shift in economic gravity is the same thing as a power shift (it is not), or that as these economic changes continue, they will either lead to a transfer of power from one hegemon to another (this is questionable) or to the creation of something now regularly (and dubiously) referred to as a new 'Asian Century'. As I will seek to show, these assertions contain serious analytical flaws. Equally flawed, I would insist, is the idea that we can make bold predictions about where the world will be in the future. As we can all attest getting the future right has in the past proven to be a fool's errand. This, I would want to argue, has important lessons for those now confidently predicting a major power shift over the coming decades. The 'rest' may now be growing fast, while the United States and the European Union (EU) languish. However, as more sober analysts have pointed out, the crisis in the West may not last forever, while the many problems facing some of the rest—including

India and China—could derail their apparently irresistible rise up the economic league table. . . .

American Economic Decline?

. . . a large part of the case in favour of the notion that a 'power shift' is underway rests on the assumption that the leading Western player—the United States of America—faces an irresistible economic decline that will, if it continues, either allow others to take advantage of its weakness or reduce its ability to lead. . . . [W]ith its share of world trade falling, its debt increasing, its economy in slowdown since 2008 and its dependency on foreign purchasers of its debt on the rise, it looks to many analysts at least as if the United States will either 'need to retrench' or, more problematically, pass on the baton to other more capable powers. . . .

There can of course be no doubting America's many economic problems. Nor should there be any doubt either that America's share of world gross domestic product (GDP) is much less today than it was, say, 25 years ago, let alone at the end of the World War II when it was the only serious player in the world capitalist system. But this is hardly the same thing as suggesting that the United States is in irreversible economic decline—now a common view—or that China has now overtaken it—an equally popular view. Even on the simplest of GDP measures, the United States is still well ahead of China. Thus, whereas China with a population of around 20 per cent of the world's total generates something between one-seventh and one-tenth of global GDP, the United States with only 6 per cent of the world's population still manages to produce between 20 and 25 per cent. Indeed, by a simple GDP measurement, the US economy remains more powerful than the next four biggest economies combined: that is to say China, Japan, Germany and the United Kingdom. . . . Furthermore, in terms of living standards, the United States continues to be ahead by a long way with an overall average 4 times higher than that of Brazil, 6 times higher than that in China and as much as 15 times higher than in India. . . .

If the United States is hardly the declining economic superpower portrayed in much of the literature today, it also continues to be able to do things that others can only dream of. In part, this is a function of its size; in part, a function of geographical luck (the United States possesses enormous quantities of oil, gas, coal and food) and in part, a function of its embedded position in the world economic system. As Carla Norloff has recently shown, despite a gradual economic decline since the end of the World War II, the United States still possesses critical features that give it what she calls 'positional advantages' over all other states. She even challenges the now fashionable view that America's hegemonic burdens are outweighing the benefits. She suggests otherwise: Washington actually reaps more than it pays out in the provision of public goods.[1] The United States also has one other, very special, advantage: the dollar. . . . Furthermore, . . . even the financial crisis has not weakened the position of the United States anywhere near as much some have assumed. Indeed, in a world where uncertainty reigns (most obviously in the EU), 'money' in its purest form has fled to safety, and nowhere is regarded as being as safe as the United States. To this extent, the financial crisis, ironically, has only affirmed US financial power rather than weakened it.[2]

We also have to judge economic power not only in terms of the size of an economy but also by the qualitative criteria of 'competitiveness'. Economies like China, India and Brazil are undoubtedly large and will no doubt get larger over time. But this does not necessarily make them competitive in relationship to most Western countries or the United States. In a 2011 survey, in fact, the United States came fourth in the world in a group of 15 countries. Moreover, 11 within the 15 were definably Western, while the other 4 included Japan, Taiwan, Hong Kong and Singapore—countries all closely tied to the West and to the United States. As for the BRICs, they came well down the list. Thus, China came in at 27, India at 51, Brazil at 58 and Russia at 63.[3] Other studies have arrived at not dissimilar conclusions concerning the qualitative gap that continues to exist between a number of the 'rising' economies and many of the more established ones, the United States, in particular. In terms of cutting-edge research in science and technology, for example, the United States continues to hold a clear lead. Indeed in 2008, the United States accounted for 40 per cent of total world research and development (R&D) spending and 38 per cent of patented new technology inventions. More significantly, scientific research produced in the United States accounted for 49 per cent of total world citations and 63 per cent of the most highly cited articles. The United States also continued to employ around 70 of the world's Nobel Prize winners and could lay claim to two-thirds of its most cited individual researchers in science and technology.[4]

Innovation is also an American strength.[5] Other countries are clearly beginning to catch up. The United States, however, is still a country that continues to innovate across the board. Critics would no doubt point to the fact that the United States is slipping down the league table. However, it still ranks fourth in the world. China meanwhile only came in at 54th in 2009, India at 56th and Brazil and Russia even further behind. Of course, this does not take account of change over the longer term, or of the fact that a country like China is making a concerted effort to build a more innovative economy.[6] But as even the Chinese would accept, it still has very long way to go. Indeed, in spite of official efforts to encourage what is termed in China a 'capacity for independent innovation', there remain several weaknesses in the Chinese political economy. . . . There is also wider political restraint as well. Innovation usually requires open debate, a capacity to challenge established truths and incentives to think the unthinkable; and none of these, to be blunt, are much in evidence in modern China today.

Finally, in terms of global economic power, the United States is still well ahead in one other vital respect: corporate strength.[7] Some of the emerging economies are beginning to catch up, and some of America's closest allies in Europe and Asia run it a good second. But the United States clearly remains in 'poll position' with American companies in 2011 constituting 4 of the top 10 corporations in the world, 14 of the top 30 and 25 of the top 50. Western companies more generally still outperform all others, with the United States and the EU together representing 6 out of the top 10 global corporations, 22 out of the top 30 and 37 out of the top 50. Some of the BRIC economies do have some very large companies with China, unsurprisingly, leading the way with 4 out of the top 10, 8 out of the top 50 and 61 out of the top 500, a remarkable achievement for a country that only 25 years ago was virtually irrelevant in the world economy. Still, as a recent Brookings study has shown, it does not follow that these companies are internationally active or should even be regarded as 'multinationals' in the true sense of that word. Indeed, 49 of the top 57 mainland companies in China remain under state control; and with a very few exceptions, the overwhelming majority all operate predominantly within the country—and for several good reasons including a shortage of managers with the necessary linguistic skills and experience of working abroad, a lack of transparency, poor global brand presence, and a very real difficulty in adapting easily to foreign legal, tax and political environments.[8]

Hard Power–Soft Power

If the United States retains some very formidable economic assets, the same can just as easily be said about its still very powerful position within the larger international system. This is no longer a fashionable view to defend of course. Indeed, a combination of an ill-judged war in Iraq, the use of torture in the 'war on terror', the near meltdown of the American financial system in 2008, and the slow recovery of the American economy since, has led many to question America's capacity either to lead others or garner support for its policies abroad. . . .

Obviously, there is something to this, which is one of the reasons why this kind of argument has proved so popular among those who now hold to the view that we are now in the midst of a 'power shift'. But one of the problems with it, clearly, is that it seriously understates how much hard power the United States can still mobilize, even after the very limited cuts proposed by President Obama. It might be intellectually fashionable to argue that military power is becoming less and less salient in an age of asymmetric war where the weak can do a great deal of damage to the strong. However, the very fact that the United States is able to mobilize the military manpower it can (currently it has more men and women under arms than it had on the eve of 9/11), can project power to every corner of the earth, is still the main provider of security in Asia and Europe and spends as much as it still does on 'defence'—about 45 per cent of the world's total—suggests that the country has a very long way to go before one can talk about it becoming less of a superpower. The military power of other states moreover does not compare, even China's with its huge standing army (which has not fought a war since the disastrous invasion of Vietnam in 1979) and its increasingly large blue water navy that now includes one aircraft carrier. Indeed, when its first aircraft carrier was finally given its first sea trials in 2011, the alarm bells went up in the region. However, China's one aircraft carrier hardly compares with America's 11 carrier groups. Nor has the ongoing modernization of China's military brought it anywhere close to US levels. Indeed the most recent figures show that the United States not only expends five times more on national security than China. Taken together, its many allies in the region (including among others Japan, South Korea, India and Australia) also spend more on their military forces than China, and do so by a significant margin—nearly US$200bn compared to China's $115bn.[9]

This in turn should alert us to yet another aspect of America's impressive position in the world: its formidably wide alliance system. . . . There might be fewer states willing to 'follow' the United States in ways that they did during the Cold War. There are also a few 'problem' countries like Pakistan, Turkey and Egypt that have increasingly difficult relations with Washington. Nonetheless, even those who have doubts about American leadership skills, still find that they have no alternative but to ally themselves with it. This is obviously true of the Europeans who can see no other security guarantor than the United States. But it is also true of key states in Latin America, Africa and Asia. If anything, it has become even more true in Asia; in fact, as China has risen, most Asian countries (including communist-led Vietnam) have demanded more, and not less, of an American presence in the region. China as a result now finds itself in the paradoxical position of having greater economic influence in Asia but fewer friends. To this degree, its growing economic power has not translated into it having more political influence as well. Nor have its heavy-handed policies in Asia helped. On the contrary, by laying claim to the South China Seas and remaining silent about the aggressive behaviour of its single ally North Korea, it has actually made America's position stronger rather than weaker. Indeed, precisely because China does not 'inspire confidence', it has been possible for the United States to be viewed by most countries in the region as that well-known 'indispensable nation' upon whose continued presence their own safety ultimately depends.

America's continued presence in Asia raises a wider question about whether 'power' in the broader sense is in fact tilting away from the West as is now so often claimed. China may well be the new engine pulling along the world economy. Its economic role in Africa, Brazil and Australia may have become crucially important. And its new middle class may be buying more and more of the high-end products that the West is only too happy to sell it. Yet, thus far, China has been much less than successful in winning friends and building relations of trust with other countries. It might be an exaggeration to say that China 'is generally held in suspicion' around the world. But China does confront some serious difficulties when interacting with others. In part, the problem is cultural. This is still a country after all that for all its new openness continues to harbour a suspicion of 'foreigners'. The overwhelming majority of its people moreover are deeply insular in outlook and have little experience, and hardly any understanding, of the world outside of Chinese borders. This is even true of many of its senior policy-makers, the bulk of whom travel abroad infrequently, do not speak foreign languages with any degree of fluency and who have been brought up politically in the hidden world of the Chinese Communist Party. There is also a larger ideological and political issue. China might be a trading superpower. But it has no vision and no sense of what it might take to become a serious superpower in a leadership position with all the responsibilities and dangers that would entail. If anything, China is extraordinarily ill-equipped to lead with its defensive, almost suspicious view of the world, and its constant reiteration of the old Westpahalian mantra that states should keep their noses out of other people's business. Nor is there much sign that it is keen to do so. In this, of course, the Chinese themselves have been perfectly candid. Our foreign policy goal, they repeat, is to create an international environment that will permit us to focus on domestic affairs and economic growth at home; and anything disturbing that derails us from this very long-term task stretching over several decades should be avoided at all costs. It is not even certain that China even regards itself as a model for others to follow. Indeed, how could it do so in a world where democracy—however imperfect—has become the political norm? People abroad may admire China for what it has achieved; a few may even hope that its rise will lead to a degree of balance in the international system. But when it imprisons dissident artists, repeatedly attacks the much admired Dalai Lama and then seeks to punish another sovereign state for an entirely independent committee awarding a peace prize to one of its citizens, this is hardly likely to win it converts in the wider world.

If China has a real problem in projecting a positive and confident picture of itself or of the world it would like to build, the same can hardly be said of the United States. . . . the 'West' for all its faults—growing inequality, ethical standards in decline and all the rest—still looks a more attractive proposition than anything else on offer. As a recent study has shown, 'soft power' is almost entirely the preserve of Western, or more precisely democratic, countries with the United States still leading a league table that includes most West European countries as well as two countries from Asia—Japan and South Korea. China on the other hand comes in 20th, just ahead of Brazil at 21st, followed by India at 27th and Russia 28th out of a total of 30 countries assessed.[10]

There are several reasons why the West continues to score well in terms of soft power, the most obvious being that Western countries have a pluralist political culture where having dissident views, will not, by and large, end up with one spending a rather long term in prison or worse. But another reason—clearly connected—has to do with its open system of higher education. Here, even the much-maligned United States continues to have great magnetic pull, nowhere more so than in China itself, judging by the enormous number of Chinese students who every year seek a place in US institutions of higher learning. Many of them may in the end return to China. However, they clearly believe that getting an education in a US college will improve their job prospects in an increasingly tough Chinese job market. Nor is this temporary 'brain drain' a mere accident of history. Indeed, one of the more obvious signs of continued Western and American strength is its university sector. Other countries and continents obviously have universities. But very few of them rank especially high in international terms. The BRIC countries in particular seem to face almost insuperable difficulties in raising standards. Brazil and India for example have no universities in the top 100, Russia only one and China a mere five—three of these being in Hong Kong. The United States, in 2011, meanwhile remained home to 8 of the top 10 ranked universities in the world, 37 of the top 50 and 58 of the top 100. Even the United Kingdom does well, having 17 ranked universities compared to a total of 13 in the whole of Asia.[11]

If standards in higher education are still being set in the West, the same can also be said about the rules and associated institutions that govern the international system more generally. Admittedly, many of the most important institutions in the world today are not functioning as well as they might and, over time, changes in the international economy will have to be reflected in the way the world is managed. The fact remains, however, that nearly all the key rules governing the global economy, and most of those dealing with critically important issues such as nuclear non-proliferation, trade liberalization, women's rights and the protection of intellectual property rights, have been laid down by, and are still more likely to be upheld by, countries in the West. Furthermore, while many of the emerging economies might have many entirely legitimate complaints about how the West has behaved in the past and how the United States still behaves now, none of them have either the desire or the capability of really challenging the West in any meaningful way. This in large part has much to do with their still very high dependency on western markets and western Foreign Direct Investment. But more importantly, it is because they realize that their own success over the past 25 years has been in some part determined by adopting broadly Western economic rules. This is not to play down their own contribution to their own success. Nor should we assume that countries like China and India have adopted a pure Western model. They have not. Nonetheless, their much heralded rise only began in earnest when they abandoned one, rather self-sufficient way of doing economics, and started the long journey towards a global economy that was western in design and market-oriented in fundamentals.

A New Asian Century?

If, as I have suggested, the West has far more global influence than many writers of late have suggested, how, then, do we explain what now seems self-evident to many analysts: that we are moving into a new Asian Century in which the West as traditionally understood will have far less wealth and altogether less power? . . . Is this merely a matter of ignorance, wishful thinking or simply a misunderstanding?

On a number of issues concerning modern Asia, there can be no serious disagreement. Its weight in the world economy has clearly got bigger. It can boast two of the BRICs—China and India. It presents major investment opportunities.

And it is home to an increasingly significant regional organization in the shape of Association of Southeast Asian Nations (ASEAN). Asia's rapid growth over the last two decades has also been accompanied by a dramatic reduction in poverty. In East Asia and the Pacific region alone, the percentage of the population now living on less than US$1.25 per day has dropped from 55 per cent in 1990 to only 17 per cent in 2006. China alone has taken nearly 200 million people out of poverty over the last 25 years.[12]

These achievements are all real enough. Moreover, when set alongside the miserable economic situation currently pertaining in many parts of Europe, they look almost miraculous. But one should beware hyperbole, especially when it comes to announcing an 'Asian Century' that has not yet arrived. Asia's weight in the world has certainly risen; but by much less than is commonly assumed. Indeed, a closer look at the figures indicates that the shift in economic power from West to East can be overstated. In 1995, for instance, Asia's total share of world GDP (in nominal terms at market exchange rates) was already 29 per cent. Fifteen years later, it was no higher. As for the now widely accepted view that Asian producers were fast acquiring an ever-larger slice of global exports, the figures indicate that the region as a whole could lay claim to 28 per cent of the total in 1995, but only 31 per cent by in 2009, a rise of only 3 per cent over 15 years. Nor do these base figures take account of other significant indicators, many of which point to important flaws in the Asian economies. The quality of Chinese products, for example, does not match world standards. And in crucial cutting-edge areas such as hardware and software technologies, the United States still dominates.[13] In short, Asia still has long way to go before it will catch up with the West—a West by the way, whose combined output is still double that of the East.[14]

If we are nowhere near arriving at a so-called Asian Century, one of the other reasons for this is that the entity we call Asia hardly exists as a collective actor. As many observers have pointed out, one of the most remarkable features of Asian political landscape is how fragmented it happens to be. Thus, many in Asia, China in particular, harbour deep resentments towards Japan. Japan in turn bitterly resents China's rise. And India has problems with nearly all of its Asian neighbours, China especially. Most Asian nations also have a very powerful sense of post-colonial identity. This not only fosters quite a degree of suspicion of each other, but also weakens any sense of common purpose.

Finally, before we can talk of a new Asian Century, we should remind ourselves that there are other parts of the world where relations between states are a good deal more settled and amicable—most notably between those countries making up the Transatlantic relationship. Asia may be rising and the BRICs emerging. However, one should not underestimate the many strengths possessed by the key states constituting the wider Transatlantic space. Even in the midst of the crisis, the United States and the EU still account for well over half of World GDP in terms of value and 40 percent in terms of purchasing power.[15] The most important international banks are also to be found in Europe and the United States. Europe and the United States moreover play host to nearly all of its major business schools; and in areas such as oil exploration, aviation and chemicals, they still lead the way. The two together are also the world's most important source of Foreign Direct Investment, and by far and away, the world's most important markets too. They also invest in each other's future in vast amounts. Indeed, in 2010, the United States invested far more in Europe than it was ever likely to do in Asia or China—three times more to be precise. Meanwhile, the EU had invested eight times more in the United States than it had in the whole of Asia. Americans today may not view Europe as being terribly exciting. And no doubt Europeans will continue to worry as to their current status in a Washington fixated on nearly everything else except the EU. But that does not make the economic relationship any the less significant. . . .

Conclusion

I have made a strong claim in this article. This challenges the notion that we are in the midst of some larger power shift. This, in my view, not only misunderstands the complex notion of what constitutes 'power', it is empirically dubious too. As I have tried to show here, the United States still has a great deal of power, much more than any other country in the world, now and for the foreseeable future. China meanwhile confronts several basic problems at home and abroad (as indeed do the other members of the so-called BRIC family). And the idea that we are moving ineluctably into what some have termed an 'Asian Century' is unsustainable. In making this case, I am not implying that the world is an entirely static place. Nor am I making a plea for the status quo. Rather, I have tried to go behind the headlines and to call things by their right name. Not only is this important for purely intellectual reasons: in my view, it is strategically important too. After all, if a country like China really does come to believe that one day it really will be ruling the world, and Americans see no alternative but to combat this in whatever way they see necessary, this could very easily lead to an increased, and in my view, a quite unnecessary escalation of tension between these two very powerful states.

I draw two other very important conclusions from the foregoing analysis. The first concerns the lessons we should be drawing from the past. Here, the Cold War looms large in my thinking. I am not naïve enough to think that it would have been easy to have avoided some form of competition between the United States and the USSR after World War II. But there is little doubt either that Western worst case thinking based on exaggerated fears of a rising Soviet Union did make the conflict far more intense and long lasting than it might have been otherwise. In the same way, though in a very different context involving a very different kind of state, there is a very real danger today that if the policymakers and analysts begin to talk up Chinese strengths without recognizing its very real limits, they could easily end up creating yet another security dilemma. . . .

Finally, I want to make a plea here for a far more subtle theory of the modern international system. Too many writers over the past few years have talked of the world as if it were like a series of billiard balls banging up against each other in some zero-like contest in which states and regions in one part of the world rise, while others in other parts of the world fall. This might make perfect sense to some realists. However, it ignores just about everything else, including the fairly self-evident fact that the modern international economy is now so interdependent that even if we accepted the perfectly reasonable idea that certain states can make relative gains here at the expense of other states there, in the end, most states—including most obviously the United States and China—have become entirely dependent on each other for their prosperity and security. To this degree, we no longer live in a world composed of clearly specified friends and well-defined enemies, but rather in one where partnership has become a necessity. Once upon a time, this way of looking at the world was branded by its critics as liberal idealism. In the twenty-first century, it has, in my view, become the highest form of realism.

Question for Review

Cox argues that forecasts of U.S. decline are overdone because the United States retains considerable power. What is his argument, and how can we reconcile that with the central message of the Posen and Kirshner selections?

Notes

1. Carla Norloff, America's Global Advantage: US Hegemony and International Co-operation (Cambridge: Cambridge University Press, 2010).

2. See Doug Stokes, 'A Post-Crisis Piper? Assessing Dollar Decline and US Primacy', Unpublished Manuscript.

3. Source: http://www3.weforum.org/docs/WEF_GloblalCompetivenessReport_2010-11.pdf

4. See: http://www.rand.org/pubs/monographs/2008/RAND_MG674.pdf

5. See 'A New Ranking of the World's Most Innovative Economies', Economist Intelligence Unit, April 2009, pp. 1–11.

6. George Kee, 'Chinese Innovation Sidesteps US crisis', Global Times, 12 August 2011.

7. The statistics in this paragraph are taken from the FT Global 500, 2011. FT Weekend Magazine, June 2011 and the Fortune's Global 500 List, 2011.

8. David Shambaugh, 'Are China's Multinational Corporations Really Multinational?' East Asia Forum Quarterly, 10 July 2012.

9. For figures on global military spending in 2012, see the SIPRI Handbook for 2012. Available at: http://en.wikipedia.org/wiki/List_of_countries_by_military_expenditures\#SIPRI_Yearbook_2012_World.27s_top_15_military_spenders

10 See Jonathan McClory, 'The New Persuaders II: A 2011 Global Ranking of Soft Power' (Institute for Government, 1 December 2011), p. 24.

11 These figures from http://www.topuniversities.com/top-100-universities-in-the-world-2011

12 These figures were obtained from 'Asia's Importance Growing in Global Economy', IMF Survey Online. Available at: http://www.imf.org/external/pubs/ft/survey/so/2010/car05120a.htm

13 Sarajit Majumdar, 'Global Power Shift—West to East?' Asia Sentinel, 9 January 2009.

14 'The Balance of Economic Power: East or Famine', The Economist, 27 February 2010, pp. 77–78.

15 See Daniel S. Hamilton and Joseph P. Quinlan, The Transatlantic Economy, 2011. (Washington DC: Centre for Transatlantic Relations, 2011) p.v.

The Future of the European Union

Stephen M. Walt

Testimony to the Committee on Foreign Affairs
Subcommittee on Europe, Eurasia and Emerging Threats
U.S. House of Representatives
Hearing on "The European Union's Future"
July 14, 2015

Mr. Chairman and members of the Committee:

It is an honor to be invited to speak with you today, in the company of these other experts. It is obviously a tumultuous time for the nations of Europe, most of whom are close allies of the United States. Because the European Union is a key trading partner, home to more than 500 million people, and tied to the United States through NATO and many other connections, its condition is of obvious importance to the United States. Trying to anticipate its future path is therefore a critical task.

Unfortunately, it is hard to be optimistic about the EU's long-term prospects. Although the EU has been a positive force in world politics for many years, it now suffers from growing structural tensions and a series of self-inflicted wounds. Its members may overcome today's challenges and continue to build an "ever-closer union," but this outcome is unlikely. Instead, the EU is more likely to face repeated crises and growing internal divisions, and we cannot rule out the possibility of gradual and irreversible disintegration. This situation is not good news for the United States, as it will make Europe a less valuable ally and increase the number of places and issues that U.S. leaders need to worry about.

To explain why I reach this depressing conclusion, I will first describe the EU's past achievements and then discuss the main sources of strain it now faces. I close by outlining several possible futures and explain why I believe the EU's best days are behind it.

Past Achievements

The European Union is in many ways a remarkable political experiment. In the aftermath of the most destructive war in history, and after centuries of recurring conflict, a generation of European leaders had the imagination and determination to conceive and create a new order based on economic integration, open borders, and the partial surrender of sovereignty to a new supranational organization. The original European Coal and Steel Community evolved to become the European Common Market, expanded to include a host of new entrants, and then deepened to become the European Union and create a common currency for some of its members.

For much of the past half-century, this collective effort encouraged economic growth, gave Europe a more coherent voice in international economic affairs, and reduced the danger of great power competition in Europe itself. The EU has also been an influential model for other states, and especially the post-communist governments in Eastern Europe. Indeed, the desire for EU membership encouraged these states to adopt critical democratic reforms following the collapse of the Soviet Union and dampened potential conflicts during this delicate transition period.

Yet despite these impressive accomplishments, the EU's present condition and future prospects are not bright. In particular, it now faces at least five fundamental challenges. Some of these challenges are problems of its own creation; others reflect broader changes in the world at large. None of them will be easy to overcome.

Sources of Strain

1. Over-Expansion

The EU is now a victim of its past successes. What began as a limited arrangement among six countries to coordinate the production and marketing of coal and steel has become an elaborate supranational organization with twenty-eight members, whose affairs are partially governed by the European Commission, the Council of Europe, the European Parliament, the European Council and its elected president, the European Court of Justice, and a host of subsidiary agencies. Each member-state retains a separate national government, however, with authority over health, police, fiscal policy, and defense and foreign policy. Today, Europe's governance arrangements make America's federal system look simple by comparison.

Moreover, as the EU has grown, its membership has become increasingly heterogeneous in terms of population, economic size, per capita income, and cultural background. At roughly €2 trillion, Germany's GDP is more than three hundred times larger than Malta's (€6 billion), while Luxemburg's per capita income is roughly eight times larger than Latvia's and five times larger than that of Greece. The geographic size, population, and natural resource endowments of the EU's member states also vary enormously, as do their cultures, religious affiliations, and national histories.

Ironically, that heterogeneity is a key reason why the EU's newest members (mostly from East and Southeastern Europe) were eager to join, and why the original members encouraged their aspirations. In essence, both parties wanted the new member states to become more like the rest of the community. But convergence between old and new members has been slow and incomplete, and the EU's governing institutions must try to accommodate and reconcile a broader array of interests, political traditions and historical experiences than it did in earlier periods.

The inevitable result is that it is harder for the EU to reach consensus on critical issues and more difficult to resolve underlying problems in a timely and effective manner.

As the EU has grown, in short, it has become more cumbersome, more divided, and less effective. It has also become less popular, with more than 70 percent of EU citizens reporting in 2013 that "their voices do not count in EU decision-making" and nearly two-thirds declaring "the EU does not understand the needs of its citizens."[1]

2. The Demise of the Warsaw Pact

The disappearance of the Soviet Union was a welcome development, but it removed one of the main motivations for European unity. Although scholars and journalists often portray the EU as a purely economic and political project, security concerns were a key part of its rationale from the start.[2] In particular, European leaders in the 1950s believed only a continental-scale economy could provide the wherewithal to counter the Soviet Union and Warsaw Pact, and economic integration was also necessary to prevent political rivalries from undermining the Western effort to keep communism from spreading. Together with NATO, therefore, European economic integration was an important component of the Western effort to contain Soviet expansion.

This security rationale faded as NATO become stronger and it disappeared entirely when the Soviet Union collapsed. The absence of a clear and present danger permitted Europe's leaders to focus more attention on individual national concerns, and devote less political capital to preserving the broader European project. EU members have repeatedly pledged to develop a "common foreign and security policy," but they have never succeeded in doing so. Today, the incoherent and inconsistent European response to events in Ukraine highlights the lack of consensus among EU governments on basic foreign policy issues.

3. The Euro Crisis

The third problem facing the EU today is the euro crisis. With hindsight, it is clear the decision to create the euro was a fateful error, as skeptics from across the political spectrum warned at the time. European leaders established a common currency for political rather than economic reasons: they sought to give new momentum to the broader goal of European unity, to bind a reunified Germany within a stronger set of European institutions, and to put Europe on a more equal footing with the United States.

But as the euro's critics emphasized, the EU did not possess the political and institutional mechanisms needed to make a currency union work. Instead, the euro's proponents simply assumed that eurozone members would abide by agreed-upon fiscal guidelines and never allow themselves to get into serious financial trouble. As Joseph Joffe, the editor of *Die Zeit*, noted back in 1997, the euro tied the disparate national economies together like cars on a locomotive and assumed that all would run at the same speed and on the same track forever.[3] The euro's architects further assumed that if these assumptions proved to be too optimistic (as indeed they did), a future crisis would force them to create the political and economic institutions they needed (e.g., common bank regulations, shared fiscal policy, a stronger central bank, and greater capacity to transfer resources from wealthy states to members in need of help).

The 2008 financial crisis exposed their follies and the EU has been preoccupied with containing the damage ever since. Seven years have passed since the crisis hit and top government officials and central bankers are still devoting countless hours to saving the common currency. They have made tentative steps toward creating slightly stronger economic institutions, but the EU is still light-years away from having the political institutions needed to sustain a genuine currency union. When Greece exits—as it almost certainly will—this event will demonstrate that the euro is not irreversible and sow new doubts about its long-term prospects.

The economic costs of the euro crisis have been enormous, but the political costs are also substantial. Every hour that Europe's leaders have spent trying to dig themselves out of this mess is an hour they could not devote to dealing with China's rise, the problem of terrorism, the consequences of the so-called Arab spring, Russia's policy in Ukraine, or any number of domestic issues. Even worse, the euro crisis has sown deep divisions within the continent itself, as debtors and creditors increasingly regard each other with a level of resentment and hostility not seen for many years. Needless to say, this situation is not what the euro's creators had in mind when they took that fateful step.

4. A Deteriorating Regional Environment

The EU is now buffeted by serious instability on its frontiers. State failures in Libya, Syria, Yemen, and parts of Africa have produced a growing flood of refugees seeking to enter the EU, while the emergence of Al Qaeda, ISIS and other extremist movements has had worrisome repercussions among a small percentage of Europe's Muslim population. While it is sometimes exaggerated, the danger of home-grown terrorism is not zero and a number of Europeans are now calling for new barriers to immigration and new limits on cross-border movements within Europe itself. If adopted, such measures would reverse the movement toward open borders that was one of the singular achievements of the 1986 Single European Act. Last but not least, continued violence in Ukraine raises new concerns about the security of the EU's eastern frontier. EU member-states have thus far been unable to agree on new measures to address any of these challenges, further underscoring the dysfunctional nature of contemporary EU decision-making.

5. The Persistence of Nationalism

The elites who created and built the EU hoped that it would transcend existing national loyalties and that its citizens would eventually identify as Europeans first and as Germans, Danes, Italians, Belgians, Spaniards, etc. second.

This transformation of loyalties has not occurred; if anything, public attitudes are headed the other way. As previously discussed, the euro crisis has exacerbated national tensions and European leaders have consistently emphasized national interests rather than the broader goal of European unity, even as they attempt to strengthen the EU's existing institutions.[4] The United Kingdom may even vote to leave the EU next year, while resurgent nationalism could lead Scotland to exit the United Kingdom. Powerful nationalist sentiments continue to simmer in Catalonia and several other regions as well.

Economic hardship and rising opposition to immigration have also fueled a resurgence of extreme right-wing movements in many European states. These movements are hostile to the core principles upon which the EU is built and their growing popularity raises further doubts about the EU's long-term future. Add to this mix Europe's unfavorable demography—its population is declining and the median age is rising rapidly—and you have a recipe for continued economic stagnation and popular discontent. If these trends bring parties such as France's National Front to power, it will make it even harder for the EU to regain its former legitimacy and restore momentum for further integration.

What Lies Ahead?

Looking forward, one can imagine at least three possible futures for the European Union. First, Europe's current leaders could follow in their prede-cessors' footsteps and find new ways to overcome the challenges identified above. Support for European integration has waxed and waned in the past, but previous European politicians eventually opted to move forward rather than let their grand experiment languish or collapse. In theory, creative and determined leadership could save the euro (with or without Greece), build the institutions needed to support a common currency, integrate immigrant populations more effectively, and adopt reforms designed to trigger more vigorous economic growth across the continent. Concerns about Russia's intentions might provide a new rationale for unity as well, and especially if the trouble in Ukraine spreads to other areas.

Unfortunately, this optimistic vision of a reinvigorated EU is unlikely to occur. There are no European leaders today with the vision and stature of a Konrad Adenauer, Charles DeGaulle, or Margaret Thatcher, and European publics are more likely to reward politicians who secure better deals for their individual countries rather than those who sacrifice narrow interests in favor of an ever-closer union. The EU's elaborate governance structures would make any serious reform effort a long and torturous process, which means even a successful resurgence is likely to take years to design and implement.

Instead of a new push for ever-greater union, therefore, the EU is more likely to simply muddle through. It will strive to contain the fallout from a Grexit, sign the Transatlantic Trade and Investment Partnership (TTIP) with the United States and pursue closer economic ties with China. If all goes well, the EU will still be in business, but its current liabilities will remain and its global influence will continue to decline.

There is a third possibility, however: the EU experiment could begin to unravel in more far-reaching ways. Greece's exit from the Eurozone will create new doubts about the euro's future, more member-states may begin to question the benefits of membership and a few (such as Greece or Hungary) might even draw closer to Moscow. Nationalist resentments could fester and deepen, authoritarian or neo-fascist leaders could come to power somewhere, and Greece or Hungary might even draw closer to Moscow. If the EU begins to unravel, the only question may be: how fast and how far?

Neither "muddling through" nor gradual collapse would be good news for the United States. Europe is not as vital a strategic interest as it was during the height of the Cold War, but it is still an important economic and military partner. Slow growth in Europe also means slower growth here in the United States, and a divided and poorer Europe will be even less helpful as the United States tries to deal with a rising China, a turbulent Middle East, or instability in sub-Saharan Africa. Problems within the EU will distract us, and reduce the time and attention US leaders can devote to other issues.

To sum up: since the end of the Second World War, tranquility and prosperity in Europe has been of enormous benefit to the United States. The European Union was not the only source of stability and economic growth in Europe, but it was a key ingredient in a world order that was overwhelmingly favorable for the United States. If the EU's best days are behind it—and there are good reasons to believe that they are—then Americans must prepare for a world that is less stable, secure, and prosperous than the one to which we have become accustomed. I hope that is not the case, but it is the most likely outcome given where we are today.

Thank you.

Question for Review

If you had to bet on the future of the European Union (EU), which of the following scenarios over the next two decades would you bet on and why: (1) the EU collapses; (2) the EU becomes an ever-more closer union; (3) the EU remains a "Europe of united states" but not a "United States of Europe."

Notes

1 (1) Pew Research Center, "Key Takeaways from the European Union Survey," May 12, 2014, at http://www.pewresearch.org/fact-tank/2014/05/12/5-key-takeaways-from-the-european-union-survey/

2 See Sebastian Rosato, *Europe United: Power Politics and the Making of the European Community* (Ithaca: Cornell University Press, 2012).

3 Joseph Joffe, "The Euro: The Engine That Couldn't," *New York Review of Books*, December 4, 1997, at http://www.nybooks.com/articles/archives/1997/dec/04/the-euro-the-engine-that-couldnt/

4 This behavior is not new; earlier steps to build stronger institutions invariably involved bargains between competing state interests. See Andrew Moravcsik, *The Choice for Europe: Social Purpose and State Power from Messina to Maastricht* (Ithaca: Cornell University Press, 1998).

Credits

Chapter 1

Page 10: Thucydides, "The Melian Dialogue" from *History of the Peloponnesian War*, translated by Rex Warner, 1954, pp. 400–408. Translation copyright © Rex Warner, 1954. Reproduced by permission of Penguin Books Ltd, Penguin Books, Ltd. (UK) and Curtis Brown, Ltd. (UK).

Page 16: Ian Hurd, "Legitimacy and Authority in International Politics", *International Organization*, 53:2 (Spring, 1999), pp. 379–408. © 1999 by the IO Foundation and the Massachusetts Institute of Technology. Used by permission of the MIT Press.

Page 19: Excerpt from *Politics Among Nations*, 6th edition: "The Struggle for Power and Peace" by Hans J. Morgenthau, edited by Kenneth W. Thompson, copyright © 1985 by Alfred A. Knopf, a division of Penguin Random House LLC. Used by permission of Alfred A. Knopf, an imprint of the Knopf Doubleday Publishing Group, a division of Penguin Random House LLC. All rights reserved.

Page 28: From J. Ann Tickner, "A Critique of Morgenthau's Principles of Political Realism" in *Gender and International Relations*, eds. Rebecca Grant and Kathleen Newland. Published by Indiana University Press. Reprinted by permission of Kathleen Newland.

Page 41: Republished with permission of Foreign Affairs, from "What is Power in Global Affairs?", Joseph S. Nye Jr, 2011; permission conveyed through Copyright Clearance Center, Inc.

Chapter 2

Page 48: Kenneth N. Waltz, *Theory of International Politics*, pp. 79–106. Reprinted by permission of Kenneth N. Waltz.

Page 70: "Anarchy and the Struggle for Power" from *The Tragedy of Great Power Politics* by John. J. Mearsheimer. Copyright © 2001 by John. J. Mearsheimer. Used by permission of W. W. Norton & company, Inc.

Page 78: Alexander Wendt, "Anarchy Is What States Make of It: The Social Construction of Power Politics", *International Organization*, 46:2 (Spring, 1992), pp. 391–425. © 1992 by the World Peace Foundation and the Massachusetts Institute of Technology. Used by permission of the MIT Press.

Chapter 3

Page 87: Thomas C. Schelling, "Game Theory: A Practitioner's Approach", *Economics and Philosophy*, Vol. 26, Issue 01, pp. 27–37, 30, 40. Copyright © 2010 by The American Political Science Association. Reprinted with the permission of Cambridge University Press.

Chapter 4

Chapter 5

Chapter 6

Chapter 7

Chapter 8

Chapter 9

Chapter 10

Chapter 11

Chapter 12

Page 434: From Alexander B. Downes, "Regime Change Doesn't Work," *Boston Review* (September/October 2011). Reproduced with permission from Alexander B. Downes.

Page 442: Hartzell, Caroline A., and Matthew Hoddie, "Crafting Peace through Power Sharing" pages 141–157, in *Crafting Peace: Power-Sharing Institutions and the Negotiated Settlement of Civil Wars, 2007.* Copyright © 2007 by The Pennsylvania State University Press. Reprinted by permission of The Pennsylvania State University Press.

Chapter 13

Page 454: Material reprinted from *Activists Beyond Borders: Advocacy Networks in International Politics* by Margaret E. Keck and Kathryn Sikkink. Copyright © 1998 by Cornell University Press. Used by permission of the publisher, Cornell University Press.

Page 461: Herbert Lin, "Cyber Conflict and National Security." Reprinted by permission of Herbert Lin.

Page 474: Steven R. Ratner, "International Law: The Trials of Global Norms," *Foreign Policy,* Issue 110 (Spring 1998), pp. 65–75. © 1998 by the Carnegie Endowment for International Peace. Reprinted with permission Foreign Policy.

Chapter 14

Page 480: Republished with permission of American Association for The Advancement of Science, from "The Tragedy of the Commons", *Science,* Moses King, Vol. 162, Issue 3859, pp. 1243–1248, © 1968; permission conveyed through Copyright Clearance Center, Inc."

Page 491: Adam Roberts and Dominik Zaum, "The U.N Security Council", from *Accountability and Reform. Selective Security: War and the United Nations Security Council Since 1945,* Adelphi Paper 395. Reprinted by permission of Taylor & Francis.

Page 500: Kenneth N. Waltz, "Globalization and Governance," *PS: Political Science and Politics,* Vol. 32, No. 4 (December 1999), pp. 693–700 with minor revisions. Copyright © 1999 by The American Political Science Association. Reprinted with the permission of Cambridge University Press.

Page 512: Republished with permission of *Foreign Affairs,* from "The Unruled World: The Case for Good Enough Global Governance", Stewart Patrick, Volume 93, Number 1, pp. 58–73, January/February 2014; permission conveyed through Copyright Clearance Center, Inc.

Page 522: Republished with permission of *Foreign Affairs,* from "The Future of the Liberal World Order," *Foreign Affairs",* G. John Ikenberry, Vol. 90, No. 3, pp. 56–68, 2011; permission conveyed through Copyright Clearance Center, Inc.

Chapter 15

Page 532: "Emerging Multipolarity: Why Should We Care?" by Barry R. Posen from *Current History,* Volume 10, Issue 721, pp. 347–352. Reprinted with permission from Current History magazine (November 1, 2009). © 2015 Current History, Inc.

Page 541: From Alan Dupont, "The Strategic Implications of Climate Change," *Survival: The IISS Quarterly*, Vol. 50, No. 3 (June–July 2008), pp. 31–47. Copyright © The International Institute for Strategic Studies. Reprinted by permission of Taylor & Francis Ltd. on behalf of The International Institute for Strategic Studies.

Page 550: "Bring Them All Back Home? Dollar Diminution and U.S. Power," Jonathan Kirshner, *The Washington Quarterly*, 36:3, Summer 2013, pp. 27–45. Reprinted by permission of Taylor & Francis Ltd. on behalf of The Washington Quarterly.

Page 560: "Power Shifts, Economic Change and the Decline of the West," Michael Cox, *International Relations*, 2012 26: 369. Reprinted by permission of Sage Publications.

Page 571: "The Future of the European Union" by Stephen M. Walt in *The European Union's Future*. Published by Committee on Foreign Affairs in 2015.